There is a road, steep and thorny, beset with perils of every kind—but yet a road: and it leads to the Heart of the Universe. I can tell you how to find Those who will show you the secret gateway that leads inward only. . . . For those who win onwards, there is reward past all telling: the power to bless and save humanity. For those who fail, there are other lives in which success may come.

HELENA PETROVNA BLAVATSKY
(discovered in her desk after her death
on May 8, 1891)

THE GUPTA VIDYA

GOD, NATURE AND MAN

THE GUPTA VIDYA

The Gupta Vidya

Volume I

God, Nature and Man

RAGHAVAN NARASIMHAN IYER

TT

Theosophy Trust Books
Norfolk, VA

The Gupta Vidya
Volume I
God, Nature and Man

by Raghavan Narasimhan Iyer
Library of Congress Control Number: 2019908542
ISBN: 978-1-7334650-0-7
10 9 8 7 6 5 4 3 2 1

Publisher's Cataloging-In-Publication Data
(Prepared by The Donohue Group, Inc.)

Names: Iyer, Raghavan, 1930-1995, author.
Title: The Gupta Vidya. Volume I, God, nature and man / Raghavan
Narasimhan Iyer.
Other Titles: God, nature and man
Description: First edition. | Norfolk, VA : Theosophy Trust Books, 2020.
| Previously published in Hermes, 1975-1989. | Includes bibliographical
references and index.
Identifiers: ISBN 9781733465007 | ISBN 9780999238271 (ebook)
Subjects: LCSH: Theosophy. | Spirituality. | Metaphysics. | Immortality. |
Consciousness.
Classification: LCC BP565.I97 G861 2020 (print) | LCC BP565.I97
(ebook) | DDC 299.934--dc23

Theosophy Trust Books
Norfolk, VA

First edition: June 20, 2020

Published and printed in the United States of America

Articles from *Hermes* may be found at https://www.theosophytrust.org

ACKNOWLEDGEMENTS

[Editor's note: the introductory materials were intended for all three volumes, and are reproduced in each volume for the reader's convenience.]

The arcane teachings in these three volumes on the Gupta Vidya were, almost entirely, delivered orally from 1949 to 1989 in India, England, Canada and the United States. The talks and answers to questions were taped and transcribed, edited and published in the journal *Hermes* (1975 - 1989), Concord Grove Press, 1407 Chapala Street, Santa Barbara. I am deeply grateful to all those who generously helped in the task of taping, transcribing, preliminary editing, proofing, composing and formatting, copy editing and printing.

I am especially indebted to Pico Iyer for his patient and superb editing, and to Elton Hall and Kirk Gradin for transferring them from the Verityper format to that of my own computer, whilst I alone am responsible for all errors and deficiencies in this work. Whatever is of value in these volumes I owe to the writings of H.P. Blavatsky, W.Q. Judge, D.K. Mavalankar, Claude St. Martin, Bhavani Shankar, Robert Crosbie and Krishna Prem, and to my Spiritual Teachers — Ramana Maharshi, B.P. Wadia, D.S. Sharma, Sarvepalli Radhakrishnan, S. Subramaniya Aiyer, Thangammal Gopalaswami Iyer, K. Swaminathan, Krishna Shastri, my parents L. Narasimhan and Lakshmi N. Iyer, and my wife Nandini.

I have also enormously benefitted over half a century from memorable conversations with honest agnostics and humane gnostics alike — Dr. J.N. Chubb of Elphinstone College, T.D. Weldon (my main Oxford Tutor), Dr. R.H. Thouless, Maude Hoffman, Hans Christofel, Christmas Humphreys, Claude Houghton, Clifford Bax, Gilbert Murray, Victor Gollancz, H.S.L. Polak, Friedrich Plank, Rabbi Rosen, Dr. John Smythies, James Laver, Lord Bertrand Russell, Bhikshu Sangharakshita, H.D. Lewis, Stephen Spender, Arne Naess, Arnold Toynbee, Julian

Huxley, David Astor, Rev. Michael Scott, Sir William Deakin, David Footman, James Joll, H.H. Price, Sir Alfred Ayer, Sir Patrick Strawson, Patrick Corbett, Geoffrey Hudson, John Plamenatz, Richard Crossman, Sir Isaiah Berlin, Guy Wint, Albert West, Pyarelal Nair, Lord Pethick-Lawrence, Viscount and Bronwen Astor, Vinoba Bhave, Fosco Maraini, Sir Richard Livingstone, Dr. Roberto Assigioli, the monk Sangye Tenzin, the Ashanti Chief in Ghana, Danilo Dolci, Bratako Ateko, Kudjo Mawudeku, Robert Hutchins, Herbert Schneider, Paul Wienpahl, Bishop James Pike, Caesar Chavez, Ian Stevenson, Svetoslav Roerich, Tenzin Gyatso (the 14th Dalai Lama), Periyavar (the late Kanchi Shankaracharya, 1894 - 1994), and Tangye Tenzin, the wise Abbot of Sera Je Monastery (Shigatze and Bylakuppe, Mysore).

This three-volume work on the *Gupta Vidya* is gratefully dedicated to The Venerable Lohan ("The Great Sacrifice"), The Maha Chohan (Arghyanath, the "Lord of Libations"), Agatsya Muni ("the Regent of Aryavarta"), Mahatma M. (Rishi Vishvamitra) and Mahatma K.H. ("Pitaguru"). They called it forth and for Them it was recorded.

March 10, 1995   R. N. I.

SHRI RAGHAVAN N. IYER

(March 10, 1930 – June 20, 1995)

He drew a circle that shut me out —
Heretic, rebel, a thing to flout.
But Love and I had the wit to win:
We drew a circle that took him in!

Edwin Markham

The spiritually penetrating essays in these three volumes were set forth for the expressed purpose of shedding the pristine light of universal Theosophy on the path of spiritual self-regeneration in the service of humanity. The Theosophical philosophy is predicated on the ageless truth that divine wisdom exists, and, most significantly, that wise beings exist who dynamically embody it in world history; that sages and seers still grace the globe and that they continually oversee the spiritual, mental, and physical evolution of man and nature. The secret Society of Sages that guides human progress periodically sends forth one of their own to sound afresh the Divine Philosophy and exemplify the spiritual life in all its richness and mystery. Such an enlightened spiritual teacher articulates eternal but forgotten truths in ingenious ways, adopting modalities that inspire the mind, release soul perception, and cut through the froth of history and the miasma of an age.

Shri Raghavan N. Iyer was a man of immense magnanimity and deep spiritual and intellectual genius. Born in Madras, India in 1930, he matriculated at the University of Bombay at the precocious age of fourteen and received his bachelor's degree in economics at age eighteen. Two years later he received the Chancellor's Gold Medal, earned his master's degree in Advanced Economics, and was selected as the Rhodes Scholar from India to Oxford University. At Oxford, he excelled in his academic studies and avidly participated in Oxford's rich social, political, and cultural life. During his undergraduate years, he eagerly joined a number of Oxford University clubs and societies. He was apparently so well-liked and respected that, in time, he was elected president of several prominent student organizations: the Oxford Social Studies Association, the Voltaire Society, and the Plotinus Society (which he also founded). His broader social sympathies and para-political concerns were served by joining and eventually becoming president of the Oxford University Peace Association and the Oxford Majlis Society (a debating society of Oxford students from South Asia that took up political issues). In 1954, he became president of the prestigious Oxford Union — perhaps the premiere debating society of his time. (Debates were usually spontaneous, witty, and packed full of appropriate references to recognizable historical figures in literature, politics, and society.) At year's end, he earned first-class honors in Philosophy, Politics, and Economics and later was awarded his master and doctorate degrees in Political Theory.

Shri Raghavan was an outstanding teacher of philosophy and politics throughout his public life. He assumed the mantle of teaching at the age of eighteen when he was appointed Fellow and Lecturer in Economics at Elphinstone College, University of Bombay. In 1956, he was appointed an Oxford don, giving tutorials in moral and political philosophy. In addition to teaching at Oxford, he lectured throughout Europe, America, and Africa, e.g., the University of Oslo in Norway (1958), the College of Europe in Belgium (1962), Erasmus Seminar in the Netherlands (1962), the University of Chicago in America (1963), and the University of Ghana in Legon (1964). His profound insights, sparkling intellectual clarity, mastery of different conceptual languages, and his infectious enthusiasm inspired thousands of students on different continents and earned him the deep respect of his contemporaries.

After accepting a professorship at the University of California (Santa Barbara) in 1965, he taught classes and seminars in political philosophy until his retirement at the age of fifty-six. His introductory classes and graduate seminars were legendary for their philosophical depth, theoretical openness, and visionary richness. His class topics were innovative and they attracted the curious, the committed, the idealist, the political realist, and the culturally disenfranchised. The most inspiring (and exacting) undergraduate courses were always enrolled to the maximum and lectures frequently ended with spontaneous standing ovations from the students. Those classes included: "Parapolitics and the City of Man", "Anarchist Thought", "Plato and the Polis", "The Dialectic from Plato to Marx", "Politics and Literature", "American Radicalism", and "The American Dream and the City of Man". His lectures were full of wit as well as wisdom and they unfailingly inspired students to cultivate an abiding confidence in themselves as learners and to become viable contributors to the emerging City of Man. His formal lectures and innumerable informal gatherings affected generations of students who later contributed to diverse fields of work, worship, and humanitarian service.

In addition to his vast and varied gifts as a teacher, Shri Raghavan Iyer was a devoted consultant and lecturer to various world organizations committed to some form of universal human betterment. While an Oxford don, he became a member of the Executive Committee for the World Association of World Federalists (The Hague) and likewise became a consultant and lecturer for the Friends International Centre (Kranj, Yugoslavia). In a similar spirit of rendering service, he became a consultant to OXFAM and accepted the temporary post of Director of Studies, UNESCO Conference on "Mutual Understanding Between the Orient and the Occident". He was also a member of The Club of Rome, The Reform Club, and The World Futures Studies Federation. In later years he became a contributing member of the Task Force appointed by U.S. President Jimmy Carter to develop "The Global 2000 Report for the President"—a call for Promethean initiatives to meet the most compelling needs of an emerging global civilization.

Over the arc of his extraordinary life, Shri Raghavan wrote numerous articles in diverse fields of thought as well as authored and edited many works that point toward an emerging global consciousness—replete with multiple challenges and stirring prospects. In 1965, he edited *The Glass Curtain between Asia and Europe.* This compilation of essays by internationally reputed historians contained a fascinating dialogue between Shri Raghavan and the world's most eminent historian at the time, Arnold Toynbee. They mutually explored Shri Raghavan's thesis that there exists an obscuring "glass curtain" between Asia and Europe that needs to be recognized and dealt with before there can be true intellectual and cultural understanding between East and West.

His most well-known and prominent books are *The Moral and Political Thought of Mahatma Gandhi* (1973) and *Parapolitics — Toward the City of Man* (1977). Each of these remarkable pioneering works is accessible to both the profound thinker and the serious inquirer, the erudite scholar and the dedicated student, the earnest seeker and the committed practitioner. Later, in 1983, he edited an extraordinary collection of spiritually inspiring readings entitled *The Jewel in the Lotus* — aptly characterized by Professor K. Swaminathan, a noted compiler of Gandhi's collected writings, as "a Universal Bible". In addition, Shri Raghavan edited and wrote luminous introductions for numerous sacred texts, including Hindu, Buddhist, Jain, Jewish, Christian, and Sufi teachings.

The deeper replenishing current of Shri Raghavan's life, however, flowed from the empyrean springs of *Theosophia.* He became a Theosophist at age ten when his father first took him to the United Lodge of Theosophists in Bombay. In time, he was introduced to the profound writings of H.P. Blavatsky and W.Q. Judge. Not long after entering the orbit of the Theosophical Movement, he made a sacred resolve to serve the Lodge of Mahatmas and increasingly assumed responsibility for forwarding the impulse of the worldwide Theosophical Cause of promoting universal brotherhood. For the rest of his life, all his efforts in the academic, social, political, and religious arenas were infused by his wholehearted devotion to the service of the Brotherhood of Bodhisattvas and to the enlightenment of the human race. This deeper, ever-present golden thread of meaning that wove together all his worldly activities became more apparent when he emigrated to America.

In 1965, Shri Raghavan moved with his wife and son to Santa Barbara, California. (His wife, Nandini, a brilliant Oxford don who received a First in Philosophy, Politics, and Economics at Oxford, went on to teach in both the Philosophy and Religious Studies departments at the University of California, Santa Barbara until her retirement. Pico, their only child, was born in Oxford in 1957. He later graduated from Oxford University and became a contributing writer to *Time* magazine and is now a noted author of inter-national standing.) Once settled in California, Shri Raghavan and Nandini founded the United Lodge of Theosophists, Santa Barbara. Beginning informally in October of 1966, the Lodge grew from fourteen initial students to over a hundred active associates. Soon after its inaugural meeting on February 18, 1969 (the death anniversary of Shri Krishna), Lodge members were invited to give talks and, in time, to co-lead Theosophy School classes for the young. In addition to evolving various modalities of giving and receiving Theosophical instruction, Shri Raghavan and Nandini founded several ancillary institutions that further served the global aims of the worldwide Theosophical Movement.

One such ancillary institution is the Institute of World Culture in Santa Barbara. On July 4, 1976—the bicentennial of the American Declaration of Independence—Shri Raghavan and Nandini co-initiated this educational non-profit organization. Its "Declaration of Interdependence" elucidates ten aims that are the visionary basis of all its intellectually and culturally enlightening programs and activities. The Institute of World Culture regularly hosts engaging seminars, forums, lectures, study circles, and film series. There is a wholesome blending of spiritual, intellectual, ethical, and cultural themes for focused thought and extensive discussion. The Institute has proved to be a culturally "consciousness expanding" experience for many and has, in its own way, contributed to a deeper appreciation of the often unsuspected power of classical and renaissance cultures to provide illuminating perspectives on a host of contemporary national and global issues.

As a forward-looking extension of his sacred obligation to serve the Theosophical Movement, Shri Raghavan founded, edited, and wrote for the golden journal *Hermes* (1975 – 1989). This wide-ranging spiritual journal was dedicated to the pristine sounding of Brahma Vach and to the spiritual regeneration of humanity. The profound articles found in *Hermes* span the spectrum of human thought from the metaphysical to the mystical, the ethical to the psychological, the spiritual to the material, the mythical to the historical. They convincingly reveal the subtle Theosophical foundations of all religions, philosophies, and sciences. They ingeniously address the chronic problems of the age and provide much needed "correctives to consciousness" in an age that tilts away from soul-saving and revitalizing ideals.

As repeatedly witnessed by close students, Shri Raghavan spoke at many different levels and freely interacted with each and all — regardless of race, creed, or condition. He exemplified — for the sake of the future — a multitude of Aquarian modalities and qualities. He was, in one sense, very Hindu: a true Brahmin — spiritual, cultured, brilliant, full of the graces that immediately remind one of ancient India and of golden ages long past. He was also very English: confident, highly educated, extremely literate, and at ease with statesmen, scientists, educators, and royalty. He was also very American: a true and fearless rebel, innovative, resourceful, visionary, and the eternal friend of the common man. But, beyond all this, he was in a much deeper sense the Universal Man, original, *sui generis* and timeless. His sympathies were always compassionately inclusive and his repeated emphasis — from first to last — was to "draw the larger circle" through universality of thought, the richness of imagination, the therapeutics of speech, and the magic of selfless action.

The wide-ranging arcane teachings in all three of these volumes were transcriptions of talks given between 1949 to 1989 in India, England, and the United States and were carefully edited by Shri Raghavan shortly before his death. When meditated upon and skillfully applied to the realm of self-chosen duties, they purify the mind, cleanse the heart, and give birth to men and women committed to creatively contributing to the universal civilization of tomorrow.

CONTENTS

IV THE SPECTRUM OF CONSCIOUSNESS

ΑUΜ

To contemplate these things is the privilege of the gods, and to do so is also the aspiration of the immortal soul of man generally, though only in a few cases is such aspiration realized.

PLATO

INTRODUCTION

GUPTA VIDYA *is like an ancient Banyan tree. Some come to sit in its shade, while others come to exchange words and seek friends. Still others come to pick fruit. Nature is generous.*

Some come to sit in the presence of teachers to receive instruction in the mighty power of real meditation, to secure help in self-examination. All are welcome.

The antiquity and enormity of the tree are beyond the capacity of any person in any period of history to enclose in a definition or formulation.

Great Teachers point beyond themselves to that which is beyond formulation, which is ineffable and indefinable. They seek to make alive and to make real for every man the priceless boon of learning truth.

RAGHAVAN N. IYER

THE GUPTA VIDYA

The universe is even as a great temple.
CLAUDE DE ST. MARTIN

The central truths of Gupta Vidya are not derived from any ancient or modern sect but represent the accumulated wisdom of the ages, the unrecorded inheritance of humanity. Its vast scheme of cosmic and human evolution furnishes all true seekers with the symbolic alphabet necessary to interpret their recurrent visions as well as the universal framework and metaphysical vocabulary, drawn from many mystics and seers, which enable them to communicate their own intuitive perceptions. All authentic mystical writings are enriched by the alchemical flavour of theosophical thought. Gupta Vidya is an integrated system of fundamental verities taught by initiates and adepts across millennia. It is the *Philosophia Perennis*, the philosophy of human perfectibility, the science of spirituality and the religion of responsibility. It is the primeval fount of myriad religious systems as well as the hidden essence and esoteric wisdom of each. Its cosmology is known as *Brahma Vidya* and its noetic psychology is known as *Atma Vidya*. Man, an immortal monad, has been able to preserve this sacred heritage through the sacrificial efforts of enlightened and compassionate individuals, or Bodhisattvas, who constitute an ancient Brotherhood. They quietly assist in the ethical evolution and spiritual development of the whole of humanity. Gupta Vidya is Divine Wisdom, transmitted and verified over aeons by the sages who belong to this secret Brotherhood.

The supreme presupposition of Gupta Vidya is an eternal substance-principle postulated as the ineffable Ground of all being. It is called a substance-principle because it becomes increasingly substantial and differentiated on the plane of manifestation, while it essentially remains a homogeneous principle in abstract space and eternal duration. The perceived universe is a complex mirroring of this Unknown Source, all finite conceptions of which are necessarily incomplete. It is the Absolute Negation of all that exists. It is Be-ness or *Sat*, the Secondless Reality, the No-thing of ancient philosophy, the 'Boundless Lir', the Unknown Beginning of Celtic cosmogony. Compared with It, all manifestation is no more than an impermanent illusion or *maya*, a kaleidoscopic medium through which the one Reality shows itself in a series of reflections. Spirit and matter are the two facets of this indivisible principle which only seem to be separate during a vast period of cosmic manifestation. They radiate from this transcendent source, yet are not causally related to It, since neither quality nor mode may properly be ascribed to It. They appear periodically on the objective plane as the opposite poles of this Reality yet they are not inherently separate, but mutually coexist as spirit-matter. In manifestation this substratum differentiates itself into seven planes of increasing density, reaching towards the region of sense data. Everywhere the root essence of homogeneous substance is the same, transforming itself by minute degrees from the most ethereal to the most gross.

The seven planes of manifestation may be seen as condensations of rarefied matter and also as living streams of intelligences — primordial rays proceeding from an invisible Spiritual Sun. All modes of activity in the Universe are internally guided by powers and potencies arrayed in an almost endless series of hierarchies, each with its exact function and precise scope of action. They are called Dhyan Chohans in Tibetan cosmogony and bear many other titles in the rich panoply of religious traditions — Angels, Devas, Dhyani Buddhas, Gods, Elohim, etc. All these are transmitting agents of cosmic Law (*rta*) which guides the evolution of each atom on every plane in space, the hierarchies varying enormously in their respective degrees of creative consciousness and monadic intelligence. As an aggregate, this immense host of forces forms the manifesting Verbum of an unmanifest Presence, constituting simultaneously the active Mind of the cosmos and its immutable Law. The idea of myriad hierarchies of intelligences animating visible Nature is a vital key to understanding all true mysticism. Many flashes of intuitive perception reveal multitudes of radiant beings elaborating the interior architecture of matter. Great mystics show a reverential recognition of the Logos or Verbum, the Army of the Voice, operating behind the screen of surface events as the noumenal cause of natural phenomena. This involves deciphering the signs of these intelligent forces by following the traces of their effects. The natural world bears the signatures of a divine archetypal world. With proper keys to archaic symbolism, the true seeker can read these signatures and recover the lost knowledge which would restore a primeval state of gnosis equivalent to that of the Gods. The letters composing the Sanskrit language are the phenomenal expressions of these finer forces, and by understanding them one could discover the root vibration, the ineffable Word, reverberating throughout the sentient world of visible Nature.

The arcane teaching concerning the Great Chain of Being in the supernatural realm continually reappears in human history as the inexhaustible fountain-head of aesthetic expression, heroic action and mystic illumination. The diverse expressions of creativity in the arts, religion and philosophy stem from this common unseen source, and the search for its origin is the hallowed mission of many a mystic and artist. The problem of tracing particulars to universals is as crucial to art as to psychology. The sevenfold classification of man's inner constitution corresponds to seven cosmic planes of being. Man is truly a microcosm and miniature copy of the macrocosm. Like the macrocosm, the individual is divine in essence, a direct radiation from the central Spiritual Sun. As pure spirit, every human being needs the vestures through which life may be experienced on differentiated planes of existence, so that one can become fully conscious of individual immortality and one's indissoluble identity with the whole. Every person is a complete reflection of the universe, revealing oneself to oneself by means of seven differentiations. In one's deepest self, the individual is *Atman,* the universal spirit which is mirrored in the luminous soul or *Buddhi.*

The light of *Buddhi* is focussed through *Manas* or impersonal intellect, the source of human individuation. These three together constitute the imperishable fire in man, the immortal Triad that undertakes an immense pilgrimage through successive incarnations to emerge as an effortlessly self-conscious agent of the divine will, the Light of the Logos, Brahma Vach.

Below this overbrooding Triad is the volatile quaternary of principles drawn from the lower planes of cosmic matter: they are *kama*, the force of blind passion and chaotic desire shared by man with animal life; *prana*, the life-current energizing the whirling atoms on the objective plane of existence; the astral paradigmatic body (*linga sharira*), the original form around which the physical molecules shape themselves, and hence the model for the physical frame (*sthula sharira*). This quaternary of principles is evanescent and changeable, established for man's use at the time of incarnation and dissolved at death into its primary constituents on their corresponding planes. The real man, the higher Triad, recedes from the physical plane to await the next incarnation. The function of each of these sheaths differs from one individual to another according to the level of spiritual development of the incarnated soul. The astral body of the Adept is of a much higher degree of resilience and purity than that of the average man. In visionaries and mystics, the sheaths intervening between the spiritual man and the brain-mind are sufficiently transparent so that they can receive communications from the overbrooding Triad in a relatively lucid manner. Man is a compound being simultaneously experiencing two worlds, inner and outer. Each person's present life experience is but a minute portion of what was witnessed by the immortal individuality in previous incarnations. Thus if men and women assiduously search within themselves, they can recover a vast heritage of knowledge spanning aeons. These memories are locked in mansions of the soul which only ardent desire and strong discipline can penetrate.

Memory is integral to consciousness and since all matter is alive and conscious, all beings from cells to deities have memory of some type. In man, memory is generally divided into four categories: physical memory, remembrance, recollection and reminiscence. In remembrance, an idea impinges upon the mind from the past by free association; in recollection, the mind deliberately searches it out. Reminiscence, however, is of another order altogether. Called 'soul-memory', it links every human being to previous lives and assures each that he or she will live again. In principle, any man or woman may recover the knowledge gained in previous incarnations and maintain continuity with the *sutratman*, the thread-soul, the eternal witness to every incarnation. There are also types of memory which are indistinguishable from prophecy, since the more one progresses towards homogeneous and rarefied planes of existence, the more past, present and future collapse into eternal duration, within the boundless perspective of which an entire cycle of manifestation may be surveyed. Such was the level of insight reached by the great seers or rishis who recorded their findings in the Vedas and other great scriptures, thus transmitting the ancient *Gupta Vidya* or 'the Secret Doctrine', fitly taken as the title of H.P. Blavatsky's monumental modern exposition of theosophical thought. Some mystics have penetrated deeply into the realms of reminiscence, bringing back the fruits of knowledge in previous lives. Greater still is the ability to enter into former and more spiritual epochs of humanity and to make those visions come alive for those who had lost all but a faint intuition of a larger sense of self.

The source and destiny of the soul's inward life fundamentally involve the entire scope of evolution. Coeval with the manifestation of the seven worlds of the cosmic plenum is the re-emergence of beings who assume once more the evolutionary pilgrimage after an immense period of rest. The emanation of matter and spirit into the objective plane of existence is but half the cycle. Its return brings all beings and forms to the bosom of absolute darkness. The period of manifestation covering trillions of years is called a *manvantara* and the corresponding period of rest, called *pralaya*, lasts for an equal duration. They are the Days and Nights of Brahmā, which were reckoned with meticulous precision by the ancient Aryans. The whole span of the *manvantara* is governed by the law of periodicity which regulates rates of activity on all planes of being. This is sometimes spoken of as 'the Great Breath' which preserves the cosmos. The essence of life is motion, growth and expansion of awareness in every atom. Each atom is at its core a monad, an expression of the highest self *(Atman)* and its vesture is the spiritual soul *(Buddhi)*. Prior to the monad's emergence in the human family, it undergoes aeons of experience in the lower kingdoms of nature, developing by natural impulse (metempsychosis) until the latent thinking faculty of *Manas* is awakened by the sacrificial efforts of beings who have risen far above the human state in *manvantaras* past. They kindle the spark of self-consciousness, making the unconscious monad a true man *(Manushya)*, capable of thought, reflection and deliberate action. The soul embarks upon a long cycle of incarnations in human form to prepare itself for entry into still greater planes of existence.

The evolutionary tide on earth is regulated by the unerring hand of cyclic law. Man passes through a series of Rounds and Races which allows him to assimilate the knowledge of every plane of existence, from the most ethereal to the most material. Man's planetary evolution describes a spiral passing from spirit into matter and returning to spirit again with a wholly self-conscious mastery of the process. Each Round is a major evolutionary period lasting many millions of years. Each Race in turn witnesses the rise and fall of continents, civilizations and nations. An earlier Race than our own, the Lemurian, lived in an idyllic Golden Age, an epoch ruled by natural religion, universal fraternity, and spontaneous devotion to spiritual teachers. Many of the myths regarding an era of childlike purity and unsullied trust in humanity's early flowering preserve the flavour of this period. As man evolved more material vestures, *kama* or passion tainted his power of thought and inflamed his irrational tendencies. The nightmare tales of Atlantean sorcerers are the heavy heirloom of contemporary humanity. The destruction of Atlantis ushered in the Aryan race of our own epoch. The Indian sages who inaugurated this period are among the torchbearers for the

humanity of our time. Intuitive mystics recognize the sacred role
of ancient India as mother and preserver of the spiritual heritage
of present humanity. The classical Indian scriptures resonate with
the authentic voice of the Verbum, uncorrupted by time and
human ignorance.

Pertinent to historical insight is the doctrine of the *yugas*, the
cycle of four epochs through which every Race passes, the Golden,
Silver, Bronze and Iron Ages. The *yugas* indicate a broad sweep of
karmic activity at any point in the life of an individual or
collection of individuals. The entire globe may not be undergoing
the same age simultaneously nor may any one individual be
necessarily in the same epoch as his social milieu. According to
Hindu calculations, *Kali Yuga* began over 5,090 years ago and will
last altogether for a total of 432,000 years. This dark age is
characterized by widespread confusion of roles, inversion of ethical
values and enormous suffering owing to spiritual blindness. Many
have celebrated the myth of the Golden Age as extolling the
plenitude of man's creative potential. The doctrine of the *yugas* is
not deterministic. It merely suggests the relative levels of
consciousness which most human beings tend to hold in common.
Thus a Golden Age vibration can be inserted into an Iron Age to
ameliorate the collective predicament of mankind. The Golden
Age surrounded human beings as a primordial state of divine
consciousness, but their own pride and ignorance precluded its
recovery. In the wonder of childhood, in archaic myths, in the
sporadic illuminations of great artists and in mystical visions, one
may discern shimmering glimpses of the Golden Age of universal
eros, the rightful original estate of humanity.

The progress of humanity in harmony with cyclic law is
facilitated by a mature grasp of karma and rebirth. These twin
doctrines of responsibility and hope unravel many of the riddles
of life and Nature. They show that every person's life and character
are the outcome of previous lives and thought patterns, that each
one is his or her own judge and executioner, and that all rise or
fall strictly by their own merits and misdeeds. Nothing is left to
chance or accident in life but everything is under the governance

of a universal law of ethical causation. Man is essentially a thinker, and all thoughts initiate causes that generate suffering or bliss. The immortal Triad endures the mistakes and follies of the turbulent quaternary until such time as it can assume its rightful stature and act freely in consonance with cosmic order and natural law. As man is constantly projecting a series of thoughts and images, individual responsibility is irrevocable. Each person is the centre of any disturbance of universal harmony and the ripples of effects must return to him. Thus the law of karma or justice signifies moral interdependence and human solidarity.

Karma must not be seen as a providential means of divine retribution but rather as a universal current touching those who bear the burden of its effects. This has been called the law of spiritual gravitation. The entire scope of man's affairs — his environment, friends, family, employment and the like — are all dictated by the needs of the soul. Karma works on the soul's behalf to provide those opportunities for knowledge and experience which would aid its progress. This concept could be expanded so as to encompass all connections with other human beings of even the most casual kind, seeing them as karmically ordained not for one's own progress but for the sake of those who struggle with the dire limitations of ignorance, poverty or despair. A deeply moving account of this trial is given in *The Hero in Man*, wherein, while walking among the wretched outcasts of Dublin, the author, George William Russell ('A.E.'), rejoices in the conviction that the benevolence he feels for each benighted soul will forge a spiritual bond through which he may help them in the future. Karma means a summons to the path of action and duty. As one cannot separate one's own karma from that of one's fellow-men, one may determine to devote one's life to the remission of the karmic burden of others.

At death the true Self or immortal Triad casts off the physical and astral bodies and is released from the thraldom of passions and desires. Its natural tropism to gravitate upwards allows it to enter the rarefied plane of consciousness where its thoughts are carried to culmination, clothed in a finer body suited to that sublime existence. This state, *devachan*, is a period of rest and assimilation between lives and the basis of the popular mythology of heaven. On the other hand, the lower quaternary languishes after death in *kamaloka*, the origin of theological dogmas concerning hell and purgatory. There it dissolves by degrees back into its primary elements at a rate determined by the cohesion given them by the narcissistic personality during life on earth. Inflamed passions and poisonous thoughts sustained for long periods of time endow this entity with a vivid, vicarious and ghoulish existence. This plane of consciousness, termed 'the Astral Light' by Eliphas Lévi, is intimately connected with the lives and thoughts of most of mankind. It is the vast slag-heap of Nature into which all selfish and evil thoughts are poured and then rebound back to pollute and contaminate human life on earth. This plane of carnalized thought tends to perpetuate the horrors of the Iron Age and condemn humanity to a state of spiritual darkness.

The crucial difference between individuals lies in whether they are enslaved by the Astral Light (the region of psyche) or whether they are capable of rising above it to a calm awareness of the wisdom and compassion latent in their higher nature, the realm of nous. Beyond the region of psychic action lies the pristine sphere of noetic awareness called *Akasha*, from which empyrean individuals could derive the inspiration needed to go forth and inaugurate a Golden Age by laying down the foundations of a regenerated civilization. Sages, past and present, saluted as Men of the Word (*Brahma Vach*), have accomplished the arduous transformation of their own natures, overcoming every vice and limitation and perfecting themselves in noetic ideation and sacrificial action. Mahatmas or Hierophants and Bodhisattvas renounce everything for the sake of suffering humanity. Solitary mystics on the ancient Bodhisattva path of service salute them as gurus, guides and preceptors and acknowledge their invisible presence as the *Guruparampara*, the sacred lineage behind their own modest labours for mankind. These wise beings are the noble trustees of the *Philosophia Perennis* and the compassionate teachers of the whole human family. The mystical pilgrimage of mankind is an authentic reflection of their ageless wisdom.

DEITY

THE SELF-EXISTENT

The Secret Doctrine establishes three fundamental propositions:

An Omnipresent, Eternal, Boundless and Immutable PRINCIPLE *on which all speculation is impossible, since it transcends the power of human conception and could only be dwarfed by any human expression or similitude. It is beyond the range and reach of thought — in the words of Mandukya, "unthinkable and unspeakable".*

To render these ideas clearer to the general reader, let him set out with the postulate that there is one absolute Reality which antecedes all manifested, conditioned being. This Infinite and Eternal Cause — dimly formulated in the "Unconscious" and "Unknowable" of current European philosophy — is the rootless root of "all that was, is, or ever shall be." It is of course devoid of all attributes and is essentially without any relation to manifested, finite Being. It is "Be-ness" rather than Being (in Sanskrit, Sat), *and is beyond all thought or speculation.*

The Secret Doctrine, i 14   H.P. BLAVATSKY

In the telling phrase of the *Book of Dzyan,* the oldest book of revelation in the Mystery Temples, the Rootless Root symbolizes the First Fundamental Truth of Gupta Vidya. It is the Unknowable for humanity, in general; it is also the unthinkable and unspeakable, especially in the Mysteries, for those who have apprehended the unknowable, who have risen beyond all temporal thoughts to the supernal realm of Divine Thought, transcended even that, and become one with TAT. It is beyond all names and forms, yet includes all, cancelling and superseding all beginnings and endings. It is beginningless, ever-existing and never dying. It is the fountainhead and origin of all Life, and of the seven kingdoms of Nature in all worlds and systems, in all stars, planets and galaxies.

It is the origin of all during a *manvantara*, the 'Day' of the great universe, which is the period of activity for every single being throughout the cosmos. It is also equally and exactly the same during the 'Night' of non-manifestation in which every being is re-absorbed into the great bosom of the Divine Ground, that which includes all and yet itself is No-thing, which is everything and nothing. Unthinkable, unspeakable, it is the Soundless Sound in the eternal Silence that transcends all sounds and silences in the manifested worlds of Nature, both visible and invisible. It encompasses the entire human kingdom and the lives of all gods, monads and atoms, beings of every kind at whatever degree of awareness, knowledge, self-knowledge, universal knowledge, universal self-knowledge or universal self-consciousness.

Beyond and behind all of these is TAT, which is ever full, and which, though boundless, is capable of emanating countless universes, and yet remains totally undepleted. One of the most thought-provoking stanzas in Sanskrit declares: *That which is ever full has taken away from it that which is ever full, and yet, it remains ever full.* It transcends all infinities and sum totals, and therefore it is known to the man of meditation, and sometimes in speech, as that which is No-thing or No-being. It is No-thing in space and time, nothing that is ever manifested, because it is eternally beyond manifest and non-manifest, being and non-being, day and night. It is beyond all contrast, beyond all divisions and dichotomies, beyond Spirit-Matter and the very division and contrast between concretized spirit and sublimated matter on all planes of existence. It is sometimes spoken of as the One Universal Existence, as in the eighth *shloka* of the *Stanzas of Dzyan*:

ALONE, THE ONE FORM OF EXISTENCE STRETCHED BOUNDLESS, INFINITE, CAUSELESS, IN DREAMLESS SLEEP; AND LIFE PULSATED UNCONSCIOUS IN UNIVERSAL SPACE, THROUGHOUT THAT ALL-PRESENCE WHICH IS SENSED BY THE "OPENED EYE" OF THE DANGMA.

It is the attributeless Absolute, whose only predication is

attribute-lessness. This, though a paradox of thought and language, is a poetical and metaphorical way of conveying what the *Mandukya Upanishad* calls "the unthinkable and unspeakable".

And yet, as the thirteenth chapter of the *Bhagavad Gita* declares, "That which is remoter than the remotest is closer than the closest." Few fitter poetical depictions of it were offered than these lines of William Blake:

> To see a World in a Grain of Sand,
> And a Heaven in a Wild Flower,
> Hold Infinity in the palm of your hand,
> And Eternity in a hour.

Here is a way of revering, honouring and saluting, but also recognizing, the Absolute without attempting to 'nail it down' by specific attributes. That which is attributeless has as many attributes as there are seeds, flowers and trees. It has, in fact, been often depicted as the Tree of Life, which includes all possible trees and all actual trees, in all possible worlds. This mighty metaphor is older than that of Blake. It is as old as thinking man. Everything represented by the hidden roots, the shoots, the trunk, the myriad branches, the myriads upon myriads of leaves, the flowers and fruits of the tree — deeply rooted in the earth and extending upward to the heavens — is significant in this hoary metaphor. It signifies the sacred function of the entire manifested cosmos. It is like a suspended bridge between the Divine Ground and all beings, and is itself expressed throughout the gamut of all existence.

The term 'Be-ness', though better than the term 'Being', is still only a poor English equivalent to the rich Sanskrit term SAT, which embraces the concepts of Being, Be-ness and Absolute Truth. SAT also encompasses the concept of Universal Absolute Consciousness, because the Absolute, though it has neither consciousness nor desire, neither wish nor thought, is absolute thought, absolute desire, absolute consciousness, absolutely all. It is each of these, and yet it is beyond them all. It cannot be limited by any single being or thing in relation to its vast, immemorial, variegated perception or perspective, vital experience or vocal description. It is beyond all of these, inexplicable, inexhaustible and impossible of definition.

This is implicit in the etymology of the English term 'absolute', which is derived from the Latin *absolutis*, 'that which is completed', 'that which is complete in itself'. Therefore it excludes nothing, it wants nothing, it lacks nothing, it needs nothing. It is all-complete and it is unfettered. Neither earthquakes nor wars, nor the ever-present cycle of destruction can have any mark or trace on it, or in any way fetter the Absolute. It is unconditional and beyond all conditions, and yet it is in all conditions intact, complete, self-sufficient, and utterly incapable of being touched or tainted, circumscribed or narrowed. It surpasses the vastest, infinite sum totals of objects and subjects in all possible worlds. The Latin *absolutus* is itself derived from the past participle of the verb *absolvere*, 'to free from', 'to complete', an etymology which suggests that it is not a static concept, nor indeed, is it dynamic, for it is endlessly at work, behind anything and everything, and therefore to be identified with the ultimate, unknowable mystery of the One Law, ceaselessly operating throughout the cosmos.

It is ever behind every single change, every single movement, all the rhythms and patterns of Nature in its intricate, inexhaustible vastness on the invisible causal as well as the visible plane. Therefore, it is ever capable of liberating anything and everything from conditionality. That liberation is known — if indeed we can talk of such knowledge — as the ending of embodied life, as a kind of death, yet in the Absolute there is neither birth or death. Nothing is ever lost, nothing is ever saved, nothing is ever begun, and nothing is ever ended, because everything that comes to be already exists in the Absolute. Everything that ceases to be continues to remain in the Absolute, otherwise there would be no continuity between *manvantaras* over immense periods of time, enormous epochs in galactic space. That which is unconditional, inexhaustible, all-complete and omnipresent is also by its inherent nature that which both seemingly binds and effectually liberates.

To the highest minds of meditation, the greatest lovers of wisdom, who have reached the pinnacle and summit of the loftiest conceivable altitude of philosophic thought, it is impossible to think about it, except with deep veneration. It is unapproachable, except by cancelling all divisions between thought, will and feeling, between head and heart, and every category of every school. All of them are dim, feeble, and at best logically limited representations of existence and reality, which are only irrelevant aspects of that which ever *is* and, therefore, by definition can never emerge into existence and never cease to be. Hence the term 'Be-ness'. The Latin term *solvere*, implying an alchemical sense of negation, comes from the Indo-European root *leu* which means 'to loosen', 'to divide', 'to cut apart', as with a pair of scissors. In conversation, human beings cut apart themselves, other human beings and the world, dividing constantly, but feebly compared with the way Nature divides all things with a daily magnificence. All our efforts to cut up, to divide and analyze the Absolute will fail because it is that which can never be divided, can never be cut up. It cannot be extended, contracted, shrunk or swallowed. No spatial metaphor can begin to characterize its essential indestructible property rooted in ever-existing self-existence. It is not only the sole Self-Existent, but it is also inclusive of all that is existent at all levels. If that is so, all words are merely invocations or petitions to burst the barriers and boundaries of finitude, fragmentation and limitation. To move towards the Absolute is continually to cancel and transcend every possible limit or characterization.

The Self-Existent is apprehended by human beings more readily in silence than in speech, in states of non-being rather than in what seem to be modes of being in a body. Spatial terms obviously can have no possible reference to the Absolute. And yet, on the visible plane, both in the sky and in the sea, we have two conspicuous, all-powerful representations of that which is incapable of limitation, that which is so deep and homogeneous that it is incapable of being understood in terms of visible motion, movements and waves. No human being who has ever reflected upon the sky or sea can fail to have some sense of the Absolute. No one who has ever reflected upon all the trees, all the birds upon this earth, all the animals, plants and minerals of every kind, all the millions upon millions of elementals that ceaselessly dance in the three kingdoms below the four visible kingdoms, can fail to recognize the vastitude and richness of the Absolute even in the realm of the manifest.

Few human beings make the effort of thought and imagination which is the prerogative of being human and think of the births of all babies on earth, not in numbers, but in terms of souls taking on bodies as part of one great pilgrimage. The ceaseless, eternal, sacred pilgrimage of all humanity is older than universes and will go on long after this universe has been destroyed. This cannot, after a point, be understood numerically in a linear way. Some other dialectical mode must be adopted. Minimally, one could think in a Shakespearean way about all tongues, all breaths, all eyes, all hands, all fingers as intimated in many magnificent statues of the Hindu gods. One would have to think in terms of myriads of humanities, and all of them gathering meaning and dignity through the experience of finitude, pain, conditionality and ignorance. At the same time, their sheer persistence through all of these limitations represents the indestructible core of divine discontent in the human soul, seeing beyond all possible experiences, constantly enacting an uncharted pilgrimage through innumerable worlds. And yet, these pilgrimages themselves are like the winking of an eye in the limitless Life of the Eye of Self-Existence of the Absolute.

Clearly, there is no insuperable difficulty in thinking intently about the First Fundamental of Gupta Vidya. But, in thinking of boundless vastitude, if one tries to do so in terms of numbers or in terms of spatial concepts of largeness, one encounters a problem. For example, if one thought of all the grains of sand upon this earth, one might as well call them infinite. And yet, one has common sense and intelligence enough to know that actually there is a finite limit to the number of all the grains of sand upon all the beaches upon this globe. And indeed, one does not have to know very much astronomy to know that there must be a finite limit to everything that is manifested, whether they be planets, stars, galaxies, galactic systems or even grains of sand. No wonder the latter is a favorite metaphor of enlightened beings like Gautama Buddha. There is no human being who cannot understand the notion of the immensity involved in what is so infinitesimally small to the naked eye, a grain of sand. The infinite in the infinitesimal can be experienced by a thinking being not just with reference to the sky and sea, but also with reference to trillions upon trillions of grains of sand. And yet, however unutterable these are in magnitude, they must actually be finite. And so too with the multitudinous strivings of all souls to characterize the Absolute, the God beyond all gods.

From this it is evident that any attempt to apprehend the Absolute in terms of an image or icon, let alone in terms of something extraneous to the cosmos and which is actually anthropomorphic — would be absurd. It would be the surest way of caricaturing the notion of Deity since, if there is any deity less than the Absolute, that would not be the highest conceivable source worthy of human adoration. Can there be a deity which is equivalent to the Absolute? 'Deity' itself is an abstract notion, and the word 'Absolute' is an imperfect term which has relativity built into it. This can be seen clearly from the use of 'absolute' in ordinary speech: any references to something that we call 'absolutely true' or 'absolutely correct', like any measure of 'absolute heat' or 'absolute cold', are relative to a particular scale of measurements or a particular system of concepts. One does not have to be highly trained in informal logic or formal mathematics to realize that these are necessary notions, but still notions that are man-made, notions that have limitation built into them.

If this is so, we can appreciate the generous assistance given by enlightened beings to limited and imperfect minds in helping them to get beyond mere spatial or numerical magnitudes and metaphors by invoking poetical speech. Poetical speech is truer,

less faulty, more evocative, even though it may involve the imagery
of the visible, tangible and spatial. The human mind is capable of
coining and formulating imagery, in art as in science, in poetry as
in mathematics, which points beyond itself. And that is why many
of the greatest *Rishis* and Sages have come as *Kavis,* Divine Poets.
They have chosen, instead of characterizing or conceptualizing the
Absolute, to celebrate it, to adore it. Therefore, all the great hymns
are magnificent acts of celebration —celebrations of life,
celebrations of the dignity of death, celebrations of the integrity
as well as the compassion of all the laws that work throughout
manifestation. The Absolute extends our view of what is known
and unknown, pointing beyond all possible pathways, to what is
essentially unknowable, transcending all knowledge and
cognition.

If there is an eternal wisdom in this universe, hidden in the very
depths of manifestation, that Eternal Wisdom, when expressed, can
only be an aspect of the Absolute. If there is universal ideation,
profound contemplation by the very greatest beings in all
evolution, that universal ideation would be seen because of their
greatness merely as a mode of participation in only a tiny portion
of the Absolute. And yet, any notion of the Absolute, with all its
vastness, its transcendence and its grandeur, would be meaningless
if it denied significance to the very least being, to the shortest-
lived insect. If the Absolute could not itself be invoked for the
sake of giving meaning and beauty, dignity and truth, to the least
particle, to whatever existed for the most fleeting second, it would
not really afford an active understanding either of life or the
cosmos. It would not be a proper function of the exercise of the
human capacity for comprehension through knowledge of life,
and therefore it would fail. All human efforts to include, as to
exclude, will necessarily fall far short of any attempt to characterize
the Absolute. The Absolute summons that in us which does not
merely want to characterize or describe, but to understand
ceaselessly, to make understanding an eternal process of
comprehensive learning, coeval with ceaseless living in a world
of constant change, under which remains an indestructible core

of changelessness. That core is in every atom, in every being, in every second, in every moment, everywhere and always.

Given this, we can see why the great metaphors of the ancient scriptures are truly invitations to deep, calm, and continuous reflection upon everything that is. The 'Boundless All', 'that which is and yet is not', 'Eternal Non-Being', 'the One Form of Existence', 'the Eternal Parent', and 'the All-Presence' are all expressions that help us because of the beauty of language, and because of the beauty of the concepts they evoke. The ubiquitous presence of Deity can no more be denied than we can deny the existence of the sun and its omnipresent light. Even if there were myriad suns and myriad worlds, the process of the diffusion of light must be analogous to what makes our living possible on this earth and our experience of the visible sun at dawn, midday and dusk. The wise celebrate the ever-present Invisible Sun even in the light of the physical world that surrounds us in our physical bodies. They thereby recognize the ever-existing, invisible Spiritual Sun that gives spiritual and mental illumination continually. The notion of life is inseparable from the notion of light, but also inseparable from cosmic electricity. There is a pulsation thrilling and throbbing even in the darkest period of non-manifestation, and that has sometimes been saluted as the Eternal Great Breath. The breathing in and breathing out of worlds and universes would itself have no meaning if there were not a ceaseless breathing at the very core of all life and light, and of all cosmic electricity.

Yet every one of these poetic notions gets tainted and tortured by the intrinsic limitations of human beings who must start with the limits of the known and extend them. To do this, they must emulate the greatest human beings, who always, the more they know, are even more aware of what they do not know. The more gnostic they are, the more agnostic they become, and the more they rejoice in the fact that the mathematics of the cosmos transcends the greatest possible representations in laws and equations, in theorems and theories. The authentic beginning of advanced thinking in the philosophy of science is the recognition, through the study of mathematical logic, set theory and mathematics, that this is intrinsically so. This is especially true today owing to the impressive work in the nineteenth century of outstanding minds who demonstrated conclusively how many infinities one could find in mathematics. One can even construct modes of non-Euclidean geometry in which an infinitude of points can still be related to what is capable of being mapped.

Impressive though this may be, it is but a small part of human knowledge, only a small representation in recent history within a limited field of a knowledge that is as old as thinking man. Many human beings have experienced this in the realm of feeling even more intensely than they have experienced it in the realm of thought. Consider the ecstasy of a child. Consider the sadness of a human being who is ready to finish a single day in the seemingly endless series of days that makes up the wheel of worldly existence. Consider the poignancy felt when nearing the moment of death, which is really no more than a transitional phase in a ceaseless journey. All of these are universal experiences of the transcendence of feeling. In all cultures, civilizations and societies, among human beings who are highly sensitive to the deeper levels and subtler vibrations of feeling, there is a firm recognition that more is said through intimation than through explicit representation in external speech or form. This is part of the poetry of human life, part of the poetry of cosmic existence.

What is unsaid is more significant and more real than what is said, because it brings us closer to the Absolute. What is thought by human beings, but thought in a way that they are not even aware of, is often closer and truer to the intrinsic nature of life itself, of consciousness and of the Absolute, than all the thoughts that they bring to the forefront of their attention, let alone the thoughts they articulate and share. There is, therefore, no sense in which a human being can expect to begin to understand the Absolute except by accepting the fact that one is born alone, lives alone and dies alone. So does everything in Nature. And yet, there is nothing in Nature that is not bound up with everything else that exists. This is true in the realm of atoms, true in the realm of plants, true in the realm of human beings. Still, there is a secret solitude to the life journey of every ant, of every fly, of every flower, and also of every human being.

The Absolute, then, is the very ground of all reality. All denials of it are meaningless, because they simply trap one in the unreal, which itself is only like a minor shadow of what is an ever-present veil upon the Absolute. To have a sense of the meaning of sacred metaphors, such as the 'All-Presence' or the 'Boundless All' is to make come alive infinitude within finitude, transcendence within immanence, boundless space within visible space, eternal duration within limited time. The Absolute is the only conceivable ground of all experience, and it must lie continuously before our physical eyes, as well as our mind's eye and our soul's eye. To make the Absolute the ground of our being, our thinking, our living and our feeling is to recognize that everything which is by its very nature limited because of language, because of gesture, because of definition, because of its captivity within space-time is merely a kind of apologetic, imperfect representation of that which is beyond representation in the realm of thought and the realm of feeling.

This is not difficult to understand. We are only speaking of what we already know, and what we know that we know. But we cannot bring what we know that we know in the depth of our being — which has sometimes been called the 'I am I' consciousness — into the realm of that which is limited. Therefore, the Absolute is that from which we are self-alienated, owing to our needlessly self-devised limitations. Ultimately, in a Platonic sense or as Shankaracharya pointed out, there is only one error, and that is the root of all errors. It is the treating of that which is ever changing as enduring, that which is unreal as real, or that which is finite as if it had a kind of indefinite extension in the realm of time. This applies to all worlds, all lives, all acts and all relationships. It applies to all religions, all philosophies, all sciences and all systems of thought. It applies to the entire gamut of what we call civilization, which is only at best like a mask upon the great secret, unspeakable, unthinkable pilgrimage of the immortal soul of all Humanity. In other words, in consciousness we can dare further and go beyond what we can construct through thoughts, words, formulations and expressions. We all know this, because most of our life is spent either in sleep or in states of consciousness where we are in no position to articulate our thoughts to anyone, or even to ourselves. Thus philosophers in the East have said that you cannot even begin to pronounce upon human nature, until you can first address yourself to Being in all states of non-manifestation, which actually far exceed, in their impact upon our finite being, what we regard as visible and temporal states.

The central truth in relation to consciousness has already been sensed in relation to matter itself in contemporary science and it was always known to the greatest philosophers. When you think of Absolute Abstract Space, Eternal Duration and Perpetual Motion, there is no manifest motion, no measurable time, no extended space, which is not puny in relation to Duration which is eternal, Motion which is ceaseless, Space which is boundless. We all have a sense of Abstract Space, Eternal Duration and Perpetual Motion; otherwise we would not be able to live. There would be no light in our eyes, no power to give life. There would be no will, no capability of what Spinoza called *conatus* — rational self-sustenance in living on and surviving, from day through night into the next day, from one life into the next life through the intermediate states between lives, let alone being able to cross the bridge between our boundaries of existence and those of all other beings now alive in worlds of embodied existence. There would be no way to cross those barriers if we absolutized our finite concepts, making them the sole basis of all knowing. The concepts to which we are ordinarily attached are partial reflections only of the elementary needs and evanescent wants of what is shadowy in comparison with the immortal, indestructible story of human consciousness. That is why, even though the notion of consciousness would be misleading in relation to the Absolute (which is better seen as a state of unconsciousness or dreamless sleep), yet consciousness itself, like space, duration and motion, is a useful working symbol for the Absolute. But by its nature it is a conditioned symbol, because the entire gamut of consciousness of all the greatest beings in all the worlds must still have a boundary in matter, in embodiment, and the Absolute must surely far transcend all boundaries.

Thus, when certain ideas are pushed far enough, we get a sense which helps to correct the finitizing tendency of the human mind, its self-imprisonment, its conditioned, habitual bondage to limiting and deceptive notions. Such notions cannot have any basis in reality or in thought when thought is sustained and truly rigorous, thorough and logical, and when philosophy is fearless and daring, questioning and searching in every possible direction. But if all our concepts are conditional, how then can the Absolute be conceived? The simple answer is that it cannot be conceived. The *Mandukya Upanishad* declares it to be inconceivable, unthinkable and unspeakable. Yet, what is so daunting in this? There are many things in ordinary life that we find unspeakable because of their ineffable grandeur, but we often attach a much deeper and stronger sense of reality to what is unspeakable than what is spoken. This is a very common experience. Certainly we did this almost constantly, until we learnt to lisp and speak in the first two or three years of life. Surely, then, to make this a peculiar problem in relation to the Absolute is itself artificial. It is philosophically a pseudo-problem. Because something is infinite, it does not mean that the human mind cannot set up series, find out ratios and factors, rates of change, and try to understand what is meant by the notion of the infinite.

In relation to the Absolute, we have the greatest scriptures, the most beautiful poetry which elevates our sights, our senses, our sensitivity and feelings. Though inconceivable, there is nothing that is worth conceiving, other than the Absolute. And we are conceiving it all the time, because it is the root of the very process of conceiving. If it is the root of the process of conceiving, then we can see how we may get artificially caught in mental cobwebs, which is the ancient description of most human thought and language.

To deny or attempt to ignore the ubiquitous importance of the Absolute is to contradict what we know when we are asleep.

Cognition of the Absolute must, by its inherent nature, only be possible owing to that core in us which itself is unconditional and capable of conceiving to the point where we transcend the limits of conceiving. We are capable of using words with the incantatory power of music, reminding us of the ever-present ground of speech, the interstices, the spaces, the silences between and within words. It is only by developing a taste for silence in sound, for the unmanifest within the manifest, for the unspoken within the spoken, the unrecorded within a world of frail and fugitive and often false recordings — that we come closer to the heartbeat that makes us human. The Absolute is characterized as the Sacred Heart of all existence because, although it is ever-present, it is at the same time unfathomable by thought or speech. It is closer to us than anything we can ever say or think, just as there is nothing more fundamental than the beating of the heart, and there is nothing around us that is more palpable, if only we would listen, than the beating of the cosmic heart. Great beings have always shown how to tune oneself to the great heart of the cosmos. They are in ceaseless meditation at all times, in a state of supreme total spiritual wakefulness known as *turiya*. Even if most human beings, by comparison, are like lisping, faltering adolescents because of their inability to contain and continue thought and consciousness to a point where the boundaries are burst, this state of *turiya* is accessible to each and every person.

Just as we took a lot of trouble to learn how to walk and talk, we cannot expect, without a lot of effort, to reverse all the habits of the imprisoning sensorium and the imprisoning finitude of embodiment. We cannot develop a taste for the sheer joy of the exhilarating experience of the Absolute without earnestly availing ourselves in meditation of the finest philosophical and poetical characterizations of the Absolute. These are always found in abundance in Sanskrit literature, wherein the Absolute is seen as not only as *Sat* and *Chit*, all consciousness and all reality, but *Ananda*, all joy — but at a level where you cannot separate any one from the others. The joy is in the *Sat*, the *Sat* is in the *Ananda*, the *Sat* and the *Ananda* are in the *Chit*. It is a ceaseless, joyous, reality-affirming ideation, which is only a kind of sharing with those who are the Builders, making manifestation possible and maintaining it, and Those who within that world of manifestation have transcended all barriers and become totally enlightened, more powerful than all the gods, than the Demiurge, than even the highest beings who maintain the realm of manifestation.

It is certainly possible for us, if only we would have the necessary courage, whole-heartedness and single-mindedness, to break through the fundamental illusion of form, and awaken the subtler senses. It is possible to open the doors and the avenues of true cognition by the immortal Monad, which is dateless and deathless and has little to do with any particular embodiment or any particular set of acts. At this point, we come to see that to revere the Absolute is to revere life itself. It is to revere all humanity and all that exists. It is to revere Nature itself, which through change, death and destruction ceaselessly regenerates itself. Thus, it is to revere the quintessential principle of continuity, the vital principle of self-regeneration which is as potent in every atom as in the Absolute itself.

The Absolute, to those who see it as *Satchitananda*, is most perceptible in the *Anu*, the Atom, but this is more fundamental than those atoms which are purely conceptual devices of modern thought. The *Atman* is the atom. *Brahman* is in the infinitesmal point of timeless, spaceless Duration-Existence, but which itself is at the heart of that which makes space and time not multi-dimensional, but actually without any dimension. This we can understand by considering the mathematics of a point, which has no extension, no length, no breadth nor thickness. And this idea itself only intimates the activity of the Absolute, which ceaselessly mirrors itself in billions upon billions upon billions of points, in a transcendental manner applicable to mind or matter, to space or time, to all possible cycles and patterns of causation and to all possible worlds.

Thus it is that the greatest and the wisest beings have always known that the way to recognize and revere the Absolute is by revering the Absolute in the here and now — in every hair on every head, in every blade of grass and everything that breathes. The God beyond all gods is in every pair of eyes. Reverence for the Absolute is a whole way of life in which we totally cooperate with the eternal heartbeat of the universe, cooperate with it through spiritual breathing, mental breathing, through a certain conscious, constant, ceaseless, boundless pulsation of eternal prostration and eternal reverence. To live in this way is to dare to challenge the unknowable and to give dignity to the process of eternal knowing and learning — which is the dialogue of the soul with itself. This is true philosophy, true speech, the true dialogue of the Self with itself. We can only talk about the Absolute when we talk to the God in ourselves, and we cannot do it suddenly if we do not do it daily. Actually, we do it all the time, but we are not aware of this. When we do it consciously, and not just with a limited notion of ourselves, but with a notion of divine Selfhood that has a place for everything that exists, the whole of life becomes a dialogue with the Absolute. That dialogue becomes the life of soul itself. The richer it is, the more rooted in the non-manifest. And, when words are spoken or acts are performed, it makes them sacred and meaningful, giving them the beauty and dignity of the Divine Dance. If this then is our understanding of it, there is nothing which could be solely relevant to the Absolute, and at the same time there is nothing which is not so relevant.

This brings us closer, then, to the Eye of the *Dangma*, the Eye of the Sage, who breathes the Absolute, fully and self-consciously — who is name and form and without name and form, who is each and every other being and yet beyond all, and who sees worlds by analogy with the day and night of every being on the physical plane. In it he sees the Day and Night of worlds and universes. To him there is no difference. It is the same process. Every time the Sage sees a human being asleep, whether a baby or an old person, it is all the same. He sees all beings asleep, all worlds asleep — because the Sage is incapable of limitation through the perceptual realm. Long ago, he went far beyond the unfolding of all the subtler senses, where there is simultaneous, instantaneous transmission of thought. Nothing can happen on a star which does not affect us, say the poets, and nothing could happen to a star which the Sage does not instantly feel.

We have, then, in the Sage a concept of living and breathing which so far transcends all possible human conceptions of perfection and enlightenment that no Sage could ever convey it fully by words or acts, gestures or postures. When Sages have spoken, whether it be Adi Shankara speaking of the *Tattvamasi mantram,* or Gautama Buddha speaking of experiencing *nirvana* in *samsara,* or K'ung Fu Tzu speaking of the Great Extreme, they have done essentially what we would do to children: provide pregnant analogies to make souls question and think. Above all, individuals must be encouraged to turn within themselves, wherein there is a richer experience, a greater realm of living, loving and knowing than they could ever find in the external realm. To begin to become sagely is to awaken the memory of the immortal soul, which has had myriads of parents, myriads of friends, myriads of co-workers, and to make all of that deeply, powerfully relevant to each and every moment, in each and every context.

Thus, Dakshinamurti, the Initiator of Initiates, the paradigm of all Sages, the supreme incarnation of Maheshwara, is himself unthinkable and unspeakable like the Absolute. To speak of the one is to speak of the other, which is why wise human beings use meditation upon the *Guruparampara,* the sacred lineage of true Sages, as a way of coming closer to the Absolute. Every child uses the help of its mother or father or an adult to learn how to walk. That is Nature's way. That is what comes naturally to the human being, and it is that which is ultimately the Only Way, the only door to greater knowledge, greater experience, profounder apprehension, deeper comprehension and, even more, to a taste or a foretaste of *Satchitananda.* If a person understood all of this, he or she would see quickly that to limit the unmanifest by the manifested, or the inexhaustible Absolute by any possible notion of a first cause or any particular limited God, would indeed be to limit Man. To limit Humanity, whether in terms of two thousand years or twenty billion years, would be equally irrelevant. It would truly be to deny the very visible facts of the cosmos and human life, thereby cutting oneself off from one's truest life, which is no other than the Divine Ground of the attributeless Absolute, the blissful state of silent, ceaseless contemplation (SAT-CHIT-ANANDA).

DEITY IN ACTION

Absolute Unity cannot pass to infinity; for infinity presupposes the limitless extension of something, and the duration of that 'something'; and the One All is like Space — which is its only mental and physical representation on this Earth, or our plane of existence — neither an object of, nor a subject to, perception. If one could suppose the Eternal Infinite All, the Omnipresent Unity, instead of being in Eternity, becoming through periodical manifestation a manifold Universe or a multiple personality, that Unity would cease to be one. Locke's idea that 'pure Space is capable of neither resistance nor Motion' — is incorrect. Space is neither a 'limitless void', nor a 'conditioned fullness', but both: being, on the plane of absolute abstraction, the ever-incognisable Deity, which is void only to finite minds, and on that of mayavic perception, the Plenum, the absolute Container of all that is, whether manifested or unmanifested: it is, therefore, that ABSOLUTE ALL.

The Secret Doctrine, i 8

It is fruitful to consider the ever-existent Absolute and everything intrinsically relative in the light of distinctions we make between unity and infinity, eternity and periodicity, the relationless and whatever is inextricably bound by relations. First of all, absolute unity is beyond infinity as spatial or temporal extension, even if boundless and endless, for it transcends polarization into infinite and finite, unbounded and bounded, which are correlative terms. It is important to grasp this truth fully and clearly, and to assimilate it completely, so that anyone can readily acknowledge the Rootless Root beyond perception and conception, images and ideas, beyond the fleeting and fickle awareness of objects and subjects, and even beyond the Creative Logos, the One Source and Ground of all manifestation. Each and every human being can say truly within the silence of the inmost heart:

I am the perceiver, the spectator, the eternal witness, intact and unmodified, attributeless, *sui generis. I am Brahman, Brahman am I.* I and the Absolute are one, always and forever, in all spaces and conditions and contexts. I am No-Thing, absolute voidness, *shunyata, nirguna brahman,* in a constant state of *nirvikalpa samadhi,* changeless amidst all change, beginingless and endless even amidst births and deaths, in a state of *parinishpanna,* supreme self-awareness as the One Self-Existent.

Secondly, the Universal Kosmic Mind ever abides, both during *pralaya* and *manvantara.* It is immutable, unmodifiable — the plenum of infinite potentials. This unconditioned consciousness becomes relative consciousness or *Mahat* periodically at every manvantaric dawn. The Mahatma, who is not only one with *Mahat* — the mind of the cosmos — but also attuned beyond *Mahat* and primordial *ahankara* to the Universal Mind, is in a state of serene *turiya,* supreme spiritual wakefulness. He is undistracted during *manvantaras,* undisturbed during *pralayas,* ever retentive — *smartava* — of the pristine vibration of the manvantaric dawn during cosmic and human evolution. This state of serene, absolute awareness is beyond all the relativities and polarities of consciousness, which are merely modifications and manifestations of the One *chit,* the Supreme Ideation behind and beyond all creation, change, and transformation.

Thirdly, if one of the ways in which we can distinguish the Absolute from the relative is that the Absolute always stands out of all relation to anything, and the relative is always in some relationship or the other, then mind at any level of manifestation will be inextricably involved in relations and relativities. Thus, apprehension and mastery of the nature of those networks of relations matters a great deal to one's effective capacity for self-transcendence. True knowledge or the highest wisdom ever sees what is essential among hosts of inessential, secondary and tertiary emanations, whilst rejecting nothing and assigning a proper place and due significance to each and every form, colour and number, polarity and relativity. Always aware of the quintessential distinction between internal and external relations, and the continuous modification of each through the other, which determines the regulated flow of *kundalini shakti* within the astral spine, the Mahatma is fully able to overcome the process of transmigration, as well as to transmute it during voluntary and partial incarnations into this world. This is *tattvajnana* — the knowledge of *tattvas* or essences — but in relation to the *adhitattva*, the one supreme element, the one Fohatic force behind all forces, the one Reality behind and beyond all appearances, from the most sublime, the most rarefied, the most ethereal, to the most mundane, the most tangible, the most immediate.

Given all this, human consciousness must move to higher levels through a steady increase in its reflective awareness of its own relations and relativities, as well as through the progressive awakening of its own fundamentally unmodified nature. In practice, these two processes are inseparable. The Immortal Spectator goes through a series of progressive awakenings from lesser to greater horizons of awareness, from derivative causes through primary causes to the Ceaseless, Causeless Cause, and from primary relations to the Three-in-One, which radiates from the ever-concealed One. The self-moving soul graduates through identification and attachment to the transient to greater identification with the "One without a second", beyond form, beyond colour and beyond all limitation. The sovereign means of this self-mastery is through threefold meditation upon indivisible *mulaprakriti* — the indestructible Root Substance — upon the unmanifested Logos, the source and synthesis of the primary seven Logoi, and upon the one Fohatic force of universal ideation behind and beyond cosmic electricity and cosmic *eros*, cosmic magnetism and cosmic radiation. Such meditation is a constant abidance in the never manifested but ever-existent Three-in-one, beyond the divine dance of the One Logos and the seven planes or forty-nine states of conscious existence.

Karma is Deity in action — the eternal, divine pulsation and breathing of the Absolute. It is the Unknowable at its Rootless

Root, but it is partly cognizable as the Law of eternal causation and ethical retribution, mirroring and maintaining the universal unity and total interdependence of all gods, monads and atoms. On the three formless *arupa* planes, and on the four planes of conditioned consciousness and modified ever-changing matter, it reflects absolute harmony, justice and compassion. These are ceaselessly mirrored in the operations and manifestations of karmic subtotals, embodied in the vestures, the ideational causation of all beings, the networks of interrelations between the seven kingdoms and all the beings therein. Karma is the progressive driving force behind all cosmic and human evolution and involution, and as such, it is inexorable, impersonal, universal, irresistible, omnipresent and omnipotent. Self-conscious monads can cooperate with this Law, but they cannot cancel or supercede it. Every instance of working against the Law, consciously or unconsciously, is an inevitable precursor of pain and suffering, disillusionment and disappointment, persisting ignorance and delusion, which must eventually culminate in self-alienation and the doom of total self-destruction. For finite minds, the operation of karma must be understood relative to past and to future, to context and condition, to planes of consciousness and states of matter. This intrinsic relativity is due to the subject-object relationship, which must vary with all planes and sub-planes, with all states and sub-states, with all globes and vestures, with all degrees of apprehension, and all levels of awareness, ranging from atoms to worlds, from infusoria to the stars and galaxies. Thus the vast order of relations is inclusive of all possible worlds, all orders of being, and all the cosmic hierarchies extending downward from Dhyanis to *devas* and *devatas,* from the Demiurge and Divine Host of Builders to all the elementals that belong to the invisible cosmos behind the visible universe.

Anyone's understanding of the Absolute and relative, as applied to the philosophy of perfection, depends upon our grasp of this fundamental theory, difficult and abstract though it may be. Perfection must be relative to the vestures and conditions experienced by monads, as well as the degrees of unconsciousness, partial self-consciousness, and even universal self-consciousness of thinking beings — ideating selves — in a world of dif-ferentiating objects and multiple agents and selves. There can be no static final perfection. Humanity can and must comprehend and enjoy the host of perfections as consummations of the repeated use of skills, of faculties, and of instruments of cognition and action. Such growth and maturation comes through self-correction, through learning from the lessons of life, and as the result of experiments with limited truth in changing contexts. Absolute perfection must pertain to universal self-consciousness in the highest possible and conceivable sense. It is meaningful precisely because of the existence and living reality of Those who have attained to that state. But even such Beings, when embodied in available vestures at any given time, and when working with the available materials on any globe or in any period of evolution, must take on the relative imperfections of the race or the age in which they incarnate. At the same time, their voluntary incarnations vindicate the promise and the possibility open to all souls of perfecting conditions and vestures, while honoring, serving and reaching out to the Knowers of the Three-in-One.

Even the mention of absolute perfection requires one to take several steps upward, metaphysically, to consider Absolute Being, Divine Thought, and the ideal Kosmos. Firstly, we are helped to consider Absolute Being by an extraordinary and challenging question raised in *The Secret Doctrine*:

> As the highest Dhyân Chohan, however, can but bow in ignorance before the awful mystery of Absolute Being; and since, even in that culmination of conscious existence — 'the merging of the individual in the universal consciousness' — to use a phrase of Fichte's — the Finite cannot conceive the Infinite, nor can it apply to its own standard of mental experiences, how can it be said that the 'Unconscious' and the Absolute can have even an instinctive impulse or hope of attaining clear self-consciousness?
>
> *The Secret Doctrine*, i 51

Here is an important reference to the error of absolute idealism in its modern form, which has tinctured philosophical thought for the past three centuries. The error of absolute idealism consists in the notion that the Absolute, being equivalent to absolute mind and absolute freedom, can be known by thought and emulated by the conscious ego, which is wholly autonomous as a mirror of the Absolute. Even Fichte fell into this error, though he saw that the infinite cannot conceive the finite, and also that, compared to what we call consciousness, the Absolute must be the Supreme Unconscious.

Schelling, on the other hand, stressed the inconceivability of the Absolute, even though he felt it must be the object of true philosophy in its search for a science of the Absolute. Hegel criticized Schelling's view as an empty abstraction, whilst Schelling in turn dismissed Hegel's attempt to ascribe absolute attributes to the Absolute as panlogicism. Hegel was concerned to distinguish between different phases in the Absolute, from supreme unconsciousness to self-consciousness. If God is asleep, how to wake him up? If the Absolute is unconscious, how to get things moving and produce self-consciousness in itself, let alone in the world? This concern of Hegel, to distinguish between different phases in the Absolute from supreme unconsciousness to self-conscious alienation from itself in the world of appearances, was prompted by his wish to describe its recovery of full self-consciousness, in history and in the world, through all its emanated rays. Hence, he felt compelled to speak unphilosophically of the Absolute as capable of becoming self-conscious, or at least of having an impulse toward self-consciousness, and he used this conception to explain the dialectical unfoldment in time and history of various phases of the Absolute.

By contrast the highest Dhyanis and all Mahatmas, who are tribeless and raceless and belong to no religion except the religion of the One, recognize the absolute transcendence by the Absolute of even absolute consciousness or Divine Thought. They there-fore stress that the highest gnosis heightens the joyous sense of wonder and reverence, the ever deepening of states of silence, and an open-ended agnosticism that sees beyond all worlds, all systems of thought, and even the highest possible conceptions of perfected human beings. The finest statement of this teaching was given by Rishi Sanatsujata in the *Mahabharata.* He explained that silence *(maunam)* is meditation, silence is the *atman,* silence is the AUM. There are clearly depths upon depths in the highest meditations and the deepest silences, and the Soundless Sound points beyond itself, just as all sounds point beyond themselves, to the Silence of the Soundless Sound. This is the unknown darkness of the Absolute, the Divine Darkness that is beyond worlds and must ever surround the Absolute in its Absoluteness. Its absoluteness is known as *parabrahman,* the emphasis being on *para* — beyond — as the *shloka* said of Buddha at the close of the *Heart Sutra:*

> *gate gate paragate parasamgate bodhi svaha*

> Gone, gone, gone beyond,
> Gone to the other shore, O Bodhi!
> So let it be.

Secondly, in relation to the exalted conceptions of Divine Thought and the ideal Kosmos, *The Secret Doctrine* states that:

> It is only with reference to the intra-cosmic soul, the ideal Kosmos in the immutable Divine Thought, that we may say: 'It never had a beginning nor will it have an end.' With regard to its body or Cosmic organization, though it cannot be said that it had a first, or will ever have a last construction, yet at each new Manvantara, its organization may be regarded as the first and last of its kind as it evolutes every time on a higher plane.
>
> *The Secret Doctrine,* i 3

Whilst there is no first or last in the appearance of worlds, epochs of manifestation, and subsequent periods of non-manifestation, the cosmic process is not a mechanical repetition of cyclical recurrence for two important reasons. First of all, the ideal Kosmos can only be partially and imperfectly reflected in any series of actual universes. And at the same time, secondly, there is a progression in awareness and in modes of substance between *manvantaras,* owing to the inexhaustible potential contained in the all-sufficient ideal Kosmos. Yet, whilst the intra-cosmic soul, the ideal Kosmos in the immutable Divine Thought, is beginingless and endless, it is not the Absolute. Divine Thought itself represents the highest knowledge accessible, beyond which lies the unknown darkness of the Absolute.

Thus, one of the highest mysteries lies in the fact that the Absolute finds its highest expression in its greatest Knowers, the wisest Beings throughout the ages. Further, this mystery is reflected in the relativity of time itself, wherein each time-bound epoch of embodied existence is dependent upon a prior case. It also represents a unique manifestation that cannot ever be exactly duplicated. In this sense, even the relative reality of each epoch of manifestation must have an immense sanctity, one which is in no way diminished by the consideration of preceding and succeeding epochs, or even by the contrast between actual manifestation and the ideal Kosmos in the Divine Thought. This is important because, when most people think of progression, they tend to think in a utilitarian and time-bound manner of succession as supersession. The latest must be the best, apparently, and is itself only a means to an end, a higher state in the future. To think in this self-contradictory way is to misunderstand completely the Absolute, the realm of the relative, and also the mysterious concepts of mirroring and inevitably incomplete incarnation. This persistent error arises out of the failure to see that the supremely transcendent Absolute is also ever present in anything and everything existent. The Absolute is universally immanent.

To take a time honoured example, much favoured by all the Rishis and Sages, who are poets and seers as well as philosophers and renouncers, the leaves of a tree are similar and also subtly different, each radiating, especially when newly sprouted, the freshness of its uniqueness. Each tree is also unique, and one can imagine that from the seed of each healthy evergreen tree, there may arise trees that are even finer or grander than those before. But the quintessential sap in every tree that springs from the seeds of its predecessor is the same. It is the primordial sap, which is inexhaustibly potent. Similarly, seekers of enlightenment have to recognize and revere the all-potent sap of the Absolute, as well as the inexhaustible fecundity of the ideal Kosmos, potentially present in the Absolute. They must venerate the inconceivable richness and diversity of unique expressions of ideal forms, as well as the ever-expanding and ever-deepening awareness of all the myriad hosts of hierarchies, from the highest and most homogenous to the lowest and most heterogenous, from *manvantara* to *manvantara*. This is what Plato meant by the statement that time is the moving image of eternity. It is a celebration of endless continuity as well as infinite diversity amidst the seeming discontinuities in the realm of appearances. To know this is to live in the Eternal Now. Every atom is sacred, and so too is every grain of dust. Just as the Absolute beyond all absolutes is sacred, so too are all the omniscient Knowers of *Brahma Vach*, regardless of all the variations among them, and even differences of degree in universal self-consciousness.

This sense of limitless sanctity throughout all manifestation brings the true seeker to the mystical and powerful idea of the Diamond Soul. One could think of and see the Diamond Soul as a shining jewel, precipitated from the Absolute into the realm of the relative, a jewel so multifaceted that all sentient beings may find means of approach by some aspect of the Light that it compassionately radiates in every direction. As Krishna, the Purna Avatar and the paradigm of all Avatars — who are all one and the same — states, "In whatever way men approach Me, in that way do I assist them." Sacred texts speak of the alchemical and therapeutic influence as well as the elixir of immortality and the philosopher's stone for highly developed souls who are ready for

further initiations into the Mysteries. The same teaching is also
behind the *trikaya* doctrine of Mahayana, the three vestures of
dharmakaya, sambhogakaya and *nirmanakaya*. The first corresponds
to the state of *nirguna brahman,* the second to the state of *saguna
brahman,* and the third to the state of Mahatmas and Bodhisattvas,
who live in this world, unseen and unknown but ever helpful to
all souls who are ready to receive the light of truth, wisdom and
compassion. At another level, there is also a similar teaching in
regard to the simultaneous triple incarnation of a perfected
enlightened being, as a transcendental Buddha, a mediating
Bodhisattva, and an incarnated Teacher of Enlightenment. All
point to the ineffable, inconceivable and inexpressible Absolute,
the supreme, transcendental Source of all light, all life and all love.

Now, the intuitive must look at Absolute and relative self-
consciousness because the Avatar is a fact. What about the Avatar
or the Mahatmas as an ideal? There is the priceless instruction:

> 'Paramârtha' is self-consciousness in Sanskrit,
> Svasamvedana, or the 'self-analysing reflection' — from
> two words, *parama* (above everything) and *artha*
> (comprehension), *Satya* meaning absolute true being,
> or *Esse.* In Tibetan Paramârthasatya is *Dondampaidenpa.*
> The opposite of this absolute reality, or actuality, is
> Samvritisatya — the relative truth only — '*Samvriti*'
> meaning 'false conception' and being the origin of
> illusion, Maya; in Tibetan *Kundzabchi-denpa,* 'illusion-
> creating appearance'.
>
> *The Secret Doctrine,* i 48

Paramarthasatya, like the Absolute, is supreme, transcendent,
universal self-consciousness, the One and Only Self-Existent
beyond all worlds and beings, all states and conditions. But
paramarthasatya is correlative with *samvrittisatya,* and thus refers
to the continual cancelling of all that is evanescent, fascinating
and enslaving. It refers to the transcendence of all that is deceptive
and alluring in the realm of appearances, relativities and relations,
the realm of relative truths, partial truths and falsehoods, of

unrealities and illusions. All these elements of *samvritti* can give rise to delusions, but nowhere more persistently and poignantly than in relation to the sin of partial and partisan selfhood, the sin of separateness from the whole and from all other parts. This can be countered by a vigorous dialectic of continual negation, such as that taught by Nagarjuna. It ever demands the voiding of all false conceptions, entities and selves, coupled with the ready willingness to enter the Supreme Void, the Divine Darkness, wherein is hidden the ineffable light that is nameless and formless, signless and shadowless. That light of the Logos, Daiviprakriti, is best worshipped in the silence of the secret sanctuary of the spiritual heart, which mirrors the compassion of the *vajrasattva*, the Diamond Soul.

Jnanayoga, the path of Divine Wisdom, involves ever-deepening levels of vision attained by the Seer, but Divine Wisdom cannot be a subject for study in any ordinary intellectual sense. It may be an object for search, however, once one awakens in oneself the desire to begin the search and learns how to sustain the light of enquiry. True enquiry must begin in self-enquiry and must persist until, as veil upon veil lifts, there is an acceptance that there will be veils upon veils behind. The pupil must persist in the progressive discovery of the distinction between the Self and non-self, willing to see that seeming life is really death, and that what seems to be non-being leads to true Being. This painful and persistent search for the one Self hidden in each and all beings, worlds and conditions will eventually lead to the recognition, at some stage of one's quest, that one is both the subject and the object of the search, because transcendent Divine Wisdom is within oneself and it is also in each and every noetic soul on its great 'pilgrimage of necessity'. Within oneself is the entrance to the sanctuary of the cosmic Heart, the Supreme Self, the omnipresent AUM who is *Ishvara*, the *paramatman*, known ultimately as *parabrahman*, the sole source and *sine qua non* of Deity in action in the manifested cosmos.

The mysterious mirroring of the Ultimate Reality is itself the mighty and magical power of *maya*, the creative capacity of the

Logos, and the source of illusory manifestation. This means that the polarity of *paramartha* and *samvritti,* of *nirvana* and *samsara,* is ultimately mayavic, and that the true path of Divine Wisdom cannot be a mere negation of manifestation as illusion. Thus the twentieth century Tamil poet Muruganar states:

> To cling to the void and neglect compassion is to fall short of the highest path. To practise compassion is not to abandon the toils of existence. He who is mighty in the practice of both passes beyond *nirvana* and *samsara.*

This Sacred Teaching is the Secret Heart of Gupta Vidya, and is central to the purest and highest Mahayana teaching of the Gelupka tradition in Tibet. It was reaffirmed in this century through silence and speech by Shri Ramana Maharshi, who urged one and all who came to him to keep searching for the origin of the 'I-thought' in asking the age-old question "Who am I?" until it dissolves in the attributeless Supreme Self in the Silence, which is Wisdom-Compassion. It alone can give the true strength to do one's *dharma,* the best one can in this world of *samsara,* whilst abiding alone, aloof and apart in the blissful awareness of the vestureless state of *nirvana,* supreme non-doing, or pure being.

Once one sees that *samsara* can be equated to *samvrittisatya,* and that *nirvana* can be equated to *paramarthasatya,* one may apprehend the nature of the Highest Path. Both *samsara* and *nirvana* are states of mind. What humanoids call this world is a state of mind. Because both *samsara* and *nirvana* are states of mind, they may therefore be seen as contrasting states of consciousness — *samvrittisatya* corresponding to the realm of relativities and relative truths, and *paramarthasatya* to the realm of the Absolute, the transcendental, the dateless and deathless, the ever existent. In deep sleep, in meditation, in times of the deepest silence and stillness and during the calm of ceaseless contemplation, anyone who is pure and patient can touch the threshold and have a taste of nirvanic completeness. While in waking consciousness and in chaotic sleep, souls are tossed upon the tempestuous waves of samsaric existence, which is transient, conditioned, provisional and probationary. It is solely meant for the soul's learning of the lessons of life.

The Highest Path must represent the dissolution of all dichotomies and dualities, and the transcendence of the very contrast between two worlds — the world of time and the world of eternity, the world of matter and the world of spirit, the world of temporal change and the world of timeless duration. If the former is only a veil upon the latter, mortality is a mask for the immortal ray of the Supreme Logos in the cosmos, and the world of appearance serves merely as a School of ceaseless renunciation and disinterested performance of duties. In it all disciples may learn the relinquishment of the acquisitive karma of results, as well as skilful means, in the sacrificial application of Divine Wisdom to each and every atom in every sphere of ever-moving life. The Path to serene enlightenment is secret and sacred because it cannot be seen from the outside, and cannot be told by words or conveyed through acts. Yet it is that to which everything points. Anything can intimate the AUM to the meditative soul in the Silence of the spiritual comradeship of those who have chosen Krishna-Christos, saluting and emulating the Knowers and Exemplars of *Brahma Vach*.

CONSCIOUSNESS
AND EXISTENCE

*The One Being is the noumenon of all the noumena
which we know must underlie phenomena, and give them
whatever shadow of reality they possess, but which we have
not the senses or the intellect to cognize at present. The impalpable atoms of gold scattered through the substance of a
ton of auriferous quartz may be imperceptible to the naked
eye of the miner, yet he knows that they are not only present
there but that they alone give his quartz any appreciable
value; and this relation of the gold to the quartz may faintly
shadow forth that of the noumenon to the phenomenon. But
the miner knows what the gold will look like when extracted
from the quartz, whereas the common mortal can form no
conception of the reality of things separated from the Maya
which veils them, and in which they are hidden. Alone
the Initiate, rich with the lore acquired by numberless
generations of his predecessors, directs the 'Eye of Dangma'
toward the essence of things in which no Maya can have any
influence. It is here that the teachings of esoteric philosophy
in relation to the Nidanas and the Four Truths become of the
greatest importance; but they are secret.*

The Secret Doctrine, i 45

In order to comprehend consciousness from the standpoint
of the cosmos as a whole, consciousness must refer to that
which exists even before a cosmos comes into being. It is that
which subsists and persists during the epochal manifestation of a
cosmos, as well as that which endures after the dissolution of the
cosmos. By analogy of the macrocosm to the microcosm, the full
consciousness of an individual must be viewed as an unbroken
stream which existed before any particular form. That stream
persists during all the vicissitudes experienced in and through
vestures occupied in relation to others ensouled by other sparks

of the Central Spiritual Sun. If that stream of consciousness is unborn and undying, unbroken and ever existing, it must also be unmodified by all that is experienced through involvement in a form, and must therefore subsist after the dissolution. Consideration of the nature of primordial consciousness is essentially the recognition of changelessness in a world of change. That which is entirely changeless is beginningless and endless, unconditionally eternal.

The eternity of pure consciousness transcends the vast, though specific, sense of eternity referred to in the *Stanzas of Dzyan*, which speak of "the Seven Eternities" comprising a *Mahakalpa*. Even to begin to contemplate this unbroken consciousness and to consider the meaning of manifestation in the light of such an eternal reality is something the human mind is scarcely prepared to do. When confronted with such a prospect, the mind, which tends to be conditioned by sense experience, by memories and anticipations, immediately begins to reflect the succession and variety of changes. As the mind is itself part of Nature and part of matter in the deepest sense, it encounters profound obstacles to the ceaseless contemplation of the changeless SAT. By itself the mind cannot generate a principle of continuity. It can only do this by negation or abstraction. Even employing the *via negativa* or *neti, neti,* negating all that is embodied and involved in events in space and time, the mind must use language which participates in the relationality of whatever exists in space-time. By abstraction, by attempting to leap beyond that language, it is also fundamentally involved in speaking in terms of an experience, but which cannot be easily rendered into the language of relationality in space-time. That language, therefore, tends to be paradoxical.

It is difficult to talk about absolute metaphysical darkness when human beings are almost constantly conditioned by the contrast of light and shade, or day and night, which by extrapolation they may apply on the cosmic plane. To transcend all this and to talk of absolute darkness is in effect to talk of "No Thing." Metaphysical darkness is the eternal matrix in which sources of light appear and disappear. It is that to which nothing is added to make light, and that which need not be subtracted from light to make darkness. It is the noumenon of both phenomenal light and darkness, remaining in the perception of even an intuitive human being as nothing more than a gray impalpable twilight. This persistent obscurity and lack of clarity will arise again and again, so long as one attempts to contemplate consciousness from the standpoint of that which is immanent and involved in vestures, that which uses language and is constantly employed to identify and re-identify, to compare and contrast objects. Yet it is possible through meditation to penetrate beyond the veil of concepts to a deeper sense of being which is beginningless and endless, unmodified by the mind. It is possible to experience oneself in relation to that which has no frame of reference in terms of space and time, no images that refer to existing or possible objects.

To rise to this level of imageless consciousness requires unremitting perseverance because one must put aside in-numerable layers and levels of language and thought. To understand this is to recognize in relation to the mind that which intuitive contemporary physicists have begun to understand about the many-layered and many-levelled structure of space. Mathematically, one can generate a multidimensional space; employing what is now known as quantum physics, one can generate models which allow, at any given time, myriads of possible worlds in reference to any single atom, electron or photon. There is thus a host of parallel pathways that can be, but are not, taken owing to the probabilistic curves that apply to the quanta of light and atoms. So too with consciousness. It is possible to use the mind to abstract away altogether from what actually exists. Yet at the same time, one may preserve a sense of being; the absence of a framework need not cause one to fade away and altogether lose one's sense of self-existence. To think in these ways is to begin to draw upon the metaphysically profound and purifying potential of space.

At the simplest level, one may, like Emerson, see the heavens as the great cleanser and purifier of consciousness. An uninformed eye sees the sky as bare space. But many people are by now aware from contemporary astrophysics that space is not totally empty, that there is matter and radiation in all the spaces between the galaxies. It is empty only by reference to the familiar space of the world of objects. Turning the idea over in the mind again, one might ask why the night sky, seemingly so empty, in fact suggests an indefinite extension in every direction, provides an intimation of a million galaxies. It seems as if there is at once some kind of structure and some kind of transcendence of all possible structures. To reflect upon these lines is to begin to approach the esoteric conception of space, which is neither a limitless void nor a conditioned fullness, but both. To persist in this thought is to raise fundamental questions about real being as opposed to embodied existence, about that which is within and without, omnipresent and invisible. By removing consciousness from its habitual confinement to narrow categories, such meditation can cleanse the mind.

Meditation must go even deeper, however, in order to generate a notion of Absolute Abstract Space without reference to subjects or objects. The point must be reached where there is a dissolution of the sense of 'I' in reference to a pristine sense of self-existence. The notion of an 'I' cannot arise unless there is already a separation in consciousness between the self within and the self as embodied, between the self in contemplation and the self that is extended without. Anyone even remotely familiar with the persistently intrusive nature of 'I'-consciousness during attempts at meditation, much less daily life, must understand the tremendous effort of abstraction, of imagination and depth needed to reverse the false order of priority which immersion in the immanent world of space-time imposes upon the pure stream of unmodified consciousness. Ego-consciousness insists upon pronouncing this or that as real. It imposes its own polarized constructions on appearances, maintaining that that which is more real is dark or empty, and has to be discovered by removing perceptible layers. In fact, however, the opposite is true. Spiritually, what is real is what is unmodified, what can never be penetrated by analysis of the differentiated realm of space-time, of subjects and objects.

From the standpoint of Spirit, everything that emerges is unreal because it is only a veil upon that which is hidden behind it, not in the manner of subtle phenomena veiled by grosser phenomena, but in the manner of noumena which transcend phenomena entirely. All phenomena, whether they seem subtle or mundane, are equally unreal. Their reality is at best a relative mode of existence, relative to the observer and to most sense-perceptions, relative to the concepts and the cogitations of individual subjects, relative to phases and states of evolving consciousness. Even more fundamental than the veil of concept is the veil of maya itself. Even to speak of maya is as mysterious and metaphysical as talking about blankness, Absolute Abstract Space, nothingness.

The doctrine of maya is really a doctrine about time and causality, about consciousness and veiling, about the many-layered nature of space. When the contemporary physicist says that the universe is space and matter, this is but a dim reflection of the ancient idea that the universe is *nirvana* and maya. There is something mayavic about matter, but there is also something at the root of matter which is pure, homogeneous and eternal. There is noumenal substance beyond maya. There is also that about space which is beyond all possible dimensions. Even thinking of space as multidimensional does not reach to the soul of the concept. Even the mathematician who conceives of space as a collection of dimensionless points, each one the reduction of the circumference of a circle when its radius is zero, gets no closer. By imagining an infinite number of such points, one can generate a sort of metaphysical mapping of dimensionless points, which could be called space. It would be quite different from the metric space of the physicist, and much more abstract than the sense of visual space obtained by the casual watcher of the skies. But even this mathematical conception of space involves one in a mapping, in the snares of a rational mind, in conventional grooves, dependent upon the relativities of space-time and the shared experience in the world of contrasting objects and cogitating subjects.

To ascend in consciousness into the realm of pure noumenal substance and Absolute Abstract Space, one must come to terms with the problem of the ego. The ego, or the sense of 'I', is that which consolidates, separates and appropriates both subject and object, nurturing a sense of possession and self-protectiveness. It is that in self-consciousness which seems to be engaged in a dubious process of preserving something, a sense of identity, but a something that turns out to be nothing in the eye of eternity. In contrast to this misplaced and misproportioned sense of ego-identity, the ancients considered even the gods, the Rishis, the Dhyani Buddhas and Manus, along with everything in this universe, as simply the periodic potencies of Brahmā-Vishnu —infinite space. Space in the ultimate sense is both infinite expansion and all-pervasiveness, infinite growth and infinite preservation. The ancients did not conceive of this cosmos as something which could expand perpetually or be totally annihilated; for them expansion, preservation and annihilation were relative to a location or *loka*. Anything which disappears or appears on one plane emerges from or is absorbed into another plane. Beginnings and endings are not final. They simply exist, relative to an observer. But according to Gupta Vidya, they are also relative to planes of consciousness inhabited by various types of observers. Many, indeed most, of these planes are beyond the powers of observation of most souls. But it is certainly possible to hypothesize them and to explore the theoretical and practical implications of depth vision in consciousness. Each plane of consciousness can only be experienced by appropriate instruments that cast onto the screen of consciousness perceptions of objects and subjects in reference to a circumscribed set of variables. Given the postulate of Absolute Abstract Space, however, no set of instruments could exhaust the possibilities of growth or of absorption and annihilation.

As soon as one begins to view this entire universe as a limitation upon potential existence, one of myriad possibilities latent within Brahmā-Vishnu as infinite space, it becomes clear that there must be an illusion about egoity. It is an illusion of indefinite preservation. In the worst and saddest cases this amounts to a strong identification with a body. This is the karma of those who abused power in declining Egypt and elsewhere, and now fall under the influence of Madison Avenue and Hollywood. Involved in body worship, craving indefinite prolongation of bodily existence, they present an extremely ugly and unnatural spectacle to the eye of the detached observer. Behind the mask of seeming glamour, few things are more hideous than clinging to a form in desperate defiance of the laws of Nature. Even these extreme cases, however, are only an exaggerated and tragic form of *tanha,* the craving to exist in an embodied form. Buddha taught that existence is suffering, that the cause of suffering is craving and that the extinction of *tanha* is *nirvana* or *moksha.*

According to the *Stanzas of Dzyan,* both the causes of the misery of existence and the seven paths to the bliss of *moksha* have a reality which is relative to a period of manifestation. In *pralaya* they are not. Speaking of the twelve *nidanas,* or causes of being — the concatenated chain of antecedent causes and successive effects through which karma and reincarnation operate — and referring also to maya — the element of illusion which enters into all finite things as a function of the limited powers of cognition with which any observer apprehends the appearances of the one hidden noumenon — H.P. Blavatsky explains *tanha* as follows:

> 'The Causes of Existence' mean not only the physical causes known to science, but the metaphysical causes, the chief of which is the desire to exist, an outcome of Nidana and Maya. This desire for a sentient life shows itself in everything, from an atom to a sun, and is a reflection of the Divine Thought propelled into objective existence, into a law that the Universe should exist. According to esoteric teaching, the real cause of that supposed desire, and of all existence, remains for ever hidden, and its first emanations are the most complete abstractions mind can conceive. These abstractions must of necessity be postulated as the cause of the material Universe which presents itself to the senses and intellect; and they underlie the secondary and subordinate powers of Nature, which,

anthropomorphized, have been worshipped as God and gods by the common herd of every age.

Ibid., i 44

Given the extreme persistence of *tanha,* it is a long and difficult evolutionary process to elevate consciousness beyond the realm of maya. Even human beings who have successfully generated a sense of selfhood independent of the body have attachments to the mind, through concepts, expectations and images. Even if they have gone beyond the *samskaras* and have begun to inhabit a realm of higher Manasic ideation, they have still, out of their love of meditation or their desire to help the human race, an inherence in form. It is so difficult to transcend *ahankara* altogether, collapsing it to a zero, that there is clearly something about this illusion which is due to the Vishnu function in the universe itself. To cooperate with this, and to plumb its pure depths, one must learn to coordinate it self-consciously with the Brahmā function of expansion. From the standpoint of Buddhist metaphysics, an obsessive concern to extinguish the sense of 'I' entirely only amounts to a form of craving for non-existence, a form of holding on to life. The same desire can exist both in a negative and a positive form. The desire to commit suicide, for example, exists in proportion to the desire to continue living.

Polarity of desire does not make the slightest difference to the intensity of craving and the intensity of conceptualization through form. This may be understood cosmically in terms of the duality of the Logos in manifestation as it incessantly acts through negative and positive, active and passive, forces. The positive force continually expands and sheds while the negative force continually gathers and fecundates. The active force falls into the veil of cosmic matter towards which it is continually attracted. This process, essential to cosmic manifestation, is the basis of limitation of consciousness in relation to manifested and differentiated matter. It is the basis, in some of the Puranic texts, for the depiction of *ahankara* as universal self-consciousness, coordinate with *Mahat* or universal mind. In these systems, however, there is a fundamental distinction between the lower forms of *ahankara,* related to an identification with a name and a form, or even individuated mind extending throughout a *manvantara,* and the highest form of *ahankara* associated with the cosmos.

Thus, owing to the universal tendency towards a mayavic inherence of consciousness in form, every human being attempting to contact the stream of pure unmodified consciousness is bound to discover certain barriers that are extremely difficult to cross, and which cannot be wholly dissolved while the capacity for incarnation still exists. Hence the rejection in Mahayana Buddhism of the desire for liberation and the necessity of cooperating with the universal sacrificial processes of the cosmos — *Adhiyajna* — in the pursuit of the Bodhisattvic ideal. With meditation one can participate through indefinite expansion in the consciousness of all beings. One can potentially be present in the consciousness of every atom, every ant, every grain of dust and every star. For most, these will merely be words, remote indeed from immediate experience. But one can nevertheless try to recognize theoretically, and beyond ordinary language, that there is an infinite possibility of expansion of the sphere of being and consciousness. In this expansion, however, it would be an error to suppose that one is doing the work oneself. In fact, one is merely becoming a vesture, a focusing instrument, of that which is intrinsic to the universe itself. Brahmā is everywhere. The creative Logos is ceaselessly breathing in and breathing out. Through this expansive force forms come into being, disappear and are replaced by new forms. Considered in its ultimate and absolute origin, this is the basis of the expansion into manifestation of what the *Stanzas of Dzyan* call "the One Form of Existence". The deliberate invocation of this expansive force is a corrective to the contracting tendency of consciousness which consolidates *ahankara* at lower levels.

Owing to *ahankara* at the level of physical name and form, human beings are, typically, terrified of death. They must instead learn to expand their consciousness and consider the myriad human beings that they once knew, or did not know, who must have been their ancestors. Where are they? Can one imagine a consciousness after the moment of death? Can one imagine a consciousness that is capable of including innumerable human beings who have disappeared as bodies and forms? One might imagine entering a gallery of ancestral photographs and understanding that none of the human beings represented there still resemble the images that portray them because their forms have all been buried or burnt. Yet if one concentrates on the pin-points of light in their eyes, one can come to see these as a kind of collective veil upon the eternal sentient rays of light that are their true natures. "Dust thou art and unto dust shalt thou return" was not spoken of that light. It was spoken of the body, not the soul.

The vivifying expansive spiritual efflux in the immortal manvantaric ray inheres in and pervades the radiant plane of *Akasha*. Gupta Vidya

> regards the Adi-Sakti — the direct emanation of Mu-laprakriti, the eternal Root of THAT, and the female aspect of the Creative Cause Brahmā, in her Akashic form of the Universal Soul — as philosophically a Maya, and the cause of human Maya. But this view does not prevent a person from believing in its existence so long as it lasts...for one Mahamanvantara; nor from applying Akasha, the radiation of Mulaprakriti, to practical pur-poses, connected as the World-Soul is with all natural phenomena, known or unknown to science.
>
> *Ibid.,* i 10

The immortality of the ray from the One Source applies only to this vast cosmic epoch. Even the highest gods — the Dhyani Buddhas, the Manus, the Rishi-Prajapati and the planetary spirits — live for only one great period of manifestation. One may think of them as forms and intelligences superior in every way to human beings, but when the *Mahamanvantara* ends, they are reabsorbed. After an existence of myriads upon myriads of years, they pass into a *laya* state, becoming sleeping points within the night of non-manifestation. In the *Mahapralaya* all the elements and hierarchies involved in manifestation become reabsorbed into the One. If this reabsorption applies to the gods, men and women can surely cooperate with it. There is, after all, nothing to be afraid of, because whatever the object of one's fears, it will eventually be dissolved. Secondly, there is nothing to depend on, because whatever the crutch of one's weaknesses, it will some time be reabsorbed.

Instead of placing one's reliance upon ultimately ephemeral forms, no matter how abstract, one should awaken and strengthen a sense of spiritual solidarity with the Great Breath. To begin to become attuned to the Great Breath in consciousness means re-educating all aspects of one's being. This demands much time and hard work owing to the vast numbers of miseducated life-atoms in one's vestures. Through *tanha* and *ahankara*, masses of these miseducated elementals conjoined with brain electricity have left astral grooves, memories of mortality and insufficiency, of limitation and finitude. Because of this fragmentation and discontinuity of consciousness, one constantly tends to look outside oneself for that upon which one may rely. Owing to this exteriorization of all the sense organs and faculties, one has virtually no acquaintance with the vast internal range of these organs. The *deva*-sight and *deva*-hearing, the sense of inner touch, are scarcely accessible to the self-crippled victims of *ahankara*. Thus, as human beings withdraw identification from the lower forms of *ahankara*, they can learn to inhabit self-consciously the stream of divine consciousness of the gods.

If even the gods exist only sempiternally, but to be reabsorbed at the end of the *Mahamanvantara*, this is certainly true of all human beings — *unless they become self-consciously immortal in spirit.* Man is greater than the gods. If one grasps the immensity of Gupta Vidya and its teaching in relation to triune SPACE, one will realize that it is not only possible to revolutionize one's thinking, feeling and breathing in relation to the vestures, raising them to a divine level. It is also possible to abide self-consciously in the Self-Existence of *Sat-Chit-Ananda*. This is the ultimate meaning of Krishna's affirmation that those who worship the gods go to the gods and "those who worship me come unto me." Beyond the realms of the gods, beyond *nidana* and *maya*, is the transcendent and absolute ground of all causality.

> The Secret Doctrine...postulates a 'One Form of Existence' as the basis and source of all things. But perhaps the phrase, the 'One Form of Existence,' is not altogether correct. The Sanskrit word is Prabhavapyaya, 'the place, or rather plane, whence emerges the origination, and into which is the resolution of all things.'...The Puranic Commentators explain it by Karana — 'Cause' — but the Esoteric philosophy, by the *ideal spirit of that cause.* It is, in its secondary stage, the Svabhavat of the Buddhist philosopher, the eternal cause and effect, omnipresent yet abstract, the self-existent plastic Essence and the root of all things, viewed in the same dual light as the Vedantin views his Parabrahm and Mulaprakriti, the one under two aspects.
>
> *Ibid.*, i 46

During the long night of non-manifestation, when the previous objective universe has dissolved into that *Karana* and is held in solution in space, which is filled with the unconscious pulsation of the Great Breath, the One Form of Existence is in causeless, dreamless sleep.

> The Father-Mother are the male and female principles in root-nature, the opposite poles that manifest in all things on every plane of Kosmos, or Spirit and Substance, in a less allegorical aspect, the resultant of which is the Universe, or the Son. They are 'once more One' when in 'The Night of Brahmā,' during Pralaya, all in the objective Universe has returned to its one primal and eternal cause, to reappear at the following Dawn — as it does periodically. 'Karana'—eternal cause—was alone. To put it more plainly: Karana is alone during the 'Nights of Brahmā.'
>
> *Ibid.*, i 41

The All-Presence of that *Karana* is sensed by the opened eye of the Dangma or Mahatma, which is one in consciousness with the ideal spirit of that cause, unrestricted and unlocatable through any relationality to the dormant planes of the sleeping cosmos. In principle, self-conscious immortality in Spirit extends beyond even cosmic epochs, beyond the sempiternity of the gods and beyond the largest cycles of involvement and reabsorption.

Pure unalloyed consciousness is unmodified by all macrocosmic and microcosmic existence, is untouched by relationality at every level of manifestation and time. This affirmation of the pure eternity of Spirit is the central teaching given to all souls who seek to enter the silence of the Divine Dark and experience the reality of the unmanifest. If one senses the possibility of rising to and remaining in that consciousness, then one will begin to awaken the mystical sense of inner touch in relation to the impalpable *Akasha*, the ethereal substratum which interpenetrates all life in every atom and form. It is through this highest and finest veil upon pure SPACE, upon Deity itself or *Parabrahm*, that the Mahatmic magic of transmutation works. The more one uses this teaching to awaken a deeper sense of reality and self-existence, the more one may comfortably dispense with all the subtle ways in which maya controls human beings through the *nidanas* and the concatenation of causes.

> Whatever plane our consciousness may be acting in, both we and the things belonging to that plane are, for the time being, our only realities. As we rise in the scale of development we perceive that during the stages through which we have passed we mistook shadows for realities, and the upward progress of the Ego is a series of progressive awakenings, each advance bringing with it the idea that now, at last, we have reached 'reality'; but only when we shall have reached the absolute Consciousness, and blended our own with it, shall we be free from the delusions produced by Maya.
>
> *Ibid.*, i 40

The realization of consciousness beyond all maya cannot conceivably be understood as a once-and-for-all process for any human being in any given incarnation. Yet if human beings have lived on earth for millions upon millions of years, distilling the pure spiritual essence of consciousness through myriad lives, they should not underestimate their noetic possibilities as men and women of meditation. By receiving the sovereign, sacrificial Teaching for the sake of serving all humanity and aiding in the divine evolution of Ideas, one may become an authentic co-worker with Nature and a true servant of "the Boundless Age" of Amitabha. By awakening the spirit of compassion, one may recover the memories of initiations in past lives that are locked in the *karana sharira*. Then one may nurture fresh flowers of devotion, AUM in action, to be consecrated to the eternal incognizable *Karana*, the ever-acting Causeless Cause.

THE LIGHT OF THE LOGOS

Each atom has seven planes of being or existence, we are taught; and each plane is governed by its specific laws of evolution and absorption. Ignorant of any, even approximate, chronological data from which to start in attempting to decide the age of our planet or the origin of the solar system, astronomers, geologists, and physicists are drifting with each new hypothesis farther and farther away from the shores of fact into the fathomless depths of speculative ontology. The Law of Analogy in the plan of structure between the trans-Solar systems and the intra-Solar planets, does not necessarily bear upon the finite conditions to which every visible body is subject, in this our plane of being. In Occult Science this law is the first and most important key to Cosmic physics; but it has to be studied in its minutest details and, 'to be turned seven times,' before one comes to understand it. Occult philosophy is the only science that can teach it.

The Secret Doctrine, i 150 - 151

T he Law of Analogy provides the primary key to philosophical comprehension and spiritual unfoldment in the sevenfold cosmos. Its noumenal core is irradiated with *Daiviprakriti*, the invisible light manifested through Ishwara, the Logos, as well as the unutterable potency of Vach, the Verbum in its supernal essence *(Para)*. The visible universe, constituted by Vach in its objective or *vaikhari* aspect, veils this core through a screen of appearances that are essentially illusory, though they endure for immense periods of manvantaric time. There is an inherent logic to the invisible cosmos, governing the internal relations that pertain to supersensuous states of consciousness and the planes of homogeneous substance. This archetypal logic also regulates the external relations of form and change in the endless series of permutations and combinations in the visible world. Only by proceeding from within without, by first gaining insight into the internality of these fundamental relations, can one fully grasp the world of external relations.

Just as ontology determines the order of knowing, so too it establishes the ethical and psychological nature of bondage and freedom. The more one is preoccupied with externalities and external relations, the more one is trapped within the realm of effects. One is captive to the mayavic succession that seems to be ever changing but also has a false stability or reflected reality. The more one is enmeshed in the web of appearances and the tyranny of the trivial, the farther one is from sovereignty, self-conquest and choice in the most fundamental sense. Lacking any self-originating power, a person caught in the maelstrom may appear to command raging forces, but this is an illusion. The person has merely become a focal point for the psychic *turba*, the emotional perturbations of enslaved beings. On the other hand, any individual could intently reflect upon the ascending triangle of the eyes and the crown of the head, and the descending triangle of the eyes and the mouth. These triads correspond to interior relations in consciousness, which may be unravelled through repeated efforts to cognize a point enclosed by an ever-moving circumference. When one begins to train the mind to think in terms of these invisible realities and the dynamic logic of their internal relations, one can come to see how forms convert into each other according to an essential mode of unfoldment. Through deepened perception, one will discover how people are caught up at the surface level of external events, but also, through daily meditation, one will penetrate conceptual representations of realities which are hidden.

Penetrating perception and sustained meditation are elusive and difficult for minds that have overdeveloped the analytic tendency to dissect and classify. This habitual inclination is bound up with *brantidarshana*, false apprehension in the realm of changing phenomena. A helpful start in the use of analogy and correspondence, vividly illustrated by George William Russell (A.E.), is to consider the hour of twilight, which corresponds in each day to the twilight of an incarnation as well as to the *sandhyas* that mark the seasons of Nature and the cycles of manifestation. Sit down calmly at twilight and starting from some awareness of the apparent passage of day into night, think of the significant transitions in states of consciousness that can be analogically applied to greater and greater scales of being. One might ponder the *Stanzas of Dzyan* which intimate extremely subtle differences which are nearly indistinguishable because of the enormous height of abstraction. Until Stanza VI, sloka 4, we have reference to that which goes beyond the solar system, applying to all possible systems in a *Mahamanvantara*. This degree of universality is largely incomprehensible to human minds conditioned by the dominant plane of consciousness and the prevailing density of the present Round. Therefore the succeeding verses apply only to our solar system, and even they are quite recondite. The practical teaching, given from the most ancient times to the person who truly wants to make a beginning, is to devote some period in the day to reflect calmly upon great cycles in reference to the cosmos, the process of incarnation and the whole of humanity. Those who do this will begin to develop an intuitive sense of the archetypal nature of what is essential in human evolution, and gradually come to discern fundamental internal relations which were previously obscured by surface appearances and unconnected events.

Of the fourfold forms of Vach, the *madhyama* form, corresponding to the Light of the Logos, is transformed by Fohat, the androgynous energy in the objective universe which connects subjective thought with the potentialities locked up in abstract matter. Imagine a person sitting before a lump of inert clay and having only a vague mental image of a pot. What is it that will connect the nebulous image of the pot in the uncollected mind of the person, who has perhaps never done any pottery before, and a mass of inert clay which in itself cannot convey anything? While there is no ostensible connection, nonetheless, if the person becomes sufficiently concentrated and intently concerned to give visible representation to the indefinite image, a point will come when the person may, out of that inward intensity, take hold of the materials at hand and it might almost seem as if the inert clay could speak. This is readily recognized by individuals who are bursting with the energy of creative imagination. The entire universe is governed by noumenal thought, which is the supreme source of all energy. It is through intensity of concentrated thought that any self-conscious being creates a current of ideation, a flow of energy that will enable some mode of manifestation to occur. Owing to this fundamental relation of pure thought to potent ideation, it is axiomatic in the arenas of creativity and choice that the more calm one is, the more dynamic one can be; the more abstract one's thought, the greater is one's capacity to create in the realm of the concrete; the more one is absorbed into the homogeneous, into the undifferentiated darkness, the greater the precision with which one can work in the realm of contrast, heterogeneity and differentiation.

The mystery of *Kriyashakti*, of creative imagination, is indeed incommunicable by a person who has truly experienced it to those who have not, but every human being, simply by remaining alive and moving about in the world, is unwittingly participating in this dynamic process of converting thought-energy into material motion. This is why most people can do many things which they cannot conceptualize. Even with perfectly ordinary movements, a person who skilfully moves in a certain way in response to an idea cannot recapitulate that movement as a connected series of discrete steps. If one tried to think out the movement ahead of time, one might even be immobilized. Everyday self-consciousness is extremely constricted through preoccupation with names and forms and events, comparisons and contrasts, but also the world of differentiation in which there seems to be a wall of separation between objects and between subjects. Owing to the common tendency to take all this for granted, the mind ossifies as an inert, static and passive recipient of impressions, for which creativity and self-sovereignty remain elusive.

To dislodge the host of habits that have become ingrained in one's modes of thought and life, it is essential to burst the boundaries of personal identity. One must intensely question the conventional conception of existence, seeking the deeper meanings of birth and death, action and inaction, day and night, not only for oneself, but also in relation to humanity and the cosmos. Exercising one's divine prerogative as a thinking being, one can choose seminal seed-ideas as the preliminary basis for impersonal meditation. Such daily reflection must ponder ideas and themes that are universal but at the same time they must be brought to bear upon the uniqueness of one's own condition, understanding and experience. By dynamizing ideas through contemplation, one comes to view the simplest acts of life in terms of the potency of ideation. Once this point is reached, although it brings the recognition that there is very much one does not know, it also awakens a longing to learn which is sufficiently strong to overcome the inertia and defeatism of ignorance. This mental posture prepares one for persistent efforts to meditate upon primal abstract ideas, which are cosmic in scope and without reference to the phenomenal world of manifestation and change.

At the initial stage, ideas like absolute abstract Space, Motion and Duration might seem to be merely figurative terms, but by repeatedly returning to these themes, by undistractedly thinking them through, the mind will stretch until it begins to conceive a state of being that transcends all familiar distinctions. One will even experience a peculiar pain, but this is a welcome sign of the beleaguered resistance of whole sets of habitual tendencies which would, if passively allowed to run their course, restrict one's horizon to a vegetative, stagnant and meaningless existence. Pain is inevitable when by intense thought, by *iccha* or inclination, and by the determination to enjoy the experience of uninterrupted continuous meditation, one compels masses of solidified elementals in the vestures to break up and disperse. As the channels become unclogged, and as one persists, these discarded elementals can be rapidly replaced through the fervour and strength of meditative practice. Subtler energies, noumenal ideas, imponderable forces, can be drawn into the voidness created by the exodus of elements which were clogging the astral channels and spiritual centres. The chief obstacle to steadfast persistence in meditation is the fear, engendered by ignorance, of non-existence. While such fear can assume pathological forms, it is an unavoidable accompaniment of any identification with the shadow that obscures the light of the Higher Self.

At the highest level light is both a precursor and a successor to the Logos, and allegorical theogony speaks of it as being both the mother and the daughter of the Logos. While the Logos is itself the *pasyanti* form of Vach, and its cosmically diffused light is the *madhyama* form, prior to both is the *Para* form of Vach correlative with *Mulaprakriti,* the noumenal Root of Nature as an aspect of *Parabrahm.* This highest aspect of Vach is an invisible supernal light latent within *Mulaprakriti,* which is not the Light of the Logos because there is not yet a creative Logos, or a manifested cosmos. *Para Vach* is a light that is potentially present within the darkness of *Mulaprakriti,* the indestructible and eternal essence of matter, which is like a vast etheric ocean of inconceivably subtle substance. When that primordial light is focused at a point, which is called the Spiritual Sun, the intense concentration of universal potential light-energy conceives the prototype of a whole system of worlds that will come into manifestation. In the subsequent process of gestation the concentrating light-centre of the Logos diffuses a light which is different from the pregenetic noumenal light that is ontologically prior to the creative Logos. The diffused Light of the Logos determines the rates of vibration and the relations between molecules and atoms throughout the evolving cosmos. Light, then, passes in and through the focusing centre of the Logos, emerging into another realm which, though dense when compared to the light that precedes the Logos, is still so subtle and ethereal that the astral senses can give no impression of it. It can only be conceived by negating sense-perception and disengaging from all sensory images of light and dark. When at a higher stage of meditation the creative Logos, the invisible centre of the cosmos, is perceived through the medium of the light that issues from it, then a critical state is reached involving the capacity of self-consciousness to release the active energy that is the propelling power of manifestation. Meditation is thus the basis of true magic.

The archetypal logic of what must be between the ever-unknowable unmanifest germ of manifestation, and the noumenal manifestation which is several degrees prior to the phenomenal world of change and appearance, intimates the combined mystery of self-existence and self-awareness. The expansion and contraction of consciousness at the highest conceivable level must correspond to primal relations between atoms and molecules, to primal sounds and colours, and to primal radiations of light. They also correspond to fundamental and ineffably subtle conceptions of being which are radically different from the sense of being that the personal consciousness assumes in relation to physical sounds, colours and contrasts of light and shade in a world of seemingly distinct subjects and objects. At its root, self-consciousness aspires to a realm of inexhaustible creativity where the possible worlds are so assuredly infinite that it is also a realm where there is a minimum of manifestation. When human beings have by initial attempts at contemplation discerned something about meditation (*dhyana*) as the basis of the entire universe of spiritual reality, they then truly begin an inward journey through ever-deepening perceptions and conceptions.

Though all the languages of the world are largely misleading, one can still find, hidden amidst the ignorantly transmitted words and sounds of shadowy beings, pale reflections of the noumenal realm of reality. Awareness of this realm, even when one is still largely captive to a shadowy and derivative sense of being, can be of immense benefit to one who really starts to withdraw inwards and increase spiritual wakefulness. Paradoxically, one has both to withdraw from what looks like activity and at the same time, instead of becoming drowsy, one has to become much more wakeful. Many people have great difficulty in doing this, because they have become so dependent for a sense of being alive upon hectic involvement in the phenomenal world of visible effects. Through engendered habits, the centres of action have become so clogged with disordered elementals associated with the sense-organs that they merely fall asleep when they try to withdraw inwards. The only recourse is to generate a profound state of wakefulness from as high a level as possible, and then decisively burn out the matrices and patterns through which the lethargy of non-learning has become consolidated.

There is a vital connection between the Logos and logic, Divine Spirit and human reason, between light and learning. In the oldest universities the mantramic motto was: *May we be illuminated.* This is deeply significant. Learning connotes the reception of light; its essential mode is always sacred, subtly erotic and spiritual. Everything that obstructs the innate willingness to learn of the immortal soul is redundant. It is merely some aspect of delusive ignorance, inert and static, but also chaotic, dark and nebulous. The immortal soul's intense desire to learn, to discover meanings potentially present in our world of seeming confusion and succession, can release the hidden creative spark. If this is sought in silence but with complete faith and through concentrated effort, it will soon become a steady flame with which one may choose, see connections and make combinations beyond those provided by the sensory realm. Without ostentation one may begin to enrich one's inner life by quickening the noetic activity of untrammelled consciousness. It is significant that even at its lowest inverted levels there is some analogy in the operation of self-consciousness to its activity on the highest planes.

The personal parasitic consciousness, fraught with false assumptions about the birth and death of the body, induces a sense of reality vampirically by drawing constant attention to itself, by being observed from the outside. This is merely the result of the acute inability at the lower level to generate or sustain a firm basis of self-existence. But there is always that slender thread in this fragmented consciousness which can be awakened through the therapeutic shock of recognizing a superior mode of cognition. Such a recognition will be painful because it becomes mandatory to dictate terms to the fickle mind and repeatedly direct it towards a seemingly distant goal. It would be better to do this at the initial stage of awakening, for the longer it is delayed, the more difficult it appears to be.

One must use this teaching constructively to create a magnetic field of noetic energy replete with living potential, wherein the power of choice is enormously strengthened, and one may see hidden possibilities in everything around. To do this effectively one must periodically void the entire scene, void any sense of self, void every lower conception. The more one can void and negate, the more one may see why, to the mystic and the Initiate, so-called bare space is much more full than seemingly populous space. One will begin to appreciate the paradoxical but compassionate recordings of advanced beings who have gained a vast experience of the sixth and fifth planes of matter and consciousness. Having spoken of the myriad forces of visible Nature as merely the differentiated aspects of absolute abstract Motion, and after intimating the modifications of the motion of the Great Law at seven invisible points, H.P. Blavatsky proceeds to depict the occult conception of negation, which is crucial to true magic.

> We have said that Laya is what Science may call the Zero-point or line; the realm of absolute negativeness, or the one real absolute Force, the NOUMENON of the Seventh State of that which we ignorantly call and recognise as 'Force'; or again the Noumenon of Undifferentiated Cosmic Substance which is itself an unreachable and unknowable object to finite perception; the root and basis of all states of objectivity and subjectivity too; the neutral axis, not one of the many aspects, but its centre.
>
> *The Secret Doctrine*, i 148

Then, after considering the concept of a "neutral centre", she adds:

> The *Primordial Atom* (anu) cannot be multiplied either in its pregenetic state, or its primogeneity; therefore it is called 'SUM TOTAL,' figuratively, of course, as that 'SUM TOTAL' is boundless. That which

> is the abyss of nothingness to the physicist, who knows
> only the world of visible causes and effects, is the
> boundless Space of the Divine *Plenum* to the Occultist.
>
> *Ibid.*, i 148

It is extremely difficult for those whose consciousness is permanently established on the highest planes to communicate with people who are systematically misled by the chaotic crowding that pertains to the fourth, the third and second planes. It is difficult to show the deluded that a vastly richer sense of reality is accessible when one negates, withdraws and meditates. Hence, the pristine and supremely benevolent Light of the Logos is sometimes compared to a supernal grace or gift that is only given to those who seek it with sufficient ardour and faith. In such comparisons there is a deeply suggestive analogy between Kwan Yin as the Divine Voice, the Mother of Mercy and Knowledge, and Kwan Yin, the noble nun in the time of Tsong-Kha-Pa. Kwan Yin's great pledge of renunciation and service is the spontaneous expression of an exalted state of consciousness, of pure compassion which in Buddhist metaphysics lies at the very heart of all reality, the cosmic Kwan Yin that is the same as Brahma Vach.

The symbolism of Kwan Yin enshrines cosmic truths which are dimly mirrored in human life everywhere. There is something of Kwan Yin in every human being. There is that audible voice of compassion, of tenderness and truth even in the most brutalized and aggressive of natures. This precious element of pure tenderness is indestructible. It is coeval with the whole of life, and without it there would be no life whatsoever. By calmly reflecting upon the ultimate source of this diffused tenderness, gentleness and compassion, one will discover that it has its own melodious and moisturizing effect upon the hidden centres of divine and human consciousness. One will readily see that it is delusion which induces hardness and harshness, inflexibility and lack of generosity. When one deeply meditates upon the well-springs of compassion in visible and invisible Nature, one can hear the Divine Voice of Vach, the verbum resonating everywhere and at all times. This is what *yogins* seek to do through severe training: to reach a point where through the *anahata,* the indestructible centre, they effortlessly experience the inaudible hum of the OM at all times. They are attuned to what the Chinese call the *Kung,* the Great Tone of Nature, which is like the *F* note but is also more than merely a particular note in the audible scale because it resonates equally through the many octaves of existence. When one experiences the constant reverberation within the human heart of that which is also at the core of the whole cosmos, then oneness with the cosmos and all of life is no longer a phrase, but the supreme fact of real existence. Lesser facts regarding separation and differentiation are seen to be unreal ripples on the surface of appearances, no longer able to interrupt one's attention. One can truly become a grateful witness to the secret work of Kwan Yin as the presiding goddess of the active forces in Nature, nourishing and sustaining all.

> She is male and female *ad libitum,* as Eve is with Adam. And she is a form of Aditi — the principle higher than *Ether* — in Akasa, the synthesis of all the forces in Nature; thus Vach and Kwan-Yin are both the magic potency of Occult sound in Nature and Ether — which 'Voice' calls forth Sien-Tchan, the illusive form of the Universe out of Chaos and the Seven Elements.
>
> *Ibid.,* i 137

The closer one approaches in meditation to the fusion of the knower, the known and the process of knowing, the greater is one's awareness of the magical potency within the noumenal forces of Nature. Ordinary understanding of forces like electricity, light, heat and sound yields some measure of control on the lower planes, yet relies upon a sharp contrast between the observer and the field of observation. When conceptualizing fields of energies and mapping them out, these are regularly treated as being outside and independent of human wills. Hence, most people, when they switch on a light, imagine that what takes place has no relation, or at best some external mechanical relation, to themselves. There are, of course, those who assuredly know that one should never switch on a light, kindle a flame, or indeed invoke any of the powers of Nature, without profound gratitude. If human beings could be taught that they should be spontaneously grateful at every point, and that they should make continual obeisance for the abundance and bounty they witness every moment, then they would become more self-consciously aware of the archetypal process which is re-enacted not only all around, but within them constantly.

Every lighting of a lamp is rich with resonances in human and universal consciousness, ranging from the incandescent manvantaric dawn to the kindling of *Manas* in incipient humanity, and even to the flashes of intuition that guide the footsore pilgrim through the labyrinth of life. To lack gratitude for any one of these is to be alienated from them all, such is the inward continuity of visible Nature. To sense no difference between the divine Light of the Logos and the modest light of the table lamp that illumines one's book, is to begin to live an inner life, because one is aware of what is going on archetypally and cosmically in reference to higher states of consciousness. This is how one inhabits that field of spiritual awakening which is the hidden force behind evolution. Setting aside the notion that the forces of Nature are generated by objective matter, or are merely modes of its apparent motion, Occult Science perceives behind phenomenal forces elemental agencies which correlate with the elements of pure primordial Matter and are directed in their action by Divine Intelligences. Drawing upon the symbolism of the chariot, H.P. Blavatsky likens the objective forces to the noise of the passing vehicle, and the elemental causes to the driver within the chariot.

> The sensation of light is like the sound of the rolling wheels — a purely phenomenal effect, having no existence outside the observer; the proximate exciting cause of the sensation is comparable to the driver — a supersensuous state of matter in motion, a Nature-Force

or Elemental. But, behind even this, stand — just as the owner of the carriage directs the driver from within — the higher and *noumenal* causes, the *Intelligences* from whose essence radiate these States of '*Mother*', generating the countless milliards of Elementals or psychic Nature-Spirits, just as every drop of water generates its physical infinitesimal Infusoria.

Ibid., i 146-147

Just as the forces of objective Nature are traceable to their origin in pre-cosmic ideation, so too are the compound elements of physical Nature the transitory offspring of the archetypal Seven Elements evolved from the one Element — *Mulaprakriti*, "the Mother" who "sleeps, yet is ever breathing". The specializations of the Seven Elements in relation to the earth represent a degree of differentiation and complexity well removed from Universal Substance, but even this stage remains *terra incognita* to those whose conception of matter is bound by the physical senses. Noting the prescient questioning by William Crookes regarding the alleged homogeneity of the chemical elements, H.P. Blavatsky indicates that the ancients were well aware of the potentialities, correlative functions and attributes of the sub-elements entering into Air, Water, Earth and Fire, and that alchemy rests upon such knowledge. The danger, as she points out, is that exclusive attention to classifying the phenomenal varieties of matter will blind one to the inherently noumenal nature of its essence. One should not make the false assumption that matter as it is known to the present senses is the only form of matter that exists. All monads involved in the crucible of evolution have been engaged with matter in other states that have nothing to do with matter as is now known. Furthermore, matter in turn will be different in the future.

If no physical intellect is capable of counting the grains of sand covering a few miles of seashore; or to fathom the ultimate nature and essence of those grains, palpable and visible on the palm of the naturalist, how can any materialist limit the laws changing the conditions and being of the atoms in primordial chaos, or know anything certain about the capabilities and potency of their atoms and molecules before and after their formation into worlds? These changeless and eternal molecules — far thicker in space than the grains on the ocean shore — may differ in their constitution along the line of their planes of existence, as the soul-substance differs from its vehicle, the body.

Ibid., i 150

To begin to understand that what are called 'water' and 'fire' are not really what Water and Fire are in their *Atma-Buddhi-Manas* is also to begin to understand oneself as an *Atma-Buddhi-Manasic* being. If one can instill this recognition and make it strong, but also appreciate that there is *Atma-Buddhi-Manas* in everything, this will bring about an immense sense of wonder and calm. All rush involves the cruelty and violence of ignorance, and produces harsh painful creakings in the astral form and aura of those who become addicted to chaotic elementals. While it is deeply uncomfortable for serene and wise souls to be in the presence of such disturbed natures, nonetheless out of unremitting devotion to the Kwan Yin in every soul, they continue ceaselessly in the sacrificial task of transferring the higher life-atoms to all in need. Once one can reach out to the noumenal intelligent causes radiating the elemental forces of Nature and generating the endless streams of subtle lives, one is touched by the fire of cosmic ideation. As these wonderful but hidden aspects of the world become real, the conception and the quality of one's life and breath undergo subtle transformations. The force inherent in a living person's breath emanates from the living and thinking entity that breathed, whether the impulse originated consciously or unconsciously. No more than any other force in Nature is breath a mode of objective matter in apparent motion. Further, the level of apperception of the sense-organs is connected with a certain level of breathing. When one becomes more sensitive and ethereal in one's perceptions, by learning to hold and make active within oneself increasingly abstract and subtle rhythms and more universal conceptions, this will refine and transmute one's breathing. One can bring about changes in the potent centres of the subtler vestures through the breaking down of habitual modes and lower levels of differentiation.

Consolidated matrices can always be dissolved by collecting their constituents back together at a *laya* point of neutral voidness, which marks where differentiation at some level stops, and where a higher level of differentiation can begin. Because there are these zero-points, one can break down a habitual scale or level of differentiation and begin another. For this reason the arcane teachings emphasize the alchemical reduction of all the elements to the original, universal Element, to the One that is the substratum of them all, the *prima materia* which is, as the seventh state of matter, total latency, total negation and total non-activity. Owing to the participation of every single element of life in the seventh plane of matter-consciousness, they are each pervaded by *laya* points, and it is always possible to void particular combinations and levels and start again. To learn to do this at will, successfully and continuously, requires a fundamental change in the tropism of one's mind and nature, patterns of reaction in thought and speech that have been cut like grooves into the psyche by persistent habit. The misuses of language and the general overuse of sound inevitably obscure the Light of the Logos and block the invisible channels of consciousness. These prevailing irregularities must be made smooth patiently and gently, with the firm recognition that all inward reform is undertaken on behalf of, and in indebtedness to, Vach and Kwan Yin. One must assume the standpoint of the owner of the carriage directing the driver from within, and as Robert Crosbie said repeatedly, "See yourself as the Perceiver." One must recognize always that the real Perceiver has nothing to do with the shadowy self, or what is too commonly verbalized.

The real Perceiver is the immortal soul, and one must strive to witness the world through its eyes alone, returning to its vantage point repeatedly until all compulsiveness and forgetfulness are overcome. Then when one ponders the sacred teachings of the *Book of Dzyan,* its voice will speak to what one is directly experiencing. One will recognize its authentic accents in accounting for the evolution and absorption of worlds, the dissociation and reassociation of lives at the most cosmic and fundamental levels. Imbued with the spirit of light and learning, and steeped in the archetypal logic of the unfoldment of the universe from within without, one will savour the analogous reflections of the Logos at every level of the world, until one comes to have a totally altered way of looking at matter and mind, space and time, motion and force, light and electricity, heat, water, air and, above all, fire. With an ever-increasing sense of the invisible world, one will recognize what is noumenal and causal within it, in relation to which the visible world is that realm in which the only point or purpose of breathing is a constant spirit of thanksgiving.

THE LOGOS AND MAN

Man was regarded in several systems as the third Logos.
The esoteric meaning of the word Logos *(speech or word,*
Verbum) *is the rendering in objective expression, as in a*
photograph, of the concealed thought. The Logos *is the mirror*
reflecting DIVINE MIND, *and the Universe is the mirror of*
the Logos, though the latter is the esse *of that Universe. As*
the Logos *reflects* all *in the Universe of Pleroma, so man*
reflects in himself all that he sees and finds in his *Universe,*
the Earth.

The Secret Doctrine, ii 25

The sacred mantram *"the Logos in the Cosmos and the God in Man"* is more than a cryptic algebraic formula for the correlation of forces between cosmic Nature and the human principles. It intimates the identity in *esse* of the ever-present matrix of all worlds and the sovereign immortal spirit of Man. The complete realization of this close union and harmonious concord is the fruition of the Hermetic discipline of conscious invocation of the Invisible Sun, which alone can unveil the manifold Logoic mystery of the Tetraktys. As there is no ultimate ontological distinction between divine and human nature, every sincere effort to comprehend the function of the triple Logoi within and beyond the cosmos involves a self-conscious awakening of the afflatus of the higher Triad in man. This primary fact of spiritual life stands behind the teaching of *The Voice of the Silence* that "Thou canst not travel on the Path before thou hast become that Path itself." In order to commence this journey properly, it is initially necessary to connect the luminous conception of the three Logoi with an elevated and expanded view of the creative activity of human intelligence. As that intelligence is progressively refined through the patient practice of *Buddhi Yoga,* one can become an alchemical apprentice aiding the divine evolution of ideas, the fohatic nerve-current of cosmic and human evolution. *Jnanasakti*, *Kriyasakti* and *Itchasakti* constitute the triune force of spiritual ideation, volition and energy.

The metaphysical meaning of the term 'logos' as "the rendering in objective expression, as in a photograph, of the concealed thought" points to the magical process of translating an idea into form. Owing to the mutual interpenetration of planes of manifestation, this archetypal activity pertains to different levels of abstraction and concretion, to essential noumena as well as to ephemeral phenomena. Ontologically, the process of Becoming requires the seeming differentiation into three Logoi: the unmanifest LOGOS, the inexhaustible Spirit of the Universe; the manifest Logos or creative Demiurge, the all-pervading Soul of the Universe; and Man representing the Third Logos. Metapsychologically, this implies the distinction between Nous — apprehending, noetic and in close affinity with τὸ ἀγαθόν (tò Agathon) — and Dianoia — comprehending, phrenic and synonymous with Logos. Even the colloquial and generic use of 'logos' by the ancient Greeks to refer to ordinary speech, thought and reason, as well as to the creative activity of artists and artisans, conveys something of the esoteric meaning. The present period of technological innovation, based upon the partial intuitions of perceptive but obscure pioneers, affords numerous analogues of Logoic function, especially in optics, microelectronics and genetics.

It is, however, not easy to discern the subtle connections between the metaphysical imagination and the critical breakthroughs in scientific thought. Intuitive perception requires the numinous intelligence implicit in the concept of 'logos' itself. Unlike the pedestrian skills involved in contemporary tests that measure one's 'intelligence quotient', but which is largely a matter of association of ideas and symbols, true intelligence is rooted in spiritual wakefulness. Spiritual perspicacity is connected with the capacity to alter perspective deliberately, and sharply contrasts with psychic fixation, passivity and monotony. Without the ability to move the mind at will, it is impossible to choose constructively between alternative currents of ideation. Since *Prajna*, wisdom and insight, summons the ability to think the right thought in the right place and time, to lack intelligence, in this sense, is to be a helpless creature of circumstances.

A practical test of real intelligence at the ordinary level is one's ability to recognize and release the intelligence of others. The tendency to underestimate the intelligence of other human beings is inevitably the mark of insufficient intelligence and the cause of needless obstructions and wasteful conflicts between people. Every ancient tradition traced the diverse modes and degrees of intelligence exhibited throughout Nature to a single universal source susceptible only to noetic apprehension. The Kabbalists, for example,

> never cease to repeat that *primal intelligence* can never be understood. It cannot be comprehended, nor can it be located, therefore it has to remain nameless and negative. Hence the Ain-Soph — the 'UNKNOWABLE' and the 'UNNAMEABLE' — which, as *it* could not be made manifest, was conceived to emanate manifesting Powers. It is then with its *emanations alone that human intellect has to, and can deal.*
>
> *The Secret Doctrine,* ii 41

And it is out of these emanations that human intellect, which is the Light of the Logos awakened to self-consciousness, is constituted. By means of this One Light the monadic stream, *Monas,* evolves through all the phases of changing form and collective intelligence. Hence, within the human kingdom the measure of growth in intelligence is one's recognition of and respect for the kindred intelligence of every other Monad, whether human in fact or incipiently. Considered from the standpoint of primal intelligence, such an incredible reservoir of untapped energy exists in virtually every human being that the ostensive differences between people pale into insignificance before the sublime grandeur of spiritual creativity, which releases the potential for self-transcendence as well as self-actualization.

Noetic intelligence involves the capacity for making creative correlations, not in terms of mechanistic categories or limited conceptions of space, time and motion. Rooted in pre-cosmic substance and pure ideation, and symbolized in its successive stages by the arcane language of sound and light and number, it is only hinted at by notions of impressing, visualizing, photographing, projecting and mirroring. This mirroring faculty in its deepest sense is the paradigmatic function of Logoic activity. The profound teaching of St. Paul that "things visible are evidence of things invisible" points to the infinite reflective potency of the Logos in Nature and in Man. It is also the theurgic activity that enables one to make ideas come alive, because without the capacity to make ideas act upon the will there is no intelligence in the noetic sense. At the most fundamental philosophical level the Logos is the mysterious heart of cosmogenesis, for genesis is no mechanical generation but rather the emergence out of the eternal into time, from *esse* into *existence*, from BE-NESS into being.

> At the commencement of a great Manvantara, Parabrahm manifests as Mulaprakriti and then as the Logos. This Logos . . . constitutes the Basis of the SUBJECT-side of manifested Being, and is the source of all manifestations of individual consciousness. Mulaprakriti or Primordial Cosmic Substance, is the foundation of the OBJECT-side of things — the basis of all objective evolution and Cosmogenesis. Force, then, does not emerge with Primordial Substance from Parabrahmic Latency. It is *the transformation into energy of the supra-conscious thought of the Logos,* infused, so to speak, into the objectivation of the latter out of potential latency in the One Reality. Hence spring the wondrous laws of matter. . . . Force *succeeds* Mulaprakriti; but *minus* Force, Mulaprakriti is for all practical intents and purposes non-existent.
>
> *Ibid.,* ii 24-25

As this process is recapitulated at more manifest levels, the Second Logos or Demiurge and the Third Logos or Man arise, each the objective expression of that degree of the concealed Thought which it reflects or mirrors in itself. With each, the triadic *esse* gives way to the sevenfold *existence*, the combination ten or ⊕ 10, numerically and geometrically representing the descent and differentiation of light into the series of hebdomadic hierarchies symbolized by π. Each universe, world or planet has its own Logos, Lord or Eye manifesting sevenfold light. In geometrical language, for any place, the Logos manifesting as Light through the hebdomadic hierarchies delimits the manifested realm as a circle whose circumference exhibits the centre through the radii. The Ray is the mysterious proportional link between centre and circumference, between the Logos and cosmos, between God and Man. It is by this sevenfold Ray alone that the evolving Monads of a world can cognize the Logos through the Demiurge. The Third Logos is Mahat, the Divine Mind, Humanity ensouled by Manasaputras.

Within every Logoic sphere there is a mirroring from the relatively abstract to the relatively concrete, from the homogeneous to the heterogeneous, the realm of noumenal light to the phenomenal region of relative darkness. For eyes and senses accustomed to the shadowy concretions of a phenomenal world, the noumenal antecedents of that world are as darkness. Understood from the side of the concealed Thought, however, the phenomena of a world are but a ceaselessly shifting *maya*, a play of lesser lights against the bright white screen of Eternity. Owing to the inertia of the physical eye and its fixation on objective images, the physical world seems to be filled with enduring forms. From a subtler noumenal standpoint all these forms are comprehended as a tremendous whirl of life-atoms, dancing in and out of relation with each other in constant accord with the essences characteristic of their more noumenal origins. To begin to see this is to sense the activity of Nous which directly apprehends archetypal noumenal realities that cannot participate in manifestation except partially, and at many removes, through a series of reflections. Nous is like a sublime light behind a series of mirrors that finally yields reflected visible light.

To enter this plane of noetic light is to arouse *Buddhi Manas* through true meditation. To emerge from that plane retaining full awareness is to perceive a world that is far more wonderful than anything uninitiated artists could imagine. With the awakened eye one would see the world noumenally as composed of rays, octaves, hosts and spheres of light.

> *The Spheres of Being, or centres of life, which are isolated nuclei breeding their men and their animals, are numberless. . . .*
>
> *The nucleoles are eternal and everlasting; the nuclei periodical and finite. The nucleoles form part of the absolute. They are the embrasures of that black impenetrable fortress, which is for ever concealed from human or even Dhyanic sight. The nuclei are the light of eternity escaping therefrom.*
>
> *It is that* LIGHT *which condenses into the forms of the 'Lords of Being' — the first and the highest of which are, collectively,* JIVATMA, *or Pratyagatma* (said figuratively to issue from Paramatma. It is the Logos of the Greek philosophers — appearing at the beginning of every new Manvantara). *From these downwards — formed from the ever-consolidating waves of that light, which becomes on the objective plane gross matter — proceed the numerous hierarchies of the Creative Forces, some formless, others having their own distinctive form, others, again, the lowest (Elementals), having no form of their own, but assuming every form according to the surrounding conditions.*
>
> *Ibid.,* ii 33-34

The path towards transcendent awakening begins for human beings on the plane of the universe which mirrors the indwelling intelligence of the Demiurgic creative Logos. Looking at the stars, asking questions, quickening the mind through thinking and rethinking, one must learn to see the universe as the diffused differentiation of a hidden light, which is itself the reflection of Divine Mind. Uninvolved in its own manifestations, that Mind may be contacted only through its pristine ray in Monadic individuality, the awakened *Buddhi Manas* capable of becoming attuned to the *Buddhi Manas* of Nature. Only when one comes closer to the Divine Mind, *Mahat,* can one apprehend the full meaning of man's extraordinary prerogative as the Third Logos. Reaching ultimately to the most exalted conception of the creative possibilities of human nature, one will discover one's spiritual heredity and deepest *dharma* in the august company of the Manus and Rishis, the Dhyanis and Bodhisattvas, the informing Intelligences animating the various centres of being. Honouring in them the manvantaric manifestation of THAT which is indefinable, incomprehensible and immutable, one will understand that "man cannot know higher beings than his own 'progenitors'."

Humanity is so bountifully endowed by the Rishis, and therefore by Nature, that it has never been able to use more than a small fraction of its splendid inheritance. Just as the visible sun releases more energy in a split-second than humanity can use in a year, the Agnishwatha Pitris and the Ever-Living Human Banyan have given humanity more gifts than it can use over any epoch. The sacred teachings glitter with myriad diamond points of apperception for awakening noetic insight. But in order to use them effectively and make them come alive, the habitual *turba* of the psychic nature must be stilled. One must be calm, wide awake, relaxed and reverential. One must be Manasically attentive, relinquishing memories and anticipations, letting go of notions of success and failure and fixations tied to personal identity. All this must be dispersed into the astral light, for it has nothing to do with the Monad during its long pilgrimage on earth.

Man is not meant to propitiate elementals or mechanically perform rituals, but rather to elevate self-consciousness and establish a proper relation with divine ideas. As with the development of any faculty, the greater the exercise, the easier it will become. If one is truly serious about maturing spiritually and gaining the cool confidence to constitute oneself a chela, then one must concentrate and incarnate sacred teachings without idle and futile speculation about one's abilities and prospects. Ability inevitably grows with application, and with it the will to further application. In time, as psychospiritual centres gradually awaken in their natural and proportional order, one will be prepared to deal with higher levels of noetic energy. In order to hold, preserve and extend them, one will have to withdraw the mind repeatedly from the proclivities and delusions of the persona. In this way noetic insight will emerge, even if imperfectly mirrored on the plane of the phrenic and the psychic. One cannot leap immediately to the pure apprehension of Nous, but one may assuredly move in that direction in waking life. As one sincerely tries, unexpected and unsought help will come in a variety of ways, enabling one to see profounder and more numinous meanings as veil upon veil is lifted. The more one uses what one knows, the more meaning will come to one's aid, with a greater continuity of ardent aspiration.

As this discipline deepens and ripens into the practice of *Buddhi Yoga,* the living lineage and divine descent of each human Ego begins to assume a more precise meaning. Just as the seven Hierarchies of the invisible Logos constitute an indivisible creative impulse, the Demiurgic Host of the sun and the seven sacred planets are a single active potency in the world of forms. As the Spiritual Sun gives life to the entire Kosmos, the sun of our solar system gives life to the planets, and these in turn give life to the earth, to man, to the various Races and Sub-Races, and to the principles of human nature:

> *The Globe, propelled onward by the Spirit of the Earth and his six assistants, gets all its vital forces, life, and powers through the medium of the seven planetary Dhyanis from the Spirit of the Sun. They are his messengers of Light and Life.*
>
> *Like each of the seven regions of the Earth, each of the seven First-born* (the primordial human groups) *receives its light and life from its own especial Dhyani — spiritually, and from the palace* (house, the planet) *of that Dhyani physically; so with the seven great Races to be born on it. The first is born under the Sun; the second under Brihaspati* (Jupiter); *the third under Lohitanga* (the 'fiery-bodied', Venus, or Sukra); *the fourth, under Soma* (the Moon, our

Globe also, the Fourth Sphere being born under and from the Moon) *and Sani, Saturn, the Krura-lochana* (evil-eyed) *and the Asita* (the dark); *the fifth, under Budha* (Mercury).

So *also with man and every 'man' in man* (every principle). *Each gets its specific quality from its primary* (the planetary spirit), *therefore every man is a septenate* (or a combination of principles, each having its origin in a quality of that special Dhyani). *Every active power or force of the earth comes to her from one of the seven Lords.*

Ibid., ii 28-29

Because Man as the Third Logos reflects in himself all that he sees and finds in his universe, the earth, the awakening of the Light of the Logos in Man is a sacred process governed by the laws of cosmogenesis. The full awakening of *Buddhi Manas* is technically impossible without coming into conscious relation with the hierarchy of the informing Intelligences connected with Mercury-Budha-Hermes. These Rishis, Mahatmas, Dhyanis and Chohans, mirroring the Divine Mind on the plane of *Aditi-Akasha*, fulfil a necessary hierophantic role in relation to spiritual humanity. This was shown, for example, in the life of the emperor Julian, who prayed to the Occult Sun every night through the intercession of Mercury. Hermes, the evocator of souls,

is symbolised in Grecian mythology by one of the *dogs* (vigilance), which watch over the celestial flock (occult wisdom), or Hermes Anubis, or again Agathodaemon. He is the Argus watching over the Earth, and which the latter mistakes for the Sun itself. . . . As says Vossius: 'All the theologians agree to say that *Mercury and the Sun are one*. . . . He was the most eloquent and the most wise of all the gods, which is not to be wondered at, since *Mercury is in such close proximity to the Wisdom and the Word of God* (the Sun) that he was confused with both.' . . . The *Hermes-Sarameyas* of the Greeks is closely related to the Hindu *Saram* and *Sarameya*, the divine watchman,

'who watches over the golden flock of stars and solar rays.'
Ibid., ii 28

As a mind-being (Manasa), every person is inherently capable of expanding, heightening and refining consciousness through the noetic potency of the light of spiritual awareness. This light is in the minds and hearts of all humanity, but unless individuals orient themselves in the direction of its source in the Spiritual Sun and recognize their kinship with all other Rays, they will not be in a mental posture that is ready to receive Divine Wisdom. To do this they will have to pass before those watchmen and vigilant protectors of Brahma Vach and show an understanding of the impersonal laws that govern the realm of Initiations into the Mysteries.

Thus, whilst it is important and instructive to grasp the doctrine of the three Logoi philosophically, it is critically necessary to make these ideas come alive through meditation and moral sensitivity. Once the neophyte touches the higher energy-fields of Akashic ideation, this vibration begins to have a powerful effect upon the astral and physical vestures, affecting everything in one's experience including sense-perceptions. As it is imperative to familiarize oneself with the forces attendant upon these alchemical changes in consciousness, one must adopt self-chosen modes of Hermetic discipline. For some this will include forms of abstinence such as wise fasting. From all it will require silence rooted in reticence, deepening and enriching calm contemplation, altering the ratio between the unmanifest and the manifest in every arena. Actually doing this is quite difficult because of the constant pressure on the defensive personality to manifest, a tendency fostered by contemporary culture and aggravated by the deadweight of atavistic habits of thought and ahankaric speech. Nonetheless, through patient persistence in thoughtful withdrawal, one will become more precise in the performance of duty and develop a depth in one's inner states of consciousness as well as one's spontaneous responses.

Cultivating profound reverence and uttermost devotion, one

may come into communion with the Spiritual Sun, seeing its Ray within oneself as the golden cord of one's being, inseparable from the Ray in every other being. Then, using the *Gayatri* every day, one will over a period of time find spiritual knowledge spontaneously arising from within. As one turns to the sacred teachings of Gupta Vidya, it will seem as if they are evocative reminders of whole areas of untapped knowledge within oneself, but which can be summoned only for the sake of helping humanity, for such knowledge is a tapestry woven from those Rays. One will be able to draw upon soul-wisdom if one truly wants to elevate and enrich the quality of one's ideation for the sake of becoming selfless, voiding any sense of egoity in the persona, and becoming a pristine ray of light focussed upon the Spiritual Sun, the Dhyanis, the Mahatmas and the moral welfare of the entire human race. This is the perennial teaching of the greatest mystics, most of whom preferred not to refer openly to the Spiritual Sun and its relation to Χρυσο-φαής Ἑρμης, Hermes of golden light, whose true name they regarded as too sacred to be pronounced. They understood that behind what many people took to be merely fanciful names and fairy stories of the stars and planets, there were divine forces, the regents of invisible globes and planets, and they knew that these correspond to actual pedigrees and powers within every single human being. By gaining an intuitive sense of reverence for all the planets, for what they represent on the inner planes, and for their correspondences in the human constitution, one may begin to break down the seeming barrier between the cosmos and oneself, between selfhood and otherness in all beings.

It is the essential metaspiritual identity of all that is the basis of the self-conscious reunion of cosmos and man. As H.P. Blavatsky stated before pointing out the stature of man as the Third Logos, the entire teaching of cosmogenesis shows

> the genesis of Gods and men taking rise in, and from, one and the same Point, which is the One Universal, Immutable, Eternal, and absolute UNITY. In its primary manifested aspect we have seen it become: (1) in the

sphere of objectivity and Physics, Primordial Substance and Force (centripetal and centrifugal, positive and negative, male and female, *etc., etc.*); (2) in the world of Metaphysics, the SPIRIT OF THE UNIVERSE, or Cosmic Ideation, called by some the LOGOS.

Ibid., ii 24

From the same indivisible point, in the most supple medium of rarefied matter in abstract space, spring forth whole lines of activity upon the subjective and objective planes. These are synthesized in human beings because of the gift of self-consciousness which both enables one to make everything that is subjective an object of meditation, and everything that is objective a resource of the immortal subject through sifting and seeing it as not-Self. When this divine faculty implicit in the androgyne Light of the Logos in man is fully developed, it is ceaseless and omnidirectional in its creative beneficence. As a transitional stepping-stone in the painful ascent for human beings who have yet to free themselves from the drugged world of self-delusion, they have to start by setting aside time for contemplation and meditation, self-study and service. By so doing, they can begin to experience an authentic sense of the true Self and void the so-called reality of the not-Self, thereby taking a crucial step towards greater and deeper continuity between different states of consciousness.

Even though an individual may remain at the initial stages for several lives, it is still to some extent possible at the moment of death, if one has prepared properly, to establish a tropism towards the Spiritual Sun. When the main motive is the good of all, it is noetic, having an affinity for τὸ ἀγαθόν *(tò Agathon)*, and there can be help from the Brotherhood of Bodhisattvas to enable one to continue the effort more fruitfully in the next life. Then one can readily choose to adopt the highest matrices for the purified imagination and for profound meditation, having to do with the Pythagorean Triangle, its mystical completion which forms the Tetraktys, and the ever-invisible First Logos.

This LOGOS is the apex of the Pythagorean triangle.
When the triangle is complete it becomes the Tetraktis,
or the Triangle in the Square, and is the dual symbol of
the four-lettered *Tetragrammaton* in the manifested
Kosmos, and of its radical triple RAY in the
unmanifested, or its *noumenon.*

Ibid., ii 24

So sacred are these ideas that discursive reasoning can only obscure
the deeper awareness of their essential meaning. Yet there will be
those extremely rare individuals who are so struck
by the theurgic teaching that it will initiate a revolutionary
transformation of consciousness and of the human temple with
all its potential powers and gifts that are accessible to the immortal
soul. Those so touched would be willing and ready to summon
the same regenerative intuitions in others. In order to energize
the motivation that will make this possible, the aspirant must
reach out with undivided consciousness to the Spiritual Sun, the
Source of all life, because any lesser motivation and inspiration
will not provide the requisite continuity of Bodhisattvic
consciousness. The root reason why many persons cannot
maintain continuity of consciousness is that they do not truly love
humanity. They may foolishly mistake hazy sentimentality for such
love, but they cannot even really love themselves until they have
repeatedly asked themselves: Who am I? If one identifies with mere
shadows, one cannot recognize the light-rays in all beings, let alone
love the light in all. It is best to acknowledge that one cannot and
then find out why. Instead of brooding upon and building up the
shadow, one has to cut through it, seeing it for what it is.
Appreciating that it is good to be alive is closer to the latent love
of humanity than strong emotions directed here and there.
Rejoicing, like Miranda in *The Tempest,* in the existence of all others
is essential to true empathy.

Exercising the sacred privilege of cheerfully discharging one's
duties towards all others can become a way of life. One should
open one's eyes to that which is beyond and above oneself,
constantly aspiring in thought towards Mahatmic consciousness.

One must reflect upon humanity as a whole in relation to the Spiritual Sun, upon the meaning of human existence, upon the majesty of human suffering, but also its baffling urgency and awesome reality. Then one will discover a genuine gratitude for being a member of the human family and an awakened capacity to love humanity and its great pilgrimage. The more one truly loves, the more one will be effortlessly drawn into a current of joyous devotion to the unthanked Teachers of self-orphaned humanity, and the more one's spiritual heart will resonate to the universal compassion of *Daiviprakriti,* the Light of the Logos. Once this point is reached, there is really no going back. One has glimpsed the Hound of Heaven. The stream is entered. Sadly, many awakened souls forfeit the great opportunity in advance by speaking too soon and, above all, by becoming voluble psychiatrists and hasty judges of their personas and their prospects. Forgetful of most of what significantly happens in their lives, they become wastefully preoccupied with grading themselves, partly because they are afraid that at the moment of death they are going to be finally graded by an arbitrary God or a hostile universe.

All such cogitation is a cowardly insult to the living inheritance of spiritual intelligence in every human soul. Instead, one must persist in silence, with patience, perseverance and humility, until one touches the irreversible current of noetic insight, *satori* and *prajna,* the Tathagata Light. When it comes even as a form of grace, it will be self-evident, and it will not allow one ever to fall back into the abyss of self-destruction. One will realize that one's transfiguration should not be articulated, and yet one will discover that one's deepest thoughts and simplest words invisibly aid others in moving in the same sunward direction. Every seeker can effectively generate the *eros* and motivation to sustain and enrich the inward continuity of consciousness and identity with all souls. Whilst one cannot rapidly recover the soul-nobility of one's spiritual ancestors, whose every thought and feeling is full of unconditional love for all living beings, one can move in the right direction. Through an honest acknowledgement and accurate assessment of exactly what is needed, one may assuredly avoid danger to the soul.

All sacred knowledge is karmically double-edged, for though it is accessible, it cannot be applied properly without simultaneously generating the suitable conditions, and if it is accessible but not used, it becomes inaccessible. This means at the most practical level that, without fear or cavil, one should sincerely try to use and apply the teachings in daily life, without excessive concern to draw elaborate inferences from instantaneous responses. Just as the Word is behind all words, what is hidden is always greater than what is revealed. But where there is the authentic attempt to reflect the concealed Thought, the Light of the Logos will guide, and the reflection will be greater than one may know. As Mahatma K.H. wrote to A.P. Sinnett:

> It is upon the serene and placid surface of the unruffled mind that the visions gathered from the invisible find a representation in the visible world. . . . It is with jealous care that we have to guard our mind-plane from all the adverse influences which daily arise in our passage through earth-life. . . . There are the powers of all Nature before you, *take what you can.*

SPACE AND
SELF-CONSCIOUSNESS

*The Occult Catechism contains the following questions
and answers:*
'What is it that ever is?' 'Space, the eternal Anupadaka.'
*'What is it that ever was?' 'The Germ in the Root.' 'What is
it that is ever coming and going?' 'The Great Breath.' 'Then,
there are three Eternals?' 'No, the three are one. That which
ever is is one, that which ever was is one, that which is ever
being and becoming is also one: and this is Space.'*
                                        The Secret Doctrine, i 11

The object of all training in ancient schools of Initiation was to bring the anchorite to a truer realization of the one eternal reality that abides behind the vast screen of manifest existence. Such a realization is not merely cognitional; it transcends all distinctions between subject and object, all conceptions of agent and field, and reaches beyond the range of all possible representations. In this spirit, enlightened preceptors provided chelas with appropriate texts and themes for reflection. Although these affirm positive lines of thought, and lead disciples to a fuller understanding of embodied life, they also involve negation and synthesis, for they integrate and resolve all elements of life into their ineffable, ineluctable origin in the unitive ground of the Real. A disciple who immerses his or her consciousness in these precisely constructed catechisms experiences and exemplifies their magical transforming power. But this capacity for transformation does not lie outside the disciple. Rather, the self-induced effort to engage in meditation is identical with the realization of the highest Self. That Self is the Real, and its foremost representation in Gupta Vidya is SPACE.

Authentic meditation demands a radical re-centering of oneself in real Being. Hence, to the question *What is it that ever is?*, the Catechism responds with the affirmation, *Space, the eternal Anupadaka. Anupadaka* is that which is parentless and beginningless. It is That before which there was nothing else. In a conceptual sense it may seem obvious that space *per se*, as distinct from its containment, is independent of the existence or non-existence of particular things that it may or may not contain. Yet existentially, it is extremely difficult to generate a sense of That which ever is. Whatever might be one's view of the age of the universe, whether conceived in terms of tens of billions of years or a billion times greater, no measure of time is commensurate with That which ever is. Since human beings cannot readily remember yesterday or clearly perceive tomorrow, their concepts of remote ages inevitably amount to little more than concrete representations extrapolated from present sense-perceptions. Such extrapolation can never extend to That which ever is — Space.

Even if it were possible to visualize the beginning of the universe as it now seems to exist, this would only be to entertain a logical and mathematical notion connected with certain conceptual maps. It would not touch that Space wherein there is even now the possibility of myriads of other universes. Even the statistically possible multiple worlds of quantum physics are apprehended as logical abstractions, rather than as ever-present potentials in ever-present Space. Nor does it help to postulate a hypothetical set of initial conditions at the commencement of the universe, and then to argue that variations within this set represent the potential of all possible universes. This merely relocates conceptual multiplicity at a remote point in the past, without touching the ontological fullness of the Space that ever is. So too, if one likes to think in future time, which is of course only a manner of speaking, one may imagine a time, billions upon billions of years in the future, when there is no earth or solar system, no galaxy and, indeed, no knowable universe. But even with the complete extinction of the universe, there is still Space and still too the potential of a myriad worlds. Each of these worlds contains certain possibilities beyond itself; none of these worlds, therefore, can exhaust the reality of Space itself.

Though the first affirmation in the Occult Catechism invites contemplation, it does not readily yield its full implications. Those implications are not supported by most of our concepts,

assumptions and attitudes in day-to-day living. After the initial
affirmation, there is in the Catechism an apt response of the chela
to the Guru, setting forth the meaning of the affirmation:

> '*Explain, oh Lanoo (disciple).*'
> '*The One is an unbroken Circle (ring) with no
> circumference, for it is nowhere and everywhere; the One is
> the boundless plane of the Circle, manifesting a diameter
> only during the manvantaric periods.*'
>
> Ibid.

The circle without circumference indicates the incognizable
Presence, Kosmos in Eternity, whilst the plane of this circle is the
Universal Soul. These two are one, the eternal *Anupadaka*. The
Sanskrit term *Anupadaka* is ordinarily translated as 'parentless', but
like every Sanskrit term, it has an untranslatable resonance, a
wealth of meanings that are only revealed in meditation. Sanskrit
is the language of the science of the future. When one hears the
word *Anupadaka,* one at first hears the prefix *Anu*. This reminds
one of that which is indescribably and indivisibly atomic. *Anu* is
also applied in reference to *brahman*. *Brahman* is in the *Anu*, and
Brahman is also beyond the greatest possible expansion of Brahmā.
It is the smallest of the small and the greatest of the great; it ever
is and it is ever present. Once the higher imagination is aroused
through the resonance of the syllable *Anu,* the idea is fused with
pada, which has to do with measure, as well as with parentage.
Together the syllables intimate that which is beyond all possible
measure and without origin, that which cannot be conceived, yet
cannot be absent from any conception. Owing to the emergence
of certain tools of measurement over the last few centuries,
modern man has begun to resemble a brash teenager, who
presumes in his ignorance to limit the whole range of possible
being. But even the momentous discovery that there are millions
of galaxies and billions of suns yields no conception of all modes
of possible existence, or indeed of all sentient self-persistence. Nor
can this reveal all possible levels and forms of matter, both
phenomenal and noumenal, or all possible rhythms and ranges

of ideation. Yet to the eye of the *Lanoo*, disciplined through meditation, the ground of all these possibilities is intimated in the mysterious *Anupadaka*.

Nowadays people tend to think of space — if they think of it at all — either as a property or as a possession providing a field for ego-assertion. Sometimes they merely connect it with the fantasies of science fiction. Space, in the geometric sense, is too often associated with bad memories of high school geometry classes or treated as the private preserve of erudite specialists. Yet those of the ancient world maintained an immense reverence for Space, which the Occult Catechism identifies with the eternal *Anupadaka*. This Space is the *Maha-Akasha* of Gupta Vidya. Space, in this sense, evokes a reverence comparable to the term 'God', before it became trivialized, anthropomorphized and reduced to a kind of cosmic father-figure. Before it was associated with some smiling universal patriarch, the term 'Deity' called forth a tremendous reverence, even as late as early Greece, let alone much earlier in Chaldea, Egypt and certainly a million years ago in ancient Aryavarta. There, one would only whisper such terms or remain silent and try to experience that which is ineffable in the sounding of the AUM.

Next, the Occult Catechism asks the question, *What is it that ever was?*, and gives the response, *The Germ in the Root.* Perhaps the rational mind wishes to respond to this second question by saying 'Space' again, because if Space ever is, of course it ever was. Yet the Catechism, through which candidates were prepared for the Mysteries by Hierophants, suggests something else. To say that Space ever is is to indicate the infinite potentiality of infinite worlds that ever exist. This limitless multiplicity is only brought together or integrated by the numinous idea of potential; our own notion of potential itself is liable to be foreshortened by our limited conceptions of the familiar world. Here, however, we are being told that there ever was, behind the multiplicity of myriad possible worlds, the Germ in the Root. This is explained by the *Lanoo* as follows:

The One is the indivisible point found nowhere,
perceived everywhere during those periods; it is the Vertical

*and the Horizontal, the Father and the Mother, the summit
and base of the Father, the two extremities of the Mother,
reaching in reality nowhere, for the One is the Ring as also
the rings that are within that Ring.*

Ibid.

The Germ in the Root, which is sometimes called the Rootless
Root, points to a single root-substance. One cannot separate even
the most abstract Space from matter, albeit an extremely abstract
matter. And one cannot separate abstract matter from spirit, which
is sometimes called the first differentiation of the Absolute. As
Mahatma K. H. explained in a letter in the nineteenth century,
"Spirit is called the ultimate sublimation of matter, and matter
the crystallization of spirit." Just as one cannot separate spirit from
matter, so too one cannot separate spirit-matter from Space. These
arcane conceptions have nothing to do with what are ordinarily
labelled time, space and form. The Catechism affirms that all these
fundamental conceptions exist inseparably in a root, in a germ.
There is an eternal rootedness within the realm of the infinite
potential of inexhaustible Space. That eternal rootedness, though
transcendent, is ever present in a germinal form; that germinal
form, therefore, is omnipresent.

This germ is as much present in any one point in
differentiated space as in any other point. It is the mystical
abstraction intimated in the Rig Vedic *Hymn to Creation* by the
phrase "the primal seed and germ of mind." It may be thought of
as the centre of a circle or a sphere, or of a series of circles and
spheres, without partiality or restriction to any one of these centres.
In ancient times, men of meditation possessed a degree of natural
impartiality towards all points in boundless space. Yet modern
man, who is a spiritual pygmy by comparison, finds it hard to grasp
such effortless impartiality. Modern man cannot even be impartial
towards his fellows; he is addicted to discrimination. The disciple
can reverse this tendency by looking to the sky, and begin to
associate the cosmos with the magnitude and breadth that modern
astronomy has revealed. The courageous meditator flies on the
wings of the porous imagination, transcending all possible
concepts of being and visualizing an infinitude of points in

inexhaustible Space, each one of which is dimensionless and frictionless. Many are prone to think of points in terms of something that appears against a blank background of emptiness or nothing. The Occult Catechism, however, offers the notion of a point within which exists all the potential that we ascribe to bare space. That potential is in a germinal form. As an entire tree is implicit within a seed, so too the whole Tree of Life, as the Kabbalists thought, is implicit within that point. And this point ever was in every atomic differentiated point of manifested life.

Grasping such a conception involves abandoning the ordinary suppositions of the mind. Those who have been treating their bodies cavalierly suddenly recognize that every point of Space, every point within and around the human form, is the same as every other, and that behind each point there is the Germ in the Root. This realization breaks down the sharp dichotomy between the animate and inanimate, and it shatters the limited notions of the self and the other. If all points are identical in their rootedness, with which point can one logically identify the Self? Is the Self the point between the eyes? Is it the point which is the light in the heart? Is it the point above the head? To ask these questions in relation to the Germ in the Root is to begin to ask what it is to be a human being and a Monad. To apprehend the Germ in the Root as that which ever was is to grasp the potential in Space of consciousness and of self-consciousness.

This represents a fundamental revolution in the very ideas of individuality and identity. As such, it goes beyond even the most advanced conceptions of twentieth century thought. Nonetheless, modern science, especially astronomy and mathematical physics, has come to a point where it must consider the relation between many possible worlds or myriads of galaxies and that which is called human life on earth. Some contemporary cosmologists think there must be a sense in which the whole universe generates the possibility of life as we know it on earth. They recognize, therefore, that life on earth is no special case. Rather, they see their own existence as conscious spectators within a vast universe as the realization of a possibility that is inherent in the foundations of that universe itself. Earlier science sought to reduce life to a fortuitous combination of chemical elements; these newer enquiries, however, concede the fundamental reality of consciousness. Whilst this does not exclude attempts to discover life on other planets, a possibility encouraged by everything known about the chemical conditions of life on earth, it does exclude the notion of life being created by some fortuitous chemical mix. Such contemporary reflections have given rise to "the anthropic principle", a phrase coined by Brandon Carter to designate a position between the crude anthropocentricism of pre-Copernican thought and the post-Einsteinian claim that all local conditions in time or space are merely random inhomogeneities. Between these two extremes the anthropic principle proposes that the existence of intelligent observers itself represents an inherent property and characteristic of cosmological and evolutionary existence. Cosmogenesis and anthropogenesis constitute two aspects of one unfolding impulse.

Whatever the eventual uses of the anthropic principle, it is, as yet, only a speculative abstraction applicable to the cosmos as a whole. Its distributive psychological significance to individual self-conscious human life has yet to be developed. The Occult Catechism teaches that nothing ever was that did not have the Germ in the Root. There was never a time or space, or even space-time, in which there was not the Germ in the Root. There has always been the possibility of consciousness and also of self-consciousness. This certainly devastates many popular assumptions. Human fears of darkness, silence, loneliness or death — fears of being forgotten or unloved — only reflect metaphysical misconceptions at the most basic level. Human beings have begun to identify themselves with the tokens through which they are re-cognized in differentiated interaction. So, they must keep touching each other to reassure one another that they exist. All of this is far removed from the reality of self-conscious existence that ever was in the Germ in the Root. Through meditation one learns to see life even where there are no systems of worlds. Self-conscious life is potentially present as the Germ in the Root even in *Maha Pralaya*.

In the Occult Catechism the disciple is also asked *What is it that is ever coming and going?* and responds, *The Great Breath.* Phenomenal and noumenal existence are pervaded by a constant activity. This process of becoming is not only a potential element present in Space, and a permanent possibility because of the Germ in the Root, but there is an actual elaboration out of all possibilities of consciousness and of self-consciousness through a continual coming and going. There seems to be something diastolic and systolic about the cosmos itself. One cannot even imagine blank space without a kind of pulsation. There is a kind of secret cosmic heart where there is an eternal inward and outward vibration, a ceaseless inbreathing and outbreathing of the Great Breath. As the Catechism explains,

> *Light in darkness and darkness in light: the 'Breath which is eternal.' It proceeds from without inwardly, when it is everywhere, and from within outwardly, when it is nowhere — (i.e., maya, one of the centres). It expands and contracts (exhalation and inhalation). When it expands the mother diffuses and scatters; when it contracts, the mother draws back and ingathers. This produces the periods of Evolution and Dissolution, Manwantara and Pralaya.*
>
> Ibid., 11-12

Even in darkness, even in inexhaustible Space abstracted away from all possible worlds, there is an everlasting energy. To call it energy, however, is not to limit it in terms of ordinary notions of energy which depend upon specific connected patterns of activity and rest. Rather, it suggests an elusive field, in which conceptions of polarity do not apply. The occult notion of Fohat, particularly in its pre-cosmic existence, is thus generally inaccessible to even highly abstract field theories. Rather, one must think in terms of a sense of rhythm or alternation, which may be symbolized in terms of a breathing in and breathing out. This vibrationality transcends all our concepts of matter, mind, existence, activity and withdrawal. The phrase 'Great Breath' is used because the original

Sanskritic etymology of the word 'breath' implies the primal vivifying power of expansion at the root of manifestation. Breath is connected with the divine perpetual motion of the *Atman*; even the single letter *A* conveys the meaning. If divine spirit is in perpetual motion, it involves a perpetual breathing in and breathing out. It cannot be visualized without the *Ah* and the indrawing into the *M*. Therefore, a deific potency grounded in the very process of becoming produces the cosmos, and this is linked to the attempt, in meditation, to transcend all forms and all limiting conceptions of motion, space and deity through the AUM.

This vibratory current underlying all active life in the cosmos is mirrored in the grandest cycles of Nature, as in the smallest. The Chinese held that it could be discerned in the sounds made by forests, rivers, great cities and the sea; they thought of it as the voice of Nature itself. It was likened to an imperceptible tone that one could learn to hear only by withdrawing attention from particular sounds. Many composers, including Beethoven in his "Pastoral Symphony," have intuited the significance of the F note in Nature. The "Pastoral Symphony" conveys a sense of the unity and ubiquity of a vibration that dances in and through all the kingdoms of elementals in Nature. The symphony is formed out of all that moves and animates the pastoral scenes of the globe. The attentive ear can detect it in the ocean, in the whistling wind, even in the silent air. All Nature's different sounds are resolved again and again into this great tone which intimates the reality of the transcendental Great Breath.

That breath itself can work at the primal level of differentiation, at which there is a vibration in the depths of the ocean of infinite Space. There is a kind of breathing in and breathing out that does not participate in the sevenfold scale applicable to differentiation, whether in relation to sound or the principles of the cosmos. Ordinarily, the human ear can only take in a certain range of sounds; therefore the ear can use only a limited scale to reach beyond those sounds into the Soundless Sound. The Voice of the Silence is present in the seemingly still reverberation within the depths of the night ocean that seasoned

sailors can experience during lonely watches. It is present too in
the noontime glory of the sun, the one great root-vibration which
is ceaselessly sounding and which is ever soundless. Every living
being has a heart that moves in sympathy with this ceaseless
pulsation, the one vibration that is the basis of all life and
compassion. In essence, every human being is like a drop, identical
to every other drop, within a vast shoreless sea of universal
existence. All beings flow within the great universal rhythm of
the Soundless Sound, the AUM throughout the ages.

After this third great affirmation, the *Lanoo* asks, *Then, there
are three Eternals?*, and the Guru responds, *No, the three are one.
That which ever is is one, that which ever was is one, that which is
ever being and becoming is also one; and this is Space.* The apparent
separation of these three highest abstractions is itself an illusion.
In reality the three are one. *Anupadaka*, the Germ in the Root,
and the Great Breath are distinct in a world of relativities only so
long as our consciousness is affected by contrasts between light
and darkness, withdrawal and involvement, waking and sleeping.
This primary dichotomy arises because our sense-organs are
constantly involved in accumulating, eliminating and recapturing
perceptions. Human beings are so immersed in a world that is
broken and disconnected in consciousness that they have lost a
sense of the fundamental unity of that world and of consciousness
and of the relation between the two. It is not merely a world of
multiplicity. It is a world of disconnectedness. Thus, even if many
worlds existed, as some scientists suggest, they would not be related
to the common concept of space on such a dualistic view, and
hence we would know nothing about them.

Ordinary conventions and criteria of meaning make it
impossible to speak meaningfully about myriad possible worlds —
unless they have some connection with our possible world of
space. Yet just because we cannot talk about them if we accept
these criteria, it does not follow that we cannot lay these criteria
aside and think about them. It is far more important that
individuals learn to meditate upon the transcendental possibility
of the existence of multiple worlds than that they learn how to

talk about them. Modern man is altogether too much engaged in attempting to communicate that which he does not comprehend; in so doing he forfeits the possibilities of learning. Modern civilization is caught up in 'show and tell', whereas the ancient world followed the principle of neither showing nor telling. They taught that one should close one's mouth, one's eyes and one's senses, and plunge into meditation. This is hard for people who have become conditioned from early childhood by 'show and tell' and who, after a point, end up cancelling all their words by the sadness and emptiness, the loneliness, in their eyes.

According to Gupta Vidya, the eyes of every human being potentially carry the wisdom of the sage and of the Pythagorean spectator, who can reflect upon each of the three hypostases, or limbs, of the Three-in-One. That Three-in-One becomes a four, because the Three-in-One plus the One becomes the divine *Tetraktys*. By thinking of each one of these distinctly, and stretching the mind beyond all formulations, one can come to think of them all together. Initially, using a phrase in each case, one must attempt to reach out into that which totally transcends the mind, seeking solidarity with the inexhaustible potential of dimensionless space which is universal consciousness and the One Life. To do this in meditation is to void the small self and to reascend in consciousness to That which ever is, ever was and ever becomes. As the Catechism explains,

> *The Germ is invisible and fiery; the Root (the plane of the circle) is cool; but during Evolution and Manwantara her garment is cold and radiant. Hot Breath is the Father who devours the progeny of the many-faced Element (heterogeneous); and leaves the single-faced ones (homogeneous). Cool breath is the Mother, who conceives, forms, brings forth, and receives them back into her bosom, to reform them at the Dawn (of the Day of Brahma, or Manwantara).*
>
> *Ibid.*, i 12

The inexhaustible potential of the Three-in-One comes to

bear fruit through the idea of the Germ in the Root in the form of the living cosmos. To dissolve the difference between oneself and that permanent possibility of becoming is to draw closer to the fountainhead and origin — the *fons et origo* — of all possible cosmic and human creativity. It is to live self-consciously as the Great Breath, the reverberation that exists even in the night of non-manifestation when there are no universes. This vibration is within every human being; when it is withdrawn from the outer vestures, the human being must prepare to die. When the sounding of the AUM is stilled, the wise know that the moment of death is approaching. Only those who have learnt to live life in spirit and not in matter can perceive this withdrawal.

The sublime unity of the Three-in-One beyond all differentiation is the ultimate and fundamental reality called SPACE. This is not only the eternal *Anupadaka,* the inexhaustible matrix of infinite potential. It is not only the Germ in the Root, present in every point of space. It is also the Great Breath, the breathing in and out of the One Life itself. In contemporary thought there is a concept of superspace, a space that is more fundamental than the astronomer's space of myriad planets and black holes. Some intuitive thinkers sense that space must be moving, like a fluidic substance, and moving not only in the extraordinary Einsteinian sense, where space moves through force upon matter. These speculations invoke a meta-topological space, which is more like a torus than like a sphere, and which has a great deal of angularity, quirkiness and unusual connectedness. If holes in space are comparable to holes in doughnuts, what of the superspace that fills the holes in space? These different levels of space are constantly shifting in relation to each other, permitting various possible modes of geometry and discrete motion of matter and energy in different circumstances.

All of this is quite distant from the discarded Newtonian view of space as a simple substance, as the fixed background against which the universe could be described and the pathways of all bodies traced out. Whilst modern thought has gone far beyond this static conception, it has attained, as yet, only an embryonic sense of the full reality of SPACE. To see the container of all possibilities, the root of all consciousness and the vibration of life as one, and to see them fully, is to have transcended *maya*. For the human being this means coming to see oneself and all other human beings as points of sentient life. Owing to their attachment to extended forms and sensation, human beings are reluctant to reduce themselves to a point. They are, therefore, cut off from the fullness of life. Only through renunciation of the self, only through lifelong meditation, can one substantially deepen one's sense of reality. One must break, within oneself, that which causes the modification of the mind and thought through *maya*. Metaphysically, there must be a universe for there to be an increased intensification of awareness, but this is at the price of breaking and making discontinuous through modification that awareness. That in the universe which modifies awareness only modifies it apparently. Though that modification might last billions upon billions of years, it can still be cancelled and transcended; there is that in every human being which is prior and posterior to all possible modifications of mind and matter.

This reality is also present in every atom, and a human being is capable of knowing what is in every atom, because the Germ in the Root is in himself or herself. It is present as an 'I', as 'I-am-I' consciousness, as a ray or point. There is, therefore, a possibility of becoming self-consciously absorbed into SPACE in the ultimate sense. Gupta Vidya commends to every aspirant daily meditation upon Space. Whatever problem the meditative seeker encounters, he is at least engaged in a process which can reduce the ignorance and misery which he creates when not meditating. The human mind is either active or passive, either moving towards self-mastery or serving as the psychic medium of universal forces made chaotic and disconnected through false identification with form. What people ordinarily call life is a mixture of living and partly living. Many people are not quite there. They drift as psychic automata conditioned by habits. They are neither fully aware of themselves nor of what they are thinking and doing. Much less are they aware of each other. They do not honour their own true thoughts, and they rarely listen to each other. Often they feel alienated and disengaged from the broader life of the human race. Sleepy, passive and acted upon by irrational forces, they are subject to constant fears about loss of identity. In short, they lack a sense of reality.

In such a world any aspirant who develops some degree of capacity for meditation in the true sense will soon be able to offer some healing help to other human beings. As soon as one tastes the joy of meditation, one will realize the truth of Krishna's affirmation, "Even a little of this practice delivereth a man from great risk." This wisdom is not merely for individual deliverance. It is the radiant living substance of the cosmos, and it underlies the lives of all. If the aspirant would become a true *Lanoo*, faithful to the Guru's compassionate wisdom, then gratitude will transform this initial joy of realization into an irreversible will to sacrificial service. Drawing into attunement with the Tathagatas, one may become a faithful servant of *Brahma Vach*, a co-worker with Nature, capable of exhaustless realization *(Svasamvedana)* of the boundless potential of the one eternal Reality.

COGNITION, BREATH AND SPEECH

In the 'Book of Hermes', Pymander, the oldest and the most spiritual of the Logoi of the Western Continent, appears to Hermes in the shape of a Fiery Dragon of 'Light, Fire, and Flame'. Pymander, the 'Thought Divine' personified, says: 'The Light is me, I am the Nous (the mind or Manu), I am thy God, and I am far older than the human principle which escapes from the shadow ('Darkness', or the concealed Deity). I am the germ of thought, the resplendent Word, *the* Son *of* God. *All that thus sees and hears in thee is the* Verbum *of the Master, it is the Thought (Mahat) which is God, the Father. The celestial Ocean, the Aether... is the* Breath *of the Father, the life-giving principle, the* Mother, *the Holy Spirit... for these are not separated, and their union is* LIFE.*

The Secret Doctrine, i 74-75

I n the compelling mystical dialogue between Pymander and Hermes, the personified Thought Divine delivers a magnificent affirmation of the descent of the fiery power of Universal Thought from the Divine Darkness to give light and life to an intelligent and intelligible cosmos. The Divine Pymander speaks as the Dragon of light, fire and flame — the resplendent Word sprung from the primal germ of thought that lies beyond being and non-being alike. Pymander represents the concealed Deity, the ubiquitous presence and vital potency of the Word, the basis of all cognition in the cosmos. Hermes represents the finest aspect of human consciousness, involved in a sublime quest for union with *Atma-Buddhi*. It is that noetic intelligence, inseparable from the Thought Divine, which is capable of resonating in devotion to the vibration of the Word from which it sprang. The sacred dialogue of Pymander and Hermes intimates the mysterious relationship between mind and speech in man and the cosmos, alluding to the significance of their interaction in the mystic path towards fusion with *Atman*. The dialogue also points to an archetypal series of correlations between diverse principles, uniting the Aether-Breath of the Father with the life-giving Holy Spirit of the Mother within the ONE LIFE.

In explicating this passage from the *Book of Hermes*, H.P. Blavatsky correlated the Thought Divine with *Mahat*, a generic term having different meanings in different contexts. In its highest meaning it conveys the Universal Mind, an ideal and pregenetic abstraction eluding any formal definition. In Gupta Vidya a fundamental distinction divides Universal Mind as the permanent possibility of Thought from the mind of a cosmos in manifestation. Ontologically prior to any set of elements that embody it in a cosmos, *Mahat* in its most primary sense is the all-pervading first Logos.

> The *Mahat* (Understanding, Universal Mind, Thought, etc.), before it manifests itself as Brahmā or Siva, appears as Vishnu, says *Sankhya Sara*; hence *Mahat* has several aspects, just as the *logos* has. *Mahat* is called the Lord, in the *Primary* Creation, and is, in this sense, Universal Cognition or *Thought Divine*.
>
> *Ibid.*, 75

Even though one may distinguish between *Mahat* as that which precedes the cosmos and *Mahat* as the cosmic mind, this distinction is essentially one of epistemological convenience. Ultimately, *Mahat* as the cosmic mind is itself only a kind of condensation or emanation, a radiation from the Universal Mind. As such, it is entirely unconnected with the emergence and disappearance of worlds. When Universal Mind is juxtaposed with the idea of thought, as in the conception of the Thought Divine, there is no reference to any discrete or individuated thinker. Rather, the Thought Divine conveys the idea of a purely transcendental Universal Cognition, without implying any linear succession in time. Like an eternal vision of the cosmos that was, is and shall be, the Thought Divine encompasses an entire series of possible creations and stages of the unfoldment of Universal Mind in manifestation. This pure self-reflection of *Mahat* at the highest level is prior to all manifestation. But it represents a plane of reality which is perpetually accessible to those awakened minds that empty themselves through meditation and learn to insert themselves self-consciously into the unmanifest ground of their own being. The ascent towards this inward realization must begin with the recognition that everything that is manifested is a reflection of that which is invisible, manifest only on subtle planes. One must learn to understand the visible in terms of that which is only perceptible to astral and higher senses. Yet even beyond those invisible planes of subtle manifestation abides that which is beyond all manifestation and prior to it ontologically. This is referred to as Universal Cognition or Thought Divine.

Universal Cognition is incapable of having any attribute and, therefore, is incapable of predication. It cannot be the subject of any verb or the referent of any adjective. Nor should it be mistaken for a noun simply because in various mystical texts it occurs as a substantive term. It is the primordial plane of pure consciousness or reality which is fundamentally so different from everything that belongs to the process of becoming that it cannot even be thought of in terms of existence. An intuition of this reality may be glimpsed through contemplation of ideas like Be-ness and pure being, which have built into them an element of self-existence in an abstract universal sense which in no way makes any reference to any process of manifestation. Nor should it be thought of in terms of any specific absence or privation of manifestation in connection with any concretized idea of *pralaya*.

Mahat as universal self-existence is beyond existence and non-existence as a pair of opposites. It is only possible to ascend to such a metaphysical idea through an extremely long and arduous course of deep meditation maintained over lifetimes. Yet if one can grant in principle that there could be such a plane of Universal Cognition, a supernal realm of Universal Ideation which is the plane of the very highest perfected beings, and that there is in this a basis for universal self-existence, then one could conceive how, through a downward reflection into the world of differentiated matter, there could arise a conception of what is called, in the Second Creation, a feeling of self-consciousness or egoism.

> 'That Mahat which was first produced is (afterwards) called *Ego-ism,* when it is born as "I", that is said to be the *second* Creation' *(Anugita,* ch. xxxvi) . . . i.e., 'when Mahat develops into the feeling of Self-Consciousness — I — then it assumes the name of Egoism', which, translated into our esoteric phraseology, means when *Mahat* is transformed into the human *Manas* (or even that of the finite gods), and becomes *Aham*-ship.
>
> *Ibid.*

The progressive unfoldment of *Mahat* is inconceivable without a parallel and coordinate development of undifferentiated matter or *Mulaprakriti.* Just as there is an essential aspect of *Mahat* that is independent of the alternation of *manvantara* and *pralaya,* there is that eternal root of all substance, the virginal veil of *Parabrahm.* Its first radiation may be conceived of as a super-astral or noumenal light, the mystical Sea of Fire of the *Stanzas of Dzyan.* This sublime ocean of primordial light, akin to Aether-*Akasha,* becomes in turn the realm of differentiated matter, the vesture of evolving *Mahat* in manifestation. The deeper this descent into manifestation, the more distorted and distorting this material medium becomes, until it reaches the stage of gross astral matter — also known as the Fiery Serpent. This transformation in the *upadhi* or basis of the field of manifestation is expressed by Plato in the *Timaeus* in terms of 'the same and the other'. Originally, there is that which is pellucid and homogeneous, inimitable and indivisible. In the descent from the highest plane, it becomes on the lower planes divided and distorted, confused and partaking of otherness. Yet it remains through all things a projection of that which is intrinsically pellucid, intrinsically homogeneous and undifferentiated. There must be a germ within the confusion of the lower astral substance that corresponds to or is consubstantial with the pure parentage of that from which it is ultimately an emanation. Hence, there is an element of illusion in the seeming separation of *Mulaprakriti* and *Daiviprakriti* during the process of manifestation from the seemingly different gross differentiated dregs of the lower planes of material existence. If one penetrates far enough into the essential ground of every point in space, one will eventually reach *Mulaprakriti*, that which is the veil upon *Parabrahm*. This absolute notion of substance has no reference to any modes of motion or forms, but represents root matter which is connected with the primary ground of *Akasha*.

As the teachings of Pymander to Hermes intimate, there is an analogy and a correspondence between these levels of the differentiation of the universal substance-principle and the levels of manifestation of Universal Cognition. There is that at the core of Universal Cognition or *Mahat* which corresponds with primordial root substance or *Mulaprakriti*, beyond all reference to manifestation and therefore, unconscious during the process of manifestation. It is neither a subject nor an object to consciousness or of consciousness. Yet it can in turn emanate, and this would be represented mystically as Divine Thought condensing into the Word or the *Verbum*. It is the cosmogonic and metaphysical basis of the mysterious relationship between speech and mind. Within the mystical Sea of Fire there is fiery substance affected by fiery ideation. The fiery cognition that is inseparable from fiery substance on the plane of the super-astral Akashic or noumenal light is the ultimate basis of the records in the library of *Akasha* that constitute the great spiritual utterances of humanity. This would be the storehouse of wisdom-consciousness, the *Alayavijnana* of the Buddhists and the supernal realm of the Vedic hymns and all the other sublime utterances that have come down in human life. All these manifestations of sacred speech have their roots in *Akasha*. Whether they are known or not in external form to particular human beings in any given period of history, they have their persisting reverberations. They endlessly reproduce themselves in multitudinous ways, permeating the processes of human evolution throughout manifestation, serving as the intelligent order of Nature sprung from divine ideation.

If an individual has some theoretical appreciation of this dual unfoldment of *Mahat* and *Mulaprakriti*, then it becomes possible to discover within one's own self-consciousness a means and method of drawing towards Universal Mind. *Egoism* must be clearly distinguished from *egotism*. Egoism is the pure sense of 'I-am-I' consciousness, bound up with the principle of individuation. It is possible to detach the pure sense of 'I' from every object and every kind of concern or conception which is centered upon a differentiated world. Through an interior discipline of concentration, which may be called the *aham* meditation, it is possible to withdraw that sense of 'I-am-I' into itself to such a degree that it can light up a field of higher awareness. This is the ultimate reason for and the basis of the imperative importance of daily meditation.

Perfected human beings are masters of ceaseless contemplation. Whilst they may be recognized as heroic individuals, engaging in courageous deeds, they are essentially men of thought, constantly plunged into deep reflection. By contrast, human beings who do not master the power of thought and the differentiations of matter in their vestures are fragmented in consciousness and at the mercy of external influences. In effect, they are slaves to the desire principle, driven by limited modes of thought towards transitory objects. This is the common plight of vast numbers of human beings, and whilst all have the opportunity in one form or another to deepen their powers of reflection in life, one who postpones the effort will undergo extraordinary difficulty. It is of vital importance that children learn how to sit down, to be quiet, to meditate and concentrate. At any age in life, one must attempt these disciplines. No matter at what level one approaches the problem, one must learn to abstract, to withdraw, to sustain intact a subtler awareness. If one can develop a capacity to enjoy ideas and to penetrate through meditation to a certain level of consciousness, this will eventually become a continuous current in one's life to which one can return again and again.

All of this amounts to a re-ascent in consciousness through the vestures of the mind towards their ultimate ground in that which is beyond manifestation. The same process may be understood in relation to the complex teaching of Gupta Vidya concerning the different aspects of breath and their relationship through speech to mind. Like everything else in arcane metaphysics, the concept of breath does not refer merely to something physical. It refers, even at the lowest level, to that which is astral, but which has its analogues all the way up to and including the highest vestures and beyond. When texts like the *Anugita* speak of the discipline of the breath or *pranayama,* they refer not to the crude physical manipulations of the breath that often pass in ignorant circles for a form of *yoga.* These physical practices are often dangerous in the extreme and invariably result from a fatal misunderstanding of the teachings. Philosophically, the breaths are rhythms and motions in the *karana sharira* or the *anandamaya kosha,* inseparable from *Buddhi.*

> In the *Anugita* a conversation is given (ch. vi, 15) between a Brahmana and his wife, on the origin of Speech and its occult properties. The wife asks how Speech came into existence, and which was prior to the other, Speech or Mind. The Brahmana tells her that the Apana *(inspirational breath)* becoming lord, changes that intelligence, which does not understand Speech or Words, into the state of Apana, and thus opens the mind.
>
> *Ibid., 94*

Inspirational breathing is important in relation to being able to aspirate properly, to speak clearly, and so to control the power of sound. To control a restless mind, for example, one could try reading aloud some passage from a sacred text. The principal thing is to forget oneself, in the lower sense. Yet this is no easy task, if only because one has spent too much time, too much energy and too much wasted breath over so many lives in lower self-meditation. Even if this is so, one can use the vestures of the lower self on behalf of a higher egoism. Through intoning sacred words, paying attention to the sound of one's own voice and the words being formulated, one may employ the power of speech to govern the restless lower mind. Because one is lending voice to intoning that which is meaningful and powerful, the practice will, after a point, prove helpful. The simplest way of doing this, honoured the world over, is by chanting. Take, for example, a single sound like "*Ram*" and continually chant it. Of course, this must be done with attention. There is a thin line between chanting "*Rama, Rama*" and chanting "*Mara, Mara*," between invoking the *Atman* and intoning 'death'.

When people take advantage of the power of sound through chanting to calm the mind, they are able to gain some relief from its restless activity. But as the *Anugita* teaches, speech which is uttered audibly is capable of affecting only the lower or movable mind. Audible speech cannot affect the immovable mind except in the case of an Adept, who is above both the immovable and movable minds and can use all energies noetically. Thus, the *Anugita* points to the important use of the power of audible speech in reference to the lower *Manas*, working through the power of recitation of texts and *mantras* to gain self-control. This is in line with the common-sense recognition that sometimes it is necessary to talk to oneself, disconnecting from one's lower *Manas* and giving oneself instructions, or in Buddha's phrase, "dictating terms to the mind." This can be helpful in strengthening the practice of one's resolves, in holding fast during difficult times, and it is also related to the practice of singing and chanting while working in order to maintain a certain rhythm. All of these are legitimate uses of speech. In the use of audible speech to govern the lower mind, that speech must originate in a self-consciousness that is superior and prior to the utterance. It must be inspired, guided by a breath that comes from a region of more subtle and universal substance and intelligence, if it is to have a harmonizing effect upon the physical and lower astral field of the personal mind and the body.

According to the *Anugita*, it is possible through the power of silent or inaudible speech to approach the realm of the immovable mind, enabling one to draw upon its powers of inspiration. Ordinarily, people find it difficult to distinguish between what they call thought and silent speech. This is because ordinary views of the power of thought are extremely vague. Hence the crucial importance of regular efforts to engage in meditation, attempting to hold ideas in the mind, if only by trying to hold sentences or stanzas from sacred texts before the mind. As one does this, one can intone the sentence in the mind, and as one intones it, one can dwell upon it. Gradually becoming one with the Teaching in the mind, one may increasingly learn to think upon it in the true sense of the word 'thought'. In this way, one can begin to apprehend both noiseless speech and the mystical process whereby it nourishes the life of the soul.

Having recounted the Teaching of the *Anugita* regarding the relationship of inaudible and audible speech to the immovable and movable mind, H.P. Blavatsky remarked:

> This allegory is at the root of the Occult law, which prescribes silence upon the knowledge of certain secret and invisible things perceptible only to the spiritual mind (the 6th sense), and which cannot be expressed by 'noisy' or uttered speech. This chapter of *Anugita* explains, says Arjuna Misra, Pranayama, or regulation of the breath in Yoga practices. . . . This story is quoted to show how inseparably connected are, in the metaphysics of old, intelligent beings, or rather 'Intelligences', with every sense or function whether physical or mental. The Occult claim that there are seven senses in man, as in nature, as there are seven states of consciousness, is corroborated in the same work, chapter vii, on Pratyahara (the restraint and regulation of the senses, Pranayama being that of the 'vital winds' or breath).
>
> *Ibid.*, 95-96

In this passage the *Anugita* affirms that the mind is the lord of the senses. Although in ordinary language one speaks of touch, taste, smell, sight and hearing as independent powers of sensation, all of these are closely interrelated with each other. Furthermore, as the *Anugita* teaches, without the mind, "the senses never shine, like an empty dwelling, or like fires the flames of which are extinct." Only through the mind are the various senses able to apprehend their respective objects. Unlike some epistemological systems which attempt to conceive the full operation of the senses independently of the mind, and then to depict the activity of the mind in relation to the senses as purely inferential, the *Anugita* points to a much more intimate relationship. Each sense is seen as a differentiation both of the abstract power of thought and the abstract principle of substance on a particular plane. There is no mind-body problem in the philosophy of Gupta Vidya. There are, instead, corresponding to different planes of Universal Cognition and *Mulaprakriti* in manifestation, different sets of senses and organs of action. By recognizing the predominance of the mind in relation to the lower astral and physical senses, it is possible through deliberation and thoughtfulness to rise above the compulsive and involuntary processes that operate through the sense-organs of the gross body. Just as audible speech can aid in calming the lower mind, so too physical movements and disciplines can aid in gaining steadiness and control on the physical and even mental plane. Physical exercise or, at another level, certain physical postures, can aid in clearing the mind and making it more direct. This can help an individual to moderate emotional extremes, to cut through a great deal of the confusion of the lower *Manas* caught up in sensory life.

> This, of course, with regard only to *mind on the sensuous plane*. Spiritual mind (the upper portion or aspect of the *impersonal* MANAS) takes no cognisance of the senses in physical man. . . . The ancients were acquainted with the correlation of forces and all the

recently discovered phenomena of mental and physical faculties and functions, with many more mysteries also.

Ibid., 96

The entire capacity to calm the lower mind through the power of audible speech or physical movement depends upon tapping a reflection of the synthesizing principle of *Buddhi*. *Buddhi* is mirrored in every object, in every sense and sense-organ. Above all, it is mirrored in the higher *Manas* itself. In turn, it is mirrored in the synthesizing power of lower *Manas*, considered as the lord of the senses. Higher *Manas* is capable of synthesizing and abstracting from all the senses, including the lower mind, which, though subtler, still exists on a plane of differentiated space, time and substance.

By invoking the power of *Buddhi*, it is possible to transcend everything in this lower realm, while at the same time giving proper value to all that is being transcended. This means recognizing that the entire realm of the lower senses is a dynamic field of minor deities and intelligences. All of these work and have their place in differentiated life, and so it is always meaningful to sanctify and revere everything in reference to the sensory plane. There is also a mirroring — in the integration of these senses and powers, these deities and intelligences — of a higher synthesis to be attained self-consciously through the union of *Manas* and *Buddhi*. As the *Anugita* teaches:

> 'There is one unmoving (life-wind or breath, the "*Yoga inhalation*," so called, which is the breath of the *One* or Higher SELF). That is the (or my) own Self, accumulated in numerous (forms).'
>
> This Breath, Voice, Self or 'Wind' (*pneuma?*) is the Synthesis of the Seven Senses, *noumenally* all minor deities and esoterically — the *septenary* and the 'Army of the VOICE.'
>
> *Ibid.*

This mysterious unmoving breath can only be experienced if one has become proficient in deep meditation, capable of remaining abstracted from the astral form for long periods of time. This, in turn, is possible only if one has learnt how to make the astral form coil down and attenuate itself, virtually destroyed at will. These are very high states indeed, but even if unattainable at present, they are well worth thinking about. Just to appreciate these possibilities is helpful in learning to master the outer vestures.

At the root of these mysteries of mind, speech and breath lies the mysterious union, spoken of by Pymander, of the celestial ocean, the Aether, the breath of the Father and the life-giving principle, the Holy Spirit or Mother, which together are LIFE. The Father-Mother-Son are One, the three-tongued flame that never dies, the immortal spiritual Triad in the cosmos and in man — the *Atma-Buddhi-Manas.* Anyone who carefully contemplates this divine unity, as conveyed by the teachings of Pymander to Hermes, will soon transcend the majority of foolish questions and doubts that arise regarding the ontology of Gupta Vidya.

> If the student bears in mind that there is but One Universal Element, which is infinite, unborn, and undying, and that all the rest — as in the world of phenomena — are but so many various differentiated aspects and transformations (correlations, they are now called) of that One, from Cosmical down to micro-cosmical effects, from super-human down to human and sub-human beings, the totality, in short, of objective existence — then the first and chief difficulty will disappear and Occult Cosmology may be mastered.
>
> *Ibid.,* 75

As people typically cannot get rid of separateness, they go on mutilating Divine Wisdom in the name of making distinctions. In reality, the entire cosmos is a series of exact correspondences, like a series of vast spherical lenses in perfect alignment and continually transmitting prismatic rays of refracted light. Since the cosmos, including human nature, is completely in order, it does not matter at what level one begins one's meditations, so long as one is inwardly attuned to a line of transmission and reflection. The source of this series of reflections and transmissions is what people often loosely call the Higher Self. It is, in reality, the spiritual fire within the human being, the *Atma-Buddhi-Manas* which is overbrooding. This cannot be tapped and its energies cannot be lent merely in providing continuity through the states of consciousness of the lower self. It cannot be drawn upon merely to hold body and soul together. It can only be tapped by a specific means of self-discipline which involves the transformation of the sense of self, the idea of 'I-am-I', from its lower application in terms of name and form to its original meaning connected with *Mahat*. This discipline requires a continual balance between the differentiated aspects of Universal Cognition and those of Universal Root Matter. Whether one thinks of this as ascending a ladder or travelling a path or any other of the symbolic metaphors available to the disciple, it connotes the cognition of synthetic relationships between *Mahat* and the Mahatmas, between *Nous*, *Daiviprakriti* and the *Verbum*. All of these are varied but precise expressions for different levels of reflection of one and the same spiritual energy or spiritual breath and fire. In every case, however expressed, it is the seventh principle in Man and the Kosmos, one with the seventh Cosmic plane, the highest Logos, the Avalokiteshvara.

THE SEVENTH PRINCIPLE

The whole difference between Buddhistic and Vedantic philosophies was that the former was a kind of Rationalistic Vedantism, *while the latter might be regarded as* transcendental *Buddhism.*

H.P. BLAVATSKY*

The juxtaposition and contrast of Buddhist philosophy as rationalistic Vedantism with Vedantic philosophy as transcendental Buddhism arises because of the different ways each attempts to represent the seventh principle in the cosmos and man, the very highest reality. In Vedanta and in Buddhism it is vital to recognize an unconditional reality which cannot possibly be characterized in any terms applicable to conditioned worlds of either subjectivity or objectivity. Absolute Reality cannot be described in terms of the states of mind of beings who experience subjectivity on the planes of differentiated matter. Nor can the Absolute be characterized in terms of properties and relations that may be predicated of moving objects in ever changing relationships on more or less differentiated planes of matter. If both philosophies are agreed upon this, the critical difference between them has to do not merely with the use of terms, but with the idea of consciousness or awareness.

In Vedanta the seventh principle is the *Jivatman.* On its own highest plane, it is a pure, unconscious and universal spirit. *Jivatman* must be seen as a pure subject independent of all possible experiences that may come to it when embodied in a world of subjects and objects. This is important in Vedanta because it provides for the possibility of a self or knower capable of apprehending, uniting with and becoming one with the Absolute. In Vedanta it is crucial to recognize that subjectivity in its highest

* "Editorial Appendix to the Aryan-Arhat Esoteric Tenets"

sense — quite independent of any notions of incarnated or even disembodied existence — belongs to the highest reality. Therefore, it is also possible in Vedanta to think in terms of *Brahman* as giving rise to Ishvara or Brahmā. Sometimes this is put in terms of a distinction between *nirguna* and *saguna Brahman,* that is, *Brahman* without attributes, but appearing as with attributes.

> It must not be thought that the name 'Brahman' is identical . . . with Brahmā or *Iswara* — the personal God. The *Upanishads* — the Vedanta Scriptures — mention no such God, and one would vainly seek in them any allusions to a conscious deity. The Brahman, or Parabrahm, the ABSOLUTE of the Vedantins, is neuter and unconscious, and has no connection with the masculine Brahmā of the Hindu Triad, or *Trimurti.* Some Orientalists rightly believe the name derived from the verb 'Brih', to *grow* or *increase,* and to be, in this sense, the *universal expansive force of nature,* the vivifying and spiritual principle, or power, spread throughout the universe and which in its collectivity is the one Absoluteness, the one Life and the only Reality.
>
> *The Theosophist,* 1884

Vedantins who use this language are still aware that the highest Deity imaginable within a scheme of manifestation is itself, in the ultimate sense, merely an appearance or a portion of the Real existing in relation to time and space during a vast period of manifestation. The conception of Brahmā or Ishvara has meaning in reference to an assemblage of worlds and beings, but it is basically rooted in nothing other than *Parabrahm.* Hence, the distinction between *Parabrahm* and Ishvara is relevant to time and what is called creation. It is a distinction helpful in understanding the gestation of a world of differentiated and conditioned existence out of an unconditioned reality.

Buddhist thought, on the other hand, is concerned that all limitations or anthropomorphic conceptions be avoided. One should not only dispense with any notion of Deity independent of or outside the world of phenomenal existence, but one should not reify consciousness, though absolute and infinite.

> The Buddhists ... deny either subjective or objective reality even to that one Self-Existence. Buddha declares that there is neither Creator nor an ABSOLUTE Being. Buddhist rationalism was ever too alive to the insuperable difficulty of admitting one absolute consciousness, as in the words of Flint — "wherever there is consciousness, there is relation, and wherever there is relation there is dualism."
>
> *Ibid.*

This concern with the temptation to anthropomorphize absolute consciousness, the moment one begins to speak of it, is reflected not only in the contrast between Buddhism and Vedanta but also within Buddhism itself. It appears in the difference between the Madhyamika school and the Yogachara school. In the latter one finds the idea of *alayavijnana,* a storehouse of collective consciousness. This idea is unacceptable to the Madhyamika school of Nagarjuna, where no reality is attributed to anything in any degree except in relation to the One. In pointing to these distinctions, H.P. Blavatsky was not merely making philosophic points about different schools, but was conveying and intimating the profound Teachings of what she called the Arhat secret doctrine. In this doctrine there is ultimately only One Element, and that element — if it is to be characterized at all in the language of consciousness — is unconscious. It is not unconscious in the sense that one might ordinarily attribute to a sleeping person or to a rock, for this sense of the term 'unconscious' is relative to limited states of consciousness in a world of differentiation. To speak of the One Element as unconscious is to imply its total transcendence of all differentiation and manifestation.

> The Arahat secret doctrine on cosmogony admits but of one absolute, indestructible, eternal, and un-created UNCONSCIOUSNESS (so to translate), of an

element (the word being used for want of a better
term) absolutely independent of everything else in the
universe; a something ever present or ubiquitous, a
Presence which ever was, is, and will be, whether there
is a God, gods, or none; whether there is a universe,
or no universe; existing during the eternal cycles of
Maha Yugs, during the *Pralayas* as during the periods of
Manvantara: and this is SPACE, the field for the operation
of eternal Forces and natural Law, the *basis* (as our
correspondent rightly calls it) upon which take place
the eternal intercorrelations of Akasa-Prakriti, guided by
the unconscious regular pulsations of *Sakti*—the breath
or power of conscious deity, the theists would say—the
eternal energy of an eternal, unconscious Law, say the
Buddhists.

Ibid.

Another way of saying this is that the one primordial
element is totally inert or passive, without any relationship
to anything outside itself. At the same time, it is absolute,
indestructible and eternal, being independent of everything in
the universe and, indeed, independent of the universe itself. It
is independent of everything that arises in space and time, and
therefore independent of worlds and *manvantaras*. It transcends
even the distinction between *manvantara* and *pralaya*, and its
being is independent of the existence of a god or gods or the entire
plenitude and panoply of forces at work in the cosmos. Hence,
it is appropriate to symbolize this one ultimate element as
Space. In Gupta Vidya Space is one of the foremost means of
representing and seeking understanding of the Absolute. This is
not space in any relational sense, but Absolute Abstract Space,
which exists eternally and transcends all distinctions between the
manifest and the unmanifest. Because it is beyond *manvantaras*
and *pralayas*, it is equivalent to Eternal Duration. One cannot even
begin to think upon this one Absolute Abstract Space, boundless
and universal, without also thinking about Eternal Duration. In
turn, both of these are related to Eternal Motion.

According to the *Esoteric Axioms of* Gupta Vidya, there is an intimate connection between Eternal Motion and individuated consciousness:

> Whatsoever quits the *Laya* (homogeneous) state becomes active conscious life. Individual consciousness emanates from, and returns into Absolute consciousness, which is eternal MOTION.
>
> "Kosmic Mind"

Eternal Motion linked to Absolute Abstract Space and Duration generates the possibility of conceiving a consciousness which is indistinguishable from unconsciousness, but which is characterizable as Absolute Consciousness. From this originates the entire realm of differentiated and individuated consciousness, the world of subjects and objects on seven different planes.

That which is ascribed here to Ishvara and to *svara* in Hindu metaphysics would be ascribed by Buddhists to the One Law or, in Tibetan terms, Fohat, which is itself the aspect of pulsation of that One Law. These differences of terminology reflect not only differences of language but also of conceptualization bearing upon the spiritual exercises in both systems. At the same time, when one understands philosophically and at the core what is crucial to each system, there is no fundamental difference between them. The difference lies in modes of characterizing the Absolute. In the one case — the Vedanta — the characterization is in terms of spirit and consciousness, while in the case of Buddhism it is in terms of space. The conception of Absolute Abstract Space is represented in Buddhist language by *maha shunyata*. This teaching may be found, for example, in the *Mantra of Voidness,* one of the great short *sutras* of Mahayana Buddhist literature and the basis of a remarkable commentary by the Tibetan Lama Geshe Rabten. He succeeded in conveying something of the transcendental and all-encompassing quality of Voidness, speaking of it in terms analogous to the Alkahest, the universal solvent of alchemical tradition.

This purifying property of space is a recurrent theme throughout the literature of Gupta Vidya. It suggests that if one really knew how to persist and to progress far enough and long enough through deep meditation in understanding the supreme absolute Void, one could totally transform one's consciousness. This means voiding all objects and subjects, everything that one knows in reference to limited periods of time, voiding all worlds and all conceptions of all possible worlds. To do this would be to rise to a level of apprehension of Voidness which is incommunicable. It can only be experienced in the deepest states of meditation.

The practice of meditation upon Voidness is crucial in Tibetan Buddhist theurgy to generating the Buddha vesture. The higher and deeper one goes into Absolute Voidness and the longer one can stay there in deep meditation, the more one will be able to come out of meditation with a total detachment and capacity to transcend this world with all its distortions, changes, illusions and delusions. One can gain an independence of everything pertaining to mayavic life as a seemingly separate individual subject in a world of discrete objects. But more than that, one will be able, through that deep meditation on universal Voidness, to gestate or generate, at a profound level and with a deep intensity of concentration, a matrix of forces simply not accessible or available on any lower plane or through any other means.

All of this was understood and practised during the golden age of Vedic religion. That which Buddhism ascribes to the realization of Voidness is ascribed in the Hindu scheme to the realization of *Brahman*. There is also a direct correlation between the release of subtle energies through inward realization of the four bodies of Brahmā, and the Buddhist teachings of the accessibility of fundamental cosmic generative forces through meditation connected with Fohat. Speaking in the symbolism of Hindu mysticism, H.P. Blavatsky pointed to the significance of the concept of *soma* in Vedic practices which seek to draw upon the energies of the highest Pitris.

A 'soma-drinker' attains the power of placing himself in direct *rapport* with the bright side of the moon, thus deriving inspiration from *the concentrated intellectual energy of the blessed ancestors*. This 'concentration', and the moon being a storehouse of that Energy, is the secret, the meaning of which must not be revealed, beyond the mere fact of mentioning the continuous pouring out upon the earth from the bright side of the orb of a certain influence.

"Thoughts on the Elementals"

Whether this profound Teaching is put in terms of spirit and universal consciousness, in terms of Space and the Void, or indeed in any other mystical terms, what is vital in understanding the Teaching is to avoid any fixity or rigidity arising through the limitations of one's mind. In whatever terms, the universal expansive force is in its collectivity the One Absoluteness, the One Life and the One Reality central to the entire Teaching of Gupta Vidya. This fusion of Absoluteness, the One Life and the One Reality is central to the doctrine of perfectibility. Those who are able to fuse these conceptions in consciousness through meditation are capable of growing into higher states of apprehension of supersensuous matter. They are also enabled to use that knowledge to produce great results in the world by the power of *kriyashakti*. This same Teaching is implicit within the conception of the *Trimurti*, a magnificent symbol of the manifested universe. When one goes beyond all possible concepts of matter, one transcends the *Trimurti*, merging back into the one Supreme Reality. One becomes capable of realizing the powers and instrumentalities of Brahmā, Vishnu and Shiva.

Within Vedanta this sublime level of spiritual realization is elucidated through specific teachings concerning different types of existence.

Vedanta postulating three kinds of existence — (1) the *paramarthika* — (*the true, the only real one*), (2) the *vyavaharika* (the practical), and (3) the *pratibhasika* (the apparent or illusory life) — makes the first *life* or *jiva*, the only truly existent one. Brahma or the ONE'S SELF is its only representative in the universe, as it is the *universal Life in toto* while the other two are but its 'phenomenal appearances', imagined and created by ignorance, and complete illusions suggested to us by our blind senses.

The Theosophist, 1884

As the only true and real existence, *Paramarthika* is related to *svasamvedana* — self-analysing consciousness — at the highest cosmic level. In representing the reality of universal self-consciousness in the Absolute, one could ascribe that universal self-consciousness to a principle or one could intuitively see that beings perfected in previous periods of manifestation, who have reached to that plane of universal self-consciousness, collectively embody *Paramarthika* even in the *mahapralaya* — the long dark night of non-manifestation.

Compared to that supreme state of universal self-consciousness, the states of *vyavaharika* and *pratibhasika* are relatively unreal. Considered in themselves, however, the point of distinguishing between them lies in the difference between penetrating illusions and being able to work through them. On the one hand, there is a capacity to recognize the unreality of the world of appearances, of all lower states of mind, of all perceptions, emotions and desires. All of these are dependent upon and connected with the external world. Yet there is a capacity not only to penetrate these illusions but also to master and appreciate them, a capacity to work in the world of appearances, even though that work, seen from a higher point of view, is itself illusory. All work, however noble and good, is still in time and ultimately has a quality of relativity. It is dependent upon a manifest field and a frame of reference. These are in turn unreal in relation to the eternal night in which the universal self-consciousness of *Brahman* connected with *Paramarthika* is to be imagined. While the realization of emptiness of *pratibhasika* existence is a great attainment, individuals who grasp the significance of *vyavaharika,* or practical existence, have an advantage over those who have merely seen through the illusory nature of life. Through mastering the modes of manifestation, they are able to work in the world of illusion along the lines of what Buddhists call the Bodhisattva vow. They can recognize more fully and freely the educational aspect of manifestation. It is essential to understand that manifestation is not meaningless just because it is unreal relative to the highest states of consciousness. Even though it is unreal, the recognition of that unreality is part of grasping the meaning of manifested existence. That meaning must be seen from the standpoint of the immortal soul and the spiritual individuality.

Without this basis of identity rooted in the ultimate and transcendental *Atman,* the ultimate abstract Buddha-nature, there can be no effective participation in the realms of illusion. The world is bound to appear to the unenlightened as a meaningless struggle for existence. Seen from the perspective of the terrace of enlightenment, however, this struggle for existence is a perpetual struggle for adjustment. In it, everything tends to harmonize and equilibrate before it assumes any shape. This is an aspect of what Buddhists call the One Law and Hindu philosophy calls *ṛta.* It is also symbolized in the great metaphor of the War in Heaven, which works on all planes. For there to be movement from a more rarefied plane of being to a more differentiated plane, there must be some kind of polarization and eventual equilibrium of contraries. To differentiate is to create a greater contrast and therefore also a greater potential field for polarity, for transformation, for adjustment, change and growth. This works not only in reference to the physical body and physical nature, but also in the astral realm. At a higher level the War in Heaven has immediate reference to the evolution of the intellectual principle in mankind.

The teachings regarding the War in Heaven and the polarization and equilibration of contraries give a metaphysical key necessary for psychological comprehension of the possibility of seeing, affecting and cooperating with this perpetual struggle for adjustment. For example, it is the basis for the adoption at a certain stage in occultism of strict rules, where one does not touch animals or human beings or certain objects, where one avoids certain kinds of activity and certain types of people, all for the purpose of self-magnetization. To create a particular kind of field it is crucial to do only those things which are compatible with that field. Most people are not ready for this, but if a person does come to this stage, certainly those changes in life would have to be made which move the plane of struggle altogether from the visible realm to much subtler and deeper aspects of the psyche and the mind affecting states of consciousness experienced in dream and deep sleep.

To make such a quantum jump from one level of apprehension and perception to a much higher level would involve putting into practice the teachings of *Jnana Yoga*. Here, within the central arena of the mind, one must renounce former pictures of oneself and the world, accepting for a period of time a painful immersion into the void or abyss which mystics call the dark night of the soul. Without such a baptism and purification, it is not possible to move to a higher level of conceptualization and imagery in relation to reality. This is actually a twofold process, requiring first the self-conscious negation of prior attachments, followed by an infusion from above and within of original creative energies ultimately flowing from the field of universal self-consciousness. In a sense, one must undo that which has been done in order to realize that which precedes all manifestation.

The process whereby individuals realize universal self-consciousness must itself conform to or be a part of the general process whereby individual consciousness emanates from and returns into Absolute Consciousness or Eternal Motion. Absolute Abstract Motion is beyond all differentiation and manifestation, but considered in its periodic aspect of cosmic motion it is the cause of all subjective and objective differentiations. H.P. Blavatsky explained this in terms of the Hindu idea of *swara*, citing and commenting on a passage from an occult treatise:

'It is the *Swara* that has given form to the *first accumulations of the divisions* of the universe; the *Swara* causes evolution and involution; the *Swara* is God, or more properly the *Great Power* itself *(Maheshwara)*. The *Swara* is the manifestation of the impression on matter of that power which in man is known to us as *the power which knows itself* (mental and *psychic* consciousness). It is to be understood that the action of this power never ceases. . . . It is unchangeable existence' — and this is the 'Motion' of the Scientists and the universal *Breath of Life* of the Occultists.

"Psychic and Noetic Action"

In other words, the ultimate power of self-consciousness, belonging to ideation and therefore to all vibrations associated with self-conscious thought, is causally prior to all the actual impressions on matter which are manifest as the phenomenal world. All matter has been impressed by derivative intelligences flowing from self-conscious ideation. In Gupta Vidya, the entire universe of manifested matter cannot be understood except in terms of the existence of self-conscious knowers, creators and builders — the hosts of the Dhyanis. In essence, the power of self-conscious creation and ideation is indestructible. In itself it cannot cease just because changes in the external field have taken place or entered a period of rest. That power is independent of the field within which it creates secondary and tertiary impressions.

To take a simple example, imagine a Sage who moves from one room, where all the objects have been magnetized by him, to another room or cave elsewhere with a different set of objects. Surely he will magnetize them just as much as the objects in his previous room were magnetized. The self-conscious power of ideation is, at this high level, quite independent of the external field in which it produces derivative impressions of various orders. That power is ultimately the One Life, the One Motion or the one universal Breath of Life, which is equated with the substratum of beginningless and endless cosmic motion. There is, then, within self-consciousness a potential level of causation far transcending all known conceptions of causality involving a complexity of factors, parameters and variables within particular fields of differentiated existence.

In the *Stanzas of Dzyan* this boundless potentiality inherent in *svara* is connected with the hypostatic descent of the One Ray into the Luminous Egg of *Hiranyagarbha*, thereby initiating the process of cosmic manifestation. This threefold hypostatic presence within the Golden Egg of Brahmā is called "the root that grows in the ocean of life." This is

> the potentiality that transforms into objective differentiated matter the universal, subjective, ubiquitous but homogeneous germ, or the eternal essence which contains the potency of abstract nature.
>
> *Transactions of the Blavatsky Lodge*

H.P. Blavatsky distinguished the purely transcendental, absolute and abstract nature of this potentiality from its manifold modes of activity in cosmic manifestation in terms of *Paramatman* and *Jivatman*:

> The Ocean of Life is . . . the 'One Life', Paramatma, when the transcendental supreme Soul is meant; and Jivatma, when we speak of the physical and animal 'breath of life' or, so to speak, the differentiated soul, that life in short, which gives being to the atom and the universe, the molecule and the man, the animal, plant, the mineral.
>
> *Ibid.*

Just as the *Jivatman* is an emanation or projection of the *Paramatman* — the transcendental supreme soul — so too the *Jivatman* emanates a breath of life essential to all gestation and growth on the physical, astral and intellectual planes. This is the fundamental formative factor in all the kingdoms of Nature, including not only the mineral, plant and animal kingdoms, but the human kingdom as well. Behind this, however, in a deeper sense directly connected to the *Paramatman*, a breath of the Divine Life is present in the power of self-consciousness.

An intimation of this presence may be glimpsed by considering the etymology of the word *Atman*, which is ordinarily spoken of as the seventh principle of human nature but which is in reality no discrete principle at all. *Svara*, the current of the life-wave in the dual process of involution and evolution, is the Spirit within the universal soul, the living basis of the laws of cosmic motion. The term *Atman*, coming as it does from the root *at*, carries the idea of Eternal Motion. In turn, the root *at* is a variant of two other roots: *ah*, containing the idea of breath, and *as*, conveying the idea of being. Thus, the eternal motion of Divine Light associated with the *Atman* is the Divine Life-Breath. It is also the basis of pure noumenal being. These roots have their origin in the sound produced by the breath of all living beings. As the primordial current of life, it is the basis of inspiration and expiration, the beating of the heart, the cycles of the seasons, the vast periods of *pralaya* and *manvantara*.

This is a tremendous truth to contemplate. It implies that anyone who has gained the power of withdrawing consciousness from the physical and astral bodies, and who has become capable of self-existence in the pure divine sphere of light surrounding every human being, is capable of tapping the higher reaches of noumenal spiritual and mental breathing. Such a Man of Meditation realizes *Brahman* and the Void beyond all beings, the perpetual motion within the depths of the ocean of Life that endures whether universes exist or not. It is beyond all formulation and characterization, beyond all schools and philosophies. It is the eternal pulsation in the Golden Egg of *Hiranyagarbha*, the eternal motion of the *Atman*, the eternal vibration within the divine sphere of Light.

PRIMEVAL SELF-GENERATION

LAKSHMINARAYANA

The primeval Father-Mother of the *Stanzas of Dzyan* is what the Hindus called Lakshmi-Narayana. In its state of pure potential in eternal duration and boundless space, it is prior to all worlds and beings. It is tellingly depicted in the *Rig Veda* as the One, the Alone, which breathes breathless by its own nature, and apart from which there is nothing whatsoever. Lakshmi-Narayana is signified by Buddhists as *Svabhavat* — noumenal, homogeneous, radiant substance — void of all attributes, but having the intrinsic, inexhaustible capacity of self-generation. More neutrally, it is the noumenon of spirit-matter, which is also the one force, the one life, and the abstract basis of all potential subjectivity and objectivity in the context of pre-cosmic ideation. The name 'Father-Mother' indicates its dynamic potential for cosmogonic creativity, and it is also known as the seven-vowelled sound, too sacred to pronounce, which must be seen as prior to all differentiation and which enshrines the ultimate mystery of all archetypal gestation.

In the Platonic or Hermetic tradition it is known as Divine Thought, prior to cosmic ideation, let alone the emergence from the ever-existent universal mind of what we call the cosmic mind, which in turn becomes *Mahat*, the supreme intelligence behind any system of worlds. It is intrinsically mysterious because of the central paradox that the boundless Absolute can neither think, will, nor feel, nor indeed take on any self-limitation, and yet, the world of differentiated objects and subjects characterizing manifestation must have an intrinsic continuity and con-substantiality with the undifferentiated, the unbounded, the indivisible. This mystery belongs to the dawn of differentiation, which precedes what we ordinarily call differentiation and at the same time suggests, such as during the dark hours at the dawn of Venus, the pristine state of the first Logos. The unmanifest Logos is pre-cosmic ideation and pre-cosmic substance, and also potential pre-cosmic force. It is all these three in one, in a state of primordial unity. If this Logos is intrinsically eternal, omnipresent and ever-existent, it cannot be brought into any temporal, causal or chronological sequence, or into any possible relationship to our world of space and time. It must be prior to all planes of matter, all states of consciousness, and all worlds of subjects and objects.

At the same time, its inconceivable transcendence does not make it less real than whatever is immanent or immediate to any set of spectators. It is, in fact, supremely real, and all that is immanent, manifest or conceivable in the realm of the manifest must be less real, or only derivatively real, in relation to it as the Rootless Root. If we can sense something of this mystery of mysteries, we should be able to rise beyond all polarity, duality and manifestation. At the same time, brooding in the silence, we should gain some idea of the ever-present ubiquity of the one endless existence beyond all change, the one life behind and beyond all life processes, the one supreme source of all. Veiled by the most noumenal essence of spirit-matter, it is boundless and inexhaustible potential, capable of gestating and also transcending infinite worlds, but incapable of being diminished or attenuated however many infinities are drawn out of it. As the Upanishads declare, "From the fullness, fullness was taken out, and fullness remained."

We may visualize it as absolute, abstract, dimensionless space; or as eternal duration; or as *Sat-Chit-Ananda* — Be-ness, consciousness, bliss; or as a Divine Darkness overbrooding the mother deep of boundless space, endless duration and ceaseless, motionless motion; or as a Soundless Sound in absolute Silence; or as a primordial Light of all lights shooting its pristine ray into the immaculate, eternal, virgin egg which seems to condense into the World Egg. All such metaphors, images and symbols, let alone words and concepts, fail to convey the incommunicable, but they intimate the mystery of self-consciousness and also of LIFE. This is archetypally true of the images in the *Stanzas of Dzyan*, which are really much more than mere images, because they are capable of sustaining an immense depth of philosophical meditation.

> DARKNESS RADIATES LIGHT, AND LIGHT DROPS ONE SOLITARY RAY INTO THE MOTHER-DEEP. THE RAY SHOOTS THROUGH THE VIRGIN EGG. THE RAY CAUSES THE ETERNAL EGG TO THRILL, AND DROP THE NON-ETERNAL GERM, WHICH CONDENSES INTO THE WORLD-EGG.
>
> *Stanzas of Dzyan*, III.3

Here we have the fundamental dynamic of Father-Mother which must point to the mystery of self-consciousness and of LIFE itself, visible and invisible. From the subtlest metaphysical interaction as depicted in the Stanzas, right down to the procreation of children, the dynamic of Father-Mother points to a universal core mystery. There is much more than a mechanical interaction at work, something much more mysterious than linear logic. *A* and *B* does not equal *AB*, but mysteriously produces *C*, or you might say *ABC*.

This same dynamic applies at all levels of being, and, by analogy and correspondence, the principles operating in this core dynamic are central to the attempt to make meaningful, inward connections in consciousness, for example, between knowledge and virtue, or between insight and energy. To understand this, one must first comprehend at some level the relevance of *Svabhavat*, spirit-matter, or Father-Mother to the mystery of LIFE itself, both invisible and visible, before turning to the deeper mystery of universal and collective human self-consciousness. Then one can turn to a scrutiny of the logic behind the dynamics of *Svabhavat* and consider its relevance to all levels of being, actual and possible. From this, one may appreciate its practical or psycho-ethical implications in making significant, unexpected connections, resolving what look like sharp contrasts, reconciling dissimilars, integrating different, disparate sectors or categories, as a way of recovering and rejoicing in the inviolable, indissoluble integrity of Being, both cosmic and human.

First of all, considering the mystery of LIFE invisible and visible, when we normally look upon any entity or process as alive, and not dead or wholly dormant, we commonly assume a persisting identity or a systemic structure. We assume some means to recognize and confirm a principle of internal growth, discernable change and persisting patterns, as well as a measure of intelligibility and indeed of intelligence in responsiveness to inner demands and outer pressures. Everything alive may be somewhat mysterious, in that philosophically, all explanations are incomplete. The total stock of all our knowledge is inadequate, and even where predictability is possible, there is an inscrutable element in reference to time and timing, and in relation to rates of change or what looks like uniformity of behaviour. If we go further and ask questions about sentience, awareness, consciousness, self-regulation and self-correction, or about possibilities of choice and probabilities of outcome, our task becomes even more difficult. But, if we raise a question not merely about all of this, or about the boundary between the living and the moribund, but actually about the intrinsic life principle itself, it is extremely difficult to cope with an issue of such generality. It overwhelms our thought and language, outstrips the finest exercise of our reason and the farthest reach of our intuition, and even surpasses the depth of our imagination. However, when we look at the etymology of the Sanskrit word *Svabhavat* — and no wonder Sanskrit is the language of the science of the future — we notice at the core of its meaning the idea of self-generation to an indefinite extent with inexhaustible potential, with immense and even immeasurable fecundity, and also its unitary nature, *sva*, as a single supreme substance or substratum, *bhava*, in a process of constant inner movement.

In the cosmogony of Gupta Vidya there is only one life, one force, one intelligence, one substance, which is the primordial one element. All of these are equivalent to each other. Just as Spinoza found the whole universe to be only one substance that equals both Nature and God, all of these are equivalent, a single substance. They, or rather IT, is prior to the distinctions between spirit and matter, and subject and object. It is prior to all differentiation and every act of conceiving, ideating or moving anything at all. It is the luminosity hidden in darkness, reposing in eternal Duration in a condition of total latency or non-manifestation. It is outside any conceivable space or time matrix, and it is unrelated to anything we may call motion or causality. And yet, it is the one and only LIFE, because there is nothing else but itself. And, it is the sole source of worlds, beings, minds, forms and prototypes of anything and everything that can come into existence. It is the ultimate mystery itself, the *mysterium tremendum* of which mystics speak. It is the mystery of non-spatial Space, non-temporal Duration and unconscious Consciousness. It is not the Absolute, but a veil upon Absoluteness, because it can potentially give rise to worlds and beings, whereas the Absolute *per se* is without any conceivable or possible relation to anything other than itself. It is pure potential which contains all possibilities, probabilities and conceivable modes of actualization, like a blank slate or screen, or an empty stage. Here, one can think of myriads upon myriads of frail and yet suggestive analogies, but none of them can remotely convey the reality of the Absolute.

Secondly, turning to the mystery of universal human self-consciousness, one may ask, What is its relationship to *Svabhavat*? Self-generation is not necessarily equivalent to self-consciousness, especially if it is innate in primordial spirit-matter or *Svabhavat*, which, though all-inclusive, homogeneous and universal, does not involve a conscious fusion of subject and object, their mutual interaction, or the union of the Knower, the Known and the process of Knowing. To put this in another way, if Father-Mother-Son are wholly one in a state of blissfully unconscious repose, it would be misleading to talk of universal self-consciousness, except as potentially present, like everything else, within it. But this approach is wholly to focus upon *Svabhavat* as the world-substance of spiritual matter, or as the plastic essence of matter which is homogeneous and prior to all differentiation. We should remember that 'the seven-skinned Mother-Father' is a symbol for all the emergent septenates, connected not only with planes of matter, but also with states of mind or being — the seven states of consciousness which correlate with seven planes of thought as well as of substance.

That is why Plato and Hermes Trismegistes would regard this Mother-Father as Divine Thought, the basis of eternal self-existence, which corresponds exactly to the older, magnificent, Hindu androgynous Lakshmi-Narayana. This would certainly be the paradigm of universal self-consciousness at the highest level of Deity, which is also the source and fount of life eternal, the light of the first Logos, sometimes called the unmanifested Logos, which is simultaneously pre-cosmic ideation, pre-cosmic root substance and primordial Fohatic force, or Daiviprakritic Light, the eternal Soundless Sound — *Nadabrahman*. The highest perfected beings are fused with, attuned to, and consubstantial with the sacred eternal Flame of universal self-consciousness, and are therefore Watchers in the night of non-manifestation. That is why the mystery of the one eternal Life itself may be seen as a radiation of the deeper or more hidden mystery of universal self-consciousness.

Thirdly, given this, we can sense the logic of the inner dynamics of *Svabhavat,* spirit-matter or Father-Mother. It is no less than the logic of primordial, ever-existent, all potent unity, the logic of the highest Logos, which is the sacred Three-in-One which, when fused with the life-light flowing from its apex and through its radiating aura, is the divine Tetraktys. It is Eternity in time, the unspeakably sacred *Ain Soph,* inseparable from that light which is the primordial *shakti,* the immaculate virgin goddess of wisdom, Sarasvati Vach, Isis Athena, the supreme truth-ideation-bliss of this inconceivably highest of states of self-existence. It is the Unity of unities, the Triad which is the father of all triads, within the boundless circle of Eternal Duration, the circle with its centre everywhere and circumference nowhere. As the secret, sacred source of noumenal life, light and electricity at the highest pre-cosmic level, it is also the noumenon of all cosmic creativity prior to, during and beyond all possible brooding, gestation and manifestation. It is eternal and yet also the source of what is ever-new, its newness being a source of endless mystical wonder in the highest contemplation of the greatest sages and seers. Its dynamism is best understood in the Platonic sense of *dynamis*, as that which is presupposed by everything else, which being subsequent to it, may best, or indeed only, be seen in relation to it as a subliminal substratum, to use a misleading Latin term. The logic and inner dynamic of spirit-matter or Father-Mother is extremely elusive, and almost impossible to pin down, formulate, or characterize.

We could readily see this if we considered the long standing difficulties for millennia in relation to the ancient, medieval and modern notions of substance, essence or being, and therefore also mind, matter, and force, or with the logic of internal and external relations which is so crucial to understanding Aether-*Akasha*. To take an illustration, the 'problem of substance' has perplexed, bewildered and eluded the best philosophical minds that the best exoteric civilizations have produced. In the writings of Aristotle, who took something occult, twisted it and then created problems for a long time after, the principle term for substance, *ousia*, was a word which for earlier Greek writers meant 'property' in the legal sense of the word, 'that which is owned'. This sense is familiar in English in the old-fashioned expression 'a man of substance', which meant a man of property. The word *ousia* also occurs in philosophical writings before Aristotle, but with a different sense. It is a synonym for *physis*, a term which can either mean the origin of a thing, its natural constitution or structure, the stuff of which things are made, or a natural kind of species. The Latin word *substantia*, from which the English term is derived, is a literal translation of the Greek *hypostasis*, 'standing under', which was, of course, important to Socrates and Plato in their formulation of the stairway of the dialectic. This term acquired its philosophical connotations in later Greek and occurs principally in controversies among Christian theologians about the real nature of Christ, the body of Christ, the *corpus christi*, the soul of Christ and so on.

A third philosophical term *hypokemenon*, 'that which

underlies' something, is used by both Plato and Aristotle to refer to that which presupposes something else, a notion having some conceptual relation to *Svabhavat*. But, to see why the 'problem of substance' became a problem, and a big one at that, one must turn to Aristotle, who said in his *Categories* that *ousia*, substance, in the truest, primary and most definite sense of the word, is that which is neither predicable of nor present in a subject. For instance, the individual man or horse is a primary *ousia* or substance. Then he said, those things are called substances within which a species of primary substances are included, and so also those things which, as genera, include the species. That is, there is more of substance in man than in the individual man. Aristotle seems to have the idea here that essences or natures are substances, and that the more qualities they comprise the more substantial they really are. The notion of essences as substances is treated at length by Aristotle in the *Metaphysics*. His doctrine of secondary substances has little to recommend it, and involves a serious logical confusion between the relations of class membership and class inclusion, as well as the notorious difficulties of the doctrine of essences.

In another sense, Aristotle held that substances can exist on their own, whilst qualities and relations can only exist as the qualities and relations of substances. Thus, X is said merely to be present in Y when X is incapable of existence apart from Y. This notion introduces a third sense of substance as that which is capable of independent existence. It is difficult enough to define clearly what one means by speaking of qualities as incapable of existence independent of substances. It is yet another thing to treat relations in the same fashion. Once we introduce the notion of relations of substances as involving dependence on other substances, we put a restriction not only on the independent existence of those relations, but also upon that of the related substances themselves, very few of which would be what they are independent of any relations. A fourth criterion of substance entertained by Aristotle is that which, whilst remaining numerically one and the same, is capable of admitting contrary qualities. This notion is developed by later philosophers into the conception of a center of change, and thus of a substratum that underlies and supports its qualities. Finally, Aristotle emphasized the notion of substance as a logical subject, that which is not asserted or predicated of a subject, but of which everything is asserted.

These various notion of substance — 1. as a concrete individual; 2. as a core of essential properties; 3. as what is capable of independent existence; 4. as a center of change; 5. as a substratum; and 6. as a logical subject — are never thoroughly worked out and reconciled in Aristotle. Most of the time he prefers the second sense: substance as a core of essential properties. But, when one thinks of *Svabhavat* — the one and only substance in Spinoza's sense, that which is self-generating, and which is the spirit of matter — one is thinking of that which cannot have any attributes because it is prior to differentiation. The object-oriented and seemingly specific Aristotelian concept of substance simply is of no help in understanding concepts like *Svabhavat*. This is a problem to this day, certainly in physics, but in all other fields as well. The ancient atomist school, founded by Leucippus and Democritus, developed by Epicurus, and expressed in its most attractive form in *De Rerum Natura* by the Roman poet Lucretius, held that the only truly real and substantial elements of Nature are the atoms out of which everything is composed. It is these that are fundamental, unchangeable, and in the last resort capable of independent existence. This is a bit closer to *Svabhavat* than the other Aristotelian conceptions of substance, yet it is not that simple, particularly when the Aristotelian notions of a concrete individual or a core of properties are substituted, in modern atomism, for the actual understandings of the classical atomists.

Now, Spinoza showed that if by substance we mean that which is fully independent in its existence, that which is in itself and is conceived through itself, then it is easy to show that there can be only one such being, which is the whole universe. Thus, Spinoza equated substance with God and Nature. This was called by Hume a 'hideous hypothesis', and it won for Spinoza the inconsistent titles of 'atheist' and 'pantheist'. Prejudice being little troubled by inconsistency, modern Christian missionaries and their apologists hurled these two epithets as rebukes against Buddhism. Having detected the same spirit in Buddhist thought that is found in Spinoza, they confidently declared Buddhists to be both atheists and pantheists. In addition, having perhaps partially grasped the earnest practical intent of Buddhist psychology, which is to force the choice between God and Mammon, they also found Buddhist thought 'pessimistic' because it so clearly came out against Mammon. Considering Spinoza in his immediate context, however, what he really did was indicate obliquely that substantiality in Descartes' sense is a matter of degree. While there may well be both thinking things —subjects or minds, and extended things — objects in space, nothing in the universe is completely independent of its environment. Subjects and objects are inevitably interdefinable, which we would readily understand today in the language of system analysis. In particular contexts, and for certain purposes, some are more dependent or more independent than others, but these attributions of independence and dependence are only relatively true.

The basic element of Leibnitz's metaphysical system was not the atom, not substance in any Aristotelian sense, but what he called the 'monad'. In his *Monadology* he defines a monad as nothing but a simple substance. There were in Pythagorean and Platonic thought references to a primordial Monad that comes out of the primeval darkness, radiates, and then disappears again into the darkness, like the Concealed Lord in Tibetan Buddhism. But when Leibnitz said that a monad is nothing but a simple substance, what he meant by 'simple' was without parts, impartite and indivisible. At the same time, his monads were supposed to be immaterial substances, invisible centres of change, as well as subjects to which predicates can be applied, observationally and conceptually. This created the problem in early twentieth century logic that a substance remaining apart from its predicates seems destitute of meaning. It is as if one were to talk to the average person of a god that neither thinks, wills or feels. Such a god is totally empty of any meaning or any reality for that person, even though the person may see the futility and philosophical absurdity of a finitized, thinking, feeling god which is merely one 'person' among many persons, but the most supreme.

Kant, who had anticipated some of these difficulties raised in twentieth century logic, approached the concept of substance metaphysically, radically transforming the terms of the discussion. In his view, the unity and permanence of substances are features that are contributed to the world of phenomena by human understanding. One can now see the relevance of this approach to contemporary particle physics, but, on the other hand, it is also applicable to the highest ordinary metaphysics. The process of observation itself, or at least its preconditions, substantializes or makes an entity out of whatever can be observed in terms of an inner unity or coherence and a possible combination of reliable predicates. Thus for Kant, substance shrinks from being a fundamental feature of the objective world to merely an aspect under which men cannot help classifying their possible experience. They cannot help themselves not because of the nature of external reality, but because of the structure of their own cognitive apparatus.

Today, there is no one unitary science, such as metaphysics or ontology, that can be looked to in the external world for a solution. On one logical interpretation, a substance is something for whose existence there are no necessary conditions. Yet, it may well be that nothing in the universe is independent of all conditions in the universe, but this then becomes an empirical question. The relation being predicated often turns out to be nothing more than the familiar notion of being a member of a group. The moment you say of X that it has a property Y, in principle it can be said to belong to or depend upon a group that has in common the property or characteristic Y. All of this chains us within complexity and the desire for intelligibility, but at the same time condemns us to the impossibility of gaining clarity, consistency and all-comprehensiveness with regard to what the *Tao Te Ching* calls 'the ten thousand things', all specific substances. None of these difficulties would arise with the conception of

Svabhavat, but to avail ourselves of it would require an equally difficult degree of abstraction from what we call either material or mental, matter or mind, and even what we call living or existence. Certainly, there can be no metaphysically or conceptually cheap solution to the predicament surrounding the 'problem of substance'.

In nineteenth century thought, Hegel attempted to resolve the nature of substance by modifying certain aspects of Leibnitzian monadology. Leibnitz had seen every monad as a subject that contains all its predicates. When one refers to a particular human being, for example, conceived as a monad, this reference theoretically includes anything and everything that anybody either now or yesterday or tomorrow could say truly and accurately about that monad. Every subject contains all its predicates. That is, a monad is an individual from the proper notion of which one should be able to deduce everything that anyone could ever say of it. Now of course, we do not even begin to do this with actual human individuals because we are stuck merely by name and form, by association, habit, memory and expectation. But, in theory, if one pushed this far enough, perhaps because one was so infinitely in love with just one person in this world, one would eventually come up against the difficulty that, however much may be predicated of this individual, there is something about him that goes beyond predication. One difficulty here is that Leibnitz attributed to his monads, which are actually epistemological subjects, the sort of identity that typically belongs to a predicate. To know something as a predicate is to know what it implies, that is, a definite set of entailments that define it. This approach is, for the reasons stated, inadequate for epistemological subjects. Like Spinoza, Hegel sought to avoid this difficulty by allowing only one individual substance, but then he went further, in the shadow of Christian theology, and called it the Absolute, the ultimate subject of every statement, which enters into everything always. But, unlike Spinoza, Hegel did not endow individuals with any real basis of independence as subjects, like a *connatus* of Spinoza, but rather left them as merely dependent aspects of the collective subjectivity of the Absolute. This then raises, for Hegel, the problem of how two different people who see differently can settle between them how and when their recognitions of the ubiquity of the Absolute tally with each other, or do not, and what to do about it.

Another version of the problem springs from the same root as the Hegelian Absolute, but in twentieth century idealist logic, is the notion of the concrete universal, which takes features of both subjects and predicates in a single entity. Whereas a monad is a subject with the characteristics of a predicate, a concrete universal is a predicate treated as a concrete individual thing. Eating, and therefore the eater, would be an example. But, in advanced formal logic, Frege insisted, there are both objects and concepts, and both are necessary if one wants to build up a mathematical or axiomatic system, or if one wants simply to make sense of the foundations of mathematics, arithmetic and number theory. For Frege objects are complete or, so to speak, saturated, and that is what makes an object an object. Whereas, a concept or a function is incomplete or unsaturated, so that a concept term is always a predicate that can be added to, enlarged and modified. Therefore, it can never become a fixed subject like an object, and the attempt to characterize, for example, persons as concrete universals is bound to be either incomplete, if sufficiently complex to be interesting, or pointless, if confined to the properly concrete.

This distinction of Frege's raises other problems in reference to logic, but already this much is enough to show how any attempts to resolve everything that exists in this world to one notion of substance or matter is as difficult, if not more so, than trying to reduce it merely to one thing that we might call mind or consciousness. This difficulty is built into our logic and into our language, and this is only to show why the problem, if one tries to understand it, let alone go deeply into it, is not an easy one. It is perfectly true that if we can sense through illumination, a flash of reason, or an intuitive apprehension which is also a form of pristine prayer or communion, the sacred logoic logic mentioned earlier, we can resolve all dichotomies, transcend all polarities, and reconcile all standpoints. Actually, we are more likely to do this in silence rather than in speech, in pauses rather than in articulations or responses. And if we do, we are likely to be able to express this only through ejaculations, through making noises like those babies make when they learn, because it is difficult to express the reconciliation or resolution we sense inwardly in our being or consciousness — some would say in our guts — in a way that can be formulated without creating more difficulty, disagreement and more problems. Hence, if one can sense some resolution through direct, immediate experience in silence, such as through love, whatever the object of devotion, then, even if one cannot put it into words and get other people's compliance or conviction, one can still retain it as something very private, but it can be as real as one chooses to make it by one's allegiance and attention.

It can also help to make original, significant, daring connections between seemingly discontinuous or totally different spheres of life. Two things may seem objectively unconnected, but if one gets into the habit of pondering upon this logoic logic, one will be surprised what sudden new connections could be made between, say, water and fire, or between earth and air, or between any two things which ordinarily seem like opposite poles. For example, if one takes maleness and femaleness as categories of thought and plunges sufficiently deeply into either of them, one will find that each is dependant upon the other, defined by the other, and that what looks initially like a contrast eventually actually becomes an absorption and also transcends the polarity itself. In slowly training oneself in this way, it will help to watch great spiritual artists, musicians and dancers enacting superbly the ever-integrating calculus of the divine dialectic, ceaselessly fusing the one and the many, the Knower, the Known and All-Knowing, in a single obeisance to the ever unknowable. It could all be put in a simple *namaste*, if behind the *namaste* there is true reverence, true universality, true love of all humanity, true respect for being human and true respect for the Divine. It could be done by a gesture, it could be done by a glance. Here one is reminded of the magnificent and unique gestures of great Teachers, both in recorded history, such as the holding up of a flower by the Buddha, and in profound literature, such as the kiss by Jesus at the time of his rejection by the Grand Inquisitor.

One should as a minimum begin by radically rethinking and continually questioning the seeming contrast between the potential and the actual. What looks potential to one person seems actual to someone else who is at another stage. Or, one could rethink the relation between what we call the passive and the active, recalling H.P. Blavatsky's statement, 'My days are my *pralayas,* my nights are my *manvantaras.*' Again, one should constantly rethink the relations between the real and the unreal, between being and becoming, between the unmanifest, the ever-manifesting and the fully manifested, and, if one is going to go even deeper into a life of mystic meditation, one must question the distinctions between what we call life and death, what we call old and young, what we regard as living and what we think to be dying, as well as upon *nirvana* and *samsara.* And, there is much to be learned by contemplating the ever rich and enigmatic relationships between the seed and the fruit, the root and the flower, which are both beautiful and challenging to the refined spiritual imagination, the mystic poet hidden in every human heart.

At the same time, whilst ceaselessly exploring and endlessly attenuating all conditioned sense of self, making a spiritual quest out of the questionings of the heart and of the head, we should ever remember the wisdom of the saying that we can best approach the mystery of life through the tree of life. In a Blakean sense one should try to see the ocean through a drop, the world through a grain of sand, eternity through an illusory moment in the eternal now, and heaven in a wild flower. To take an exalted example, one may salute the sacred fires within the crystalline globe of mystic initiation, rejoicing in the thought, like Mahatma K.H., that in every granitic rock or grain of sand there is a magnificent crystallization of the invisible flame of Supreme Spirit. It is in the bright crystals, but it is also in what looks like hard rock. Every particle conceals the magically perfect insemination by *Mahapurusha*, the *uttamapurusha* in the sacred womb of Aditi-*Akasha*. To complicate the metaphor, and to be both brahminical and rabbinical, imagine *Mahapurusha* in the sacred womb of Aditi-*Akasha* with what the ancient Kabbalist called the closed eye of *En Soph* in the blazing light of the Divine Darkness. These incredibly powerful pregnant metaphors suggest a reversal of the polarities and inversions of our modes, negating the karma creating thoughts, words and reactions with which we are totally congested, and which we dare to make the basis of judgments and decisions with a false finality and pseudo-solemnity that would be comic were it not so pathetic. It is quite extraordinary how far inversion can go creating a situation where one is actually completely closed to the magnificent open-texture of even dawn and midnight, of the great globe of the earth, and of the starry universe, let alone the proemial Kosmos that can be contemplated as the embryo of all possible universes.

Each and every time we take anything for granted, we are petrifying instead of crystallizing. When Mahatma K.H. spoke of the crystallization of the flame of Spirit in granite or sand, he also referred to petrification, which works through fear and produces the opposite result. Crystallization depends upon the right degree of temperature, and upon cooling at the correct time at a certain rate. Nature does this quite extraordinary heating and cooling best, blending them together to produce a particular kind of crystal. Here, one is reminded of the magnificent metaphor of the old Lama who wordlessly shows a young boy a magnificent crystal Buddha, revealing to him the radiance in the crystal that brings it alive, making matter perfectly synchronous with the causally prior crystalline beauty of being and thought of the Buddha-state. Then, if one thinks of the seven primary crystalline geometries, which are like Akashic cell types in biology, one may begin to intuit something extraordinary, that the fiery seed of the purest metaphysical poetry, of Vedic speech, lies concealed, waiting to be ignited, within every mute monad immersed in the universal pilgrimage of all LIFE. This is what is really going on in and around us all the time.

If we can think and feel deeply enough about this, we will understand why participation in embodied existence is a great illusion — and indeed can be extremely delusive — if it is not offset by even more time spent in silent communion that counterbalances the amount of involvement through visible participation. This is the real reason and the spiritual imperative behind the need to rethink the relation between the visible and the invisible, the seemingly substantial and the truly real, the spoken and the unspoken, the reactive and the self-generating, the world of mayavic form and the cosmos of spirit-matter, *Svabhavat*, the mystical Father-Mother. Because the external and sensory is the embodiment of the non-existent and the unreal, it will be eternally true that more can be suggested of the real than said, that more can be conveyed of it through gesture than through specific expressions. The language of the soul is in the light of the eyes, but it also resonates through every life atom within the human being. To realize it in fullness is to become a witness to the highest mysteries of adamantine perfectibility, to master the Divine Creative power of *Kriyashakti*, and to become one with the crystalline radiance of the Logos within and beyond the eternal Father-Mother.

DATELESS AND DEATHLESS

Having taken as a bow the great weapon of the Secret Teaching, one should fix in it the arrow sharpened by constant Meditation. Drawing it with a mind filled with That (Brahman) *penetrate, O bright youth, that Immutable Mark.*

The pranava (AUM) *is the bow; the arrow is the self; Brahman is said to be the mark. With heedfulness It is to be penetrated. Become one with It as the arrow in the mark.*

Mundaka Upanishad

Dateless and deathless, the intricate impulse works its will.

RUPERT BROOKE

To become a man of meditation is to master the Science of Spirituality, which may be approached by any aspirant who is in earnest pursuit of the ageless truth. All human beings are consubstantial with the very highest in the cosmos. All human beings are also continuously interacting, through the ceaseless flux and efflux of life-atoms in their enveloping vestures, with everything that exists. This dual participation in time and timelessness is central to the attempt of any person to raise his or her sights, to arouse the power of spiritual awakening, to go beyond all categories, including even the subtlest intellectual conceptions. The essence of the inmost core of being, the self, is inseparable from the Self of the whole and the Self in each and all. Whenever a person makes such an attempt, he is not in the same position as at any other moment. No human being can be sundered from other human selves owing to the constant interaction of life-atoms, and every human soul participates, in principle and in practice, in all the states of being of all beings that are now alive, or were embodied upon this earth.

From this enormous universal perspective, one can see that most ordinary thinking, even concerning spiritual life, is way off centre, what the Hopi Indians called *koyaanisqatsi,* out of balance, reeling, badly requiring radical readjustment. It is based upon an emphasis on a minute portion of oneself bound up with present preoccupations and feelings, passing emotions and desires. Owing to limited specific aims, people hold extremely foreshortened, fragmented and distorted conceptions of themselves. When this fact is coupled with the endemic tendency to manufacture a delusive personality out of habits, wants, memories and fears, one comes to see that most so-called human life is a sorry disappointment to the immortal soul. Yet, whilst every human being must live in the world for the sake of spiritual growth — for there can be no growth without participation — no human being need be lost. Every human being must to some extent participate in the world of illusion, in the whirl of change, and therefore in the realm of ever-conflicting and ever-changing thoughts, feelings and desires. This does not, however, alter the fundamental fact that every human being is perpetually rooted in That which is beyond all time and worlds.

In the Upanishads this paradox is portrayed by the metaphor of two birds in a tree — the one busily pecking at the tree's fruits, the other serenely watching from above. One's true Self is a spectator in eternity, seeing everything from a universal and eternal standpoint that is unmodified by mental conceptions and undisturbed by fleeting emotions. It is witness to the captivity of the other bird in the world of illusions, a participating and fragmented mind, which is by turns passive and assertive, frightened and aggressive, grasping and gasping. Once one recognizes that there is a deeper core in one's being which does not become involved in the world of time, change and reaction, but is able to reflect upon the entirety of what happens to all the lower vestures, then one begins to recognize in oneself a principle of transcendence and a true basis of aspiration.

There is no unbridgeable gap between the two perspectives. The potential awareness in the bird that is caught in illusions of the other bird as its true Self will make a crucial difference in its ability to relativate its plane of perception. From the perspective of the Science of Spirituality, which is grounded in the ontology of objective idealism, everything in the universe is the result of ideation. All forms, at every level, are, at root, expressions or manifestations of pure ideas. Two important consequences follow from this: first of all, there is an interpenetration of all worlds through ideas; and secondly, there is in every human being a power to step aside from self. Through ideation, one can abstract and remove oneself from seeming captivity to the world, and instead of doing this involuntarily through sleep or death, or intermittently through emotional or intellectual ecstasy, one can learn to do this consciously, constructively and as a matter of spiritual discipline.

If one can think this through, not merely in relation to specific contexts and particular situations, but in terms of all manifested existence and the entire sphere of objective phenomena, one will come to see that there is an illusion inherent in the manifested world itself, and that its relative reality is only the result of ideational participation, involvement through a lesser ideation, by the Self in that world. In other words, though the metaphor of the two birds or selves is helpful, one is, in reality, only one being with the power of ideation. The concept of the scale of ideation, ranging from the absolute and abstract to the particular and concrete, is directly reflected in the constitution of the human mind. The distinction between the divine intelligence of higher *Manas* and the personal ray of the same mind is really a difference between sets or classes of perceptions. One can look at anything passively by comparing and contrasting, obsessively, and from within a narrow spatio-temporal framework. Or one can loosen the framework and look at the same thing from a larger perspective, in relation to the distant past and what may be in the dawning future, in relation to what is deceptively near or far, but also in relation to certain intimate feelings and enduring convictions that are actually much closer to oneself than the dominant emotions or *idée fixe* of any particular context.

These capacities to alter perspectives, to expand horizons and to deepen perceptions all spring from the fundamental capacity to ideate. At its very deepest core, the Self is eternally ideating and eternally watching, but this vital truth is obscured by the extent to which one becomes wholly identified with the participating and reacting self. The projected ray, itself the product and proof of the power of ideation, becomes permeable to external sights and forces which appear to be inescapable because they affect one's inner feelings, states of mind and persisting moods. Affecting one's astral system and the extent to which it is stretched or strained or loosened, this immersion in and identification with lesser planes of ideation distorts one's tone of voice and spreads a film over one's vision, clouding everything one sees.

All of this represents an obscuration of one's true Self that is the effect of complex karma. But when one begins to be able to recognize this and understand what one has done to oneself through neglect of true meditation over lifetimes, one can move away from this initial duality and seek the beginnings of authentic meditation upon the OM. Celebration of the OM is the central thread of the spiritual path and of the quintessential Hermetic current. Celebration of hymns of praise to the OM is the axis around which the entire work of the Great Lodge of Mahatmas turns, and it is a celebration on behalf of and among intrepid individuals who are willing to become men and women of meditation, deeply conscious of what the highest level of OM represents. The OM is the highest that one can conceive. The unbroken current of meditation of the true Self is also the supreme resource behind the whole of manifestation and THAT which is beyond manifestation itself. It is *Nada Brahman*, the divine resonance that becomes the vibrant vesture of the divine radiance of the Light of the unmanifested Logos.

At its highest level, AUM is the Soundless Sound which becomes the medium of transmission for the Ineffable Light. The AUM is also the origin of sound in the world of manifestation, the most sacred syllable, the hierophantic leader of all prayers and chants, and the most important subject of all meditation. Thus, it may be seen in two ways. As a single letter uttered with one articulation, it is the OM, the symbol of the Supreme Spirit. One should imagine this as a constant, omnipresent sounding, capable of being consciously sounded within the consecrated temple of the human form. One should imagine it superimposed on all other sounds, all other vibrations, all other thoughts and feelings. To do so is to cooperate consciously with the great cosmic sounding of the One Resonance, but within the sphere and temple of one's own invisible vestures. OM is the Supreme Spirit, *Ishvara*, the Most High.

Considered as the triliteral word AUM, consisting of the three letters A, U and M, as well as the crucial silent stoppage, it implies all the archetypal trinities and triplicities inherent in the manifesting Tetraktys. It signifies the three Vedas and the Vedanta. It connotes the three primary states of human consciousness, which are at one simple level waking, sleeping and deep sleep; it also includes *turiya*, the state of supreme spiritual wakefulness. It pertains to the three divisions of the universe invoked in the *Gayatri* — *bhur*, which is the most material and visible realm, *bhuvah*, which is the indwelling, invisible counterpart of the visible, and *svah*, which is transcendental, ethereal and celestial in comparison with all that is astral and earthy. It is essentially the Trimurti, the three ruling deities Brahmā, Vishnu and Shiva, the mighty agents of creation, preservation and destruction, the three principal attributes of the One Supreme Reality, which is *Sat-Chit-Ananda*, the fusion of Truth, Ideation and Bliss. In this sense, AUM embraces the entire cosmos as emanated and controlled by the Supreme Spirit, the *Paramatman* which is a pristine, primeval radiation from the Divine Ground, *Parabrahman*.

At the highest, most para-cosmic and universal level, the Sacred Word is both the One and the Three-in-One. It is the OM, the single homogeneous sound which, whether uttered or unuttered, is the supreme sound, the One Sound behind all other sounds. As the pristine vesture of the one unmanifested Logoic Light, it is the source of all vibrations. It can also be seen as the triune AUM because, as human beings, all individuals are triune in nature and connected with the triune aspects of the cosmos — the physical, the astral and the ethereal. AUM can also be related to the three aspects or interpenetrating phases of one single continuous activity which involves creation, preservation, destruction and regeneration. Just as one can postulate that Deity is independent of and prior to all worlds, and the universe itself, so too one can cognize the mirroring of Deity in Nature, in the cosmos, in the process of manifestation, as the triune AUM, which is the source of all the many variegated combinations, permutations, collections and associations of vibrations that are involved on all planes of life. By deliberately moving away from the dualism of two selves, and towards the interrelated vibrations of the two AUMs, which are really one and the same, one may come to cognize the unmanifest behind the manifest, the substratum behind the mutable, and the indwelling, unmanifest, ever-existing spiritual source of life, light and energy behind the cosmic dance of Deity. It is ceaselessly at play, continually working through vast, immense multiplicity, constantly harmonizing, sifting and selecting, but also perpetually dissolving and destroying forms, and reaffirming endlessly the inmost, imperishable essence of Life.

Thus, the *Maitrayana Brahmana Upanishad* speaks of the OM as:

> The *Udgitha*, called *Pranava*, the leader, the bright,
> the sleepless, free from old age and death, three-footed,
> consisting of three letters and likewise to be known as
> fivefold, placed in the cave of the heart.

It is the end and aim of the deepest undercurrent of constant meditation, beyond all borrowed vestures and finite faculties, and one with the Highest Self. As an ardent apprentice in the science of meditation upon the AUM, one might start one's day by thinking of it in relation to the dawn of manifestation, corresponding to the moment when one awakens, arises from sleep and begins one's duties in waking existence. One could return to it around midday, again at sunset and again before going to sleep. Thus, one could give oneself four significant moments

during the day, four precious opportunities to reaffirm the dateless
and deathless, the bright, the bodiless, the indestructible, the
immortal and invulnerable as one's inmost Self and the inmost
Self of all that exists, but also as THAT *(TAT)* which transcends
the cosmos. If one aspires to adore the AUM, worship it, commune
with it and become one with it, then the more one can
contemplate it, chant it, feel with it and for it, the more one
could think about it — thinking until one loses oneself in the
thought and feeling of its nature — the better for one's constant
current of meditation.

The *Maitrayana Brahmana Upanishad* gives further food for
reflection upon the object of worship, explaining that:

> In the beginning *Brahman* was all this. He was one,
> and infinite.... The Highest Self is not to be fixed, he
> is unlimited, unborn, not to be reasoned about, not to
> be conceived. He is like the ether, everywhere, and at
> the destruction of the Universe, he alone is awake. Thus
> from that ether he wakes all this world, which consists
> of thought only, and by him alone is all this meditated
> on, and in him it is dissolved.

In other words, thinking about that Highest Self, one can fuse
the three functions of the meditator, the act of meditating and
the object of meditation. He is the object of meditation, but He
is also the subject of meditation who gives the power to meditate.
His self-subsisting essence is the sustenance of the power of
meditation. The way in which the subject, the object and the
activity of meditation are fused in Him as the Three-in-One
represents the entire invisible, unmanifest universe veiled by the
manifest cosmos. And that is true of each and every human being.
Once one begins to focus on TAT which is all that exists, as in the
wonderful songs of the poet-sage Namalvar, one will be drowned
in Him. These people, those people, this man, that man, this
woman, that woman — none of these have any meaning other
than Him. All hands are His hands, all feet are His feet, all eyes

are His eyes, all minds are His mind. Everything thrills and throbs in the AUM because of the one indwelling, universal, ever-existent Light of the Logos. As the Upanishad says:

> His is that luminous form which shines in the sun, and the manifold light in the smokeless fire. . . . He who is in the fire, and he who is in the heart, and he who is in the sun, they are one and the same. He who knows this becomes one with the One.

The sole prerogative and higher privilege of being human is the possibility of knowing, celebrating and adoring the Universal Self and beholding its triune nature within and behind all subjects and objects, as well as all their interconnections. To know that Self is to fuse everything ceaselessly and yet remain apart, alone and ever awake in the Night of Non-Manifestation, apart from the entire masquerade of manifestation.

W.Q. Judge states, in commenting upon these passages from the *Maitrayana Brahmana Upanishad,* that

> . . . 'to know' this does not mean to merely apprehend the statement, but actually become personally acquainted with it by interior experience. And this is difficult. But it is to be sought after. And the first step is to attempt to realize universal brotherhood, for when one becomes identified with the One, who is all, he 'participates in the souls of all creatures'; surely then the first step in the path is universal brotherhood.
>
> *The Path,* May 1886

To experience the elusive ideal of universal brotherhood as actual conscious participation in the souls of all creatures means thinking through as many lives as possible from the standpoint of souls going through the school of experience and seeing all of them within a single universal pilgrimage. In another place, Judge underscores the intimate connection between ethically and psychologically inserting oneself into the pilgrimage of Humanity and the quickening of the power of meditation in the awakened soul:

> If we do all our acts, small and great, every moment, for the sake of the whole human race, as representing the Supreme Spirit, then every cell and fibre of the body and inner man will be turned in one direction, resulting in perfect concentration.
>
> *Irish Theosophist*, July 1883

This fusion of thought, will and feeling, cognition and concentration, volition and empathy, so crucial to the activation of the true potency of meditation, is virtually impossible when predicated upon the nebulous notion of the personal self. But when seen as the living solidarity of all souls, all selves, all beings, in the one universal pilgrimage, it becomes buoyant and effortless, joyous and expansive.

This is the golden thread inspiring and sustaining alchemical self-regeneration through meditation, and it lies at the core of the sacred meaning of the *Gayatri*, the holiest of all *mantras*, which begins with the deathless AUM and ends with the dateless OM.

> The object of this prayer is that we may carry out our whole duty, after becoming acquainted with the truth, while we are on our journey to thy Sacred Seat. This is our pilgrimage, not of one, not selfishly, not alone, but the whole of humanity. For the sacred seat is that place where all meet, where alone are all one. It is when and where the three great sounds of the first word of the prayer merge into one soundless sound. This is the only proper prayer, the sole saving aspiration.
>
> *The Path*, January 1893

One can thus see that the very stance of an individual soul trying to become one with the Higher Self is only a way of stating what could equally be stated from the other side. The same process could also be seen as that of the universal Self entering into the receptive seeker, more fully suffusing every cell and atom of the surrendering devotee. The *Gayatri* invokes the True Sun of the Highest Self to unveil itself and illumine one's entire being. This hidden element of divine grace is vital to the operation of consecration, prayer and meditation because one's determination to learn the truth includes a fearless recognition that there is that which hides or veils it from one's vision. Only when the projected ray subordinates and surrenders itself to its divine parent can there be a release of intense, ardent, longing aspiration for the Supreme Truth, for the one Source, for the sacred seat of the ever-invisible, ever-existent Fire, which is the fountainhead of all Mystery Fires, ceaselessly burning throughout *manvantara* and *pralaya,* unaltered by the whole universe and unmodified by all conditioned existence.

If this is inaccessible, it arises from the karma of past deeds, which have left the brain substance and fibres of one's being too opaque and too sluggish to respond to higher vibrations. If one is mired in a life of careless indifference and recalcitrant ignorance, unable to cooperate with the universal processes of Divine Life, it means that in the past one did not cooperate with and adore the Greater Mysteries, but settled instead for something small and tawdry, a delusive spell of self-adoration. Such a life creates a film or veil that estranges one's own feelings from the feelings of others, one's own concerns from the concerns of the universal pilgrimage of humanity. Failing in the custody and care of the divine flame within, one falls into that fickle carelessness which produces endemic passivity, extinguishing full awareness and plunging one into irresponsibility and the aimless drift of self-indulgence amidst the highs and lows of the insecure self. One becomes blinded and bound by a fundamental ignorance of the self-destructive, self-doomed nature of such an episodic existence, where the sacred power of mind is dragged down and made to enlist in the slavery of consciousness to the senses, to false distinctions between inner and outer, and also to an extremely narrow, ephemeral and unreal conception of space and time. Far from aiding the *persona* in its desperate plight, this infusion of a volatile mentality only serves to feed the vultures of the insatiable cravings, and stokes the fires of multiplicity which can only produce a kind of chaotic screen that fogs, confuses and smokes out the light of true reason, hindering the hearing of the Soundless Sound. At best, there lingers a subliminal echo which can haunt but cannot heal. Thus all past karma has created a kind of captivity and a failure to understand illusions as illusions, yet this bondage is masked by a pessimistic pseudo-objectivity that declares a false finality to the conditioning of consciousness and a depressing fixity to the state of enslavement to delusion.

That is why it is so crucial that in the very act of adoration, using the *Gayatri,* one utters a tremendous cry of the soul, which is a cry of spiritual freedom. But such a cry is useless at the moment of death. It is to be made now or never, by those who use the *Gayatri* unfailingly; it is a cry for clarity, a cry that the veil may fall, that the scales may drop from one's eyes, and that the obscuration of one's being may be dispelled. Therefore, it takes the form of the sound '*Unveil!*'. Judge, in translating the *Gayatri,* has deliberately fused its actual meaning with a very powerful mantra in the *Isha Upanishad,* producing a ringing rendition which conveys the full force of the invocation:

> AUM. Unveil, O Thou who givest sustenance to the Universe, from whom all proceed, to whom all must return, that face of the True Sun now hidden by a vase of golden light, that we may see the truth and do our whole duty on our journey to thy sacred seat. OM.

The vase of golden light is the *Hiranyagarbha,* the cosmic sphere of Light around the secret, sacred Sun which is the true source of all enlightenment, all ideation, and all divine and supra-mental energy. It is only reflected at a very limited level in the physical sun, which is the source of what people call physical life or pranic vitality, and also what they call light. That light, however, appears bright only in contrast to physical darkness, and it is only an illusory light compared with the ineffable Light of the Divine Darkness that is the essential nature of the unmanifest Logos. Whilst the physical sun gives all the energy that people ordinarily understand, that pervasive energy must necessarily participate in the law of conservation and must also be subject to the law of entropy. The ineffable Light of the Logos, by contrast, is inconsumable and inexhaustible: it can only be the object of the highest ideation of a *Manasa*, an immortal thinking being who can light up the flame that is its priceless share in the universal fire of *Mahat*.

The *Gayatri* can be extremely potent if it is used regularly every day, but it can only work when it is invoked on behalf of all living beings. It can become daily more intense as a regular act, a request or prayer, a kind of petition for grace arising out of the depths of the hidden hearts of the human race. Then it becomes a form of manifestation capable of summoning and activating the sacrificial ladder, along which travel the high Dhyanis, Devas and Hierarchies that move up and down the great rainbow bridge invoked by all the Vedic hymns. Being the *Matriveda*, the mother of the Vedas, the *Gayatri* is venerated as the highest possible *mantra*. It enables every human being to reach out on behalf of all Humanity, ardently to the One Source. By doing this again and again, one becomes attuned to that to which one appeals, and familiar with the descent of the Divine Light and the shedding of its supernal grace.

If human beings start to use the *Gayatri* daily whilst their motives are yet sullied, they are in awesome danger. They risk summoning forces that will be too strong to resist or to regulate, and they will need the ever-present protection of the Rishis and Mahatmas, who are likened in Upanishadic metaphor to the ribs of an umbrella sheltering all beneath. Every human being holds the handle of this umbrella, but its ribs belong to all Humanity, for they represent the highest hierarchies of enlightened human beings who are conscious instruments of the Cosmic Will. They are the supreme divine agents of the One Law, the One Life and the One Light, and through their boundless compassion they can protect and provide opportunities to human beings, who suffer from glaring gaps between their moral stature and their mental aspiration, between their spiritual strength and their emotional stamina, between their longing for union and their communion with the One. The compassion of perfected human beings gives strength to the weak. And it gives hope to those who are sometimes awed or made afraid by the enormity of their undertaking.

Yet, whilst this allegorical umbrella provides a measure of assured protection to the fallible aspirant, enlightened beings cannot vicariously substitute for the self-conscious effort each individual must make for himself or herself to maintain the mysterious thread of life's meditation as a constant vibration. There must, however, be honesty and moral courage in recognizing the avoidable gaps in one's practice, and a clarity in discerning tendencies that make one vulnerable to delusion through likes and dislikes, delusive affections and false dependencies. One must become vigilant against the simian tricks that memory plays, and against the perverse tendency to misuse the power of thought to produce rationales which only consolidate the discontinuities in oneself. All of these persist as concessions to that part of oneself which is drowsy, lazy, cowardly and terrified of the Light; that part which is terrified of standing up confidently and moving apart from the inert mass of most beings. Before one can become a true man or woman of meditation, and so a true servant of Humanity, one must first become, in a Pauline sense, separated out of the astral and psychic plane — a being without external signs of slavish connections with human beings. One must go through the Isolation of the immortal soul, a painful period of withdrawal from lesser supports. Only then can one attain the height of what is possible, reaching the pristine source that is above the head, and that, once touched, eventually sets aflame the thousands of latent centres that are in the head, the legendary Tree of Light, Life and Cosmic Electricity in Man.

Long before this turning-point is reached, one must render reliable the steady effort to meditate. Thus it is said that if one cannot initially meditate upon the most abstract themes, one should begin by meditating upon meditation itself. Meditate upon the great Masters of Meditation, enjoying the very thought of the Buddhas of Contemplation, self-luminous beings who are masters of compassion and ceaselessly radiate currents of beneficence. In the very enjoyment of meditating upon the galaxy of Dhyanis and the host of Mahatmas, one will elevate oneself, expanding one's horizon, one's sense of kinship and one's conception of the human family. One will be thrilled that the human family can include such a vast array of self-resplendent beings, and one will begin to see this world anew.

Then, when one earnestly meditates and finds multiple obstructions arising, one will be able to see them for what they are and honestly trace them to their origins in forgetfulness, indolence and cowardice. At the same time, one will understand that the very ability one has gained to stand apart from these shadows is itself rooted in a recognition of that which is all-knowing, unforgetful, ever awake, courageous, free, untrammelled and universally self-conscious. Even though one's deeper Self must be repeatedly invoked, one will still find a certain joy arising in oneself, a certain natural desire flowing out of deep love for that universal Self. This is the true source of all other loves and the only thing that can ultimately give meaning to all one's other altruistic urges. It is the wellspring of one's empathy for all life, for all the kingdoms of Nature, for what is in every stone and plant and tree. It is that in oneself which can resonate to the rising sun, can respond to the setting sun, and can echo back to the invisible Midnight Sun. All these are but veiled expressions of a deeper universal current of energy which is compassionate, which is sacrificial, and which is consciously emanated by the Masters of Light and Love, Compassion and Wisdom.

When one begins to develop a natural joy, hunger, longing and love for this mystic meditation, one will find that it acts as an eliminator. Many of one's lesser longings will simply fall away, and one's vanity, delusion and ego-projection will be revealed and emptied out. Yet, what was good and true at the core of them will never be lost, for that is an outflow of the fount of universal love which belongs to the *Paramatman*, the universal Self. If this meditation is real, it should arouse and deepen one's capacity to be one-pointed — single-minded and single-hearted — able to concentrate upon the appointed task at hand and able to consecrate it for the good of all. Letting go of all results, reducing one's participation in fantasy, anticipation and regret, one will become more fully engaged, more fully active and wide awake. With this, a great deal of what before looked to be oneself will become exteriorized, come out and fall away. It will all show itself for what it is — a mask, a veil. And layer by layer, veil upon veil of false selfhood will fall away until nothing remains but the one ineffable Light. It is beginningless and endless. It is the Light that is hidden in the Divine Darkness, behind all worlds, beings and manifestations. It is the One Light behind every spark of aspiration and every spark of truth, beauty and goodness in each and every being in existence. It is the Light of which Jesus spoke when he said, "If thine eye be single, thy body shall be full of Light", and it is the Light spoken of by Krishna as the lighting up in oneself of the Supreme Saviour, who then becomes visible. Let each fearless pilgrim soul meditate upon that Light which lives in all as the Highest Self. Let each devotee concentrate upon it in adoration, surrendering and subordinating all to that one fiery Self. And let each heroic seeker after undying truth will to work for its eternal habitation in every human heart.

*   *   *   *   *

> *And now thy Self is lost in* SELF, *Thyself unto* THYSELF, *merged in* THAT SELF *from which thou first didst radiate.*
>
> *Where is thy individuality, Lanoo, where the Lanoo himself? It is the spark lost in the fire, the drop within the ocean, the ever-present ray become the All and the eternal radiance.*
>
> *And now, Lanoo, thou art the doer and the witness, the radiator and the radiation, Light in the Sound, and the Sound in the Light.*
>
> The Voice of the Silence

EVOLUTION
AND
INVOLUTION

CONSCIOUSNESS
AND FORM

Worlds and men were in turn formed and destroyed,
under the law of evolution *and* from pre-existing
material, *until both the planets and their men, in our case
our Earth and its animal and human races, became what
they are now in the present cycle: opposite polar forces, an
equilibrized compound of Spirit and Matter, of the positive
and the negative, of the male and the female. . . . There was
a spiritual, a psychic, an intellectual, and an animal
evolution, from the highest to the lowest, as well as a physical
development — from the simple and homogeneous, up to
the more complex and heterogeneous; though not quite on
the lines traced for us by the modern evolutionists. This
double evolution in two contrary directions, required various
ages, of diverse natures and degrees of spirituality and
intellectuality, to fabricate the being now known as man.*

The Secret Doctrine, ii 84, 87

Ancient wisdom, unlike modern thought, successfully
bridges the recondite concepts of evolution, history and
individual growth. It sees all three as continuous,
contiguous components of a single metaphysical process whereby
spirit and matter are interwoven in a cyclic movement that
transcends time, while providing the basis of all self-conscious
human growth. The metaphysics of Gupta Vidya points to the
interrelationship of *Purusha* and *Prakriti* in the proemial and
pregenetic dawn of manifestation as the foundation for all the
subsequent and more complex dualities of life. Prior to all worlds
and all beings, the one universal Substance-Principle is the radiant
ground upon which all processes of composition and balance,
polarity and development, must occur. The pregenetic logic of
manifestation, evolution and development is equivalent to the

mystical presence of the Logos at every point of the cosmos, producing, preserving and transforming its distributive and collective life. This logic cannot be understood, however, through any idea of creation *ex nihilo* or through linear progression upward from some sort of primeval slime. To accommodate the idea of pure consciousness and pure substance prior to all possible manifestations in the realm of form and transformation, it is essential to meditate upon that which was in the beginning, that which is, and that which will be forevermore.

In the language of the first fundamental principle of Gupta Vidya, it is characterized as Absolute Space, Absolute Duration and Absolute Motion, from which arise Pre-cosmic Ideation and Pre-cosmic Substance. The starting-point of thought must be removed to a point which is prior to all worlds, all beings and all existence as we know it, a realm of primordial Being. From this starting-point, one may recognize that there is an ontology prior to the logic of all development. To understand that prior ontology is crucial if one is even to begin to conceptualize the logic of growth, development and evolution, and also to comprehend that all subsequent processes in manifested space and time must perpetually reiterate that ontology. There is a constant balance between consciousness and form, spirit and matter, on diverse levels of manifestation, leading up to the present human kingdom and onward towards human perfection. Before this balance can culminate in the present human kingdom on the physical plane, it must be struck on the astral plane. This concerns the arrangement of atoms and organic forces on a causal level which eventuates in the positive polarity associated with the male vesture and the negative polarity associated with the female. The astral process is itself a reflection of more abstract processes, reflected in turn in the completed and concrete forms of the physical plane.

The primary principle of dynamic balance, which precedes both beings and worlds, is central to the doctrine of double evolution. The direction in which unfoldment takes place in the realm of consciousness is different from the direction in which development takes place in the realm of substance. Thus, when duality supervenes in the realm of manifestation, there is a tension between pairs of opposites and between contrary polarities. There is, therefore, a profound need for balance in consciousness, balance in astral substance and correlations of atoms, and also balance on the physical plane. One line of evolution, which is connected with the unfoldment of consciousness, may be seen in terms of a line extended from above below. Everything that is in existence is a reflection of that which exists in a state of pure being on a more primary plane of prototypical substance and primeval ideation. This is the ancient Hermetic teaching. To understand the descent in consciousness from prototypical germs to ramifying forms, it is necessary to recognize that this descent involves the spiritual, the psychic, the intellectual and also that which is called physical evolution. In this sequence the psychic mediates between the spiritual and the intellectual.

When the light-essence of spiritual energy comes down to a certain level of differentiation, it casts a glow or aura with a capacity for diffusion. This is the psychic extension of what is spiritually present in seed form in the realm of noumena. It is the psychic emanation of the spiritual, and it is prior to all phenomena. It is also prior to the intellectual, because once intelligence has become differentiated, it must become associated with structures and pathways of development at all levels and in all kingdoms. The specialization of intelligence must come after the more nebulous condition of the psychic, which itself is an outgrowth of the general spiritual condition. This intellectual specialization makes possible evolution up to the animal kingdom, from the elemental kingdoms through the mineral and the vegetable to all the complex forms that have emerged over an immense period of time in the animal world. The animal kingdom itself includes a vast range of mammals, fishes, insects, birds and other phyla that make up the whole spectrum of animate existence. All of these are the result of the progressive condensation and specialization of consciousness.

On the other side of double evolution, viewed not from the standpoint of consciousness but from that of substance, is a movement from the simple and homogeneous to the elaborate and complex. This progress towards heterogeneity is what is sensed and studied by modern evolutionary science. Its great pioneers in the nineteenth century speculated about protoplasm or *monera* and other primal essences in an effort to find out how the logic of development could be understood. How, they asked, can one trace the protean diversity of form to something which is extremely primary and comparatively simple? It is not possible, however, to understand the development of complexity out of simplicity without understanding the progressive specialization of consciousness. Hence the doctrine of double evolution in contrary directions, with its various stages and ages of development bringing about the multi-layered and multi-faceted being now known as Man. Having once grasped the inter-relationship between the immense development from the simple to the complex in the realm of substance and the descent of consciousness through specialization from above below, one must attempt to understand human development and growth in the same terms.

Philosophically, there is no sharp separation between Deity, Nature and Man; the problem is to understand human development without anthropomorphizing Deity and Nature, yet also without imposing upon Man any mechanistic model or rigid teleology. Instead, appropriate meaning must be given to human existence in the dual terms of the descent of spirit into matter and the ascent of form towards the unmanifest.

> Furthermore, the one absolute, ever acting and never erring law, which proceeds on the same lines from one eternity (or Manvantara) to the other — ever furnishing an ascending scale for the manifested, or that which we call the great Illusion (*Maha-Maya*), but plunging Spirit deeper and deeper into materiality on the one hand, and then *redeeming it through flesh* and liberating it — this law, we say, uses for these purposes the Beings from other and

higher planes, men, or *Minds* (Manus), in accordance
with their Karmic exigencies.

Ibid., 87-88

This dual process of unfoldment and evolution, from the standpoint of consciousness and substance, does not occur either mechanically or automatically. It is characteristic of modern so-called scientific theories that they establish law-like regularities at the expense of creating automatism. This tendency arises because contemporary science is, in part, trapped by the explanatory force of the concept of causality. Whilst this was especially true of nineteenth century science, it is a predicament which is, fortunately, being eased somewhat by the development of quantum mechanics and particle physics, wherein it is impossible to cling to seventeenth century conceptions of cause. Nonetheless, once emphasis is placed upon explanation in terms of causal antecedents, one creates a constricted alternative to earlier religious explanations of Man which were largely teleological. There are ghostly echoes in modern evolutionary theory and in post-Aristotelian biology of earlier teleological systems. They often arbitrarily assume that in every organism there is not only intelligence, but also some pre-determined tendency towards some pre-established goal. To view life in this manner is, of course, to look at phenomena from a different point of view than that which is suggested by the concepts of law-like recurrence and antecedent causes.

Gupta Vidya avoids the false dichotomy between mechanistic causal processes of becoming and an imposed teleology seeking to define all things in terms of purposes and outcomes. Instead, it assigns a primary and active role to creative imagination. This implies that the evolutionary process cannot be explained or characterized, whether in terms of the descent of spirit into matter or in terms of the increasing complexities of matter, without the direct involvement of great minds. Beings, once human and perfected in former periods of evolution, become crucial in furthering this evolutionary process and in giving it a redemptive force. This essential point in ancient philosophy is directly at odds with all modern scientific explanations. Furthermore, it confronts modern thought with the complex conception of the pre-Christian world regarding the nature of Deity and pantheons of gods. Central to that world view is the role of myriads of minds, beings which are superhuman and are fully perfected from earlier periods of evolution. Viewed in this context, human beings now evolving on earth are potentially gods, and were, during the Third Root Race, conscious of their divine ancestry.

All of this is a tremendous challenge to received religion and recent dogmas of science. In diverse ways, it is necessary to accommodate the intervention of mind-beings in evolution, who, out of their capacity for creative imagination, play a crucial part in giving direction and focus to ideation and making it act upon the realm of form. In the light of this fundamental Teaching, it is essential to see every single human being as a fallen god. If human beings in the Third Root Race were like gods, then in the process of evolution human beings have become so much caught, through concretizing intelligence, in matter that their spiritual senses have significantly receded. They have become alienated from their true natures. Complex and difficult enough to understand in their metaphysical and meta-psychological origins, men have become compounded riddles to themselves through their own self-obscuration. Nonetheless, those very perfected beings who were present at the dawn of humanity on this globe still preside over seemingly orphaned humanity. Hence, throughout ancient thought the keys to the mystery of Man have always been present and within the reach of anyone who is sincere and in earnest in the arduous search for self-knowledge.

How precise and true is Plato's expression, how profound and philosophical his remark on the (human) soul or EGO, when he defined it as 'a compound of the *same* and the *other*.' ... It is the '*same* and the *other*,' as the great Initiate-Philosopher said; for the EGO (the 'Higher Self' when merged with and in the Divine

Monad) is Man, and yet the *same* as the 'OTHER', the Angel in him incarnated, as the same with the universal MAHAT.

Ibid., 88

Their consciousness confined through identification with grosser forms, human beings have become alienated from their highest possibilities. They may have achieved a sense of continuity and identity on a lower plane, but at the expense of a close connection with their deeper and larger selfhood. This risk is inherent in the very process of developing and specializing a concentrated egoity or sense of 'I' in relation to a name and a body, particular conditions and memories, desires and expectations. All of this involves exercising the principle of 'I-ness', *ahankara,* in ways that generate a sense of reality, but also bind down egoity in the realm of differentiated manifestation. As a result, there is an acute frustration for that pure essence which is the angel in man. This is the *Atma-Buddhi* overbrooding *Manas.*

Through identification with *kama,* the sensorium and the *linga sharira* or astral form, *Manas* has become beclouded. Therefore, *Atma-Buddhi,* though it is inseparable from pure thought and ideation, pure *Manas* and egoity, overbroods incarnated *Manas* but only at a distance. There is a persistent alienation from active Manasic self-consciousness owing to its involvement through matter and desire with the world of differentiation. There is an agonizing separation of *Manas* from its true estate where it is one with *Atma-Buddhi.* To be one with *Atma-Buddhi* also means to be one with *Mahat,* the cosmic mind and universal consciousness. Put in another way, the alienation of the individual from the universal is repeated within the individual in a body. This becomes a protracted alienation between the Atma-Buddhic Monad in its pure state and the embodied consciousness, whereby *Manas* has been deflected and captured by *kama.* The meta-psychological process is reflected in the embodied consciousness as the illusion of separate objects and subjects.

All of this makes poignant the idea of spirit plunging deeper and deeper into material existence and then redeeming it. This does not happen automatically. Once human beings are plunged, through their claustrophobic egoity, into the world of sensation and matter, they are painfully alienated from their true selves. Unless they recognize that fact and do something to mitigate and counter their overactive tendency towards kamamanasic thought, they cannot free themselves. Unless they deliberately take steps to withdraw from identification with name and form (*namarupa*) through meditation, through abstraction and silence, through calmness and negating the illusions of the world and the false self, they will be unable to cooperate with the redemptive function of spirit. What is true of cosmic evolution on universal terms is also true of humanity at the individual and collective level. Mankind is involved in a metaphysical Fall and a potential redemption at the individual level.

Every human being must discover his true identity by asking, "Who am I?" He must initially recognize the falsity and absurdity of identifying with any mask or persona. Yet this is precisely the tendency of exteriorized language and lower manasic cerebration. All of this must be thought through and negated. He must seek to realize in daily experience the meditative state which Patanjali calls the condition of the Spectator without a spectacle. To realize this state is to experience pure 'I-am-I' consciousness without any reference to being a subject separate from other subjects or any identification with an object in a field of differentiated objects.

Owing to the long history of each human being in incarnation, the attainment of this high degree of abstraction requires a great deal of systematic work upon the vestures. To develop the capacity to give a sense of reality to pure being, apart from all desire and memory, without expectation or attachment to the temporal processes of past, present and future, requires a purification and transmutation of the life-atoms constituting the astral and physical vestures. This alchemical process of self-purification and transmutation must itself be a deliberate and self-conscious embodiment of the principles of double evolution.

It is, therefore, essential to understand that

> every atom and molecule in the Universe is both
> *life-giving* and *death-giving* to that form, inasmuch as it
> builds by aggregation universes and the ephemeral
> vehicles ready to receive the transmigrating soul, and
> as eternally destroys and changes the *forms* and expels
> those souls from their temporary abodes. It creates and
> kills; it is self-generating and self-destroying; it brings
> into being, and annihilates, that mystery of mysteries —
> the *living body* of man, animal, or plant, every second
> in time and space; and it generates equally life and
> death, beauty and ugliness, good and bad, and even
> the agreeable and disagreeable, the beneficent and
> maleficent sensations.
>
> *Ibid.*, i 261

Rather than being rigidly Manichaean, one must recognize that
at the core of the life-process there is that which is both life-giving
and death-dealing. There is that which has both the Vishnu
function (of providing continuity) and the Shiva function (of
destroying and regenerating). Which of these functions is relevant
at any precise moment in relation to any particular circumstance
depends upon the meaning of events to the immortal Manasic
Ego in its relation to *Atma-Buddhi.* The meaning of outward events
in life is determined by their mental correlations, and these
meanings may be seized only through a heightened state of mental
ripeness. The Occult Catechism expresses this in terms of the
relationship between the Atma-Buddhic Monad — the 'Double
Dragon' — and the world of manifested form through the
mediation of *Manas.*

> *For the 'Double Dragon' has no hold upon the mere
> form. It is like the breeze where there is no tree or branch to
> receive and harbour it. It cannot affect the form where there
> is no agent of transmission* (Manas, 'Mind') *and the form
> knows it not.*
>
> *Ibid.*, ii 57

The agent of mental and moral transmission which is crucial to all human life might be called the selector. Every human soul as a self-conscious being has the capacity to perfect the power of choice and so become morally fully conscious. Those beings which presided self-consciously over the dawn of humanity on the earth are just such perfected human beings. Morally, they are so sensitive that they do not even like to breathe if there is the remotest possibility that by doing so they may hurt another being. Towards this ideal, all moral consciousness must aspire. Ultimately, no one has any right to breathe unless by doing so he positively blesses all beings. This morality is very distant from the amorality of the Kali Age, the age of annihilation and kama-rupic shells, souls thronging the exits of the great theatre of human existence. Nevertheless, this highest conception of choice and of the capacity to energize the breath with the spiritual will and the beneficent impulse of universal compassion is central to the humanity of the future. It is the inherent mode of perfected beings, who cooperate with Nature in the processes of evolution, history and the growth of individual human beings. The challenge before men and women who would aid the unfoldment of the civilization of the future is to realize within themselves the presence of these creative powers of imagination and the redemptive capacity of the spiritual will when employed in the service of others.

Every human being involved in a physical form is aided by the logic of the life cycle of that form in perceiving opportunities for inward growth. The physical form observes certain laws of growth and disintegration. Every human being until the age of thirty-five experiences a period wherein the fiery lives constituting that form sacrifice themselves to produce and sustain the complex life of the body. Thus, they act as builders impeding the activity of potential destroyers, a process that mirrors the evolutionary development of complex forms out of simple homogeneous substances. At the same time, there is in individual human life a descent of spirit into matter, first as the overbrooding of the Atma-Buddhic Monad and then as the incarnation of the Manasic principle. As the self-conscious intelligence of the human being matures, the complex differentiation and perfection of the human form proceeds to its culmination.

As in the series of globes and races in the earth chain there is a theatre for the universal descent and ascent of spirit in relation to material form, so too the individual is involved in a dual ascent and descent, moving in opposite directions from the physical and spiritual standpoints. Up to the age of thirty-five the specialization and descent of spirit into matter is accomplished by the differentiation and ascent of matter into complex form. Thereafter the opposite processes begin to take hold. From age thirty-five to age seventy, broadly speaking, there is a physical disintegration of form accompanied by a progressive possibility of spirit freeing itself from the prison-house of matter. The descent or decline of material form on the side of substance is accompanied by the potential ascent of spirit which is capable of self-consciously elevating matter.

The opportunity afforded by the physical life cycle to every human being is truly to experience deliberately the process of spiritual ascent. From this it is possible to understand why human beings should learn early how to cooperate with the productive, conservative and regenerating impulses inherent in physical form. When one is young, one should not behave as an old person who has already learnt what there is to learn from life. Instead, one should attempt to master the discipline of conservation of energy so that he may, after the age of thirty-five, make a disciplined use of energies and seize the opportunities that accompany the loosening of the grip of form over consciousness. Owing to the complex karmic legacy that each human being brings into incarnation, one must learn, as soon as one realizes the magnitude of the problem, to relax and renounce the tenacious hold of the body and physical sensory life upon oneself. One must free the mind from attention-getting and from the demands of the physical senses. The aim of Manasic living is to become more capable, through meditation, of spiritual creation and generation, of *Kriyashakti*. This is the power of spontaneous generation and spiritual action which is inherent in the cosmos and exemplified by the highest perfected human beings. Just as it has been an essential component in the evolution of humanity up to the present period, it is the *sine qua non* of future human development, both individual and collective.

It is the prerogative of human beings to aid the spiritual evolution of ideas. This means learning to release the benevolent potency of spiritual ideation and the spiritual will. Thus, individuals can help to light up the latent divine intelligence in life-atoms, in forms and stones, in vegetables, plants and animals. Human beings are continually involved with all of these, especially through the three elemental kingdoms, which are rapid transmitters across the entire globe of all the impressions that human beings give out. Naturally, human beings are also able to draw out the latent divine intelligence in the minds and hearts of other human beings. To work with this process means to perceive, by analogy and correspondence, that what in the physical plane can be sacrificial and compassionate action under the laws of cycles and the tutelage of the lower Pitris is, in reference to the higher planes, that which involves the free choice, the conscious attention and the deliberate selection of human beings. The human capacity to aid in the lower evolution of Nature is a direct reflection of the human capacity to participate in the higher evolution of Manasic self-consciousness. Naturally, those beings who are perfected in *Manas* enjoy an effortless command over the lower elements of Nature. This moral solidarity of Nature and Humanity draws attention to the central importance of ethical consciousness.

Ethics sharpens one's conception of how to select what is really necessary to do. This is the central Manasic function of the selector, the refined sense of *svadharma,* the sense of one's true sphere of spiritual obligation. Manasic maturity can be realized only through a renunciation of the false doctrine of vicarious atonement and the vampirical elements in consciousness which arise out of envy. There is that in lower *manas* affected by the unbalanced operation of *kama* which would seek to deny light to others, to steal light from them or to steal its way into the true light without merit or service. Unless one tries to expunge these tendencies from one's nature, one will pay heavily at the moment of death. The innate possession by human beings of the Manasic capacity should inherently lead them to pass on anything they know. Without regard to the possibility of misuse, one must take the risk, like the Manasaputras, and seek to pass on to others what one has received as a free gift oneself. This will be the natural tendency of mature individuals who have deeply thought about the enormous debt of gratitude they owe towards higher beings who have given and continue to give so much to present humanity.

Through the continuous activity of the Logos in manifestation, every human being has received a priceless inheritance of specialized intellectual function and highly differentiated complex vehicles and instruments. To understand this immense privilege and potential of human incarnation is to rethink one's entire concept of what is vampirical and what is constructive in the use of the energies of man. As a ray of the Logos, every human being resides in divine space as a point in *Akasha,* capable of focussing the highest energies. As a ray of the Logos, every human Monad is capable of releasing, through sound, vibrations with mental and physical correlations that can aid in the forward movement of evolution. The indissoluble unity of the Logos in the cosmos and the God in man is magically enshrined in the mantram AUM MANI PADME HUM. The archetypal music of the spheres resonates in human consciousness, however limited the instruments of human music. All human thought, speech and action involves the gods, and all are capable of aiding or hindering the onward evolution of Nature and Man. Hence, in viewing the complex compound being of Man, the *Anugita* declares:

'The indestructible and the destructible, such is the double manifestation of the Self. Of these the indestructible is the existent (the true essence or nature of Self, the underlying principles). The manifestation as an individual (or entity) is called the destructible.'

Thus speaks the ASCETIC in Anugita; and also: 'Every
one who is twice-born (initiated) knows such is the
teaching of the ancients. . . . Space is the first
entity. . . . Now Space (*Akâsa*, or the noumenon of
Ether) has one quality . . . and that is sound
only . . . and the qualities of sound are Shadga,
Rishabha, Gândhâra, Madhyama, Panchama, and
beyond these five Nishâda and Dhaivata'; (the Hindu
gamut). These seven notes of the scale are the principles
of sound.

Ibid., i 534

These principles of sound are the elements and factors of
the activity of the Logos in manifestation. They correlate with
colours and planets, with principles in Man and Nature, with
degrees of differentiation of light and substance. Therefore, they
correlate with states of consciousness and degrees of specialization
in intelligence. Through an appreciation of the music of the Logos
there can be an apprehension of noetic magic in its highest sense.
The Logoic differentiations of Akashic ideation on the plane of
Mahat are the basis of the specialization of intelligence and its
mastery over the development of complex forms in substance.
Whether through mathematics or music, through metaphysics
or movement, human beings can learn something about the
intonations and reflections of the divine process. Ultimately, the
great prerogative of self-conscious Monads is to rise higher than
all the evolved hierarchies in Nature. There is a deep sense in
which every human soul is no less than TAT. Humanity is capable,
therefore, of a degree of individuation of the universal divine
principle both in consciousness and in substance that is equivalent
to becoming a Dhyani, a son of the gods. Through perfection in
Karuna, universal compassion, man is capable of *Prajna,* Divine
Wisdom. Through mastery of all the combinations of sound in
light flowing forth from the Divine Darkness and the Soundless
Sound, man is capable of drawing into the neutral layer —
the attributeless substratum of all differentiations of sound
corresponding to *Mulaprakriti,* the Eternal Father-Mother — root

matter and root ideation. Having become *achyuta* and established in consciousness of Absolute Space, Duration and Motion, the perfected Bodhisattva becomes the unswerving servant of Amitabha, the Boundless Age, in the endless cycles of evolution.

EVOLUTION AND CONSCIOUSNESS

We see a flower slowly developing from a bud, and the bud from its seed. But whence the latter, with all its predetermined programme of physical transformation, and its invisible, therefore spiritual *forces which gradually develop its form, colour, and odour? The word* evolution *speaks for itself. The germ of the present human race must have preëxisted in the parent of this race, as the seed, in which lies hidden the flower of next summer, was developed in the capsule of its parent flower.*

The Secret Doctrine, ii xvi

The twelve *Stanzas of Dzyan* on anthropogenesis, like the seven *Stanzas* on cosmogenesis, are accompanied by interwoven Commentary and supplemented by elaborate elucidations of myth and symbol, of science and philosophy. To gain a clear comprehension of the overall framework is difficult partially because it was meant to be difficult. There are numerous blinds, overlapping statements and various interlocking classifications which use terms differently in distinct contexts. There is a code language in *The Secret Doctrine,* which is meant to arouse Buddhic intuition and to nullify the tendency of lower *Manas* to consolidate categories, classifications and even concepts. As an initial aid in gaining a broad picture of human evolution, H.P. Blavatsky gives at the beginning a brief account of the five continents which more or less roughly correspond with the five Root Races through which humanity has passed on this globe in reaching its present stage. If one sees the entirety of involution and evolution in the form of a circle, humanity as a whole has come down over half the circle and has begun to ascend back to its pristine source. This critical stage is represented by the Fifth Sub-Race of the Fifth Root Race in the Fourth Round. The purpose of understanding this entire scheme is to see more clearly the varied ways in which every human being today is bound up with all other human beings who ever lived or will live in the future.

It is not enough to do this vaguely in terms of some fuzzy proposition about what Feuerbach called 'the species nature of humanity.' Rather, it must be done in terms that are significant from the standpoint of sentient beings, human souls that have lived and struggled, learnt and forgotten, erred, picked up the thread again, expanded consciousness, assumed contraction of consciousness involuntarily and voluntarily, by mutual impact in a multitude of conditions and contexts. In order to convey a vast gamut of possible relations between externality and internal states of consciousness, H.P. Blavatsky sets out the broad scheme of Continents and Races, beginning with the Imperishable Sacred Isle of the Blessed:

> This 'Sacred Land'. . . is stated never to have shared the fate of the other continents; because it is the only one whose destiny it is to last from the beginning to the end of the Manvantara throughout each Round. It is the cradle of the first man and the dwelling of the last *divine* mortal, chosen as a *Sishta* for the future seed of humanity. Of this mysterious and sacred land very little can be said, except, perhaps, according to a poetical expression in one of the Commentaries, that the 'polestar has its watchful eye upon it, from the dawn to the close of the twilight of "a day" of the GREAT BREATH.'
>
> *The Secret Doctrine,* ii 6

The proper study of mankind is Man, declared the poet Pope. This is a mighty venture into the range and reach of human consciousness. The intuitive individual who turns inward, giving reality to the secret wisdom within the sanctuary of immortal consciousness, will necessarily turn back far beyond the confines of recorded and unrecorded history, beyond manifested events and finite memory. One must thus return to the primal fount of one's deepest kinship with enlightened beings on the Imperishable Sacred Land who were the divine guardians that nursed and protected the First Root Race. No poetical description, philosophical account or scientific scheme could do justice to that primordial state of collective consciousness. It is not to be located in the mists of antiquity, but lies in a realm transcending ordinary conceptions of past, present and future, perpetually present during the vast epoch of a *manvantara*. This is the noumenal basis for all theological or poetical conceptions of paradisaic consciousness.

In the para-temporal sequence of human evolution we are then told of the legendary home of the Second Race:

> The 'HYPERBOREAN' will be the name chosen for the Second Continent, the land which stretched out its promontories southward and westward from the North Pole to receive the Second Race, and comprised the whole of what is now known as Northern Asia. Such was the name given by the oldest Greeks to the far-off and mysterious region, whither their tradition made Apollo the 'Hyperborean' travel every year. *Astronomically,* Apollo is of course the Sun. . . .
>
> But *historically,* or better, perhaps, ethnologically and geologically, the meaning is different. The land of the Hyperboreans, the country that extended beyond Boreas, the frozen-hearted god of snows and hurricanes, who loved to slumber heavily on the chain of Mount Riphaeus, was neither an ideal country, as surmised by the mythologists, nor yet a land in the neighbourhood of Scythia and the Danube. It was a real Continent, a *bonâ-fide* land which knew no winter in those early days, nor have its sorry remains more than one night and day during the year, even now. The nocturnal shadows never fall upon it, said the Greeks; for it is the *land of the Gods,* the favourite abode of Apollo, the god of light, and its inhabitants are his beloved priests and servants.
>
> *The Secret Doctrine,* ii 7

Then we have the Third Continent in which the Third Root Race came to experience the first stirrings of self-conscious awakening. It is designated as 'Lemuria', a name invented by P.L. Sclater, who held on zoological grounds that there was once a continent which extended from Madagascar to Ceylon and Sumatra, including some portions of what is now Africa. This gigantic continent stretching from the Indian Ocean to Australia and beyond has almost entirely disappeared, leaving only some of its highest points as scattered islands.

Next we have the Fourth Continent, now called Atlantis, the first 'historical' land, which together with the Fourth Race, passed through markedly different phases. Following the era of the Fourth Root Race, a period as long as five million years, the Fifth Root Race, to which present humanity belongs, began a million years ago with its First Sub-Race in ancient India. Atlantis was originally much vaster than the last large fragment which disappeared about 850,000 years ago. Geologically, the Fifth Continent should be America, but H.P. Blavatsky says, "as it is situated at the Antipodes, it is Europe and Asia Minor, almost coeval with it, which are generally referred to by the Indo-Aryan Occultists as the fifth." The classification of the Continents follows the order of evolution of the Races, not the geological appearance of the Continents. Nor do the present configurations of land masses indicate the past relations of Races.

> There was a time when the delta of Egypt and Northern Africa belonged to Europe, before the formation of the Straits of Gibraltar, and a further upheaval of the continent, changed entirely the face of the map of Europe. The last serious change occurred some 12,000 years ago, and was followed by the submersion of Plato's little Atlantic island, which he calls Atlantis after its parent continent.
>
> *The Secret Doctrine*, ii 8-9

Any accurate appreciation of philosophical anthropogenesis and its spiritual implications must be consonant with cosmogenesis. One must work back from the fourth globe, our own earth, to its earliest inheritances which connect with the entire solar system. This is not only true on the physical plane, but also simultaneously on the invisible planes. This is difficult to understand but it is crucial if one is to make sense of the cosmic scale on which interact internal and external evolution. The nineteenth century conception of material evolution represented a considerable improvement upon the fragmented and arbitrary conceptions of creation which persisted among the credulous and the bigoted. This advance was accompanied by resuscitated cultural theories harking back to classical notions that were pre-Socratic, Platonic and Aristotelian. Nonetheless, it externalized, on the basis of a restrictive view of evidence, the fundamental concepts of mutation, change and chance, and organic growth. In order to accommodate a richer view of evolution even in the external world, and a much more formidable programme of internal evolution in consciousness, thoughtful individuals have to see beyond the orthodoxies of science and of religion. They need to draw freely upon their own subjective experiences in seeking and gaining self-knowledge. The process must be conceived as open-textured, admitting of fructification from the realm of ideation to the region of event. This demands the deliberate extension of the horizon of growth and the potentials in all human beings. The study of human nature must be undertaken in a disciplined manner that is both logical and also intuitively corresponds to that which is integral to cosmic evolution. The metaphysical power to abstract and to visualize has to be aroused if one seriously intends to make sense of human evolution in a universe of infinite unmanifest potentiality.

The methodology of Gupta Vidya is linked to the process of self-regeneration. It focuses upon the purification and perfection of the vestures of the aspirant *pari passu* with the unfolding of perceptual mysteries. It is, therefore, inseparable from the actual course of human evolution itself. It is, in fact, evolution made self-conscious. In its conceptual framework, it mirrors the living matrix of both cosmos and man, and in practice it teaches the macrocosmic and microcosmic application of the different keys of interpretation to myths and symbols. These often offer hints about the vibrations connecting different parts of the universe and different parts of the human constitution. Anyone who begins to appreciate the richer classifications of the ancient world, especially in Sanskrit but also in Greek, will refuse to be bound by any simplistic cardboard categories such as 'mind' and 'body', 'irrational' and 'rational'. These are of little help in understanding the complex interaction between the cosmic and the atomic. Every human being has the same evolutionary task as every other human being who ever lived, lives now or will live in the future. In this pilgrimage there are ancient guidelines in cutting through the clutter of detail and getting to the core of noetic consciousness.

Owing to centuries of mutilation of the higher faculties by dogmatic religion and materialistic science, many people do not have metaphysical imagination. In mass society many find it difficult to generate abstract ideas or to sustain constructive thought. All too often persons get threatened if confronted by any idea that has no immediate concrete reference to their personal self-image. This sad condition demonstrates the inherited damage to consciousness which is transmitted, and even aggravated, by contemporary media. To correct this will require tremendous courage and compassion, and also great wisdom in altering the plasticity of the human mind. Eventually this subtle transformation will require that every human being make some effort to think metaphysically. After a point, what is initially difficult becomes easier, and suddenly a whole group of people who were once completely bewildered by metaphysical abstractions awaken a dormant aptitude for the exercise of creative imagination. The metaphysical must connect with the mystical.

Those who truly seek to prepare themselves for discipleship must choose a mode of life which can help to maintain an increasing continuity of consciousness. Using the method of analogy and correspondence, one will find that *The Secret Doctrine* is replete with instruction concerning meditation and self-study, about how to understand other human beings, and how to make a constructive difference to the collective karma of the human race. Each human being, every day and night, has microcosmic choices and opportunities which, if calmly understood from the perspective of the macrocosmic, enables an honest seeker to be truly helpful to the Brotherhood of Bodhisattvas. In the early stages this would be mostly unconscious to the lower mind, but entirely clear to the immortal soul. Even small differences wrought in the moral choices one makes by night and day can unlock doors for vast numbers of human beings and open pathways which will be relevant to the Races to come and the Aquarian civilization of the future. Aspiring disciples will find that sometimes just by taking a phrase or a sentence and writing it out, reflecting upon it and sincerely attempting to apply it to themselves, trying to use it at dawn, midday, the twilight hour or late at night, but always so that one may become the better able to help and serve the whole of the human race, they will tap the inexhaustible resources of *Akasha*.

It is certainly possible to establish a strong nucleus of spiritual seekers who can imbibe the elixir of Divine Wisdom. One is automatically unable to glimpse the secrets of Nature if one is not of the right frame of mind, does not have the proper motivation or does not have the proper mental posture of a disciple. But if one does have even a modicum of these, one will receive intimations from unseen helpers as to how to make Hermetic wisdom come alive and become an alchemical, ambrosial source for self-transmutation. Speaking of winged Mercury as the perpetual companion of the Sun of Wisdom, H.P. Blavatsky pointed to the profound mysteries in human consciousness which are vitally relevant to *sushupti, dhyana* and *turiya*:

> He was the leader of and the evocator of Souls, the 'great Magician' and the Hierophant. Virgil depicts him as taking 'his wand to evoke from Orcus the souls plunged therein'. . . . He is the golden-coloured Mercury, the χρυσοφαὴς Ἑρμῆς whom the Hierophants forbade to name. He is symbolised in Grecian

mythology by one of the *dogs* (vigilance), which watch
over the celestial flock (occult wisdom), or Hermes
Anubis, or again Agathodæmon. He is the Argus
watching over the Earth, and which the latter mistakes
for the Sun itself. It is through the intercession of
Mercury that the Emperor Julian prayed to the Occult
Sun every night; for, as says Vossius: 'All the theologians
agree to say that *Mercury and the Sun are one.* . . . He
was the most eloquent and the most wise of all the gods,
which is not to be wondered at, since *Mercury is in such
close proximity to the Wisdom and the Word of God* (the
Sun). . . . '

The Secret Doctrine, ii 28

Through daily meditation upon the Spiritual Sun, *Buddhi* is
aroused and sheds its light upon the noumenal meaning of
experience, the internal relations in human consciousness which
are connected with the external conditions of material evolution.
Hermetic wisdom bridges the gap between ideation, image and
form, between universal Spirit and differentiated matter, between
the cosmic and the human, between the abstract and the concrete.
Meaningful correlations between noumenal causes and
disconnected events are sensed in *sushupti*, dreamless sleep.
Dhyana or meditation dissolves the boundaries of the separative
self and prepares the awakened individual to attain unbroken
continuity of consciousness. The process of evolution is reversed,
the illusory succession of events is shattered by insight, and
spiritual wakefulness *(turiya)* is eventually experienced. When this
becomes an unbroken state of ceaseless contemplation,
enlightenment is possible and all life may be experienced with
therapeutic skill, the firmness of the caduceus, the fire of
compassion.

EVOLUTION AND KARMA

*It now becomes plain that there exists in Nature a triple
evolutionary scheme, for the formation of the three
periodical Upadhis; or rather three separate schemes of
evolution, which in our system are inextricably interwoven
and interblended at every point. These are the Monadic (or
spiritual), the intellectual, and the physical evolutions. These
three are the finite aspects or the reflections on the field of
Cosmic Illusion of ATMA, the seventh, the ONE REALITY
. . . . Each of these three systems has its own laws, and is
ruled and guided by the different sets of the highest Dhyanis
or 'Logoi'. Each is represented in the constitution of man,
the Microcosm of the great Macrocosm; and it is the union
of these three streams in him which makes him the complex
being he now is.*

The Secret Doctrine, i 181

Man and Nature, *Atman* and *Brahman,* are One in their
transcendental origin, but threefold in their
manvantaric manifestations through interlocking
planes of consciousness and form. The mystery of the Three-
in-One is mirrored in the archetypal mode of instruction
exemplified by Gautama Buddha, who shed the pristine light of
Bodhisattvic Wisdom upon the span of all three worlds, teaching
devas, men and gods. The complex riddle of human nature
inscribed in the sevenfold vestures of man and Nature can only
be deciphered through a progressive comprehension of all its
interconnected links ranging from the homogeneous planes of
arupa ideation to the most material planes of differentiated form.
The complete union of *karuna* and *prajna,* of compassion and self-
knowledge, depends upon the all-inclusive integration of every
element and atom participating in the cyclic sweep of cosmic
evolution. Under the supreme decree of eternal harmony, all that
lives forms a single community and brotherhood, bound together

and governed by the law of Karma.

Within that vast programme, each evolving unit is joined to every other by laws of collective and distributive action, and it is upon the correct understanding of these coordinate links, inherent in the interrelationships of the embodied vestures, that the further spiritual growth of humanity depends. In practice, and in time, this requires the seeker self-consciously to differentiate and comprehend the origin, functions and virtues of each of the principles in man. To acquire skill in action, the logic of the programme of evolution must first be seen in terms of its triadic nature, and then applied, with moral discrimination, according to the laws of analogy and correspondence, within each of the seven kingdoms of Nature. Through *tapas* and ascetic striving, guided by devotion to the Mahatmas and rooted in a vision of the Bodhisattvic ideal, each pilgrim-soul can discover and unlock the mysteries hidden within the microcosmic world of the visible and largely invisible vestures.

Examined from the standpoint of individual effort, this task may be seen as a progressive and painful, though extremely rewarding, process of inserting personal existence into universal human history and ultimately into cosmic evolution. For the student of *The Secret Doctrine*, this may be put in terms of the fusion of cosmogenesis with anthropogenesis through entry into the path of *The Voice of the Silence*. Acquisition of a dialectical understanding of the operation of Karma, in its triple operation in the spiritual, intellectual and physical fields, arises from an awareness of eternity in time which yields that timeliness in conduct spoken of by Krishna as renunciation in action and by Buddha as skilful means.

As a starting-point, one must come to see that the diverse rules and laws applying to the different kingdoms of Nature and their coordinate schemes of evolution are inseparable expressions of one universal law of growth. Whether put in terms of the relationship between the Unmanifest Logos and the diverse Logoi operating on different planes, or in terms of the differentiations of Spirit and Matter out of one homogeneous Substance-Principle, the complex structures and varied modes of growth participated in by human beings represent a single triadic process. In the language of the Commentaries upon the *Book of Dzyan,* this central principle is put in terms of the magnetic attraction exercised by the model of the Heavenly Man over every spark of sentient life evolving throughout the infinitudes of space.

> 1. *'Every form on earth, and every speck (atom) in Space strives in its efforts towards self-formation to follow the model placed for it in the* 'HEAVENLY MAN'. . . . *Its (the atom's) involution and evolution, its external and internal growth and development, have all one and the same object — man; man, as the highest physical and ultimate form on this earth; the* MONAD, *in its absolute totality and awakened condition — as the culmination of the divine incarnations on Earth.'*
>
> The Secret Doctrine, i 183

This is a general law applicable to the whole of life, from the tiniest atom to the most massive form, all of which evolve from Akashic prototypes that are like seeds within the Cosmic Egg of Brahmā, the container of the Heavenly Man. As in the awesome metaphor of the Ashwatha tree, with its roots in heaven and its branches and leaves below on the planes of manifestation, life proceeds from formlessness into form and ever seeks to return through the circulation of its essences and elixirs to its transcendental source.

For all human beings in the present period of evolution, spiritual growth consists in awakening noetic awareness of formless spiritual essences, a process of Manasic maturation which requires precise apprehension of the different sets of Dhyanis and ancestors involved in the complex karmic heredity of humanity. The ascent to Monadic awakening culminating in self-conscious divinity proceeds *pari passu* with an increasing participation in the sacrificial descent of the Light of the Logos into the human temple. Humanity is the beneficiary of vast processes of evolution that were completed on preceding globes both in the present earth chain and in the previous chain of globes known to us as the

moon chain. Like dwarfs seated upon the shoulders of giants, men
and women of the present enjoy the privilege of self-conscious
existence and survey the grand prospects of future evolution only
because of the sacrifice of Mahatmas and Dhyanis throughout
ages without number. Metaphysically, there is neither a beginning
nor an end to the series of vast epochs of manifestation, and the
significance of reaching the man-stage of evolution lies in the
prerogative and potential of becoming a co-worker with Nature,
with Amitabha, the Boundless Age.

Terrestrial evolution may be conceptually divided into three
streams, corresponding to the Monadic, the intellectual and the
physical components set forth in Gupta Vidya. The phrase
'Monadic evolution' points to the emergence of successively higher
phases of spiritual activity of the metaphysically indivisible unit
called the Monad, or the *Atma-Buddhi*. In reality, that Monad is
not subject to change or alteration, but is the constantly presiding
divine presence at the heart of the sphere of mayavic and samsaric
existence. In its highest sense, the MONAD is single and impartite,
and the conception of a plurality of Monads is merely a
terminological convenience within the veil of illusion. Pythagoras
taught that the MONAD, having radiated Divine Light, retires into
the Divine Darkness.

Although Monadic evolution is spoken of as equivalent
to spiritual evolution, both Spirit and Matter, with all their
differentiations, are ultimately One, inseparable from meta-Spirit
or *Atman*. Nonetheless, within the planes of differentiated
existence and consciousness, it is helpful to distinguish the realized
degrees of universality and individuation of consciousness
attributable to the evolving sparks of the One Life. Hence, in
the metaphysics of *The Secret Doctrine* there is a fundamental
distinction between the hosts of solar and lunar Monads,
the *Agnishwatha* and *Barhishad* Pitris. Within the stream of
intellectual evolution, and associated with the Solar or *Manasa*
Dhyanis, are to be found the exalted bestowers of self-conscious
intelligence upon incipient humanity. Within the stream of
physical evolution and associated with the building of the mortal

vestures of man are to be found the hosts of the lunar Pitris. Whilst it is possible to distinguish the ancestry and attributes of the various principles of sevenfold man, ultimately there is only One Principle — the *Atman.*

The development of humanity in the present series of globes began at a point like the intersection of cosmogenesis and anthropogenesis. As the sevenfold theatre of evolution known as the earth emerged from *pralaya,* and the Fohatic life-wave began to quicken the sleeping centres, those Monads from the moon chain which had attained the highest degree of physical evolution on the old chain commenced their activity in the first of the new worlds. Restricted in their degree of Monadic activity to the fourth plane, these builders of form were capable of recapitulating evolutionary development only up to the incipient human-germ stage. Progressively, over the first three and one-half Rounds of the development of the earth chain, these lunar Dhyanis unfolded, through the power of instinctual intelligence, the *rupas* that constitute the lower kingdoms of Nature.

Viewed from the Monadic standpoint, this process is equivalent to a descent or involution of Spirit into Matter, of consciousness into form. Viewed from the standpoint of *Prakriti,* it is a process of elevation of the undifferentiated life-essence characterizing the elemental kingdoms through stages and degrees of refinement, corresponding to a progressive permeability to the Atmic light. By the mid-point of the present or Fourth Round, this process of the working up of substance into incipient human form reached its culmination. It was at this juncture that the preferred forms became the vehicles of already self-conscious Monads associated with the intellectual stream of evolution. This point is depicted thus in the Commentaries upon the *Stanzas of Dzyan*:

> 2. *'The Dhyanis (Pitris) are those who have evolved their* BHUTA *(doubles) from themselves, which* RUPA *(form) has become the vehicle of monads (seventh and sixth principles) that had completed their cycle of transmigration in the three preceding Kalpas (Rounds). Then, they (the*

*astral doubles) became the men of the first Human Race of
the Round. But they were not complete, and were senseless.'*
Ibid., i 183

After this long period of gestation, the prepared *rupas* became
the vehicles of Solar Monads through the lighting up of *Manas,*
which occurred over eighteen million years ago. To understand
this awakening of consciousness, one must clearly distinguish
between the evolution of intelligence and the development of
form. Although, for the sake of our comprehension, it is helpful
to speak of lunar Monads reaching the human germ stage in
earlier Rounds, and to speak of incipient human Monads
throughout the early phases of the Fourth Round, it must be
understood that these references are to beings which are human
in form though not in consciousness. Further, the emanation of
the fires of Manasic awareness into these incipient forms should
not be understood as the entry of Monads into forms which are
already occupied by other Monads. It is like the successive passage
of two rays of light through the same aperture; the ray has become
intensified, rather than multiplied. Referring to this mystery, Jesus
said: "I and my Father in heaven are One."

True human existence presupposes the inherent possession
of the higher *arupa* fires of Manasic awareness. Amongst the
Agnishwatha custodians of the sacred fire, distinctions may be
drawn between those who had attained full enlightenment in
prior periods of manifestation and those who had not yet
completed the task of intellectual human self-evolution during
the Rounds of the moon chain. There is a further distinction
between those differentiations of the Monadic essence which only
reached the incipient human stage in the middle of the Fourth
Round of the present globe and which only entered upon the
stage of human existence on that globe, and the former two classes
of human beings. It is upon the correct understanding of the
karmic attainment of each of these three classes of human beings
that a proper understanding of justice and injustice in human
life depends.

Much contemporary confusion between the spiritual and the intellectual, between the intellectual and the physical, is due to the unwarranted degree to which human consciousness is presently limited by attachment to the outward plane of sensory existence. As a result, wandering into the astral regions is often mistaken for awakening to spiritual consciousness, whilst intellectual life is reduced to an inductive enumeration of empirical particulars. *The Secret Doctrine* devotes considerable attention to the development by the lunar Dhyanis of the ethereal vestures underlying physical evolution. The student must understand that the region of outward sensation is a reflection of the lowest, or seventh, component of the astral; the realm of the lunar Pitris comprises the entirety of the lower four planes of existence. Hence, the ethereal lunar Dhyanis evolved out of themselves astral doubles. This process of subtle development proceeded from within without throughout the entirety of the first three Rounds, beginning with the most developed lunar Monads and eventually including all those less developed Monads which would enter the human kingdom on the present globe.

By the beginning of the Fourth Round, incipient humanity was essentially complete as an astral type, though as yet lacking in self-consciousness. During the Fourth Round, with each successive Race and Sub-Race, up until the beginning of the Fifth Race, there has been a progressive consolidation of the external form surrounding the astral double, the *linga sarira*. Corresponding to this process, and running parallel with it simultaneously, was a progressive adaptation of the physical form and structure of the fauna of the earth as the latter passed through its stages of geologic formation. Altogether, there was a tremendous consolidation of matter which produced a connection between the astral and the physical that has an important bearing on the porosity of the evolving brain to the Light of the *Atman*.

Given this broad understanding of the development of human form through the activity of the lunar Pitris, most of the inheritance of humanity from the early Rounds, and indeed the early Races of the present Round, lies hidden within the casement of the physical form. Existing on subtler planes of matter and consciousness, the evolving humanity of the early Rounds was largely ethereal. Subsequent to the incarnation of the *Manasa* Dhyanis into the waiting forms in the Third Root Race, at what is called the balance point in a series of Races and Rounds, the development of the inner astral man has proceeded along different lines. Yet, owing to the tremendous debasement of human consciousness during the Fourth Root Race, both the nature of the transformations affecting the ethereal vestures, and even the very existence of those vestures, have become obscured to human awareness. Hence, the deeper meaning of these interior processes and their vital relevance to the intellectual evolution of humanity are virtually *terra incognita* to present humanity. Recognizing the blindness of contemporary awareness, the Commentaries state:

> 3. '*The inner, now concealed, man, was then (in the beginnings) the external man. The progeny of the Dhyanis (Pitris), he was "the son like unto his father." Like the lotus, whose external shape assumes gradually the form of the model within itself, so did the form of man in the beginning evolve from within without. After the cycle in which man began to procreate his species after the fashion of the present animal kingdom, it became the reverse. The human fœtus follows now in its transformations all the forms that the physical frame of man had assumed throughout the three Kalpas (Rounds) during the tentative efforts at plastic formation around the Monad by senseless, because imperfect, matter, in her blind wanderings. In the present age, the physical embryo is a plant, a reptile, an animal, before it finally becomes man, evolving within himself his own ethereal counterpart, in his turn. In the beginning it was that counterpart (astral man) which, being senseless, got entangled in the meshes of matter.*'
>
> *Ibid.,* i 184

This passage points to the underlying karmic continuity

within the entire scheme of evolution and also to the crucial significance of the difference between its physical and intellectual components. Whilst the development of the inner astral man was the result of the sacrifice of the lunar Dhyanis through the early Rounds, the development of self-conscious individuality was the result of the Great Sacrifice of the *Manasa* Dhyanis, who lit up in every incipient human Monad the power of choice, the potency of intelligent conscious reflection in the human mind of the Universal Mind. Humanity, in the great height of its Golden Age over eighteen million years ago, was in a state of mystic meditation attuned to the universal host of Creative Fires which had come down as a single, beneficent initiatory Presence. This glorious truth and lost light has come down in every myth and tradition of all the tribes of humanity, including those who, alas, concretized and misused the sacred Teachings at terrible karmic cost to themselves. The principle that humanity is the progeny of the Dhyanis, "the son like unto his father," grown lotus-like from a seed within, has a dual and a triple meaning. In relation to the early Rounds, it refers to the process of formation and consolidation of the astral around the *sishta* or seeds of future human form borne by the lunar Dhyanis. Commencing with the descent of the *Manasa* Dhyanis in the Third Root Race, it refers to the flowering of the self-conscious powers of intellection around the bright ray of the descending *Manasa*.

Fundamentally, unfoldment *from within without* is the archetypal mode of growth on the spiritual plane. Both the ascent of the astral form and the descent of the higher principles are interrelated aspects of a single process of equilibration between the poles of Spirit and Matter. The lotus plant, each seed of which contains a complete blueprint of the full flower, provides through its phanerogamic growth a perfect model of the spiritual mode. In every spiritual system, therefore, the lotus is venerated, and various spiritual centres in man, as well as the cosmic centres of life-giving and death-dealing forces, have been compared to lotuses.

During the eighteen and three-quarter million years since

the awakening of *Manas,* the modes of creativity and birth have
shifted from the androgyne state of the earlier human races to
the present separation of the sexes. The earlier Races of humanity,
likened symbolically to dragons and to eggs, reproduced
themselves by those agencies and means which are now somewhat
familiar to students of biology through the study of various non-
human species. With this shift, there was a reversal in the mode
of development of form. Under the current scheme, embryogenesis recapitulates the entire series of forms assumed by the
evolving astral form of man during the early Rounds. Here,
however, it is important to recall the mantram — 'Nature unaided
fails'. Despite the marvellous complexity and variety of forms
evolved by the lunar Pitris in the stream of physical evolution, it
is simply impossible for these material agencies to produce a
human being. It is for this reason, incidentally, that no amount
of genetic manipulation can produce anything other than a
Frankenstein's monster. To produce a human being, something
more is needed than is contained in the karmic and genetic
programme of material evolution.

The attainment of human consciousness can only come
about through the descent of self-conscious beings perfected
in prior periods of evolution. Hence, there is universal awe and
reverence for the entire host of these beings, all of whom
gathered around their Chief, Dakshinamurti, the Initiator of
Initiates, and came down into the forming worlds of the earth
chain. Fully perfected in previous *manvantaras,* their presence
in these worlds is solely for the sake of presiding over the
programme of intelligent human evolution. Reverence for the
Manasas is the hallmark of the degree of human evolution of
the soul; the more highly evolved an individual human being,
the more readily does it display a spontaneous devotion
towards Mahatmas and Gurus. Such is the natural tropism of
human consciousness.

During this early Golden Age of humanity, when all alike
felt the luminous presence of the *Agnishwathas* within, human
beings at the same time enjoyed the use of the ethereal vestures,

with their marvellous powers, evolved from the lower kingdoms. That these powers and faculties are now atrophied, and virtually unknown to present humanity, is the karmic consequence of the misuse of knowledge in the Lemuro-Atlantean and especially in the later Atlantean Fourth Root Race. Whilst the involvement of Spirit into Matter in the first three Rounds and in the early Races of the Fourth Round was a necessary aspect of the karmic programme of evolution, the self-conscious degradation of Manasic intelligence, through identification with the lunar forms, was not. The enormous liability of human beings to recurrent types of psychic and physical disease, as compared to the inhabitants of the animal kingdoms, is a direct consequence of this needless fall into matter. Grave though these susceptibilities may seem, however, they are of little import when compared to the spiritual consequences of the Fall — the closing of the Third Eye and the loss of awareness of the *Agnishwatha* Pitris.

Given the self-imposed burden of spiritual as well as psychic blindness, it is not surprising, though still tragic, that humanity is scarcely aware of, much less able to respond to, the challenge of the transformations being wrought by cyclic law within its mental and material vestures. In order to regain initiative as a Manasic being, one must grasp the deeper significance of the fact that, prior to the descent of the *Manasas* and prior to the separation of the sexes, the entire programme of human development was *from within without,* and that after this point, human development began with the recapitulation of the entire physical scheme of evolution within the mother's womb. Thus, on the physical plane, ontogeny recapitulates phylogeny, but only up to the point attained by mindless lunar evolution over eighteen million years ago. Therefore, for the past eighteen million years, through the power of self-evolution, human beings have had to gestate out of their astral bodies, by a process of separation and self-training, the embryo of that which will become, over many lives in the future, an Adept.

H.P. Blavatsky took trouble to explain in a veiled way the secret and complex Teachings of threefold evolution to those who did not have access to Sanskrit, Chaldean or other ancient languages and texts, and those who could not use the arcane symbol systems to benefit from the wisdom of the enlightened. This Teaching is essentially different from any seventeenth century idea of human rationality or eighteenth century doctrine of human progress or Victorian doctrine of complacent optimism. This ancient Teaching is directed towards millions of years in the future and millions of years in the past, and its principal lesson, which should be more comprehensible in an age of computers, is that in this cosmic programme the minutest difference that is made every moment has tremendous bearing upon what happens through exponential curves over millions of years.

Once one truly understands human evolution, as distinct from the instinctual and involuntary evolution of the lower kingdoms, one can also grasp the warning implicit in the esoteric Teaching that the cycle of metempsychosis for human Monads is closed at this point of the Fourth Round and the Fifth Root Race. It is technically impossible for human beings who totally fail to be human to take bodies in the animal kingdom. Hence, the tragic prospect awaiting those who cannot make full and proper use of the Manasic principle is eventual annihilation. Thus, one can also come to appreciate the enormous compassion of the Teachers in the nineteenth century when, since 1848, the muddy torrents of *kamaloka* broke loose. Owing to nefarious practices of mediumship in séances and elsewhere, and through an obsessive and excessive concern with lunar ancestors, there was at that time a vast outpouring of *bhuts* and elementaries from the dregs of the astral plane. This same year, termed by some historians as "that wonderful year", witnessed a great variety of outbreaks and upheavals throughout all the countries of Europe. Owing to the appalling karma of 1848, great compassion was shown in the partial transmission of Teachings which had always been locked in the secret sanctuaries, and this in itself heightened the karma of human beings.

If one now looks back to the Victorian Age, it is evident that events did not work out as many people had hoped. Indeed, even in the last ten years of the nineteenth century, a death-blow was given to the Victorian Age. By the First World War the Victorian order, which had been so much taken for granted, had collapsed. In the Second World War the entire old European order collapsed. Now we are witnessing the culmination of the ancient Karma of Israel. All of this is part of the programme of Karma which is no respecter of personal emotions, likes or dislikes, or the sectarian predilections of human beings through excessive attachment to external forms.

There is a tremendous logic to the precipitation of karma in the programme of cyclic evolution. That logic is on the side of every immortal soul. It is not on the side of the ratiocinative mind. It is not on the side of *kamamanas*. It is unequivocally on the side of *Buddhi Manas*. Therefore, every human being's urge to transcend the boundaries of the personal self, and every human being's deep desire (which is expressed every night in *sushupti*, and which may be strengthened through daily meditation) to come closer to the One Flame, to the Light of the Logos in the heart, is truly blessed. But if one wanders in the opposite direction, one risks much and it would be the height of unwisdom. The Avatar quickens life amongst those who are responsive, but the Avatar also quickens the doom of those who are unwilling to avail themselves of the Light. This is evident to the intuition of growing numbers of souls throughout the world who wish to remain in the forward current of human evolution which gives birth, and not be caught up in that reverse current which propels into the vortex whatever is inconsistent with the humanity of the future.

This implies a decisive moment of choice for humanity; the power of choice is the hallmark of Manasic existence, and its intelligent exercise gives true self-respect. To meet the trials of the future, it is helpful to have some conception of the excellences inherent in humanity. The *lakshanas* displayed by the early Races can and will become the norms of the future Races. Each human being has participated in the spiritual civilization of the Third Root Race when

in the beginning, mankind were morally and physically
the types and prototypes of our present Race, and of
our human dignity, by their beauty of form, regularity
of feature, cranial development, nobility of sentiments,
heroic impulses, and grandeur of ideal conception.

Ibid., i 185

These are the marks of human potential and perfectibility of
which every human being has been capable for over eighteen
million years. Over that span, alas, a small minority of mankind
has become involved in psycho-physical inversion and

the gradual debasement and degradation of man,
morally and physically, can be readily traced throughout
the ethnological transformation down to our time.

Ibid.

Even where this process of degradation leads to the
permanent withdrawal of the soul from the human tenement, the
withdrawal of the ray back into its parent source and the
consequent need for the One Flame to emanate a new ray totally
disconnected from the prior series of incarnations, there is no
wastage. Even so unspiritual and materialistic a lunar form would
be made use of in the programme of Karma, serving as a vesture
for those Monads delayed in their entry into the human kingdom
until the Fifth Round through the ancient sin of the mindless.
Such is the karmic economy in nature that the astral vestures
vacated by failed human beings will form the karmic compensation of those Monads held back from human life and
imprisoned in anthropoid forms, owing to the omissions and
delays of selfish egos in the Third Root Race. As the anthropoids
die out during the latter part of the Fifth Root Race, their Monads
will pass into the astral forms of the Sixth and Seventh Races of
this Round. Then, in the Fifth Round, these Monads will enter
directly the stream of Manasic intellectual evolution and be
welcomed into the human family.

Distant though this age millions of years away may seem to

ordinary mortals, to the eye of the Initiate it is like tomorrow. Strange and arcane as these Teachings may seem to an intelligence caught in the dark folds of matter, they are inevitable consequences of the universal decree of harmony and justice governing the sweep of cyclic evolution. Yet, for those courageous pilgrim-souls who want to take seriously the Pledge of Kwan Yin — the Bodhisattvic vow to aid every sentient being caught in the bonds of samsaric existence — the intricate and elegant complexities of Monadic, intellectual and physical evolution must be understood and mastered in their applications throughout the three worlds. For the aspirant to godlike Wisdom and Divine Compassion, everything turns upon the conception of space, time and consciousness. If one would rise above the ocean of *samsara*, above the fourth plane, and choose the path of renunciation, one must enter the boundless void and eternal motion of the *Atman*, and become the willing servant of the One Law of Compassion and Sacrifice, *mahakaruna* and *mahayajna*.

SPIRIT, MIND AND MATTER

The 'midway point of evolution' is that stage where the astral prototypes definitely begin to pass into the physical, and thus become subject to the differentiating agencies now operative around us. Physical causation supervenes immediately on the assumption of 'coats of skin' — i.e., the physiological equipment in general. The forms of Men and mammalia previous to the separation of sexes are woven out of astral matter, and possess a structure utterly unlike that of the physical organisms, which eat, drink, digest, etc., etc., etc. The known physiological contrivances in organisms were almost entirely evolved subsequently to the incipient physicalization of the 7 Root-Types out of the astral — during the 'midway halt' between the two planes of existence. Hardly had the 'ground-plan' of evolution been limned out in these ancestral types, than the influence of the accessory terrestrial laws, familiar to us, supervened, resulting in the whole crop of mammalian species. Æons of slow differentiation were, however, required to effect this end.

The Secret Doctrine, ii 736

Human beings hold within themselves the keys to their own growth, both as individuals and as a species. The chief gain behind the resuscitation of the concept of evolution, since the nineteenth century, is the greater sense of human responsibility towards the whole of Nature. Understood rightly, the idea of spiritual evolution opens up avenues of authentic creativity which are also the means of fulfilment of the sacrificial *dharma* of humanity. To see the basis of moral responsibility and human freedom in the idea of evolution, however, one must let go the baggage of anthropomorphic religion and materialistic notions of Nature. In the long run, it makes little difference whether one conceives of man as the adventitious special creation of a supernatural god or as the equally adventitious product of a fortuitous concurrence of atoms. In either case, one has divorced quintessential self-consciousness from the root of Nature. One view regards the position of humanity in Nature as a kind of Babylonian captivity, to be resented and endured until the arrival of an unsolicited apocalypse and an undeserved deliverance. The other sees mankind as a transitory quirk of cosmic probabilities, like a wave formed in and out of the waters of the open sea, which seems engaged in a struggle for survival and stasis that is ultimately as meaningless to itself as to the element into which it will again be dissolved. Each of these views distorts the fundamental Teaching of Gupta Vidya.

Ancient wisdom holds that there is a fiery spark of divinity latent in every human being, and that each person can, through the quickening of that fire, rise in consciousness to a condition exalted above but never alienated from all the intelligent hosts and hierarchies of differentiated Nature. This realization of freedom involves no break in the moral solidarity between Man and Nature. Rather, it is accomplished through steps of sacrifice towards all other beings. Nor is there anything accidental about the power which involves Man in differentiated Nature and which makes possible his mastery of it. That power is the radiant light-energy of the *Atman,* reflected and refracted in all the planes and principles of Nature and Man. Nor is there, according to ancient wisdom, anything fortuitous about the origin of Man. All humanity and all Nature are sprung from the same root substance. That substance is not blind and inert but refulgent with intelligence, suffused with the divine radiant energy of the *Atman.* Thus, the substantial solidarity of humanity and the rest of Nature is equally a moral and intelligent solidarity with all living beings. There is no gap between the human sense of self-consciousness and purpose and the cooperative and compassionate impulses that guide all of Nature.

Any account of the evolution of Man and Nature which does justice to both must strike a balance between the unique and essential meaning of human existence and the uninterrupted continuity of Man and Nature. Typically, orthodox religious theories of the origin of Man tend to isolate humanity from Nature, whilst modern biological accounts of human evolution tend to obliterate the precise role of human self-consciousness in Nature. Philosophically, both accounts treat human existence as accidental. In the one case, Man is the product of an arbitrary act of an anthropomorphic god superimposed upon Nature; in the other, Man is the result of an arbitrary accident of atoms. Neither view establishes any real connection in principle between Man and Nature.

> The occult doctrine, is, we think, more logical. It teaches a cyclic, never varying law in nature, the latter having no personal, 'special design', but acting on a uniform plan that prevails through the whole manvantaric period and deals with the land worm as it deals with man. Neither the one nor the other have sought to come into being, hence both are under the same evolutionary law, and both have to progress according to Karmic law. Both have started from the same neutral centre of Life and both have to re-merge into it at the consummation of the cycle.
>
> *Ibid.*, 261

The term 'evolutionary law' may be thought of as a bridge between immortal, divine and unmodified self-existence in eternity and the complex, differentiated realm of time-bound existence and circumstance. Evolutionary law bridges eternity and form, expanding the germinal potential in the neutral centre of Life into a series of manifestations in time and space. Yet the nature and potentiality of that centre cannot be deduced or derived through any enumeration of the forms or transformations of form that arise from it. Instead, it is necessary to rise in consciousness to a direct cognition of that centre through a universalization of one's consciousness. From that pristine perspective one can survey the vast panoply of forms in Nature, experiencing their continuity from within without. Whilst Gupta Vidya rejects materialized conceptions of biological evolution, it has always held that the human form, and all its parts, originated through a series of transformations that are perfectly continuous with the rest of Nature.

> It is not those who teach the transformation of the mineral atom through crystallization — which is the same function, and bears the same relation to its *inorganic* (so-called) *upadhi* (or basis) as the formation of *cells* to their organic *nuclei*, through plant, insect and animal into man — it is not they who will reject this theory, as it will finally lead to the recognition of a Universal Deity in nature, ever-present and as ever invisible, and unknowable, and of *intra*-Cosmic gods, who all were men.
>
> *Ibid.*, 255

Perfected human intelligence is an integral part of Nature, inextricably interwoven with all its many processes of transformation. Thus, the differentiations of Nature are by no means incompatible with the uninterrupted solidarity of Man and Nature. In a sense, anthropomorphic religion suffers from a false sense of modesty. Perfected human intelligence is vastly more important in Nature than human beings are readily able to conceive. At the same time, human intelligence is a sacrificial expression of universal divine intelligence, and its purposes are simply part of universal Logoic volition. Whilst nineteenth century evolutionary theorists may have sought to reject the cruder teleologies of medieval religion, they still viewed the categories of volition in narrowly personal terms, and so could not conceive that the impersonal fabric of Nature was the veil of the divine intelligence in Man.

> The whole trouble is this: neither physiologists nor pathologists *will* recognize that the cell-germinating substance (the *cytoblastema*) and the mother-lye from

which crystals originate, are one and the same essence,
save in differentiation for purposes.

Ibid.

It is the differentiation and elaboration out of itself of that essence which produces the panoply of gross and subtle forms in Nature. The logic of the process of crystallization in the mineral kingdom is analogous to the logic of the process of the elaboration and formation, out of organic nuclei, of cells. The transformations of primal vital energy into morphological units in the kingdoms of Nature, together with the processes of metamorphosis taking place in those kingdoms, are invariably the expression of a unified law of evolution. That law, however, is not single and simple, but complex and composite. This much should surely suggest itself to even the casual observer of the physical universe. It is still more obvious if one considers all the intricate developments of intelligence on the invisible planes of abstract ideation and astral substance which witness the interplay of potentials and powers that give rise to every possible type of being. Innumerable are the species of being unknown to us at this point in evolution, either because those forms have disappeared or because those beings have withdrawn from the sight of human beings as constituted at present.

When one thinks of the living expression of the philosophic problem of the One and the many, one will naturally become suspicious of any simple linear theory of merely physical evolution. This, of course, was the problem with the early models of evolution developed in the nineteenth century, particularly Darwin's. Drawing upon a variant of simple Aristotelian teleology, Darwin's model benefited from the method of classification pioneered by the great Swedish biologist, Linnaeus. Darwin himself, out of his wealth of observation, tried to put all these different species into a single simple theory. He himself was a remarkably curious man, a true naturalist, who became an ardent explorer and a voracious reader. Like other leading thinkers of his day, he was aware that neither geological nor biological formations, neither flora nor fauna, were unchanging. But as soon as he sought to put their present varieties and past transformations into a single theory, he became entangled in gross over-simplification. Unfortunately, Darwinists are strangers to the tentativeness that Darwin himself rightly felt towards his own formulations.

Darwin was primarily concerned to describe a mechanism broad enough to account for the variation among the types of life. This fascination with mechanical processes, and the effort to impose them upon life at every level, was characteristic of nineteenth century thought. Alfred Wallace, who wrote at the same time as Darwin, developed an alternative model of biological evolution somewhat influenced by the thought of Lamarck. Working on the Continent, Lamarck had pointed towards the existence of some kind of inward impulse within living forms which works gradually to transform them. The celebrated paradigm of this process is found in the giraffe, which, by reaching upward over a long period of time, somehow willed itself to lengthen its neck. According to Lamarck, this had to be explained by some internal factor in evolution, something not reducible to the lottery of heredity or to the cruel vagaries of the environment. This innate creative impulse in Nature, Lamarck believed, could be exercised by a creature in its life, thereby affecting subsequent generations. To some extent, these ideas interested Wallace, who attempted to integrate them into his own account of the precarious evolutionary struggle for survival. But all Lamarckian theories of evolution which seek to connect learning with biological transformation must eventually come to terms with the "learner's paradox" set forth by Plato in *Meno.*

Unless one approaches the problem of learning, whether in man or beast, with a philosophic clarity, it will appear that learning is either impossible or unnecessary. As a result of empirical thinking over the past century, very few theorists, however interested in the ideas of Lamarck, have been able to formulate convincingly the idea of an intelligent inward principle in evolution. Instead, they have largely succumbed to reductionist, behavioural accounts of individual learning that cannot do justice to the processes of evolutionary transformation. Darwin himself, though capable of understanding some things outside a model of monistic materialism, was nonetheless not metaphysically inclined. In the end, he had a deep intellectual fascination with the problem of subduing the largest possible amount of empirical evidence to a single general hypothesis which would explain the struggle for existence and survival in an ever-changing environment. Thereby, he unwittingly provided a tremendous brake upon modern man's reverence for the rich complexity of Nature. It is therefore common for Darwinians to point to the variety of forms of life as a kind of wastage in Nature. Since the variety of Nature is seen as the random result of a mechanical process, it is impossible to attribute meaning to any of its specific products. The appearance and disappearance of species are seen as random incidents in the wastrel career of prodigal Nature.

Gupta Vidya, by contrast, conceives of evolution as having a unified plan and a unitary logic. But it does not think of that evolution as linear. Instead, it depicts a complex cyclic unfoldment from the invisible to the visible. Based upon a theory of different planes of consciousness and different states of matter, it holds that there must be a continuity between these planes extending from the divine Monad. This source is the Logos in the Divine Darkness, before worlds are emanated, which encompasses all the forms, both subtle and gross, within those worlds. There must be a continuity between the supreme potential of many worlds in that divine pre-existing cosmic Logos and the intelligence that one finds in the smallest insect. Every living and changing creature is connected to the primary differentiations on the plane of *Akasha*. Given the primal Logoic radiation at the root of the cosmos, there is subsequently an evolutionary process connecting the most spiritual and the most physical, the most abstract and the most concrete, the most eternal and the most ephemeral. It accommodates different rates of growth on different planes of consciousness and matter. This can be understood only if one refuses to imprison oneself within a hard-and-fast dichotomy between ideation and substance, spirit and matter, consciousness and form. One must recognize that there is one unitary essence which, at different levels, generates the polarity and interplay of spirit and matter. In fact,

> There are several 'protyles' in Nature, correspond-
> ing to the various planes of matter. The two sub-physical
> elemental kingdoms, the plane of mind (*manas*, the fifth
> state matter), as also that of Buddhi (sixth state matter),
> are each and all evolved from one of the six 'protyles'
> which constitute the basis of the Object-Universe. The
> three 'states', so-called of our terrestrial matter, known
> as the 'solid', 'liquid', and 'gaseous', are only, in
> strict accuracy, SUB-states. As to the former reality of
> the descent into the physical, which culminated in
> physiological man and animal, we have a palpable
> testimony in the fact of the so-called spiritualistic
> 'materializations'.
>
> *Ibid.*, 737

Ultimately, spirit is matter in its subtlest sense; matter is spirit in its densest sense. There is One Universal Life, force, energy, essence, which transcends all the dichotomies that arise from the physical senses. Owing to the conditioning of human consciousness through its physical activity, the very means of recognizing what is visible or gross or specific or concrete, in opposition to that which is general, abstract, invisible and ethereal, is distorted and dichotomized. When perception is full, these false divisions are discarded. Instead, one can perceive the multiple and intertwined lines of evolution, understand their relation to each other and to their unmanifest origin. To detect this continuity within the kaleidoscopic variety of living forms is to recognize the meaning of different forms and different rates of progress.

This reflection upon the unreality of the polarity between consciousness and form must not be allowed to ossify into a static idealism. Instead, it should be the starting-point for a meditation upon the possible changes in the relationship between spirit and matter in manifestation. For it is through an understanding of this shifting dynamic balance that one may discover the keys of self-conscious creativity and evolutionary growth. The sense of evolutionary initiative which is involved here is so metaphysical that it must initially be understood in terms of some supremely suggestive metaphor. Hence all those traditions which conceive of Nature as a consummate artist, or the Logos as the grand architect of the universe. The potential in invisible Nature includes ideation and subtle energy, the spiritual will to create which is identified with Kamadeva, the creative power of that which was at the very dawn of manifestation. This creative designing energy in the heart of the cosmos does not act arbitrarily and then disappear. Once released, it becomes present in every member of an entire series of transformations. It continues to abide within every spiritual atom and Monad. The atomic energy of the atoms of the physical plane is merely a reflection of the One Universal Life-energy that is inherent in the subtlest planes of substance and ideation. In every subtle atom in Nature, there is memory, will and sensation.

Naturally, these terms should not be understood in the narrow context of mundane human expressions of sensation, memory and will. To do so would be to corrupt philosophic pantheism into crude idolatry. Even during the nineteenth century, vitalism was seen as a major conceptual alternative to mechanism. Whilst contemporary thinkers are little closer to understanding life-atoms and the life principle in universal Nature, micro-biologists and particle physicists are becoming progressively impressed by the immense intricacy and complex intelligence that is reflected in every single particle, atom and cell. But still they cannot make sense of this at the micro or at the macro level. How is the intelligence in the atom to be connected to the intelligence in the human brain and heart? By beginning with the metaphor of the artist, the designer and the architect, who marshals matter in line with the designs of intelligence, who produces forms with beauty, merit and function, one can gain some sense of the needed continuity between spirit and matter. It is necessary, however, to go beyond the stage of imaginative metaphor if one would understand the evolution of natural forms of life. One cannot cooperate with Nature until one solves the riddle of that creativity within one's own inner vestures.

The design and formation of the living being is a complex process occupying myriads and myriads of years of a gradual descent of spirit into matter, an involvement of consciousness in form. In principle this process is no different from that known to creative human beings who meditate upon some germinal plan. They know that the great work of imagination and creativity extends over many lifetimes. It requires evolving oneself, evolving other human beings and evolving new modes and new possibilities. True human creativity starts at a fluidic proemial level, free of over-elaborate detail. It intensifies the central idea behind the vision until, working in time with the cycles of Nature, there comes a gradual shaping and consolidation. The imagination can be bodied forth into the manifest form of the vision. In order to retain a high degree of fidelity to the original idea while achieving precise degrees of concretion, there must be a continuous purging and purification of the field of motivation and ideation. Above all, there must be a tremendous mastery, through the use of silence and secrecy, over all the invisible forces that are auspicious to gestation. To work in this way is to emulate Nature. Nature works in secret, especially on the causal plane, just as seeds in the soil germinate below the surface. Within these invisible processes there is a mysterious absorption and osmosis of subtle light-energies from the sun and the moon. Living forms on earth are nourished not merely by the visible physical soil, but also by the magnetosphere surrounding the earth.

If this is true of the good gardener of Nature working on the physical plane, it is doubly true of the wisdom of Nature throughout the evolutionary process. Prior to the present Round and to the present physical plane, Nature traced out the astral prototypes of all her kingdoms in subtler fields of matter. Before the shifting balance of spirit and matter reached the midpoint of evolution, Akashic ideation was translated by the Lunar Pitris into the astral matrix that is presently veiled by a thin veneer of physical form.

The fish evolved into an amphibian — a frog —
in the *shadows* of ponds, and man passed through all
his metamorphoses on this Globe in the Third Round
as he did in this, his Fourth Cycle. The Third Round
types contributed to the formation of the types in this
one. On strict analogy, the cycle of Seven Rounds in
their work of the gradual formation of man through
every kingdom of Nature, are repeated on a
microscopical scale in the first seven months of
gestation of a future human being. Let the student think
over and work out this analogy. As the seven months'
old unborn baby, though quite ready, yet needs two
months more in which to acquire strength and
consolidate; so man, having perfected his evolution
during seven Rounds, remains two periods more in the
womb of mother- Nature before he is born, or rather
reborn a Dhyani, still more perfect than he was before
he launched forth as a Monad on the newly built chain
of worlds. Let the student ponder over this mystery, and
then he will easily convince himself that, as there are
also physical links between many classes, so there are
precise domains wherein the astral merges into physical
evolution.

Ibid., 257

It is possible for Man, involved in the highest demiurgic
creativity of *Kriyashakti,* to emulate this process of Nature. Rooted
in the silence and secrecy of the unmanifest, one may self-
consciously unite oneself with and draw upon the divine creative
agencies that are at the origin of Man and the cosmos. To
understand this is to place the entire physical plane in proper
perspective, gaining a fresh insight into its aggregate continuity
with subtler planes of matter. As soon as one acquires a direct
sense of the meaning of the involution of spirit into matter, one's
conception of evolution is transformed. One is no longer
concerned with quixotically tracing out physical continuities
between fossil forms and questing for missing links. Instead, one's
attention will be redirected from the past towards the future, and

towards human possibilities as yet unrealized. This is a tremendous challenge to the imagination. It restores the idea of the plenitude of potential in Nature, and it rescues one from Epimethean empiricism. All too often, the effort to seek explanations amounts to nothing more than a concern to explain away what exists. At best, such efforts may help to codify and classify natural forms imperfectly; never can it help one to create and anticipate the myriad possibilities within the mind of Nature and matter. This much is clear, both philosophically and practically. Those who become classifiers and historians of design are hardly ever those who create or design themselves. To study and serve Nature is not at all the same as classifying and categorizing her. Like the medieval authors of angelologies or the collectors of butterflies, too many people suppose that classification is comprehension. Mutilation of Nature does not amount to mastery over her.

The Promethean task of the future evolution of humanity has nothing to do with such lifeless and destructive mis-conceptions. It involves the rejection of all linear thinking captivated by exterior forms. One must learn to think of evolution on multiple lines, to distinguish between the spiritual, intellectual and material threads of evolution in Nature. Cosmogenesis and anthropogenesis must be seen in terms of eternal duration and periodic time. Gupta Vidya teaches of seven Rounds or circlings of seven globes, six of which are invisible to perceivers on any one plane. Since present humanity is on the fourth globe of the earth chain, the first three and the last three globes of that chain are invisible to present humanity. Human beings see only that which is consubstantial with the physical senses. Through limits of perception they run the danger of foreclosing the possibilities of Nature. To counter this, one must develop a sense of the larger picture. One must gain some theoretical understanding of the seven Rounds, which extend over millions upon millions of years and provide arenas for gradual evolution to take place on a series of planes of matter. Before the nineteenth century, Western thinkers found it virtually impossible to conceive of either Man or Nature as older than about six thousand years. Nowadays it is becoming easier to contemplate that some anthropoid forms associated with the evolution of man existed nearly eighteen million years ago. All such developments are helpful. They are still, however, far from any clear recognition that human intelligence antedates the origin of the solar system. The entire field of over eighteen million years of self-conscious human existence upon this earth is but a tiny fragment in relation to all the Rounds involved in the earth chain and the even vaster expanse of cosmic evolution in general.

Nevertheless, a careful study of the Teachings of Gupta Vidya in regard to the Rounds and Races of humanity on the present earth can be of great help in restoring individual initiative. Unlike any unilinear theory of evolution restricted to the physical plane, the cyclic interplay of spirit and matter in manifestation carries with it an inherent sense of timing and opportunity. Considered broadly, humanity is at the mid-point of an immense evolution. There has been a vast descent of spirit into matter and there will be an equally vast reascent of matter into spirit. If one studies a diagram of the seven globes of the earth chain arranged in a circle, one may intuit something which applies not only to the long period of human evolution but also to the life cycles of a single individual. The same evolutionary logic is equally applicable to the conscious spiritual growth of the individual. Instead of seeing the descent of spirit into matter in terms of some sort of Fall linked to sin, one should come to see human beings as gods who are fallen only in the sense that they have become obscured. They have through the density of matter merely become forgetful. This should be seen as a sacred and sacrificial process necessary for evolution to work itself out fully on the plane of physical matter. To see this, however, is also to understand that there is another side to the process.

If there is an involution of spirit into matter, there must be an evolution of spirit out of matter which carries with it all beings in a conscious return to the source. This return to the source is enacted at a microcosmic level every time a human being meditates, but it can be done much more self-consciously. To do this, to become one with the true 'Maker' within oneself, one must die to the cries and pleadings, the fascination and noise, of the exterior physical world. The tragedy of many people is that they find no reason to be glamorized by the world, but at the same time they remain terrified of the inner life. They shy away from the solitary depths of meditation. Fearful of their own fallibility, lacking confidence in themselves and Nature, they are lost between two worlds.

This confusion may be understood as the collective effect of the reversal of momentum from involution to evolution. If one had a cooler understanding of the logic of the process, one could see that the gradual descent of spirit into matter which occupied the first three Rounds and the first half of the Fourth Round is now being replaced by the opposite process. Because humanity is now in the Fifth Root Race out of seven Races in the Fourth Round, it is already somewhat past the midpoint. If one would serve the evolutionary future of mankind, one must withdraw attention from the creation of the cosmos and man in the past and redirect it to the future. If one would move forward in evolution, one must grasp the fundamental shift that is taking place between

> the transformations through which man passed on the descending arc — which is centrifugal for spirit and centripetal for matter — and those he prepares to go through, henceforward, on his ascending path, which will reverse the direction of the two forces — viz., matter will become centrifugal and spirit centripetal.
>
> *Ibid.*, 261

During the descending cycles of manifestation, spirit works centrifugally by diffusion of light in every direction. Matter, on the other hand, works by concentration and condensation, becoming harder and denser and absorbing into itself various essences. This process confuses human beings. They experience a distinct gap between spirit and matter, are seemingly caught in what is purely the shadowy side or external aspect of Nature. But having passed the midpoint at which astral potentials are merged into physical forms, humanity is moving towards a comparable future point when physical existence will dissipate and evaporate through a remerging into subtle substance. On the ascending arc of the process, matter will become what spirit was. Matter will become more etherealized, looser and less concrete. It will begin to etherealize itself; spirit, on the other hand, will be characterized by greater freedom in inner concentration. As spirit is freeing itself from confinement in the grossest matter while matter is etherealizing itself, consciousness is becoming more individuated on the plane of ideation, yet more universal in its sentient contact with all of manifestation. Spirit is drawing itself more and more inwardly into itself, and so recovering the pristine potential and potency of the Logos that was and is at the heart of all life and Nature. If the descending arc of evolution is compared philosophically to the One becoming the many, then the ascending arc may be viewed as the many rebecoming the One. This applies to universal collective consciousness, spanning all humanity and every kingdom of life, as well as to every human life.

The possibilities of individual growth and refinement of consciousness are coextensive with the evolutionary and involutionary possibilities of Nature as a whole. This will never be grasped by a merely retrospective and materialistic view of evolution. It is the persistent challenge that lies before the pioneers of the humanity of the future. Guided by the brilliant light of the Avataric star, pilgrim humanity is even now embarking upon the long, slow, upward return journey to its divine origins. In the far distant future, in the Seventh Race of the Seventh Round, every unit will reawaken to the divine unity and the divine wisdom that underlies the cosmos and Man will be restored. Even now, for those with an eye to the future, there is a perceptible brightening in the hidden heart of humanity. New modes and models are being gestated in the *Akasha*. These may be perceived through the silence of devotion and meditation by all those who wish to make themselves the true servants of humanity and the wise custodians of Nature's rich resources.

THE FIRES OF CREATION

"After the changeless (*avikâra*) immutable nature (*Essence, sadaikarûpa*) had awakened and changed (*differentiated*) into (*a state of*) causality (*avayakta*), and from cause (*Karana*) had become its own discrete effect (*vyakta*), from invisible it became visible. The smallest of the small (*the most atomic of atoms, or aniyâmsam aniyâsam*) became one and the many (*ekanekârûpa*); and producing the Universe produced also the Fourth Loka (*our Earth*) in the garland of the seven lotuses. The Achyuta then became the Chyuta."

The Secret Doctrine, ii 46-47

The archetypal evolutionary process, moving from the *arupa* planes of the unmanifest into the sevenfold worlds of form, enshrines the sacred mystery of creativity, divine and human. Creation is the ceaseless action of concentrated will acting upon cosmic matter, calling forth the primordial Divine Light and Eternal Fire latent within it. The noumenal quality of the outcome depends upon the degree of abstraction of volition and visualization and the corresponding depth of potential energy that is released. Beginning with the incognizable and imperishable *Brahman*, Hindu cosmogony depicts the gestation by Brahmā of four bodies — *Ratri* (night), *Ahan* (day), *Sandhya* (evening twilight) and *Jyotsna* (dawn). Through Dhyana Yoga, the supreme absorption of thought into its inmost self, Brahmā proceeds to construct the manifold orders of beings ranging from the highest *asuras* to the varied denizens of the differentiated worlds — Gods, Pitris and mankind. These four orders of beings are essentially correlated with the seven Hierarchies, each of which has its own creative role and distinct modality in the invisible and visible worlds, and all of which are integrally present in the sevenfold constitution of man.

The oldest Aryan philosophy associates the three highest

arupa groups with the Agnishwatha, the Solar Pitris or divine ancestors of humanity, and assigns their potency to the purely formless and invisible Fire of the Central Spiritual Sun. This primordial Fire, one and threefold, is metaphysically prior to the septenary fire of the manifested universe, just as pre-cosmic Fohat is but a potential creative power in the unmanifested universe, preceding the differentiation of the triple One into the many and the awakening of the active seven creative forces of Nature. Similarly, Kamadeva is the first conscious and all-embracing desire for universal good, as well as the primordial feeling of infinite tender compassion, love and mercy that arose in the consciousness of the creative One Force when it came into life and being as a Ray from the Absolute. According to the Vedic Sages, it is the sacred bond between entity and non-entity, pellucid *Manas* and pure *Atma-Buddhi*, before it is transformed into the magnetic attraction between forms. Thus the creative powers of the Agnishwatha *arupa* Hosts are already implicit in *Daiviprakriti*, the Light of the unmanifest Logos, itself the product of the purely noumenal impress of Divine Thought upon pre-cosmic Root Substance.

The Sons of Fire and Wisdom are the hidden root of spiritual humanity and endow Man with the sovereign afflatus of *Atma-Buddhi-Manas*. They originate every Fohatic potency in the human principles, each of which seems to act as a living force summoned by will and desire, through which the relatively subjective continuously affects the relatively objective. Gupta Vidya teaches that these Fire-devas, engendered through the body of *Ratri* or Night, and known variously as Agni-Rudras, Kumaras, Gandharvas and Adityas, are at once the entire host of perfected Rishis, Munis and Nirmanakayas from previous *manvantaras*, as well as the personified sacred fires of the most occult powers of Nature. They are Agni, the first son of Brahmā, his three descendants and their forty-five sons by Aditi-Daksha's daughters, forty-nine fires in all. As the Kumara-Makaras they are linked to Kamadeva, *Aja* and *Atma-bhu*, unborn and self-existent, and one with Agni. As virgin ascetics they direct the six *shaktis* of *Mahamaya*, synthesized by the seventh, *Daiviprakriti,* in the work of cyclic evolution, and endow nascent humanity with *Manas,* which is capable of reflecting the forty-nine fires through *Kriyashakti.* Through this magical power of concentrated imagination and will, capable of producing perceptible results out of the inherent energy of ideas, the Kumaras created, during the Third Root Race, the Sons of Will and Yoga. Creating first the Seed of Divine Knowledge and then the Host of ancestors of all the Arhats and Mahatmas of the succeeding Races, the self-conscious Monads of the Nirmanakayas of past *manvantaras* entered the sheaths they themselves had formed by *Kriyashakti.*

Although reduced to a distant echo and dim reflection by the corruptions of anthropomorphic religion, a classic example of *Kriyashakti* in exoteric scripture is the *Fiat Lux* of *Genesis* in the Old Testament. In the East there is a beautiful tradition, whereby as soon as anyone puts on a light in the evening, all inwardly salute that light and the privilege of being able to perceive and to use it. Even though many levels of reflection removed from the pristine Light of the Logos, which defies every effort to capture it in any equation, visible light inevitably inspires gratitude in human beings in need. No wonder great universities adopted as their motto mantramic affirmations like 'May we be illuminated', echoing the ancient invocation of the *Katha Upanishad.* Any person privileged to enter the sacred soil of any place wherein lies the possibility of preparing for some level of illumination in the sciences and arts is thrice-blessed, for all of these may be traced to the original instruction of infant humanity by its Divine Teachers. Nevertheless, what is true of horses is even more true of men and women: you may take them to water but you can neither make them drink nor can you drink for them. To drink of the waters of wisdom requires even more willingness, cheerfulness and concentrated self-training than that evidently required to learn a musical instrument, to learn to paint or sculpt, or to learn to fashion out of the resources of nature foods and artifacts for the nourishment and benefit of others. All arts involve the essential ingredients of concentration and imagination, combined with care and precision to enable one person to do something worthwhile for others. They all intimate a central logic to creativity, whether in literature, thought or human relationships and communication. When this numinous ordering is absent or obscured, there is a wasteful production of deformed shadows which only serve to separate and estrange human beings from each other through misunderstanding, instead of assisting the communion of minds, the understanding of hearts and the cooperation of wills in the realm of constructive action.

The divine gift of *Kriyashakti* is potentially present in the will of every human being, but it lies latent and even, alas, atrophied owing to the neglect, misuse and abuse of creative faculties in past lives, all of which prevent the tapping of its energy and power. Nor can this condition be abruptly changed. Just as it would be irresponsible in the extreme to allow a child or a fool to play with explosives or to come near high voltage equipment, it would be indefensible to give an unready human being easy access to spiritual wisdom and divine theurgy. The sad consequence could only be moral and mental harm to oneself and others, damage to future incarnations or, at worst, the tragedy of soul-destruction. Yet, in the realm of spiritual knowledge there is a natural protection rather like that in the complex code languages of modern science where, as Einstein knew, fewer people than can be counted on one's fingers will truly understand the fundamental equations of the most advanced theories. If this is fortunate in such areas as nuclear physics, laser technology and genetics, how much more so in regard to spiritual knowledge. Even so, there is a wealth of teaching in the *Stanzas of Dzyan* concerning the hidden logic of birth and growth, especially in the accounts of the development of the seven Races, which is relevant to understanding the complex mystery of creativity locked in the principles of man. The vastitude of suggestions, clues, hints and bare intimations will suggest to the slightest spark of the intuition that these overlapping and shifting frameworks can guide the aroused imagination towards the archetypal logic of Nature which reflects the primordial germ of thought in the Divine Mind. Initially, creativity seems to the enquirer to be a temporal sequence of successive stages and distinct interactions between beings only because the enquirer's state of awareness is almost wholly conditioned by differentiation in space and time.

It is helpful to recognize three archetypal phases in abstract creativity. The first is represented as a changeless potentiality in bare space, the *avikara* condition of immutable Nature, or *sadaikarupa*. The second phase is represented as the awakening out of the first, through an initial imperceptible differentiation, of a state of potential causality, the *avayakta* stage. The third phase involves the interconnection of cause, or *karana*, with discrete effects — *vyakta*. This must not be understood in terms of typical sense-bound notions of visible causes and separate results since it has to do with the origination of the visible within the invisible. Yet it is that invisible, indiscrete and eternal potentiality which, in a sense, becomes its own discrete effect, the purely spiritual atom becoming the One and the many and producing thereby the manifested worlds, including the globes of our earth. Like Solomon's temple, the temple of truth is built by invisible hands; from the visible effects alone nothing significant can be inferred in reference to true creativity. Those who either do not use their eyes sufficiently to see the sky, or merely employ visual images as the sole basis for inferences about results, will involuntarily incarnate again and again, trapped in the *maya* of visible phenomena.

Progress in human thought and the advent of true creativity in human affairs require the powers of philosophic abstraction, prolonged concentration and noetic meditation. It is essential to enter the invisible realm of germinating seed ideas and, like the good gardener, to learn to work with and through Nature. Disinterested in visible results, which are but the flowers of yesterday, one must learn to wait patiently for the cyclic harvest, sustaining a lightness of heart, an ardent love for the soil and a joyous gratitude for the generosity of Nature. The good gardener is the paradigm of the wise man or woman confirmed in a perception of invisible reality, in which there is always both a boundless potential and the germinating seeds. Beginning on the noumenal plane, the series of causes has its representation on the invisible plane of abstract mathematical form, and also in the secret core of the orderly if gradual progression in the realm of the visible. This hidden logic of creativity, birth and growth from invisible seeds is mirrored in the wisdom of natural forms, such as in the ever-increasing concentric rings of trees. Anyone who has contemplated the rings of an ancient pine or mighty oak, and seen how the steady growth of Nature follows her own seasons without reference to the vagaries of human emotion, can begin to appreciate how the smallest of the small, the *aniyamsam aniyasam*, becomes the One and the many, *ekanekarupa*. There is an immediate connection between the *Atman* in and beyond all, and the most minute of the myriads of invisible atoms within every single living form.

The highest sees through the eyes of the lowest. Hence the Kriyashaktic power of creative imagination lies waiting to be aroused in every Manasic being, but this requires the uttermost refinement of faith, will and desire through *Buddhi Yoga*. In conveying the process whereby Brahmā constructs his four bodies by concentrating his mind into itself, and then 'thinks of himself' as the progenitor of the world, H.P. Blavatsky refers to this as *Kriyashakti*.

> This *thinking of oneself* as this, that, or the other, is the chief factor in the production of every kind of psychic or even physical phenomena. The words 'whosoever shall say to this mountain be thou removed and cast into the sea, and *shall not doubt* . . . that thing will come to pass,' are no vain words. Only the word 'faith' ought to be translated by WILL. Faith without Will is like a wind-mill without *wind* — barren of results.
>
> *The Secret Doctrine,* ii 59

True faith and spiritual will have nothing to do with blind acceptance or petty wilfulness bound by likes and dislikes. They point instead to mental control, concentrated determination and unbounded effortless confidence which can be brought together in a mystic marriage or fusion of the higher faculties. One must gain an intuitive understanding of why Kamadeva-Agni, the primordial fiery spirit of compassion, allegorically the son of Dharma (sacred moral duty and justice) and Shraddha (faith), carries the sign of Makara on his banner. Apart from the sublime motive of universal compassion, the faculties of the Higher Triad in man cannot awaken to self-conscious creativity. But once the current is touched, then, out of noetic love for universal good, out of deep feeling and intense thought upon a firm basis that is impersonal, controlled and calm, one can release a current of ideation that can heal and help, bless and guide, any human being receptive and responsive to the power of that current.

Once this point is reached, one is prepared to pursue the exacting theoretical and practical discipline of occult science. The classifications of the principles of Man and Nature into septenary sets take on a living immediacy beyond any merely intellectual notions regarding rainbows, musical scales, days of the week, or any of the other septenates known to the casual observer. As the factor number of the *manvantaras*, 7 is critical to the whole of manifestation and to all human progress. Divided into the 3 and the 4, it is representative of both the Hierarchies and the various Pitris from which the human principles are derived through the Logos or Word. Proceeding from the Circle of Divine Thought to its Diameter, the Word containing π and the inmost logic of the Hierarchies in its ineffable nature, indiscrete fire becomes liquid fire, giving rise to the myriad centres of life — the union of Thought and the Word. As 7 is the number of Union, 3 is that of Light and 4 that of Life. In the human principles the higher three are born from the fiery Agnishwatha Pitris, the Asuras born from *Ratri*, the body of Night of Brahmā. The fourfold human body of illusion is formed by the inferior hosts of Barhishad Pitris, born from *Sandhya*, the body of Twilight of Brahmā. Until the Fire-devas incarnate into the prepared forms of the mindless Third Root Race, the Atma-Buddhic Monads of incipient humanity cannot attain self-consciousness. As the *Stanzas* explain:

'It is from the material Worlds that descend they, who fashion physical man at the new Manvantaras. They are inferior Lha (Spirits), possessed of a dual body (an astral within an ethereal form). *They are the fashioners and creators of our body of illusion.'* . . .

'Into the forms projected by the Lha (Pitris) *the two letters* (the Monad, called also "the Double Dragon") *descend from the spheres of expectation. But they are like a roof with no walls, nor pillars to rest upon.'* . . .

'Man needs four flames and three fires to become one on Earth, and he requires the essence of the forty-nine fires to be perfect. It is those who have deserted the Superior Spheres, the Gods of Will, who complete the Manu of illusion. For the "Double Dragon" has no hold upon the mere form. It is like the breeze where there is no tree or branch to receive and harbour it. It cannot affect the form where there is no agent of transmission (Manas, 'Mind') *and the form knows it not.'*

'In the highest worlds, the three are one, on Earth (at first) the one becomes two. They are like the two (side) lines of a triangle that has lost its bottom line — which is the third fire.'

Ibid., ii 57

Human perfection requires the self-conscious mastery of the forty-nine fires, that is, the full alchemical union of *Manas,* which reflects the forty-nine fires, with *Atma-Buddhi.* Beyond the simple spectrum and septenary scale, with its division between three primary and four secondary colours and tones, there is a far more intricate and intertwined matrix of light and sound. Just so, the full complexity of the fiery hebdomadic Heart of the Dhyan Chohanic body, the Agnishwathas, is mirrored in the human principles, and even in the physical heart with its three higher divisions and four lower cavities. Every effort to gain continuity of consciousness in thought, dispassionate strength of will and deeper compassion in feeling, when pursued over seven days, seven years or seven lives, has a direct bearing upon the inward awakening of the creative fires of the Higher Triad. Similarly, all fragmentation of consciousness, personal wilfulness and selfish motivation is a form of mental and spiritual illness requiring the self-administered medicine of conscience and contemplation. In fact, every therapeutic measure of health, such as temperature, blood pressure, pulse and respiration rate is but a visible analogue of inner conditions, just as the art of physical medicine is the transference to the visible plane, by invisible Adepts, of the therapeutics of spiritual wisdom, for the sake of relieving humanity of some of its mental and physical pain.

The restoration of the spiritual health of humanity requires a renewal of the integrity of the operation of the four flames and three fires. Essentially, every person is an indivisible unitary being. Though it is possible to distinguish thought, will and feeling (or head, hands and heart, at another level) for the sake of understanding, these are not separable in fact, any more than the circulations of blood, plasma and spinal fluid can be severed from each other in the living body without producing a corpse. Similarly, without the highest faculties or fires that are mirrored in the simplest aspects of human life and being, one cannot have an integrated unitary human nature. This is why *The Voice of the Silence* calls those who are not yet awakened to the integrity of creative spiritual consciousness the 'living dead'. Nevertheless, one may make an initial approach to the teaching of the correlation between *Atman, Buddhi* and *Manas,* Spirit, Soul and Mind in man, and the three modes of fire connected with the Hierarchies. According to the veiled parables of the *Puranas*:

> The 'Three Fires', Pavaka, Pavamâna, and Suchi, who had forty-five sons, who, with their three fathers and their Father Agni, constitute the 49 fires. Pavamâna (fire produced by friction) is the parent of the *fire of the Asuras*; Suchi (Solar fire) is the parent of the fire of the gods; and Pavaka (electric fire) is the father of the fire of the *Pitris*. . . . But this is an explanation on the material and the terrestrial plane. The flames are evanescent and only periodical; the fires — eternal in their triple unity. They correspond to the *four* lower, and the *three* higher human principles.
>
> *Ibid.*

Pavamana, the fire produced by friction, involves a differentiation of substance, implying knowledge of complementarity and polarity in reference to the substances involved, as well as persistence. On the physical plane, friction represents that without which engines will not run, but also that because of which they will not run forever. In theogony, friction is produced by Visvakarman using the *pramantha*, or fire drill, and the swastika to produce Agni amidst *maya*. Cosmically, the *Pavamana* fire is correlated with soul, and is the parent of the fire of the Asuras. Metaphysically, it means union between *Buddhi* and *Manas*, the latter merging partially into and becoming part of the Atma-Buddhic monad. Physically, it relates to the creative spark or germ that fructifies and generates the human being. Psychologically, it points to the possibility through meditation of betrothing idea and feeling, consecrating and invoking them together, and using their offspring of thoughts, volitions and feelings in daily life. Through repeated attempts one may refine this union of idea and feeling, deepening it by abstraction, meditation and imagination, until it acquires a mystical depth, breadth and continuity. Mystically, the *Tretagni* is obtained by the attrition of fire-sticks made of Ashwatha wood, whose lengths equal the metre of the *Gayatri*.

Suchi, the solar fire, is 'the drinker of waters'. Cosmically, it corresponds to Spirit, and it is the parent of the fire of the gods. Typically, human beings are only able to touch this solar fire in *sushupti*, which accounts for the serene beauty, purity and defencelessness reflected in the face of someone in deep sleep. It is the source of the ineffable and elusive radiance which mothers and midwives sense at the overwhelming and unique moment of birth of every baby, each of whom sounds the Word in some form. In theogony the Gandharvas are the aggregate powers of the solar fire and constitute its forces, and under their leader, Narada, they teach the secrets of heaven to mortals. Mystically connected with *soma*, and psychically with the *sushumna* solar ray prized by yogis, they are spiritually and physically the noumenal and phenomenal causes of sound. By making one's entire life revolve around one's most noble ideals and aspirations on behalf of all humanity, maintaining the impulse with a continuity that transforms consciousness, one may make the higher aspects of the *Suchi* fire a living reality. Filled with secret joy and happiness, and exempt from the lunar waxing and waning of passion and animal instinct, one can constantly show compassion to others not so privileged as to be at all times eternally young and cheerful. Once it is aroused as a spark in the core of the invisible heart, the *Anahata* or indestructible centre, the solar fire will then burn as the constant steady flame of an entire life, making it into a poem, a song, even a symphony.

The *Pavaka* electric fire is connected with the latent intelligence in every elemental atom. The eternal motion of the *Atman* is mirrored at the level of maximum differentiation in the unerring, instinctual motion and power of life in every single atomic constituent of all forms, organisms, constructs and kingdoms. Cosmically, electric fire correlates with the body, and is the parent of the *Kavyavahana* fire of the Barhishad Pitris. It is called electric fire because it can only work through a positive and negative pole, such as the head and feet of a human being or the north and south poles of the earth. These two centres act as the storehouse, receptacle and liberators of cosmic and terrestrial vital electricity. In the solar-selenic radiance of the *aurora borealis* and *australis*, the Fohatic forces working at the poles display characteristic qualities of *Akasha*, air and fire, that is, sound, touch and light or colour. The mysterious magnetosphere of the earth, with equatorial, ecliptic and tropical circles, contains a mystical key to the primeval revelation of the Vedas to those Rishis who first saw, then heard, the songs of their Fathers. Through the influence of alchemical writers like Boehme, much was learnt during the nineteenth century regarding electricity on the physical plane, but as contemporary theories readily acknowledge, there are many hidden aspects of what is called electricity, the essential nature of which is sensed but largely unknown. The ancients gave great importance to electricity in its relation to self-purification through self-magnetization. This has to do not merely with physical hygiene, but with all modes of pollution and cleanliness affecting the body, brain and heart. Many people instinctively feel a wish to bathe after various kinds of debasing encounters, but one cannot produce a metaphysically and karmically purifying result through physical means alone. Nevertheless, if the abstract is made the basis of the external, through meditation, then spiritual knowledge and devotion can purify one's nature from within without, from above below.

These sacred fires are the priceless inheritance of every human being but this inheritance must be claimed by each individually. The integrity of the universe and the evolutionary logic of creativity, birth and growth must be accepted and examined in each avenue of one's life before they can be discovered within one's higher nature. As the dual progeny of the Solar and Lunar Pitris, man must discover how to incarnate the solar in the lunar, raise Agni in *maya*, thus aiding the forward impulse of Manasic evolution. The lunar realm is not wholly and inherently inimical to man. Indeed, this could not be so except in some absurd Manichean scheme which totally divorces the sun from the moon. The new and full moons, the eclipses regulated by Rahu and Ketu, and the twenty-eight days of the lunar month, associated in one sense with the twenty-eight *nakshatrams* and in another with the twenty-eight stars of Makara, contain keys crucial to making the solar relevant to the lower lunar light. Without penetrating these mysteries to the core, enlightenment understood as the total consummation of wisdom in action remains inaccessible to a human being. In essence, this means disengaging the sense of self from Indu, the psycho-physical moon, and discovering the occult nature of Soma, the spiritual regent of the invisible moon, and the father, by Tara, of Budha — Wisdom.

According to the ancient allegory of the war in heaven, this mystical marriage symbolizes the rejection of anthropomorphic religion in favour of the pursuit of inner wisdom. From the exoteric standpoint, this rebellion implies a fall from divine grace, but esoterically it is the revolt of *Manas* against bondage to the lower, albeit ethereal, creative hosts born from the *rupa* bodies of

Brahmā. The original and metaphysical 'fall', by which the Achyuta become Chyuta, refers to the initial and inevitable differentiation of the universal spiritual light of cosmic ideation. This is the Mahatic light incarnated by the Sons of Wisdom into humanity through the power of *Kriyashakti*. It is this same power, the spirit of Divine Wisdom in man, the Manasic spirit, which taught man the secret of creation on the Kriyashaktic plane and procreation on the earthly plane, which led him on the path towards self-conscious immortality. That this provoked the wrath and envy of those polluted by anthropomorphic self-worship can scarcely be blamed upon the Kumaras and Agnishwathas, the spiritual benefactors of intellectual humanity. Hence the so-called fall of Adam and Eve, the rebellion of spiritual intelligence against the inertia of matter, marks the turning point in the movement from consciousness to self-consciousness and then towards universal self-consciousness. The cloying dogmas of original sin and demonology are nothing but the sorry legacy of self-mutilation, self-murder and perverse ingratitude perpetrated by those who live as if they matter more than universal good. Atlantean sorcerers inverted and misused spiritual knowledge and power, proliferated excuses and sought to shed their karmic debts on others. In the end, however, they will be wholly eclipsed in their own ever-lengthening shadows as they walk away from the sun.

Spiritual growth depends upon the daily, hourly and constant practice of walking towards the sun. No matter how heavy and footsore the pilgrim through self-imposed karmic burdens from the past, it is always possible to take gentle steps towards the light, to thrill at the thought that others are doing the same, and to learn from them and love them as companions on the Path. As understood by philosophers like Kant and sages like Buddha, no one can force another to reverse the tendency towards inertia. Hence Buddha regarded the production of a permanent change in the life of an individual human being as the highest magic. But this magical ignition of *Bodhichitta* involves the consent, cooperation and gratitude, the questioning and intensity, as well as the love, devotion and compassion of that human being in wanting to pass on and transcend the separative sense of self. Without a spark of these spiritual qualities, it is not possible to realize the justice and magnificence of human life. It is central to the entire teaching of Gupta Vidya that whilst metaphysical differentiation through consciousness is indispensable for there even to be self-consciousness, this is fundamentally different from the difficulty for a ray of spirit, when encased in matter, to rebel against inertia. There are many modes of inertia — spiritual inertia which is the refusal to climb, mental inertia which is the refusal to think, moral inertia which is the refusal to take a vow or make a resolve, psychic inertia which is a refusal to be awake and responsive to the rhythms of nature and the extraordinary gifts of human life. None of these can be blamed upon the metaphysical differentiation of consciousness, and the purported second fall itself marks the awakening of that questioning spirit which is the signature of humanity's divine origin and is essential to overcoming all inertia.

The ancients were masters of the art of self-questioning and interrogating Nature. They knew, as does every great scientist or artist, that if one knows how to ask, and how to wait, Nature will never refuse to speak. This is above all true in the realms of philosophic religion and spiritual enlightenment. From the start, the pilgrim who enters a period of probation must see the whole of human existence as a profound process of learning, loving and living. From that initial stance, maintained through a lifetime of suffering and growth, one can come to the greater beatitudes of the mystery of self-enlightenment, whereby one is prepared to enter the antechamber of the temple of spiritual initiation into the primordial and eternal Wisdom of the Mahatmas and the Bodhisattvas, the Teachers and Friends of the human race.

THE CANDLE OF VISION

The latent aspiration to light up the candle of vision derives from that light itself. This constitutes the indestructible hope of humanity. Herein is a redemptive truth amidst painful conditions of obscuration in which shallow conceptions of reality leave so many without the minimum means for psychological survival. The smoke of delusion rises from the fire of craving and fills the surrounding atmosphere, inducing a drowsy heaviness which makes clear thinking impossible. It inhibits cool concentration upon the correct performance of even simple tasks, and prevents people from exchanging honest words of warmth. Beyond this mental darkness shines *Buddhi*, the divine spark in the secret heart, the light of spiritual discernment, the core of the calmest noetic awareness attainable by every human soul. Even in the hour of extreme hopelessness a person may seek authentic glimmerings of devotion to a dateless and deathless reality hidden behind the veils of matter. Such moments of awakening could become the basis of lighting up one's latent higher consciousness that overbroods the shadowy personal self identified with a name and form and a network of illusions.

The hope of self-transformation cannot become self-sustaining without a firm foundation in philosophical principles. Until the mind is raised to that level of concentration and universalization where it can retain impersonal truths as living realities within its storehouse of thoughts, it cannot become a pure mirror of cosmic ideation. Unless the heart is nourished by a never-ceasing love for beings other than one's little self, there is a sterile lack of creativity. The great theosophist and poet, George William Russell ('A.E.'), recognized that unless the imagination is purified by being withdrawn from self-satisfying fantasy, and reaches beyond itself, it will be impossible to light up the pristine ray of true vision. A mature honesty is needed in our appraisal of our self-limiting mentality, our frantic emotions which exaggerate our shadowy self-love and our weaknesses of will which hinder continuity of consciousness. Such self-scrutiny can use the light of higher analysis to burn out those crystallized accretions in the astral vehicle which prevent the candle of vision from becoming a stable source of illumination.

When alight, the candle in the heart is capable of shining with a powerful flame, descended from on high, deathless and indestructible. The Spiritual Sun in every man, the *Atman,* is the eternal witness, unconditioned and free, independent of any thing or being and self-sustaining, streaming forth through the light of *Buddhi.* Every human being is capable of understanding these ideas because each is an immortal soul that has been through a long pilgrimage of over eighteen million years. All men and women are fallen divinities. Each must have a sufficient desire to light up the path, but not for one's own sake. Any who seek the vision for themselves alone will never find it. This is the law of life and nature, and it is equally the law of humanity. People may steal their way through adventitious aids such as herbs or drugs into what they imagine as "magic casements in faery lands forlorn". Poets like Keats spoke meaningfully about the power of divine dreaming, but though this may induce intermittent participation in the supernal realm of imagination — "Many goodly kingdoms have I seen and they stretch both far and wide," — such fortuitous flights cannot light up the candle permanently as a steady flame in the surrounding darkness.

Nature's laws, which are impartial and impersonal, are served by a long lineage of illustrious teachers, the Guruparampara. As a boy of seventeen, A.E. came to sense this, and later spoke of his inmost experience in his remarkable book, *The Candle of Vision.* His authentic account could give hope to all the sad victims of a social system that compounds common weaknesses, portraying like a magnifying mirror the scars that so many would like to forget. A.E. knew that which all true poets and mystics see: the Golden Age is here and now. It is not lost in the past and it is not latent in futurity. If it is not recognized here and now, one will not know what it means. Whoever, throughout the regenerating cycles of the seasons, cannot see nature in her Golden Age, will not become a cheerful servant of those enlightened beings who have perfected the powers of compassion, concentration, and the spiritual will. This force is not directed towards earthly results, but it is precise and infallible in relation to universal and supreme good. Anyone may become a helper, but each must first become a learner from nature. A.E. tried to do this and wrote about his efforts:

> I was aged about sixteen or seventeen years, when I, the slackest and least ideal of boys, with my life already made dark by those desires of body and heart which we so soon learn to taint our youth, became aware of a mysterious life quickening within my life. Looking back I know not of anything in friendship, anything I had read, to call this forth. It was, I thought, self-begotten. I began to be astonished with myself, for, walking along country roads, intense and passionate imaginations of another world, of an interior nature began to over-power me. They were like strangers who suddenly enter a house, who brush aside the doorkeeper, and who will not be denied. Soon I knew they were the rightful owners and heirs of the house of the body, and the doorkeeper was only one who was for a time in charge, who had neglected his duty, and who had pretended to ownership. The boy who existed before was an alien. He hid himself when the pilgrim of eternity took up his abode in the dwelling. Yet, whenever the true owner was absent, the sly creature reappeared and boasted himself as master once more.

A.E. knew that it was difficult, but he did not give up. Men who have silently suffered for the sake of others do not give up, while those who have never known real suffering rarely get started. Whether in ghettos or in so-called smooth places, those who have truly known pain realize that there is no panacea. Others forfeit the fruit of their sufferings by anodynes which prevent any permanent learning of lessons. Those who persist, as A.E. quietly persisted, come to know what the ancient teachers taught: that no man need ever despair if he will only persevere. "I remember incidents rather than moods, vision more than ecstasy. How can I now, passed away from myself and long at other labours, speak of what I felt in those years when thought was turned to the spirit, and no duty had as yet constrained me to equal outward effort?" He then experienced what many people now sense but before which they find themselves bewildered and feel unworthy:

> I came to feel akin to those ancestors of the Aryan in remote spiritual dawns when Earth first extended its consciousness into humanity. In that primal ecstasy and golden age was born that grand spiritual tradition which still remains embodied in Veda and Upanishad, in Persian and Egyptian myth, and which trails glimmering with colour and romance over our own Celtic legends. I had but a faint glow of that which to the ancestors was full light. I could not enter that Radiance they entered yet Earth seemed to me bathed in an aether of Deity. I felt at times as one raised from the dead, made virginal and pure, who renews exquisite intimacies with the divine companions, with Earth, Water, Air and Fire. To breathe was to inhale magical elixirs.

We all know of places where to breathe the beneficent scents of Nature is a sacred privilege. In those who are receptive, they arouse soul memories of another age, when spiritual Teachers were able to walk openly and teach many. These Initiates are always at work but in ways that are only sensed by those who love the whole of humanity and are willing to persist in their secret search. "To touch Earth was to feel the influx of power as with one who had touched the mantle of the Lord." Anyone who plants a tree in a proper spirit knows what this means. Perhaps the best therapy for people in trouble is to become patient gardeners. "Thought, from whatever it set out, for ever led to the heavenly city." Anyone who has a beautiful thought can make it his true friend, taking him further in quest of the heavenly city. Despite falling and stumbling, one can start anew. A.E. knew that all deep feelings are incommunicable. We become awkward when we try to express them. We do not know how to command the appropriate utterance for our deepest feelings. We have no words to express a thousand distinctions clear to the spiritual sense. If I tell of my exaltation to another, who has not felt this himself, it is explicable to that person as the joy in perfect health, and he translates into lower terms what is the speech of the gods to men. It is impossible to convey that which in its inviolate core we must most honour, and to do it proper homage means that we will never treat it as our exclusive possession. The moment we think the vision is only ours, we degrade our life and treat our spiritual discoveries like parcels of real estate which can be owned and fenced. In the spiritual realm there is neither property nor appropriation, and only those who do not appropriate are ready to receive. A.E. learnt from his friend, William Quan Judge, the teaching enshrined in that injunction of the *Ishopanishad* which subsequently became the favourite of another seeker, M.K. Gandhi: "Renounce the whole world and then enjoy it."

We must live as if there is a tremendous sanctity to everything we touch — bathing is a sacrament, eating is sacred, sharing the presence of other human beings is a privilege. These are among the forgotten truths which need to be re-kindled in contemporary society, but through quiet compassion for those who are weak and sick and not through empty talk of soul-force. The innate decencies of ancient cultures can be brought into a vibrant conception of soul-civility in daily life. Individuals become truly cultivated by learning to greet the whole of life with respect and reverence. Those who deeply think about this and want to make radical changes in their lives would be willing to bid a firm farewell to the shallow conventionalities of a decadent culture. It is cruel and wrong to mock human beings caught up in it. It is necessary to feel compassion but at the same time to assume a position of non-cooperation with those who revel in the feverish celebration of all that is false. This requires the cool courage which comes through serene contemplation.

When one calmly reflects upon something beautiful, some vision of the future, noble ideas and images, a plenitude of thoughts arise and one's imagination takes wings. It soars upwards like Shelley's skylark and then descends to that point in space and time where, in the words of Shakespeare, it can give "local habitation and a name" to resonant images. This is a mirroring of the divine activity of the mighty Masters of creative imagination who ceaselessly work with precision, purity and perfect control for the sake of universal good. Many poets and creative artists in moments of inspiration have intimations of their spiritual consciousness. Similarly, all men and women enter every night into a sublime state of dreamless consciousness where even for a few moments they enjoy glimpses of divine wisdom. These then become filtered through the *kama manas* — the desiring and rationalizing mind attached to a false sense of self — so that on waking up there is a vague feeling that something wonderful came to one in sleep. But there is also a painful awareness of its loss. Before going to sleep one should prepare one's mind, body and heart, and, above all, one's own highest longings for union with the immortal and sovereign spirit. With assiduity in devotion and in practice, one can eventually enter at will into the state of pure, universal consciousness. In the beginning, if one would like to test oneself, one may go to sleep with one idea and see if it can be maintained intact throughout sleep so that one wakes up with that idea. In this way, one can attain an increasing measure of continuity of consciousness in daily life.

Those who submit themselves to tests of this calibre know that the journey is arduous but that every effort counts. Again and again, a point is reached upon the path where suddenly stasis and control are lost because one finds waves upon waves of titanic psychic energy flooding in upon the mind. One sees various images that are dark and fearful as well as fascinatingly beautiful images. These have some relative truth but no real spiritual knowledge as they are feeble compensations for the frustrations of living. At the same time, they may be long shadows cast by divine visions which are always self-transcending. A.E. speaks of this when he depicts Dante's vision of Beatrice. One sees an endless variety of seemingly lovely pictures of women or men, and ethereal entities of every kind. But they do not add any meaning to a person's life or bring one any closer to other human beings. If one keeps the chela's daily ledger, one will detect significant patterns over a period of time. Through recognition of these patterns one will gain some clues in relation to one's unconscious fantasies and fears, whether they originated in childhood or in previous lives. One may also discover clues concerning the recent past as well as the present.

The more one reads inspired passages in scripture and poetry, the more one nourishes oneself with noble ideas and images, the more the imagination will be enriched and intensified. In 1964 the National Association of Independent Schools selected R.K. Narayan's *Gods and Heroes* as one of the ten books most effective with school children in America. Many such books have since been published on the myths and legends of ancient cultures. In the education of the future, as well as now for those under-developed minds, unwarmed hearts and famished souls who never had this enrichment in childhood, books could be chosen which evoke ennobling images. Psychologists in France have commented upon the profound feeling for purity among adolescents all over the world. The purer the force of love, the more sacred every expression becomes. Purification of the imagination is most needed in an age of profanation. The only way a person ever learns is, in Gandhi's phrase, by making experiments with truth in daily encounters.

As the imagination is stirred and the candle of vision is initially lighted, the flame reveals inverted images of objects. If we could conduct in consciousness Newton's experiment and put two mirrors one beside the other, the inverted images would re-invert themselves. There are seven planes of consciousness, and human beings in general live mostly below the fourth. Plato taught that there are successive reflections, and every image is a reflection of that which is prior to it. The neo-Platonists stressed that the visible man is an imperfect shadow of his true self. Every time we think, "This is me", we must recognize that what we see is merely a mayavic shadow of that which is behind it. A human being is rather like the Egyptian sphinx. What do the face and the form of the sphinx suggest about the human soul? What does it convey about the long journey and divine descent of the immortal soul of man, through its projected ray, into a series of vehicles and incarnations? At the highest level, a human being is a self-conscious monad within a translucent alabaster vase, suffused with golden light. The monad is imprisoned within grosser sheaths, which result in obscuration, distortion and fragmentation of consciousness.

At the beginning of our quest for clarity of vision, it is very important to determine carefully the subject of meditation. We must choose the finest, noblest ideas that we can find as themes for calm reflection. Those who have made the ascent many times and descend with ease, take off and land with complete control, do not need to discriminate strenuously among objects as they enter readily into states of consciousness that transcend names and forms, objects and beings. When they meditate deeply on the colourless, attributeless light of *Atman,* they are able to see the one light not only in every colour but in every one of the sub-colours. They can see it in all its permutations and combinations, and make precise discriminations in regard to moral qualities, because colouring has to do with the moral propensities of classes of elementals which are modifications of a single homogeneous substance. When a man of meditation gains complete control over that homogeneous substance beyond form, colour and limitation, then he has effortless command over *Kriyashakti,* the creative power of ideation and imagination.

Two metaphors could be of help here, used both by Emerson in his essay on friendship, and by A.E. A true friend is as luminous as the diamond, but also as variegated as an opal. A.E. similarly spoke about the clarity of the diamond and the colouring of the opal when communicating his own experience:

So did I feel one warm summer day lying idly on
the hillside, not then thinking of anything but the sun-
light, and how sweet it was to drowse there, when, suddenly, I felt a fiery heart throb, and knew it was personal
and intimate, and started with every sense dilated and
intent, and turned inwards, and I heard first a music as
of bells going away, away into that wondrous underland
whither, as legend relates, the Danaan gods withdrew;
and then the heart of the hills was opened to me, and
I knew there was no hill for those who were there, and
they were unconscious of the ponderous mountain piled
above the palaces of light, and the winds were sparkling
and diamond clear, yet full of colour as an opal, as they
glittered through the valley, and I knew the Golden Age
was all about me, and it was we who had been blind to
it but that it had never passed away from the world.

THE DESCENT OF MANAS

Lead the life necessary for the acquisition of such knowledge and powers, and Wisdom will come to you naturally. Whenever you are able to attune your consciousness to any of the seven chords of 'Universal Consciousness', those chords that run along the sounding-board of Kosmos, vibrating from one Eternity to another; when you have studied thoroughly 'the music of the Spheres', then only will you become quite free to share your knowledge with those with whom it is safe to do so. Meanwhile be prudent. . . . Do not attempt to unveil the secret of being and non-being to those unable to see the hidden meaning of Apollo's HEPTACHORD — *the lyre of the radiant god, in each of the seven strings of which dwelleth the Spirit, Soul and Astral body of the Kosmos, whose shell only has now fallen into the hands of Modern Science. . . . Let rather the planetary chains and other super- and sub-cosmic mysteries remain a dreamland for those who can neither see, nor yet believe that others can.*

The Secret Doctrine, i 167

T he complex teachings concerning states and planes of consciousness, invisible globes and chains of worlds, and the evolutionary pilgrimage of Monads, may be grasped through meditation upon the fundamental axiom that Law and Deity are one. It is also necessary to notice the septenary principle in terms of which the Logos emanates everything in manifested Nature. It must be seen at the outset that there is an essential difference between the three highest planes — belonging to the Archetypal Kosmos — and the four lower planes of the world of formation. The latter, along with everything that exists as a manifesting entity, comprises the various sevenfold chains of globes. Further, since virtually all human beings primarily function by using five senses appropriate only to the most material of those globes, their terrestrial eyes betray them into a needlessly narrow and restricted view of Nature and what is 'natural'. Seeing illusory forms, sharp contrasts and seeming divergences at the grossest level, the unwary experience an intense feeling of separateness and a false sense of confinement in their vestures and relationships. Given this sad predicament, a mental bridge must be consciously extended from the lower planes to the metaphysical verities which are shrouded in invisible Nature, the heavens above, and even beyond. Outside metaphysics, neither occult philosophy nor spiritual progress are possible. Only when the seed ideas of the Gupta Vidya are vivified through meditation and nourished by *praxis* can they serve as the hidden roots of an expansive consciousness delicately attuned to the deeper purposes of soul-evolution, the music of the spheres and the heartbeat of the human race.

The marriage of meditation and duty gives birth to the Bodhisattva ideal of renunciation through service. This is the sacred and archetypal meaning of *dhyana, dharma* and *karuna,* which are all magically fused in *bodhichitta,* the jewel in the lotus, God in Man as in the cosmos. Originally anchored in the notion of "that which holds", dharma is the self-sustaining factor in Nature through which self-conscious beings in a world of change are able to support themselves in the realm of action by a sublime idea common to a variety of simple tasks, and relevant to humane relationships of every sort. When the power and potency of dharma are invoked through voluntary sacrifices and sacred pledges, through self-chosen obligations and consequent trials, duty becomes a self-validating principle shining by its own light, independent of anything outside it. Those alone who are unequivocally committed to dharma, and who have passed through preliminary initiations, can profit from the secret teachings proffered to them. Each and every sincere aspirant on the path of duty can truly hope to discover the guiding light and sovereign talisman of selfless service. But, as a Master has intimated, if the disciple would perceive even the dim silhouette of one of the 'planets' on the higher planes, he has to first throw off the thin clouds of astral matter that stand between him and the next plane. Krishna in the *Bhagavad Gita* stressed the critical shift from a sense of duty supported by social structures to a self-consecrated conception of dharma, whereby human beings are continually defining themselves and shedding the light of self-conscious thought within the radius of their obligations to others and to themselves.

Virtually all the practical difficulties encountered in the daily performance of duty — such as trivialization, routinization and staleness — may be traced to the force of habit and the hypnosis of automatism on the astral plane. Whenever one is passive, one is far from spiritually awake, and hardly functioning from a universal standpoint in the local habitations of particulars. But, if through joyous meditation one secures an elevated basis for one's emanations into the world, then one's words and actions directed toward other beings reflect a reverence for them as immortal souls. One can also help to enhance the latent self-consciousness in all the life-atoms of the seven kingdoms of Nature. Such capacities are not superogatory gifts in rare human beings at this stage in evolution, but rather basic obligations for all. Since the commencement of the Fourth Round all the lower kingdoms of Nature have vitally depended upon man for their continued development and collective evolution. The summoning of elementals into potent and creative combinations is the theurgic task of human benevolence, noetic deliberation and calm continuity of spiritual purpose. Individuals who come to understand this process will discover an ease and lightness in the pilgrimage of life that seem paradoxical to others who are burdened by a dour sense of duty. Sadly, those who are already weighted down by their own muddled misconceptions often aggravate this burden through compulsive speech, complaining about kindred souls and against life itself.

Occultism begins when one ceases from all complaints, tortuous games and cowardly delay, and instead silently resolves to come to terms with the manifold karma of an incarnation.

Rather than infecting and polluting the elementals of one's astral photosphere by excessive statements of intention, idle speculation and resentment of supposedly external duties, one must embrace the initially painful recognition that duty is inherent to one's status as a human being. Even a week of wise and cool reflection upon the dharma of being human and potentially divine can lighten a lifetime, but those who do not even make this effort will never understand the point. On the contrary, they strangely seem to enjoy wallowing in guilt and self-pity, and thus, as they chew the cud of their ill-digested ideas and stew in the acid juices of their bitterness, they further weaken the fragile connection between the overbrooding Triad and the manifesting quaternary. Whereas, as soon as one takes a firm stand upon what is truly human, and through deep thought and meditation cuts to the core of essential self-respect and inescapable responsibility to the whole of life, one can create a passage in that aspect of *Manas* which is conjoined to the lower principles, through which the light of *Buddhi* can illumine the field of duty. Thus *Kurukshetra* becomes *Dharma-kshetra*.

The criterion of whatever is genuinely Buddhic is that it is effortlessly self-sustaining. *Buddhi*, as a human principle, correlates with exalted planes of consciousness and ethereal globes of the earth chain, which are impermeable to the discontinuities of thought and feeling that inhibit terrestrial cerebration and emotion. The sense of separation and fragmentation engendered on the lowest plane weakens the will and dulls the mind by rendering the electrical connection with the immortal Triad fitful and inconstant. Spiritual will is generated by and works through seminal ideas. The more one allows the mind to soak in the sublimely abstract, until this is more real than anything else, the more one is able in a Promethean way to direct the flow of consciousness through concentrated thought. Such meditative purification strengthens the spiritual will and provides continuous inspiration in the daily performance of duty. When one becomes familiar with its cleansing effects, one will look forward to every encounter with the spiritual, and even in brief spells of leisure one's mind will naturally turn to sacred themes. Those who freely benefit from this mental discipline are truly fortunate in their simplicity of stance. Without taking anything for granted, they cherish the profound privilege of contemplating and reaffirming the fundamental principles of spiritual life. They are thereby protected against the errors of futile speculation, and against complex attempts to reconcile the irreconcilable by adapting the spiritual sciences to material conceptions. By honouring the basic rules and sharpening discernment through practice, they stay within the forward current and gain true self-respect. They recognize that the mere thought of falling away from it, through foisting blame upon the external world, rapidly destroys the sacred foundation of discipleship.

Men and women, in general, may not be able all at once to live purely by the power of thought and ideation. But if even a small number of people make an honest effort to do so, lending beauty and significance to their days in the knowledge that others are doing the same, a strong magnetic field may be generated whereby weaker brethren would be held up, whilst those who build strength would not be brought down by the weakest links in the chain. Everyone could be pulled up together; there would be a proper balancing because different people experience the different cycles of moods at different times. If their minds and hearts are focussed upon the collective effort, if they feel part of and have inserted themselves into a larger whole reflecting the will and the wisdom of Shamballa, the mighty Brotherhood of Bodhisattvas, then they will move in dulcet harmony with the Demiurgic Mind of the cosmos. They will taste the rapture of self-conscious participation in the Divine Motion of noumenal reality, the awesome Dance of Shiva as well as the playful sport of Krishna and the *gopis*.

To a *sadhaka* or seeker who thinks in this archetypal mode, the sole reason for skilfully performing any act in life is to render gentle and gracious service to others, to human beings as well as to life-atoms. There is, for example, no other metaphysically sound reason to clean and care for one's physical body than the duty one owes oneself as a trustee of Nature and a servant of Humanity. If one grasps the idea of Monadic evolution metaphysically, and not merely statistically or speculatively, it will be evident that there are myriad opportunities daily for engaging in sacrificial acts of service to others. It is the exalted privilege of a self-conscious Monad to be able to serve all life-atoms through the concentrated power of compassionate thought. The humanity of the future will readily associate its healing exposure to the mellow light of the early morning sun, or its cool enjoyment of pellucid water, with a vivid awareness of invisible beings that are magically fused in a divine dance. Bringing Buddhic perception to creative acts, they will balance the antipodes of human nature, suffusing the most ordinary and simple tasks with the exhilarating fragrance of veiled serenity.

Once a person becomes adept in this art of service, the whole of life becomes a song of ceaseless and silent sacrifice, the true 'music of the spheres' intimating the mystery of Apollo's lyre. A point is soon reached at which one can scarcely believe that one could waste a single hour brooding over the shadowy self, though one will recognize that this is precisely what one did in life after life of ignorance, even in the presence of the Divine Wisdom and its loving exemplars. Then one will appreciate what the wise have always taught, that anyone who misuses, let alone flouts and betrays, a great opportunity, will not in any future life be able to come into a close relationship with any Spiritual Teacher. Where such laws are involved, nothing happens merely for the first time; whenever the karma of groups of people sharing abnormal tendencies brings them together in order to work them off, these tendencies will be made to look normal. The souls concerned may, when they are brought together, actually convert their condition into a general theory of the world, thus reinforcing and absolutizing their abject ignorance. Then, for those who toil for the restoration of the rhythms that are natural to the human heart, there is what a Master called "uphill work and swimming in *adversus flumen.*" He asked why the West should learn from the East that which can never meet the requirements of the special tastes of aesthetics. He then spoke of the formidable difficulties encountered by them in every attempt made to explain arcane metaphysics to the Western mind. Stressing the intimate connection between occult philosophy and true metaphysics, H.P. Blavatsky conceded:

> It is like trying to explain the aspirations and affections, the love and the hatred, the most private and sacred workings in the soul and mind of the living man, by an anatomical description of the chest and brain of his dead body.
>
> *The Secret Doctrine*, i 169-170

The arcane teachings of the sevenfold nature of the earth and humanity are not offered for the sake of those who would "nail every shadow to the wall". Nor are they intended to be reconciled with the conceptions of a modern science which cannot acknowledge any matter except that which falls under the purview of the corporeal senses. The esoteric teaching regarding septenary chains is intended for those who are dedicated to the sacrificial awakening of spiritual intuition in the service of all, and those who are prepared to make Buddhic application of Divine Wisdom in daily life. For example, it is the enigmatic teaching of *The Secret Doctrine* that the moon which is seen by the physical eye is a corpse, and that this moon, together with all the physical planets, is visible in this way only because it belongs to a particular plane of perception. But if each visible world is part of a chain and there are six invisible globes which are involved in the causal forces associated with each planet, it is important especially to understand the relation between the moon and the earth. This is analogous to the relationship between the astral when it is saturated by *kama* and that aspect of the astral which is ensouled by *prana,* or life-energy. We often notice that a mentally healthy individual is full of life and therefore very cheerful and generous, reaching out to others, due to this natural energy within the astral-physical body, the energy of *prana.* But there is also that aspect of the astral which is affected by lunar forces, by obsessional thoughts, and yet is constantly fluctuating like the visible moon.

What is going on within the human being is causally connected with the relations between the different invisible aspects of the visible planets. The moon, as the ancients knew, is much older than the earth, being but the visible remnant of an entire chain of globes that was the parent of the earth chain. And therefore even though what we see as the visible moon does not look, certainly unlike the sun, to be a parent of the earth, nonetheless what we see is the representative of the corpse, the *kama rupa* of an entire lunar chain of globes, the higher principles of which have long since passed into the earth chain. Beings on earth have astral forms because these vestures are themselves the progeny of the lesser Pitris, the lunar ancestors. As the lunar chain was dying out in its last Round, it sent all its energy and 'principles' into a neutral centre of latent force, a *laya* centre, thereby informing a new nucleus of undifferentiated substance and calling it to active life. The lunar ancestors are also connected with the ancestral germ that was transmitted over an immense period of time and makes even physical conception possible. Metaphysically, everything physical is actually astral, so the process of conception has its roots in aspects of astral form, matter and substance which go back to the lunar Pitris. Therefore there is a direct sense in which terrestrial humans are able to function as sevenfold beings only because of this inheritance, which is a mixed blessing.

Because many human beings have identified with their physical bodies despite the fact that they are self-conscious beings, they have forgotten both their divine inheritance and their myriad debts, even on the physical plane, to those who went before. While some older cultures may have been preoccupied with ancestor worship, modern societies are almost blind to what they owe to the lunar Pitris. If they were true to this inheritance, they would have a greater grasp of the right use of all the senses, because these would all be recognized as vital powers, the reflections of divine potencies upon the astral plane. This would bring a sense of the sacred to the use of sight, hearing, taste, smell and touch. Instead, there is constant abuse of all the sense-perceptions and therefore there is a sense in which people are vampirizing the lunar Pitris, living upon them without acknowledgement, misusing the energies derived from them. This neglect of duty entails a costly vulnerability to the *kama rupa* of the moon which goes through its own cyclical changes, appearing on the physical plane as the waxing and waning of the physical moon in its mutual relations with the sun and earth. Behind this visible process lies a whole set of disintegrating tendencies which were discarded as unusable from an earlier period of evolution, but which exercise a powerful negative effect upon those vulnerable to them through the misuse of their own energies.

Such people are recognizable by their appalling lack of natural gratitude. The idea that all life is an expression of gratitude through service and duty, which is entirely natural to solar beings, seems strange to them because it brings back bad memories of base ingratitude in other lives. Familiar with gratitude merely as a passing emotion, they can hardly resonate to Pliny's teaching that the whole earth is a kind nurse and mother to mankind, and its elements are not at all inimical to mortals. Their moral and spiritual deficiency goes back to the lost continent of Atlantis, wherein they were engrossed in utilizing spiritual knowledge for the sake of self-aggrandisement. As a result, there was enormous damage to the Third Eye, which then closed. Therefore they now experience a technical difficulty in being intuitive, as well as in conserving, consolidating or controlling astral tendencies. Owing to their alienation from their spiritual heritage through the astral damage they have done to themselves, they tend to concoct theories which purport to disprove the possibility or use of any metaphysical intuition at all in the human race. Meanwhile, they remain subject to the affinities they have formed with classes of elementals, shells and elementaries, and hence to the sullen state of depressed consciousness that is their inescapable karma. What they must learn, and what their karma affords them the opportunity to learn, is that they exist solely for the sake of reaching out to something larger than themselves. If through the initially painful recognition of their own awesome responsibility and austere duty they learn this lesson, it will work to the long-term good of the soul. But if they indulge and engage in this perverse and cyclical state of mind, they are only prolonging the karma that goes back to other lives.

Individuals must one day come to see that in a universe of Law all human qualities are connected with cosmic sources and forces. Nothing is accidental. A person cannot be a silent worshipper of the Spiritual Sun and cannot constantly think of it without always being full of optimism and benevolence. On the other hand, one cannot be caught in the meshes of cynicism and pessimism without having connected oneself to the dark side of the moon through *adharma* and the persistent misuse of powers. In Kali Yuga there are many such souls, and though they desperately need help, and do not know how to help themselves, they try to lay down the conditions of life for all. Harming and even destroying each other in their ignorance, they use up human bodies, and in extreme cases through annihilation there is a compassionate release of the immortal Triad altogether from the astral form so that another cycle of incarnations may be initiated by the Triad. The soulless shell that is left behind is dominated by the perverse energies of the tortuous mind, and only dissipates after it goes through a terrible torment. Long before this extreme condition, there are warnings and whispers by the divine Triad, and if these last chances are taken promptly, there can be a gradual restoration. If they are not taken they may be given again, though each time the signals will be fainter. But if they are repeatedly flouted, doom is inevitable.

Seen in this light, much that goes on in human life in the name of rationalizations and ideologies, much that is repeated again and again as a form of inefficient self-hypnosis, amounts to nothing but a pathetic and soul-destroying denial of the meaning and justice of life. If people persist in this despite abundant evidence to the contrary, they are only rendering irreversible their own passage down the lunar path of self-destruction. In the presence of the solar light everything is rapidly intensified. If one receives and becomes a sacrificial user of the life-giving current of the wisdom, at whatever level, this is sane. Every authentic effort counts. It is not so important to take a constant inventory of where one comes out; what is vital is the refusal to give up on the effort and the steadfast will to maintain a strong line of courageous conviction, inserting oneself into a larger and larger perspective. If one does not do this, one will accentuate the opposite tendencies. Such is the nature of light. In the presence of light energy the dark will necessarily be activated, and all the ghouls and vampires, all the nefarious elements connected with doomed sorcerers, will deposit themselves in the astral corpus, the *linga sharira*. Truly, it is for the sake of all souls that such occult teachings as the correspondences of human principles and planetary globes are given out, not for the amusement of dilettantes or the derision of scoffers.

> 'Gratification of curiosity is the end of knowledge for some men,' was said by Bacon, who was as right in postulating this truism, as those who were familiar with it before him were right in hedging off WISDOM from Knowledge, and tracing limits to that which is to be given out at one time.... Remember: —
>
> ... knowledge dwells
> In heads replete with thoughts of other men,
> Wisdom in minds attentive to their own....
>
> Ibid., i 165

The mind that is able to absorb Divine Wisdom is itself an inherently pure substance which can reflect the light of Spirit. But when it is continually used in association with the voracious sense-organs of an astral form chained to a physical body, in order to feed the appetites, the desires, the fancies and the tyrannical will of the boisterous elements that make up the persona, the mind gravitates downwards. This may be called the lunar activity of the mind, whereas when the mind draws upwards to the *Buddhi*, it is solar. When the mind ascends towards the Spiritual Sun, becoming itself a great luminous globe close to the causal realm, this is the mysterious sacrifice of *Manas*. Also, because *Manas* has come down one plane there is acute awareness and imperious intelligence in the fickle world of materiality. Hence there is a solemn responsibility for all thoughts and sensory consciousness in a world of contrast, differentiation and moral choice. Owing to the descent of *Manas* down one plane, all life is ethical, therapeutic and probationary, from the impartial standpoint of the immortal soul.

The test of being truly human is to see everything as involving ethical issues. The moment one starts to see all life as fraught with extremely complex choices which invoke the highest and profoundest morality that is concerned with soul-evolution, linking consciousness with motive and the welfare of every single soul in its pilgrimage, one discovers an exalted concept of ethical sensitivity, far superior to the ersatz notions of right and wrong in conventional morals. At best, these dicta embody worldly wisdom based on the past, and are only able to support social expediency and, occasionally, certain good habits. True morality involves the direction, either upward or downward, that is given to every single life-atom. Its enormous scope encompasses the vast sweep of the Root Races of humanity, which "commence with the Ethereal and end with the spiritual on the double line of physical and moral evolution — from the beginning of the terrestrial round to its close." The moral task of the immortal soul summons it in a great sacrifice, for it takes the daunting risk of descent into a restricting vesture of clay. Its awareness is lent in the direction of differentiation and disunity, the direction of potential death through discord, doubt and despair. This materialization of the spiritual energies belonging to mind takes place macrocosmically and microcosmically, involving both the principles of sevenfold man and the globes of the planetary chain. ". . . It is a case of descent into matter, the adjustment — in both the mystic and physical senses — of the two, and their interblending for the great coming 'struggle of life' that awaits both *entities*."

Dynamically, only the *Atman* and *Buddhi* are of the spiritual plane because they have an eternally self-sustaining light-energy. The *Atman* is in perpetual motion and *Buddhi* is the diffused but indestructible light of the *Atman*. *Atman* and *Buddhi* do not typically incarnate in human beings. If they did, human beings would be gods. But before human beings can become gods, they must become heroes. For them to become heroes they must enter the thought-sphere of *Manas* and elevate it towards higher altitudes. This is what Buddha meant by dictating terms to the mind, made captive through craving to the world-illusion. In this paradigmatically human arena most testing takes place on a plane that is invisible to the persona. As a result, people without a sense of morality rooted in *Manas* suppose that they are not being tested, or that they can get away with mental dishonesty and sanctimonious hypocrisy. But if, as in Edward Bellamy's strange story, all human beings were endowed with telepathy, there would be a quick ending to furtiveness and religiosity since all particularized thoughts would be instantly known to all. No doubt there would be deeper secrets locked up in *Atma-Buddhi* — but there would be a much purer mode of communication because a great deal of the humbug masquerading behind the mask of self-righteousness would be transparent. There would be no room for deceptive façades and moral evasion. This is only a pale anticipation of the state of consciousness of civilizations yet far in the future, in the Fifth and the Sixth Rounds, when the state of consciousness would be so exalted, that beings enigmatically referred to as Sixth Rounders like Buddha or Shankara, or Fifth Rounders like Plato and Confucius, would represent the average of those future humanities. The entry of such beings into the Fourth Round, like raindrops that presage the monsoon, must remain mysterious. Such beings speak in terms of experience concerning invisible realities, using language to intimate and evoke latent perceptions in human beings who, even in the Fourth Round, have not taken full advantage of the Fifth Race, which is archetypally characterized by pure thought.

Rationality and reason, in the best sense, constantly look for universality and effortlessly practise the Golden Rule, never expecting of another what one dare not expect of oneself, always putting oneself to the test and eschewing all negative judgements of others. By these criteria, many human beings have fallen below the potential of the fifth sub-race of the Fifth Root Race of the Fourth Round, and behind even the powers of thought of its first sub-race. This abnormally retarded condition is quite independent of Kali Yuga, and goes back to the fourth sub-race as well as to the Fourth Root Race. It is a strong persistent shadow which again and again obscures a variety of individuals. An individual may make progress in three lives upon the Path and may have the good fortune to be in the presence of Teachers and co-disciples whose consciousness is naturally magnanimous, and who naturally represent the graces of the Golden Age. But the fourth time around this individual could be pursued by the dweller on the threshold, by the conglomeration of all the terrible tendencies which had not been worked out and which go back to an earlier incarnation. When it comes, it has to be faced, and the light of Spirit must be heroically reaffirmed in the midst of the worldly maelstrom.

Manasic or ethical evolution rests on a fundamental distinction between what is self-sustaining, enduring and indestructible in the spiritual realm, and what is changing, evanescent and discontinuous in the material realm. Because of the downward movement of thought from the spiritual plane into the material plane and upward back to the spiritual plane, there is a constant possibility of the crass materializing of the spiritual, the effete etherealizing of the material. When a human being wakes up to the practical and profound alchemical implications of the metaphysical teaching that every moment one has the opportunity either to choose ethereal and refined conceptions or the opposite, then the doctrine of the seven globes comes alive. One can take even the most worldly material events and lend them beauty, significance and meaning from the standpoint of the immortal soul through the power of Manasic consecration. For the noetic mind it is natural even to take the most trivial subject and to give it a deeper meaning, whereas the mind caught in the coils of *kama* can take even sacred themes and constantly concretize them. Those who understand what is really at stake and who begin to reflect upon etherealization versus concretization could then look at their feelings, their thoughts, and particularly their words, to find out how much they are raising consciousness and how often they are lowering it. The tone of voice becomes important; the light in the eyes becomes relevant; one's first thought on waking and one's last thought before speaking become valuable tests. When the spiritual life becomes real in these ways, life itself is transformed, enriched, elevated, even beatified.

H.P. Blavatsky urges, as do the Mahatmas, that people become aware of these tendencies. Again and again the Masters of the East have written with great pain about the difficulty of teaching spiritual wisdom to a materialistic age because of the constant danger of over-categorization, over-definition and concretization, which are real dangers that affect what happens to the Teachings. While some of this is due to materialization of terms, obscuring the meanings behind the veil of words, the real problem is in consciousness, not language. The difference in the end is between Wisdom and knowledge, between the Sun and the planets, between the *Atman* and the other principles. Without the Soul Science, Gupta Vidya, the Secret Wisdom, and Atma Vidya, Spiritual Self-knowledge, all the other facets of occult learning will be useless. They will merely become mechanical activities, mixed up with psychic fantasy. Although they may increase the operation of instinctual behaviour, and be often mistaken for the spiritual, they will have little to do with the spiritual, least of all with fully self-conscious spiritual impulses.

> Without the help of Atma-Vidya, the other three remain no better than *surface* sciences, geometrical magnitudes having length and breadth, but no thickness. They are like the soul, limbs, and mind of a

sleeping man: capable of mechanical motions, of chaotic dreams and even sleep-walking, of producing visible effects, but stimulated by instinctual not intellectual causes, least of all by fully conscious spiritual impulses.

The Secret Doctrine, i 169

The great danger is that if one is caught up in the exoteric form of the esoteric teaching, through lack of meditation, inattention to duty, and insufficient assimilation of the ideal of sacrifice rooted in metaphysical understanding, one will merely activate a lunar astral form and generate the *kama rupa* of a disciple. In other words, everything will become merely the mimetics of mechanical motions. On the other hand, if one is truly in search of the immortal soul, viewing spiritual realities and seminal ideas as one's true invisible companions, then one will be constantly probing into the hidden depths of one's own nature in silence with calmness, serenity, contentment and cheerfulness. One will deepen and strengthen whatever elements of these qualities one can already find within, always putting the onus upon oneself, and never on the side of others or on the side of discontent, psychic noise and petulant complaint. The sovereign responsibility and golden opportunity in the use of this teaching are great because if it is applied in earnest each day, it will infallibly deepen all one's perceptions. Seeing beyond the outer surface of terrestrial life to the inmost depths of every other human soul, one will truly become a friend and a helper of the entire human race.

AS ABOVE, SO BELOW

Thus is repeated on Earth the mystery enacted,
according to the Seers, on the divine plane. The 'Son' of the
immaculate Celestial Virgin (or the undifferentiated cosmic
protyle, Matter in its infinitude) is born again on Earth as
the Son of the terrestrial Eve — our mother Earth, and
becomes Humanity as a total — past, present, and future —
for Jehovah or Jod-he-vau-he is androgyne, or both male and
female. Above, the Son is the whole KOSMOS; *below, he is*
MANKIND.

The Secret Doctrine, i 60

The mystery of immaculate conception is inherently inseparable from the magic of the Tetraktys, which, Pythagoras taught, is too sacred to be spoken of and should rather be the subject of profound meditation over a lifetime. "The triad or triangle becomes Tetraktys, the Sacred Pythagorean number, the perfect Square, and a 6-faced cube on Earth." The Tetraktys is incarnated by the enlightened being, the Initiate, who is more than *Atma-Buddhi-Manas.* If the Initiate were only *Atma-Buddhi-Manas,* he would be on so high a plane of universal consciousness that he would hardly be able to incarnate. The Initiate is *Atma-Buddhi-Manas* plus the visualized essence extracted from all the lower principles and planes so as to serve as a stable focus for the immortal Triad in space and time. The Initiate permanently synthesizes individuation and universalization. The universal principles are brought together through *Buddhi* in an individuated, perfected instrument, which exemplifies the Tetraktys. This exalted condition is founded upon the metaphysical axiom in all spiritual growth that the higher one ascends, the more one's sense of being is essentially a mode of participation in cosmic principles. *Atma-Buddhi-Manas* cannot incarnate in personal consciousness as long as its dominant concerns are almost entirely bound up with pleasure and pain, fame and shame, gain and loss. These evanescent if hectic preoccupations bind together the *skandhas* and colour the composite vestures, producing an illusory panorama which people commonly call life, but which is viewed by the Adept as the night of nescience. The only way one can activate the higher faculties is by a conscious and continuous attunement to universal principles. *Atman* is an unconditionally universal essence, while *Buddhi* is connected with *Mahabuddhi* and *Manas* derives from *Mahat*.

The Mahatma is one whose mind has become "like a becalmed and boundless ocean" — the ocean of cosmic ideation — and whose heart has become the hebdomad, the Dhyan Chohanic heart that pulses at the core of all manifestation. The uninitiated cannot understand this owing to the tenacious sense of separateness that attaches to the personality but which is entirely inapplicable to the Adept. The Adept cannot be sundered from the whole of Nature, but is truly, as in Leonardo's diagram, the man within the man, the enlightened cosmic man that overbroods man as a unit and whose unity is mirrored in that unit. The *Atma-Buddhi-Manas* of the Adept is necessarily inseparable from the *Atma-Buddhi-Manas* of individual human beings. The Adept is verily the spiritual soul of all humanity.

Human beings represent varying degrees of self-consciousness in inverse proportion to their personal attachment to the limited modes of life available in the world of sensation. Like assertive adolescents, they are engrossed in the *Mahamaya*, partly because they wholly identify with name and form and pant with thirst for embodied life and an ever-present fear of pain and deprivation. Yet, while the human condition is characterized by *avidya*, all individuals are fundamentally light-rays from the same luminous source. They are most likely to experience their essential humanity in deep sleep, where even those who are demons by day become like little children.

According to the Upanishadic teachings, all phenomenal distinctions disappear in deep sleep. There is no father and no mother; there is no husband and no wife, no brother and no sister, no enemy and no friend; there is neither young nor old, neither male nor female. The distinctions that people make entirely disappear in *sushupti*. During deep sleep the soul is able to speak its own language, what Erich Fromm called "the forgotten language", which was once known as the language of the gods. This is the language of unconditioned consciousness in which our pristine humanity comes into its own. Human beings are most assured when they are least deluded. The Mahatma is totally free from all delusion and can fathom the secret heart, the pulsing reverberation of the whole of humanity that gives its forward impulse to evolution.

When spiritual knowledge becomes conscious awareness, wisdom through use, Gupta Vidya becomes *Paramarthasatya*. *Paramartha* is the ultimate comprehension of *Satya*, the truth of all things, of *Sat*, pure being, the ideal universe. *Paramarthasatya* is consummate comprehension of the noumenal universe that does not manifest but is the Divine Ground spoken of by mystics, which is latent in *Hiranyagarbha*, the divine bosom, and animated by *Mahat*, divine thought. The mystery of immaculate conception has to do with the paradox that the most fully incarnated being is also the least incarnated. While this is too enigmatic to reduce to discursive logic, it is intuitively clear that the more complete the incarnation, the less is the being involved in incarnation in the sense of attachment to so-called living. The paradox is deeply enshrined in the mystery of the immaculate conception:

> The Primordial Substance had not yet passed out of its precosmic latency into differentiated objectivity, or even become the (to man, so far,) invisible Protyle of Science. But, as the hour strikes and it becomes receptive of the Fohatic impress of the Divine Thought (the Logos, or the male aspect of the Anima Mundi, Alaya) — its heart opens. It differentiates, and the THREE (Father, Mother, Son) are transformed into four. Herein lies the origin of the double mystery of the Trinity and the immaculate Conception.
>
> *The Secret Doctrine*, i 58

At the dawn of manifestation, *Mulaprakriti*, the Germ, which is the Father-Mother potentially and the point in every atom, is latent in cosmic substance. When the Germ is awakened by the descending ray, Divine Thought becomes the inseminating force which activates the sleeping energy within every life-atom. Then the three become the four through the transformation of the primordial Triad in a pure state of Parabrahmic latency into a creative Logos that lights up and makes *Mulaprakriti* radiant. It thereby becomes *Daiviprakriti*, also known as Brahma Vach, Divine Wisdom, the Verbum, the Word, the Light of the Logos. This gives rise to the manifest universe. The same idea is found in Aryasanga's *Precepts for Yoga* in a metaphorical form, indicating that absolute Unity may not be comprehensible to the individual unless that absolute Unity is seen in relation to primordial, indestructible matter and also in relation to eternal duration:

> If thou wouldest believe in the Power which acts within the root of a plant, or imagine the root concealed under the soil, thou hast to think of its stalk or trunk and of its leaves and flowers. Thou canst not imagine that Power independently of these objects. Life can be known only by the Tree of Life.
>
> *Ibid.,* i 58

To visualize the invisible Root, it is easier to think as well of the massive trunk and its many branches. This is a cosmic analogue to something that can be actualized within the human constitution, as suggested by Bhavani Shankar in his Commentary on the *Gita*. It is veiled in the sacred teaching of the lotus, which is "the product of heat (fire) and water (vapour or Ether)". Lotus plants are phanerogamous, containing in their seeds complete representations, as prototypes, of the future plant. The lotus is a representation in the vegetable kingdom of a sacred macrocosmic mystery, which is why the spiritual centres in the human constitution have from the most ancient times been compared to lotuses. Bhavani Shankar speaks of the thousand-petalled lotus in the brain, which is also referred to in the *Bhagavad Gita* and which symbolizes the radiance and the richness of the energy-field that is latent in human beings. The Guru can activate the spiritual seed in the disciple who is ready. This would also have a bearing upon the mystery of the caduceus. When a disciple has reached a moment of ripeness in inward development, it is possible for active *Buddhi,* or what is called in *The Voice of the Silence, Kundalini,* that mysterious energy which flows through two alternating currents intertwined, to become a reality. Thus a creative fusion of consciousness can be attained wherein the Third Eye may open, the eye for which there is no past, present or future, the eye of spiritual vision, of universal wisdom and of inner enlightenment, the eye of Shiva, the eye of Dangma.

In metaphysical language it is possible, when cognizer, cognized and cognition are one, for absolute consciousness to become a pervasive reality in the life of a perfected human being through *Paramarthasatya,* through Divine Wisdom embodied and manifested. Such a man is called a sage, a *muni,* in whom there is such a vast expansion of individual self-consciousness that it has become universal self-consciousness. This is also expressed in terms of the noumenal realm of *Akasha,* which is connected with the subliminal astral light, sometimes called in mythic language the immaculate virgin mother. It is Sarasvati, the Light of the Logos, the goddess of wisdom, Sephira in the Kabbalah, the mother of the Sephiroth. These are different words for the divine sphere of universal consciousness that is the elixir of immortality, which may pour like rain into the receptacle of the clear mind undarkened by personality and raised to the realm of pure receptivity. Shankaracharya differed here from the Dvaita schools, which put strong emphasis upon devotion but in terms of the gap between God and man. Shankara taught that man is one with God, that *Atman* is *Brahman* and that devotion is simply a return to one's true nature. The simulacrum of devotion fostered by orthodox religion, which puts strong emphasis upon one's own insignificance and inability to do anything at all, is fundamentally different from that self-energizing devotion which is like breathing.

Real devotion is a return to one's true nature. All human souls in the Third Root Race were natural exemplars of humanity, and were joyously devoted. In the infancy of the human race immortal souls did not know any way other than devotion and harmony, which is why devotion has often been compared to the child state. Any other mental posture was unnatural to them. To discover one's true nature through *jnana* is also to release that true devotion which may bring back the spiritual knowledge that was one's own in many former lives. True devotion is a fusion between the chela and the Guru, the mind and the heart of the disciple becoming totally attuned to the mind and the heart of the Teacher. So great is the luminous beauty of this state of total attunement that it is a shining paradigm of the immemorial teaching of Divine Wisdom and the sacred process of initiation. Mystics have conveyed this in many ways because it is a state that is understandable at some level by every human being who has the hidden spark which helps to recognize the flame that intimates the fire. As there is a spark of true devotion in each human heart, so there is *Buddhi* in every human being, even though latent and reflected in *kama*. If *Buddhi* is the seed of the Buddha, the lighting up of *Buddhi*, the spark of devotion, in vast multitudes of human beings is the alchemical function of all spiritual Teachers. They come to awaken soul-memories in human beings who have forgotten and fallen from their pristine state, soul-memories of what they essentially are and what they self-consciously could become.

It is a metaphysical axiom of Eastern psychology that something can cease to exist and still be. The analogy is given of hydrogen and oxygen which exist independently as gases, but in water they seem to have disappeared, though they are still there. This is an apt analogy to what happens to the entire universe in *pralaya*, when it goes to sleep, ceases to be. Imagine a state of supreme stillness such as in the depths of the ocean or when it is well past midnight and one is meditating upon the midnight sun. One can also visualize the veiled full moon on the first day of the new moon. Such analogies suggest that one can generate a sense of reality which is not dependent upon Nature's photographs and the astral light, which is sometimes called Nature's infinite negative. Beyond these periodical manifestations there is the living, breathing stillness, the divine darkness, the absolute unconscious consciousness which is within the secret heart of Nature. During *pralaya* the universe seems to have gone to sleep. The archetypal noumenal matrices in thought that lie behind all manifest forms are reabsorbed into the supreme consciousness. If there is to be unbroken continuity between one *manvantara* and another and also through *pralaya*, analogous to self-conscious continuity between one incarnation and another through *devachan*, there must be a sense in which this process is analogous to the rhythmic inhaling and the exhaling of breath.

If it is possible to make a meaningful analogy with the long periods between *manvantaras* and the intervals between incarnations as well as the silences between breaths, there must be some profound secret here which contains the clue to conscious immortality. Human beings get caught in the processes of emanation and involution, which is why they are obscured. Physiologically it is a losing race against clock-time because they are dying faster than they are recharging themselves. This is the result on the physical plane of what takes place in consciousness. On the mental plane they are not absorbing ideas, that is, they are not meditating, not reflecting, and are receiving impressions in such a chaotic rush that the mind is like a worn-out record that is overused. They are making use of only a minute percentage of their potential brain-energy and even less their heart-energy. They will remain spiritual paupers, living far below their capacity, until they restore a natural rhythm in the relation between what they receive and what they give out.

Krishna teaches in the *Gita* that both receiving and giving may be seen as sacrificial. If the idea of sacrifice is linked up to what is inhaled, which is a form of receiving from outside, then it is clear that one is continually benefiting from the sacrifice of Nature. Exhalation is also a mode of sacrifice because every time one breathes one is giving to the world. Much of this is erratic and involuntary since most people's minds are not cooperating with their lungs. The personal mind tends to ruin whatever knowledge it has by possessiveness. That is not true of breathing, which goes on all the time and, while it is sometimes disordered, it also has its recurring rhythms. The breath should become less hurried and short, deeper and more gentle, until it is non-violent and sacrificial. Through carelessness in speech the greatest harm is done to breathing and to eating, but if one is alert and mindful, pausing with quiet gratitude periodically and rhythmically, then one moves away from a polarized activity towards a triune motion. Instead of taking in and throwing out, one takes in, holds, and then gives. As one's rhythms become triune in breathing, this becomes a conscious reflection of Brahmā-Vishnu-Shiva, *Atma-Buddhi-Manas*. If one also keeps in mind the *Atma-Buddhi-Manas* of the life-atoms that one is dealing with, this will deepen continuity and ultimately transform and revolutionize the rhythm of one's life. These simple considerations are supremely practical examples of Buddhic analogy and correspondence between the cosmic and the human.

The authentic teachings of Gupta Vidya are always intended to awaken slumbering intuition. Those who learn to profit from the gift begin to find that there is great Buddhic wisdom concealed therein as the inheritance of future races. By contact with what is Buddhic, one's own *Buddhi* is stirred. By concentrating on retention, which is connected with continuity of consciousness, there can be a strengthening of the *antaskarana* bridge between nous and psyche, the immortal and the mortal, the universal and the particular, the infinite and the finite, the transcendental and the temporal, eternal duration and present time. When the first steps are taken upon the Path, the disciple's heart will quicken to a sense of the joyous mystery of the immaculate incarnation of the light of the Logos in the whole of humanity.

Saith the Great Law: "In order to become the KNOWER of ALL SELF, thou hast first of SELF to be the knower."

To reach the knowledge of that SELF, thou hast to give up Self to Non-Self, Being to Non-Being, and then thou canst repose between the wings of the GREAT BIRD. Aye, sweet is rest between the wings of that which is not born, nor dies, but is the AUM throughout eternal ages.

The Voice of the Silence

CREATIVE EMANATION

Throughout these infinite orbs of mingling light,
Of which yon earth is one, is wide diffused
A spirit of activity and life,
That knows no term, cessation, or decay;
That fades not when the lamp of earthly life,
Extinguished in the dampness of the grave,
Awhile there slumbers, more than when the babe
In the dim newness of its being feels
The impulses of sublunary things,
And all is wonder to unpractised sense:
But, active, steadfast, and eternal, still
Guides the fierce whirlwind, in the tempest roars,
Cheers in the day, breathes in the balmy groves,
Strengthens in health, and poisons in disease;
And in the storm of change, that ceaselessly
Rolls round the eternal universe, and shakes
Its undecaying battlement, presides,
Apportioning with irresistible law
The place each spring of its machine shall fill;
. . . .
No atom of this turbulence fulfils
A vague and unnecessitated task,
Or acts but as it must and ought to act.

PERCY BYSSHE SHELLEY

Beyond conception and imagination, beyond all categories and concepts, feelings and emotions, is THAT (TAT) — attributeless and without limitations. Unbounded by either frontier or horizon, It cannot be modified by anything anterior or external to It. The great teaching of the Upanishads and of Shri Shankaracharya is that every human being is inherently capable of cancelling all conditions of place and time. Each individual can rise to a transcendental awareness unconfined by perspectives and objects of perception. For a human being, a

Manasa, to become self-consciously aware of the whole is to recover a primordial freedom which can neither be bought nor bartered, because it never enters into the external relations of the world, into particular forms and differentiations. A person can regain an indefinable, inalienable originality which springs from the source of all manifestation. Every human being is an original who can never be fully revealed in any finite series of concrete expressions. He can never be understood from the outside, and he is more than what he senses, feels or thinks. He is far more than all the confused and blurred vibrations arising from his brain-mind, ensnared by myriad cords of delusive desire. Every person is essentially and eternally TAT, and to affirm it in consciousness, to give it the silent strength of a potent force for regeneration, is the greatest service anyone could render for the sake of all.

With this sublime teaching, which invokes the primeval and never-ceasing power of self-regeneration in the universe and in oneself, how is one to connect it to life in the world? What is its meaning in terms of existence as a personality, a name and a form, with relationships and obligations, with debts and liabilities? If one ponders such questions, then one must intently reflect upon how entire universes could emerge from TAT. It is not adequate merely to accept the fact that these universes cannot exhaust or have any external relationship to TAT — one must ask how there could arise the staggering array of galactic clusters, galaxies, stars, solar systems, manifold forms of life-energy, light rays, and all the binding chains of causality in recorded and unrecorded history. What significance do these have, if any, in relation to TAT? Is there a cosmic basis for the decision to rearrange one's circumstances, to recreate not only one's life but one's manifesting self, allowing what is dying in oneself to die and what is gestating to be born? Out of dying embers can one kindle the fire of a new self which may find — in the realm of manifestation — meaning in life and relationships, and discover unending modes of expressing the divine within?

To begin this process of questioning, it is helpful to reflect upon an archetypal cosmic triad. Between the vast manifold of a universe of differentiations and TAT, there is the mediation of a triadic force operating ceaselessly in manifestation. One aspect of it is creative, another aspect is preservative, while a third aspect is destructive and simultaneously regenerative. This is the Trimurti of ancient Hindu tradition — Brahmā , Vishnu, Shiva. The term 'Brahmā' derives from the root *brih*, 'to expand'. There is an expansive force that is ever at work in Nature and in history. It manifests in certain individuals more than others because they have a proper relationship to that universal power of expansion. Anything which merely contrasts, limits, and consolidates the claustrophobic condition of self-limitation, is not protected, sustained or supported by the ever-expansive force of the creative Logos in the cosmos, the god in man. Anything in man which is not universifiable or sharable — which cannot be spread or cannot give rise to growth in others — is not of the nature of life-energy, but rather of the nature of *tamas,* inert and stagnant. The prison-house, the clay tenement of personal life, is the shadowy projection of a crippling sense of self, repeatedly involved in ossification and death. Physiologically, every human being is caught in a futile effort to beat the entropic demise of the body. It is dying faster than it can be rejuvenated. This is an extremely significant truth in the region of gross matter, dispelling the pseudo-coherence and false entitative nature of what one thinks is real and with which one identifies.

The Trimurti is continuously at work in Nature and in man. In the ancient tradition of India its divine ground is called *Brahman* — without qualities, inconceivable and beyond all possible characterization. Out of *Brahman* (TAT), there emerges Brahmā, the logoic force which is both spirit and matter and the fountain of creativity. It is the Invisible Sun, the transcendental source of illumination and energy, as well as the power of vivification and growth. It is the generator of electricity and magnetism and their complex transformations, working continually in a universe of constant transmutation. The creative Logos can only be cognized by those faculties which are superior to the physical sensorium, and which are capable of being activated by the powers of mental concentration and deep meditation, of controlled imagination and cool visualization. Through these faculties human beings can gain access within themselves, in the deepest recesses of thought and feeling, to their own abundant share of inexhaustible creativity. A man is as creative as he chooses or wills to be. He is as vital as is his capacity for constructive thought, which depends upon his firmness in setting aside the negative, self-cancelling and mutually contradictory mental currents which pass for thinking but are no more than chaotic cerebration. A man is as original as is his determination to replace what Shelley called "Fancy's thin creation" by seminal mental acts of the imagination carrying within themselves the sovereign power of self-sustenance. Such acts can evoke and emanate a multitude of creative energies flowing as a living, continuous stream of light from one central source of ideation, which is effectively tapped through daily meditations.

This fundamental teaching could be fruitfully applied to the extent that it is understood not only in relation to oneself but also in relation to everything that exists, especially beyond the curtain of sense-perception. One can make come alive in consciousness the invisible processes of growth in Nature and enter into an intimate relationship with what is alive, burgeoning and ceaselessly circulating. In contemporary society, people impoverish themselves through compulsive misuse of the power of speech, ignorant misdirection of the power of thought, and sad dissipation of the power of imagination in futile and sterile fancy. They thus cut off contact with their godlike resources and become like batteries that are largely drained of energy. Too many people sit and complain, hoping for some sudden miracle. One may feel compassion especially for those who know that to be self-destructive is, by definition, to be insensitive to help from outside. The tragedy of weakness of will is evident on all sides.

It is by no means unthinkable that there should be, both in principle and in practice, human beings who have perfected their faculties in relation to their vestures. For them there are no barriers in the realm of thought. They can make things happen which would baffle the boldest minds of the age. They could affect the climate at will, project themselves in many different places, materialize objects, supersede gravitational fields, and perform so-called miracles. Yet they always work under laws of Nature, with full knowledge of causes and consequences. All their doings are diverse forms of tribute to the inexhaustible power of the creative Logos. The grander their gifts, the greater their obeisance to the sacred source of creativity. They know that every human being is a god potentially, capable of viewing the universe as a vast field responsive to the powers of concentrated thought, conserved energy, chastened imagination and purified will. One could affect the whole for good or for ill. One could work with Nature to elevate all beings in accordance with the forward impulse of evolution, which excludes none and includes all in the progressive ascent of self-consciousness, culminating in enlightenment. Or one could work against Nature, and then one's creativity is a nine days' wonder, a pathetic instance of monumental waste, a pyramid of misspent energy, a tragic desecration of the prerogatives of thought and imagination.

While vast creative powers are recognized by many as potentially present, most do not understand why they are not generally accessible. Suppose one pictures a single, superhuman Creator who lawlessly and arbitrarily manufactures a universe. Then one will see the whole of Nature simply as a capricious catalogue of created things which have no innate power of creativity, but are merely inert objects spewed forth from this gigantic being, this sultan in the sky who is conceived as an anthropomorphic God. One would then view every man or woman as a helpless creature for whom the beginning of wisdom is abject fear of that almighty potentate. This is a dismal picture of the world, but it is one that cannot be discarded easily. People may say they do not believe it any more, but it has infiltrated their consciousness. As a result, it is difficult to dislodge, especially when one takes into account previous lives of involvement with gross and degrading conceptions of this kind. Instead of rejoicing in the richness of material Nature, one tends to regard it as insentient. Instead of celebrating the creative energy of the Logos, one grovels before a grotesque image and sorry substitute for the Godhead. Instead of seeing oneself as a creative being responsible for the entire stream of emanations flowing from oneself, one attempts to abdicate responsibility, seeking scapegoats because of feeling that one has lost before having started. As an original sinner, a weak worm who somehow needs to be saved, one is afraid of being damned, and pursues a frantic lifestyle unconsciously based upon a paranoid theology where Big Brother is watching and His name is interchangeably 'Devil' or 'God' — one is never quite sure which. Such human beings become so furtive that they have scarcely any relation to the dignity and stature of the mighty benefactors of mankind.

A radical revision of facile theocentric thought is necessary. If we can conceive of a realm of unmanifest, primordial matter that is ontologically prior to all energic fields, then we could view heat, light, electricity, magnetism, sound, colour and number as interrelated expressions of a single source. In its deepest and subtlest aspect, this primordial substratum of matter is suffused with a vast potential which partly manifests as what we call the universe. Thus there is vastly more energy in the cosmos than the whole of humanity can use. Electricity existed long before men invented ways to harness it, and is in fact coeval with manifestation. Long before men constructed thermodynamic theories, heat energy existed, subject to definite laws. It was also always true that everything that came into existence could not be easily converted into another form of energy with perfect efficiency. Every time something is given out, it cannot be taken back in its original form. Generally, before men were able to formulate theoretically their own approximations of the laws of Nature, the processes of Nature worked in accordance with archetypal principles which had a fundamental logic that was fully understood by Adepts. Their wisdom suggests that each and every person can benefit by calmly reflecting upon his own inherent potential power of creativity and also upon the fact that he has unlimited access to the undifferentiated field of primordial matter.

One can activate in that homogeneous noetic substratum whatever great idea one chooses as the subject of disciplined meditation and release it as an emanation, by the force of an impersonal and unselfish desire, into a universe of manifestation. In regard to all such acts of creative will, unselfish motive is crucial. Without an understanding of metaphysics, the precondition of altruism would appear to be an arbitrary moralistic injunction. This, however, is to be mistaken in one's comprehension of the cosmos. A person who is handling explosive material, regardless of how he acts in other contexts, must be cool and deliberate. If he is nervously thinking of himself while handling it, he is liable to be blown up. Even a selfish manipulator makes allowances for other people when driving on the road. One may say he does it out of necessity. Sometimes he may do it with panache; sometimes he may do it simply to show that he is human. There is no reason why, whatever the smallness in a person, if he has some familiarity with immense forces, he cannot summon a modicum of coolness, calm and self-forgetfulness. A man concentrated on doing a complex repair job has temporarily to forget himself. A person intent on handling potent forces has to have both knowledge and calmness at some level. It is no different in regard to the far more awesome powers of invisible Nature which operate under laws that are extraordinarily difficult to grasp, but which are known and mastered by wise beings who belong to the Brotherhood of Bodhisattvas.

For them there are no miracles: there is only Law. Through self-conscious thought, will and imagination, they fuse wisdom and compassion in focussing universal, selfless desires. Their love streams forth abundantly in every direction to every being alive. They are effortlessly capable of handling the vastitude of creative possibilities of the cosmos. They always work with Nature and never against it because they have gained complete mastery over the creative will as well as the massive burden of cosmic responsibility. As long as there is an inexhaustible creative potential and, simultaneously, entropy supervenes in a law-governed realm of matter, there is need both for the capacity to harness unexplored creativity and the constant recognition that all products of creativity have limits and parameters. However grand, they must end; however great, they cannot last forever. Not only that: they entail consequences for which someone must assume responsibility, because Nature returns to human beings what they have done to and with it. If one stresses that Nature is giving back solely the consequences of other men's actions, this only means that one does not really want to take much responsibility. Masters of Wisdom and Compassion voluntarily assume responsibility without appropriating the free will of any person or atoning for anyone's sins. Taking responsibility for the whole world, they can shoulder it, and in assuming that uncircumscribed responsibility, they define themselves. The more one is responsible for the consequences of acts, the more one can recognize the practical importance of the philosophical distinction between creation and emanation.

To create is to tap the inexhaustible source of creativity, but when that creativity flows in a continuous stream in time and space, it manifests as a series of emanations. Creativity is like the tremendous energy locked within the sun, only a portion of which emanates. It streams forth in rays, and thereby gives life and light to all beings. Those who are gratefully self-conscious about what they receive, benefit more, because they come into closer relationship with thought-fields prior to the physical forms of transmission of light-energy. The physical sun is only an expression of an analogous source that generates light, life, energy and warmth through the immense power of ideation of a host of divine beings who stream forth emanations in unison. What unites them is their constant reverence and silent worship of TAT, which is beyond all, beyond the logoic source of manifestation itself, and beyond all possible worlds of manifestation. They constantly send forth streams of thought-energies which collectively constitute the highest creative potencies in the cosmos.

Any man who spends a lot of time in the heat of the sun

will get sunburnt; he will find he gets a headache; he will learn that he can neither look at the brilliant light directly nor use even a little of it at any time. He will get rapidly fatigued because he does not have an adequate receptivity to solar light and energy. So too, a person may think that he seeks the company of the great Bodhisattvas, but would actually be unable to handle it if he were in their presence. It would be too 'hot' for him. The only way in which he could manage it would be if one of them chose, out of compassion, deliberately to shield most of his light-energy, and out of the tiny portion that he manifests, helped to raise consciousness wherever needed. This voluntary self-restriction of energy is suggested in a Hindu fable about the sun. It is said that no woman could marry the sun-god because she would get burnt up if she came too close. Out of compassion, the Sun withheld most of his energy for the sake of entering into a relationship with the mythic bride who represents Nature. The Logos cannot enter into a direct relationship with Nature except through a portion or reflection of itself. This is analogous to the partial emanation of the light of the sun in a single day.

The doctrine of emanation preserves the continuity of the expressed with the unexpressed, and also the necessary finitude of what is expressed in relation to the infinity of unlimited potentiality. This philosophical idea is profoundly important for those who apply it to themselves. If one is divine in essence, then intrinsically one's energy and potentiality are inexhaustible. But at the same time, one also exists as an ever-changing physical body, where there is constant movement in complex molecular, cellular and organic structures of life-energy, and a continuous interaction with everything else. In that realm one must necessarily lose. One dies faster than one lives. Not to know this is not to grow up. But one can still make good use of one's knowledge of the inexhaustible creative energy within. Having grown up and accepted that existence as a physical body and personality is but a shadowy portion of what one really is, one can appreciate why this minute portion is mortal. Cooperating with the process of dying, one is happy to be dying every moment. Where this is understood, people can join together and aid each other. They may conspire — breathe together — to activate their latent creative wills, somewhat emulating the Brotherhood of Bodhisattvas, who sustain a mighty field of creative force that is benevolent and beneficent, giving appropriate channels of expression to the vast spiritual energies of the cosmos. The work of the Brotherhood of Bodhisattvas is to remind men of what they inwardly know but which they do not realize they have forgotten. To know it truly is to be so aware of it at all times that nothing else counts as knowledge. This is the oldest teaching in regard to creative emanation. After his compassionate enactment of the universal vision, of the incredible beauty in the universe of manifestation, springing from a single source of creativity, Krishna declares:

> But what, O Arjuna, hast thou to do with so much knowledge as this? I established this whole universe with a single portion of myself, and remain separate.

ORDER IN CHAOS

The harmony of Nature consists in symphonious discord.
D.K. Mavalankar

All human beings can transcend qualities and qualifications relative to the standpoints of myriad observers. Each could move closer to an illimitable Reality which is without attributes, without lights and without shadows. The truly reflective individual reaches beyond every self-limitation to a compelling vision of the noumenal source of reality which is inexhaustible in its energic potentiality and its immense possibilities. He daily completes his duties in a manner that reflects, though intermittently and incompletely, a richer conception of the Self and of its manifestation in the world. He is serious about situating himself in relation to the vast world of temporality from the vantage point of that which is beyond time and space. He is willing to live as if there were something more important than could ever be communicated, more profound than could ever be seen, more permanent than could ever be felt. He participates in the ineffable depths of feeling; he touches the realm of the unconditioned in thought, sensing an apprehension of reality and existence beyond all possible expression. Its sole testimony is his own rapt silence in tune with the music of the spheres, the Verbum into which all sounds are ceaselessly resolved. Such a man begins to become attuned to the Great Breath of Nature. He sees the rise and fall of the ocean and hears the whistling of the wind, the torrential sweep of a cyclonic force, the rustling of leaves and the murmuring of forests. The ever-changing expressions in Nature are rhythmic though episodic alternations of a single process, from which he feels detached, but in which he is intimately involved without being wholly enclosed.

The exemplifications of the sacred teaching TAT TVAM ASI are as varied as the modes in which diverse Monads can make it come alive. A person may hear all his life about this teaching, and even repeat every day, "THAT Thou Art", "I am that universal SELF", "I am the Self of all creatures." Nonetheless, the teaching avails him naught. He cannot make that teaching come alive if he cannot think and act in terms of that affirmation, if he cannot correct and control his trains of associative thought. He cannot order his feelings or discriminate and discipline them out of the welter of reactive reflex emotions that well up within him until he asserts his own sovereignty as a thinker in the kingdom of his own sensations. He must retain that teaching precisely when it is most difficult to hold — when there are lesser vibrations, discordant notes, the cacophony of so-called conversation, the chaos and discontinuities of fragmentary consciousness that we call civilization and all meaningless social interaction. Unless, in the midst of this, he retains, preserves and reaffirms the great teaching, it avails him naught. Every person needs more than an initial reflection upon the meaning of his affirmation. He must understand the shifting polarities of existence, must see a connection between these and the shimmering polarities of his own feeling-nature, mental states, moods and responses to the world. He must see why he is buffeted like a storm-driven boat, why he is tossed in a state of flux, why his motion is so disordered and disharmonious. He must ask why his mind never seems to discover a resting place, why his own lunar nature finds no sea of tranquillity. He needs to know why he cannot find within his personal consciousness anything that can clearly mirror his partial awareness of the reality of the injunction: *THAT Thou Art*. This requires *svasamvedana*, the self-analyzing reflection that involves a calm separation of competing elements in his own nature.

The seeker must be willing to order all his tendencies into sets and investigate their connections, and the ways in which they intensify, cancel and nullify each other. If he genuinely strives to gain control over his own shadow — the name and form in which he masquerades and through which he plays out a variety of roles — he must ask in what meaningful sense he can translate his dim awareness that he is more than the sum-total of his changing appearances and clumsy manifestations, such that he could make it credible. He could affect the environment around him, not to convince other shadows or to seek reinforcement from other weak human beings, but rather to look at the sky without fear, and to move under the sun without guilt, to walk amid trees with dignity and climb without confusion. He can move within the world of tumultuous alarms and jungle noises with a confident conviction that there is the possibility within himself and all others of rediscovering, however painfully, the dignity and divinity in man. He must become a man rooted in meditation. To the extent to which he is honest about the confusion in his own nature and in the world as it is reflected in him, he must also be rooted in faith, willing to believe in himself against the empirical evidence. Since other people will not believe in him against the evidence, if he cannot, he is lost. Then increasingly his loneliness will not be sharable; his awkward, pitiable pleas for help will go in vain. He will have to live with the torturing awareness that his personal chaos is of little interest to anyone else. Some may intervene in his life purportedly to help him, though more often, perhaps, to seek such help as they can; others, merely out of habit through compulsive speech, gesturing and posturing in the name of friendship. This phantasmagoria will make no difference to the burgeoning discontent within him in relation to his own disorder, disintegration and disequilibrium. How can a person be a part of the contemporary social scene and not share in the contemporary chaos of surrounding disintegration?

The individual must begin where he is amidst the disorder around him and, recognizing an isomorphic disorder within himself, must courageously ask himself whether this universe has meaning. Is it merely a random, discordant motion of atoms, molecules, cells, planets, galaxies and galactic clusters — an interrupted chaos? To ask the question sincerely is to realize that his knowledge is insufficient to make any such assertion about the universe. Even in times of imminent social disintegration there are voices and visions, prophetic intimations of forgotten truths.

These forgotten truths need no mere verbal affirmation nor resuscitation under the influence of hallucinogenic drugs — they need to be used as the basis of a new conception of life and of man as part of Nature. They must be made the basis of an ordering principle which an individual can consciously introduce into his own life. Not to know this is to be insensitive to the present historical moment. In the contemporary world there has been an enormous mixing of karmas. The over-arching karma is concealed under the mingling of lesser karmas. A thoughtful person might look back at his ancestry and be willing to acknowledge diverse antecedents. He might see it beyond praise and blame, as important independent of judgements. He may even take a certain pride in self-consciously recovering something of its story. Another man might not want to regress in history, but be willing to look forward and discern that in relation to the coming century all societies and individuals are equal in that they all must be agnostic. Adepts and Bodhisattvas, on the other hand, know what the cyclic law will allow, not merely in the coming century, but in millennia from now. The gap is very great between Initiates who can make exact calculations and the greatest men of our age, who are no different from the most ignorant man in their inability to know indubitably anything about the future.

Any person can self-consciously recover his membership in the commonwealth of mankind by taking to himself the best that he can extract and utilize from the great religions, cultures, races, literatures, languages, schools of thought, learning, art and excellence. He may not become another Leonardo da Vinci. Nevertheless, the range of choice is vast. The eclectic nature of the possible combinations for a man is very real. He has a freedom that did not belong to persons in the last century. He can make his own combination of influences from the past, and they can become his own by use. He can become a self-conscious keeper of the archives of mankind in his life. He can become a custodian of the precious jewels of the great religions, a preserver of the meanings of myths and monuments, an enjoyer of the grand banquet of human excellence, and a worthy recipient of the gifts of past and present. The Brotherhood of Bodhisattvas does this constantly. They are the guardians of records of all that is quintessential to the human family over millions of years. They are the preservers of primordial truths. They still re-enact the sublime utterances that we call the *Rig Veda*, that are known in the chants of the great scriptures. And because of their persistent preservation, orphan humanity is not abandoned. They enable those in the forefront of the human race in their capacity for universalization, individuation, sacrifice and heroic commitment to emerge from the multitudes and to become servants in the vast Army of the Voice.

It is possible for any man or woman to enter into that ancient fellowship of those who seek to become the servants of the great preservers of the secret records of antiquity. Krishna taught Arjuna in the fourth chapter of the *Bhagavad Gita* that after the greatest — now forgotten — civilizations of long ago came and went, "the mighty spiritual art" was lost. Though it was lost, collectively speaking, it was never lost to all because these hierophants assiduously preserved it. It has been called the Wisdom-Religion. It is the divine wisdom maintained by those few who embody it, who are its self-conscious custodians, tribeless and raceless, genuinely free men proud to belong to the family of Man. They differ from the exhaustless potentiality of the Divine Mind only as divine thought differs from divine ideation. It is the difference between a library and men who in using the library and in reflecting and ideating upon its books, magically bring them to life. Are there any clues in the Wisdom-Religion of humanity that a person might use as an ordering principle, while remaining aware of the chaos in his own psychic nature? There are, if he follows *The Voice of the Silence*: "Now bend thy head and listen well, O Bodhisattva — Compassion speaks and saith: 'Can there be bliss when all that lives must suffer? Shalt thou be saved and hear the whole world cry?'" If one ardently wishes to understand the heart of the universe, one must initially be willing to put oneself in the position of other people. This is a precondition for all spiritual teaching.

It is only to the learner that Gupta Vidya can speak, only to the man willing to make the initial act of minimal compassion, to see the world as a whole and to feel what all humanity might be feeling. He cannot tell whether his perceptions are wholly accurate. But if he observes, learns and reflects, he will begin to see that there is a connection between the invisible worlds in which innumerable beings live as centres of consciousness, and what he can see in the sweeping screen of Nature itself. Human consciousness — the power of thought, the power of visualization, the power of imagination — though it be repeatedly defeated, repeatedly degraded, is nonetheless indestructible. The faculty of self-conscious awareness in the human being never seems to be exhausted, even by the whole catalogue of abuse of that power.

Although we may see only the frothy misuse of consciousness, the energy that keeps men alive is a collective power, what has been called "the mighty magic of *prakriti*." Behind every expression of life-energy by every human being is a vast ocean of consciousness in motion, affecting and agitating everything that moves, while itself remaining unmoved. Vishnu seated upon a coiled serpent in a boundless ocean resembles the man for whom the universe is simply a minute portion of himself, a lotus emanating from his navel. The one absolute existence and the universal ground of being, consciousness and motion, so far from being exhausted in systems of manifested life and intelligence, is unaffected by them. Yet somewhere, somehow, it is involved in maintaining the order and sustaining the law that governs existence. All universes and all systems are but subsystems of one inconceivably vast cosmos. All of them are an expression of one Law, and there is something archetypally true and primordially present in that Law which, inherent in the very nature of the one reality, only partially participates in the manifested world.

This has been deftly conveyed by poets and philosophers in graphic descriptions of the heavenly orbs, of the awe that they feel in relation to ontological plenitude. They had a certain proper reverence for the process of life itself, beyond the capacity for formulating categories, for crucifying the ineluctable wonder of manifested existence. How, then, can a person in his or her own daily life employ a conception of infinitely diverse beings — going through seemingly endless development, with most stages unknown and invisible, and passing through all of these as part of one single process? How can one conceive of life-energies streaming forth from a single, indivisible source of ever-active consciousness, itself inexhaustible? Not with the finite mind, nor with the help of ordinary language, nor by analogies with our false feelings of separateness, nor with labels attached to names and forms. Yet, there have been those who have made this conception the basis for their own deliberate attempt to erect order out of chaos by reflecting upon something fundamental to it.

That fundamental principle is an x factor in every equation. 'Vishnu' is derived from a Sanskrit root meaning 'to pervade'. If there is a universe, there is an all-pervading presence sustaining it. If there is a power that is both all-pervading and self-sustaining, that gives unity to diversity and continuity to change, it is integrally present in everything and at the same time is involved in a ceaseless reordering in a dynamic universe of ceaseless change. This archetypal principle moves towards dynamic equilibrium and purposive homeostasis. *The Voice of the Silence* teaches: "The wheel of the Good Law moves swiftly on. It grinds by night and day. . . . Its wheel revolves for all, the humble and the proud." It makes no distinctions between men. Man-made distinctions are irrelevant to the great chain of being, this constantly revolving wheel of life. Archetypally, it involves beginnings and origins. It involves growth, decay, sickness and error, and is also a principle of health. It is not, however, a principle of immortality. There are life-giving forces that are as strong as the death-dealing forces of entropy and decay. So one might describe it as an anti-entropic principle without which beings could not exist. And if all beings share one thing in common — that they exist — and if they themselves do not exhaust the potential power of the consciousness which they reflect and modify, then the existence which is shared by all beings is one. Existence, when pondered by the mind, is an illuminative field for consciousness.

A person could reflect consciously upon the lives of other people, upon the lives of animals and of stars. What is that power of self-maintenance that belongs to none exclusively yet is shared by all? It may seem to have a beginning and an end in time and space because every event must have a terminus. And yet the process itself continues, and ceaselessly continues. It defies description, baffles analysis, participates in the wonder and enigma of life. The central informing intelligence continually restores equilibrium whenever it is disturbed. It continually consolidates wherever there are forces of disintegration, thus enabling continuity to take place within all the fragmentary interruptions upon the scene of things. Vishnu is the one great shoreless conscious existence. It is beyond forms, and yet manifests in the entire kaleidoscope of images. And it is, when made the object of meditation, the one great field of consciousness, with the rays, sets, ranks and beings of different grades and different powers manifested in relation to their latent potential power of perception. It is a vast world with a central source of luminous intelligence. In relation to that which is in all beings, one can light up the universe and see its fullness. But one cannot see the fullness of the universe unless one is willing to withdraw excessive valuation from particular things. Unless a person is willing to negate that to which he has attached too much reality, he will never be able to apprehend the whole field of existence. *The enemy of the inexhaustible preserving power of consciousness is disproportion and excess in our horizon of perception* — the tyranny of objects in the false sense of selfhood that we create out of our exaggerations of every kind.

Can human beings, while involved in matters that are overvalued and therefore false, still participate in the masquerade for reasons they cannot formulate, through feelings they cannot express? When a person begins not merely to live but to respond to life, seeing what life means for so many others, despite the illusory nature of all life's formulations, he then begins to see the underlying rhythm amidst all chaotic and disordered expressions.

Beyond the categories that men impose upon manifested life, it keeps the great wheel revolving and the world in motion. When a person wants to understand this in his own life, he has to ask, what, out of his illusions and exaggerations, are the causes sown each hour on the plane of thought and feeling and of word and deed which will necessarily involve him in the balancing process of Nature. In the end, a person has only one choice in terms of the pervasive Vishnu principle in Nature: either he becomes an ally of Vishnu, anticipates the balancing that life is going to do, or he is the involuntary victim of the balancing process. What is true for a man is true for a family, a race, a nation or a world. Otherwise, the inexhaustibility of the potential of deity would have no meaning. Men and women on one particular planet may feel justified in holding permanently to an ethnocentric view of the universe as revolving around their own nation and race, and a view of social life as entirely explicable in terms of an epiphenomenal externalization existing solely for self. The psychology of this perspective ultimately collapses, for it involves an agonizing and self-destructive logic, and yet it is the logic by which many persons live, thereby limiting themselves, if not consciousness. An individual may think that he is favouring the universe by existing; he has no conception of the self with which to handle his legitimate dislike of himself. But worse, he thinks that the self he dislikes is the only self. If he could see that there are significant omissions in his viewpoint of what is too vast to be held in consciousness, but also of what is too minute to have been noticed by him, then he would know that unless he gives himself time to reflect and space to feel what Nature is telling him, he will never be able to hear the Voice of the Silence. The Voice of the Silence would ask him, "Shalt thou be saved and hear the whole world cry?"

The masquerade of maya maintains itself because compassion is at its core. It is a great school of life and there is a strange kind of learning in which consciousness is involved and every individual is a learner. All sense-organs are gateways of learning and observation. Generally, one is smoked out, one's capacity to absorb is inadequate in relation to the stimuli. One is in a state of spiritual and intellectual hypoglycemia. One cannot handle the information that the universe, the world and life daily present to one's consciousness. One must consciously sift so as to introduce order into the chaos of one's self-awareness. One needs a fresh standpoint. One might consider last week's events from the viewpoint of a future historian. One might ask, as Maslow did before his death, how one will appear to one's grandson. One might gauge oneself from the standpoint of an acquaintance of twenty years ago. In the end one will have to assume the firmer standpoint of the unconditioned, uninvolved Self, in relation to which the sense of personal self is an absurd lie. In terms of that, one can then discover life's priorities. And then one can persist in asking the question in relation to different aspects of oneself, bringing them into *chidakasam*, the field of cosmic consciousness. What was previously fascinating becomes irrelevant. What was previously significant becomes monotonous. There is something else which is real, if incommunicable. And, by reflecting again and again upon the essential amidst a mass of inessentials, one begins to rehearse within the universe of one's own being the movement of the great revolving wheel of the Law. In the words of *The Voice of the Silence*, "The worthless husks it drives from out the golden grain, the refuse from the flour."

A man can self-consciously do with his own life what the wheel does with the universe. When Buddha attained enlightenment, he was truly in a position to give a deliberate turn to the great wheel. A man can initiate a forward impulse in history and do it deliberately, because he knows enough about the little wheel of his own personal consciousness, and about the many wheels of the many selves that mesh together in the great wheel of existence. As a man sifts from inessentials an essential core by which he consciously intends to live, he recovers the seed of Buddhahood, an acute sense of kinship with everything that lives and breathes. A person does so when he meditates on existence as a whole and merges his own selfhood into that vaster being. "'Great Sifter' is the name of the 'Heart Doctrine.'" It is a teaching which helps one consciously to sift, just as Nature ceaselessly sifts. "The hand of Karma guides the wheel; the revolutions mark the beatings of the karmic heart." When a person consciously discriminates, he works with Nature without awaiting karma's disciplinary measures. He anticipates the Law and is unafraid. A man can do this in relation to a whole collectivity that we call a nation or a historical period (though those who do so are so rare that Hegel called them world-historical individuals). When a person sifts for himself and for the sake of others, while also observing and learning from the process as a whole, he discovers that the ordering principle of Vishnu is ceaselessly balancing out in Nature. Life will be balanced out. Compassion, the Law of Laws, requires justice in Nature and in time. If a person knows this, he can proportion his perception of life, events and himself in a perspective that can safeguard against discontinuity and dissolution. Even if it protects an illusion, it is an illusion that he sees through — he is neither involved in nor trapped by it.

The more something is illusory, the more it needs to be reinforced from outside and the more that reinforcing will fail in the end. But the more something is real, the more it is self-validating, the more it reinforces itself, the more it revolves like a wheel that once put in motion will keep revolving, though not forever. But when a man, remembering the original affirmation — THAT Thou Art — places his consciousness beyond the whole process of manifestation, then, like a Buddha he places himself beyond the great revolutions of the cosmic wheel. He remains awake during the period of non-manifestation. He has little need to pay tribute to the world of manifested existence. Indifferent to perfection in time, such a man enjoys that kind of consciousness which is neither bliss nor pain, but rather pure awareness, for which we have no adequate concepts or analogies. Such a person, like Vishnu, floats upon the ocean of life. He sees all conditioned existence simply as one small lotus spilling out of one portion of himself while he himself is not caught in the motion of *prakriti*. This, of course, is a very high ideal. In the wisdom of the ancients we encounter the highest ideas of human self-government, difficult to embody, and even more difficult because many today are afraid of the very words 'self-control' and 'discipline'. How could such persons be ready for discipleship?

If there is a discipline that is intrinsic to Nature itself, then a person who reflects that discipline must be natural and disciplined as well. What is unnatural or undisciplined simply represents deviations from the processes of Nature. At the root of Nature is a continuing reordering in diversity of unity, a reordering in a hierarchical form. That hierarchical governance in Nature can accommodate unity, equality and fraternity. It is very difficult to understand in ordinary human terms the symmetry and organization, the interdependence and the harmony of, for example, a forest of redwood trees. In the past these redwood forests were preserved in the great economy of Nature by forest fires. After man stepped in, wanton denuding of the landscape was followed by a desire to preserve the big redwood trees. The wish to preserve disallowed forest fires, and as a consequence, the young trees cannot grow. Something in the economy of the redwood forest has been lost in man's very attempt to preserve it. There is something natural about the emergence of a young tree; if it needs space to express itself, some other vegetation must go. A forest fire is a kind of sacrifice. Therefore, we need a third term to mediate between the words 'natural' and 'discipline' — the word 'sacrifice'. All life is a disciplined form of sacrifice in its purest economy. Human wills imposing upon each other create an inequitable distribution of sacrifices, with the result that a human being must maintain himself precariously between the two horns of a dilemma. Either somebody will discipline him, and so antagonize him. Or he will be very natural and antagonize others. Once a person chooses a discipline, it becomes natural for him to live it out. And only those who really know a discipline can fully appreciate its improvisations and innovations, sustained by a tremendous accumulation of sacrificial devotion to the discipline, so that all effort becomes as natural as breathing. A disciple is a person who says, "I am willing to train myself in a discipline that has an immemorial lineage, in which there are many participants, and in which I am ultimately answerable only to myself. But in relation to that discipline I am willing to take a vow, to make a pledge and to bind myself to a commitment that is irrevocable." Only through an irrevocable commitment can a man or woman begin to walk the Path that leads through a series of painful struggles, deaths and rebirths towards the exalted position of the truly free soul, the soul that is fully awake.

Cosmic order may be a threatening subject for the cowardly, but for the Buddhas collectively it is the basis upon which they maintain a principle of concord and unanimity to guide and to guard existence. This idea has been lost to many because of the deified — and eventually mummified — notion of Buddhahood. Yet there are men so perfect in relation to humanity that they collectively constitute a guardian wall, a kind of academy that through ceaseless contemplation maintains the moral government of the universe. Theirs is an extremely exalted position which a person can only understand after much preparation. When a person deeply meditates upon it, he comes to see that there is within the universe an archetypal conception of an ideal society, a utopian kingdom, the kingdom of God on earth, heaven in time. In every person some soul-awareness survives of the grandeur of the golden conception of King-Initiates, themselves the most disciplined beings imaginable, who are so far from being threatened by differences of rank, grade and degree that they observe them constantly with a delicate deference and a magnificent enjoyment. Sometimes they are known as the fathers of the human race; at other times as its elder brothers. Sometimes they are called the Sons of Wisdom because of their own relationship to *Mahat*, the manifested Logos. That conception is so far removed from our own age that it cannot be readily accommodated in our lives. Yet it may serve as a model upon which individuals can base an architectonic vision of a new social order.

The Marquis de Condorcet in the eighteenth century predicted a time when the sun would shine only for those human beings free from dependence upon everything external to them, those who have wholly acknowledged the sovereignty of divine reason within them. That time will not blossom for all mankind for hundreds of millennia. But that time has surely come for a sufficient number of men and women to enact an *Akashic* model of what the future holds for all. A man becomes a man of ideation when he uses the ideas represented by the Wisdom-Religion, even though he cannot preserve them and use them with the spiritual potency that once innately belonged to him. Every time he uses them, he becomes more alive, more capable of withstanding the buffetings of change. He gains more continuity of consciousness. He moves from the realm of the unreal to the Real, from darkness to Light, from death to Immortality. His is the great compassion shown in sharing some wisdom with those who truly wish to make serious effort toward self-renovation in their lives on the basis of the eternal verities of Brahma Vach.

CEASELESS DISSOLUTION

The world is like a burning house that is forever being destroyed and forever being rebuilt.

GAUTAMA BUDDHA

Ceaseless dissolution is a necessary condition of any world of manifestation, lest it be the only possible world and lest Time be a tyrant determining life arbitrarily and externally. *Nitya pralaya* means constant, continuous change, mostly imperceptible, taking place at the atomic level. Human beings, as ever-changing, anti-entropic beings, can take advantage of the cycles of constant change creatively, but this demands sacrifice. Nature's manifestation of ceaseless movement is, in its deepest sense, wholly invisible and inaudible. An ancient Rishi compared eternal motion — the Great Breath — to an unconscious pulsation in the depths of the ocean. Rivers and streams empty themselves into the ocean, after passing through immense changes in their torrential rush, while turbulent storms brood over its surface. Yet beyond and beneath all this is undemonstrative, undisturbed, ever-continuous change. In relation to what is unmanifest or unconscious at the human level, every rhythm of change is creative. People find autumn beautiful, as the trees shed their leaves, because they resonate to what is hidden, and they can pass through the winter with a sense of what was before and what is to come.

Individuals who yearn to live in harmony with the great patterns and processes of Nature, soon discover that most of life consists of exaggerations. We have been trained to identify ourselves with a name, and to inflate our own importance. We are even tacitly required to pretend somehow that we are immortal on the physical plane — falsity lies at the very core of living as a personality. It is a yardstick of spiritual progress that we have today reached a point where some people think it is insufficient to go through school, get married, have children, and work at jobs. Others, going through similar experiences, may be intensely excited, irradiated, transformed. One person is decaying, while another experiences the thrill of coming to birth. One person is withdrawing and retreating, while another is coming forward with the joy of creativity, releasing what he or she has to give to the world. To honour the integrity of Nature is to make each particular person and thing of name and form unimportant, but at the same time to recover a sense of excitement about the whole process. None of us can readily make the whole world beautiful and exciting. There are so many human beings, so many pulsing hearts, so many struggling souls, so many people in search of knowledge and truth. Yet when we try to formulate and capture what is real, what is precious and meaningful, let alone what is sacred in our lives, we fail. These points of failure can be seen as necessary to growth and change in the ratio and relationship between the unmanifest and the manifest in our lives.

Daytime is the time of manifestation. Even the most selfish human being, when fast asleep, shows an innocence and vulnerability, a return into a realm of pure potential. This makes one think not merely of what was or might have been, but even more, of what might be. It is during the period of non-manifestation that one prepares to make the period of manifestation creative. Creative attempts must have beginnings and ends, and any exaggerations in the middle engender frustration and disillusionment through their falsity. The process is sacrificial, engaged in for its own sake, without knowing how or even if it helps other human beings. We are often most helpful to each other when we least know it; our silences teach more than our speech, and when we speak it is what we do not say that may affect another human being for the good. Even when we show our worst side to another human being, that person, out of the simple need to live with self-respect, may see behind the tragic waste some potential good. This is an act of faith in the invisible.

A person who starts to see life in this manner knows, as the great sages have taught, that beginnings and endings are unknown and only the middle is evident. Such a person attempts to live without grabbing at the answers of life or demanding that everything be instantly explained, for he sees each life as one night at the theatre. The chain of nights is a long pilgrimage with many roles ranging from Puck to Prospero. Do we need a rigid teleology fixed on some arbitrary sense of purpose? The moment we accept one, there is falsity. Purpose must be progressively self-discovered. No one can tell another, "This is the point of living for you." Sages do the opposite. They do not tell the secret a soul has to discover. From the standpoint of wise beings, the vast and ceaseless sacrifice of the whole of evolution for some ever-discovered, ever-created purpose, is never complete. The point of one's life might not be known except at the moment of death, but one can know if one has allowed the whole of one's life to prepare for that moment. For each human being it is true, "Your time has yet to come." There is no sense in trying, on the basis of ill-understood judgements in the past, on the assumption of one's separateness, entitativeness, or supposed physical immortality, to anticipate and capture in advance the moment of awakening that is yet to come. At the same time, one dare not shut the door simply by habit or inertia, by prejudice or obstinacy, by pride or perversity, to some great moment of satori, some shattering peak experience. If all the flowers, trees and leaves of Nature behaved in that way, we would not see the cycles of growth, change, decay and above all the majestic beauty of the silent night, when nothing seems to change and all is absorbed back into the abyss. To understand human lives in the same way, it is necessary to preserve a due reverence for the unseen, unmanifest and undiscovered, as well as for that which is waiting to be known, waiting to be loved — within oneself and resonant to that which is deep and hidden in the heart of another.

Life is no cruel burden imposed upon human beings by some capricious external power, but rather a festival in which there is continual learning and living and loving. But these cannot occur without unlearning, unloving and undoing the excess and illusion of the past. It is a cleansing process of transmission and continuity;

it is, ultimately, a great sacrifice. Instead of sacrificing ignorantly and impulsively, unwittingly and feebly, one can make everything one has to offer count in the larger context of the vast, ceaseless sacrifice. This can be known only in solitude, at dawn or sunset, in meditation or during deep sleep, wherever one draws within the very depths of one's inmost self and feels closer to the core of every being. It is known to Krishna and Buddha and all the Mahatmas of boundless compassion who are such magnificent evergreen examples of sacrifice, with both the great fruit of immense, painfully won experience, the wisdom born of suffering and struggle, and also with the eyes of a child capable of looking with wonder and freshness at every moment. Like the poet, "Look thy last on all things lovely." Look at every moment as if it will never come again. At the same time, do not live by breathless, feverish anticipation. Live at a distance from what men who hug this painted veil call life, and then one will discover that there is a deeper life. There are others who have gone before in that undiscovered country of the unmanifest. There are those who have kept the fires burning through the long night of history, through the cycles of rise and fall of cultures and civilizations, who have stood apart from Atlantis and Athens, from the great pyramids of Egypt and Central America, who have contemplated on the banks of the Ganges and watched over the temples and the pagodas of the East, because they knew that these were part of a larger sacred history which will unfold itself through millennia in the future.

So great is the power of sacrifice when raised to this level of detachment, foresight and withdrawal, that the very thought of it makes everything beautiful. It makes all the small, fumbling attempts at sacrifice by awkward and ignorant human beings retain some echo of meaning, a saving grace, and points to a profounder meaning which when discovered cannot be told. When understood, it can be shared but cannot be spelt out. In learning of this universal sacrifice, it is natural to want to make a decisive change in our lives. We become disgusted with cowardly escapism, fearful of everything but always wanting to preach and dogmatize at others. We wish to start again. This is painful and poignant, but when we have been through it, we can sympathize with others who are also trying to create change within a social context where there is more abortion than creation. Because we remember our past selves and our protracted struggles, we can make our life meaningful to another person trying to do the same. Paradoxically, in highly complex social structures, there is more passivity than anywhere else in the world. This takes the form of endless fantasizing, producing a compensatory life which is partly a dark secret, but also partly the only sense of subjective reality accessible. It involves endless hopings: suddenly a miracle will take place; suddenly everything will change; suddenly one will get a billion dollars; suddenly the most perfect woman or man will come and rescue one from the bottomless pit of self-hatred and usher one into the Garden of Eden; suddenly a perfect ruler will arrive upon the political scene and lead us all into a new age. Yet for all this, endless reinforcement is needed; we do not really believe in our own fantasizing. It is tiring; we feel guilty. So, Nature gently admonishes, "Now, go to sleep."

Shakespeare described sleep as "Nature's second course." What we experience during the day is the first course. This is very suggestive, because our understanding depends upon our readiness. But the second course requires more than mere readiness. It requires forgetfulness. If we cannot do it naturally, Nature will compel us. Nature's second course is for those who are open to assimilation. To say, "I do not know the meaning of life. I do not understand everything which took place. I have tried to study my day; I have also tried to prepare myself for tomorrow. But, beyond a point, I must say, 'Stop!' to the analytical mind, to give myself a chance to be rested, to be nourished within" — this is Nature's second course. If one has rushed through events during the day, to be in an eventless state of dreamless sleep is restful. If one has been too worldly and enmeshed in words during the day, to be in a wordless state of sleep is soothing. If one has been agitated and tense, overactive and energetic, or extremely drowsy, to fall into the rhythms of deep sleep is refreshing. What is Nature's third course? At a superficial level one might think it is like dessert. It is that happiness, sweetness and fulfilment which you somehow expect to complete the picture. One thinks one is entitled to it because one has a constitutional right, but, in fact, it is never what one hoped it might be, and one never knows whether someone else is getting a better serving. One is liable to be mistaken. If one merely tolerates the first course, keeping in mind that there is a second, and inwardly negates one's experience, cutting out the excess while at the same time, out of the chaos of impressions, trying to initiate a gentle, subtle change, then one will begin to make discoveries. One will discover eternity in time. One begins to discover how *nitya pralaya* works in the large and in the small, in the macrocosm and microcosm. One discovers that changes do not come in lumpy categories with labels. The profoundest changes are interstitial, imperceptible and subtle. There is no guarantee that a person involved in a series of events will be the best person to understand their significance. This is why it is difficult to initiate change, why people oscillate between abortive attempts at making real changes, only to repeatedly fall back into passivity while endlessly looking for external reinforcement. One becomes a fatigued machine. If one is extremely assertive and ruthless as well, one runs the risk of becoming soulless.

The paradox is that only when a person can see through the maya of apparent changes to the ever changeless, can he initiate real change. If you suddenly found out from your doctor that you have three days to live, how would you initiate change? It would seem impossible to amend all the things that should have been put right long ago. But out of the very necessity, a person may, in a Kierkegaardian sense, will the good. He may single-mindedly do the one thing he was supposed to do and meant to do all along but which, for a multitude of reasons, he put off. This, of course, is an extreme example. The wise do not wait for the imminence of death to adopt this attitude. The supremely wise have overcome this a long time ago, and do not wait until Monday morning to begin the week, but by Friday evening have thought out their week from Saturday to Friday. They do not wait for next month or next year to think of what should be done then. The wise think now in terms of what should be done in the coming century, within the limits of Karma, the circumference of all options of all human beings. This distance of vision and perspective is the gap separating Mahatmas from ordinary human beings. We allow ourselves to live with the gap every day, and yet we wonder why we are walking backwards, why we cannot hear the music of what is really happening in the contemporary historical moment, why we are left behind by the great initiatives of our time. It is a terrible mistake to write daily one's obituary — and to do it badly. If people want to put themselves into perspective, make their own efforts, and accept their unimportance, they may be of service. The Mahatmas work at all times through all humanity. The question is not, "Can they use me?" but, "Am I open? Am I ready?" The greatest changes have precise timing and come when the ripeness is greatest. Because people in general do not know this, Hegel thought human beings as a rule were victims of illusions. Very few become true individuals, heroic pioneers and makers of the future. But all human beings can put themselves in line, out of the best and truest accessible in their lives, with those who are the great knowers and the great makers of the destinies of humanity.

In a well-ordered society, with sages at the helm, the whole of life and education would be precisely structured in a way that nurtured this possibility for human beings. In the classical Hindu scheme, the first fourteen years of life are filled with so much to enrich, purify and sustain the imagination that before the libido is released, one is ready for it. One knows what to do with the vitality and the *eros*, the creative urge welling within, because one is not suddenly confronted with it, irrationally, impulsively, blindly and awkwardly. Between fourteen and twenty-one one develops the power of reason. Well before twenty-eight one has so sharpened the faculty of discrimination that one does not wait until growing old to be wise. If all of these are done, then in a Platonic sense one might hope that at thirty-five a person could have the synthesizing eye where there is a balancing of all the parts of one's nature, and where all the faculties are there for use in a certain correct relationship with each other. One can make sense of oneself and one's life only by making oneself a zero, making oneself utterly unimportant wherever and whenever needed, in order to be an invisible, initiating helper of others. Well before thirty-five one knows that one cannot do everything.

You can start with small beginnings. Tomorrow you have to see someone for some reason. Right now you could ask yourself, "What is the best that I can bring to that encounter?" You cannot answer this question without also asking, "Now, what is it like to be that other person? What is it like to have lived his life or her life?" Having posed these questions, you could then ask, "How could I best receive what that person has to bring to the occasion?" Finally you might say, "Well, I cannot think about this anymore; I must leave the rest to what happens." If you train yourself to do this, you reach a point where you can assimilate each experience *ante rem,* archetypally, in advance of that experience. This is not to say that you know everything that is going to happen or that everything moves like mechanical clockwork. Only the weaker side of a human being wants guarantees. There will always be the unpredictable, to be handled at the time in the context. In fact, very often we have the opposite experience. When we are told something in advance, we really do not know what we will do. Suddenly we are put in the situation and we have an idea. If we learn to assimilate in advance, our powers of absorption are strengthened. We can retain more, can select more constructively and creatively, and can carry through more effectively throughout the rest of life.

This method is grounded in the nature of the cosmos. If there is entropy, man is not automatically anti-entropic. This is not true even at the level of physical survival and biological evolution. If we are to be anti-entropic, we must get to the very core of the laws that make entropy significant and constructive. *Nitya pralaya* cannot be separated from *nitya sargha*; continuous destruction is inseparable from continuous creation. But because we are spoilt as children and as adults by the tendency to want instant gratification, instant proof, instant everything — thus showing our infinite unimportance — so, too, we are victims caught in a bazaar of clamorous claims and counter-claims utterly irrelevant to true history. In certain arenas this cannot be done, such as war. There is an integrity that men in major theatres of war recognize, because there is no time there for pseudo-analysis or dithering. War is a shadowy reflection of the methods that characterize, at the highest level, cosmic evolution, the methods of the Army of the Voice, of the Brotherhood of Bodhisattvas. They act now in relation to hundreds of millennia from now. Those who think in this incredibly precise manner with so vast and impersonal a perspective know the tides of the times yet stand apart from them. They recognize great moments when they occur. This is the gulf between Divine Wisdom and the ordinary person. It makes a huge difference if one trains oneself to assimilate in advance, but one equally needs to correct oneself. One needs to eschew over-anticipation, because if one is trapped in it, one is not ready to experience, still less to assimilate. If one does not get down to doing with natural simplicity the most elementary things that need to be done, one will never reach to the summits where the Brotherhood of Bodhisattvas stand, ideate and work.

Although there can be no vicarious assimilation, there can be learning. But usually one is more interested in reinforcement and ego validation than in genuine learning. Can one sit before the *Bhagavad Gita* or any sacred text, thinking of Krishna, Buddha or Christ? Can one think of the sun in the morning and see behind and beyond the veil of the visible sun to the invisible sun, the ceaseless source of life, light and energy on all planes? Can one seek the heart of the One Ground which is beginningless and endless? The person who really does this assimilates the very core in a posture that is neither too high nor too low, reducing the muddle and clearing side issues out of the way. Such a person acts with authenticity, truth-value, relevance, and the capacity to connect what is to come with what went before.

This represents a radical mode of thinking and living. It

means living without regret or anticipation, neither in the past nor in the future. It is to live in the present, but because the present is ever elusive, it is to live in eternal duration. One is focussed upon the imminent present which looks towards the imminent future in terms of the boundless past and the endless future. Ultimately, this is to live in terms of that which cannot be categorized in terms of past, present and future. There are periods of richness, periods of withdrawal and periods of purging all that had to be experienced at the differentiated heterogeneous level of fragmented and divided space. They are all drawn back into homogeneous, unbroken, undivided space-time, a realm of consciousness which is the sole creative source, like sleep by night and the solitary watch during the long night of non-manifestation of universes. It is also like the period between incarnations when there is a return by the immortal soul to its divine primordial state. Those who make this state of pure awareness the basis for their daily meditation will see analogies at many levels between these great periods. They will become beings of true self-consciousness.

Where others see obstacles, they see opportunities; where many see scarcity, they see plenitude; where many compete as if in overcrowded space, they see interstices, openings, room for many more. In time this becomes a way of breathing. The Mahatmas are ceaselessly in tune with the Great Breath. They are free from the tyranny of time, not only in regard to what we call day and night, life and death, or the huge expanses of *manvantaras* and *pralayas*, but free from every possible categorization of the process. They have become one with the One without a second, the One that never manifests, which is in every single atom, yet which is beyond all possible forms and is the great source of all beginnings, all endings, and all reachings by human beings for transcendence, all hungerings of the human heart for something authentic, and all attempts by human minds for more fundamental knowledge. This is the source of that forward impulse in the Self towards infinite expansion, towards ineffable transcendence, and also towards spiritual immortality in time and space, through becoming an embodiment of that which has no dissolution of any kind, while the atoms are ceaselessly involved in the permutations of *pralaya*. *Svasamvedana*, Self-knowing, is the sole basis for constant and serene attunement to *Paramarthasatya*, universal and abiding Self-consciousness.

> *All is impermanent in man except the pure bright essence of Alaya. Man is its crystal ray; a beam of light immaculate within, a form of clay material upon the lower surface. That beam is thy life-guide and thy true Self, the Watcher and the silent Thinker, the victim of thy lower Self. Thy Soul cannot be hurt but through thy erring body; control and master both, and thou art safe when crossing to the nearing "Gate of Balance".*
>
> The Voice of the Silence

JIVA AND SELF-GENERATION

THE ONE RAY MULTIPLIES THE SMALLER RAYS. LIFE
PRECEDES FORM, AND LIFE SURVIVES THE LAST ATOM
(of Form, Stula-sarira, external body). THROUGH THE
COUNTLESS RAYS THE LIFE-RAY, THE ONE, LIKE A THREAD
THROUGH MANY BEADS *(pearls).*

The Secret Doctrine, i 222

The archaic *Stanzas of Dzyan* present a symbolic statement of the archetypal process of becoming throughout all planes and in all spheres of manifestation. It is none other than that through which the One becomes the many while remaining the One within the many. At the highest level of abstraction, surpassing both subtle and sensory perceptions, as well as all the conceptions of the materializing mind, the one pure Ray of primordial Light out of the absolute Darkness is said to multiply the smaller rays. This is a symbolic representation of the quintessential logic of differentiation, the logic of divine descent and manvantaric manifestation. There is in this fundamental logic a mirroring of the miraculous nature of birth on every plane. Gestation and growth on every plane is rooted in the universal solidarity of all life. That solidarity is much more than a physical fact or a psychic sentiment. It is a moral and metaphysical framework within which takes place all transformation of form and consciousness.

The symbolic code language of Gupta Vidya contains the fundamental challenge of Divine Wisdom to modern thought. Through elaboration and ramification, modern thought has created a vast conceptual structure of explanation and thus unravelled many secondary processes of causation. Yet, at the same time, modern thought cannot explain so basic a phenomenon as how a foetus emerges and develops from a single minute cell. Despite all the popular clichés about the extension of life through genetic engineering, the fundamental mystery of the embryo remains. Similarly, modern thought has little to say about the metaphysical mystery of the One or the psychological mystery of the Ego. In all three, there is the same challenge. The mystery of the One is a challenge to metaphysics and meditation. In meditating, one gathers within oneself all the many rays, archetypally collected into the primary seven and then merged into one central invisible point. Through repeated effort, one can thus experience something of that state of consciousness which is prior to differentiation. This is an experience of the metaphysical Void, but it is different from the experience of deep sleep because one retains full self-consciousness.

The challenge is to imagine what it would be like in the Divine Darkness, where there is no thing and no forms. Then one must imagine that within the germ of divine thought within the Divine Darkness there may arise one ray of ideational energy which contains the potentiality of the entire cosmos. From that one ray one must imagine an entire ordered array of progressive elaborations and manifestations. This is symbolized in the language of the Kabbalah by the phrase "thrones, powers and principalities". These refer to all the subtle hosts of invisible Nature. In meditation one must reach beyond all of them to the One. Then one will be able to accommodate all these thrones and powers and principalities, the manifold hierarchies involved in multiplication of the one ray, within the folds of hebdomadic and unitary life. Although this is a challenge to metaphysics, it can only be met through deep meditation.

The mystery of the one Ego was intimated by Plato, who said that the human soul was a compound of the *same* and the *other*. This is the mystery of that which is different from, yet consubstantial with, that which it reflects. This mystery poses a profound challenge to one's deepest sense of 'I-am-I' consciousness. At the root, 'I-am-I' consciousness involves a total negation of all time and form, and of all identification with memories, sensations, expectations and anticipations. It can also abstract from all that exists in the realm of appearances and thus experience pure being, which is indivisible and universal. How, then, is 'I-am-I' consciousness different from Deity itself? That is, one might say, the ultimate mystery of the Sphinx, the riddle that has to be unravelled by each human soul, not in sleep or dreams and not after death, but through intense reflection in waking consciousness. This abstraction of meaning from experience must be achieved through introspection, through identification with other hearts and minds and souls, and also through the intimate knowledge of all the life-atoms that ceaselessly circulate between all beings. The soul must acquire a working acquaintance with the pantheistic conception of Deity in Nature. To solve the problem of the Ego in its entirety is the fundamental challenge of meta-psychology.

Both of these problems, the problem of the One in relation to the many and the problem of the same and the other in relation to the 'I-am-I' consciousness, are replicated and reflected within the mystery of the embryo, the foetus and the germinal cell. H.P. Blavatsky posed the challenge to biological thought by asking

> whether it seems *unnatural,* least of all 'supernatural', to any one of us, when we consider that process known as the growth and development of a foetus into a healthy baby weighing several pounds — evolves from what? From the segmentation of an infinitesimally small ovum and a spermatozoon; and afterwards we see that baby develop into a six-foot man!
>
> *Ibid.,* 222

The mysteries of embryology are inseparable from those of cosmology. The philosophy of Gupta Vidya is fundamentally based upon the ultimate analogy in every process of manifestation between the most cosmic and the most atomic, between the divine and the human. Hence, the *Stanzas of Dzyan,* in depicting the origin of the cosmos, contain innumerable references to *Hiranyagarbha* — the cosmic egg. They speak of the primeval gestation within the waters of space, and explain how the entire spectrum of worlds emerges from a point in the germ to yield manifestation as we know it. These cosmological processes are truly difficult to comprehend, for they raise fundamental questions which cannot be answered merely through some pious reference to the heavens or through intellectual imagery. Unfortunately, this is all that pseudo-religious and pseudo-philosophic traditions have done, and they have therefore failed to answer the challenges of universal cosmogenesis and anthropogenesis. If one grasped the integrity of the universal processes that give rise both to Nature and Man, then one would understand that these questions are no easier to answer than parallel questions about the human body and physical birth. Since Deity, Man and Nature are philosophically inseparable, one cannot comprehend the origin of the cosmos, the origin of humanity or the birth of a single baby independently of each other. One needs to regain a sense of wonder that something so infinitesimally small as an initial germinal cell can give rise to a full-grown human being.

H.P. Blavatsky proceeded to develop and sharpen the mysteries which embryology poses by crediting modern thought with an approximate understanding of

> the atomic and physical expansion from the microscopically small into something very large, from the — to the naked eye — unseen, into the visible and objective. Science has provided for all this; and, I dare say, her theories, embryological, biological, and physiological, are correct enough so far as exact observation of the material goes. Nevertheless, the two chief difficulties of the science of embryology — namely, what are the forces at work in the formation of the foetus, and the *cause* of 'hereditary transmission' of likeness, physical, moral or mental —have never been properly answered; nor will they ever be solved till the day when scientists condescend to accept the Occult theories.
>
> *Ibid.*, 222-223

If, in other words, one wishes to give a systematic account of the process of immense expansion that goes on in the development of the foetus, one must have a knowledge of different planes and subplanes of matter, mind and consciousness. One must also develop an account of the interactions of these agencies and forces during the different stages of the development of the foetus, and give a philosophically coherent account of the processes of transmission of likeness, through which active forces promote actual growth. In commenting upon one of the more intuitive developments of nineteenth century biology, H.P. Blavatsky praised Professor Weissmann and his view of the ancestral germ-cell operating on the physical plane. She made a vital distinction between this physical plasm and a spiritual plasm. If one accepts the notion of an ancestral germinal cell which is through its very substance the agent of transmission over an immense period of time, then one must ask at what point man becomes endowed with that cell. Suggesting the metaphysical mystery of *Jiva* or cosmic life-energy, she stated:

> Complete the physical plasm . . . the 'Germinal Cell' of man with all its material potentialities, with the 'spiritual plasm', so to say, or the fluid that contains the five lower principles of the six-principled Dhyan — and you have the secret, if you are spiritual enough to understand it.
>
> *Ibid.*, 224

Such fundamental questions cannot be answered on the basis of inductive methods and within the confining categories of modern thought. No experimental science, however systematic and complicated, can penetrate the ontology of the process of becoming. A poet or mystic, using metaphors, can often come much closer to invoking a sense of the mystery of that process, as, for example, when Rupert Brooke wrote, "Dateless and deathless . . . the intricate impulse works its will." Poetic intuition intimates something intrinsic and inherent to the life process, something that is extremely fertile, extremely complex and intelligent, yet unerringly precise. The vision of mystics and poets touches that which is beginningless and endless in life, that which eludes all categories, formulas and equations.

The substantial and independent nature of the life principle is one of the fundamental tenets of Gupta Vidya. Behind all the myriads upon myriads of phenomena of life in form subsists that which is prior, and also posterior, to all forms. The continuity of this life-essence is expressed in the concept of the *sutratman* or life-thread, the essence of which is like a ray originating or penetrating innumerable embodiments. It is also likened to a drop which is an integral part of a vast indivisible ocean of life-energy or *Jiva*. Universal Life at the macrocosmic level must be understood on its own — independent of function, independent of manifestation and independent of form. This marks a fundamental point of divergence between the methods of modern knowledge and the modes of Divine Wisdom. According to arcane science, life alone can understand life. One must experience through meditation what it is to give birth to an idea, to a current of ideation which can then produce a powerful electrical vibration in the *Akasha*. This process of abstraction in the unseen universe stirs up all that is latent and consubstantial with an authentically universal idea, and which can thereby work over immense periods of time through many minds and in many forms.

To comprehend this brings one closer to the magic of Bodhisattvas and Mahatmas, as well as to the powers of creation, spontaneous generation and gestation that are inherent to Universal Life. Only in this way can one begin to apprehend something of the inexhaustible ocean of life. In order to begin to understand what it means to give birth to an idea, one might meditate upon the architectonic process of evolution from a minute germ into a foetus. To think deeply and profoundly about this would involve thinking about all the stages through which the foetus passes, by analogy with the cosmic process. Then, though one may not immediately approach the mystery of embryology or cosmology, one will begin to experience something of the logic of that process of becoming which the *Stanzas of Dzyan* put in terms of the one Ray multiplying the smaller rays. This is the universal and archetypal mode of the manifestation of life which precedes form and which survives the last atom of form. For the human being, that process must be intuited and experienced within the noetic mind before it can be understood in its reflected forms.

Once one gains some experience of this inward process of life, then one can understand that seemingly familiar reflections of life on the gross physical plane are in fact profoundly mysterious, unfamiliar and wonderful. From an occult standpoint the gestation of the human physical foetus is almost totally misunderstood by contemporary biology. Since, for example, contemporary biology is completely ignorant of the processes of the involution of spirit into matter through successive rounds and globes of the earth chain, its observation that embryogenesis follows the lines of phylogenesis is inaccurate. Gupta Vidya is totally at odds with contemporary evolutionism and particularly with Darwinian and neo-Darwinian ideas. It holds that the human species is much older than all the fauna that have gone through so many transformations on the physical earth plane. Whilst agreeing that there is not a single animal today which exists as it did millions of years ago, it nonetheless holds that the human form is indeed identical to the human form that existed long before all the fauna of the mammalian kingdom came into existence. Further, there is that within the human form which is archetypal in a cosmic and divine sense.

It is, not surprisingly, extremely difficult for contemporary human beings to understand the sanctity of the human form or to recognize the body as a divine temple. They are too engrossed in sense-perceptions and too engaged in the desacralization of the human body, which starts with the abuse of sex even before puberty. Yet the body is in truth the most divine phenomenon in the universe. If humanity knew this during the golden age of the Third Root Race, it certainly lost sight of it a long time ago. Yet the nature and development of the physical human form is inseparable from the inner growth of man. Pointing to the supercilious attitude of contemporary humanity to its own physical embodiment, H.P. Blavatsky remarked:

> If this physical phenomenon astonishes no one, except in so far as it puzzles the Embryologists, why should our intellectual and inner growth, the evolution of the human-spiritual to the Divine-Spiritual, be regarded as, or seem, more impossible than the other?
>
> *Ibid.*, 223-224

If a foetus and eventually a human form can develop from a cell, why cannot human beings develop their subtle spiritual vestures in a similar manner? What is the nature of that spiritual germinal cell which can be energized by meditation and which can unfold to the full glory of human perfection? If one asks how a basis of continuity and transmission of physical life came to exist in man, one can also seek the origin and nature of that spiritual plasm within the universal history of the human race. This is connected with the mysteries of the embodiment in matter of the Dhyanis. It is not something which only took place long ago, but a continuing fact of manifested life. H.P. Blavatsky quoted from a work on occult embryology as follows:

> When the seed of the animal man is cast into the soil of the animal woman, the seed cannot germinate unless it has been fructified by the five virtues (the fluid of, or the emanation from the principles) of the six-fold Heavenly man. Wherefore the Microcosm is represented as a Pentagon, within the Hexagon Star, the 'Macrocosm'.
>
> *Ibid.*, 224

Thus, there is actually involved in the birth of a physical human being that which is quite independent of physical procreation and physical passion. It involves the cosmic hierarchies, the divine elements within the invisible theogony of the universe that constitute the Dhyani Buddhas. Some of the Dhyani Buddhas are involved with the lower principles and hence with the physical processes of gestation and conception. Others have much higher functions in relation to universal life. All are relevant to the life of the microcosm within the macrocosm, the pentagon within the hexagonal star. All are somehow reflected in the process of embryogenesis and involved in the unfoldment of consciousness that takes place throughout the life cycle of the human being. In fact, there is no point in the experience of any human being that does not involve the hosts of Dhyanis. This may be understood by grasping the fact that life as an abstract universal essence is present in all its potency in every one of its differentiations. Again quoting from the same source, H.P. Blavatsky continued:

> 'The functions of *Jiva* on this Earth are of a five-fold character. In the mineral atom it is connected with the lowest principles of the Spirits of the Earth (the six-fold Dhyanis); in the vegetable particle, with their second —the *Prana* (life); in the animal, with all these plus the third and the fourth; in man, the germ must receive the fruition of all the five. Otherwise he will be born no higher than an animal'; namely, a congenital idiot. Thus in man alone the *Jiva* is complete. As to his seventh principle, it is but one of the Beams of the Universal Sun. Each rational creature receives only the temporary loan of that which has to return to its source; while his physical body is shaped by the lowest terrestrial lives, through physical, chemical, and physiological evolution.
>
> *Ibid.*

It is crucial that *Jiva* not be narrowed down to its aspects on the lower planes of manifestation. It is true that there is life in the infusoria, the bacteria and the minutiae of every atomic point in manifestation. Hence the doctrine that every microscopic form is composed of billions upon billions of 'lives'. There is also life in each of the seven kingdoms. There is life in the elemental kingdom composed of sylphs, salamanders, undines and gnomes — the elementals connected with the elements below the mineral. There is life in the stone and in rock, and there is life in the vegetable kingdom, marked by the emergence of sensation on a subtler plane than the cohesion characteristic of the mineral kingdom. In what may be thought of as an analogue to vision, there is the osmosis by plants of light. The light that a plant receives from the midnight sky and in the early hours of the dawn, the light it receives from the moon and the sun, are all different aspects of *Jiva* in relation to the vegetable kingdom. The same life process is at work in complex and diverse ways throughout the animal kingdom.

Other aspects of *Jiva* cannot be equated with anything that comes out of the entire process from below, up to and through the animal kingdom. Otherwise, the human form would be nothing more than a Frankenstein monster. There is nothing in contemporary knowledge that can remotely imagine what it is that makes such a fundamental distinction between a living animal form and a living human being. There is nothing, in fact, in contemporary knowledge which can distinguish even between a living body and a robot or automaton, so impoverished are its conceptions of life and motion. The assumption of a vital essence or principle is not, in itself, sufficient for such distinctions, since the life-fluid or Paracelsian *Liquor Vitae* differs between the animal and the human kingdoms. That aspect of *Jiva* which circulates in the human body sustaining its vitality is a gift of the higher Dhyanis, a flow of noumenal, self-conscious intelligence. Because this distinctively human vitality is not directly involved in physical manifestation, it is virtually unknown to human beings. Yet it can be recognized through its absence, or when there is a danger of losing it. It is that which vitalizes, brings to birth and releases the spiritual will. It is that which lights up the creative energy of the higher imagination and that which belongs to the power of ideation and intention. It is that power of the human monad capable of impressing desire with a form and with an intelligence.

It is that life which is given by the power of ideas, and hence it is connected over the long process of history with what is called education.

It is the central thread of the slow, painful and imperfect process of soul instruction. Though liable to inversion and corruption, it remains the central process of unfoldment through which alone there can be a release of what would otherwise remain a merely latent potential within humanity. Life in this higher sense is inseparable from the power to choose and to reflect, the capacity to concentrate and connect. This power of synthesis is so crucial, even in its physical reflection at the level of the limbic system in the brain, that even a small amount of damage to that part of the physical vesture can result in paranoia or schizophrenia. Millions upon millions of people alive today experience an intense splitting of the thought process. They cannot anymore connect or coordinate; they cannot show full awareness of beginnings, middles and endings. Instead, they are merely involved in an immense proliferation of images without control or coordination.

Paradoxically, awareness of and participation in *Jiva*, or life in this highest sense, can only be increased by non-manifestation. That is why people cannot understand it. On the one hand, without sleep the human body would die. It is only in sleep and the quietude of the sensory apparatus, especially the lower physical senses, that the spiritual senses have any chance at all in the ordinary human being. It is only through sleep that there is a real osmosis, a connection, with the higher vestures. Without sleep there would be death. The physical form is the product of inward vitality or *Jiva*, and not the reverse. Therefore,

> The animal tissues, . . . from the moment of the birth of the Entity, are regulated, strengthened, and *fed* by it. It descends in a larger supply to vegetation in the *Sushumna* sun-ray which lights and feeds the moon, and it is through her beams that it pours its light upon, and penetrates man and animal, more during their sleep and rest, than when they are in full activity.
>
> *Ibid.*, 537

Without this process of inward nourishment and restoration through sleep, there would be no resistance to the intense excitation of nervous energy, connected with the vital fluid, which ultimately comes from the Spiritual Sun and is therefore, on its lower plane, extremely destructive if uncontained. Where there is no discipline or no shielding of that energy, it gives rise to extreme fatigue and drains all human life.

> This is called nervous excitation, but no one, except Occultists, knows the reason of such nervous per-turbation or explains the *primary* causes of it. The 'principle of Life' may kill *when too exuberant,* as also when there is too little of it. But this principle on the manifested (or our) plane is but the effect and the result of the *intelligent action* of the 'Host' — collectively, Principle — the manifesting LIFE and LIGHT. It is itself subordinate to, and emanates from the ever-invisible, eternal and Absolute ONE LIFE in a descending and a re-ascending scale of hierarchic degrees — a true septenary ladder, with SOUND (or the Logos) at the upper end and the Vidyadharas (the inferior Pitris) at the lower.
>
> *Ibid.,* 539

To be able to release the higher *Jiva,* one must become extremely calm and quiet, capable of sitting for hours doing nothing — not even thinking in any strenuous sense — but receiving. One must be wide awake, attuning oneself to the Spiritual Sun, to the regents of the sacred planets, and to the spirits of the elements — to the spirit of fire, of air, of water and of earth, and above all of Aether-*Akasha.* Only when one becomes a man of silence, a man of meditation capable of remaining still and wide awake while abstracted from even the subtlest sensations, can one come any closer to experiencing what *The Voice of the Silence* calls ALL-THOUGHT. Only by mastering the mind can one intelligently guide through the fifth principle, or *Manas,* the second principle of the universal soul, the vital force in Nature which circulates through man. When one has mastered these inferior potencies, one can experience the subtle fiery substance of *Akasha,* Nature's infinite library. Through introspection and silence, through oceanic calm, one can increase one's spiritual life-energy, which is the highest *Jiva.* To do this is to emulate those Vidyadharas who are esoterically the hierarchy that endows man, in the Third Root Race, with self-consciousness. These Siddhas are beings "affluent in devotion" and exemplars of the highest and holiest communion with the Logos.

To intuit and assimilate their presence in oneself, one must learn to sit in the silence of one's own meditation, without projects or pencils, pens or tape recorders, icons or insignia. All apparatus must go. One must simply reflect, beginning with a *bija sutra,* a sacred mantram. Then one can commune with all those beings in evolution who are wealthy in the power of adoration. They are those who so rejoice and adore others above and beyond them that through that adoration they release divine *Eros* in the highest sense, the power of divine adoration and worshipful prostration. Through the thrill of that inward adoration and mental prostration, the opposite of the self-made man's crude conceit, it is possible to tap and release spiritual energy. That energy comes out of communion with the collective hosts of light-beings who are involved in endowing human beings with the highest vital energies and powers.

It is in this sense that *Jiva* is complete only in man. And yet even this *Jiva* is independent of the highest Atmic light connected with the seventh principle, which may be likened to one of the rays or beams of the Central Spiritual Sun. The ultimate spiritual origin of life is intimated in the cryptic code language called Sanskrit by *Jivatman,* which suggests the whole of the universe in a single word. If one truly understood the many dimensions of *Jiva* and the many hierarchies to which it is connected, and if one also understood something about spiritual life and the Spiritual Sun, one would be able to understand the *Atman* as perpetual motion, and to grasp the continuity between the radiations of the Central Spiritual Sun and the pulsations at the heart of the solar system.

> '*The Sun is the heart of the Solar World (System) and
> its brain is hidden behind the (visible) Sun. From thence,
> sensation is radiated into every nerve-centre of the great body,
> and the waves of the life-essence flow into each artery and
> vein. . . . The planets are its limbs and pulses'. . . .* 'The Sun
> *in abscondito* being thus the storehouse of our little
> Kosmos, self-generating its vital fluid, and ever receiving
> as much as it gives out', and the *visible* Sun only a
> *window cut into the real* Solar palace and presence, which
> reflects, however, faithfully the interior work.
>
> Thus, there is a regular circulation of the vital fluid
> throughout our system, of which the Sun is the heart —
> the same as the circulation of the blood of the human
> body — during the manvantaric solar period, or life.
>
> *Ibid., 541*

The mystery of the *Jivatman* encompasses the mystery of the
cosmos, the Ego and the embryo. It is the most powerful motor
of spiritual energy, tapped by *yogins* through the power of vows
upheld intact over lifetimes of meditation. It is the essence of
immortal life which may be drawn upon through penance,
through *tapas*, through true repentance and through compassion.
It is the living essence of the Kwan-Yin Pledge, one with the
spiritual life-energy and spiritual will, the spiritual plasm of occult
cosmology. It is altogether beyond terrestrial perception and the
seeming reality of animal existence. It is beyond the ethereality
of the lesser gods. It is that which is ever present and primordial,
indestructible and omnipotent. It is the fluid in *Akasha*, the very
energy that circulates in the highest beings in manifestation,
released through renunciation and devotion, sacrifice and
meditation. It is, in essence, immortal life in spirit, the mystical
Logos permeating the cosmos, and the divine Presence in every
human heart.

RESONANCE AND VIBRATION

> *As the aggregate sound of nature is shown to be a single definite tone, a keynote vibrating from and through eternity; having an undeniable existence* per se *yet possessing an appreciable pitch but for 'the acutely fine ear' — so the definite harmony or disharmony of man's external nature is seen by the observant to depend wholly on the character of the keynote struck for the* outer *by* inner *man. It is the spiritual* EGO *or* SELF *that serves as the fundamental base, determining the tone of the whole life of man — that most capricious, uncertain and variable of all instruments, and which more than any other needs constant tuning; it is its voice alone, which like the sub-base of an organ underlies the melody of his whole life.*
>
> *The Theosophist,* January 1882   H.P. BLAVATSKY

The entire cosmos is a complex matrix of sound and light vibrations. Every element in our world and every kingdom of beings derives its essential nature from the keynote resonating as the basis of its consciousness. All primary questions concerning origins and destiny turn upon the rate of vibration, the plane of matter and state of consciousness, and corresponding conceptions of space, time and motion. Beyond the planes of manifestation and prior to the primal differentiation of spirit and matter lies the one invariant and all-potential vibration of the *Paramatman,* which through its radiation gives periodic form and substance to the septenary cosmos. It is necessary to discard the false notion that each human being is somewhat like a machine or a self-contained box. As the universal vibration of the One Life is at the core of every living form, no being in the universe is entirely dependent upon any external source of motion. Owing to the transcendental commonality of consciousness, all beings are inevitably involved in a universal system of mutual interdependence.

Whilst mechanistic models of Man and Nature, popular in the seventeenth century, served to stress the order of Nature, they nonetheless contributed to the false notion that each person is separate and identifiable with a body construed as a self-contained mechanical unit. Today, however, no one who is well-informed even at a simple level about electronics can think in this way. To take a contemporary analogy, it is more plausible to think of oneself as a collection of receiving and transmitting centres, capable of self-attunement to a wide variety of vibrations in the universe. Even the elusive concept of a unified field theory corresponds on the physical plane to the metaphysical idea of the eternal motion of the *Atman.*

The idea of universal vibratory consciousness must be linked to the concept of ethical responsibility if it is to be of help to human beings in daily life. The idea of instantaneous inter-dependence of all beings must be joined to the ideal of continuity of consciousness through variegated experiences. Memory must be linked to motion. Since the eighteenth century and the development of the mechanical theory of heat, all physical conceptions and models of memory have been circumscribed by the doctrine of entropy. In this view, all motions exist on the same plane and are therefore subject to mutual interference and obscuration, gradually tending to the increase of chaos and confusion. In such a scheme, it is inconceivable that any vibratory motion could be preserved intact over any long period of time. This itself is a consequence of the assumption that all things are moved from outside, and that, being subject to conflicting external influences, no single body can remain in a constant vibratory state of motion. For theories of memory, this implies that any matrix wherein memory resides must be constantly subject to corruption and forgetfulness. Thus ethical responsibility is ephemeral and all learning is inevitably undone by entropy.

In various popularized versions, especially in the social sciences and in psychology, the mechanical theory of heat has come to resemble an *a priori* road-block barring all conceptions of universal responsibility and continuity of consciousness.

Conceptually, it is important to recognize that the law of entropy applies only to closed systems having no access to additional sources of energy. Philosophically and psychologically, it is crucial to see that these sources of energy might just as well be internal as external.

The ethical significance of the problem of memory and forgetfulness was stressed by both Plato and Shankara. Plato held that all learning is recollection, whilst Shankara said that the negligence of recollection is death. But unlike contemporary mechanists, they held that learning and life are capable of enormous conscious extension. These abundant possibilities are connected with the Vedic conception of fire, the pristine symbol of wisdom and the immortality of spirit, as well as with the primal heat of Kamadeva associated with the manvantaric awakening of the manifested universe. According to Gupta Vidya, the universe is not a closed system but is instead pervaded by the immanence of its purely transcendental radiation. This immanence, which is realized in the fullest enlightenment, is reflected within the universe in an ordered series of planes and sub-planes of consciousness and matter. On each of these planes, objective existence and subjective relationship correlate with characteristics of space, time and motion defining that plane. Each plane, however, stands as the effect of a more noumenal plane whilst at the same time serving as the causal basis of a yet more differentiated plane, all within the overall limits of a vast gamut of manvantaric manifestation. Life on the highest noumenal plane is consciousness of the illimitable ground of all possible differentiated existence.

As the highest noumenal vibrations in the cosmos are themselves constantly sustained by the unmanifest eternal motion of the *Atman*, human beings can strengthen and maintain fidelity to those vibrations through self-transcendence and self-purification. Each vibratory state of consciousness on every plane is a reflected resonance of the highest noumenal states of consciousness and hence of Atma Vidya. This is the meaning of the occult axiom: *The highest sees through the eyes of the lowest.* Yet to realize this self-consciously, it is necessary to work with secondary and tertiary vibrations. The term 'self-reference' actually refers to a process in consciousness whereby a vibratory matrix of long or short duration is established on a plane or sub-plane that is subjective when compared to the apparent content or basis of the reference. In this way, all self-conscious activity on an objective plane has a tendency to establish or reinforce subjective matrices on relatively subjective planes. These matrices, which do not decay through the mere passage of time on more objective planes, form the basis of memory — and hence of continuity of consciousness and ethical responsibility. As H. P. Blavatsky explains:

> Nothing that takes place, no manifestation however rapid or weak, can ever be lost from the *Skandhic* record of a man's life. Not the smallest sensation, the most trifling action, impulse, thought, impression, or deed, can fade or go out from, or in the Universe. We may think it unregistered by our memory, unperceived by our consciousness, yet it will still be recorded on the tablets of the astral light.
>
> *Lucifer,* October 1891

This implies that every feeling and every thought, however unequivocal or guilt-ridden, everything that one has known within the privacy of one's own solitude, has been recorded in a universal computer. Every visible and invisible manifestation is somewhere recorded. Manifestation itself is a process of unfoldment from within without; but insofar as human beings operate from without within, they do not grasp the nature of the inward matrices of their own manifestation. Nothing that is recorded may be lost or erased. No angel or saviour can alter or edit the karmic record. No sensation or act is too trifling to be registered. This is a staggering fact. Normally, in their egocentricity most people see every occurrence in relation to their own likes and dislikes.

Gupta Vidya, however, affirms that the most trivial element of experience of any single being, and particularly human beings, is permanently retained in a kind of universal brain. But whereas mechanistic information resides on media that are external to the being generating and deploying that information, karmic information resides within the subtle vestures of the being itself. It consists of conscious vibrations, feeling-tones, colorations of attitudes, flavours of actions, aromas of characters, all of which are elements of one's conscious existence. Every vibration in manifestation, from the last vibration of the Seventh Eternity at the end of *pralaya* and the first flutter of manvantaric dawn, to the supple creative light witnessed in the final *sandhya* before *pralaya*, is alive and suffused with the consciousness of the One Life. Every field of objective sensation springs from the differentiated Dhyani-energies of that One Life in manifestation intimated by those mystics who speak of the aroma of lifetimes being preserved in the *sutratman*. For human beings, the cycle of incarnation involves a continual disintegration of everything below the fourth plane, and a continual recording of everything in the living *Akasha* and astral light. Light itself, as vibration, is life.

Once this is understood, it is clear that there can be no flight from the cosmos or escape from the past. No agency of vicarious atonement can rewrite the record for any being. One's response to this realization is itself a decisive step in consciousness with immense karmic consequences. To some the very idea may seem sinister. This is the result of an absurd adolescent escapism that has been reinforced by self-appointed external authorities using false dogmas to trade in human weakness. This is not only unscientific and arbitrary, but also dangerous. It is characteristic of all systems which are unphilosophical but employ religious and occasionally pseudo-scientific language, including behaviourism. Anything and everything which tends to erode the sense of ethical responsibility is false. Anything which addresses human beings in terms of their enormous responsibility for all that they have emanated and initiated is true. Yet this still provides only one, though basic, criterion — responsibility and irresponsibility. We need a more complex conception offering an account of the degrees and interactions of responsibilities. Without it, one's conception of individuality will remain truncated, while one's concern with karma will be perverted into an interest in salvation and damnation.

To understand the operation of karma and memory across lifetimes, it will help to consider situations where there is a loss of memory within a single lifetime, and the nature of the opportunities afforded by the recovery of memory. For example:

> There are cases on record of long months and years of insanity, of long days of fever when almost everything done or said, was done and said unconsciously. Yet when the patients recovered they remembered occasionally their words and deeds and very fully. *Unconscious* cerebration is a phenomenon on this plane and may hold good so far as the personal mind is concerned.
>
> *Ibid.*

Such an abrupt break in personal memory can be prompted by fever, the influence of drugs, psychic spells, madness, infatuation, terror and fear. Similar though less serious lesions in memory occur through impulsive talk, automatic action or daydreaming, through intensity of emotion or confusion of thought. All of these processes involve the spiritual nerve-currents of the subtlest vesture, which affect in turn the intellectual nerve-currents of the mind-vesture, and, ultimately, the astral nerves and the physiological form. All of the vestures resonate and respond to each other ceaselessly, whether one notices it or not. Thus, in comparison with the self-consciousness of an Adept, human beings are behaving thoughtlessly, unselfconsciously or semiconsciously most of the time. When they suddenly recall what they have been doing after a spell of oblivion, they are often terrified of confronting themselves or any honest human being.

Perhaps, however, one will not be afraid and wish to run away when confronted with the implications of one's past actions. In proportion to one's commitment to the pursuit of integrity before the traumatic episode, one will be relieved to remember what one actually did. Though shamed and shocked to discover one's actions, one can refine moral sensitivity through a chastening experience. Instead of fleeing from memory, one will gladly receive the help needed to prevent recurrences in the future. Like Immanuel Kant, who said that he was grateful to be awakened from the nonage of his dogmatic slumbers, individuals seeking participation in the humanity of the future will make every effort to overcome the unconscious cerebration of the personal mind. This unconscious cerebration — so boring, so inconvenient and so pervasive — is entirely at odds with the quickening of the Race-mind that is taking place in the present cycle. Beings will either become automata or more wide awake, morally and spiritually. The only effective contribution individuals can make to the future is through bringing ethical awareness to the centre of one's consciousness, making it the basis of every act and every attitude. If one fails to do this, one's awareness will become frenetic and manic, and certainly not honourable. Self-respect is only possible through the acquisition of moral self-consciousness, for that is the only basis of the fearlessness required to face alternatives. Only when this is possible can one look at one's accounts and have the courage to change the line of action and thus to rectify them.

Yet if all of this is only applied to the personal mind and to personal memory and consciousness, it will only yield an ego-centered sense of ethics and moral awareness. In becoming concerned with one's motives and moral life, one should not just become more preoccupied with oneself. Meta-psychologically, holding oneself up as a victim of the world is little different from holding oneself up as entirely responsible for the whole world. If one forgets that other people are moral agents, and sees them only as puppets upon the stage of one's moral life, one becomes outwardly permissive, yet inwardly self-righteous. In a position of responsibility, yesterday's libertine becomes today's tyrant. Whilst powerless, the crypto-power maniac is content to play the role of the victim, acting out martyrdom whilst wallowing in judge-mentalism. But it is rapidly becoming impossible to live unless one truly loves other human beings and lives for them. Unless one can learn to live for children, one cannot live for the future.

Nor is this merely a matter of words or exhilarated emotions. It is a function of one's capacity to hold a transcendental vibration in one's consciousness, thereby giving life to what is real and turning away from what is dying with no fear, but with calm compassion. Only thus can the subjective matrix of personal self-reference be dissolved from above below.

Collective humanity is presently undergoing a crisis that is both painful and fortunate. During this psychological Vietnamization of the world, there is no escape. There are corpses, shells, wounded and deformed beings everywhere in the astral light. They may seem to be other people, but they all affect elements in oneself which are distorted and deformed. This is not actually new; a noble seer like H.P. Blavatsky spoke in the nineteenth century of modern civilization being a necropolis. The Rishi sees astral forms and auras not in some psychic way but calmly and consistently, everywhere and all the time. Without the slightest disturbance to his or her state of consciousness, everything is known and nothing is hidden. Naturally, the eyes of a seer are eyes of deep wisdom and immense compassion for humanity. And when the seer speaks, it is from a universal standpoint.

> Behold the Hosts of Souls. Watch how they hover o'er the stormy sea of human life, and how, exhausted, bleeding, broken-winged, they drop one after other on the swelling waves. Tossed by the fierce winds, chased by the gale, they drift into the eddies and disappear within the first great vortex.
>
> *The Voice of the Silence*

This vision of the spiritual travail of humanity, caught in the darkness of loneliness and despair, of spiritual failure and desperation, is overwhelming. It cannot be either understood or assimilated by personal consciousness, but requires a universal vision of karma and human experience. Authentic impersonality in consciousness must be restored, whether through contemplation of the vastitude of starry Nature, through adoration of heroic figures and scenes in distant epochs or through meditation upon universal ideas. To connect oneself to the fathomless resources of the akashic light, one will need a conception of the karmic recording process which goes beyond any analogy to the individual brain or a computer. Instead, one must conceive of every atom in every blade of grass as intimately and eternally involved with every other sentient atom throughout the whole cosmos. This is difficult to conceive of because of the immense thoughtlessness, callousness and insensitivity of much human interaction. Caught up in their self-conceptions, individuals imagine that they are isolated in consciousness from each other, or if they take interaction seriously, they tend to blame each other for the disturbances they experience. To counter this narrow view, one might re-read some of the great plays of Shakespeare: in the great duet between the frightened apprentice Macbeth and the more accomplished black magician, Lady Macbeth, who nonetheless goes mad in terror at the end, we see the agitation of nature consonant with human beings. Not only is there a resonant response to every human emotion on the sounding-board of Nature, but one may even, if perceptive, discern in these responses of Nature the archetypal processes that envelop the human individual in birth and in death.

Kama loka and *devachan* are objective resonances of human consciousness; as permanent possibilities in nature they are present everywhere and always. If, with all their implications regarding soul-memory and the cycle of reincarnation, they are not perceived continuously, it is because human beings are so isolated in their personal awareness and bodily identification that they are blind to the causal matrices they are continually elaborating. Without overcoming this obscuration of consciousness it is not possible to consult the book of memory and the book of judgement at the dawn and twilight of incarnation in a constructive manner. During life, individual karma and memory must be inserted into the vast living fabric of visible and invisible Nature, which is conscious and responsive at every point, having nothing to do with any mechanistic conceptions of the recording of information.

> Personal memory is a fiction of the physiologist. There are cells in our brain that receive and convey sensations and impressions but this once done, their mission is accomplished. These cells of the supposed "organ of memory" are the *receivers* and *conveyors* of all the pictures and impressions of the past, not their *retainers*. Under various conditions and stimuli, they can receive instantaneously the reflection of these astral images back again, and this is called *memory, recollection, remembrance*; but they do not preserve them. . . . But the Universal Memory preserves every motion, the slightest wave and feeling that ripples the waves of differentiated nature, of man or of the Universe.
>
> *Lucifer*, October 1891

Once one understands that in universal memory everything is not only recorded but felt, one can no longer hold to a separative concept of ethics. Instead, one will turn to the perspective of the poets, the seers, the Great Compassionaters who have always taught that every thought affects every plant and every star. Whilst caught up in a separative conception of ethics, one may hold oneself responsible for hurting another person, but not necessarily every leaf and plant on earth. Yet, when human beings generate maleficent vibrations, every element in Nature is wounded. Innumerable ripples reach out throughout all differentiated Nature, and they are all preserved in the universal memory, not merely as information about individual lives, but as part of the constitutive basis for living beings in general. When this observation is coupled with a consideration of the problem of unconscious cerebration, at the level of the personal mind, the entire nature of the quest for continuity of consciousness is transformed. Instead of simply insisting to oneself that one should be more responsible or more effective, that one should learn from past failures so as to acquire virtue in an egocentric sense, such personal conceptions are supplanted by a sensitivity to universal responsibility, universal causation and the operation of karmic law within the framework of universal unity.

The Wheel of the Good Law revolves for all at all times. If individuals are not aware of everything that is emanating out of them and creating effects throughout the whole of nature, this is because they are indulging in their own vibrations in a self-protective or egotistic manner. Whether positive or negative, one's feelings nonetheless affect the overall vibratory field of life in which all living beings live, move and have their being. Unlike mechanical means of recording, which make a frozen image of the motion that produced them, the karmic preservation of vibrations preserves the actual motion itself. Because karma works regardless of whether one knows about it or not, everything produces irreversible consequences that return upon oneself quite independently of whether one remembers producing the causes or not. Since one is ceaselessly interacting with everything else and constantly sending out and receiving back karmic vibrations, human life on the objective plane is perilous. Depending upon one's past thoughts, feelings and actions, the universe can be a hazardous place. To conceive of all this in terms of a limited and egotistical notion of security, particularly on the outer physical plane, is simply to reflect an ignorant fear of karma grounded in lack of self-consciousness. Measures of self-protection, locking oneself behind doors, are only hopeless and delusive stunts. Owing to the integrity of karma and the universal memory, there is no place to hide from the consequences of one's actions.

These fearful and self-righteous responses to the lessons of karma are bound up with the standpoint of a finite differentiated self-limiting personal consciousness. If one could become capable of burning out the sense of separateness of personal identity, and become attuned to universal life and feeling, universal thought and consciousness, with universal memory which receives all action, one could become karmaless. Such is the paradox of karma and memory. *The more limited one's self-reference, the more one feels karma and the more one fears it. The more universal one's sense of self*

the more one becomes all karma and even karmaless. To resonate to
the universal naturally implies that whenever there is a quiver of
pain anywhere in the world, which is constantly witnessing birth
and death, that pain is going to be felt. The pain of every being is
relevant to the universal memory and in meditation the greater
height and breadth of one's perspective is going to draw one into
contact with all this pain. It is not possible to draw the tremendous
range of manifestation self-consciously into awareness without at
the same time experiencing all karma, without learning to respond
compassionately to every sigh of everything that lives and breathes.
At the same time one becomes karmaless because the conception
of a personal karma associated with the limited self no longer
has any meaning. One is no longer subject to personal reaction
in terms of likes and dislikes, but instead lets go of everything
personal and lives only in the universal. Therefore, there are no
residues to sustain the matrix of personal self-identity.

To become karmaless is to become an Adept, fulfilling every
single responsibility completely whilst having no debt to
discharge. At any given time, becoming aware of something
undone, of something not returned, one is able to amend and
redress the balance. Desiring nothing for oneself, the plenitude
and bounty of boundless being may be given away to others.
Unconcerned about the accrual of merit, one is free from the
insidious separateness of moral self-satisfaction and complacency
connected with the idea of being virtuous. All of this is burnt
out, and one needs no thanks from others, oneself or the universe
itself. Instead, one creates spontaneous rhythms of breathing
which keep one moving with full attention from one duty to the
next without residues and with no inherence in the *linga shariram.*
This is what it means to reduce the lunar form to a zero at will,
to attenuate the coil in the spleen, reducing it to ashes and leaving
only the seed for the makers of your vesture.

All of this is far removed from the sort of egotistical self-
absorption that many people believe is equivalent to spiritual life.
Many people recognize at some level that they are going in the
opposite direction, but they do not know what to do about it.

Instead of moving in the direction of serene joyous self-transcendence combined with courageous acceptance of karma and human pain, they are becoming more and more preoccupied with success and failure. They re-enact everything to do with personal likes and dislikes but do so on a more subtle plane bound up with individuality. They walk backwards. No one, at this point in evolution, is doing this for the first time. If people are in this position, it is because they have been there before in other lives. Possessing knowledge, they made mistakes, but they do not now remember what they did because their consciousness is obscured by the consolidated ego. This creates a hardening of the apertures of the soul, as if a stone were blocking the free flow of energies from above the head down through the spine to the toes. As a consequence their consciousness and their memory are bound in a sphere of small radius. The only way to cut these bonds is to determine to learn from all karma, and then to treat everyone as a teacher.

Every experience of pain should be taken as an opportunity for learning. A preoccupation with salvation should be converted into a dedication to the endless process of learning. This cannot be done with a frenetic violence that only reinstantiates egotism. Instead it is better to sit back sometimes and reflect upon what has happened. When it does not interfere with evident duties, it is good to take time to ask oneself: "Which way am I going? What kind of person am I becoming? Why did this happen? Why did I do these things? Why didn't I have more control over my speech? Why do I have such egotistic reactions and such hostility towards innocent people? What do I ultimately value and what do I ultimately want to become? Who am I?" This self-questioning should not be undertaken in a self-accusatory mood, but rather with a meta-psychological calmness rooted in the contemplation of metaphysical ideas. It aims to get to root causes through *dianoia* and to prepare the questioner for authentic learning.

As all consciousness on every sub-plane of the seven planes of the universe derives from the *Atman*, even if one's efforts to learn originate on the plane of personal existence, they invoke a sacred and universal vibration. The earnest desire to learn inevitably strengthens the *antaskarana* bridge. It is not possible to become altruistic overnight and very few can master karma, but all can become true learners and experience the joy of continuous learning. The more one learns, the humbler one will be in coming to judgements about other human beings or in issuing indictments of nations, races and institutions. Whilst sensing a great deal that is wrong, one will be moved to find out where one can do those little things that add up to something that is clean and right. One will become more of an observer and learner, suddenly finding the world to be a vast and generous school. Then one will become more attentive to the invisible layers of this cosmic university, noticing its invisible classrooms with invisible textbooks and invisible beings involved in teaching and learning. One will notice that people cannot say what is keeping them alive, because they do not remember when awake what they experienced in deep sleep. One will realize that it is impossible to understand, and therefore to judge any human being from the outside. Only when one learns to look upon others with love and compassion rooted in a sense of the mystery of the Ego is it possible to learn from all.

What applies to others applies to oneself. While becoming humble towards other beings, one can become fearless in one's own quest for the truth, rejecting all evasions and excuses. As one becomes rooted in a life dedicated to learning, one's whole conception of memory and of what it is important to remember will change. When the primary concern is to do justice, there can be no fear to remember anything, but at the same time there will be no tendency to indulge in a great deal of memory which is useless. Above all, it will be important to keep green and fresh the memory of the moment of spiritual birth, the moment of spiritual awakening and initiation at the most minor level. Pride in one's soul-memory is not a matter of detail and information, but rather of a vibratory current of consciousness. Whether this is put in terms of the posture of the *shravaka,* the *lanoo* disciple, the devotee and searcher after truth, or the pilgrim-soul, self-conscious fidelity to this vibration is crucial to soul-memory. By maintaining this vibration intact, it is possible to begin to shift the emphasis in the fields of one's karma. These fields are not related to each other like the rooms of a house, but rather as the butter, the milk and the water before the churning. They are the interwoven resonances of the one primal vibration of the invisible Word, and the science of karma is the discovery of their hidden correspondences in oneself and throughout the visible and invisible cosmos.

As soon as one constitutes oneself an apprentice to this science, even in the most probationary way, one naturally becomes a silent adorer of the mighty peaks in human evolution, beings of boundless love and compassion, who are not sitting somewhere else, and who are not merely appearing at certain times as Teachers, but who are always present and working in subtle ways. Suddenly one becomes aware that there is a great deal hidden which one did not fully understand, and that at various moments in one's life one has been spoken to by human beings overbrooded by their Dhyanis. To have received such profound help from any other human being and to realize the meaning of the event is at once to begin to revere the ceaseless relevance of karmaless beings in a world of painful learning, of extremely slow but real progress, where, by modest increments, humanity moves in ways that are authentic, unseen and unmanifest.

Through strengthening thought, memory and choice, one will become relaxed in reference to likes and dislikes, but in extreme earnest in relation to truth. That is why one enjoys the privilege of human existence. Like Ivan in Dostoevsky's *The Brothers Karamazov*, one will seek to know the meaning of life and the cause of the persistence of pain and sorrow. By inserting the purpose of one's life and the sweet aroma of one's spiritual striving into the universal stream of spiritual evolution, one may earn in time the privilege of coming into the presence of the Guru. Having established within oneself a firm standpoint of authentic human responsibility, one will be ready to commence the study of universal compassionate action.

IDENTITY AND
INTERACTION

Space is the real world, while our world is an artificial one. It is the One Unity throughout its infinitude: in its bottomless depths as on its illusive surface; a surface studded with countless phenomenal Universes, systems and mirage-like worlds. Nevertheless, to the Eastern Occultist, who is an objective Idealist at the bottom, in the real world, which is a Unity of Forces, there is 'a connection of all matter in the plenum', as Leibnitz would say.

The Secret Doctrine, i 615

Most people think of space as a barren void, occupied at various points by diverse living and non-living entities. The vibrant life and dynamic interactions of these entities are usually seen as a complex web of causation wherein previous conditions bring about, through intermediate modes of transmission of energy, the present and future states of things. The persistence of discrete entities through time and their capacity for intense interaction with each other are both attributed to the more or less abstract material of which they are composed and the varying forces with which they are endowed. In such a conception, space itself is a purely neutral venue, capable, according to Locke, of neither resistance nor motion. The passive proscenium of Nature plays no part in the drama that unfolds among the entities making up the universe. From this perspective, the geometrical division of space into points is understood as a conceptual convenience that permits a description of the careers of entities in terms of spatial coordinates, but has no bearing upon the origin of those entities or the significance of their interactions.

Nothing could be farther from the truth. The points comprising space are the real entities, the noumena of all things, and the origin of their epiphenomenal embodiment and material interaction. Beginning with the abstract Primordial Point, the successive orders of concretion within the geometric manifold of Space are identical with the series of states of existence sometimes spoken of as planes of consciousness and substance. The totality of these states constitutes the cosmos. The manifold points in each of these derivative and differentiated spaces are equivalent to a host of beings, and the limits and possibilities of their interactions are a function of the geometric characteristics of the space in which they exist as points.

Space includes myriads upon myriads of entities, invisible beings far beyond man's ability to comprehend, classify or even conceive. What is ordinarily called the world of manifestation is only an appearance, a skin that conceals the real activity of hosts of invisible beings in invisible space. Every point of every class is connected with every other point, and all points are essentially identical with the First Point. Known variously as the Divine Unmanifest Logos, the Pythagorean *Monas* and as *Anu*, the Primordial Atom, that Point is a nucleolus of Spirit-Matter. In the most fundamental sense, it is the metaphysical cosmos, and within the evolving elaboration of its intricate geometry all beings live, move and have their being. Within this cosmos all distinctions of subject and object, form and function, entity and environment, identity and interaction, have only a relative validity, legitimated by the degree of differentiation of the particular plane of existence and limited by the ultimate identity of all points with the One Point. Thus, each point-being is a distinct perspective in consciousness, with a definite horizon of potential action and interaction.

> Esoteric philosophy, teaching an *objective* Idealism — though it regards the objective Universe and all in it as *Maya*, temporary illusion — draws a practical distinction between collective illusion, *Mahamaya*, from the purely metaphysical standpoint, and the objective relations in it between various conscious *Egos* so long as this illusion lasts.
>
> *Ibid.*, 631

This arcane conception of Space as the real world and a unity of forces finds its partial expression in the philosophies of Leibniz and Spinoza. During the nineteenth century, elements of this perspective began to enter into the speculations of modern science, particularly in the work of Sir William Crookes. While giving generous praise to Crookes for his tremendous intellectual daring, H.P. Blavatsky deliberately inserted an idea from the ancient world which was far ahead of even the most daring notions of the nineteenth century. Going to the core of the question of the nature of the organization of matter into form, she quoted Plutarch as saying, "An idea is a *being* incorporeal, which has no subsistence by itself, but gives figure and form unto shapeless matter, and *becomes the cause of the manifestation.*" As Plutarch, like Plato, was an Initiate, the idea to which he refers was, in effect, a noumenal world of archetypal forms, which serve as the prototypes upon which the entire phenomenal world is modelled. Understood in this way, an idea is a much more dynamic notion than can usually be brought to that word since Locke. In contrast to the lacklustre conceptions of modern thought, ideas in ancient philosophy were held to involve an activity that affects, moulds and directs material particles or atoms.

Ideas have the potency of ideation belonging to the Divine Mind subsisting on the substratum of *Akasha,* the infinite negative field of all form, all possible ideation and all thoughts that may arise throughout a *manvantara* in any sphere of manifestation. In this profound and creative view of thought and ideation, it is not possible to separate ideas from elementals. An idea, when pondered upon, gives form to matter, attracting to itself — according to its nature — different classes of elementals. When this process occurs with sufficiently intense emotion, energy or will, the resulting aggregate of elementals assumes a definite shape. Then the idea becomes not just an incorporeal formless being in abstract space, but an incorporeal being that is enclosed corporeally in a more concrete space. Such forms, though invisible to the physical senses, are discrete entities on the astral plane. Through a similar process these may then give way, through the power of thought, to visible, dynamic forms in physical space. Thus, the potency of thought and the reality of ideas is the starting point of the Platonic conception of the universe as a living geometry in repose.

Crookes's great strength was in his courageous challenging of the prevailing notion of an element. More than simply questioning a particular physical interpretation of the concept of atoms as units of chemical combination, he challenged the hitherto unquestioned assumption that chemical atoms are themselves incapable of further subdivision. He refused to admit that the periodic table of elements, which successfully accounted for many of the chemical properties of physical compounds, included the ultimate elements of chemistry. Thus, Crookes anticipated much of what came to be discovered early in the twentieth century concerning the atomic constitution of physical matter. Now, of course, there are many subdivisions in the realm of subatomic physics, all of which were completely unknown in the nineteenth century, and virtually inconceivable in terms of nineteenth-century conceptions of atoms. Despite this radical reformulation of the science of chemistry and despite the tremendous advances that have been made in confirmation of what Crookes pointed out, the essential challenge implicit in his thought goes far beyond anything that has already happened. That challenge was made not merely in relation to the finality of any particular scheme of classification of constituents of matter, but also to the absolute conviction that there is ultimately a fundamental element or Protyle. Though still unknown to science, this must eventually be discovered.

In her analysis, H.P. Blavatsky complimented Crookes on having set out two postulates. The first of these, the possible existence of a Protyle, was argued for extensively by Crookes and was held by him to be connected with the nineteenth-century conception of 'radiant matter'. The second recognizes that if there is such a Protyle, then there must be an "internal action akin to cooling, operating slowly in the protyle". Consider, for example, the behaviour of crystals, which require heating and cooling for their dissolution. But quite apart from crystals, which are, after all, only particular visible geometrical forms, Crookes's postulate regarding internal action echoes the doctrines of the ancient Gupta Vidya. If one goes behind all that is regarded as possible phenomena on the material plane, penetrating to the notion of a root matter or primordial Protyle, it must be possible to relate this Protyle to all manifestation. There must be some process of development within the pregenetic stage of manifestation that corresponds to internal activity in the Protyle and can be represented as a kind of cooling. Gupta Vidya designates this substance-principle as the Father-Mother, and speaks of the hot and cold breaths within this principle as governing the processes of creation and dissolution through expansion and contraction. This is only an analogical account, but it does presuppose the existence of antecedent forms of energy having periodic cycles of ebb and swell, rest and activity. Once one grants such a possibility even in relation to the primordial Protyle, one grants the possibility of a potential release, through cooling, of that which is latent.

Important as these two postulates of Crookes are, they must be supplemented by a third postulate, which is essential as a point of departure of esoteric science. This third postulate is that there is no such thing in Nature as an inorganic substance, or that whatever is seemingly inorganic is merely in a state of profound lethargy. If awakened, even the atoms within a stone become dynamic. In the course of Nature, this awakening takes place in cycles through Fohatic impulses. On a very wide scale, this progressive activation of points of life has to do with the differences between various Rounds and Races. But this awakening can also take place through the self-conscious intervention of an Adept. With sufficient knowledge, in theory and practice, of the inner nature of things, an Adept can, through concentrated ideation, quicken the sleeping atoms in any body.

Given this potential, it is necessary to rethink altogether our customary distinctions between organic and inorganic. Like Leibniz, one must come to see the ubiquity and inexorable nature of the principle of continuity throughout all manifestation. Like Leibniz, one must acknowledge the continuity between mind and matter that is either obscured or missing in Cartesian thought. For Descartes, matter is characterized by extension in space, while mind is characterized by the power of thought. Whereas matter is held to be capable of interacting with matter, and mind can interact with mind, the radical difference between thought and extension, between mind and matter, creates a fundamentally dualistic system with a 'mind-body problem'. In such a system, 'force' is merely that which acts upon bodies from outside; all motion is understood as imparted motion, according to a Newtonian scheme.

Both Leibniz and Spinoza were in sharp disagreement with the Cartesian system. Spinoza argued that everything that exists ultimately derives from one homogeneous substance. By its essential nature, that substance has two necessary attributes, which may be put in terms of mind and matter, thought and extension. The one substance in the system of Spinoza corresponds to spirit-matter, the one substance-principle of Gupta Vidya. That substance-principle is able to manifest and maintain a myriad of modes of existence. Each of these modes has latent the power of preserving its own being; every mode of the one substance can maintain itself by its own inherent power of self-maintenance. Man, however, is that distinctive mode of substance which is capable of developing the power of reason. Therefore, man, as a mode of the one substance, is a rational being capable of preserving himself and seeing the world as it is through understanding what are the logically necessary preconditions and relations for all these modes of the one substance to exist. Through this capacity to comprehend the world and its laws of necessity, man can come closer to God. For Spinoza, God equals that one substance. Thus, through participating in the power of ideation, man is able to recognize, adore and apprehend the nature of the one divine substance.

Like Spinoza, Leibniz refused to absolutize the concept of Cartesian extension, but unlike Spinoza, who emphasized the principle of a single substance, Leibniz elaborated the proposition that everything that exists must be seen in terms of monads that are like mathematical points. Leibniz was influenced by the Pythagorean conception of the *Monas,* by Giordano Bruno's conception of monads and by the thought of Jan van Helmont. Each of Leibniz's monads is without extension, each has within itself a vital energy or entelechy, capable of moving it towards a full realization of what is potential within it. The whole of existence may be seen in terms of millions upon millions of monads, each a simple, incorporeal and indestructible spiritual unit or substance. These monads are inaccessible to all changes from without, but through the internal activity of the entelechy, capable of active expression of the essential nature of substance. Every monad, at any given time, contains within itself the sum total of all its possible states, past, present and future. All of these are implicit in the present condition of the monad. The extent to which a monad will be able to realize its potential is determined by the clarity or obscuration of its intelligence. Every monad is a mirror of the totality of monads, and yet each monad is self-contained. Monads differ from each other not in relation to their essential capacity but in regard to their greater or lesser clarity in mirroring the whole.

A number of analogies link Leibniz's conception of the monads and the contemporary conception of the atom. In sharp contrast to contemporary ideas, Leibniz saw no gap between mind and matter. He began with the conception of a force which is implicit in the formal position or nature of the monad. It is in this sense that he compared the monad to a mathematical point. This itself is a crucial conception, rich in implications concerning the hierarchies of structure in the universe. Leibniz, who, together with Newton, invented the differential calculus, was well aware of the potential power of the proliferation of points in infinite series and sets. Leibniz wished to point out that there is no way by which one can ever put an arbitrary limit to that which is regarded as irreducible because any mathematical extension can, in fact, be further subdivided. This, however, does not preclude the recognition of mathematical points which cannot be subdivided. Leibniz conceived the actual existence of such points in metaphysical space as monads. Monads are not entirely like mathematical points, except that they lack all extension. One may think of them, for the convenience of understanding, as logical constructions. For Leibniz, however, they were much more than that. Being a metaphysician, he acknowledged that there are metaphysical dimensions to space which define the essential realms, interior to the monad, within which it is capable of development without reference to anything external. As a commentator on Leibniz remarked:

> Leibniz endowed them with an infinite extension in the direction of their metaphysical dimension. After having lost sight of them in the world of space, the mind has, as it were, to dive into a metaphysical world to find and grasp the real essence of what appears in space merely as a mathematical point. . . . As a cone stands on its point, or a perpendicular straight line cuts a horizontal plane only in one mathematical point, but may extend infinitely in height and depth, so the essences *of things real* have only a punctual existence in this physical world of space; but have an infinite depth of inner life in the metaphysical world of thought.
>
> *Ibid.*, 628

Though well aware of the limits of Leibniz's conceptual vocabulary and of his constricted religious teleology, H.P. Blavatsky nonetheless praised Leibniz for providing a major alternative to the Cartesian system. His monadology not only connected mind and matter, but also offered a fundamentally different conception of force and motion in relation to matter from that accessible through a crude Newtonian scheme. Force becomes an active principle that inhabits mind and moves matter, and it may be seen as mediating between the two. In the Leibnizian system the entelechy is locked within each monad, but in Gupta Vidya the ray of Divine Thought in each Atma-Buddhic monad is, in its ultimate metaphysical nature, absolutely universal and un-circumscribed. Nevertheless, there is in Leibniz a very profound system which certainly could serve to change one's view of motion and inertia.

In the Newtonian system, the physical world is seen entirely in terms of relations between particles which impart motion to each other from without. Inertia is the tendency of an object to resist changes in its state of motion, whether by speeding up, slowing down or changing direction. Motion is simply change of position in space. All interaction is understood in terms of the collision of objects with various velocities and inertias, resulting in various reactions evident in their changes of states of motion. The capacity of one body to alter the state of motion of another is referred to as a force. It is essential to this view that all action and interaction is accomplished through external contact of bodies. There is no 'action at a distance' in the Newtonian scheme. In Leibniz, however, the interior activity of the monad involves a quite different notion of the actualization of potential. Thus Leibniz, unlike Newton, did not analyse force and motion purely in terms of categories of physical geometry. Nor was he committed, like Newton, to a conception of physical space as purely neutral in relation to motion. Leibniz's conception of the abstract internal relations of monads is consistent with a conception of a series of progressively more abstract spaces, tending towards the conception of metaphysical Space.

Whilst all monads possess the same essential internal capacity for action, they are not all equally conscious or all equally capable of acting. To account for this variety among monads, it is necessary to join certain elements of Spinoza's philosophy to Leibniz's monadology. Leibniz sought to encompass the entire range of mentality — including unconsciousness, partial unconsciousness and semi-consciousness, all the way to full consciousness — through the conception of apperception. Apperception is consciousness of perception. Therefore, apperception involves going beyond the mere capacity to experience sensation or even an awareness of one's capacity to know what one is doing. This awareness that one is, in fact, perceiving becomes in itself a crucial element in perception.

H.P. Blavatsky preferred to use the word 'apperception' more in the sense of 'semi-consciousness'. This she attributed to the entire field of monads and atoms, it being the one thing in common between them all. She tended to reserve the term 'perception' for those ranges of monadic activity which encompass self-consciousness. The vast hosts of merely apperceptive monads constitute the semi-conscious vestures of other monads which are partially or fully self-conscious. In this series of ordered hierarchies, the less-developed monads constitute a kind of clothing for the gods. In Gupta Vidya the gods are not personal beings or vast elemental congeries of *devas,* but are rather *arupa* and *rupa* Dhyanis. The highest among these are fully perfected self-conscious beings, who stand at the head of the various cosmic hierarchies and can therefore clothe themselves in monads and atoms. In Spinoza's terms, these are beings who have realized the full wisdom of necessity and thereby have plumbed to the depths the mysteries of the one universal substance. Through this critical modification in Leibniz's system, one may avoid settling for the conversion of the Pythagorean supreme *Monas* into a personal God. It is questionable how much Leibniz really wanted to support the conception of a personal God, and how much of his accommodation in this area was due to a sense of prudence in relation to the Church. Nevertheless, by joining the two systems, one can preserve all the advantages of Spinoza's form of subjective pantheism — with its acceptance of the multiplicity of modes of substance — and the advantages of Leibniz's objective pantheism, with its metaphysical scheme of abstract monadic individuation. By seeing these as two aspects of a single universal substance one will come to recognize that there corresponds to monads and atoms hosts of Dhyanis or gods in the sense of universal self-conscious beings.

Clearly, such conceptions go far beyond any merely rational conceptions of prototypes in Nature. At the same time, they demand a fundamental concept of continuity that accommodates all possible forms of matter and degrees of mentality. Such a conception must span not only the manifest realms of existence but also the unmanifest. It must accommodate the essence of matter which is pure Spirit. Seen from the standpoint of metaphysical continuity, all differentiations within metaphysical space are movements from lower to higher subdivisions of Spirit-Matter. In Gupta Vidya, what is demanded of the principle of continuity is that it must encompass everything that is potential in the unmanifest. It must, therefore, be much more systematic and thorough-going than anything that could be generated through a rationalist metaphysical system. Further, within the framework of such a principle it would be necessary to generate a totally different notion of motion, one which transcends the dichotomy between manifest activity and apparent rest that is derived from the movement of objects and material particles in what is thought to be blank or empty space. For the occultist and the theurgist, there is tremendous activity going on in the interstellar and interplanetary spaces. In these seeming voids, shoals upon shoals of scintillas, atomic or monadic souls, wheel and whirl in endless spirals. That activity takes place on so vast and fundamental a cosmic scale that it is constantly affecting the manifested world in ways that cannot be explained in terms of the conventional categories of mind, matter or motion.

All of this is, therefore, *terra incognita* to modern science. If it is true, then the individual would be well advised to see how much wisdom there is in the metaphysical notion so well summed up by Philo Judaeus: "The air is at all times full of invisible souls." Human beings are constantly in touch with vast congeries of invisible lives, elementals and also gods. Every point in any space is the focus of energies that ultimately are commanded by Dhyanis or perfected beings. While this entire way of looking at the world is far beyond the frontiers of existing knowledge, it is, at the same time, hospitable to the earnest enquirer who is honestly capable of doing full justice to the wisdom of the ancients. All the ancient cosmogonies, which are now often misconstrued as atheistic systems, assigned a central and active place to the notion of gods.

These cosmogonies were only atheistic in that they dispensed altogether with the notion of some whimsical creator or single maker of the whole. The entire spectrum of ancient thought was a celebration of the possibilities of human perfectibility in a cosmos governed by Dhyanis. Furthermore, all the great hymns and *mantrams* of the ancient Aryans embody an exact knowledge of the basis of the conscious command by the perfected human being of gods, monads and atoms. It lies within the potentiality of man to attain an unlimited perspective at the very apex of the cosmos. There is no conception of perfectibility or sovereignty higher than that open to the perfected human being.

GESTATION AND GROWTH

In the Sankhya philosophy, Purusha (spirit) is spoken of as something impotent unless he mounts on the shoulders of Prakriti (matter), which, left alone, is — senseless. But in the secret philosophy they are viewed as graduated. Though one and the same thing in their origin, Spirit and Matter, when once they are on the plane of differentiation, begin each of them their evolutionary progress in contrary directions — Spirit falling gradually into matter, and the latter ascending to its original condition, that of a pure spiritual substance. Both are inseparable, yet ever separated. In polarity, on the physical plane, two like poles will always repel each other, while the negative and the positive are mutually attracted, so do Spirit and Matter stand to each other — the two poles of the same homogeneous substance, the root-principle of the universe.

The Secret Doctrine, i 247

Outside Divine Darkness, sensed though not seen by the opened eye of Shiva, the graduated polarities of Spirit-Matter pervade all manifestation. The light vitalizing and illuminating each plane of manifestation is the shadow of supersensuous matter in motion upon a more noumenal plane. From above below, from within without, the Verbum stirs the entire gamut of rhythmic resonances in the responsive centres of life, causing them to shine forth from the darkness in the myriad rainbow hues of their differentiated existence. The timeless symmetries of sound and silence, motion and rest, darkness and light, upon the *arupa* planes are dimly echoed in the consciousness and conduct of beings caught in the cyclic round of birth and death upon the *rupa* planes. Whatever their partial perceptions of good and evil, of merit and demerit, nothing in manifest Nature is so good that it casts no shadow, nor so evil that it does not have its bright side.

The progressive attainment of Divine Wisdom through noetic discrimination is not aided by crude Manichaean distinctions which vainly seek to relegate complex factors in Nature to one side or the other of a concretized moral dichotomy. Students of Gupta Vidya are initially vulnerable to just this sort of moralistic over-simplification, especially when they mistakenly surmise that the arcane Teachings suggest that the sun is good and that the moon is bad. This confusion has many roots. First and foremost, it stems from hastiness of thought which itself is the karmic consequence of entrenched error inherited from past lives. Impatience makes the cool comprehension of the elusive and subtle interaction between the solar and the lunar more arduous than necessary. When this facile misconception is perpetuated, it further restricts the range of thought to the merely literal and physical parameters of the problem. Given the vastness and grandeur of even the physical universe, with its circling systems of galaxies, stars and planets, it is foolish to give undue importance to the visible sun and physical moon and thereby compress lofty philosophic conceptions of darkness and light into these two familiar orbs.

Nonetheless, so long as the earth revolves around the sun, so long as there are days and nights, so long as there are four seasons, there is a distinct value in the twelve signs of the zodiac and in the division of the lunar month into twenty-eight days. There is a deeper significance to the broad division of the lunar month into the waxing and waning phases, and in the arrangement of its twenty-eight days in four sets of seven, each of which has its intrinsic logic. This has been sensed in mature cultures, and the simplest calendars and almanacs available to people everywhere provide basic information to make practical use of these intervals. The deeper mysteries of the archetypal divisions of the lunar month are not readily accessible, and would be of little use to most people without an intensive period of preparation involving even the more superficial aspects of this cycle.

Essentially, the new moon is a time for purification and gestation, whereas the full moon is for abnegation and *tapas*. The greater the purification through mystic meditation during the phase of the new moon, the greater can be the silent ripening of spiritual insight during the two weeks of the waxing moon. The waning half of the moon, far from being bad, finds its value in the intensification of self-study, the letting go of illusions. The aim of those who would wisely work with the cycles and rhythms of Nature should be to make this period of renunciation a preparation for entry into a broadened and deepened cycle of learning and letting go. Thus, throughout the world, men and women observe the onset of the new moon and the full moon with fasting and deep meditation, seeking a self-conscious connection with the supple forces in Nature that foster inward growth. At this point in human evolution, and especially in the so-called developed societies of the West, individuals are fortunate if they find they can make use of the ever-recurrent succession of the seasons and months. It would be well-nigh impossible to find many persons with sufficient spiritual awareness to be ready to make use of the mystical potentials of the lunar month — for example, those marked by its eleventh day.

During the present Impulsion of the 1975 Cycle every seeker can make use of the simplest facts of Gupta Vidya in daily life. Each aspirant can exchange psychic delusions for spiritual facts, so that the name of Theosophy does not become synonymous with self-deception, but rather with honest study, deep meditation and self-regenerating ethics. The degradation of the term 'Theosophy' early in this century must be corrected and reversed, so that the theosophist becomes one who is known for true knowledge based upon authentic experience and self-testing. The sorting out of cumulative confusion concerning the solar and the lunar is an essential part of this painful process of self-correction. The removal of mental confusion requires some grasp of the subtle connection between the lunar and the solar and the suggestive ways in which the solar light works through lunar substance. One must first recognize that all the human Monads of the present earth chain participated in the moon chain, which ended over three and a half Rounds ago. Before this vast period of terrestrial evolution, the hosts of Monads in their various stages of evolutionary advance that are now part of the earth chain were then active, at different levels, on the sevenfold moon chain.

Any meaningful reference to the lunar necessarily involves a reference to a previous field of evolution as complex and differentiated, as full of potential refinement and growth, as the present earth chain. The physical moon that is seen in the sky is a reflection of the disintegrating corpse of the lowest globe of that chain. It is a shadowy remnant of a once vast and vital arena of Monadic evolution. Beyond the peculiar relevance of this particular moon to the present earth, a more general meaning and metaphysical function are associated with the indispensable role of lunar predecessors when involution and evolution are viewed from the broader standpoint of an endless series of planetary chains, each linked with its successor in unbroken continuity.

> Within the strict terms of Simultaneity Theory, succession is not considered as a physically objective phenomenon, but as a subjective one. . . . It is only in consciousness, it seems, that we experience time at all. . . . In a dream there is no time, and succession is all changed about, and cause and effect are all mixed together. In myth and legend there is no time. . . . When the mystic makes the reconnection of his reason and his unconscious, he sees all becoming as one being, and understands the eternal return. . . .
>
> Our model of the cosmos must be as inexhaustible as the cosmos, [with] a complexity that includes not only duration but creation, not only being but becoming, not only geometry but ethics.
>
> *The Dispossessed*   Ursula LeGuin

Individual integrity is damaged if one falls prey to an undue fascination with the physical corpse of the moon chain. Such a fascination and even obsession, associated with the Witches of Thessaly and similar coteries elsewhere, is the unwholesome consequence of those human beings millions of years ago who used the dark half of the moon for nefarious practices. Even now, the mere mention of such malodorous practices provokes a quickening of attention. But it is this strangely perverse if fear-ridden fascination with evil which is the prolific source of evil. There should, rather, be a fearlessness in looking at the excreted dregs of human life, but only in the light of a genuine desire to develop a secure taste for the best spiritual food for the soul. One will find no such compulsive fascination with evil amongst high souls. There is only a deeply felt pain that such tragic phenomena have taken place or persist in the present, coupled with the compassionate desire and will to alleviate the immense suffering attendant upon such maleficent practices. High souls are magnetically drawn to the ineffable Light of the Spiritual Sun. Those who, alas, find themselves unconsciously drawn to the shadowy side of human life should expel once and for all this degrading and polluting fascination from their lunar minds. Anyone who has widely travelled and witnessed repellent scenes of human depravity through the stern eyes of universal compassion can only be saddened that such sordid places exist and also recognize that there is nothing novel or exciting about them. Heliopolis may be sought even in the midst of the necropolis; there is Shamballa in Myalba, Nirvana within Samsara.

Whilst everything emanating from the misuse of human faculties is indeed depressing, this can hardly be blamed upon the moon, which is also sevenfold. Perhaps it could be blamed upon the lunar corpse, which throws off a pernicious influence. Even this, however, is not all bad, and has its enigmatic effects upon the tides of the ocean, which are immensely helpful to mariners and so essential to life on the shore. Every process in Nature is imbued with inexplicable compassion, and even that which is slowly disintegrating has its therapeutic function. People should not be preoccupied with cadavers and corpses; but if seen in the right light with the right motive, even these ghoulish concerns may result in some good. Many people are insanely afraid of their own deaths; and their horror of corpses is partly the outcome of their abject fear of the 'living dead'. These soulless beings may have some fascination for the fearful personality. The entire subject, like everything connected with the mystery of the pilgrim-soul, is somewhat inscrutable. One must preserve a certain reticence, recognize one's puzzlement, accepting that it will long remain, owing to the complexity of the connection between the solar and the lunar and its important implications in relation to the varied hosts of Pitris linked with the evolution of humanity.

Some sense of the enormous difficulty in grasping the complex teachings of Gupta Vidya concerning the hosts of solar and lunar Pitris may be gained through an analogy with the awesome developments in modern science. Over the past one hundred years there has been such an untidy expansion of theoretical understanding in fields like physics and chemistry, biology and medicine, that scarcely half a dozen individuals in the world in any of these fields can claim to have a coherent perspective on the complex pattern of development taking place in his or her respective specialty. The scope of investigation and discovery has become so vast, even in a sub-field such as particle physics, that the leading experts in these fields are dismayed by the proliferation and lack of synthesis. If this is true for the best minds of the century, it is even more so for ordinary individuals attempting to understand the trends of thought at the present time. Even though the conceptual complexity in these realms of empirical enquiry overtaxes the foremost theorists, so that none can safely predict even the broad course of subsequent developments over the coming century, very little in this vast expansion of knowledge is anything more than a hit-and-miss approach to the *ABCs* of Gupta Vidya.

There is an immense and immeasurable gap between the Divine Wisdom of the Mahatmas and the progressive formulations of modern man. One of the many purposes of *Isis Unveiled* and *The Secret Doctrine* was to put modern man in his proper place, to teach him humility before the stars, and before the Himalayan heights of Divine Wisdom. The hollow presumption of modern man has unfortunately produced hosts of bewildered victims, the foremost of which is himself. Through taking pride in what amounts to bleak ignorance, modern man blunts the higher faculties of the soul, blocking the Third Eye and rendering the spinal cord incapable of restoring the flow of the divine afflatus. These are profoundly serious maladies, but if there is a recognition of the fundamental direction and flow of human evolution, there can be a constructive healing which will have its therapeutic effects in future incarnations. In a world where numerous people are spiritually and astrally deformed, one must recognize one's own ignorance and resolve to take up the ethical challenge offered by the Teachings to stand erect as a *Manasa,* a thinking being.

One must come to see that one's inner posture is improved through mental prostration before the spiritual benefactors of mankind. Far from shrinking from outward physical deformity, high souls may even take birth in deformed bodies so as to help those deformed outwardly and inwardly through their own ignorance, inversion and perversity. It is nearly impossible to tell the spiritual degree of a human being from outward signs. No empirical observation of physical deformity or mental disturbance is an everyday guide to the inner nature of the Ego inhabiting a mortal vesture. It is the height of delusion for anyone inhabiting a seemingly healthy physical form, which may only be the veil over a virtually moribund inner nature, to make judgements, based upon a harsh sense of separateness, of other human souls from their external appearance. It is precisely this persistent sense of separateness which characterizes the lunar Monad, whilst an authentic sense of universality is the recognizable mark of the solar Monad. This important distinction parallels the essential difference between the derivative light of the lunar and the self-generated nature of the light of the solar. In terms of the human principles, this corresponds to the crucial difference between the higher individuality — the nous, or matter-moving mind — and the personality or psyche, which is reactive or passive in relation to a field of derivative light.

The capacities for self-determination, creative initiative and noetic choice implicit in the concept of ethical responsibility are the insignia of the immortal individuality in man. Hence, as ancient seers and modern sages have taught, the assumption of full responsibility is the beginning of selflessness, true participation in universality. Whilst it is the hope of the Mahatmas that a few pioneering souls will become selfless servants of the human race at this point in human evolution, any would-be aspirants must first prepare themselves by becoming fully responsible under karma. In a spineless culture there may be some passing merit in packaged programmes to bolster self-confidence and self-assertion, but these are commonly vitiated by the greed of both sponsors and participants, and in any event can never substitute for true self-reliance and moral courage based upon deep meditation and honest self-study. Unlike costly weekend workshops, meditation and self-study can be embarked upon at any time by anyone; they are not only less taxing on one's pocketbook, but also more challenging psychologically.

By inserting oneself into a programme of regular meditation and proper self-study, one can insulate oneself from the nefarious influences of the moon, enter the Light of the Spiritual Sun, and in time, take advantage of that lunar element which corresponds to the elixir deposited by the sun in the moon. This is channelled through the *sushumna* ray in the spinal column.

> One of the names of the moon in Sanskrit is Soma. . . . A 'soma-drinker' attains the power of placing himself in direct *rapport* with the bright side of the moon, thus deriving inspiration from *the concentrated intellectual energy of the blessed ancestors.* . . .
>
> This which seems one stream (to the ignorant) is of a *dual nature* — one giving life and wisdom, the other being lethal. He *who can separate the former from the latter, as Kalahamsa separated the milk from the water, which was mixed with it, thus showing great wisdom* — will have his reward.
>
> H.P. BLAVATSKY

Something of the meaning of this mysterious alchemical process can be glimpsed by contemplating the threefold nature of *ahankara,* which at its highest level is universal I-am-I consciousness. At its lowest level, the *ahankara* associated with the lunar self or the illusory personality should be made to serve as the necessary focal point of the magnetic field within which the manasic self-consciousness gains proficiency in the exercise of moral responsibility. As the overbrooding individuality learns to master its projected rays, the ephemeral astral forms of its successive incarnations are gradually replaced by a purified and permanent astral vesture. The integration of the immortal individuality into the Universal Self involves still greater mysteries.

In conveying the contributions of the various classes of Pitris to the sevenfold constitution of Manu, the Thinker, the *Stanzas of Dzyan* touch upon the mystical side of the moon.

> WHO FORMS HIM? THE SEVEN LIVES; AND THE ONE
> LIFE. WHO COMPLETES HIM? THE FIVEFOLD LHA. AND
> WHO PERFECTS THE LAST BODY? FISH, SIN, AND SOMA.
> *The Secret Doctrine,* i 238

Commenting upon this passage, H.P. Blavatsky points both to its meaning in terms of arcane symbolism and its vital importance for the future evolution of humanity.

> 'Who forms Manu (the Man) and who forms his body? The LIFE and the LIVES. Sin and the MOON.' Here Manu stands for the spiritual, heavenly man, the real and non-dying EGO in us, which is the direct emanation of the 'One Life' or the Absolute Deity. As to our outward physical bodies, the house of the tabernacle of the Soul, the Doctrine teaches a strange lesson; so strange that unless thoroughly explained and as rightly comprehended, it is only the exact Science of the future that is destined to vindicate the theory fully.
> *The Secret Doctrine,* i 248

Here the term 'sin' does not mean what it currently connotes in the English language, but is a Chaldean conception having a precise if hidden relation to the moon, as well as being its symbolic equivalent. 'Sin' does not merely refer to the physical moon, but rather to the Chaldean moon-god who was the lord of wisdom and of the calendar. The ancient Hindus and Chaldeans understood the vital relationship between the moon and the principles of gestation and growth. They comprehended something of the spiritual aspect of the moon symbolized in the lunar crescent found on the forehead of true *yogins* and on the mighty brow of the Mahayogin Shiva. Manu represents the Heavenly Man, the Father of the human race, who through his mystic meditation gives of the very essence of his divine vesture that which becomes the real and non-dying Ego of every human being. The indestructible spark of the indestructible fire is the deathless Self in every human being. After the Monad-Jiva, the meta-spiritual ray and breath of the Absolute Homogeneity, has been shot down into the very depths of differentiation, and gradually worked its way up through the regions of form aided by the ethereal prototypes provided by the lunar Pitris, the divine self-conscious intelligence of the Heavenly Man enters the waiting tabernacle and lights therein the sacred fire. This divine descent can take place only in coordination with the completion of the work of the lunar Pitris.

Whilst the Monad-Jiva spirals downward into the depths of differentiated matter,

> the lower Dhyan-Chohans . . . are evolving *pari passu* with it on a higher and more spiritual plane, descending also relatively into matter on their own plane of consciousness, when, after having reached a certain point, they will meet the incarnating senseless monad, encased in the lowest matter, and blending the two potencies, Spirit and Matter, the union will produce that terrestrial symbol of the 'Heavenly Man' in space — PERFECT MAN.
>
> *Ibid.*, i 247

When from a potential androgyne man has become separated into male and female, then he is endowed with the principle of manasic self-consciousness. Thus, the creation of the animal-man and the creation of Divine Man are joined, Perfect Man in terrestrial space and time becoming the living symbol of the Heavenly Man, the transcendental archetype.

The complete and correct understanding of these mysteries can be acquired only through a mastery of the one exact science, the mathematics of the soul, which is exclusively in the custody of the Lodge of Mahatmas. This evidently cannot be taught to all and sundry, but glimpses of it may be shared with the most awakened souls of the age who can use it to help human evolution. This is very much an integral part of the programme of the Theosophical Movement, but like any other factor in spiritual life, can never be understood from outside. In order to begin to participate in this work, one must change one's very idea of the ratio between the invisible and the visible and increase the ratio of the unmanifest to the manifest, thereby creating an intense inner life through meditation. When the inner life becomes rich and replete in contrast to outer life (which only represents a small portion of oneself), true asceticism begins. Even if the vibrant sense of an inner life can only be maintained briefly each day, and needs to be sustained through participation with others also consecrated to the cause of universal enlightenment, one can, by working with others who are helping themselves, learn to work with natural cycles. In this it does not matter if one is a beginner, as long as one is starting in the right direction. It is indeed possible to gain the benediction of the presiding regents of different days — of Mercury-Hermes on Wednesday, of Surya the Sun on Sunday, of Shiva, Saturn-Kronos, on Saturday — and use this to strengthen the inner life. One could learn to use the benediction of Venus-Shukra on Friday, consecrated to higher thought, in order to learn to concentrate all one's energies around a still centre in mystic meditation. Becoming motionless within that mystic centre, remaining apart and aloof, one may begin to sense what is meant by standing aside from all the worlds that emanate out of the Divine Vesture, the invisible form of the Logos.

What the unmanifest Logos provides ceaselessly through the

manifestation of the seven Logoi is re-enacted again and again in Monadic evolution. It may be re-enacted by each ray of the Logos in every human life. Even though extremely difficult, during any incarnation in which there is an awakening to the divine immortal nature — with the body as a temple and the vesture as an energy field — the Triad above the head can come closer to the fontanelle and evoke from the light in the heart, *anahata,* a continuous current of light-energy which may refine and elevate all one's life-atoms. Such a current could not ceaselessly flow without strenuous training and wise guidance over many lives. Indeed, nothing worthwhile is ever possible without the Grace of the Guru. That help is ever available to every human being on earth in deep sleep. No being on earth is neglected. Every being in the depths of deep sleep, if even for only a moment, comes into that hinterland of the Gods, the Sages, the Rishis and the Initiator of Initiates, Dakshinamurti. The Light of the Logos is ever available in every life-atom to every being on earth throughout its seven kingdoms. There is no point in all of space beyond the purview of the flashing gaze of the Eye of Dangma.

To honour this most precious Teaching is to be propelled forward in evolution and to receive immortal life-energy, or, if one receives it and does not use it, to be thrown backwards. In either case, the consequence is dependent upon the power of choice of *Manas,* the self-conscious freedom exercised by the individual, on behalf of what is strong or of what is weak. The strong must lift the weak, whilst the sick and the perverse must be let go. Every human being must choose between the baser, pathological and paranoid elements in the psyche, and the finer, purer and more selfless elements in his nature. The two are as incompatible as terrestrial fire and water. The cosmic fire of Agni is, however, correlated with the luminous waters of space called *Akasha.* All the physical elements are mere visible representations of the true spiritual essences existing on the higher noumenal planes.

None of the terrestrial elements is good or bad in itself, but each has its place in the formation, nourishment and disintegration of mortal forms. This much is owed to modern science; it has gone farther in the past ninety years than in the preceding three centuries in dispelling rigid and concretized conceptions of material nature and its elements. Such knowledge still lies beyond the mental capacity of many human beings, and even then, it remains worlds away from a full understanding of Spirit-Matter — the One Life. Life pervades the entire universe, whether slumbering in the atoms of dust or awakened to divine consciousness in a perfected Bodhisattva. Gradually, over the ensuing centuries and millennia, humanity will awaken to an Aquarian awareness of the fire of the One Life burning within its every unit. Meta-biology and meta-chemistry will flourish when particle physics is ensouled by unitary metaphysics and enriched by the ontological logic of integration and differentiation.

The perception and comprehension of mankind will be progressively transformed by the power of Buddhic intuition, vivifying and brightening the sight of the now dormant Eye of the Soul. This cannot take place without the deliberate use of the powers of thought and self-consciousness to create new matrices of ideation and to break up and discard the calcified accretions of past ignorance which blind the soul. As H.P. Blavatsky noted, Louis Pasteur was wise in his time to observe that microbic life can sustain itself by both aerobic and anaerobic processes, thus indicating the independence of the vital potency from external environments. Through each of its distributive units life builds and unbuilds, creates and destroys, every organic form from the most minute to the most macrocosmic. Integration and disintegration of form proceed hand-in-hand with the differentiation and synthesis of consciousness throughout all the octaves of manifestation from the formless worlds built up out of the divine elements to the shadowy realm of physical existence. All alike are impelled from within by the *Shabdabrahman*, the Divine Sound surrounded by the supernal light of the *Gayatri*, the immortal pulse in the secret heart — the Sound in the Light and the Light in the Sound.

PURITY AND POLLUTION

Every 'Round' (on the descending scale) is but a repetition in a more concrete form of the Round which preceded it, as every globe — down to our fourth sphere (the actual earth) — is a grosser and more material copy of the more shadowy sphere which precedes it in their successive order, on the three higher planes. On its way upwards on the ascending arc, Evolution spiritualises and etherealises, so to speak, the general nature of all, bringing it on to a level with the plane on which the twin globe on the opposite side is placed; the result being, that when the seventh globe is reached (in whatever Round) the nature of everything that is evolving returns to the condition it was in at its starting point — plus, every time, a new and superior degree in the states of consciousness.

The Secret Doctrine, i 232

The archetypal image of man as the sacred seven-leaved Saptaparna plant suggests the sublime integrity of human development, encompassing the spiritual, mental, moral and astro-physical spheres of existence. The heart of the Man-Plant is the *sutratman*, the thread-soul spun from the distilled essence of the diverse experiences of the threefold *Atma-Buddhi-Manas* in its repeated incarnations in the lower quaternary. The triadic heart of hebdomadic humanity mirrors the complex differentiation of the triple Logoi which takes place at the dawn of cosmic manifestation. But to comprehend the correlation between the ONE, the twofold and the threefold in the cosmos, between *Atma*, *Atma-Buddhi* and *Atma-Buddhi-Manas* in man, one must understand the cyclic processes of evolution throughout the hierarchies and kingdoms of Nature. In particular, one must appreciate, morally and spiritually, the immense scope and vital significance of human self-consciousness. Unless and until human beings overcome their unnaturally protracted fascination with the lunar aspects of their evolutionary ancestry, they will be unable to discern their present predicament or discover their true status as conscious participants in the cosmic process.

The complex ills of contemporary humanity result from a long history of abdication of responsibility in consciousness. Many souls have assuredly utilized the prerogative of self-consciousness to move closer to enlightenment, whilst others have already irreversibly fallen off the human path during this epoch of manifestation. The great bulk of humanity has failed to meet its fundamental obligations to the rest of Nature. In order to understand this collective karma, it is necessary to see human existence within the broader context of cyclic evolution. The earth, as the common theatre of evolution, is comprised of a circle of seven stages or globes, around which the evolutionary life-impulse passes seven times, each immense circling of the seven globes constituting one of the seven Rounds. Each stage of activity in each of the successive Rounds provides for the development of certain states of consciousness which correspond to the plane of matter correlative with that stage. As the Atma-Buddhic Monads engaged in this process are themselves divisible into seven kingdoms falling under seven hierarchies of being, owing to their attained development in earlier periods of evolution, their internal and external relations to each other vary enormously in the different cycles of terrestrial activity.

Whilst all the elements of this vast and variegated process are ontologically reducible to one absolute substance-principle, no mere assertion of this metaphysical reduction will generate a sense of ethical responsibility. Instead, what is needed is a shrewd comprehension of the intimate relationship between the partially awakened self-conscious human Monad and the hosts of unself-conscious Monads which constitute the vestures of man and the deceptive veils of external Nature. In regard to the laws that apply to the elemental kingdoms, H.P. Blavatsky cited the work of Henry Pratt, who sketched the Kabbalistic teaching:

> They held that . . . Spirit and Matter of cor-
> responding opacity and density tended to coalesce; and

that the resultant created Spirits, in the disembodied state, were constituted on a scale in which the differing opacities and transparencies of Elemental or uncreated Spirit were reproduced. And that these Spirits in the disembodied state attracted, appropriated, digested and assimilated Elemental Spirit and Elemental Matter whose condition was conformed to their own.

Ibid., 234

The greater the purity and ethereality of a human being's vestures, the greater will be the transparency of the Buddhic light of the *Atman*. When the vestures are composed of a very fine set of filtering elementals, light will shine through them without obscuration. The capacity to focus the light of universal awareness resides in *Manas*. When acting naturally, *Manas* chooses universal themes for focussing the noumenal light of *Atma-Buddhi*. This means that *Manas* tends to levitate, to rise upwards higher and higher, towards ever-expanding perspectives upon consciousness, matter and energy. At the same time, as is all too evident, *Manas* can, through its projected ray, get locked within the lower sensorium, the mundane class of promiscuous perceptions connected with name and form, comparison and contrast, status and security, novelty and curiosity, all that is evanescent and illusive. This in itself is a result of the impure quality and leaky texture of the lower vestures, especially of the astral form. Through recurrent patterns of temporizing thought, strong associations are forged between a human being and vampirizing sub-classes of the elemental kingdoms. Through these profane alliances, the embodied human consciousness is drawn into sterile fields of suffocating material existence, following the destructive lines of its carnal attractions. These conditions vary tremendously, as Pratt suggested:

... there is a wide difference in the condition of created Spirits; and in the intimate association between the Spirit-world and the world of Matter, the more opaque Spirits in the disembodied state were drawn towards the more dense parts of the material world, and therefore tended towards the centre of the Earth, where they found the conditions most suited to their state; while the more transparent Spirits passed into the surrounding aura of the planet, the more rarefied finding their home in its satellite.

Ibid.

This clearly connotes that not all human beings live in the same dimension of space-time. They may be grouped according to divergent states of consciousness; hence there could be within a single family, within a community, certainly within a nation, people representing differences of consciousness so vast that they constitute a virtual sub-species of humanity. In the most propitious cases these beings, having achieved a certain level of personal invulnerability, would always be universalizing and elevating themselves. But others, despite the best will in the world, have consolidated or inherited extremely tenacious tendencies that push them constantly towards the shadow-play of the physical senses. They are, therefore, blinded to the joyous possibilities of what would otherwise be the natural upward arc of the metaphysical imagination. Human beings of all sorts may be characterized in terms of these marked divergences in consciousness which invariably reflect the closeness or looseness of the relation between the immortal triad and the mutable quaternary, between spiritual will and material ossification. *What might be called a human being's basic level of self-consciousness is directly proportional to that Monad's evolution as an independent centre of primordial formless intelligence.* In any particular case, the degree of this noetic individuation is a direct function of how that ray of self-consciousness has, over a period of eighteen million years, used life-atoms and the vestures, either universalizing itself or failing to do so. This is the secret history of every human soul.

Looked at in the aggregate, all immortal souls presently experiencing the complexities of this earth chain in the Fourth Round are themselves the inheritors of an evolution that goes back to prior Rounds and earlier periods of evolution. In the first three Rounds, before reaching the stage of nascent self-consciousness, every Monad would have acquired a wealth of spiritual experiences in ethereal vestures, all of which is part of the universal memory of mankind. Each unfolding Round of evolution is like a day of Brahmā, composed of one revolution of the wheel of the planetary chain or one circling of the Monadic Hosts around the seven globes. In the Fourth Round, human evolution reaches the high-point of physical development, crowning its work with the development of the perfect physical vesture. This point of maximum involution of spirit into matter represents the fullest development of physical consciousness. After attaining this threshold, evolution begins its return movement towards spirit. In this vast perspective of human evolution, humanity has already passed that point of intense involvement in differentiation at the atomic and molecular level. This is evident in the subtlety and refinement of the human cellular structure, nervous system and specialized organs. There is an immeasurable gap between, for example, the human hand and an animal's paw. Each human being carries in his hands and other organs instruments that are the product of an extraordinary specialization of natural intelligence. But this privilege — having a hand with a firm thumb, five fingers and all its mounds corresponding to the different planets — is too little considered and too often taken for granted.

Even those fortunate enough to have had access to the arcane teachings regarding Rounds and globes, the correspondences and analogies between Nature and Man, have neglected this meditation. Though supposedly liberated from both theistic and materialistic conceptions of evolution, they have succumbed to superficial views of spirituality. Few, if any, have thought to connect the ten virtues with the twice-five fingers of the two hands. However many have reflected upon the phrase "constitutionally incapable of deviating from the right path", few have tried to understand irreversibility even on the physical plane, to recognize that it might apply to leading a little child by the hand across precipitous terrain. There is no point in being *more or less* reliable when guiding a child along the edge of an abyss; one needs nothing less than absolute irreversible stability. Gandhi understood this well and tirelessly attempted to impress it upon his followers. Even disregarding so extreme a case, one can remind oneself that such a firm stability is the indispensable basis of industrial civilization. People must be prompt and reliable in going about their work. No matter how much they may be driven by lesser or distracting motives, they either turn up at work at a certain time or accept, and expect, the inevitable consequences. This works all the way through Nature and society, so much so that it is taken to be common sense. The difficulty, then, is for people to bring to bear this stringent sense of reliability upon the inner life, with its whirling thoughts, chaotic feelings and everyday moral choices.

The fundamental problem is to generate a sufficient sense of reality for the inner pilgrimage when it is freely chosen and when it is neither baited by external rewards nor buffeted by internal fears. Not all human beings are the same in this regard. Some need the stimulus of fear more than others. This is due to the aggregate character of all the impressions they have made upon the life-atoms in their vestures during their incarnations over the past eighteen million years. At any given time, through one's predominant state of consciousness, one establishes a link with elementals, which on different planes belong by affinity to quite different classes. They themselves function in groups and are connected with the five visible and two invisible elements of Nature. They are also therefore connected, by analogy, with other globes of the earth chain, and are consubstantial with matter, either in a rarefied form corresponding to the first three Rounds or in an extremely dense state connected with the point of maximum differentiation in the Fourth Round.

Viewed in a larger time scale than is ordinarily accessible to human beings, the entire process of Nature is circular; every Round on the descending scale is but a more concrete repetition of the one preceding it. Similarly, every globe within a Round on the descending arc is a materialized copy of a more ethereal sphere which preceded it in the successive descents of consciousness through the three higher planes of the earth chain. On the fourth globe in the Fourth Round, humanity has completed the involutionary arc of this process and is now engaged in the difficult push upwards and inwards towards the source of all life-energy. The immense suffering of present humanity comes from the lapses of irresponsible beings who lost touch with the great evolutionary thrust. Regardless of the exact nature of these collective failures of prior civilizations, and regardless of the particular burdens that these failures have placed on present humanity, it is now necessary for all human beings to learn to move upwards self-consciously in the ascending arc.

In practice, this means that human beings must acquire greater control over their conscious energies, a much greater capacity to withdraw from external stimuli and deformed images. This internal refinement of consciousness is the method of evolution itself, which acts to spiritualize and etherealize the complex nature of all beings, bringing them successively on to the levels of the globes in the descending arc of evolution. Thus, on the ascending arc the fifth globe corresponds to the third globe of the descending arc, the sixth to the second and the seventh to the first. A corresponding relationship exists between the Rounds themselves. This upward process is essentially the sublimation of matter and its impressibility by intelligence, which is the constructive function of thinking beings in the creative use of matter. The general sum-total of impulse given by thought to matter includes the laser-sharp contributions of legions of Adepts as well as the more haphazard effusions of millions of laggard souls. Without being an Adept, it is impossible to assess the awesome nature of this sum-total. Most human beings are, by definition, active at a middle level of consciousness and therefore are unable to understand the enormous range of alchemy that arises in human experience. They touch only a minute segment of meaningful experience in any given lifetime. Whilst the humanity of a particular Race and Round will act under a general limiting curve of consciousness, present humanity falls far short in optimizing its opportunities under the curves that apply to it, and this is largely through compulsive identification with lower classes of elementals negatively impressed in the past.

For the *Manasa*, the pure self-conscious intelligence burning brightly in the divine sphere of every human Monad, there is no inherent difficulty in understanding the nature of embodied experience. Yet for the incarnated ray, the personality, merely to talk of SAT, to talk of the eternal bliss experienced by the higher Triad, does nothing to bring about the progress of the Monad as a sevenfold being. On the contrary, idle and egotistic speech about spirituality precipitates the terrible dead weight of religious orthodoxy which stultifies human aspiration. The selfish desire for liberation, the warped assumptions of self-righteous judgementalism and the delusion that human souls can somehow opt out of the cosmic programme have never been a part of the true esoteric Teaching. What is true, however, and comprehensible is that any human being can by deep meditation, by noble association and by good fellowship learn to apply the sacred Teachings at some level, gaining brief though nourishing glimpses of spiritual realities. When through moral perseverance such moments are threaded together, they may become the basis of lines of noetic ideation which will have a definite bearing upon the quality of astral vesture and the degree of refinement one will possess in the next life. Given the great sum-total of thoughts and choices made over eighteen million years, no human being can make an abrupt or marked difference to these factors in one brief incarnation. Half of life is spent in sleep, childhood and old age; there is hardly sufficient time and continuity of effort to make a radical difference to one's vestures in the next life. But there is time enough to change the direction of one's consciousness, the type of impression one is continually making upon elementals, and the pattern which one can extend and refine in future incarnations. After successive lifetimes of such endeavour, it is possible to create a refined and pellucid brain-mind, exquisitely tuned centres in the astral form, immediately responsive to the highest aspirations, to the most impersonal ideation.

As so few have grasped the logic and the mathematics of the Teachings of the Brotherhood of Mahatmas, many have, alas, grossly oversimplified the doctrine of Adeptship and cheapened the notion of chelaship. They never asked themselves how, if over eighteen million years they had made themselves what they were, they could expect in one short lifetime to become so different from all others. Perhaps they thought of elementals as nothing more than a convenient category of explanation for unusual phenomena, with no application to the most intimate details of mundane experience. Nonetheless, the fact remains that every human being has an inheritance of karma extending back over eighteen million years, and Nature is not about to exchange its integrity for the wishful thinking of would-be neophytes. Every human being needs to realize the texture of the sevenfold vestures and to refine them to a degree that is coordinate with the entire Fourth Round and to the Races within that Round. In the far distant future, in the Fifth Round, will come the decisive moment of choice after which no one can go any farther who has not already become benevolent and altruistic, not just in intention or on one plane, but at the primary level of root-consciousness, at the level of polarity of life-atoms. A human being who has not done this will not be able to go beyond the Fifth Round at a certain threshold.

This is the crucial juncture which is being anticipated by analogy in the Fifth Race of the Fourth Round right now. Owing to the enormous retardation in evolution in the past, it became absolutely necessary for the original vibration of the Planetary Spirit, the Avataric vibration of eighteen million years ago, of a million years ago in the time of Rama, of five thousand years ago in the time of Krishna, to be resoundingly struck again so that the resultant karma would force a widespread quickening of choice. In this way, those who cannot really keep pace may be eased out of the human form, and what would otherwise be resolved in the Fifth Round through a titanic struggle between benevolent and malevolent magic may be facilitated at this point in the Fifth Race.

This compelling necessity makes the compassionate programme of the Bodhisattvas crucial and indeed indispensable. Selfish dreams of salvation have no place in our philanthropic work for the humanity of the future. It is altogether inadequate to entertain some vague intellectual awareness that there is SAT. To live SAT, to impress every life-atom with SAT, is to become a Magus. As Gandhi understood from the ancient Indian texts, to be able to exemplify one great act of *saccakriya*, with the potent energy of pure altruistic truth, is to release so powerful a force that it can radically transform the consciousness of a myriad souls and minds over great spans of space and time. This is the perpetual theurgy enacted by the Brotherhood of Bodhisattvas. Even to apprentice oneself in this benevolent art requires lifetimes of rigorous mental and moral training. Knowing at one level that there is SAT in no way dispenses with the immensity and complexity of this programme. Whosoever hopes or tries to circumvent this necessarily arduous course has simply not begun to understand the profound Teaching concerning cosmic hierarchies.

The psychic complement of selfish salvationism and shallow spirituality is the equally destructive view that there is something inescapably evil about the physical body. There is very little to choose between orthodox religion, which condemns the physical body, and empirical pseudo-science, which refuses to really respect the human form. From the standpoint of the Wisdom Religion the physical body is a temple. Materialist and religious creedalists alike, whether prating of original sin or taking pride in mechanistic innovation, degrade the most divine form on earth. If children learnt to revere their bodies before the age of puberty, there would result a cultural revolution of fundamental proportions. As one of the Mahatmas explained in the last century:

Man (physically) is a compound of all the kingdoms, and spiritually — his individuality is no worse for being shut up within the casing of an ant

than it is for being inside a king. It is not the *outward*
or physical shape that dishonours and pollutes the five
principles — but the *mental* perversity. Then it is but
at his fourth round, when arrived at the full possession
of his *Kama*-energy and completely matured, that man
becomes *fully responsible,* as at the *sixth* he may become
a *Buddha* and at the seventh before the Pralaya — a
'Dhyan Chohan'.

MAHATMA M.

The root of all retardation is the persistent refusal to learn,
to revere elders and to keep still. If children do not learn silence
and respect, they have learnt nothing. Reverence must be instilled
so firmly that it prevails in adolescence against that cowardly
minority which is endemically perverse owing to its protracted
inability to use its creative faculties. This perversity is a kind of
demoniac defiance, often a desperate desire for inordinate
attention; but it is also sometimes the influence emanating from
the astral light of the soulless beings who are increasingly
converging with the decay of the old order. Congregating in the
so-called centres of urban civilizations and of global tourism, they
have nothing but a total contempt for everything that lives and
breathes. Individuals must learn to shield themselves against these
appalling and polluting influences.

The mental perversity referred to by Mahatma M. goes back
over the last five million years to Atlantis. In the Fifth Root Race
it is wholly abnormal, because by the end of the Fourth Race it
was largely eradicated. There was a tremendous victory and as a
result of the tragedy of what transpired in those closing million
years of the Atlantean race, the wise deliberately sought to lay
down the great norms and patterns of human life at the
foundation of the Fifth Root Race. The complex codes of Manu
spring from this era over a million years ago. The archetypal
injunctions regarding the duties of family life, reverence for elders,
mutual responsibility between social orders, and the correct
participation through gratitude and devotion in the Guru-chela
relation were all exemplified and set down by the divine law-givers

at the inception of the present Race. Everything in present humanity that is truly ethical and based upon divine wisdom goes back to that origin, though obscured in its inner meaning through the course of time and through the hypocritical misuse of sacred teachings by people enthralled by external forms. So great has been the recrudescence of Atlantean pride and wilfulness that the mighty victory of light over darkness at the inception of the Fifth Root Race has been eclipsed in the consciousness of many human beings. Many have wavered and wandered under the karmic pressure of atavistic tendencies, so that they are now altogether too suggestible to the forces of superstition, materialism and self-destruction.

One must clearly delineate the moral lines within the fivefold field of the middle human principles. The only authentic mental standpoint to take is that of total responsibility for oneself, never descending to transfer blame to anything outside oneself. The right discipline for the present and coming age is that of 'the mango principle' enunciated in *The Voice of the Silence*. One must learn to be as soft as that fruit's pulp to the woes and limitations of others, and as hard as its stone to one's own weaknesses and limitations. Only by doing this can one gain the inner firmness and moral strength needed to withdraw consciously from the astral form, and eventually to dissipate that form at will. This in itself is a high stage of development, and it cannot be attained until one has paid one's debts to other human beings. Even where one is still carrying debts to others both mentally and morally, it should still be possible to be profoundly grateful and responsible in relation to one's opportunities as a self-conscious Monad. Nothing less is being aimed at than the fullest possible recovery of the true meaning of the word 'man'. Derived from *manushya*, 'the thinker', it is man alone in Nature who is capable of keeping his head erect, capable of standing firm, capable of having a straight spine and above all capable of consciously directing benevolence towards all beings. But before one can gain full control over, or some comprehension of, the ultimate destination, one must set one's inward course in the right direction. Every human being is intuitively capable of knowing whether one is going in the right direction or not.

The forward march of human evolution has nothing to do with cowardliness or evasion, with pseudo-chelaship or nefarious manipulations. These belong to the murderers of souls, whether they parade themselves in the garb of science or sexology, psychology or religion. Every decent human being will have a natural distaste towards these grotesque mockeries of human life which only serve to weaken human responsibility. But those who consult their own consciences will discover a natural sympathy with that essential tendency in nature which evinces a progressive march towards self-mastery. They will learn to discern a design and compassion in the activity of the apparently blind forces in the vastitude of visible and hidden Nature. They will learn to appreciate the intimate adaptations of natural form to intelligent purpose; through their joyous meditations, they will learn how to assist evolution onwards from within. Rejecting all irrational conceptions of evolution based upon truncated categories, they will begin to cherish the beauty and integrity of the continual process of sifting that is spiritual evolution.

Though sharp in their immediate results and distressing to the inflated personal shadow, the tests of karma are entirely moral. In the long run they can only serve to instruct humanity in the dual law of universal justice and unconditional compassion. Those who willingly submit themselves to these ethical tests and who become freely capable of breathing for the sake of others will earn an entitlement to share in the resplendently noetic civilization of the future. Those who do not will be spewed forth by Nature. Under the ancient though eternally young Avataric impulse of the Aquarian Age, there is challenge, guidance and protection for every human being who aspires to work truly on behalf of the humanity of the future. The choice belongs to each and all.

ASCENT AND DESCENT

Not even the light which comes down nearest to the earth from the sun is mixed with anything nor does it admit dirt and defilement, but remains wholly pure and without stain and free from external influences among all existing things.

EMPEROR JULIAN

T he logic of a pregenetic unity to the cosmos requires that we adopt some principle of real or apparent division of aspects, entities and qualities in existence. Metaphysically, this principle is found in the concept of a triad of divine aspects. Arithmetically, the number *1* gives the notion of number, *2* the idea of duplication, and *3* the concept of elaboration, that is, permutation and combination. Geometrically, the point and the line can generate a triangle, the simplest enclosure of space in a plane. But the idea of rotation — in this case, the rotation of an isosceles triangle about an axis from the apex through the centre of its base — produces the cone or vortex, the origin of three-dimensional space. Ontologically, the triad implies an inner side (called Spirit by G.W. Russell — 'A.E.'), an outer side (the material medium of spirit) and a dynamic principle which draws the two together. In theosophical literature, this third element is sometimes called *Fohat,* the active aspect of spirit from the standpoint of matter, and the energetic aspect of matter from the standpoint of spirit. If effects can never be completely alienated from their causes, the unity present at the advent of existence will be found at every level of its unfoldment, and *a fortiori* the triad is implicit in everything from a universe to a grain of sand.

The spiritual alchemy of the Renaissance was rooted in the premise that every base metal was essentially gold *ab ovo* made gross by the infusion of a chaotic, derivative, aqueous element — metalline organization obscuring gold's archetypal structure.

Transmutation is the process of purifying the base metal of the aqueous element until only the natural gold remains. Alchemists knew well that aurifaction is shadowed by aurifiction, the production of a metallic substance which assumes some of the external characteristics of gold, usually by mixing minute quantities of gold with lesser metals. Along with transmutation, decisive tests for genuineness of results were performed. Moral aurifiction will be exposed on the psychic plane by its fascination with images and on the plane of action by the projection of appearances. Both may contain a golden residuum in a crude alloy, but unless the tests for gold are known, one will as likely seize upon the lesser as the true metal. The concept of transmutation (along with a constellation of interrelated and supporting ideas) can apply *mutatis mutandis* to the cosmos, the psychic nature of man and the path to illumination. Spiritual alchemy enunciates the view that there is a correspondence between physical and spiritual nature, and a continuous interaction between them.

A.E. perceived the purest spiritual nature within and throughout the grossest material nature. To the extent that a particular permutation of the two natures imposes itself, under law and circumstance, upon our consciousness it becomes real to us. Similarly, the degree of will we apply to a particular level of the interrelated aspects of the Unknowable determines the clarity of appearance which that level must assume. The psyche, as a complex of thought, will and feeling, changes under these internal and external impulses, and each psychic state is strictly correlated with some level of substance. If the senses are instruments of the power of perception, then there are senses for different levels of being and consciousness that can be experienced. The mystic path is the conscious and willing activation of subtler senses so that the psyche may become fully aware of what it always implicitly reflects.

> In that mysterious journeying from time to
> eternity, where the soul moves on to ever higher planes
> of its own being, there must be many transformations

> of the psyche. Something I think goes with it from this
> world to that other. 'The gods feed upon men.'
> Something comes back with it from Heaven to Earth.
> 'The gods nourish us.'
>
> *Song and Its Fountains*

The ascent and descent of the psyche is the illumination of
the soul at different levels and interstices. The psyche aspires; the
nous inspires.

> As our aspiration is, so is our inspiration. The
> higher nature takes our fragmentary knowledge,
> thought, experience, and our aspiration, which is
> sacrifice, and it is transfigured, made whole and
> returned to us. What is earth-born is lifted up and
> perfected, shot through and through with the light of
> that higher world where the psyche nigh to its divine
> root imagines the perfection or truth in all things.
> Much must be lost of that transcendental lucidity and
> beauty of the heavenly consciousness when the psyche
> sinks through murky clouds of desire back to the body
> again. But something returns.
>
> *Ibid.*

The transient ascents of the psyche are not ephemeral events, for
the illumination of the psyche works a change in its nature. True
rapprochement of the psyche with the divine root clarifies its
obscuration so that it reflects the higher light more adequately.
"Our inspiration will be as our aspiration."

A.E.'s convictions sprang from his own experience and a
steadfast concern to make use of the analogies and correspondences which flooded into his awareness. Ordinary waking
thought is insufficient to provide the existential and experimental
basis for understanding the process of consciousness.

> Intuition, feeling, thought are too swift in their
> coming and going, too elusive for a decisive argument

over their nature. Though they may shake us by what they import, though what they in an instant hint at may be sacred to us, their coming and going are too swift for precise thought about themselves. In normal thought the fusion between inner and outer is so swift that it deceives the most attentive sense into the idea of unity, and we come to believe that there is no other creator of thought than the thinker who resides in the brain, who is with us from moment to moment, and we do not know what rays from how many quarters of the heavens are focussed on the burning point of consciousness.

Ibid.

Unaware of the elemental denizens pervading waking consciousness, much less the specific effects of collective and individual patterns of thought upon ourselves, we cannot discern their nature. In the subjective dream state, however, we make discoveries.

In dream there is a dramatic sundering of the psyche. One part of us is seer and another is creator. The seer of dream is unconscious of creation. He looks on the forms which appear as he might look on a crowd drawn together by impulses not of his creation. He does not think all this when he dreams, but, when he wakens and remembers, he knows that the creator of dream had a magical power transcending anything which he could do in his waking state. It can project crowds of figures, set them in motion, make them to move with perfect naturalness, and wear the fitting expression for the deeds they do. Yet in the waking state of the dreamer, let him be given canvas, paints and brushes, and he might boggle as a child would over the drawing of a figure. The creator in dream is swift inconceivably. What seems a long dream to the seer of dream often takes place in an instant, and may be caused by sound or touch which wakens him. Transformations, too, take

place in dream which suggest a genius to which psychic
substance is instantly malleable.

Ibid.

The psyche, when released through withdrawal from the
constraints of concrete matter, operates upon a subtle material
medium commensurate with itself. Psychic substance readily takes
the impress of intellect and the psyche witnesses instant
presentments and elaborations. The seer is unaware of doing
anything, and therefore one suspects a superior intelligent force
operating in this medium.

> The seer in dreams is apart from the creator. It is
> not unreasonable to surmise an intellectual creator able
> to work magically upon psychic substance. Sometimes,
> indeed, at the apex of dream I have almost surprised
> the creator of it peering in upon me as if it desired by
> these miracles to allure me to discovery of itself. In the
> exploration of dream we acquire some knowledge of
> the working of the psyche. And at times in the making
> of poetry I have been able to discover the true creator
> of the poem withdrawn far within from the waking
> consciousness. The poem seemed like an oracle
> delivered to the waking self from some dweller or genie
> in the innermost.
>
> *Ibid.*

A.E. knew from his theosophical studies that at least seven kinds
of dreams could be distinguished, and that the dreams he
frequently experienced intimated a higher awareness than he
found readily accessible.

> Whence come vision and high imagination? I think
> they come from a centre of consciousness behind the
> sphere of dream. Here I pass from experience to rely
> on intuition and the wisdom of others. It is to the seers
> who wrote the Upanishads I turn for illumination. They

speak of four states of soul — waking, dreaming, deep
sleep and spirit waking — the last a state in which the
spirit is unsleeping in its ecstasy of infinite vision.

Ibid.

The last state — *Turiya* — is outside the order of the other
three, and is that in which spirit is at once seer and creator, and
where seeing is the activity of shedding the light that is the *prima
materia* of creation. Since all four states are implicit at every level
of consciousness, the perceptive mystery of creation is present in
every dream. When the psyche is unobscured by preconception
and fascination, it is illuminated and hence becomes the seer —
a condition more readily recognized in the dream state than in
either waking consciousness or deep and traceless sleep. The seer
in the psyche cannot see the creator precisely because it is
that creator itself. Since its activity is less pellucid than pure spirit,
it is the channel of both seership and creation. Poetry can
emerge from states of varying illumination because this light of
conscious awareness is also the sound of understanding. *The
Voice of the Silence* addresses one who has become a master of
samadhi — the state of faultless vision — in terms of light and
sound.

> And now, Lanoo, thou art the doer and the witness,
> the radiator and the radiation, Light in the Sound, and
> the Sound in the Light.

When this sovereign state of consciousness free from all change
and interruption is reached, the text declares:

> Behold! thou hast become the Light, thou hast
> become the Sound, thou art thy Master and thy God.
> Thou art THYSELF the object of thy search: the VOICE
> unbroken, that resounds throughout eternities, exempt
> from change, from sin exempt, the Seven Sounds in one,
> THE VOICE OF THE SILENCE.

A.E. never claimed to achieve in consciousness such irreversible and transcendent heights. But he touched chords in the psyche which evoked deep spiritual resonances and gave meaning to the Upanishadic teaching.

> But for a moment I understood what power might be in sound or incantation. It made me understand a little those mystics who speak of travelling up a Jacob's Ladder of Sound to the Logos, the fountain of all melody. I found later if meditation on the Spirit is prolonged and profound enough we enter on a state where our being is musical, not a music heard without but felt within as if the soul itself had become music, or had drawn nigh to the ray of the Logos, the Master Singer, and was for that instant part of its multitudinous song.
>
> *Song and Its Fountains*

Like Socrates, who taught the way to beauty itself by recounting the words of Diotima, A.E. took sufficient steps on the Path of Infinite Promise to be able to affirm it with confidence.

> I am a far exile from that great glory, and can but peer through a dusky transparency to a greater light than the light of day. That greater light shines behind and through the psyche. It is the light of spirit which transcends the psyche as the psyche in its own world transcends the terrestrial ego. The psyche has a dual nature, for in part it is earth-bound, and in part it clings to the ancient spirit. . . . While I could comprehend a little about the nature of the psyche, I could not apprehend at all the spirit which transcends the soul, for, as the seers said of it, it is eternal, invisible and universal. Yet because it is universal we are haunted by it in every motion of mind. It is at the end of every way. It is present in sunlight.
>
> *Ibid.*

A.E.'s meditations were all intent on the discovery of the nature of soul and spirit, and his own poetic singing constituted an array of oracles from the psyche — partial, eclipsed by external trappings of phrase and circumstance, and bound by limited vision.

> Yet they themselves may pay reverence to the voices of conscience or of intuition which alone are oracles out of undiscovered depths in their own being, and intuition and conscience may utter themselves in song as well as in fugitive illuminations of mind, heart or will.
>
> *Ibid.*

The consciousness of the seer, when controlled and focussed by a profound philosophical and psychological framework, could import glimpses of pure and undiffused light from loftier realms.

> Just as the needle-point of a nerve in the eye is sensitive to light from the whole of the heavens spread above us, so at moments we feel that all knowledge is within us. But we have not yet evolved mind to be the perfect instrument to mirror universal mind as the eye mirrors infinitudes of light and darkness. But out of that centre in us through which all the threads of the universe are drawn there may come at times flashes of super-nature.
>
> *Ibid.*

Within the aurifiction of his varied visions and dreams, A.E. perceived the possibilities of the aurifaction of true seership and touched that great work within the laboratory of his own endeavours. Even more important than the content of his visions is his method for achieving an elusive transforming awareness.

> I do not think we shall ever come to truth otherwise than by such gropings in the cave of the soul,

when with shut eyes we are in a dim illuminated darkness, and seek through transient transparencies to peer into the profundities of being.

Ibid.

INVOLUTION

The Vedic Aryans were quite familiar with mysteries of sound and colour. Mental *correlations of the two senses of 'sight' and 'hearing' were as common a fact in their days, as that of a man in our own seeing objective things before him with eyes wide open at noon. Any student of Occultism, the youngest of* chelas *who has just begun reading* esoterically *his Vedas, can suspect what the real phenomenon means; simply* — a cyclic return of human organisms to their primitive form *during the 3rd and even the 4th Root Races of what is known as the* Antediluvian periods.

The Theosophist, April 1886   H.P. BLAVATSKY

The contemporary renaissance of primordial spirituality is a necessary function of collective cyclic law and concerted individual resolve. Within the triadic framework of human evolution, the relative balance of the monadic, mental and physical components varies with the cycles and sub-cycles of Race evolution through the Rounds. At the same time, the rich fabric of Nature itself and the cumulative rapidity of karmic precipitation of events initiate significant changes according to the parameters of the *yugas.* The inherent complexity of the Manvantaric scheme cannot be reduced to a simplistic model. Yet there do exist fundamental axioms of cyclic evolution which may be applied with Buddhic discrimination to the shifting circumstances and opportunities presented by the moving locus of human growth. Witnessed from the standpoint of Eternal Duration, the entire changing universe is but a kaleidoscopic reflection of divine thought in the Divine Mind. Witnessed from the standpoint of the compassionate hosts of Bodhisattvas freely incarnated in evolving manifestation, the transformations of time, of *pravritti* and *nivritti,* are a perpetual yet progressive re-enactment of a single cosmic archetype.

Each and every cycle of existence may be grasped in relation to that which Ever Is, that which was in the beginning and which will be at the end, for it is ever becoming. To the apprehension of the Rishi mystically attuned to Brahma Vach, cyclic events are, one and all, circumscribed within the principle that the first shall be the last, and the last shall be the greatest. For the individual seeker this principle helps to unravel not only the cycles and subcycles of birth and death, but also the mysteries of self-conscious self-insertion into the broader cycles of Race evolution.

Since the inception of Manasic humanity upon this globe over eighteen million years ago, and through every successive transformation of the myriad faculties of man, the Mahatmas have maintained intact the integrity of the Mysteries for the sake of the spiritual enlightenment of humanity. Gupta Vidya is a comprehensive framework of initiations into the spiritual and psychological mysteries that underlie human evolution. In every civilization throughout the past eighteen million years, the sacred fires of the Mysteries have been preserved in sanctuaries for groups of enlightened seekers who fulfil the preparatory conditions for spiritual wisdom, having taken vows and undergone a period of probationary self-training resulting in the incomparable strength of moral purity and mental reliability. Through deep meditation each aspirant must acquire a capacity for effortless resonance with the minds and hearts of all other aspirants, and thereby learn to come closer to *Mahat,* the cosmic Mind behind manifested Nature and the great hebdomadal Heart of all humanity. Without such systematic self-training — in personal invulnerability, impermeability to lower titanic forces, and a quickened sense of the immortality of the soul — it is not possible for the *lanoo-shravaka* to become fully attuned to the collective mind and heart of the human race.

In order to become a candidate for initiation into the Mysteries, it is necessary to draw closer to the living centre of universal humanity, and therefore to draw apart from mundane concerns. In practice, this means developing the capacity to withdraw from the sensorium and to enter transcendental states of consciousness through meditation based upon intensified powers of concentration, calm contemplation and a greater continuity of consciousness in Spirit. Mystically, this means attuning oneself to the music of the spheres and becoming able to listen, amidst diverse temporal circumstances, to the Soundless Sound, the Voice of the Silence. Such an awakening to the reality and presence of Spirit implies a retraining and refining of the senses, bringing about a fundamental alteration in their polarity. Each of the sensory faculties has its ultimate origin in one of the seven Dhyani-energies that constitute in their aggregate the Logos. On the universal plane these seven centres have virtually unlimited creative potential, but in their restricted reflections on the astral and physical planes the range and reach of each are severely restricted. They are limited not only by the intrinsic properties of matter and the radius of perception appropriate to the sense-organs on the physical plane, but also by the insufficient use of the sensory powers by individuals under karma.

There is, therefore, an enormous variation amongst human beings in the perception of colour and sound, a variation based on their relative capacities to use sight and hearing. There is a further variation in the capacity of individuals to correlate the entire set of sense-organs and sensory faculties in daily life. The mystical seeker, concerned to awaken the compassionate creative capacity of the higher faculties, must turn from a half-life of outwardness to a full life of inwardness. By progressively withdrawing attention from the phenomenal plane, and intensifying the power of concentration combined with *vairagya*, he must detach his mind from the world and the concerns of the separative self. As he does this, the polarity of the *linga sharira*, the astral form, which is the seat of the subtle sensory powers, will change. There follows a gradual unfoldment from within without, bringing an attunement to supersensuous spheres of consciousness and a correlative extension and integration of the range and scope of perception.

This inward mystical development, the process of involution (*nivritti*), must be understood in relation to the overall collective development of humanity throughout the Rounds and Races. Otherwise the aspirant may fall prey to the fatal delusion called individual progress. Because everyday consciousness has fragmented so violently in the present period of evolution, most human beings are highly susceptible to psychic intoxication when confronted with the enormous potential of the inner senses. Without a firm grasp of the cyclic laws pertaining to the evolution and involution of the sensory faculties, they can scarcely hope to avoid a disastrous moral inversion of their aspirations when met with the first stirrings of their dormant power.

Specifically, the future awakening of the sixth and seventh senses represents a cyclic return of the wave of human evolution to a degree of spirituality shared by all of humanity in prior Rounds and Races. A future era in which sight and hearing are experienced as mental correlates is prefigured in that distant age pointed to by the Vedas wherein radiancy and colour, light and sound, sight and hearing, were synonymous terms. Assembling both philological evidence that all representations and conceptions of light and sound are found to have their derivation from the same roots, and mythological evidence of the correlation between the deities of light and the divine singers of the Vedic hymns, H.P. Blavatsky spoke of that time when all the senses were united.

Beginning with the First Root Race of the present Fourth Round on this globe, the evolution of primitive humanity on the physical plane proceeded through the development of one of the seven senses in each of the successive Sub-Races. The separation of the senses characteristic of humanity in the Fifth Root Race represents a later and transitory stage of development which will eventually be resolved through a return to an earlier integrity of the faculties.

> *Human* speech, as known to us, came into being
> in the Root-race that preceded ours — the *Fourth* or the
> 'Atlantean' — at the very beginning of it, in sub-race
> No. 1; and simultaneously with it were developed
> *sight* — as a physical sense — while the four other senses

(with the two additional — the 6th and 7th — of which science knows nothing as yet) — remained in their latent, undeveloped state as physical senses, although fully developed as spiritual faculties. Our sense of *hearing* developed only in the 3rd sub-races. . . . 'Sound is *seen* before it is heard', — says the book of *Kiu-ti*. The flash of lightning precedes the clap of thunder. As ages went by mankind fell with every new generation lower and lower *into matter*, the physical smothering the spiritual, until the whole set of senses — that had formed during the first three Root-races but one SENSE, namely, *spiritual perception* — finally fell asunder to form henceforth five distinct senses.

The Theosophist, April 1886   H.P. BLAVATSKY

This paradigmatic and dominant mode of cognition characterized the entire Third Root Race and extended into the early periods of the Fourth Root Race. The gradual differentiation and subsequent fragmentation of spiritual perception into the present set of five senses all occurred during the present Fourth Round. This is of critical importance in comprehending the relationship between mental or self-conscious Manasic evolution and the development of the physical vestures. The full implications of these past periods in the present Round cannot be understood, however, until they are placed in the yet larger perspective of the overall balance between spirituality and mentality as affected by the cycling of the Rounds. Before the unfoldment of self-consciousness in the Fourth Round, the incipient humanity of the Third Round was characterized by a supernal and ethereal quality of vesture and form which pervaded the use of all the inner sense-organs in the Third Round.

In the words of one in whom live Truth and Wisdom . . . 'in the 1st half of the 3rd Round the primordial spirituality of man was eclipsed, because over-shadowed by nascent mentality'; Humanity was on its *descending arc* in the first half of that round and in the last half on its ascending arc: *i.e.*, 'his (man's) *gigantic*

> stature had decreased and his body improved in texture;
> and he had become a more rational being though still
> more an ape than a *Deva*-man'.
>
> *Ibid.*

Thus, in the Third Root Race of the present Round, as self-consciousness dawned, humanity was in a state of blissful primordial spirituality. Human beings felt effortlessly at one with one another on the plane of divine ideation, universal compassion and spiritual will owing to the extraordinary intensity of spiritual perception. This authentic aboriginal condition of humanity is associated with the Eye of Dangma, the Third Eye of spiritual insight and vision.

Just as the nascent mentality of mankind eclipsed primordial spirituality in the Third Round, so too in the present Round, during the Fourth Root Race, there was a tremendous heightening of mental development focussed upon increasingly differentiated planes of existence. This allowed for a quickening of *kama manas* in relation to the world of objects and subjects, of comparison and contrast. As a result, there was also a corresponding decline in the intuitive faculties of self-conscious human beings, and a corresponding weakening of the centres of spiritual perception. Whilst this process represents the natural descent of spirituality into materiality, the identification with form over essence poses the central challenge to the dawning powers of noetic Manasic intelligence. Yet during the Fourth Root Race, and accompanying the natural development of mental and spiritual powers, many classes of souls misused these powers chiefly in the service of the egotistical self. Consequently, disappearance and atrophy befell the eye of spiritual wisdom. In the chilling statement of the *Stanzas of Dzyan*, "The Third Eye closed."

Since this spiritual and mental self-degradation over five million years ago, the physical organ of spiritual perception has receded deep within the brain and there has been an extraordinary difficulty in the human organism to restore its spiritual vision. Since the beginning of the Fifth Root Race over a million years ago, the powers of mental awareness and self-consciousness — particularly the power of mental apprehension through meditation — have quickened. When human beings through meditation become capable of gaining control over the power of thought and of directing thought-forms, *Manas* is heightened. Owing to the karma of the Fourth Root Race, the humanity of the present Fifth Sub-Race of the Fifth Root Race has experienced considerable difficulty maintaining itself in pace with the forefront of human evolution. Contrary to the natural degree of progress at this point in the manvantaric scheme, many are unable to control their emotional nature and continue falling back into a relative state of mental obscuration through assigning an excessive sense of reality to the separative self and the world of sensory objects. Through the overdeveloped principle of kamic desire, and an undernourished resistance to those conflicts that erode the power of mental concentration, humanity has sunk to the nadir of its spiritual development. Through fragmentation of consciousness, through inability to stay still, through inability to concentrate, to engage in self-transcendence and to learn, vast numbers of human beings have become needlessly handicapped both morally and spiritually.

Yet, an honest and humble individual can still take advantage of the inherent possibilities of the scheme of cyclic human evolution. A vanguard of heroic forerunners will always extend the horizon of human potential. Through effortless empathy they will spontaneously show a concern for the weak and act on a sympathy for the sick and retarded. And through their compassion they will constantly reawaken the latent *Buddhi*, a spiritual love in human beings for fellow men and women. It has always been, and it always will be, possible to arouse the latent sense of empathy for other human beings; thus it will always be possible to arouse reflected *Buddhi*. And thus spiritual perception can be heightened and the lost eye awakened. The present karmic condition of humanity is serious, but it is by no means desperate. Even extremely materialistic people, upon encountering the evidence of other and ancient civilizations, immediately or through friends who can tell them of undreamt possibilities, can continually extend their sense of the horizon of human potential.

This capacity for buoyancy and ascent, inherent in human nature, reflects the primordial spirituality of the human race. This works continuously but can become intensified and deliberate only through conscious resolve. Few people today are in a position to become monks, capable of a spiritual discipline more demanding and more complete than anything within the secular realms of music or mathematics. Yet, just as in these arenas one can increase an appreciation of mathematics without becoming a genius or a love of music without becoming a performer, so too one can develop a sense of spiritual excitement without being an adept. Whatever his or her limitations, everyone can reach out through admiration to those who extend the horizon of human potential, and everyone can shatter walls of separateness and loneliness which otherwise loom like a gloomy curse. So long as the forces of unity are greater than the forces of disunity, so long as the forces of light are potentially greater than those of darkness, so long as the forces of love are more potent than those of hate, there is hope for humanity. Even the most apathetic classes of souls can unwittingly benefit from the more advanced souls of humanity. Through this continuous process of reciprocal interdependent quickening of potentials, there is a collective preparation for the future. And even if the full flowering of that future and the restoration in its fullness of the primordial spirituality of man may be a hundred thousand — or a million — years away, it is already evident in some extraordinary individuals. Many children can see sounds and hear sights, drawing the two senses together, with responses to vibrations that their parents cannot apprehend. Such individuals are seminal forerunners for the future, souls naturally attuned to that spiritual perception which is the germ of the sixth sense.

All the senses must be controlled and directed by self-conscious *Manas*. It is only through concentrated thought enriched by deep meditation, in silence and secrecy in the quiet hours of the day, that one may gather into oneself the spiritual forces of the cycle, and form a coherent inner body of meditation. By preparing for sleep and by coming out of it with a strong current of ideation, one can quicken the spiritual will and release the faculties, skills and knowledge of the soul which would otherwise be locked up. Not every age, and hence not every incarnation, is equally filled with opportunities for inward development; thus, access to spiritual teachings at those moments when the opportunities are great is a privilege indeed. The present decade is such a time because it is a period when those who will link themselves up to the humanity of the future can, and must, intensify their spiritual current of ideation. Those who cannot keep pace with the forward march of human evolution will accordingly be much more deranged and disordered than they otherwise might be. Nonetheless, all this occurs under karma; all the teaching of cosmic and cyclic evolution is designed to help the individual to insert himself or herself into the larger perspective. When more and more individuals come to see that they cannot separate their own individual growth from universal enlightenment, they will become more and more selfless and relaxed, cheerfully shedding the unnecessary weight of excessive concern for the personality. In the archetypal instruction of *The Voice of the Silence*:

> Thou shalt not separate thy being from BEING, and the rest, but merge the Ocean in the drop, the drop within the Ocean.
> So shalt thou be in full accord with all that lives; bear love to men as though they were thy brother-pupils, disciples of one Teacher, the sons of one sweet mother.
> Of teachers there are many; the MASTER-SOUL is one, Alaya, the Universal Soul. Live in that MASTER as ITS ray in thee. Live in thy fellows as they live in IT.

In the vast pilgrimage of each individual ray there are certain moments when it is necessary to go up or down, to go forward and selflessly merge with all humanity, or to slip backwards towards the imprisoning vortices of self-destruction in negative meditation. In such moments of choice, it is impossible to avoid the pain and suffering naturally attendant upon every true birth. One cannot be reborn into the new type of humanity unless one is willing to die as the old Adam, the old creature of habits given to spiritual paranoia, mental drowsiness and psychic daydreaming. This tattered shell must be replaced from within the voidness of one's own meditation by the embryo of the person of tomorrow.

> We are in the 5th race, and we have already passed the turning or *axial* point of our 'sub-race cycle'. Eventually as the current phenomena and the increase of sensitive organisms in our age go to prove, this Humanity will be moving swiftly on the path of pure spirituality, and will reach the apex (of *our* Race) at the end of the 7th sub-race. In plainer and *fuller* language ... we shall be, at that period, on the same degree of spirituality that belonged to, and was natural in, the 1st sub-race of the 3rd *Root-race* of the FOURTH Round; and the second half of it (or that half in which we now are) will be, owing to the law of correspondence, on parallel lines with the *first* half of the THIRD Round.
>
> *Theosophist*, April 1886   H.P. BLAVATSKY

The quickening of spiritual perception and the restoration of the primordial spirituality of the First Sub-Race of the Third Root Race by the end of the present Fifth Root Race are not nearly so distant as they may seem to human beings as yet unprepared in consciousness to slough off old skins. Indeed, they are the vital components of the Logoic impulse of the Aquarian Age. The incapacity of human beings in general to recognize the immanence of the restoration of archetypal spiritual humanity is bound up with their ostrich-like obsession with life in a physical form. The difficulty of extricating oneself from this mental obscuration is aggravated for many by the accelerated pace of karmic precipitation during the present Kali Yuga. This *yuga*, which has already passed away over five thousand of its four hundred and thirty-two thousand years, is a relatively short time when seen from the perspective of the Root Races and Sub-Races. It will indeed end before the completion of the present Fifth Root Race, and be followed by an ascent through the *yugas* towards the Satya Yuga, the whole process proceeding *pari passu* with the development of the final Sub-Races of the present Root Race.

The four *yugas* may be understood in terms of a descent from the most golden age to the most decadent, followed by a reascent to a golden age that represents a spiralling spiritual advance over the starting-point of the cycle. But these *yugas* do not mechanically and automatically apply to all human beings in the same way. Babies, for example, are not in Kali Yuga, but rather experience something like a Satya Yuga, albeit briefly. The *yugas* are relative to states of consciousness, and since all people even in a single city are on different planes of consciousness, their states of mind vary dramatically according to the dominant concerns of what may be called their line of life's meditation. So too they vary in their capacity to control the twenty-eight-day cycle of the moon and to master the cycles of the seasons of nature. Whether it be for a day, a week or an entire year, individuals must therefore train themselves to adapt their plastic mental potency to the prevailing conditions of periodic phenomena. Through the noumenal power of resolve they can always establish counterbalancing measures capable of producing successively higher levels of equilibrium.

For those capable of taking and adhering to vows, Kali Yuga affords a great opportunity. In other times one may postpone the results of one's actions; in Kali Yuga the results return very rapidly. Many people, experiencing this intensification of karma, have developed elaborate theories regarding the pace of change in the modern era, culture shock, future shock and the like; in truth, it is simply the result of an acceleration in the vortex of precipitation in Kali Yuga. When this factor is compounded by the embryonic forces of the Aquarian Age, everything happens much faster within a month, within a week, or even within a day, than was considered possible a century ago. Souls either lose their spiritual vibration more quickly, or hold a vibration and move much faster with it.

They can more rapidly descend into a lower state of consciousness or more speedily ascend to a higher state of consciousness. As in mountain climbing, the higher one goes, the greater the danger of giddiness and falling, and the more precipitous the potential fall the higher and more rarefied the atmosphere in which it takes place. But if one maintains steadiness in the thin air of higher altitudes, one's perspective may suddenly expand. This is true both on the mental and physical planes; in Kali Yuga karmic causes may be rapidly exhausted, and illusions rapidly destroyed. Opportunities are thus unusually abundant.

As more and more individuals experience this rapid destruction of illusions, they can experience many more lifetimes within a single incarnation than ever before. As the consequences of a fall are much more serious and severe in Kali Yuga, so too the possibilities of spiritual self-regeneration are much more golden. Because humanity will soon find itself at a level corresponding to the First Sub-Race of the Third Root Race, the ability to participate self-consciously in the self-regeneration of humanity will require the awakening of trans-rational powers of apprehension. Since the latter half of the present Round corresponds to the first half of the Third Round, renascent primordial spirituality has already begun to overshadow and eclipse the actual mentality, the cold human reason, characteristic of the earlier eras of the Fourth Round. Anticipations of this tendency have grown increasingly strong, so that in many individuals spiritual intuition outruns mental capacity or analytic facility. Many either do not take the lower mind seriously, or will not subject what is valuable in their lives to the narrow tests of analysis. Psychoanalysts or other types of analysts seem increasingly unnecessary, as people work out their problems on their own, often by simply preserving their intuitions in the face of adversity. There is also a growing awareness of the reality of spiritual vibrations. In so far as people think of themselves as starved for affection, they put an enormous and double-edged emphasis upon the feeling nature. As this makes them more passive, it makes them more vulnerable, more removed from their spiritual toughness and mental strength. But it also kindles a sense of empathy and sensitivity, and allows them to unfold more intuitive insight.

As the work of the present cycle proceeds, and the ratios affecting the quality of souls taking incarnation are shifted upwards, towards the mystically inclined, even the outward character of humanity will witness a gradual shift of tonality and colour. Already, the contemporary emphasis upon tenderness and sensitivity has begun to shift attention away from the equations of aggressiveness and success, of success and happiness. Like a Neanderthal monster, the loud-mouthed, over-assertive personality is being replaced by a new kind of soul whose ideal is a delicacy of perception. The bullies of old have lost their fascination for the great mass of human beings and are able to reinforce themselves in their desperation only by ganging together in cowardly cliques. Like museum pieces or relics, they conceal their weakness only by frightening those who are so foolish as to be predisposed to be frightened by them. It would be wiser for individuals to concentrate their attention upon that which is truly significant for the forward march of human evolution. Here as elsewhere everything is a function of spiritual attention; one can either set one's vision upon the stars or else bury it in the sand. One can either raise one's senses to the potential richness of human evolution, or lower them to the enslaving excrescences of the past. Now more than ever before vast numbers of human beings are choosing the former and setting their sights upon a higher consciousness more and more.

Spiritual endurance can only be acquired by rethinking one's whole life and by reshaping one's psyche. This requires enormous courage and deep resolve. One can either remain captive to the endless recurrence of old mistakes, or guide oneself firmly in the opposite direction. At seasonal times of renewal, it is possible to reaffirm and renew one's spiritual resolutions. It is always possible to tap the infinite resources of the primordial spirituality of the human race, and thereby draw into the current of the Mahatmas and Bodhisattvas who live eternally, regenerating the world and its humanity. Yet every resolve is tested during karmically necessary subsequent descents into materiality and form. Those strong in the power of meditation can, at the end of a month, look back at their New Year's resolutions and assess their progress. With each succeeding week, month and season they can reaffirm their resolutions, progressively strengthening within themselves the ladder of ascent in consciousness. Others may momentarily or entirely forget their resolves, and find themselves waiting for the next new year. There will always be some who are carried away by a momentary enthusiasm, and others who choose to stay with their decisions and cooperate with the forward march of human evolution into the indefinite and infinite future. So long as human beings are self-conscious and have the power of choice, nothing is automatic. Because spirituality progressively dominates over materiality, it is becoming increasingly more difficult and disastrous to stand still or regress. If individuals do not self-consciously insert themselves into the archetype of the humanity of the future, they are confronted after death by the increasingly precarious technical problem of finding vestures for their further human incarnations.

Those who awaken and use compassionately the higher powers of creative reason and imagination will be blessed to find themselves able to incarnate in future civilizations where collective enlightenment and spiritual advance proceed swiftly. Others, less able or willing to take advantage of sacred privileges and opportunities, will find themselves wrapt in the protective folds of spiritually and mentally sluggish cycles. Throughout human evolution, the mathematical law of karma works ceaselessly, setting limits and affording opportunities. The twin threads of justice and mercy are the warp and woof of karma, weaving the dominant patterns which determine the overall changes, mutations and transformations in human consciousness. Each human being has the opportunity to awaken and restore an awareness of the primordial mystery of Spirit, and joyfully enter the reascending stream of human consciousness as it spirals back to its eternal source.

THE SPECTRUM
OF CONSCIOUSNESS

THE SPECTRUM
OF CONSCIOUSNESS

Differentiated matter existing in the Solar System (let us not touch the whole Kosmos) in seven different conditions, and Pragna, or the capacity of perception, existing likewise in seven different aspects corresponding to the seven conditions of matter, there must necessarily be seven states of consciousness in man; and according to the greater or smaller development of these states, the systems of religions and philosophies were schemed out.

The Secret Doctrine, ii 597

O f all the arcane axioms of Gupta Vidya, none is more fundamental than that which declares both spirit and matter to be merely different aspects of a single reality. Upon this vital assumption depend the complex systems of correspondences which link together the cosmic and the human spheres of existence. In different religious and mystical traditions, it is archetypally represented as the triple unity of the integrative power of perception, the homogeneous field of primordial matter and the boundless potential of universal consciousness. These three form an abstract Three-in-One, a talismanic key to both the macrocosm and the microcosm. One cannot, however, avail oneself of the rich stream of intuitions accessible through this triadic conception merely by holding a static image of it before the mind's eye. Rather, one must learn to direct one's attention to some invisible, intangible point suspended within and beyond that Triad. If possible, one may conceive of that point in relation to metaphysical space, metaphorically depicted by the Hermetic circle without circumference. Just as a pendulum depends upon a mathematical point in space that cannot be known ostensibly but which is a logical necessity for comprehending its motion, so too the highest conceivable Three-in-One must be approached with close attention to such a metaphysical point lying beyond it. Only thus can a complete system of axioms, presuppositions and postulates expressed within the abstruse conception of the Three-in-One be glimpsed in their dynamic unity. Otherwise, the discursive mind will dissect the symbol and substitute its fragmented parts for an authentic understanding of the original whole.

Witnessed in intense meditation by the inward eye of the soul, the Three-in-One reveals reality as a dual stream of subjects and objects arising from, and ever united in, a single source. Manifest reality may be seen either from the standpoint of ideation and consciousness or from the standpoint of the material substratum of form. These twin perspectives have a more than merely intellectual significance. They represent a fundamental ontological dualism that pervades and is coextensive with manifestation. At the same time, they are both together a superimposition upon the unmanifest, impartite, unnameable Reality. This central presupposition is crucial to all theophilosophy and to Advaita Vedanta. It means that both in the universe and in man there is a single stream of consciousness, having seven different aspects, comparable to a single material substance having seven different modes or forms. All manifestation may be depicted from the standpoint of pure subjectivity, in terms of seven different states of consciousness, or from the standpoint of substance, in terms of seven planes of differentiation. That primordial substance is inherently undifferentiated, just as that unitary consciousness is essentially unlimited by any single state.

What is true of the entire cosmos is also true of the individual human being. A human being may be characterized in terms of consciousness, operating through various centres, and displaying a vast range from latent universal self-consciousness — realized in perfected human beings — to automatic, almost unconscious, cerebration in the physical human vesture. Within this hebdomadic spectrum of states of consciousness is a critical core of self-consciousness capable of varying degrees of relativity and universalization. Below this sphere of self-consciousness there is also a complex set of degrees and relativities, corresponding to all the states of consciousness realized in the other six kingdoms of Nature. Thus, all human beings may be characterized in terms of consciousness, with its seven dimensions and seven archetypal centres of activity. Equally, human beings may also be characterized in terms of a fundamental substance or matter which is differentiated in seven different ways on seven different planes.

There is an immense complexity in human nature seen under the aspect of form and matter corresponding perfectly to the enormous complexity experienced by human beings under the aspect of consciousness. No doubt most of human nature, both in relation to consciousness and to form, is latent in activity owing to human ignorance of its own abundant inheritance. This means that the degree of the human being's self-consciousness is also the degree to which one is able to gain access to the full range of form and consciousness potential within the different vestures.

The moment one realizes that both the universe and the human being may be characterized in this sevenfold manner, one must also recognize that there is an inescapable interconnection between these two alternative perspectives. Thus, if one speaks in terms of consciousness not vaguely but precisely, one must make reference to a field or sphere or plane of consciousness. In this way, all descriptions of consciousness point to substance and form. Likewise, if one speaks in terms of matter, one must refer to planes of matter and their differentiation, and each of these will correspond to different possibilities and powers of perception. Every plane of differentiated matter corresponds to a spectrum of possibilities of perception, whether or not there are beings to perceive. It is also perfectly meaningful to assume that some beings can freely experience those myriad possibilities in consciousness. In effect, the interdependent nature of the open-textured concepts of consciousness and substance points immediately to the necessity of a range of beings with different degrees of perceptivity. Nor should one set any arbitrary limit in advance upon the range of possible perceivers existing on all planes of the universe. There is a common danger, owing to anthropocentric or egocentric conceptions, that human beings will falsely delimit the possibilities of perception and perceivers in the cosmos. This error of self-limitation does not, of course, have any legislative effect upon the cosmos. Instead, it only serves to cut human beings off from possibilities of perception that lie latent within themselves, and from the possibility of any relationship with beings who have mastered or glimpsed the sublime capacities of perception.

In order to assimilate the inward meaning of these far-reaching presuppositions about the close relationship of spirit and matter, substance and consciousness, perception and the cosmos, one may begin by meditating upon potent mantrams provided in the Teachings of Gupta Vidya — for example, the proposition that *Light is Life and both are electricity.* Whatever formulation or corollary one chooses for meditation, one must apply it to oneself. If one does not do this, one is engaging merely in some form of verbal sophistry, which will avail one naught at the time of death. As soon as one truly grasps an idea, however, and begins to apply it to oneself, one will experience some degree of exhilarating release from the cloying conception of the compulsive personality. To see oneself in terms of a universal idea, even to a modest degree, is to realize that one is not a body, a name or a bundle of social successes and conventionally described weaknesses. Such pseudo-ideas cannot help an individual to awaken self-consciousness from the assured standpoint of immortality. The true immortal Perceiver, the God in man, is in itself without a form and beyond all states of consciousness. It is like the invisible apex or mysterious source of the dual stream of consciousness and form. To move up these streams towards it, one must work upon one's instruments, increasing their receptivity to the subtle vibrations of spiritual will and ideation. True spiritual aspiration encompasses the entire living stream of consciousness and form. It requires that one begin to take one's life into one's own hands. One must learn, in an inward sense, to stand up and be counted and noticed by those who are concerned with the spiritual evolution of humanity and by the Teacher of humanity on earth. This is the auspicious beginning of spiritual growth.

To understand this better — from a more metaphysical and a more magical point of view — it is useful to look at this triad of perception, consciousness and form from the standpoint of Advaita Vedanta. Speaking of the triple aspect of the divine principle in the cosmos — the unmanifested Logos, universal (latent) ideation and universal (or cosmic) active intelligence — H.P. Blavatsky explained:

> The Adwaitee Vedantic philosophy classifies this as the highest trinity, or rather the Trinitarian aspect of Chinmatra (Parabrahmam), explained by them as the 'bare potentiality of Pragna' — the power or the capacity that gives rise to perception; Chidakasam, the infinite field or plane of Universal Consciousness; and Asath (Mulaprakriti), or undifferentiated matter.
>
> *Ibid.*

In one sense, this highest Triad exists as a focal point within the field of universal, latent ideation. In another sense, it is a pure metaphysical abstraction encompassing the possibilities of perception, consciousness and form in their entirety. Thus *Chinmatra* is a synonym of *Parabrahmam*, the Absolute. *Chinmatra* has to do with *Chit*, the capacity to conceive, the capacity to maintain conscious perception and the capacity to form any conception at all. *Chit* is the limitless ground of the power to think and ideate. It is also much more than that. The term *Chinmatra* refers to a perfectly universal set of all possibilities of perception, reaching beyond the compass of any system of ideation and form. It is an extraordinarily profound metaphysical conception in the original philosophy of Advaita Vedanta. These Vedantins in the ancient world were not fascinated with the visual universe, despite its magnitude and grandeur, but rather directed their attention to the inconceivable sum-total of all possible states of consciousness of all possible perceiving beings on all possible planes of consciousness in all possible worlds. There has been nothing vaster or more sublime than this primary conception of the pre-genetic, pre-cosmic unity of the divine All in any of the subsequent systems of philosophy and religion in recorded history.

The richness of the idea of *Chinmatra* can only be understood if it is unfolded in its triple aspects. First of all, there is the bare potentiality of *Prajna*, which corresponds in the cosmos to the unmanifested Logos and in man corresponds to the universal spirit or *Atman*. Every human being and everything that exists is overbrooded by the *Atman*, the sole and single universal Spirit. Every existing thing, every mind that functions, originates from one source, which itself is single but unmanifest, and that is the unmanifested Logos. Not only is that Logos far more fundamental than any concretized notion of God, but it also transcends any view of the manifested Logos in relation to a particular system of worlds. Owing to its transcendental and unmanifest nature, that Logos contains the bare potentiality of *Prajna. Prajna* refers to wisdom, but it is also much more than that. It refers to cognition itself. More than that, it refers to all possible cognition by all possible minds and actual monads in all kingdoms in all possible worlds. Such a staggering conception of the pure power and possibility of perception dispenses with any dependency of perception upon what is now called the mind-brain. *Prajna* in its abstract aspect refers to the capacity which itself gives rise to the power of perception. Even the power to perceive is itself dependent, both logically and ontologically, upon that which is prior to it. This causal ground of all possible perception is the bare potentiality of *Prajna*, the unmanifested Logos and the *Atman*.

The second aspect or standpoint connected with the trinitarian conception of *Chinmatra* is *Chidakasha*, the infinite field or plane of universal consciousness. If it is possible to speak of the power to perceive as having a reality that is prior to all specific possible varieties of perception, it is also possible to speak of an equally boundless and universal plane of consciousness prior to any particular states or differentiations of active conscious awareness. This field or matrix must not only accommodate the intelligence in a cell or a plant, but also that in a Dhyani Buddha or a Mahatma. From the incipient infusoria to the highest perfected beings, all their modes and states of consciousness must be accommodated within a single unified field of latent ideation. This is the basic presupposition of the overarching law of continuity between the highest and the lowest throughout visible and invisible Nature. The universal unity of abstract *Prajna* is mirrored in the unbroken continuity of the subjective plane of *Chidakasha*. This continuity is the basis of the possibility of interaction, contact and communication — both voluntary and involuntary — between all perceiving beings in a universe of form. If one can gain a conceptual glimpse of this unmodified ground of consciousness preceding all differentiated states of consciousness, one will gain a crucial clue regarding the possibility of instantaneous transmission of energies, currents and vibrations throughout the cosmic field.

Chidakasha is a pure abstraction in relation to all differentiated states of consciousness and therefore seems to be pure unconsciousness from any and every limited perspective. Nevertheless, it is the basis of the ever-present possibility of functioning fields of consciousness within both Nature and Man. So great and incomprehensible are the latent energies of divine ideation inherent in *Chidakasha* that it is impossible to begin even to imagine them by any form of exoteric deduction or induction, conventional mathematics or logic. Even the most grandiose unified force fields imagined by the modern sciences do not remotely approach the coherence, continuity and potentiality of *Chidakasha*. *The Voice of the Silence* intimates the awesome grandeur of this theurgic conception when it speaks of a Master holding "life and death in his strong hand", declaring that "the living power made free in him, that power which is HIMSELF, can raise the tabernacle of illusion high above the Gods, above great Brahm and Indra". It is all too evident that most human beings have only barely begun to grasp the ABCs of human potential.

Finally, one may look at *Chinmatra* from the standpoint of undifferentiated substance — *Mulaprakriti* or *Asat*. This pure root matter is absolutely eternal and indestructible. It is ever existent, prior to all manifested worlds. It goes beyond the dissolution of worlds, enduring throughout the dark night of *Maha Pralaya*, representing the bare potentiality of differentiated form in a world. Just as *Prajna* and *Chidakasha* far transcend both the known and knowable limits of perception and consciousness, *Mulaprakriti* is an abstract conception of substance transcending all existing worlds within and without the solar system and the entire visible plane. More than this, *Mulaprakriti* represents the pristine possibility of coherence underlying any modes of objectivity apprehended on any plane of consciousness by any perceiver. It is prior to the substance of the astral plane and prior to those substantial grounds that support the various invisible globes of the terrestrial chain and other planetary chains throughout the cosmos. *Mulaprakriti* is unlimited by any set of possible worlds of form perceived by actual beings through various states of consciousness.

All three of these conceptions — *Prajna*, *Chidakasha* and *Mulaprakriti* — taken singly or together as the trinitarian *Chinmatra-Parabrahmam*, are gifts transmitted to future humanity through the mysterious power of sound by the ideation of ancient Adepts responsible for the formulation of the Advaita Vedanta system. Initially, it is more important to grasp the conceptual meaning of these terms than to be able to use them in ordinary discourse. Whilst some guidance is given with regard to their pronunciation so that they will not be massacred, it is still more important to meditate upon their meaning. Eventually, as the Sanskritization of human thought and language proceeds, a point will come when it will be both necessary and productive to learn the true pronunciation of such terms. It is impossible to separate the original ideational vibration with which high beings endowed such terms from a full understanding of their meaning. Mind and matter are joined. For the most Fohatic, creative activity known to human beings is to use the power of sound to bring together intention and visible action on a plane of consciousness and form. Words have the power to fuse form and image, mind and matter, theory and practice. In the civilization of the future children will learn the privilege of sounding words with a view towards communicating true meanings in the heart. That future will become realized as everyone learns to bridge mind and matter through sound.

There is no higher way of bridging mind and matter than the *AUM*, the Soundless Sound. Even if one cannot pronounce it aloud, one may reflect upon *AUM*. In this there is no West or East. There is not a single human being on earth who cannot engage in deep reflection upon the opening of the mouth, the holding of the breath and the closing of the mouth. To engage in this meditation is to begin to reflect upon the origin, the maintenance and the dissolution of the cosmos, upon the beginning of human life on earth in any incarnation, the continuance of that life, and the graceful ending of life at the solemn moment when death comes as a deliverer and friend. Brahmā, Vishnu and Shiva, creation, preservation and destruction-regeneration, apply to the cosmos as they apply to man. They are perfectly expressed in the *AUM*, the Soundless Sound; therein lies not just the act of bridging mind and matter, but the possibility of bridging mind and matter on the most universal plane. Hence, it is the basis of the most fundamental, lasting and irreversible effect, and of the highest magic.

The mystical power of sound to bridge the dual streams of ideation and form is the basis for the progressive awakening of the pure potency of the Perceiver. Mystically, the inward and sacrificial invocation of the Soundless Sound awakens the noetic intelligence that in turn lights up the higher centres in the human being. Within the array of human vestures there are many centres of latent life-energy; at the most fundamental and archetypal level, however, there are seven such centres. Each of these is connected with many others, and there are myriad centres throughout the human brain, heart and spinal column. Throughout the entire body, at the tips of the fingers and the toes, at the top of the head, there are numerous centres beyond reckoning. All of these centres may be affected either from without within and from below above or from within without and from above below. Many of these centres can be involuntarily affected by forces external to oneself.

What is internal and what is external is a matter of refinement of perspective. Many forces that human beings ordinarily regard as internal — thoughts, images and emotions — are nevertheless external to the immortal soul. This is because the personality's conception of internality and externality is based upon merely visual perceptions. On the other hand, these same centres can be affected voluntarily by that which is within and from above. They can be consciously affected by the life-impulse, the monadic essence and stream of energy that knits together all the centres in the entire human temple. The centres can be strongly affected as a result of deliberation, spiritual resolve and a fundamental willingness to initiate and take the initiative, the highest prerogative of the human being. The inward release of noetic intelligence through the sacrificial use of sacred sound is the pre-eminent means of bringing about such a radical self-transformation.

To understand this, one must understand noetic intelligence in relation to the principles of human nature and in relation to the triad of perception, ideation and form. The capacity of noetic intelligence to light up the various centres in the human constitution throws light upon the mystery of the power to perceive, *Prajna*. Normally, one cannot distinguish the power to perceive from one's perceptions. If one wants to know how good one's eyesight is, for example, one makes a test by trying to determine how well one sees objects at a distance; if one is at an optician's office, one tests how well one can see the letters lower down on the chart. The way one knows how well one can see is dependent upon one's capacity to recognize differentiated objects of perception. Yet such a test is limited in its significance because one knows that one sees differently at different times of day, and even differently depending upon the state of one's metabolism. Hence, any precise measure of the power to see based upon a circumscribed performance in relation to a few selected objects is expedient but inadequate. Even the physical organ of vision, the eye, is mysterious. Doctors know that it is the quickest organ to heal. There is a mystical relationship between the clear substance of the eye and the principle of *Akasha*. There are cognate mysteries surrounding all the other senses and their organs on the physical plane. In short, it is impossible to limit the potential of the power to perceive purely in terms of any finite, tangible list or set of objects of perception. The power to perceive must go far beyond mere objects of perception on any particular plane, especially the physical. Thus, the power to see belongs not to the physical eye but to the immortal soul. Just as there is physical sight, there is also astral sight, mental sight and spiritual sight.

On each of these planes of consciousness, the power of perception must transcend all its possible objects — astral, mental and spiritual. For example, the power to perceive must include the elasticity, resilience and flexibility to alter perspective or to move from one object of perception to another. A simple illustration of this can be found in the field of vision. At one moment one may perceive through the eyes a particular person, and then through moving the eyes one may shift to perceiving another person at another moment in time. Certainly, the power of visual perception is there while one is looking at the first person, and it is also there while one is looking at the second person. But while one is rapidly moving one's head from one person to the other, does one have the power to perceive? It would make no sense to say that the power to perceive existed only when the eyes were focussed upon a particular person and not when the eyes were moving. Thus the power of visual perception exists even when there is no particular visual perception taking place. The power of visual perception is independent of any focus upon any specific object. Understood even in this rudimentary way in relation to the physical plane, one can clearly comprehend that the power to perceive involves more than focus and fixation on an object. It involves more than any particular collection or set of subjective impressions. It involves the capacity of apprehension in relation to a field or space. This applies not only to physical perception, but also to astral and mental perception.

On the physical and astral planes, the power to perceive is focussed on objects. On the mental plane it is focussed on subjects.

On the spiritual plane it is focussed on an entire field. This synthesis of subject and object on the plane of spirit totally transcends all ordinary modes of sensation and discursive cognition. That is why people find it so difficult to understand the fact that for the highest beings, for Mahatmas and Buddhas, immersed in the deepest meditation, there are no individual human beings. From the standpoint of Buddha, the *Prajnaparamita Sutras* affirm, there are no beings to be saved. This does not mean that there is no stream of benevolent ideation flowing forth from a Buddha towards all beings. But there is no particularization and no specific relationship formed between such a high being and any one X or Y or Z. Tragically, many were mistaken over the last century in thinking that they could form, as separate beings, some exclusive relationship with Mahatmas and Buddhas. In their misconceptions they presumed to drag Mahatmas down to their own level. This, of course, is impossible, and the only fruit of their misconceptions was their own disappointment at the moment of death. Lacking any real conception of the arcane Teachings, they could not draw closer to the wisdom and compassion, the horizon and presence, of the Teachers. True spiritual intuition is an unbroken stream of universal perception, rooted in an unmodified awareness of the boundless and unmanifest ground of all existence. Just as the radiance of the sun is to be understood, if at all, from its mysterious central point outward, and not through any interactions with matter by its rays, so too the exalted state of the Buddhas and Mahatmas can only be apprehended inwardly in relation to the mystery of *Parabrahmam*.

One may draw closer to the mystery of the Perceiver only by grasping fundamental propositions which are both universal and metaphysical, and then by applying them to oneself. Using them to deepen one's own meditation, one may use them to adore and venerate the great beings that preside over the fortunes of humanity, without remotely seeking to drag them down to one's present condition. One must realize that within oneself and within them the power to perceive is an intrinsic, indwelling faculty inherent in the cosmos. It ultimately comes from the Logos, but not from the unmanifested Logos *per se*: it comes from the Three-in-One. It comes from the unmanifested Logos, universal ideation and active intelligence, the universal medium for the expression and manifestation of ideation. Put in terms of the human principles, it comes from *Atma, Buddhi* and *Manas*. It does not come from *Atma* alone except in the sense that everything comes under and from the Light of *Atma*, which itself reflects the Light of the Logos. Once one understands this, one can come to see the vital importance of *Buddhi* and noetic ideation within the cosmic and human triads.

Noetic intelligence is the Light of the Logos, the luminosity of universal ideation, which has the potentiality of becoming the light of active intelligence. This light is potentially present in the unmanifested Logos. Applying this to the human principles, noetic intelligence is the light of *Buddhi* which is capable of being actively focussed by *Manas* and which potentially exists in the *Atma*. This follows as soon as one grasps the meaning of the word 'noetic', derived from the term *Nous*, which is the universal mind — the field within which Fohat plants the elementary germs, the Monads and atoms, that consciously ensoul all forms in the manifested cosmos. In the cosmos as in Man, the Perceiver, the Witness and Spectator, governs and guides intelligent and sentient life through the Fohatic power of Buddhic-noetic ideation. Like Krishna-Shiva seated immobile in the hearts of all beings, the mysterious power of the Perceiver causes all beings to revolve. They are all contained in him, but he is not contained in them. Such is the sublime mystery of the Three-in-One.

THE SCOPE OF
SELF-CONSCIOUSNESS

In sober truth, . . . every 'Spirit' so-called is either a disembodied or a future man. As from the highest Archangel (Dhyan Chohan) down to the last conscious 'Builder' (the inferior class of Spiritual Entities), all such are men, *having lived aeons ago, in other Manvantaras, on this or other Spheres; so the inferior, semi-intelligent and non-intelligent Elementals — are all* future men. *That fact alone — that a Spirit is endowed with intelligence — is a proof to the Occultist that that Being must have been a* man, *and acquired his knowledge and intelligence throughout the human cycle. There is but one indivisible and absolute Omniscience and Intelligence in the Universe, and this thrills throughout every atom and infinitesimal point of the whole finite Kosmos which hath no bounds, and which people call* SPACE, *considered independently of anything contained in it.*

The Secret Doctrine, i 277

Self-consciousness is the Gordian knot of both philosophical psychology and arcane metaphysics. Its paradoxes can be unravelled only through a discipline that combines sacrificial action and meditation. As the aspirant proceeds along these parallel lines, recondite evolutionary mysteries will reveal themselves to the awakening spiritual sight. Beyond and beneath all of these, present both at the beginning and at the end of the quest, lies the riddle of Being and Non-Being, the crux of the process of infinite perfectibility within eternal divine harmony. Each stage along the way reveals fresh beginnings and tentative illuminations, all revolving around the talismanic question, "Who am I?" and its ever-enigmatic response from the depths of divine consciousness, *"THAT thou art."* This timeless dialogue between the divine soul and its projected ray is repeated over myriad lives in countless diverse forms. It is the quintessential enquiry of enquiries, comprehending the divine and the mundane while serving as the archetype of every science and every symbolic system. Although this enquiry is perennially and universally relevant, it truly demands an ever-deepening sense of detachment and an ever-expanding feeling of compassion for all humanity. The restoration of the dual sense of individual dignity and human solidarity is a primary object of the Aquarian Age and a necessary prelude to participation in the succeeding age of Makara, of magical creativity.

The development of self-conscious humanity on earth began well over eighteen million years ago, following a much longer period of development during the first three-and-a-half Rounds of the earth chain. Throughout this vast period, successive ethereal hierarchies fashioned the sentient but non-intelligent vestures of future mankind. With each succeeding Round and globe, a different class of Builders evolved out of itself more and more dense shadowy projections. During the early portion of the present Fourth Round, the sixth group or hierarchy, counting downward from spirit, evolved out of itself the filmy astral vestures of the future physical man. The seventh, or lowest, hierarchy then gradually formed and condensed the physical body of animal man upon the ethereal frame. Neither the sixth hierarchy, which is connected with ethereal gods, nor the seventh hierarchy, which is connected with vast numbers of terrestrial spirits or elementals, was capable of completing self-conscious intelligent man. Thus, it became the task of the fifth hierarchy, the mysterious beings that preside over the constellation Makara, to inform the empty and ethereal animal form, creating out of it the rational man. This in itself is an awesome mystery which may be understood only through meditation and, ultimately, initiation.

At a preliminary level the quintessential aspect of self-consciousness is conveyed in a statement from *The Voice of the Silence* which compares disciples to the strings of the soul-echoing *vina,* and mankind as a whole to its sounding board. The hand that plucks the string of the *vina* is likened to the great World-

Soul. The simultaneous attunement of the disciples to the World-Soul and to all humanity intimates the essential characteristic of Manasic self-consciousness. One may view human beings as links in a chain or members of an orchestra, each having a separate function. All are complementary and interdependent in their functions, yet none are equivalent in their degrees of consciousness or concentration. The third violinist in the orchestra might, for example, be an inspiration in his selflessness and concentration although musically he performs only a modest role within the whole. Indeed, the being who is high in self-consciousness is distinguished by a regular and refined ability to think of the whole. Through the powers of concentration and choice any self-conscious being can heighten the essential function of being human, which is the crystalline capacity to mirror the cosmos. Thus, whilst all human beings participate to some extent in a vague sense of solidarity, some become such effortless exemplars of cosmic solidarity that they release a potent force for human brotherhood. This capacity derives from meditation and altruism over many previous lives. The more lives devoted through meditation to heightening the power of *Manas*, the more lives devoted through renunciation to suffusing *Manas* with Buddhic compassion, the greater the degree of noetic discernment. The deeper this discernment, the stronger the sense of duty in the world, and the willingness in finite time to summon one's best and highest energies.

Employing the powers of individuality for the sake of universal unity depends on the Manasaputras, the fifth hierarchy, which preside over the constellation Makara. It is the unique capacity of the exalted beings of this hierarchy to be able to function at the highest metaphysical level while at the same time incarnating on and commanding the terrestrial plane, thus self-consciously bridging the celestial and the terrestrial. H.P. Blavatsky pointed out:

> The Fifth group is a very mysterious one, as it is
> connected with the Microcosmic Pentagon, the five-

pointed star representing man. In India and Egypt these Dhyanis were connected with the Crocodile, and their abode is in Capricornus. These are convertible terms in Indian astrology, as this (tenth) sign of the Zodiac is called Makara, loosely translated 'crocodile.' The word itself is occultly interpreted in various ways, as will be shown further on. In Egypt the defunct man — whose symbol is the pentagram or the five-pointed star, the points of which represent the limbs of a man — was shown emblematically transformed into a crocodile: Sebakh or Sevekh 'or seventh', . . . showing it as having been the type of intelligence, is a dragon in reality, not a crocodile. He is the 'Dragon of Wisdom' or Manas, the 'Human Soul', Mind, the Intelligent principle, called in our esoteric philosophy the 'Fifth' principle.

Ibid., 219

Egyptian symbolism, which echoes the arcane Gupta Vidya and anticipates the Christian notion of resurrection, depicts in the *Book of the Dead* the *osirification* of the soul. In this account, which has more to do with spiritual birth than physical death, the Manasic soul is represented under the glyph of a crocodile-headed god. This crocodile, or *Manas*, is represented as choosing a life ahead and descending through a ray which is a sacrifice, a self-imprisonment voluntarily chosen. After the death of the physical body, the crocodile is shown sifting out the quintessence of its life, through an impartial, impersonal and mathematically accurate judgement, balancing the soul's inherent claim to self-conscious immortality in the scales of justice against a feather, representing truth. In their higher periods the Egyptians emphasized the extreme precision of the mathematics of karma, which resembles the cosmic computer programme permeating all vestures. In this judgement, which is welcomed by the immortal soul, there is no room for vicarious atonement, gratuitous absolution or any escape into cowardliness, whether occasioned by individual ignorance or pseudo-religious priestcraft.

Whatever the system of symbolic representation, every

ancient account of the origin of human self-consciousness points
to the mystery of incarnation, the mystery of the descent of the
highest beings into terrestrial life, and the retention of spiritual
knowledge as spiritual memory in the midst of a world of change,
illusion and flux. This is the quintessential characteristic of the
fifth hierarchy which could not be fulfilled by either the fourth,
the sixth or the seventh group. The relationship between the
highest *arupa* hierarchies and the human principles is conveyed
in the Japanese system of symbolism in which a kind of celestial
anthropogenesis precedes cosmogenesis. In the esoteric wisdom
one usually begins with cosmogenesis and comes down through
anthropogenesis, in order to grasp the successive connections
between the cosmic hierarchies; in the Japanese system, devised
as a convenient mode for disseminating the Teachings while
preserving the significant connections, purely cosmic principles
are represented by personages that are archetypal embodiments
of human principles. Thus, terms are used that apply to the human
constitution, but not specifically to humanity.

> When all was as yet Chaos (*Kon-ton*) three spiritual
> Beings appeared on the stage of future creation: (1) *Ame
> no ani naka nushi no Kami*, 'Divine Monarch of the
> Central Heaven'; (2) *Taka mi onosubi no Kami*, 'Exalted,
> imperial Divine offspring of Heaven and the Earth'; and
> (3) *Kamu mi musubi no Kami*, 'Offspring of the Gods,'
> simply.
> These were without form or substance (our *arupa*
> triad), as neither the celestial nor the terrestrial
> substance had yet differentiated, 'nor had the essence
> of things been formed.'
>
> *Ibid.*, 214

This account may be correlated with a passage from the
Commentary on the *Stanzas of Dzyan*:

> '*The first after the "One" is divine Fire; the second, Fire
> and Aether; the third is composed of Fire, Aether and Water;*

the fourth of Fire, Aether, Water, and Air.' The One is not concerned with Man-bearing globes, but with the inner invisible Spheres. 'The "First-Born" are the LIFE, *the heart and pulse of the Universe; the Second are its* MIND *or Consciousness.'*

Ibid., 216

Combining the two accounts, there is first the divine Flame, the 'One' which is prior to the sequence, from which are lit the three descending groups or hierarchies. Seen cosmically, the first is Atmic or divine fire. The second group is fire and ether, *Atma-Buddhi,* the light of the *Paramatman* diffused throughout the cosmos as its spiritual soul, *Daiviprakriti,* the Light of the unmanifested Logos become in differentiation Fohat or the Seven Sons. From these twofold monadic units emanate the threefold composed of fire, ether and water, correlative with the *Atma-Buddhi-Manas,* fusing the three-in-one into a triad that is capable of connecting itself with a quaternary through incarnation. Succeeding these three is the fourth group comprised of fire, ether, water and air, which provides the invisible grounding of the higher three spiritual principles of the cosmos into a diffused kind of aura that permeates and surrounds the whole globe. All these hierarchies have their analogues within the human being, because they represent a separation between the celestial and the terrestrial, but, as the Japanese understood, they do not give the capacity to link the celestial with the terrestrial. This belongs to the fifth hierarchy. Hence the sacredness of Makara-Capricorn.

There is a mysterious anagrammatic connection between Makara and Kumara, the host of virgin ascetics and *yogins* presided over by Shiva-Saturn. The term 'Makara' itself is a composite of *ma,* meaning 'five', and *kara,* meaning 'hand' or 'side'. Thus, Makaram is the same as Panchakaram, or the pentagon, the five-pointed star linking heaven and earth through the divine proportion. There is a symmetry and logic to the human body, to man standing straight with his arms and legs stretched out, as in Leonardo da Vinci's drawing of the terrestrial man within the universal man. In the present zodiacal system Makara is the tenth sign, connected with the idea of the cosmos as bounded by pentagons, though in the older zodiac Makara was the eighth sign, connected with the eight faces bounding space, a reference to the *lokapalas*. The significance of man as a five-pointed star, a microcosmic reflection of the macrocosm, lies in his capacity to realize his solidarity with the fifth host of Dhyan Chohans, the Kumaras. If, when man stands erect, he is governed by that which enters through the crown of the head from above below, he is a *Manusha*, capable of firm resolve. By raising his spiritual vision, he can at once look heavenward towards the empyrean and enclose the entire cosmos within his creative imagination. At the same time, if he is also full of love for the earth upon which all beings live and move, he can consciously bridge the most celestial with the most terrestrial elements in Nature. It is this profoundly sacrificial privilege that is given to man by the fifth hierarchy, the Kumaras or Agnishwatha Pitris. The esoteric name of this solar host, the endowers of man with self-consciousness, is *Pranidananath*, Lords of Persevering Ceaseless Devotion, a designation which points to the true meaning of the later Greek term *philosophia* or love of wisdom.

Kamadeva, the Vedic Logos, is Atma-Bhu — unborn and self-existent — one with Agni, and also Makara-Ketu — he who bears the emblem of Makara on his banner. The Kumaras, sprung from Kamadeva, preside through Makara over the birth of the spiritual microcosm as well as the dissolution of the physical universe and its passage into the realm of the spiritual. Mysteriously, Mara, the mocking demon of illusion and the god of darkness and death, is yet another name for Kamadeva, the Vedic Logos, and the unconscious quickener of the birth of the spiritual. Rising like a crocodile out of the waters of the sacred river of life to greet the fiery rays of the rising sun, Makara and the host of the Kumaras are the archetype of nascent intelligent humanity and its infinite capacity for perfectibility. The cosmic glyph of Makara is that of the waves, which resembles the letter *M* and is doubled in the sign of Aquarius. Its geometric emblem is the pentagram, the sign of spiritual and physical health in the Pythagorean School, and a symbol of the divine descent and universal solidarity of humanity.

The full significance of the five-pointed star only emerges when it is inscribed within the six-pointed star, but this cannot be understood unless one has first mastered the five. This is the point at which human beings must begin, for humanity is now in the Fifth Sub-Race of the Fifth Root Race of the Fourth Round. Through incarnation and the lessons of karma, one must come to comprehend all that is implicit in five, as well as in five doubled, which yields ten, the perfect number.

> The fifth group of the celestial Beings is supposed to contain in itself the dual attributes of both the spiritual and physical aspects of the Universe; the two poles, so to say, of Mahat the Universal Intelligence, and the dual nature of man, the spiritual and the physical. Hence its number Five, multiplied and made into ten, connecting it with *Makara*, the 10th sign of the Zodiac.
>
> *Ibid.*, 221

If man is seen from this standpoint, as a monadic and Manasic being, a bridge between the cosmic and the sub-human, the enormous importance of self-consciously bridging the two poles naturally follows. Aspiration, idealism and resolve may be fused into fidelity to the best and highest that one knows within oneself. Through this fidelity, the most sacred of all virtues, it is possible to use the *antaskarana* bridge. Only thus can one invite the descent of the Dhyanis, the overbrooding triad within the temple of the human form. It is, therefore, vital to understand both the nature of human individuality and its difference, conceived in relation to the fifth hierarchy, from any sense of individuality connected with the lower hierarchies. On these lower levels, individuality is the characteristic of the entire hierarchy, and not of its individual units, and hence it has nothing to do with identification with particular units, but only with broader planes. At the higher stages of spiritual initiation, the human being necessarily must dispel the sense of a distinct individuality, but first he must entirely transcend the passions of the personality, as well as the illusory identification with name and form. This itself will occupy several lifetimes and is essential before the full awakening of true individuality.

The deep sense of separateness and the seeming cohesiveness in the personality are due to the diffused Fohatic action of differentiated *kama* operating within the *kama rupa*. The cosmic potency acting on the differentiated planes has a dual manifestation as Lakshmi-Kali, its black and white sides. Long before the pristine electro-spiritual Buddhic force of compassion can be released self-consciously, and the higher powers of the soul unlocked, all attachments to form through inverted desire must be transcended. The more progress one makes in this direction, the more one can at first generate a Manasic identity, a sense of 'I-am-I', a sense of being a ray independent of the *rupa*. Then it is possible through meditation to draw oneself towards the Spiritual Sun and to recognize the unity of all the rays that come out of that One Sun, all the living ones, all the streams projected on the cosmic screen of illusion from the absolute life. Thus one strengthens the spiritual fibres of the *karana sharira*, the causal body. This is the task of discipleship, and it demands effort over successive lives.

The highest beings, who transcend individuality, are quite different from the Dhyanis who have no individuality because they function only in terms of the collective. These latter belong, one might say, to a grouping that has a single function. They participate in a kind of higher specialization of cosmic intelligence and they have no separate will. This is not the same as the conscious capacity of the perfected human will to attune itself to that which is the transcendent source of all the Dhyanis. If one truly masters the egotistic desires and delusions of the personality, one can become effortlessly capable of non-separateness in consciousness. By pledging oneself to be a true apprentice on the path of daily meditation, one may develop increased continuity of consciousness, and so establish a noble line of life's meditation. Eventually, one may be able to envisage *Dhyana*, true ceaseless contemplation.

The arduous task of transcending and subduing the personality is a preparation for exercising the supreme prerogative of being human. The immense Logoic potential of human perfection and its virtually unlimited power of benevolence are thus conveyed by H.P. Blavatsky:

> Man being a compound of the essences of all those celestial Hierarchies may succeed in making himself, as such, superior, in one sense, to any hierarchy or class, or even combination of them. 'Man can neither propitiate nor command the *Devas*,' it is said. But, by paralyzing his lower personality, and arriving thereby at the full knowledge of the *non-separateness* of his higher SELF from the One absolute SELF, man can, even during his terrestrial life, become as 'One of Us.' Thus it is, by eating of the fruit of knowledge which dispels ignorance, that man becomes like one of the Elohim or the Dhyanis; and once on *their* plane the Spirit of Solidarity and perfect Harmony, which reigns in every Hierarchy, must extend over him and protect him in every particular.
>
> *Ibid.*, 276

Here the terms 'superior' and 'inferior' are relative to one's perspective.

If by superior one means 'closest to the One', then the highest beings will be the *arupa* forces, the Ah-Hi, the first three descending groups. But if by superior one refers to the capacity of perfected human beings operating in the middle realm to bring down the highest vibration and to infuse it into all beings, then, of course, an entirely different perspective emerges. It is in this sense that the Avatar is far superior to the Mahatma, although he is seemingly incarnated. At the level of non-incarnation, such comparisons can hardly apply. The essential capacity to become an active embodiment of universal divine compassion is the mighty prospect of perfectibility for all immortal souls alike. By the power of meditation and devotion, they can all become coworshippers of the highest in Nature, the highest within their own hearts, and the highest in all beings. Thus they can become able to handle at will all the subcolours of the spectrum through the one light of the Central Spiritual Sun.

Owing to the gift of self-consciousness through the Kumaras, every human being has the potent capacity of sacred speech. Each and every human being may meditate upon the Gayatri, and through the creative potency of sound evoke the spiritual light of the Invisible Sun on behalf of all beings. This means that every human soul can, to some degree, attune itself to what Pythagoras called the music of the spheres. Though totally inaudible to the outer human ear, it is a sound so intense, so profound, that it reverberates constantly through the cosmos. Akashic sound and the primordial light of the Central Spiritual Sun are a primordial vibration reflected in the AUM, and also mirrored in *bhur, bhuvah* and *svah*, the three worlds invoked at the beginning of the Gayatri. Ultimately, that light is *Daiviprakriti*, awakened within *Hiranya-garbha* by the first ray of the Divine Darkness in the precosmic dawn. It is this light, quickening the fiery ethereal waters of space, which is greeted by the Kumaras as the light of their true selves.

> 'When the ONE becomes two, the three-fold appears': to wit, when the One Eternal drops its reflection into the region of Manifestation, that reflection, 'the Ray,' differentiates the 'Water of Space'; . . . 'Chaos ceases, through the effulgence of the Ray of Primordial light dissipating total darkness by the help of the great magic power of the WORD of the (Central) Sun.' . . . issuing from the DEEP, . . . the divine Universal Soul in its manifested aspect . . . Narayana, the Purusha, *'concealed in Akasa and present in Ether.'*
>
> *Ibid.*, 231

There is, then, a mysterious sound, neither the AUM nor the sounds in the Gayatri, which is the Verbum, the Word of the Central Spiritual Sun dissipating the primordial darkness.

Perfected human beings can thus live, move and breathe in and through *Akasha*. These are the true Men of Meditation, self-governed Sages constantly attuned to the vibration of the One Flame. By ceaselessly negating all mayavic manifestation, they affirm its true meaning going back to the precosmic and primordial darkness that is prior to the dawn of manifestation, and even precedes the distinction of Being and Non-Being. Having gone back to that state of undifferentiated oneness, they can penetrate the world of manifestation without illusion. They can bear witness to the hidden essences and meanings, the hidden possibilities and promises, concealed within *Akasha* and partially present in ether.

Exemplifying the sacred existential connection between "Who am I?" and *"THAT thou art,"* they serve as the antaskaranic bridge which, when crossed, makes of man a god, "creating him a Bodhisattva, son of the Dhyanis." Masters of all the living elements from the *Atman* to the physical form, they are the bearers of the immutable, indestructible and deathless vibration of Eternal Life that is even present within the great Night of non-manifestation. The heart of universal self-conscious intelligence, the Brotherhood of Bodhisattvas ever remain the invisible allies of every human being aspiring through sacrifice and renunciation to the effective service of the whole of humanity.

> *Where is thy individuality, Lanoo, where the Lanoo himself? It is the spark lost in the fire, the drop within the ocean, the ever-present ray become the All and the eternal radiance.*
>
> *And now, Lanoo, thou art the doer and the witness, the radiator and the radiation, Light in the Sound, and the Sound in the Light.*
>
> The Voice of the Silence

GODS, MONADS AND ATOMS

In the realm of the Esoteric sciences the unit divided
ad infinitum, *instead of losing its unity, approaches with*
every division the planes of the only eternal REALITY. The
eye of the SEER can follow and behold it in all its pregenetic
glory.

H.P. BLAVATSKY

The student of *The Secret Doctrine* senses the vast depths of meaning and possibility intimated in the sacred teaching concerning gods, monads and atoms. Very few begin to connect, however tentatively, the apprehension they may have of themselves, as finite human beings, with the divine dimensions of the immortal monad. What is needed, if one is to discover the immense storehouse of wisdom and beneficent compassion that is the substratum of Nature and the inheritance of every human being, is a comprehensible point of convergence between our mortal lives and our divine natures. Here we may be helped by *The Voice of the Silence*, which refers to three halls in which every human being lives and through which he moves and passes, in the passage of day into night and back into day. Through this regular recapitulation in miniature of the greater revolutions of the soul, we may begin to discern the deeper mystery of the monad that extends far beyond the limits of the temporal world.

Let us start with the waking world. According to *The Voice of the Silence*, it is the hall of *avidya*, ignorance in a pristine, philosophical sense. It is the hall in which shadows flit through existence, living in a state of psychic tension. Reacting to external stimuli, they interact not in a creative, self-conscious and cooperative manner but rather as bundles of emotion interacting with other bundles of emotion. The vast, terrible vortex swells until any person caught up in it is held captive to a very limited sense of reality. He either tries to impose his illusions upon someone else (which is impossible to the extent to which the other person has a modicum of self-respect) or dramatizes and exaggerates to the utmost limit the minimum core of truth hidden within the ever growing balloon of his own fantasy existence. Hardly any authentic communication takes place, let alone any true communion between human beings in the so-called waking world.

In the *Bhagavad Gita* Krishna declared that what men call day is seen by the sage as the night of ignorance. As Buddha taught, human beings are asleep, daydreaming or half-awake. They are not alive in the sense in which only those who have a continuous conscious existence in spirit are alive. They are not alive as light-beings, who in the silent sanctuary of their own inmost consciousness are aware of their own living link with the invisible Spiritual Sun, the source of all light and life. They populate a world in which men are caught up in the realities of other men, but which are no more than shared illusions.

If one looked at the waking world only in this way, there would be something wrong. The waking world is not merely a collective projection from the subjective imaginations of human beings. We know that the waking world is also the arena in which we find seeds becoming plants and trees bearing flowers. It is the realm of rhythmic manifestation in visible Nature, in which the falling leaves of autumn have a fragrance, flavour and beauty of their own. Even in the depths of the winter snow there is some affirmation of the unity that is reflected from above below. Every seed, every tree, every plant, indeed every living thing and being bears some sort of witness to a noumenal reality. Clearly, we cannot view this world solely from the standpoint of the mental illusion of half-awake men.

It is also a world of whirling atoms, atoms which swirl in and around men, with a complexity of seemingly conflicting and chaotic movement. To the mind of the discerning seer, to the awakened senses of the man who is at peace within himself and open to the great mind and heart of Nature, this dance of atoms is a song, a majestic and magnificent symphony. There is an ordered relationship between the past, the present and the future through a process of movement that parallels an archetypal logic hidden behind the sensory screen. The waking world — the hall of ignorance, a tower of Babel for limited human minds — when seen in terms of the great mind of Nature is a world of manifested wisdom. It is a world of objective reality which is beautiful because it intimates a deeper reality that is hidden. Nature in this sense, to the eye of the silent seer, is like the goddess Isis, unveiling partly the mystery of creation. The sacrificial compassion that is in the very depths of her bosom will ever remain hidden and cannot be understood except by becoming one with it, like the child that is a foetus within the womb of the mother. Atoms interact in a colligious way when human minds, like automata, become the purveyors and the conveyors of colliding atoms. But in Nature as a whole, atoms move in a very different way. In this we may find a pointer to the fact that humanity is growing up, even in the most adolescent parts of the world (those enamoured of the gadgetry and glitter of material goals and technological splendour). Humanity is growing up because men and women are coming to see that there is a poignant contrast between what Nature, though misused, still teaches in terms of symmetry, opulence and generosity, and the stingy littleness and limitations of the structures created by ignorant human beings.

The second hall is the hall of learning, in which there are beautiful flowers, although under every flower a serpent is coiled. It is the psychical realm. People enter it when they take drugs. Some enter it without any adventitious aids just because they are psychically sensitive, mentally passive, or given to protracted day-dreaming. It is also a state of consciousness into which all men enter during sleep, when the brain of the physical body is less active and more rested. It is possible, at that time, for the astral realm to become more real to embodied consciousness as it withdraws from the sensorium and the cerebrum. This is a state in which one sees sights and sounds or titillating visions. It is a realm of colours.

All these colours vary according to the subjective feeling-state of the perceiver. What is terrifying to one could be beautiful to another. It is comparable to the domain of aesthetics, where there is something incommunicable and irreducibly unique about each person's appreciation of particular music or particular colours. No two human beings can honestly have the same authentic responses in reference to sounds or colours. This realm is treacherous because unless there are criteria, unless as an individuating, thinking being one is able to sift and select, weigh, accept and give meaning to images and events, one is lost. One is liable to be misled. At its highest level great mystics enter into trance states that are extremely beautiful, and yet, when they come out of those states they can mistranslate. They have been through something real, but when they make claims or when they attempt descriptions, they are liable to an understandable falsification, a natural exaggeration, or at best an inability to convey deeper truths that are impersonal and universifiable, usable by varieties of men in varieties of conditions.

To understand this in terms of monads, one might say that all monads are reflecting mirrors. It is possible for every monad to reflect only partially because every monad is involved in a modification of cognition, like a lens that is linked up with an aperture which is a limitation upon it. This could be misleading, because in metaphysical space in every atom and within the mind of every man there is the capacity to release the true monadic reflection which is a diamond light, many-faceted and symmetrical. But that is only possible in the context of a larger vision, a wider perspective in which one is aware of that which does not enter into any perspective or into any conditioned awareness in the mind. This is very difficult to comprehend in ordinary terms. It is as though there is a constant, if muffled, awareness of that which is behind and beyond manifestation. Because of that awareness there is a capacity to control perception in relation to limited perspectives, cognition in relation to limited conditions. One can handle secondary causes, truncated periods of time, spatially limited planes of differentiated matter or phenomenal causation.

To put this in another way, a person could look back to ten years ago and find out what are the connections he could make between his achievements and faults as a thinking human being, between his insights and his hangups of ten years ago, and then connect them with effects apparent today. Another man may not be able to do this over ten years but only over the last year. A truly wise man will be able to connect not only in relation to that which was incipient at the beginning but also, paradoxically, in relation to what came before it. That implies he will also be able to read so much meaning in one day, in one hour, and make so many connections, that for him each moment could become a mirror of eternity. In one hour he could read the vaster life-stories of men. This is possible because all atoms have an indwelling essence which is unmodified and unconditioned, which partakes of the limitless light of the one source of the whole of manifestation.

The second hall, the psychic realm, is a burden and a drag upon human beings, and especially for those who attempt to force or steal their way into it by drugs — a terrible tragedy. On the other hand, a wise being could go through those states at will, see under every flower a serpent coiled, and not be captive to anything in it. This is because monads vary in their capacity to reflect, in what Leibniz called their apperceptive function.

The third hall is the hall of wisdom, for human monads the most important. If a person is earnestly concerned to do something about his whole life, to become self-consciously engaged in self-transformation, to seek and to use divine wisdom, he is requesting during waking life whatever will help him to bring back from deep sleep that which is buried somewhere within him and which he truly knows. There is a realm of unfading light where there are no shadows. It is like standing directly under the sun and casting no shadow. To stand directly under the noonday sun in all its blazing glory is difficult. Standing directly under it, looking straight ahead, one cannot see it. One has to sense it with the mind's eye.

This is a supernal realm where one is no longer captive to

those externalities of the waking world which involve interactions of atoms and all those relationships which arise when monads are brought together. It is the kingdom of the gods. It is the sphere of pure, divine, direct perception where there is no separation between the knower, the known and the process of knowing. This might be put in terms of a luminous pyramid. A human being can acquire a balance between what he knows, the process of knowing and, above all, his own sense of awareness of himself as a knower. Yet he is growing and always reaching in each of these three areas towards that which is beyond — beyond the known, beyond himself as a knower, and beyond all conceivable processes of knowing. Long before he can enter into and become one with that mathematical point at the radiant apex of the pyramid, he can learn to look towards it and stand within the triad. When he can do this self-consciously, then for him that blissful state of deep sleep is also an illusion. He has to go beyond it. To enjoy the riches of that state is a response that is very soothing for the limited human being. Immortal individuals, however, who transcend all states of consciousness conditioned by polarities, can at will live always in *turiya*, the state of total wakefulness of the gods.

In one sense the theosophical view of 'gods' refers to those myriads of fine points of radiant matter which represent the ethereal side of nature that has not yet become human. They are often personified in the old myths as sylphs, salamanders and undines, fairies, gods and goddesses. But the principal theosophical use of the term 'god' is that a god is a fully self-conscious being, one who has effortlessly intelligent control over all the centres of his being. He is completely awake, secure in self-enlightenment. This implies that he can apprehend the relativities of all reality. He can freely enter into the world of a child. He can understand the illusion of an unhappy man obsessed with wealth or fame or power. He is capable of sharing the illusion of someone who confounds hectic physical activity with love. He is able to empathize with the victims of all kinds of illusions whilst none of these has any hold over him. He sees to the core of that causal point around which false forms and intricate illusions gather. He has mastered the art of living among, and entering into relations with, many monads with limited perspectives and feeling utterly one with those engrossed in their own limited realities. He can assist them through his awareness of that which is beyond, serving as a spiritual parent-teacher who can arouse in them the longings of the heart, the aspirations of the soul, the hopes of the mind for a fuller sense of reality, a larger life.

Such a god-man inhabits the hall of wisdom, the universal field of ideation underlying the great storehouse which could be seen either collectively or distributively. Collectively, it is like a luminous and boundless ether or pure *akasha*. On the one hand, we have the whole of the astral light, sometimes called "Nature's infinite negative", on which everything is recorded and reflected but in reverse. Corresponding to this there is at the upper pole of manifestation a cosmic, fiery, single substance or primal principle, which underlies all states and substances. There is a pure imprinting upon a cosmic cerebellum or upon the memory bank of a cosmic computer, to use an initial but misleading analogy. One could see this storehouse as everywhere and nowhere. For example, we might say of a great musician that when he composes there is no place in particular from which he is drawing inspiration. Or it is everywhere. Or it could be anywhere. It is anywhere for each great musician in each particular mood. In some way, any point is part of that boundless plane. Every human being has potential access to the universal plane of cosmic ideation upon which are recorded all archetypal realities, and hence the statement of *Ecclesiastes*, "There is nothing new under the sun." There is nothing new for one who truly stands under the sun.

Distributively, we know that all men and women are not equally able to retain continually in consciousness an awareness of what is important. They forget, they falter, and they sink. After a point they are like wounded soldiers with battered minds, bruised hearts, and actual abscesses, so that even their capacity to receive is distorted. They are like broken-down wireless sets — not clean, but rusted — in which the battery is almost dead. This is a pitiful state. There could only be hope for every human being if there is somewhere within his own nature, in the very depths of his consciousness, that which corresponds to the cosmic storehouse. This can be discovered by each one only through making divine wisdom a living power in his life, because it concerns that which is unspeakable — unspeakably sacred. There is in every man that sovereign touchstone by which he can read the eternal tablets. But before he is ready to do this he must be willing to go through a process of preliminary separation, a purgation of matter, a purification of mind.

We are told in the *Chaldean Book of Numbers* that the Blessed Ones have naught to do with the purgations of gross matter. In their terrestrial forms they may participate in all the cycles of growth that have to do with the body. They know when the centres of light in the body need help from the hierarchies of Nature. They are quite willing to take from Nature and give it as food to the body. They know how to take care of the instrument though they have no sense of identity in that instrument. They do not self-consciously participate in the purgations of matter. When individuals reach that point in consciousness, they become beings who are living continually in a state of self-conscious ideation on universal and transcending themes, any one of which can be crystallized around one seed idea on which each day could be made to revolve. Such a person can contact the crystalline purity of *Akasa* through any one of the many crystals that are available and knows that there are abundant, plentiful seed ideas in great books or even in the stutterings of a child. He can see the germ in the embryo of a hidden crystal. He is able, out of his own self-conscious development of his god-like plastic potency (that of creative imagination), to enter consciously into that pristine relation with points of contact everywhere in matter and in other minds, which enables him to tap at will any atom.

The great seer constantly discerns scintillating atoms and cascading sparks. For him the universe is gloriously alive and ineffably beautiful. He can also see with compassion the lengthening shadows that arise out of the whiners, the moaners, the complainers and the self-hating murderers of the sacred gift of human speech. He can see it all in perspective because he has become a self-conscious embodiment of that which is beyond colour, beyond form, beyond limitations. He has come to bestride the bird of life. He has become the soundless sound, and hence can make himself responsive, amidst the cacophony of the earth, to the music of the spheres. This is the very grand prospect that the universe holds for us. Any and every man, as a fallen god, could recover his divine estate, but he could not do it by phoniness or by limiting through his own constricted awareness those at whose feet he must silently sit and learn — the Great Masters of Wisdom and Compassion. Ever present on earth, they constitute a sacred current which cyclically under law at certain moments, when the need and the pain of mankind is acute, descends from their own midst and lights up minds that are ready to be lit up.

To engage in the preliminary purification necessary for entering into the universal storehouse requires immense discrimination, for what is true of human consciousness is true of the whole library of Nature. Both the exalted and corrupt are impressed there as living atomic and elemental vibrations. Hence, in the old days, cultures like the Brahminical or the Jewish, out of their own vestiges of forgotten wisdom, set up rules concerning how to bathe, how to eat, what to touch, rules in relation to minimizing contamination and minimizing pollution in human contact. Anyone who reveres his physical body as a temple of which he is the trustee, and which is the temple of a living god, is going to regard his body as deeply sacred and precious. Every contact, every emanation outgoing and ingoing that he is involved with will be examined in every context, in every kind of situation. Real men who have attained this stage of total responsibility are so compassionate, so free from any form of selfishness, subtle pride or snobbery, that they can use the science of sacred knowledge as a healing art, consciously receiving negative vibrations and sending them back purified with a powerfully beneficent impulse. This is why they cannot be imitated. Initiators provide deep wisdom and lesser men make rules, trying through imitation of the initiators to cut losses. It works up to a point, but a time comes when it works no longer.

Self-conscious human beings have deliberately to provide for themselves their own means, not merely of protection, but even more of beneficent reaching out to others and warding off, without any ill will towards the source of pollution, all those influences that are unwholesome. This requires a high degree of self-knowledge. Perhaps the simplest way in which any person could begin is to start with the idea of self-magnetization. He should do this not merely out of the limited sense of privacy that he attaches to his own house or his own bedroom, because that simply reinforces the illusion that somehow he is cut off. He may be in his bedroom and be much closer to *kama loka* and the astral light than if he were sitting in Place Pigalle in Paris. It depends on the quality and the stance of one's accumulated past thoughts. This is why the merely physical could be misleading. But if we sincerely reflected upon and sedulously practised self-magnetization, we would find that there is not a human being — and here we can learn from children — who could not truly regard his vestures as precious.

Children manage to make the most of those things which they invest with love and affection. A teddy bear could become a protecting Buddha for a loving child who knows how to treat that teddy bear. Grownups lose their living link with a kind of magical knowledge from the past. A very interesting couple, Peter Opie and his wife, wrote a fascinating book on the games that school children play. They found that all over the world little children play certain games that they do not learn from the dominant thought-forms of their particular culture, but which games are archetypal, like throwbacks to earlier times — reminders and re-enactments of forgotten rituals from the past. The universe of fairy tales, folklore and myth is a universe of recapitulation, especially at that level of innocence which we associate with children.

All over Nature there are many iridescent points of contact with the all-potent compassion of the Dhyanis — cosmic forces, light-beings, energy-giving *arupa* radiations directed by spiritual will. We have, for example, the suggestive story of that great Initiate, Rama, who, when he passed through a forest, happened to see a squirrel. He merely placed three fingers upon the squirrel and the squirrels in that part of the world forever after had three markings. The whole of Nature represents the immense magnificence of the ideation and compassion of beings who are so much more powerful than all those sad and drunken souls that may have impressed matter with negative thought. There is deep meaning to the teaching that a little bit of theurgy is a dangerous thing because it makes you afraid, but that more of it makes you fearless. When you have enough of it, you come to see that the universe is good; that in this universe the energies of life are stronger than the engines of death, that the potencies of light are greater than the terrors of the shade. You come to see, above all, that truth prevails ever and always and that at every point in each atom there is an imprint of truth. Therefore every person can recapitulate in his inmost being, through his contact with any point of matter, that truth which is a pure mirror of the universal truth in the universal mind, and which is in the universal substance from which all the many differentiations of thought, substance and form are emanated.

This union of the human monad with divine ideation in the womb of universal substance is ultimately connected with the mystery of the sacred Tetraktis, which no man could ever solve until he becomes one with the object of his search, until he re-becomes a god. The highest spiritual knowledge is always the most elusive. At the same time a person must begin at some point, as does every triangle. There is a deep sense in which every point in space-time has some affinity with one central point and must emanate from that *laya* point in any one *mahamanvantara* or great period of manifestation. Therefore, the Pythagorean *Monas* signified the One — the One that went into the darkness after inaugurating a world. It retreated and withdrew in silence and secrecy, disappearing into the darkness. The Leibnizian monads, by contrast, are those minute indivisible, mathematical points in metaphysical space which are in abundance and which could be compared, by philosophical intuition, to mirrors. But what is philosophical intuition to a noble mind is realized self-knowledge to a sage. He actually knows that these are living mirrors. The issue then is one of the living and the dead. Leibniz spoke of the *entelechy*, the indwelling light principle within every one of these monads, a core point that is hidden and invisible, which could release tremendous energy. Since *The Secret Doctrine* was written, we have learned more of this, at great cost to humanity, in the splitting of the atom. Since then, fortunately, while men have been enormously curious to know more and go beyond the hydrogen atom, they find that the door is shut. So it will be, and just as well, because men may dangerously misuse this sacred knowledge.

There is a profound sense in which we have to assert at each point, "Let me start with the simplest use that I can make of this teaching for the sake of becoming a better human being. This means being a better son or daughter, a better father or mother, a better husband or wife, a better householder, a better neighbour, a better servant of my fellowmen." This sounds difficult — it is perhaps asking too much of this materialistic culture at this point of time, but it is only asking for the ABC's. If a man does not begin right where he is and in his primary arenas of obligation and relationship, he will never really be able to embody the starting point of the triangle that he must form. Every time he makes a beginning, every time he establishes a point, very soon two other points arise. In human consciousness they are like a pair of opposites: the manic and the depressive, pleasure and pain, fame and ignominy, loss and gain. The mind oscillates towards polarities in every kind of context, condition and situation. What is misleading about this divisive polarity of the duad, seen from the standpoint of separation and integration, is that when one is caught in it one thinks that there is no way out. In fact, there always is. There is always one because there is a tomorrow. There is always one because even the greatest gloom cannot last forever. Men discover, like Ivan Denisovich in prison, that out of extreme pain they can release insights simply through noticing that there are other human beings in prison, that one can treat a prison like a university, that one can learn from all the potential teachers who are lying in chains around the prison.

Initially one learns for the sake of establishing one's own sense of dignity against other men, but that kind of learning stops very soon. Otherwise, we fall into the state of many men whose learning is short-circuited and confines them forever in those kinds of judgments which in the end say more about them than the world. They fear the infallible judgment of the law which at the moment of death they will recognize. But when men continue to learn, they come to enjoy learning. They learn what is good. They are on the side of every other man, and when they are, they reap an incredible harvest. They find that all limiting systems of learning are nothing in relation to the much greater storehouse of Nature, the endless labyrinth of instruction wherein each instruction radiates with crystalline clarity in an unending series that is part of the School of Life. To be able to do this we have to get out of the confinement of the duad, which has to do with the line and its movement. But in fact, unless there is only going to be one triangle, the line, though finite, is not final. It is not merely the base of a specific triangle. That line, while it is superior to drawing two parallel lines at the two points, must itself in turn be the beginning of further growth and new movement.

Gupta Vidya, as the source and synthesis of science, religion and philosophy, is able to bring together the gods of religion, the monads of philosophy and the atoms of science. It connects them through that archetypal philosophical logic and geometrical theogony which contains the clue to growth throughout the whole of life and which a person could use for growth within himself, using his own growing intuition and insight into the *Sutratman* — the golden thread — of the Wisdom-Religion to find out the golden thread in himself. The most important teaching in relation to all of this is continuity. Leibniz knew this at one philosophical level. He wanted to stress the continuity of Nature. In religion, a discontinuity emerged between gods and men, and therefore religions became the opposite of what they were originally intended to be. They were meant to affirm the unity and continuity of all life, and the continuity of sages, seers, prophets and divine teachers with every single living human being, not at one point of time in a particularized revelation but in an endless revelation, a ceaseless contact, a continual fellowship with all that lives and breathes.

Continuity in the realm of atoms would be more enigmatic to discover because a person, by maintaining continuity of consciousness, has to become a self-conscious transmuter of atoms who regroups and rearranges them in superior patterns. When he does, then he can truly renovate his own vestures. He can at will enter into relationship with anything and everything in Nature. He can do that because he stands outside, detached from and uninvolved in the great stream of ever becoming. He has become a man of meditation. He has become one who is untouched by troubles, one who is free from lesser allegiances and detached in the very depths of his being and consciousness. He has become the One — the One that is not merely behind but beyond the many, and is forever hidden.

We will never understand the mystery of the sacred Tetraktys until we can first draw an imaginary but deep line in the brain between the Ever Incognizable and the One manifested which is also hidden. Unless we can form this metaphysical line in the very depths of consciousness, between the noumenal and the manifested, we will not be able to understand the triangle as a diagram, much less as a moving image, a dynamic instrument for deliberate self-transformation, for taking control over mod- ifications and differentiations. Eventually it can become a basis for emanating in every direction into a boundless universe, infinite streams of scintilla — scintillating thought-forms and scintillating points of light-energy — so that one becomes both free and at the same time supremely self-conscious. One is free from all limitations and ties but is a voluntary and self-conscious servant of the great wheel of the law (Dharma), so that one tries to give a turning to the wheel, to remain useful in the great movement of the wheel by moving to its central point. One does not feel the motion of the wheel because at the centre of the great wheel of conditioned existence there is changelessness. With a motionless mind, with a heart so soaked in the ocean of compassion that it does not feel the ripples and waves, it is possible for a man to become one with the All and then relate to those whom he can help in their own pilgrimage. He can point beyond them and beyond himself to that towards which all human beings must eventually go. Where they self-consciously move in that direction like sore-footed but determined pilgrims, he becomes for them, and they become for yet others, pathfinders and forerunners, heralds of a world unborn, yet to come, but already here for those who have created it.

MIRRORING THE MACROCOSM

In the first place revere the Immortal Gods as they are established and ordained by the Law.

Reverence the Oath. In the next place revere the Heroes who are full of goodness and light.

Honour likewise the Terrestrial Daimons by rendering them the worship lawfully due to them.

Honour likewise thy father and thy mother, and thy nearest relations.

Of all the rest of mankind, make him thy friend who distinguishes himself by his virtue. Always give ear to his mild exhortations, and take example from his virtuous and useful actions. Refrain, as far as you can, from spurning thy friend for a slight fault, for power surrounds necessity. . . .

Never set thy hand to the work, till thou hast first prayed the Gods to accomplish what thou art going to begin.

When thou hast made this habit familiar to thee, thou wilt know the constitution of the Immortal Gods and of men; even how far the different Beings extend, and what contains and binds them together.

Thou shalt likewise know, in accord with Cosmic Order, that the nature of this Universe is in all things alike, so that thou shalt not hope what thou oughtest not to hope; and nothing in this world shall be hid from thee.

The Golden Verses of Pythagoras

S panning the centuries and continents, from the myths of hoary antiquity to the cogitations of modern man, certain primeval ideas and intuitions may be dimly discerned. These underlie the views held among different civilizations regarding hierarchies of beings and levels of evolution, the laws of nature and the central harmony of the cosmos, and human obligations which are rooted in a recognition of moral responsibility and are realized in a variety of relationships. There have been numerous theories concerning the citizen's political and social obligations; there have been innumerable formulations of the norms of individual excellence and collective progress. These provide the philosophical and ethical foundations of culture and society. In our century man has to re-learn the ancient, archetypal truth that he is a microcosm, a world in himself, the mirror of an invisible universe that is around and beyond him.

An educated person who does not recognize the value of reverence for Nature, for Nature's laws and for one's fellow men, cannot be regarded as a cultured individual. Intuitive thinkers of our time, like Dr. Albert Schweitzer, have realized that the collapse of civilizations came about in the past when men and women had lost their reverence for life, their sense of joy in adventure, their spirit of wonder and humility.

> Reverence for life which I apply to my own existence, and reverence for life which keeps me in a temper of devotion to other existence than mine, interpenetrate each other.

The nature of this interpenetration cannot be fully grasped unless we regard man, as did Pythagoras and Pico della Mirandola, as "the measure of all things". Man is the centre of a series of concentric circles, of little worlds extending from the 'here and now' to the infinite expanse of Space and Time. Man is a microcosm in many senses and in different dimensions of his complete individuality. His family is a small macrocosm, the range and heritage and hereditary character of which he reflects in his own being. Each day in his life is like a miniature aeon during which he emanates and absorbs fresh currents of thought and energy. As a citizen, man reproduces the attitudes and characteristics of his neighbourhood, his locality, his village or city, his province and his country. As a member of present-day humanity and of the contemporary world, man embodies the trends and forces that constitute the matrix of this great macrocosm. Man's life in a particular personality reveals the spirit of the age to which he belongs.

This manifold microcosmic nature of man gives rise to the complex of interactions between local and global, ephemeral and enduring cultures. A truly and fully cultured man is able to absorb the beneficial currents that flow from all directions and at all times; he perceives the beauty of the great macrocosm within the boundaries of the small; he enjoys the grandeur of lasting realities amidst the flux of fleeting illusions and shadows. He takes the whole universe for his province, regards the world as a city, considers humanity as his family. Like Goethe's Faust, he apostrophizes the passing moment: "Stay! How wonderful thou art!" In appreciating art, music and literature he compares the unfamiliar with the familiar and proceeds from the known to the unknown, showing an awareness, however slight, of the patterns and rhythms of Nature, the cosmic dance of the elements, the changing positions of the stars, the strange music of the spheres, the mighty magic of *prakriti* (matter). Recognizing that in every speck in space and in every form of matter is to be found the motion of invisible intelligences, of *devas* (gods) and *devatas* (Nature spirits), he pays honour first to the Immortal Gods of whom Pythagoras spoke, of whom Plotinus wrote in his fifth *Ennead*:

> For them all things are transparent, and there is nothing dark or impenetrable, but everyone is manifest to everyone internally, and all things are manifest; for light is manifest to light. For everyone has all things in himself and sees all things in another; so that all things are everywhere and all is all and each is all, and the glory is infinite. Each of them is great, since the small also is great. In heaven the sun is all the stars, and again each and all are the sun. One thing in each is prominent above the rest; for it also shows forth all. There a pure movement reigns; but that which produces the movement, not being a stranger to it, does not trouble it. Rest is also perfect there, because no principle of agitation mingles with it.

Reverencing those cosmic intelligences which we call Gods of Wisdom, we are able to see the Order that "hath established Their Choirs". We can attempt to mirror on earth that Divine Harmony or *Rta* and its action or Karma by reordering our social institutions in terms of Dharma, the Law of Duty, the Religion of Works, and *Swaraj*, the Rule of the One Self. In the memorable words of the sixth Book of *The Republic* of Plato:

> . . . are not those who are verily and indeed wanting in the knowledge of the true being of each thing, and who have in their souls no clear pattern, and are unable as with a painter's eye to look at the absolute truth and to that original to repair, and having perfect vision of the other world to order the laws about beauty, goodness, justice in this, if not already ordered, and to guard and preserve the order of them — are not such persons, I ask, simply blind?
>
> For he, Adeimantus, whose mind is fixed upon true being, has surely no time to look down upon the affairs of earth, or to be filled with malice and envy, contending against men; his eye is ever directed towards things fixed and immutable, which he 'sees neither injuring nor injured by one another, but all in order moving according to reason; these he imitates, and to these he will, as far as he can, conform himself. Can a man help imitating that with which he holds reverential converse?

This is a magnificent ideal, difficult to conceive, apparently impossible to achieve. In continuing to strive to draw nearer to this glorious goal, we are inspired by those "Heroes full of goodness and light" and the "Terrestrial Daimons" to whom, according to Pythagoras, we must pay "the worship lawfully due to them". Every person should endeavour to enter into inmost communion with the hero-souls of all lands and eras who still live, especially in their own immortal works. As Plutarch says, in his life of Aratus:

But surely a man in whom, to use Pindar's words, 'the noble spirit naturally displays itself as inherited from sires', and who, like those, patterns his life after the fairest examples in his family line — for such men it will be good fortune to be reminded of their noblest pro-genitors, ever and anon hearing the story of them, or telling it themselves. For it is not that they lack noble qualities of their own and make their reputation dependent on their praises of others, nay rather, they associate their own careers with the careers of their great ancestors, whom they hail both as founders of their line and as directors of their lives . . . For it is the lover of himself, and not the lover of goodness, who thinks himself always superior to others.

It is necessary to celebrate not only the lives of the "Heroes full of goodness and light" but also the thoughts and writings of the "Terrestrial Daimons" of our age and of the past. Plutarch wrote both the *Lives* and the *Morals*, the former setting forth to us, from an ideal point of view, what the ancient world had accomplished in the world of action, and the other, in like manner, what it had aimed at and accomplished in the world of thought. Even in the *Lives*, Plutarch is far more the moralist than the historian. A study of the archetypal ideas underlying human culture and the offering of homage to gods, adepts and geniuses are not ends in themselves but ways in which we can make of ourselves men and women of culture, of enlightenment and grace. Self-culture is in itself not the final goal, but only the means by which we can become the servants and custodians of the ideals that inspire and sustain the whole world.

Pythagoras offered the distilled wisdom of the ancients when he said:

Above all things, respect thyself.
Never do anything which thou dost not understand; but learn all thou oughtest to know, and by that means thou wilt lead a very pleasant life.

> Examine all things well, leaving thyself always to
> be guided and directed by the understanding that comes
> from above, and that ought to hold the reins.

Integrity, uprightness and self-respect — these are the very roots of real culture. Intelligent, deliberative action and an awareness of the norms of goodness and beauty (of what the Greeks called *arete*) — these constitute the fragrance or aroma of culture, the "sweetness and light" of which Matthew Arnold wrote. The joy of silent contemplation and the repose of a lofty, well-controlled mind — these are the fruits of culture, the harvest of prolonged cultivation. Cultural development, whether individual or collective, is a continuing process, a creative activity, an exciting pursuit. As Plotinus counsels in his very first *Ennead*:

> Withdraw into yourself and look. And if you do not find yourself beautiful as yet, do as does the creator of a statue that is to be made beautiful; he cuts away here, he smooths there, he makes this line lighter, this other purer, until he has shown a beautiful face upon his statue. So do you also cut away all that is excessive, straighten all that is crooked, bring light to all that is shadowed, labour to make all glow with beauty; and do not cease chiselling your statue until there shall shine out on you the godlike splendour of virtue, until you shall see the final goodness surely established in the stainless shrine.

Great and enduring changes in the world in which we live cannot come through the efforts of partisan politicians unless they are inspired and directed by the wider vision of seers, poets and artists. The concept and goal of a united world community have been foreshadowed by a long line of creative writers, especially poets, from the earliest eras. In our own epoch, several leading writers have shown a lively sense of their social responsibilities. In his fine Presidential Address in 1953 to the Amsterdam Congress of the International P.E.N., Charles Morgan appealed to the writers assembled

> not to take peace for granted but to live each hour of it fully and without fear. Above all let us not allow the name of peace to be taken in vain and perverted to the uses of terror. If its sands are running out, so are the sands of our lives. That is not a reason to allow our faith to disintegrate or our pens to tremble in our hands.

Admittedly, writers, like sensitive seismographs, are peculiarly responsive to the prevalent horrors and imminent terrors of our time. But the very immensity of the dangers that loom before us and the time ahead, according to Charles Morgan, should be "a means of grace":

> It deprives materialism of its profit and tyranny of its power. It is a reason to love and to be at peace. It is an amnesty to all the imprisonments of the mind; it empties out all the philosophies of disintegration.

It would be a betrayal of their mission if writers refused to rise above the unprecedented predicament of humanity and provide creative stimulus and spiritual sustenance to the untapped moral and mental potentials of a world in search for global solidarity. Lewis Mumford sensed the magnitude of this new imperative in his *In the Name of Sanity*. In his chapter entitled "Mirrors of Violence", he declared:

> If our civilization is not to produce greater holocausts, our writers will have to become something more than merely mirrors of its violence and dis-integration; they, through their own efforts, will have to regain the initiative for the human person and the forces of life, chaining up the demons we have allowed to run loose, and releasing the angels and ministers of grace we have shamefacedly — and shamefully —

incarcerated. For the writer is still a maker, a creator, not merely a recorder of fact, but above all an interpreter of possibilities. His intuitions of the future may still give body to a better world and help start our civilization on a fresh cycle of adventure and effort. The writer of our time must find within himself the wholeness that is now lacking in his society. He must be capable of interpreting life in all its dimensions, particularly in the dimensions the last century has neglected; restoring reason to the irrational, purpose to the defeatists and drifters, value to the nihilists, hope to those sinking in despair.

Inquire of the earth, the air, and the water, of the secrets they hold for you. The development of your inner senses will enable you to do this.

Inquire of the holy ones of the earth of the secrets they hold for you. The conquering of the desires of the outer senses will give you the right to do this.

Inquire of the inmost, the one, of its final secret which it holds for you through the ages.

Light on the Path

SPIRITUAL PROGENITORS

'The Kumaras,' explains an esoteric text, 'are the Dhyanis, derived immediately from the supreme Principle, who reappear in the Vaivasvata Manu period, for the progress of mankind.' . . . In the esoteric teaching, they are the progenitors of the true spiritual SELF in the physical man — the higher Prajapati, while the Pitris, or lower Prajapati, are no more than the fathers of the model, or type of his physical form, made 'in their image.'

. . . Sanat-Sujata, — the chief of the Kumaras — is called Ambhamsi, 'Waters,' — according to the commentary on Vishnu Purana. Why? Because the 'Waters' is another name of the 'Great Deep,' the primordial Waters of Space or Chaos, and also means 'Mother,' Amba, meaning Aditi and Akasa, the Celestial Virgin-Mother of the visible universe.

The Secret Doctrine, i 456-60

Aditi-Vach, the goddess of speech, sound and wisdom, and the Dhyanic Host of the Kumaras, born directly from the night of non-manifestation, are closely connected. Aditi is primordial Chaos, equivalent to *Mulaprakriti*, pre-cosmic root substance and the mystic mother of all the manifested gods. The Kumaras, variously the eldest mind-born sons of Brahmā and the offspring of Shiva, are the Logoic host of the highest spiritual intelligences radiating from the darkness of *Parabrahm*. Together they are the highest cognizable foundation of the first *arupa* world, from which emanate all the successive hosts and hierarchies, all the successive circles and cycles, of manifested theogony. Beyond this mystery lies the incomprehensible and infinite ocean of abstract divinity. Beneath or within it float the ordered worlds of time, like particles of dust in a sunbeam, for the radiant ocean of space is suffused with the light of the Central Spiritual Sun. The Akashic waters are alive with

Daiviprakriti, the Light of the Logos; all its innumerable centres of differentiated intelligence thrill and pulsate to its eternal motion. In it the three aspects of the ever unknowable, unspeakable and uncreate Absolute — spiritual wisdom, creative magic and evolutionary impulse — are one.

In every pilgrim-soul there is a ray of the bright essence of that divine ocean, partless and pure, unsullied by thick obscuring folds of matter. Each human being is in principle capable of seeking the inward path in consciousness because each human being is in essence a spark of Kumaric wisdom. The self-conscious realization of this sublime inheritance is the aim and object of every authentic philosophy, science and religion. It is the compassionate keynote of every system of allegory, glyph and symbol offered by Avatars and Adepts for the guidance of orphan humanity. All of these have their archetype and origin in the *Stanzas of Dzyan*, which traces directly the inauguration of humanity on earth over eighteen million years ago. *The Book of Dzyan* may be grasped only through meditation, an immersion in the steady stream of universal ideation. Indeed, the wisdom, magic and growth that it reveals and embodies are themselves aspects of meditation in the highest sense.

This may be seen through reflection upon one of the oldest symbols for the process of creation, wherein the cosmos is said to be gestated out of the meditative ideation of the Logos. In fact, the deepest possible meditation pursued by the student of Dzyan and the supernal creative activity of the Logos are not merely similar, but identical. Hence, the *Stanzas* offer innumerable keys to the mystical nature of meditation. But all too often, through a dwarfed and separative sense of self, students exteriorize the grand processes intimated in the *Stanzas*. Mistaking an intellectual formalism for Buddhic understanding, they unwittingly subvert themselves and fail to develop a line of life's meditation. But one who is willing to set aside aimless analytic speculation, and to begin in earnest generating a line of meditation that transects the cycle of one's life from birth to death, may put to good use the mysterious symbolism of the *Stanzas*.

> The great mother lay with △ and the │ and the
> ☐, the second │ and the ☆ in her bosom, ready to
> bring them forth, the valient sons of the ☐ △ │ │ (or
> 4,320,000, the Cycle) whose two elders are the ◯ and
> the • (Point).
>
> Ibid., 434

In this mystical representation of the origin of the cosmos, Aditi is shown as containing the prototypical divine principles, the triad, the line and the square, each of which becomes the next and all of which are one with each other. This refers to the mystery of the Tetraktys, the unity of the four forms of Vach, the underlying unity of the triple Logoi, the inseparability of *Mulaprakriti, Purusha* and *Prakriti,* and the divine origin of the sacred formless square equivalent to the Host of the Kumaras. The Commentary then speaks of the second line and the five-pointed star, which are distinct from the three, the one and the four, but are still contained in Aditi-Vach. Then in the phrase "bring them forth", it speaks of the four, the three and the two, the archetypal basis of all cyclic existence, depicting them as the sons of two elders, which are the circle and the point. Instead of engaging in tortuous geometric and numerical speculations, one may deeply ponder upon the circle and the point.

In meditation one may expand the circle, while reducing one's sense of identity to a point. Thus one may begin to meditate truly upon the point in the circle. Once established in this discipline, one may proceed deeper and deeper, always moving towards the ideal of the circle with centre everywhere and circumference nowhere. As one does this, the depths of one's consciousness will increase, giving a detachment from the detailed events of time and allowing a growing insight into the archetypal forms that are eternally inscribed upon every cycle.

The sequence of figures — the triangle, the line, the square, the second line and the five-pointed star — is self-evidently connected with π, 3.1415. . ., the ratio of the circumference of the circle to its diameter. Given a point and a circle, the numbers and figures of π follow immediately in a geometrical context. In meta-geometry, the Tetraktys represents the synthesis, or the host unified in the Logos and the point. Here in the relationship between *Shabdabrahman* and the heavenly hosts of hierarchies active in cyclic manifestation, a vital and valuable key is given to creativity and magic through meditation. Anyone seriously engaged in using this key will hardly speak about it. But everyone is invited to deepen reverence for mystic nature and its magical modes, and to attempt to understand what meditation upon this most primordial and archetypal process would be like. Because it is the most primordial process in Nature, it can endlessly repeat and re-enact itself, for it is the very process of creation. There can be no true human creativity outside this process, and it is the living basis of all human magic through meditation. Beginners need not worry about their incapacity or unreadiness, but should instead spend their lives adoring its practitioners and masters. Even such authentic adoration partakes of the process.

The one archetypal process of creation is re-enacted in every cycle of manifested life. From a metaphysical standpoint events in time are all equally distant from eternity. Meta-psychologically, this distance is a function of one's degree of spiritual con-sciousness, dwindling to zero in the case of the Mahatma. Instead of looking back to distant events in the dawn of manifestation, Mahatmas continuously meditate and ideate in that very dawn, imparting its energies directly and unmodified to the dif-ferentiated worlds of cyclic existence.

> At the beginning of every cycle of 4,320,000, the *Seven* (or, as some nations had it, eight) great gods, descended to establish the new order of things and give the impetus to the new cycle. That *eighth* god was the unifying *Circle* or LOGOS, separated and made distinct from its host, in exoteric dogma, just as the three divine hypostases of the ancient Greeks are now considered

in the Churches as three distinct *personae*. 'The MIGHTY
ONES perform their great works, and leave behind them
everlasting monuments to commemorate their visit,
every time they penetrate within our mayavic veil
(atmosphere); says a Commentary.

Ibid., 434-35

From the highest standpoint, once the keynote of a cycle is
struck, once its foundations are correctly laid, the entire work of
that cycle is finished. What is done in this highest sense ever recurs,
summoning the hierarchies in a specific manner for untold
millennia to come. This century itself is significant only because
it represents the coda of a dark story started more than two
thousand years ago and the beginning of a cycle that will finally
and irreversibly overcome the needless dragging out of old
Atlantean karma generated over five million years. This is the true
meaning of the 1975 Cycle. So powerful is this shift in the Akashic
matrix of the world that men and women everywhere who
become, in some degree, masters of adoration will, unknown to
themselves, become initiated in ways that affect their subtler
vestures.

Slowly, over the coming centuries, the consciousness of
children will shift, the classes of human souls in incarnation will
alter. Gradually, the regressive karma of Atlantean ingratitude will
be displaced, and orphan humanity will rediscover its true spiritual
ancestors. Right perception of these Kumaric progenitors cannot
come through any form of external worship but only through
deep meditation and an increased capacity to perceive formless
spiritual essences. The primordial seven are, at root, like the Ah-Hi
and Oeaohoo. Their secret names are unpronounceable, although
their mystery names go back to the monosyllabic vowel speech
of the Third Root Race, which was the language of incantation
and invocation among the highest magicians in the great mystery
temples. These names are like living abstract essences, like rays of
light or pure colours. Many people who have either naturally or
unnaturally entered the psychic realm recognize that there is much
more to the spectrum than is revealed by physical sight. But the

perception of pure colour in meditation far transcends the psychic realm and can only be compared with perceiving, clearly and distinctively, the fourteen colours of the rainbow or registering fourteen different notes on the piano at once. Yet the physical separation between sound and colour is an illusion.

In order to develop the subtle senses necessary for the perception of formless spiritual essences, one must learn to see all of the seven colours in each of the seven primary colours, and to hear all of the seven notes in each of the primary notes. Sometimes people experience such nuances when they hear the quarter tones in Indian music or the subtle harmonies of Bach's fugues. But unfortunately, they do not comprehend the experience, because their consciousness is too bound up with the lower mind. Worse still, they begin to talk about their experience and so corrupt it completely. It is only appropriate to speak of something which one has put to work ethically in one's life. In the humanity of the future this will be one of the common-sense rules of life.

In the present and in the centuries leading up to the major transformation in consciousness that is now taking place, there have been many false starts and inverted expectations. Whilst the ideal of universal and lifelong learning has central relevance to the future, the system of mass education that has developed is its antithesis. It has brought about the breakdown of old feudal structures, particularly their concern with lifelong loyalty, craftsmanship, humble apprenticeship to a master. The Renaissance affirmation of the dignity of man had nothing to do with the noisy pseudo-egalitarianism of the present, in which almost everyone proclaims an opinion on everything. The anticipations and stirrings in the *Akasha* have quickened the lunar tendencies in human beings, trapping the unwary in a process of lunar homogenization and ferment. Those who, under karma, were unwise enough not to preserve their balance when they felt the new inward promptings have been made by Nature to subserve the purely lunar function of producing a new kind of physical man.

As this preparatory work draws to its conclusion, solar beings will descend. These beings will be as awesome as the Grand Canyon. They will speak very little and have nothing to do with external appearances. They will not be disguised from each other, but will remain invisible to those who persist in being *chelas* to Madison Avenue and Hollywood or pseudo-initiates in junior high school. In the last century, William Q. Judge spoke of a time when America will develop a coffee-coloured civilization. What is taking place in America already is only a small portion of that which is taking place throughout the globe, and even this is a re-enactment of what has happened again and again throughout evolution. In every such cycle, especially in Kali Yuga, the tail tends to wag the dog at first, the lunar seems to obscure the solar. But the lunar is necessary for the homogenization and aggregation of lives on the lower planes. As with the original lighting-up of *Manas* over eighteen million years ago, the lunar vestures must be prepared before the solar descent can take place.

Abstract differences of degree and plane apply to the solar hosts and to the Kumaric progenitors of the spiritual Self. Because the Kumaras have to do with formless essences, they are ultimately connected with the Ah-Hi, but as the Ah-Hi, they could not give *Manas*. It was only when the Ah-Hi descended to the third plane that there could be *Mahat* and *Manas*. Only then could they become Manasaputras, capable of informing and entering into the ethereal vestures of human beings. These differentiations are intimated, indeed embodied for Initiates, in sacred mantrams, such as the fourfold *Pranava*, the AUM with its different pronunciations, and the *Vyahritis* in *Om, Bhur, Bhuva, Swar*. The most potent mantrams were always given in secret, never to be revealed, for they conveyed profound mysteries such as the true relation between Saturn and the sun. All great mantrams are means of tapping the subtle energies of the primordial seven, the magical potencies of formless essences. To approach magical wisdom, human beings must go beyond conventional conceptions of good and evil, rooting themselves in pure selflessness as men and women of meditation and effortless compassion. They must become invulnerable to insecurity and remain steadfast in their vows.

When human beings become true individuals and enjoyers of meditation, they become capable in contemplation of entering the sanctuary of the heart. First stabilizing consciousness at the hidden point between the eyes, they may then greet the lustrous point within the heart, connecting the two as a preparation for the ascent inwards and upwards towards that which is beyond all the centres. To do this in fact and in consciousness is to restore one's relationship to the Kumaras and to the realm of subtle spiritual energies which can only be experienced by becoming a person of silence. Impervious to sympathy games, never speaking to a single person about one's resolves, only talking out of necessity, one must generate the courage to go into the darkness, and to confront the demons within. To do so is to help more human beings than any mode of exoteric action can. If one is sincere in one's resolve, the Kumaras will help.

The Kumaras, who are the mind-born sons of Brahma-Rudra or Shiva, are the higher Prajapati, the progenitors of the true spiritual Self of man. Theirs is the abstract power of intelligent self-conscious creation; the lower powers of creativity, represented by the hosts of the lunar *pitris,* are only pale shadowy reflections. One's true heredity as a human being has nothing to do with one's father or mother on the physical plane. The physical form, which we owe to our parents, is only the chariot or garment of the real man. A human being's authentic heredity has to do with the *karana sharira,* the invisible permanent vesture transcending the cycles of birth and death. All the vestures of a human being come from progenitors, even though they are called human principles. Every form employed in living Nature must have its origin in classes of lives which can be assigned to hierarchies underlying the vestures and connected with different classes of progenitors. The Kumaras are the source of the true invisible spiritual vesture of every human being, a vesture which proceeds from a germ, just as the physical body is gestated in the embryo out of what initially resembles a germ. So too on the higher plane, the *karana sharira* emanates out of a germ, which is referred to mystically as the ancestral germ.

All human beings may be divided into seven broad sets which go back over eighteen million years to ancestors present at the lighting-up of *Manas*. Though the subject of spiritual heredity is very deep and difficult, one who fulfils the qualifications and needs that knowledge will be instructed by the Guru in what he is meant to know about numbers, days or planets. But in this age only a handful develop to the point where they need that kind of knowledge. Although and because a vast amount of Teaching has been delivered, helping to loosen and challenge old structures, the unwary imagine they know a good deal more than they really know. Although many talk about spiritual rays and invisible beings, true knowledge of these mysteries is preserved in silence and secrecy. Any human being who has abused such knowledge has condemned himself or herself to the extremely difficult task of working back to that primordial posture of initiation. Over eighteen million years many human beings are in this position, finding nothing else to do but painstakingly and thoroughly undo their misdeeds of the past. As Jesus taught, not one iota of the law shall pass away.

Whatever one's sins and mistakes, the rectification of one's life is akin to a rediscovery of innocence, a re-entry into the child state. Purity can be recovered, first of all, by freedom from tortuous analysis and narcissism. All schemes of self-reform that rely upon self-assertion and confession only aggravate the problem. One's real task is to see that there is no problem, that one must forget oneself. One must, in short, become like a child, learning to listen to other people, smiling at others, doing one's own work, and refusing to create problems for oneself. Those who are encouraged to talk about themselves when ill only become more ill. Lunar usurpers begin to drive the solar forces farther and farther from their consciousness. In the spiritual life, where every soul is placed on probation the moment he or she approaches the Teachings, self-concern is even more fatal. The moment one anticipates the end of one's probation, the period of one's probation is enormously extended. Such is the law, and one must never forget that behind the Avatar are mathematical magicians called

Mahatmas. Acting with infallible precision, they invite the approach of every aspiring soul in direct proportion to his or her degree of self-forgetfulness.

At the head of the host of virgin ascetics called the Kumaras stands Maha Shiva, the Mahayogin, the supreme exemplar of effortless asceticism and the highest creative meditation.

> Siva-Rudra is the Destroyer, as Vishnu is the preserver; and both are the regenerators of spiritual as well as of physical nature. To live as a plant, the *seed* must die. To live as a conscious entity in the Eternity, the passions and senses of man must first DIE before his body does. 'To live is to die and to die is to live,' has been too little understood in the West. Siva, the *destroyer,* is the *creator* and the Saviour of Spiritual man, as he is the good gardener of nature. He weeds out the plants, human and cosmic, and kills the passions of the physical, to call to life the perceptions of the spiritual, man.
>
> *Ibid.,* 459

Shiva is the destroyer of passions and of the physical senses, which are constant impediments to the development of higher spiritual perceptions and to the growth of the inner spiritual man. The more desperately a human being tries to stave off ageing, the more rapidly Shiva will destroy that being. Shiva wants every human being to grow older and to die, so that by suffering he may learn that there is no other true dharma for a human being than to overcome illusion. Nature shows this all the time. If a plant is to grow, the seed must die, and if there is to be fruit for the harvest and for succeeding years, the plant must die. To live as a conscious entity in eternity, one must kill out *tanha,* the powerful force impelling beings into involuntary reincarnation. If no self-conscious effort is made during life to overcome this force, then even the small element of choice that one might have had at the moment of death is weakened. Nothing is sadder than to see the old encouraged to cling to life and to fear death. This corrupting tendency is derived from the decadent period of fallen Egyptian civilization. Whether disguised as pseudo-science or pseudo-medicine or pseudo-religion, it is nothing more than a piteous selfishness bound up with the delusion of carnal immortality.

To live as a conscious human being is to make more room for others, and this is what the present cycle is intended to teach. Every human being must come to live in the recognition that other and finer human beings will follow him. This lesson is particularly acute in the so-called modern civilization of the West, with its false and illusive conceptions of history and progress. Every time the lesson of gratitude to ancestors and benefactors has been taught over the last centuries, it has been forgotten. It is not enough to give ritual thanks one day each year. One must learn ceaseless gratitude to ancestors and a continuous sense of obligation to descendants. This does not involve transferring one's anxieties onto children. They should rather be greeted as souls and shown by example how joyous true discipline can be. Otherwise, by the age of thirteen, children will become mother superiors, witches, pontificators, constantly engaged in passing judgements. This is awful enough amongst those who have never had the advantage of association with Gupta Vidya; those who know something of its pristine philosophy and persist in gossip and image-crippling are on the way to becoming grey magicians and worse. Jesus said it all two thousand years ago, but millions of people since then, twisting and abusing his name, failed to take in the central lesson.

To live is to die, to make more room for others. One must age gracefully, must start letting go by the age of twenty-eight, if one wants to learn how to do so at the moment of death. One must learn to cooperate with Shiva, the destroyer, who is also the creator and saviour of spiritual man, the good gardener of Nature. Through this cooperation will come a sifting of the unnecessary, a cleansing of thought, a rhythm of breathing. It will become easier to focus the mind. The more one develops a strong sense of external duty, the more one can cultivate a living awareness of the internal necessities of the soul. Long before one is prepared to engage in direct occult training, with its magical wisdom and spiritual creativity, one must learn to act economically, lightly and precisely, in a manner that refines one's spiritual nature and diffuses benevolence.

By becoming a devotee of Shiva the soul has a better chance to connect with the mind, to use the mind as a creative instrument, and to govern the body as a faithful vehicle. One will know that the soul is at work through the heart when one's capacity for loving others grows to such an extent that one has no thought of oneself. There will be a gradual diminution of the passions and an increase in the perceptions of the spiritual man. Contemporary fascination with Tantra is merely a way of evading the issue of celibacy. Those caught up in it will not develop the Third Eye; they will instead be incinerated, for there is no fooling around in the realm of spiritual fire. Go slow, but do not compensate. Shiva teaches the anchorite to be totally honest, he is the friend of that in oneself which is cheerfully modest but morally courageous.

Everyone is invited, through meditation, contemplation and adoration to enjoy the universe, to savour the Akashic waters of space, to gaze upon the depths of the midnight sky. But while appreciating all of these, one must seek to reach beyond them to the Nameless and Ineffable. The more one does so, the more one will gain an inward awareness of the reality of the divine ocean of radiant wisdom. One will become a person whose tastes change, who is free of externals, who has become inwardly wide awake. In this spiritual wakefulness one will grow in reverence for the wisdom, the magic and the potential of growth sacrificially offered by the Kumaras to every living atom in resonant space. This is the restoration of the pristine splendour of the Kumaras, the progressive realization of the Logos in the cosmos and the God in man.

THE HERO IN MAN

The air is full of souls.
PHILO JUDAEUS

The homeless tribe of mystics, the fraternity of spiritual exiles, inherit the ancient title *mystikos*, from *mystes* — those whose eyes and lips are closed, who have entered into the Mysteries. Its sacred verities can neither be fully articulated nor wholly validated in any language. The unmanifest may be suggested and shrouded by the manifest, and the mystic experiences this through his endeavours to translate his insights from the region of things felt to the region of things understood. The mystic's eyes are necessarily closed to the mundane world in as much as they intently and inwardly gaze upon the hidden realm of supersensuous realities. The mystic's lips are sealed — even in eloquent speech — because of the unutterable beauty of beatific experience and the transcendent glow of transfiguring insight. Authentic mystical awareness is markedly different from the varied forms of fantasy and reverie. Mystical experience is essentially noetic, rooted in the cognitive capacity for enlarged comprehension of noumenal truths, rather than the rush of emotion or the randomness of memory. Though the mystic path is etched across the awesome vault of infinite duration, each mystical experience is an event in time, transient, limited by a fragile beginning and a frustrating end. The experience is also episodic in that the temporal and captive consciousness of the individual cannot control it. In the enigmatic language of the Upanishads, the *Atman* — the universal overbrooding Spirit — shows itself to whom it will. Daydreams and fantasy, though they share the wayward charm of evanescent but joyous wonder, do not convey the ethical consequences of a deep mystic experience. In the presence of the magnanimous sweep of the mystic vision, a natural self-effacement fuses with a profound sense of self-completion. One becomes a selfless participant in the silent sacrifice of invisible and visible nature, in which each part has clarity and significance in relation to every other part, all sharing the diffused light of an architectonic unity.

The mystic senses the priceless privilege of being alive and the sacredness of breathing; awareness of this sanctified continuity of all life affects every thought and act, at least during 'peak experiences'. The fragmentation and discontinuity in consciousness of the vast majority of mankind — gaps between thought and feeling, idea and image, sensibility and sense, belief and knowledge — are integrated in the mystic's self-awareness. Sensing a fundamental continuity within himself, the mystic witnesses an equally vibrant solidarity between individuals. What is possible for one person to discover is possible for another, however adverse conditions may appear. The intense flashes of awareness that the mystic is privileged to enjoy are stepping stones on the path of awakening, most of which are trod in silence.

Within the historical tradition of sages, saints and seers, a few, like St. John of the Cross, St. Teresa, Bernard of Clairvaux, as well as the author of *The Cloud of Unknowing*, speak of actual experiences encountered upon the mystical way. Other sources, such as the writings of G.W. Russell (A.E.), *The Voice of the Silence* and *Light on the Path*, characterize the phases of the mystic path without attention to details of particular experiences. Still other influential thinkers, Plato and Plotinus, Shankara and Eckhart, elaborated the metaphysical framework and philosophical underpinnings of the path itself. A.E. presents an account of his haunting visions both directly, in works like *The Candle of Vision*, and metaphorically in stories and poems like "A Strange Awakening" and "A Priestess of the Woods", interwoven with thoughts on the nature of the universe and man's relation to it. He affirms that anyone who wills it can awaken spiritual insight within himself.

So the lover of Earth obtains his reward, and little by little the veil is lifted of an inexhaustible beauty and majesty. It may be he will be tranced in some spiritual communion, or will find his being overflowing into the being of the elements, or become aware that they are breathing their life into his own. Or Earth may become on an instant, all faery to him, and earth and air resound with the music of its invisible people. Or the trees and rocks may waver before his eyes and become transparent, revealing what creatures were hidden from him by the curtain, and he will know as the ancients did of dryad and hamadryad, of genii of wood and mountain. Or earth may suddenly blaze about him with supernatural light in some lonely spot amid the hills, and he will find he stands as the prophet in a place that is holy ground, and he may breathe the intoxicating exhalations as did the sibyls of old. Or his love may hurry him away in dream to share in deeper mysteries, and he may see the palace chambers of nature where the wise ones dwell in secret, looking out over the nations, breathing power into this man's heart or that man's brain, on any who appear to their vision to wear the colour of truth. So gradually the earth lover realises the golden world is all about him in imperishable beauty, and he may pass from the vision to the profounder beauty of being, and know an eternal love is within and around him, pressing upon him and sustaining with infinite tenderness his body, his soul and his spirit.

The Candle of Vision

A.E.'s mysticism emphasizes understanding through love, and he embroiders mystical naturalism with suggestions of the rich void beyond and throughout nature. He emphasizes man's identity with all nature because he sees the soul in nature and in humanity. "The great heart of the earth is full of laughter", one of his characters says, "do not put yourselves apart from its joy, for its soul is your soul and its joy is your true being." As the veil of visible nature is dissolved before the mystic's sight, time itself is seen as an illusion from a metaphysical standpoint. Consciousness is expanded or constricted by its apprehension of time. The mystic senses a vibration prior to visible nature, though insofar as it is expressible, it too has a beginning and an end. Mystical experience is timeless though located in time, and the mystic is hard pressed to describe the crossings between the unmanifest and the manifest. Speaking of the hour of twilight as a metaphor for that time when "the Mystic shall be at home", A.E. calls it "the hour for memory".

> Wherever it is spent, whether in the dusky room or walking home through the blue evening, all things grow strangely softened and united; the magic of the old world reappears. The commonplace streets take on something of the grandeur and solemnity of starlit avenues of Egyptian temples; the public squares in the mingled glow and gloom grow beautiful as the Indian grove where Sakuntala wandered with her maidens; the children chase each other through the dusky shrubberies, as they flee past they look at us with long remembered glances: lulled by the silence, we forget a little while the hard edges of the material and remember that we are *spirits*.

When the horizon set by one's awareness of time is foreshortened, memory is reduced to recent particulars redolent with echoes of childhood remembrance. As that horizon is expanded through a sense of eternity, recollection arises with a profound awareness of mythic time, and the soul gazes within the archaic history of humanity. Soul-memory exhibits natural affinities to strange dreams, insignificant in detail yet suggesting a cosmic drama in which each creature plays an appropriate role. Soul-memory also portrays to waking consciousness what would otherwise be witnessed only in *sushupti* or Devachan. If most individuals see nature as a static created world comprising myriad separate entities, the mystic beholds *natura naturans*, a dynamic process constantly unleashing creative energies.

The mystical experience is grounded in the commonality of human life.

> For this in truth it seems to me to mean: all knowledge is a revelation of the self to the self, and our deepest comprehension of the seemingly apart divine is also our furthest inroad to self-knowledge; Prometheus, Christ, are in every heart; the story of one is the story of all; the Titan and the Crucified are humanity.
>
> *The Hero in Man*

Precisely because Christ is incarnate in all humanity, every human being has golden moments and mystical glimpses, yet because Prometheus is bound for ever within us, such moments and glimpses are obliterated in waking life through indulgence, egotism, obsession with results and the concern for salvation. And if these barriers to deeper unity are bypassed without genuine self-transcendence, they become still stronger obstacles: passivity, aggression, fantasy and malignant interference in the lives of others. To thread passing moments into a continuous current in life, one must hold firmly to a selfless line of thought and motivation.

> ... these moods, though lit up by intuitions of the true, are too partial, they belong too much to the twilight of the heart, they have too dreamy a temper to serve us well in life. We should wish rather for our thoughts a directness such as to the messengers of the gods, swift, beautiful, flashing presences bent on purposes well understood.
>
> *Ibid.*

One's mind must be prepared and alert. One needs to identify with the whole of nature so as to become inconspicuous as a persona, yet ever vigilant and willing to follow the injunction given in *The Voice of the Silence*:

> Thy Soul has to become as the ripe mango fruit: as soft and sweet as its bright golden pulp for others'

woes, as hard as that fruit's stone for thine own throes
and sorrows.

Although this lies far ahead of contemporary humanity, there is
a fundamental continuity between the mystic's unwavering vision
of the Hero in man and everyday experience, through the idea of
sacrifice on behalf of the wretched of the earth.

> Now if the aim of the mystic be to fuse into one
> all moods made separate by time, would not the daily
> harvesting of wisdom render unnecessary the long
> Devachanic years? No second harvest could be reaped
> from fields where the sheaves are already garnered. Thus
> disregarding the fruits of action, we could work like
> those who have made the Great Sacrifice, for whom
> even Nirvana is no resting place. Worlds may awaken
> in nebulous glory, pass through their phases of self-
> conscious existence and sink again to sleep, but these
> tireless workers continue their age-long task of help.
> Their motive we do not know, but in some secret depth
> of our being we feel that there could be nothing nobler,
> and thinking this we have devoted the twilight hour to
> the understanding of their nature.
>
> *The Hour of Twilight*

When the Ever-Unknowable reflects itself in the process
of manifestation, the root substance-principle, the absolute
Archaeus, unfolds itself as the invisible and visible cosmos in three
hypostases. The first may be called Spirit, transcendent and
overbrooding; the second, matter, the immanent side of nature;
while the third, connecting these two at every point, might be
likened materially to electricity and spiritually to mind. This third
term is the impersonal intelligence of number and ratio, geometric
form and arithmetic progression. The basic triad is present at every
level of being, for Spirit expresses itself through matter — like the
partially revealed dancer in the Dance of the Seven Veils — while
matter lives and is transformed only under the vivifying impulse

of Spirit. Both join in innumerable permutations and elaborations of the initial threefold Word, fused in cosmic intelligence *(Mahat)* which is also cosmic law *(Ṛta)*. In the sphere of self-consciousness, this triad can be qualitatively defined as Wisdom *(Prajna)*, Compassion *(Karuna)* and Intelligence *(Buddhi)*. Each depends upon the others for its own level of purity, clarity and activity. The elaboration of the primal Word is the movement from homogeneity to heterogeneity, from subtle to gross, from potential to actual, and from subjective to objective. The creative energy enshrined in the Word is pure *eros,* and its every expression reveals as well as masks its more fundamental nature. Hence every level of being finds light and darkness, the greater and the lesser, knowledge and relative ignorance, in ceaseless contraction. The urge to manifest is the urge to objectify, to take form, to exist in time, rather than to abide in eternity. At the spiritual level, this impulsion is towards individuation, but at the natal level it is the desire to live as an ego; psychophysically it is the thirst for life.

The mystic retraces this gestation of consciousness and returns, self-consciously and spiritually awake, to its source. He experiences, understands and controls the avenues leading from personal and individual existence to cosmic and universal consciousness. Self-transformation requires self-knowledge at every stage, a path fraught with dangers. The mystic recognizes that "knowledge is power" but also knows that power corrupts the unwary. He must make compassion his own. Only then will persistent effort and unremitting vigilance lead to supreme wisdom. A.E. depicted the quest as lying

> ... between the darkness of earth and the light of spiritual self-consciousness, that the Master in each of us draws in and absorbs the rarest and best of experiences, love, self-forgetfulness, aspiration, and out of these distils the subtle essence of wisdom, so that he who struggles in pain for his fellows, when he wakens again on earth is endowed with the

tradition of that which we call self-sacrifice, but which is in reality the proclamation of our own universal nature.

Ibid.

This passage is similar to that from the rich silence of dreamless sleep, where all personal consciousness is dissolved, through the veneer of chaotic images in the transition from dreams to the waking state. But self-created enemies lie along the uncharted paths waiting to mislead and destroy the pilgrim who glimpses the golden summit in the distance but ignores the steep ravines and rocky ledges between himself and that glorious height. Ethereal sights may be mistaken for divine intimations, misleading the erratic seer. In the archetypal story "A Priestess of the Woods", the daughter of a magician learns about the elemental intelligences of Nature.

> She saw deeper things also; as a little child, wrapped up in her bearskin, she watched with awe her father engaged in mystic rites; when around him the airy legions gathered from the populous elements, the Spirits he ruled and the Spirits he bowed down before; fleeting nebulous things white as foam coming forth from the great deep who fled away at the waving of his hand; and rarer the great sons of fire.

But her father died before she learned about more than superficial signs and appearances. Her knowledge of the spirits of the earth was sufficient to make her priestess, but she knew nothing of the formless orders and divine principles. In the course of time, her message was reduced to the repeated warning of the dangers of becoming linked to gnomes, sylphs, salamanders and undines. She saw how men utterly enslave themselves to elemental intelligences through seeking worldly delights, and how they bargain away their lives for momentary gain. There is law in nature, and to violate its orders is necessarily to call forth recompense. Yet she could teach nothing that confers a greater vision, a larger perspective, a fuller hope.

When a young man passing through the forest heard her compelling discourse to the woodland fold, he took up his lyre and sang:

> I never heed by waste or wood,
>   The cry of fay or faery thing
> Who tell of their own solitude;
>   Above them all my soul is king.

Though angered by the intrusion, the eyes of the youth dazzled the young priestess with the secrecy of joy. Fearlessly he told her: "Your priestess speaks but half truths, her eyes have seen but her heart does not know . . . The great heart of earth is full of laughter; do not put yourselves apart from its joy, for its soul is your soul and its joy is your true being." She could not counter his confident affirmation, so she bowed down before it, telling her people, "His wisdom may be truer; it is more beautiful than the knowledge we inherit."

Though she maintained her vigils and cleaved to her knowledge, her heart dwelt upon a deeper mystery. Her dominion over Nature spirits ebbed, and with it her life. Life is structured by a lesser mystery, and her awakening was accompanied by a release from incarnate life itself. The young priestess, despite her ignorant elemental worship, was pure, and so her heart was touched. Those more travelled on the spiritual path may not find awakening to a deeper life so easy, for their images of the goal may involve conditional aspiration, residual desires for unearthly sensations and incomplete knowledge. The gods have many names and titles, each signifying some level and form of manifestation. The celestial Aphrodite points beyond herself to *Alaya*, compassion absolute, which, like boundless space, encompasses all things arising in it but favours none. She also appears as the terrestrial Venus of Plato's *Symposium*, who satisfies every desire without quenching the endless thirst of desire itself.

In "A Tragedy in the Temple" Asur entered the service of the Temple of Isthar wherein a friend blew to flames the mystic fire which already smouldered within him, but became attracted to her sidereal form.

> 'Brother,' he said, 'I am haunted by a vision, by a
> child of the stars as lovely as Isthar's self; she visits my
> dreaming hours, she dazzles me with strange graces, she
> bewilders with unspeakable longing. Sometimes I know,
> I must go to her, though I perish. When I see her I forget
> all else and I have will to resist no longer. The vast and
> lonely inspiration of the desert departs from my
> thought, she and the jewel-light she lives in blot it out.'

The tendencies and habits of lifetimes do not easily melt away under the heat of religious fervour. As the pilgrim-soul approaches the gateway to the arduous spiritual path, all which must perish in the divine fire precipitates the conflict between the aspirant's will to merge in the universal light and all temporal traits. This fierce struggle has been portrayed as the great battle in the *Bhagavad Gita,* shown in the Buddha's final contest with Mara before his Enlightenment, and depicted in the Psalms as the valley of the shadow of death. Mara-Lilith waits at the entrance to the mystic path to fascinate and terrify the lonely wayfarer. At the portal of the 'assembling', the King of the Maras, the *Maha Mara,* stands trying to blind the candidate by the radiance of his 'Jewel' *(The Voice of the Silence).*

Asur's friend could not help him, not understanding how the jewel of Mara is formed from all the lurking passions which agitate the dark recesses of worldly consciousness. But in a dream he saw the dreadful prospect:

> 'The form of Asur moved towards a light streaming
> from a grotto, I could see within it burning gigantic
> flowers. On one, as on a throne, a figure of weird and
> wonderful beauty was seated. I was thrilled with a
> dreadful horror, I thought of the race of Liliths, and
> some long-forgotten and tragic legends rose up in my
> memory of these beings whose soul is but a single and

terrible passion; whose love too fierce for feebler lives to endure, brings death or madness to men. . . . I saw her in all her terrible beauty. From her head a radiance of feathered flame spread out like the plume of a peacock, it was spotted with gold and green and citron dyes, she raised her arms upward, her robe, semi-transparent, purple and starred over with a jewel lustre, fell in vaporous folds to her feet like the drift of a waterfall.

For anyone not unconditionally devoted to the diamond light of formless spirit, this opalescent glamour exercises a fatal fascination. When his friend next saw Asur, "his face was as white as the moon, his eyes only reflected the light".

The dominion of Mara-Lilith is limited to the weaknesses of human beings. In A.E's "The Cave of Lilith" the temptress tells a sage:

> I, here in my caves between the valley and the height, blind the eyes of all who would pass. Those who by chance go forth to you, come back to me again, and but one in ten thousand passes on. My illusions are sweeter to them than truth. I offer every soul its own shadow. I pay them their own price. I have grown rich, though the simple shepherds of old gave me birth. Men have made me; the mortals have made me immortal. I rose up like a vapour from their first dreams, and every sign since then and every laugh remains with me. I am made of hopes and fears. The subtle princes lay out their plans of conquest in my caves, and there the hero dreams, and there the lovers of all time write in flames their history. I am wise, holding all experience, to tempt, to blind, to terrify. None shall pass by.

The sage knows that desire attaches itself to objects which must decay and perish, and that much sorrow ensues. When suffering becomes so intense that it touches the inmost depths, the soul searches for a profounder joy. "When desire dies the swift and invisible will awakens", the sage replies. Those who have entered the cave of Lilith emerge again, never to go back.

"The Secret of Power" depicts the war within and without the individual over his destiny. Light and darkness are qualities embodied by beings. In a universe where magic is possible — where Nature's secret operations may be learnt — both good and evil magicians exist, and both exert their magnetism on the soul.

> Two figures awful in their power opposed each other; the frail being wavering between them both. It alone wavered, for they were silent, resolute and knit in the conflict of the will; they stirred not a hand nor a foot; there was only a still quivering now and then as of intense effort, but they made no other movement. . . . Here were the culminations of the human, towering images of the good and evil man may aspire to. I looked at the face of the evil adept. His bright red-brown eyes burned with a strange radiance of power; I felt an answering emotion of pride, of personal intoxication, of psychic richness rise up within me gazing upon him. His face was archetypal; the abstract passion which eluded men in the features of many people I knew, was here declared, exultant, defiant, giantesque; it seemed to leap like fire, to be free. . . . I withdrew my gaze from this face and turned it on the other. An aura of pale soft blue was around this figure through which gleamed an underlight as of universal gold. . . . I caught a glimpse of a face godlike in its calm, terrible in the beauty of a life we know only in dreams, with strength which is the end of the hero's toil, which belongs to the many times martyred soul; yet not far away nor in the past was its power, it was the might of life which exists eternally.

All desire is an aspect of love. In "A Talk by the Euphrates" Merodach the priest explains:

There are two kinds of love men know of. There is one which begins with a sudden sharp delight — it dies away into infinite tones of sorrow. There is a love which wakes up amid dead things: it is chill at first, but it takes root, it warms, it expands, it lays hold of universal joys. So the man loves: so the God loves. Those who know this divine love are wise indeed. They love not one or another: they are love itself.

Universal love is the philosopher's stone, reducing all things to their essence because it is consubstantial with the *prima materia,* the core of the cosmos. Personal love may warm but it is partial, while the greater love identifies with and affects every condition. In "The Meditation of Ananda" the monk comes to feel this love for all creatures flowing through him.

From his heart he went out to them. Love, a fierce and tender flame, arose; pity, a breath from the vast; sympathy, born of unity. This triple fire sent forth its rays; they surrounded those dark souls; they pervaded them; they beat down oppression.

The divine magic of universal love invisibly affects beings everywhere. Kind acts by others may be sparked by Ananda's love, though unknown to the doers or to him. Magic is a force of Nature directed by self-conscious intelligence, and its exercise affects all nature for better or for ill. As a science, magic involves exact knowledge, but as an art, it must be either wisdom or sorcery. In time this becomes an ultimate question for the soul. Will its sorrows be merged with the sorrows of humanity, as in "A Strange Awakening", so that the gloom of the world is dispelled by the pristine light of the Spiritual Sun, or will suffering only drive the soul to a ferocious, demonic pride, leading it to join the company of Dostoevsky's Grand Inquisitor? A.E. saw that one dare not experience joy and hear the whole world cry in pain, that the quest is completed successfully only when one helps to lead others to its goal. "The Midnight Blossom" expresses this great affirmation:

'Brother,' said Varunna, 'here is the hope of the world. Though many seek only for the eternal joy, yet the cry you heard has been heard by great ones who have turned backwards, called by these beseeching voices. The small old path stretching far away leads through many wonderful beings to the place of Brahma. There is the first fountain, the world of beautiful silence, the light which has been undimmed since the beginning of time. But turning backwards from the gate the small old path winds away into the world of men, and it enters every sorrowful heart. This is the way the great ones go.'

THE DAIMON

Great Zeus, Father of men, you would deliver them all
from the evils that oppress them, if you would show them
what is the Daimon of whom they make use.

PYTHAGORAS

In the ancient world the term 'genius' essentially meant the tutelary spirit, the *daimon,* of every person. The philosophic conviction that each human being is guarded by his or her own spiritual genius was strongly held in Roman times. In the literature of the Renaissance, we encounter the phrase 'evil genius', reflecting the growing awareness that there is a sort of specialization and concentration, a peculiar intensity that marks the perversity, cunning and cynical defiance of the person who has become his or her own conspicuous enemy. For example, a self-tormented individual may often start with a good intention and at some level wish to convey generosity out of a sincere spirit. Yet whenever such a person seeks to express his or her feeling in language or gesture, it is so twisted and truncated that it is a deformed shadow of the original intent. There is an appalling awkwardness, a tragic distortion; something compulsive intervenes. This sad state of affairs is connected with the tortuous inversions of *kama manas,* the rationalizing mind enslaved by nebulous desires. With the complex mutations and disillusionments of self-consciousness, the term 'genius', originally applied to every individual's tutelary spirit, is pejoratively restricted to the evil embodiment of the soul of concentrated cunning.

In contemporary society, a shrunken notion of genius has emerged from the egalitarian concern to categorize beings in terms of some limiting and standardized concept of intelligence. Individuals with exceptional intellectual ability or creative skill in any sphere — whether in music or mathematics or whatever — cannot be readily accounted for under the conventional rules or in routinized ways. Since these anomalies cannot be ascribed to the typical educational process and established modes of training, such persons stand apart as inexplicable phenomena or fortuitous freaks. Applied only to seeming exceptions, the word 'genius' simply signifies the refusal to think more about them, for lack of any instructive explanation that pertains to human potential.

The classical conception of *daimonion ti* internalized the influences external to the spirit and objectified its inner demands, thus maintaining a dynamic balance between man and god. The belief in *daimones* as mediating spirits between gods and men was customary in ancient Athens and sacrosanct in Vedic India. Socrates regarded the intervention of the *daimon* — what Gandhi called his 'inner voice', which sometimes spoke to him and remained silent at other times to his deep despair — not so much as a command laid down on the human spirit by an external power as "an absolute law of the spirit itself," to quote Hegel's terms for the sacred task of the Delphic oracle. To make this interior voice wholly subjective is to destroy its spiritual character and distort the position claimed by Socrates and Gandhi. For a few pre-Socratic writers and for some Indian mystics, the daimon or *devata* was no more than the genius or overbrooding spirit unique to each person. If we adopt a facile rationalist attitude and take the daimon merely as an inflated metaphor for a familiar psychological process, thus denying it all transcendence and regarding it simply as a pathological oddity, a hallucination or a paranoid or hysterical symptom, we are, in fact, denying that it is an instrument of any meaningful communication and leaving Gandhi and Socrates, and many of the great mystics, enclosed in themselves, in a sort of autarchy, a pathetic state of self-deception. Even if we wish to deny the objective reality of the mystic's experience, which is strictly no easier than to affirm it, it is both unnecessary and presumptuous to deny categorically its subjective validity, or the veracity and testimony of the mystics.

Theosophically, there is a meticulous precision to the proper use of the word 'genius'. An essay by H.P. Blavatsky on the subject of genius stresses a significant distinction between *Manas* and *Buddhi. Buddhi,* or divine discernment, is the centrifugal principle of expansive sympathy together with an exalted feeling for the fitness of things, for archetypal justice and for architectonic proportion. On the other hand, *Manas* is the cool capacity for total concentration, bringing together to one centre the potential power of thought and the active energy of ideation, which in itself is unrestricted, unconditional and boundless. In individuals completely ruled by *Buddhi,* understood as the pure and potent diffusion of the universal Logoic light of the *Atman, Manas* is a translucent mirror for the untrammelled manifestation of *Atma-Buddhi.* Such individuals are gods — luminous beings who literally are not involved in the shadowy world of manifestation through identification with the lower principles. They are, so to speak, standing above and behind their visible selves and are aloof from the mayavic masquerade in limited space and clock-time. Their consciousness is one with TAT, which is utterly unmanifest, while simultaneously they have a vigilant and discerning awareness of the patterns and possibilities in chains of causes and consequences inherent in the shadow-play in which their radiant personalities are apparently manifest. They are exemplars of godlike freedom.

Creative genius, with its intermittent sparks, may be shown by those in whom the divine Triad is not fully activated and in total control, but who are moving significantly in that direction. When higher *Manas,* the self-reproductive power of unconditioned consciousness or of pure, formless ideation, is able to subordinate memory patterns, references to the past, and the illusion of time broken up into little bits, then the individual is functioning as a *Manushya* — Man thinking. Such beings may be truly termed 'geniuses', not if they merely function in this way intermittently or sporadically, but if they can do so consciously and continuously. They maintain complete control and pellucid awareness of the pleasing illusions brought to them by sense impressions and thrown up by those internal images of external impressions which are edited memory traces. They are amusedly aware of all these but are not at all bound up in them. They pass through earthly settings and scenarios without experiencing any compulsive self-involvement.

A spiritual genius is a magnanimous person able to function at all times in terms of a pure individuality that has no involvement, either through attachment or repulsion, in the myriad pairs of opposites and the many vicissitudes of change in the world. In such enlightened individuals the lower *Manas*, the more specialized reflecting intelligence which participates in the concepts, categories and languages shared among human beings, is an obedient and precise instrument of the higher *Manas*. A genius knows the archetypal logic of the relation between the unknowable, the unmanifest and the manifest. At the same time he could use elementary deductive logic with one part of his intelligence, observe the rules of inference, weigh in his mind the relative worth of the premises, but he would do all this with a detached lightness and timely effectiveness. He knows that it is a gross and shadowy representation, a kind of monkey trick in relation to the archetypal logic of the universe, which most people simply cannot grasp owing to their preoccupation with externalities. The spiritual genius is a thinking being who is without any adherence to past, present or future or any allegiance to name and form. He is wholly free from any inward mental involvement in the illusions of those who cling to exaggerated and emaciated tokens of reality. At the same time he can see these in perspective, without aversion or alienation, and he can participate compassionately with others in the temporal duties of mundane existence. Such a person is markedly different from what is conventionally seen as genius.

No disproportionate development in any one direction can be explained except as a throwback to skills secured in previous incarnations. Although one may suddenly be able to tap such abilities, they have no intrinsic moral significance and no internal relationship to higher consciousness. Higher Manasic or spiritual genius is ever involved in the morality of all things, requiring continual reference to motivation and thought. A person in whom the daimon shines forth is aware of every thought as it arises, and of everything implicit in its translation into a series of acts. He is always able to see the difference between primary and secondary orders of causation. When most people, whether in relation to a war or a crisis in personal or collective life, are talking moralistically, they are merely being intensely emotional and wondering whom to blame. They are not functioning as fully thinking beings. Others, who are partially capable of true thought, may still be caught up in externalities, trying to explain events in terms of the linear sequence of past trends. A higher Manasic being will see at the very core of this vast complexity a single and central illusion inherent in a false conception of the changing relationship between the actor, his mental framework, and other beings. Seeing that, he would know that all the rest is bound to follow.

Higher Manasic genius is vitally aware of the necessities of things, while simultaneously seeing all these necessities as relative realities. They are even somewhat absurd in relation to the supreme oneness of all beings, which is behind and beyond manifestation. Consciously rooted in his constant awareness of his immortal individuality as a spirit-soul, he lives in eternity and is not ensnared by the illusions of time. One cannot reach this lofty condition merely by rushing in one direction. One may move towards it partly, but whether one moves towards it by stages or embodies it fully in all contexts, it works in every direction because it partakes of unconditional energy. There can be no hit-and-miss development along this path. Memories from previous lives could play a part in this, because one cannot fully be a genius in one way at a certain time and not at another time in a different context. Fundamentally, to be moving towards genius is for something to be happening to oneself that is omnidirectional. It connotes the ability to look at a vast collection of beings and simultaneously see in relation to any of them that which represents their own possibility of transcendence of their own relative illusions. At the same time, the daimon allows one to maintain an equal distance from every one of a multitude of relative illusions. At first, one may only be able to do this at a certain level, and cannot move from this plane suddenly to the height of genius.

Even to reflect upon the myriad-minded conception of spiritual genius, the descent of the daimon, would be helpful because one could begin to use it as an authentic spiritual intelligence test. It might also be called an illusion test, where one sees one's own life, makeup, and reactions in terms of the exaggerations, falsities and absurdities, as well as the partialities, involved in one's moral responses, emotional reactions and so-called intellectuality. When one can break up all of these and see them for what they are, one is making a beginning in the direction of spiritual genius. This may be done by taking the opaque, brittle, blurred and confused nature that one thinks is one's exclusive and only self and which we are afraid we dare not face, and confronting it with the luminous portrait of the lustrous man of spiritual genius, the true exemplar of moral excellence, mental brilliance and intuitive insight.

It is only when human beings can deliberately think away from limiting conceptions of energy, and a purely physicalist view of breathing and infusing, that they can begin to understand what was involved in the original meaning of the term 'spiritual.' Owing to the concretization of concepts that has taken place over a long time, it is more helpful to see the word 'spiritual' in terms of its equivalent in Sanskrit, the language of the gods. The spirit is *Atman*. The word *Atman* in its etymology refers to eternal motion. Spirit is that which is eternally in movement and yet is never caught in any form nor ever expressed in any set of conditions. It may also aid in resuscitating one's conception of spirit to make a mental image, such as is sometimes evoked when one looks at the soft, mellow light over the ocean after a rain. If one looks at the ocean and sees the soft and supple light, one can gain subtle intimations of how what is showing is suggestive of something which is not being shown. This is like the mystical allusions to the bright light of the sun hidden within the dark depths. Such thoughts and images evoke an awareness that what we are seeing is like a partial yet perceptible intimation of that which can never be manifest to the mind which is modified by the sensorium.

Perpetual motion has very little relationship even to the finest and most abstract concepts in contemporary science, or to the subtlest conception of light-energy that one can possibly bring to mind. It is even subtler than that, and it can enable us to imagine better what is involved in the term 'spiritual'. We could think in terms of the night of non-manifestation where there are no universes, no solar systems, nothing in existence, and see that there is a tremendous rhythmic activity, in an undifferentiated medium of matter, of potential ideation which a Rishi once compared to the pulsations in the very depths of the vast, unconscious ocean. Behind and beyond all the surface movements — the ebb and flow of tides, the ripples or the patterns in formation — one must try to imagine what the depths of the ocean are like, not merely at a distance out from oneself, but also at a distance downwards from the surface. We can imagine an ineffable stillness and peace which is accompanied by the most rhythmic pulsations and imperceptible movements. Then we are coming closer to understanding the conception of a boundless and changeless ocean of spiritual light, which has nothing to do with forms as we know them, with sounds as we hear them, with thoughts as we think them, with any concept of identity of existence as we normally experience it, obscuring the light and the voice of the daimon.

If one wants to make functionally meaningful the ancient classifications of human principles, it is necessary to keep moving, by a continual negation through a series of increasingly accurate approximations, to what is implicit in words like *Atman, Buddhi, Manas*, or in a term like 'spiritual'. In the end one must move far away from any definable conceptions of infinity and eternity, which have a certain relativistic shadow cast upon them by all our narrower categories of space and time. The same applies even more in regard to motion and causality. One has to keep moving by trying to make an image, continuing to contemplate, to hold the mind upon an abstract idea which is unbounded. When one comes closer to it, renounce it and start all over again until one really makes void the sense of the self as the container of consciousness, which comes in one's way quite apart from what is inherited and what is shared in language. This can only be done in solitude and by closer communion with the daimon. When a person has made the effort alone, he will come to know that he has truly done it if he can also do it silently in the presence of others. It is necessarily something that has to be attempted again and again in a variety of conditions. In all of them one is experiencing an awareness of the unconditional, not of the unconditional merely as a negative contrast to particularized conditions, but as the realm of creative potentiality in terms of which all conditions are but incomplete representations. A profound and fundamental re-inversion of standpoint is needed to commence the ascent through the conditioned circles of necessity, onwards towards reunion with the spiritual daimon that was in the beginning, and to rebecome self-consciously the presiding spiritual genius of one's own evolution as an integral unit indissolubly united with the whole of Nature and humanity.

ELEMENTALS

The universe is worked and guided from within outwards. As above so it is below, as in heaven so on earth; and man — the microcosm and miniature copy of the macrocosm — is the living witness to this Universal Law and to the mode of its action. We see that every external motion, act, gesture, whether voluntary or mechanical, organic or mental, is produced and preceded by internal feeling or emotion, will or volition, and thought or mind. . . . The whole Kosmos is guided, controlled, and animated by almost endless series of Hierarchies of sentient Beings, each having a mission to perform, and who — whether we give to them one name or another, and call them Dhyan-Chohans or Angels — are 'messengers' in the sense only that they are the agents of Karmic and Cosmic Laws. They vary infinitely in their respective degrees of consciousness and intelligence. . . .

Man . . . being a compound of the essences of all those celestial Hierarchies may succeed in making himself, as such, superior, in one sense, to any hierarchy or class, or even combination of them.

The Secret Doctrine, i 274-76

The metaphysical basis of the doctrine of elementals is essential to understanding the relationship of man to the world. Both man and Nature are composed of a complex congeries of elemental entities endowed with character and perceptible form by continuous streams of ideation originating in Universal Mind. Virtually everything perceived by man, virtually every faculty of action, is such an aggregate of elementals. All the various modes and modulations of active and passive intelligence in man exist and subsist within these fields of elementals, and no aspect of human life is comprehensible without some grasp of elemental existence. Sensation, for example, which is ordinarily thought of in a purely external way, has another side to it when seen from the standpoint of the immortal soul, and this involves the intimate presence of hosts of elementals composing the very organs of sensation and mind.

The entire quest for enlightenment and self-conscious immortality cannot be understood without careful examination of the relationship of human beings to elementals. It is necessary to know where elementals reside and how their inherent modes of activity relate to the different principles in man. Sometimes people who speculate about the hidden side of Nature and human life, either inspired by folklore or a dabbling in the occult, develop a fascination with elementals and inadequately theorize about them. Usually they do not see any significance to elementals beyond their connection with the *prana* principle; this, however, is grossly inadequate and unhelpful, if not downright dangerous, particularly when coupled with lower yogic practices or mediumistic tendencies.

An authentic approach to the doctrine of elementals must be motivated by a desire to regenerate oneself on behalf of all. Both wisdom and compassion are needed if one would master the ways in which a human being may work upon elementals and also be acted upon by them. In practice, this is an extremely intimate and detailed enquiry involving all the most basic activities of daily life. The real nature of home and possessions, of eating and sleeping, and of every other aspect of life is bound up with elementals. Naturally, this includes questions of physical and psychological disease and health, with all the fads and fancies, popular and private, that accompany them. Problems of drugs and depression, along with the other ailments of the age for which there are no available remedies, are bound up with the interactions of the human and elemental worlds. No amount of mechanistic manipulation by doctors, therapists, specialists or religious counsellors will be of any avail in curing these ills of individuals and society; all ignore the fundamental nature of human malaise.

Real human welfare and well-being proceed from within without, beginning in the mind and heart and enacted through responsibility in thought and speech before they are reflected in outward action. The collective regeneration of society, therefore, depends upon the efforts of individuals to regenerate themselves fundamentally — first at the level of their basic self-consciousness, and later in relation to their vestures. Working outward from what one thinks of oneself, this regeneration must involve existing elementals in one's own being and will have definite effects upon everything with which one has contact and relationship. One must do this without falling into increasing self-obsession. One must sustain a universal motive. Merely building a fortress around one's own virtue is incompatible with teaching elementals and giving them the sort of beneficial impress that makes them a healing force in society. To avoid this moralistic delusion and still carry out the work of self-regeneration, one must insert the effort to overcome one's own sins and failings into the most universal context of human suffering. One must feel one's own pain as inseparable from the pain of every atom, every elemental and every human being involved in the collective human pilgrimage. Instead of hiding in fear or withdrawing from it, one must remain sensitive to that universal pain and so become as wide awake as Buddha.

Metaphysically, the doctrine of elementals encompasses the wide range of *devas* and *devatas,* gods and demigods, on seven different planes of differentiated cosmic substance. Extending far beyond medieval lore about gnomes, sylphs, salamanders and undines, the true teaching concerning elementals begins with the root processes by which thought impresses matter with form through Fohat. Much of this teaching is secret, but any aspirant seeking aid in the acquisition of self-mastery will find considerable help in the sacred texts of all the authentic spiritual traditions of the world. These, however, must be approached from the standpoint of the philosophy of perfectibility and the science of spirituality, with no quarter given to blind superstition and stale dogmatism. At the most fundamental philosophical level, the doctrine of elementals is indeed magical and mystical, but this magic is noetic and Akashic. It has nothing to do with the morass of grey psychic practices that pass for magic among pseudo-occultists. Instead, one must begin with meditation upon the abstract Point and the Zero Principle. (See *The Gupta Vidya*, Vol. III: *The Pilgrimage of Humanity*). Without a firmer grasp of principles and without a true mental confrontation with fundamental ideas, it is impossible to understand and use the teaching of elementals for the benefit of the world. Without these rigorous basics, one can only fall prey to secondary and tertiary emanations and so become coiled in nefarious practices and sorcery.

A secure beginning can be found in the recognition that a fully self-conscious sevenfold being is unique. Such a being is the crown of creation, the full embodiment of the macrocosm in the microcosm. In a very specific sense man is, at the essential core of his being, a pure and immaculate crystallized ray of light-energy. This light ultimately represents the radiation of universal self-consciousness, the light that brings together all the gods and all the hierarchies. It goes beyond all colours and numbers to the one clear white light, the secondless light hidden in the divine darkness and silence. Thus man is one with the rootless root of the cosmos, a differentiated being compounded of every conceivable element in every one of the kingdoms of Nature. All the seven kingdoms are in a human being. This, of course, involves not only the physical body, but a series of vestures or *upadhis* on several different planes. In all the vestures of the human being, there is not a single element of any of the kingdoms of Nature, or any of the elemental forces, that is not already present.

This complexity in human nature, spanning the unmanifest and the manifest, is the basis of the paradox that man is both the potential crown of creation and its curse. In the whole of creation, sevenfold man is the unique possessor of the pristine light which precedes, differentiates and integrates, but also transcends, the entire spectrum of colours, sounds, forces, energies and vibrations. At the very core, man is deific and divine. Yet this does not make man sublime or spiritual in a way that stones and animals are not, for the deific breath and the divine afflatus of the One Life is everywhere and in everything. What is crucial about Man is that he is the possessor of self-consciousness through the gift of the *Manasas* and Agnishwatta Pitris, a particular class of the highest gods involving the second and third of the four classes below the first. Man is thus able to synthesize and transcend all the elementals.

Since man at the core possesses a thread of self-consciousness antedating embodied life, man is the integrator of all life. This is, in a sense, what contemporary astronomy and cosmology have come to recognize in studying the hosts of stars and galaxies. They have begun to speak of an anthropic principle in Nature. This is not to be confused with the outdated and parochial notion of an anthropocentric universe. Rather, it is the recognition that one cannot understand life, even at the level of physical chemistry, or in reference to primordial matter on distant planets, without seeing it as part of a vast chain that must ultimately culminate in what we call the human being. Naturally, what is called 'human' on this earth is not necessarily the only possible mode of human being. There could be examples of other, vastly more developed, types of human beings on other planets. Indeed, when one takes into account the possible variations in consciousness connected with the possible modes of human existence, there could be human beings existing not only on other planets, but on other planes of matter, perhaps even now invisibly present on this earth.

To say that man is the microcosm of the macrocosm, whilst having the power of integration that accommodates the maximum diversity of elements throughout Nature, means that man is in fact a cosmos. Whilst that cosmos is deific at the core, it is also so vast that it would be hardly surprising if, at some stage, that cosmos were mostly chaotic. Man is a victim of his inability to master this cosmic complexity within himself. This task demands so high a degree of dignity, integrity, fidelity and control rooted in self-conscious awareness that most people flee at the mere thought of it. They would rather go to sleep or forget about it, exchanging their human prerogative for daydreams, contributing tamasic elementals to hapless rocks and stones. Hence the paradox of the human condition. When man resigns from the difficult work of self-mastery, he abandons his essential place in Nature. The illustrious Pico della Mirandola called man the pivot of Nature. This idea, sadly neglected or falsely interpreted since then, was central to the seven-century cycle of the Theosophical Movement initiated by Tsong-Kha-Pa in Tibet. That cycle has now returned to its original point, and the future unfoldment of spiritual humanity rests upon the restoration of the true dignity of man.

If man, who is the pivot of Nature, abdicates his role, he becomes a curse upon creation, more hellish and demonic than anything that exists in the external realms of Nature, or anything depicted by Hieronymus Bosch and the *tankas* of Tibet. Even the most ghastly tales of goblins, monsters, giants and fiends cannot compare with the actual evil that can exist within a human being. Certainly, one will never find anything in visible and invisible Nature that outdoes the terrifying evil of which human beings are capable. This does not, however, make man into a weak, miserable worm; it makes him into a depraved being, damned of human evolution, and a veritable devil. Deific at the core, man inhabits a cosmos which all too easily becomes a chaos. The most appalling aspects of the demonic side of man have to do with the larger story of lost continents and vanished races, eras when spiritual powers were deliberately misused. Every time a failed human being becomes an elementary, he becomes, as a disembodied entity, an agent responsible for more harm on earth than anything else that exists. This is an invisible but real and terrifying fact of modern civilization, involving all the victims of wars and all the bitter, frustrated victims of accidents, murders, executions and suicides.

If this is metaphysically true, however frightening, it is important to understand what will stimulate and give incentive and motive to a human being to rediscover divinity and dignity. What will strengthen a person, so that he will not abdicate responsibility? First of all, he must relinquish one of the greatest fictions besetting contemporary human beings: the Cartesian

belief in an abyss between mind and matter. Gupta Vidya teaches
that spirit is sublimated matter and matter is condensed spirit.
There is no point in space where there is not a spark of universal
spirit, and there is not a set of particles derived from primordial
substance which is not alive with divine intelligence. The seeming
gap between mind and matter is an illusion created by the
sensorium. In one sense, this illusion is the cost of physical
incarnation: human beings are imprisoned, and indeed self-
entombed, in a body, according to the old Orphic and Platonic
accounts. To some degree, this is an inevitable result of taking birth
in a limited body, even though the best available in natural
evolution. Nonetheless, it is not required by the programme of
Nature that human beings become so inextricably caught up in
the sensorium that they succumb to a fragmentation of themselves
and the world. It is not necessary that their minds become so
cluttered with nouns that they forget verbs, and lose through
language all sense of their spiritual vitality. This corruption of
thought through language has led most human beings to create
a false sense of identity which is actually a dominant elemental.
This offspring of pseudo-self-consciousness is made up of the
lower four elements — earth, air, fire and water, both gross and
astral — and it goes by the name of Mr. X or Ms. Y. The tragedy is
that the souls who have conjured these elementals out of their
identification with the sensorium mistake them for their own real
natures, and confuse the elemental apparitions created by other
souls for real human beings.

It is difficult for souls to wake up from this collectively
reinforced delusion and recognize these elemental projections for
what they are. It is especially hard at this time, when people have
nothing but a fugitive sense of clinging to a personality and when
the once-compelling names and forms of the past mean so little.
The elementals people mistake for themselves know only one law
and one language — that of survival at any cost and of self before
all else. When one adds to this the competitiveness and callousness
of modern society, one gets an elemental of truly monstrous
proportions. No amount of external makeup will hide the

hideousness of that elemental. Such an elemental form, as Buddha taught, is ultimately a composite entity that must be broken up. It has no enduring existence but belongs to the false, parasitic and derivative 'I'. Only by denying a sense of 'I' to this elemental can one release the true sense of 'I-am-I' consciousness in the universal light, at the same time releasing these elementals from the torture of bondage to the delusions and modes of selfishness. Even though human beings may torture elementals for a while, they cannot do so indefinitely. In the long run, they are stronger and more powerful than their captor, who is actually the weak pseudo-man or pseudo-'I', full of sound and fury and signifying nothing. Such a nature lacks the strength of genuine human thought. It is inherently cowardly, unable to do anything against the elementals; the elementals will get their revenge over a period of time.

All elementals are themselves specialized completely within one or other of the elements. This fact, which could work to the advantage of the higher sovereign spirit in man as the integrator of all the elements, becomes the exact opposite in the case of the delusive ego struggling for self-perpetuation. Such a being falls prey to a pathetic and impotent enslavement to elementals that are more intelligent, precise and concentrated than itself. Because these elementals are pure in their fiery, watery, airy or earthy nature, they have an integrity of action that cannot be diverted for long by the twisted deceptions of the false ego. They will eventually wreak their revenge for having been misappropriated on behalf of separative delusions through one form or another of ill health, mental sickness or depression.

Whilst the insecure will fix on this predicament merely as it applies to them, the rectification of wrongs involving the elemental kingdoms is actually an enormous process encompassing the globe. At this time, owing to the Avataric impulse, all the hosts of elementals have been immensely stirred up and hastened in precipitating their revenge on their torturers. The object is to get these people off the face of the earth, so that there will no longer be such a preponderance of selfish beings.

This may be the only alternative to nuclear annihilation if the earth is to be repopulated by real human beings, beings who know how to breathe gratefully just for the privilege of the air. This is an extraordinary time, calling for the reversal of long ages of degradation of the idea of Man and the freeing of Nature from an intolerable regime of domination by selfishness. Put in Christian terms, this means the reversal of the corrupt doctrines of original sin and vicarious atonement, which have obscured the true teaching of Jesus about the perfectibility of man. To understand this reversing process, one has to bring in the invisible world of devils and demons, the idea of a personal god and much else. This is a much older story than the brief history of Christianity and it has happened to every religion.

To come into line with the forward movement of spiritual humanity, individuals must bring about in themselves a fundamental transformation of mind. Through an irreversible *metanoia*, they must calmly and surely overcome the dichotomy between mind and matter, rooting their consciousness in that which is beyond all differentiation. That is why meditation is no longer a luxury, but has become a necessity for survival. Simply recognizing this, however, does not mean that it will be easy or that it will work. If the only meditation one knows is on one's lower self — the elemental — how can one expect that elemental to forget itself? That is impossible. For such beings it is not merely difficult to meditate; it is actually to ask for too much too soon in cases that are too far gone. But even though they seem to be many, they are still a microscopic minority of the whole of the human family. They are powerful because their poisonous pollution can spread fast and wide, weakening lukewarm, irresolute people in the middle who are not really doing any thinking. They can fool themselves for a while, fudging the issue of choice and responsibility, but they are eventually going to be sucked into the vortex of the times and go one way or the other.

All of this should be understood as following from the metaphysical basis of the doctrine of elementals. It is a crucial, if

painful, part of its practical application to the psychological and
meta-psychological life of incarnated human souls. Yet there is
much more to the teaching of elementals than its application to
the lower principles of human nature. Elementals, at the highest
level, are the most etheric, divine elements that exist. They are
sparks of divine flame. This is a part of the secret teachings that
is only comprehensible through initiation. Yet one can understand
theoretically that the Sons of Agni, the divine flame, are the
highest beings in evolution, and that they released myriads of
sparks of fiery intelligence which then, *pari passu* with the
differentiation of primordial substance, became the elemental
world of Nature. This process included the creation of a kind of
elemental prototype of the human being, but one that will not
consolidate or become self-conscious by itself. This must await
the descent of the *Manasas.* Still other elementals remain
permanently in the rarefied realm of *Akasha,* higher than the
aether, let alone the lower astral light. It is these hosts that Shelley
intimated in his poetry. They are invulnerable, all-powerful and
omnipresent.

Elementals reach out to the highest aspects of existence,
which is why it is extremely misleading to link elementals merely
to one principle, such as *prana,* in sevenfold man. All life-energy
works through all life-atoms; there is, therefore, a life-current
existing in human nature which may be called *prana.* It is a sort
of sum-total or quantum of life-energy within the metabolic
system of the human body or, more correctly, within the astral
body. It flows in that body like a fluidic current, and one might
say that the elementals participate actively in it, as if swimming
in an ocean of pranic life-energy. This is where they get their life.
They are repeatedly refreshed by it, especially during sleep, and
this is how they regenerate themselves. Nonetheless, the elementals
belong to each and every one of the human principles except the
Atman.

Only if one understands this can one appreciate the
enormous breadth of the doctrine of elementals. At the highest
end, it includes what are called the gods in exoteric theologies,

hosts of the finest beings in existence, though they are not self-conscious human beings. If they were self-conscious human beings in a previous *manvantara*, they have gone beyond that and only have a collective function, like that ascribed to the Dhyani Buddhas and archangels. At the same time, elementals include the three kingdoms below the mineral kingdom. Paracelsus gave, perhaps, the best summation of the metaphysics of elementals and their connection with man when he said, "Man lives in the exterior elements, and the Elementals live in the interior elements." Through the mind turning outward, man becomes fragmented and abdicates his throne. Becoming totally caught up in the external details of life, man is living, so to speak, outside his own true home. In this sense he is an exile. His body is no longer his temple, for he has cast himself out of it. In truth all the elementals live within that temple, in the interior elements.

Looked at in this way, elementals may be seen to be close to the essential aspects of a human being, in every one of the senses, on every plane and in every vesture. The human mind has its own elementals, which one may call mental elementals if one likes, though in fact they are airy elementals. On the physical plane, man has mostly earthy elementals. Within each principle, there are further subdivisions, so that there are earthy-fire elementals, airy-fire elementals and so on. Even this traditional language of the elements is awkward and misleading at best, since the true meanings of these divisions and subdivisions cannot be correlated with merely visual data, much less with the ever-changing atomic language of modern science. Whatever the linguistic problem, however, there should be no difficulty in seeing that one is really speaking of a vast, shoreless, boundless etheric field populated by billions of elementals. This is the true population of the cosmos, far more numerous than human beings or any other organic beings in any of the kingdoms of Nature. This being so, there is no way that one can even begin to understand human life apart from elementals. All daily activities of human life thus take on a fresh colouration and vitality, a magical potency involved with invisible, interior kingdoms. Every thought, every breath, every feeling and especially every word is filled with magic. Every instant, one either blesses or curses, elevates or degrades, hosts of elementals; every moment, one either sinks downward towards the demonic or soars upward towards the presence of the Blessed.

If thou would'st not be slain by them, then must thou harmless make thy own creations, the children of thy thoughts, unseen, impalpable, that swarm 'round humankind, the progeny and heirs to man and his terrestrial spoils. Thou hast to study the voidness of the seeming full, the fullness of the seeming void. O fearless Aspirant, look deep within the well of thine own heart, and answer. Knowest thou of Self the powers, O thou perceiver of external shadows?

The Voice of the Silence

THE SEVEN DEADLY SINS

I. THE HISTORICAL CONTEXT

He that is without sin among you, let him cast the first stone.
John 8:7

Throughout Christian history, sin has functioned as the Archimedean lever of orthodox Christian morality. From the patristic period to the close of the Middle Ages, sin and its progeny exercised the imaginations of laymen and theologians alike, so much so that European society and culture are unintelligible to those unacquainted with sin. From the refinements of scholastic philosophy to the exuberance of popular fancy, sin functioned as a common measure of man for all alike and in every arena. Suffice it to say, this is not the case in the twentieth century. Indeed, any enquiry today into the seven deadly sins must have a certain quaintness which would itself be entirely unintelligible to an officer of the Inquisition. Even where there were doubts about the right response to sin and even its detailed nature, there was no more doubt of its reality in general than there is today regarding notions like progress. To enquire into sin today can, however, be instructive. Sin is, so to speak, a geologic formation in human history, largely obscured by recent deposits of events, but still there, not far beneath the social surface and obtruding visibly in certain places. To understand it in the past is to understand something of the supports of the present, as well as certain possibilities for the future. Not to understand it is like being haunted by the ghosts of dead ideas.

The Christian notion of sin is, naturally, a successor to previous cultural conceptions. In particular, as one can see through the derivations of terms in the Indo-European tongues, sin and the sins reflect a crystallization of moral ideas around certain aspects of human nature and action. Activities and conditions that were morally neutral became charged with the electric force of sin and salvation, while other elements of human life once regarded as central to spirituality and ethics fell into conceptual and practical eclipse. Since the Renaissance and the Reformation, sin has been displaced by other conceptions and modalities, disclosing the pre-Christian era in a light that was not accessible during the period of Christian dominance, and also putting the era of sin in a not entirely favourable perspective. Hence, one can begin to examine the concept of sin not simply as a possession of Christianity and not simply as the precursor of certain contemporary moral and spiritual ideas, but as a specific approach to the articulation of elements in human life which antedate Christianity and also will be a part of the future. Viewed in this manner, one may ask what sorts of conceptions and ideas about human nature were assembled into the notion of sin. How were they modified in the process? What is there in the history of the idea of sin that illumines the timeless elements of human nature? And is there some way in which the collective experience of sin, the cultural living out of the idea over centuries, can be assimilated to serve the needs of the present?

These and other related questions could be given a sharper focus by attaching a more specific meaning to the idea of contemporary moral and spiritual need. In particular, owing to the massive and pervasive violence of the twentieth century in every sphere, from the political to the social and psychological, it would be helpful to explore the historic development of the idea of sin and then to apply this enquiry to an understanding of violence. Despite the moral anomie of the present century, the idea of violence comes as close as any to arousing a universal moral concern comparable to that evoked by sin in earlier centuries. At least, like sin, violence is scarcely valued for its own sake. This cannot be said, however, for each of the seven modes of action and attitude identified in the past as deadly sins. Pride, for example, is often treated as an integral component of self-respect, a definite contemporary good. Gluttony, though not good for health and perhaps unattractive to spectators, certainly has its unabashed coterie. Such facts underline the necessity of recovering the historical meanings and content of sin and the seven deadly sins before attempting to relate them to contemporary moral realities such as pervasive violence. If one merely engages in perfunctory reflections on pride, avarice and the rest, this will neglect totally the force and substance of their lost status. Thus, one would overlook the longer-term threads of moral meaning once expressed in the notion of sin and now surrounding the notion of violence.

To begin with the linguistic evidence, 'sin' comes from the Latin *sons*, 'guilty', (stem *sont-*, 'existing', 'real'), originally meaning 'real'. It is akin to the Old Norse *sannr*, 'true', 'guilty', from which come *santh* and eventually 'sooth' or 'the truth'. In Latin thought, according to Curtius, "Language regards the *guilty* man as the man *who it was*." The Old High German *sin*, 'to be', has the zero-grade form *snt-ia*, 'that which is', from the Latin root *esse*, 'to be', the Latin *est*, 'he is', the Greek *esti*, 'he is', the Sanskrit *asti*, 'he is', and perhaps also the Sanskrit *satya*, 'true' and 'real'. (The twenty-first letter of the Hebrew alphabet is *sin*, a variant of *shen*, 'tooth', from the shape of the letter, but is not related to the Indo-European 'sin'. Also, Sin, or *zu-en*, the Sumerian moon god, often rendered as *en-zu*, 'lord of wisdom', is unrelated to the term 'sin'. Furthermore, the relation to the Latin *sinister*, 'left', 'evil' and 'inauspicious', is an etymological speculation of unknown merit.)

In Greek thought there is a significant distinction between the early Homeric conception of sinister acts which vitiate the relation between the agent and his or her environment, and the later conception of sinful acts considered in themselves morally wrong and hence offensive to the gods. Whereas the first meaning seems akin to the idea of ritual impurity, the second idea definitely involves the notion of moral misconduct. Thus, Theognis said that *hubris* — overweening disregard of the rights of others — arises out of *koros* — a satiety such as when too much wealth attends a base man. Sophocles added that *hubris* results in a moral and prudential blindness, *ate*, where the evil appears good. Aeschylus explored the relation between such deeds and the rectifying principle of *nemesis* acting over successive generations, whilst the Orphics and Pythagoreans depicted its activity through successive reincarnations of the soul. In Roman thought there is also an older non-moral notion (*scelus* — ill luck attendant upon violation of taboos — and *vitium* — a shortcoming in the performance of a ritual), which later gave way to a moral notion attached to misdeeds. Virgil portrayed heaven, hell and purgatory as the exclusive theatres for the experience of the consequences of moral misdeeds. Perhaps, like Plato, he thought misdeeds were equilibrated in both this world and the afterlife, but he was often misunderstood by Christian thinkers who took a one-life view.

In the New Testament the Greek term translated as 'sin' is *hamartia*. It comes from the root *hamart* and the verb *hamartano*, originally meaning 'to miss', 'to miss the mark', and by extension 'to fail', 'to go wrong', 'to be deprived of', 'to lose', 'to err', 'to do wrong' or 'to sin'. As a substantive *hamartia* means generally 'failure', 'fault', 'sin' or 'error' with most Greek authors, but also includes 'bodily defect' and 'malady' as well as 'guilt', 'prone to error', 'erring in mind' and 'distraught'. In the four canonical Gospels, the term *hamartia* occurs three times in *Matthew*, all in contexts speaking of the forgiveness of sins. It occurs fourteen times in *John*, where it is likened to a form of blindness or incapacity and is connected to the ideas of forgiveness and non-condemnation. It occurs not at all in *Mark* or *Luke*. In the *Acts* and various letters there are about eighty occurrences. This distribution suggests that *hamartia* was perhaps a Gnostic term of reference, so far as the Gospels are concerned, and a point of interest or concern more to the disciples than it was to Jesus. Certainly he never speaks of *hamartia* in a harsh or violent manner.

In subsequent history the Latin term *peccatum*, from the verb *peccare*, meaning 'to stumble', 'to commit a fault' and thus 'to sin', became the principal designation for sin in Christian theology. It is found, for example, in the formula of confession, "*Peccavi*," meaning "I have sinned." The Latin verb derives from *peccus*, 'stumbling', 'having an injured foot', itself from the comparative form *pejor*, 'worse', of the verbal root *ped*, meaning 'to fall'. This is the same root as the noun *ped*, 'foot', and traces to the Greek stem *pod*, 'foot', and the Sanskrit *pada*, 'foot', and *padyate,* 'he goes' or 'he falls'. The same family also produces the English 'pejorative', 'impair' and 'pessimism'.

The enumeration of the seven deadly sins as specific categories of active moral transgression took place sporadically through the general development of Christian theology. While a popular notion in the Patristic period, it did not gain a precise and permanent delineation, probably because of the open texture of theological disputation. In principle, the deadly sins are the causes of other and lesser forms of sin. They are fatal to spiritual progress. The distinction between mortal and venial sins is not a distinction of content such as separates the seven deadly sins from each other. Rather, as in the writings of St. Augustine, it is a juridical distinction of degree of gravity in any sinful act. Mortal sins are either sins serious in any instance or lesser sins so aggravated in their circumstance or degree of wilfulness as to become grave. Mortal sins involve spiritual death and the loss of divine grace. Venial sins are slight offenses against divine law in less important matters, or offenses in grave matters but done without reflection or without the full consent of the will. Actual sin is traceable to the will of the sinner, whereas original sin *(peccatum originale)* is an hereditary defect transmitted from generation to generation as a consequence of the choices made by the first members of the human race.

The classification of sins was ordinarily, during the Middle Ages, part of a system of classification of virtues and vices. Whilst such efforts owed something to classical Greek ideas, they were also varied and distinctly Christian. In the twelfth century monastics like Bernard of Clairvaux and mystics like St. Hildegard of Bingen presented rich visionary descriptions of personified virtues and vices. Hildegard, in her *Liber Vitae Meritorum,* described "cowardly sloth":

> *Ignavia* had a human head, but its left ear was like the ear of a hare, and so large as to cover the head. Its body and bones were worm-like, apparently without bones; and it spoke trembling.

She was also witness to the hellish consequences of various sins:

> I saw a hollow mountain full of fire and vipers, with a little opening; and near it a horrible cold place crawling with scorpions. The souls of those guilty of envy and malice suffer here, passing for relief from the one place to the other.

Thus, through an array of boiling pitch, sulphur, swamps, icy rivers, tormenting dragons, fiery pavements, sharp-toothed worms, hails of fire and ice and scourges of sharpened flails, Hildegard traced out a catalogue of the varieties of sin and their consequences.

With equal imagination, Alanus Magnus de Insulis, in his complex religious allegory *Anticlaudianus*, showed man protected by a host of more than a dozen virtues, clothed in the seven arts, and engaged in a complex struggle against a corresponding host of besetting sins and vices. Nature calls upon the celestial council of her sisters to aid in forming a perfect work. Led by Concord, they come forth to help — Peace, Plenty, Favour, Youth, Laughter (banisher of mental mists), Shame, Modesty, Reason (the measure of the good), Honesty, Dignity, Prudence, Piety, Faith, Virtue and Nobility. Despite all this assistance, Nature can produce only the mortal, albeit perfect, body of man. The soul demands a divine artificer. Reason praises their plan to place a new Lucifer upon the earth to be the champion of all the virtues against vice, and he urges the celestial council to send an emissary to Heaven to request divine assistance. Prudence-*Phronesis* agrees to go, and Wisdom forms for her a chariot out of the seven arts: Grammar, Logic, Rhetoric, Arithmetic, Music, Geometry and Astronomy. Reason attaches the five senses to the chariot and then mounts it as its charioteer. He is able to bring Prudence-*Phronesis* to the gate of Heaven, but can go no further. There, Theology, the Queen of the Pole, takes Prudence into her care and conveys her, supported by Faith, into the Presence. She cannot bear the vision directly, but must look into a reflecting glass, wherein she adores and

worships the eternal and divine All. Then she explains Nature's
plight and asks for aid. Mind is summoned and ordered to fashion
the new form and type of the human mind. Mind constructs the
precious form in the reflecting glass, including in it all the graces
of the patriarchs. Then the new form is ensouled and Prudence-
Phronesis is entrusted with it. She returns in the chariot with
Reason to the celestial council of Nature, where Concord unites
the human mind with the mortal, though perfect, vesture formed
by Nature.

   Unfortunately, when news of this new creature reaches Alecto
in Tartarus, she is enraged. She summons the masters of every
sin — Injury, Fraud, Penury, Theft, Rapine, Fury, Anger, Hate,
Discord, Strife, Disease, Melancholy, Lust, Wantonness, Need,
Fear and Old Age. She exhorts them to destroy this new creature
who threatens their dominions. First, Folly — accompanied by her
helpers, Sloth, Gaming, Idle Jesting, Ease and Sleep — attacks the
man, but the virtues with which he is endowed repel the assault.
So it goes until the final onslaught by Impiety, Fraud and Avarice,
but the man, protected by all the virtues of Nature, by Reason
and all its arts, and above all by his divine mind, prevails. Love
and Virtue banish Vice and Discord, and the earth adorned by
man springs forth in flowering abundance. With this, Alanus
closes, observing that all good flows from the invisible and
unmanifest source of All.

   The doctrinal structuring of this profusion of mystical and
literary variety into a standardized set of seven deadly sins had
begun earlier with St. Ambrose and St. Augustine, who spoke of
pride, avarice, anger, gluttony and unchastity, as well as envy,
vainglory, gloominess (*tristitia*) and indifference (*acedia*, from the
Greek *akedos*, 'heedlessness'). It was Aquinas who, in his *Summa
Theologica*, depicted a systematic series of seven specific virtues,
coupled with corresponding gifts, and opposed by seven specific
vices or sins. In this scheme there are three theological virtues —
fides, *spes* and *caritas* — and four cardinal virtues — *prudentia*,
iustitia, *fortitudo* and *temperantia*. *Fides*, 'faith', is accompanied by
the gifts of *intellectus* and *scientia* and opposed by the vices of

infidelitas, haeresis, apostasia, blasphemia and *caecitas mentis* ('spiritual blindness'). *Spes,* 'hope', has *timor* as its corresponding gift and *desperatio* and *praesumptio* as its opposing vices. *Caritas,* 'charity', is accompanied by the gifts of *dilectio, gaudium, pax, misericordia, beneficentia, eleemosyna* and *correctio fraterna.* It is opposed by the vices of *odium, acedia, invidia, discordia, contentio, skhisma, bellum, rixa, seditio* and *scandalum.*

Then comes the first of the purely moral cardinal virtues, *prudentia,* 'prudence', which is accompanied by the gift of *consilium* and opposed by the vices of *imprudentia* and *neglegentia. Iustitia,* 'justice', the second cardinal virtue, has as its general gift *pieta* and is opposed to *iniustitia.* It comprehends ten lesser virtues as its parts. First comes *religio,* enacted through *devotio, oratio, adoratio, sacrificium, oblatio, decumae, votum* and *iuramentum,* and opposed by *superstitio, idolatria, tentatio Dei, periurium, sacrilegium* and *simonia.* Second is *pietas,* 'piety', along with its opposite, *impietas.* Third is *observantia,* enacted through *dulia,* 'service', and *oboedientia* and opposed by *inoboedientia.* Fourth comes *gratia* and its opposite, *ingratitudo.* Fifth is *vindicatio* or 'punishment'. Sixth is *veritas,* 'truth', opposed by *hypocrisis, iactantia,* 'boasting', and *ironia.* Seventh is *amicitia,* coupled with the vices of *adulatio* and *litigium.* The ninth is *liberalitas,* and its vices are *avaritia* and *prodigalitas.* The tenth and last of these virtues subordinate to *iustitia* is *epieikeia* or *aequitas.* Then comes the third of the cardinal virtues, *fortitudo,* enacted through *martyrium* and opposed by the vices of *intimiditas* and *audacia. Fortitudo* has four subordinate parts — *magnanimitas, magnificentia, patientia* and *perseverantia* — each with the evident opposing vice. Finally, the fourth cardinal virtue, *temperantia,* 'temperance', has as its opposite, *intemperantia,* along with the lesser constituents *verecundia, honestas, abstinentia, sobrietas, castitas, clementia, modestia* and *humilitas,* each of these having in turn its own appropriate vice. Despite the complexity of this system, or perhaps because of it, it did not lead to a popular designation of the virtues and vices, although it endorsed the idea that the mystical number seven should be employed in enumerating the sins.

When the King James translation of the Greek New Testament was done, the following terms emerged as the English names of the seven deadly sins: pride, covetousness, lust, anger, gluttony, envy and sloth.

1. *Pride*: From the Anglo-Saxon *prut*, 'proud'; the Old French *prod*, 'valiant', 'notable', 'loyal', as in *prud'homme*; the Late Latin *prode*, 'advantageous'; and the Latin *prodesse*, 'to be beneficial'; the compound *pro* + *esse*, literally 'to be before'. *Pro*, 'before', is from the Greek *pro*, 'before', 'ahead', and akin to the Sanskrit *pra-*, 'before', 'forward'. In *Mark* 7:22, *huperephania*, 'haughtiness', is spoken of as one of the things that come out of a man, thus polluting him. There are two other references to pride in the Epistles.

2. *Covetousness*: From the Old French *coveitier*, 'to desire'; the Latin *cupiditas*, 'desirousness', and *cupere*, 'to desire'; the Greek *kapnos*, 'smoke' (from which comes the Latin *vapor*, 'steam'); and the Sanskrit *kupyati*, 'he swells with rage', 'he is angry', having to do with smoking, boiling, emotional agitation and violent motion. In *Mark* 7:22, *pleonezia*, 'taking more than one's share', is included in the list of things that come out of a man, thereby polluting him. In *Luke* 12:15, the same term is used when Jesus points out that abundance in life does not arise from possessions. This and similar terms for covetousness occur about fifteen times in the non-Gospel portions of the New Testament. (The term 'avarice', which is now often preferred to 'covetousness', is not part of the vocabulary of the King James version. It is a Latin term, *avaritia*, 'covetousness', from the verb *avere*, 'to long for', 'to covet', and *avidus*, 'avid', related to the Greek *enees*, 'gentle', and the Sanskrit *avati*, 'he favours'. Similarly, 'greed', from the Gothic *gredus*, 'to hunger', and the Old English *giernan*, 'to yearn', and the Old Norse *gjarn*, 'eager' or 'willing', is not a common term in the King James and does not occur at all in the four Gospels. Its Latin roots are *horiri* and *hortari*, 'to urge', 'to encourage' and 'to cheer', from the Greek *khairein*, 'to rejoice', or 'to enjoy', and the Sanskrit *haryati*, 'he likes' or 'he yearns for'.)

3. *Lust*: From the Anglo-Saxon *lust*, 'pleasure'; the Old Norse

losti, 'sexual desire'; the Medieval Latin *lasciviosus*, 'wanton', 'lustful'; the Latin *lascivus*, 'wanton', originally 'playful' as applied to children and animals; the Greek *laste*, 'a wanton woman', *lasthe*, 'a mockery', and *lilaiesthai*, 'to yearn'; and the Sanskrit *lasati*, 'he plays', and *lalasas*, 'desirous'. There is no reference to lust in the four Gospels. However, the terms *orezis*, 'appetite', *epithumetas*, 'desire of the heart', and *hedone*, 'pleasure', occur about two dozen times in the Epistles, almost always in a negative context.

4. *Anger*: From the Old Norse *angr*, 'sorrow', 'distress', and *angra*, 'to grieve'; akin to Old English *enge*, 'narrow', and the Germanic *angst* and *angust*, 'anxiety'; the Latin *angor*, 'strangling', 'tight', 'anguished', and *angere*, 'to distress', 'to strangle'; the Greek *agkhein*, 'to squeeze', 'to embrace', 'to strangle'; and the Sanskrit *amhas*, 'anxiety'. There is one reference, in *Mark* 3:5, to *orges*, 'irritation', (on the part of Jesus) in the four Gospels. There are two other references to anger in the *Epistles*.

5. *Gluttony*: From the Middle English *glotonie*, 'gluttony'; the Middle French *glotoier*, 'to eat greedily'; the Old French *gloton*, 'a glutton'; the Latin *glutto*, 'a glutton', derived from *gluttire*, 'to swallow', from *gula*, 'the throat' or 'gullet' (see 'gullible'); and the Greek *delear*, 'a bait', and *deleazo*, 'to entice' or 'catch by bait'. In *Matthew* 11:19 and *Luke* 7:34, Jesus, contrasting the crowd's reactions to himself and John the Baptist, says that they regard him as a *phagos*, 'a glutton' or 'man given to eating' (unlike John, who neither ate nor drank). There is no other mention of gluttony in the New Testament.

6. *Envy*: From the Old French *envie*, 'envy'; the Latin *invidere*, 'to look at askance' or 'to see with malice', from *in*, a prefix connoting an intensification of the term modified, and *videre*, 'to look' or 'to see', hence 'to look intensively'; with the Latin root *videre* arising from the Greek *eidos*, 'form', and *idea*, 'appearance' or 'idea', and eventually the Sanskrit *veda* and *vidya*, expressing 'knowledge' and 'vision'. Both *Matthew* 27:18 and *Mark* 15:10 refer to the *phthonon*, 'envy' or 'ill-will', towards Jesus of the crowd that chose to have Barabbas freed instead of Jesus. There are a dozen references to envy in the non-Gospel portions.

7. *Sloth*: From the Middle English *slowthe*, 'sloth'; the Old English *slaw*, the Old Saxon *sleu* and the Old High German *sleo*, 'slow', 'dull' or 'blunt'; and perhaps allied to the Latin *laevus* and the Greek *laios*, 'the left', and the Sanskrit *srevayati*, 'he causes to fail'. In *Matthew* 25:26, Jesus uses the term *okneros*, 'shrinking' or 'hesitating', to refer, in the parable of the talents, to the man who hid his portion under the ground out of fear. There are two other references to sloth in the Epistles. (Among Catholic writers, the Late Latin Aquinan term *acedia*, 'sloth', is sometimes preferred to the Saxon term. *Acedia* stems directly from the Greek *akedos*, 'careless', from *a*, 'not', and *kedos*, 'care', 'grief' and 'anxiety', derived from the Avestan *sadra*, 'sorrow'.)

Generally, there is no enumeration or theory of the seven deadly sins in the New Testament. Pride, covetousness, gluttony and sloth are the only ones mentioned directly by Jesus. Even these are passing single references. Of these four deadly sins, pride and sloth are each mentioned only a few times in the non-Gospel portions of the New Testament. Gluttony is totally neglected in the Epistles. Only covetousness seems to be a major concern, receiving mention in approximately twelve places. Anger and envy as such are not spoken of by Jesus at all, although they are mentioned in the Gospels. In the Epistles, however, envy is mentioned twelve times. Lust, which is not even mentioned in the Gospels, is referred to more than twenty-four times in the various Epistles. Overall, Jesus pays little direct attention either to sin or to the species of sin, whilst the disciples, particularly in the Epistles, draw a great deal more attention to sin and, in particular, lust, covetousness and envy. Such, at least, is the testimony of the Greek text of the New Testament as rendered in the King James Version.

It is at this point, where the seven deadly sins receive their authoritative delineation in the English language, that their significance began to wane. The forces of the Renaissance and the Reformation initiated the fundamental moral mutation in European culture that led to modernity. The England of Queen Elizabeth gave way to the England of King James, and it was not so long from there to the Long Parliament. There and elsewhere people started to take a less sacrosanct view of sin and the seven deadly sins. Most important, the effort to reground morality independent of theological conceptions had taken root. It is not necessary here to go into the post-history of the notion of sin, which includes both the reaction against it as well as the effort to salvage some meaning out of it, and a great deal else. Rather, this is the point at which the structure of the concept should be examined, internally, in relation to what went before, and in relation to the present conception of violence.

II. SIN AND VIOLENCE

One of the most striking facts about sin and its division into seven cardinal forms is the general historical disarray and lack of agreement on this point. Perhaps the list of the seven deadly sins has been reasonably stable in the English language for the past three hundred years precisely because the topic has no longer been a focus of active cultural interest. Certainly, in the preceding sixteen hundred years the list varied immensely. Put in another way, despite the efforts of systematizers, there was no broadly accepted basis for an exhaustive classification of the sins, or of the virtues, for that matter. No doubt there is something arbitrary about any scheme of classification. For example, to say that all directions may be defined in terms of north, south, east and west is not to argue that they must be so defined. Yet from a certain perspective that is readily reached by most human beings, in relation to their idea of location on the earth, this seems an orderly and exhaustive scheme. Unlike the four cardinal directions, the seven deadly sins enjoyed no such widespread self-evidence. Even the division into seven seems to have been but a self-conscious effort to reflect the intellectual ways of classical antiquity, but without a compelling grasp of its logic.

When Plato has Socrates refer, without argument, to the four cardinal virtues as Justice, Wisdom, Courage and Temperance, he does so with a definite basis for the division in mind. Each mode of *arete* or 'excellence' exists as a quality or property of a human faculty, or relationship of faculties, which enables it to perform its natural function well. Thus, Wisdom is the virtue of the mind. Courage is the virtue of the spirited nature. Temperance is not the virtue of the appetitive nature, but rather its agreeable governance by the higher faculties. Justice is the principle that each faculty in man should perform the function which it is, by nature, suited to perform — nothing in excess or defect of this mean. Justice is thus the principle of virtue itself. This relationship between the system of psychology and the system of ethics is crucial to the Platonic view of man. It is more than an analogy. It is a primary basis for connecting human welfare and meanings with the broader activities of Nature, since the elements of the human psyche are inseparably derived from Nature, including its root ordering principle or *logos* and its fundamental moving causes or *theoi*. Hence, human virtues and vices represent aspects of the art of living well or ill, which is founded upon a knowledge of the psyche in the *kosmos*. The same principles can be traced out in Orphic and Pythagorean thought, as well as in Buddhist philosophy. To put it in borrowed Christian terms, simply to draw out the contrast with Christian orthodoxy, because man is God moving as Nature, when man realizes God as himself he is the master of Nature.

This is a view not easily accommodated to the Augustinian formula of the two cities and the burden of irredeemable sin. At the same time, there is in the Augustinian view a clear division of the human constitution into body and soul, and this serves the purposes of moral classification by giving a clear locus to sin. Since, *contra* Pelagius, no set of virtues can offset the alienation from God, the *peccatum originale* represented by incarnation into the bodily nature, there is really no theoretical point to a classification of the moral faculties of the incarnated soul. Thus, there is equally no sound basis for a systematic classification of sins and vices. There is simply the chthonic mass of sin irredeemably divorced from the ordering influence of the Deity, and from which the soul must be plucked by the instrumentalities of grace and the sacraments. Hence, even if there is in the seven deadly sins an imitation of classical schemes of the virtues and vices, there is not the psychology to make this borrowing consistent over centuries. This, however, was not felt as a disadvantage. In fact, the absence of the niceties of Graeco-Roman philosophies could be understood as a more forthright and less effete coming to grips with the hydra-headed problem of sin.

It is now clear that sin is quite different and much more intractable than any of the moral disorders contemplated in the classical world. The very shifts in the meanings of terms used to describe these disorders, as well as the fact of moral disorder itself, show it. The juridical and accusatory flavour of sin as guilt; the conversion of the mild and even pitiable *hamartia*, missing the mark, into a heavy moral pejorative; and the adoption of the relatively innocuous *peccus*, stumbling, to express the irredeemable moral fall of man, all suggest a hardening of moral categories and attitudes. Despite the absence of any such attitude on the part of Jesus in the New Testament, who only mentions sin as something to be forgiven or left behind, later writers lent sin monumental proportions, making it a prime focus of thought, speech, action, even meditative prayer, and above all, moral education. In fact, there seems to be a kind of violence brought into the notion of sin that was not part of the classical conception of moral failings or part of the Gospels.

A comparison with Buddhism is helpful, wherein the monk is encouraged to meditate with courage and compassion upon the sufferings of birth, death, sickness and error. It would alter the entire aura of the Buddhist way of life to substitute 'original sin' for 'error'. It would be almost as though one were to give up the hope of enlightenment and submerge the consciousness in a dark mass. The same point could be made by examining the Platonic notion of ignorance or the Hindu conception of *avidya*. It would be foolish to argue that these are categories shallow in their implications for moral life, but they do not convey the almost stifling sense of heaviness of sin. Perhaps it was the relative lightness or unburdened nature of a number of Eastern moral cultures that left morally serious Europeans, missionaries and laymen alike, with the impression that non-Europeans lacked a proper sense of morality. But then again, the average twelfth-century resident of Paris would probably have a similar complaint about the contemporary residents of London or Los Angeles.

If we turn to the particular deadly sins, several curious points emerge. For example, pride, which heads some orthodox lists and is omitted from others, is now more admired as a virtue than a vice. This is because nobody thinks, anymore, of the terrible fall of Adam and Eve from grace when they speak of "pride of accomplishment", "proud parents" or the like. Nor are they thinking of the Greek *hubris*. Generally, like most of the seven deadly sins, pride is today simply one among a host of psychological or behavioural states which are relatively acceptable or unacceptable, depending upon circumstances. It is simply difficult to put oneself in Lucifer's putative position and get a sense of what awful thing the medieval mind saw in him. Worse yet, from an orthodox standpoint, the Renaissance restored a portion of the classical admiration for Lucifer-Prometheus, so that the supposed arch-villain of pride is converted into a folk hero of sorts against the violent depredations and tortures of the Inquisition. To say that a heretic was "proud as Lucifer" became a compliment among individuals committed to the spread of light and learning in the Renaissance. Since the word 'pride' itself had originally meant 'valiant', 'loyal' and 'notable', one wonders whether the entire history of pride as a deadly sin is actually a history of the removal from power of various prominent nobles who opposed the social and political advance of the Church. The saying "Pride cometh before a fall" may have been used more as a political *verbum sapienti* than as a principle in moral philosophy. The issue of pride is still complex, as the Shelleys show — Mary pointing to the darker side in Frankenstein and Percy to the brighter in *Prometheus Unbound*. Victor Frankenstein, like Faust, seems more a case of *hubris* than of Adamic disobedience. There is no one for Victor to disobey. Yet he does display an arrogant disregard for other men and even Nature, releasing violent forces beyond his control. His pride has become an accepted token of the new *hubris* and the threat of violent doom it wantonly imposes on masses of human beings.

Covetousness too has undergone a sea change in the modern era. As a term, it has largely died out, to be replaced by 'avarice' and more commonly by 'greed'. Where the original term pointed to a psychological state of being smoked out by the boiling of one's desires, modern attention, as in so many things, has moved to the correlative exterior object. Greed is defined in relation to material possessions, not interior ferment. Desire is generally accepted as necessary, and seen as requiring not elimination but equitable management in relation to resources and expectations. There is support in the New Testament for this concern with equity in relation to covetousness, though usually the term connotes an unregulated appetite. The contemporary Gandhian maxim that the world has enough for man's need, but not his greed, points to the significance of old-fashioned covetousness. It was also Gandhi who said that poverty, the consequence of some people taking more than their share of the commonwealth, was the worst form of violence. It may be some time, however, before mental and spiritual poverty and dispossession are recognized along with their corresponding modes of violence, owing to our contemporary concentration on externals, itself a symptom of inner poverty. The violent attempts of the have-too-muches to dominate and enslave the have-not-enoughs is central to covetousness in any age. Psychologically, it is a failure of self-government of the appetites by humanity, a loss of Platonic temperance or *sophrosyne*, resulting in a self-destructive civil war.

Of all the seven deadly sins, lust seems to be the one most widely rejected today as a failing, and therefore most commonly embraced in practice. The theory of repression is set forth as a proof of the unhealthiness and impossibility of overcoming lust. Hence lust is generally held to be a mistaken and outmoded category, representative of an era of ignorance about human nature. The fact that lust was not originally restricted to the sphere of sexuality, but applied to the entire field of pleasure and pain, is now ignored. It began to be ignored, though for different reasons, from the time of Augustine. Thus, the classical meaning of lust is considerably narrowed in orthodox thought, even as compared with its meaning in the New Testament. Actually, Mill and Bentham could be seen as restorers of the full conception of lust, except that they came to praise pleasure, not to overcome it. Even Mill, however, speaks of higher pleasures, suggesting that physical pleasures represent a kind of inferior good. But in the democracy of the contemporary psyche, it is difficult to make the case against any pleasure that seeks its day, and even pains vie for equal consideration. The notion that attraction and aversion have some end beyond themselves is difficult to grasp, and the discussion of them is often pitched at the most vulgar level, in the name of honesty and accuracy. This sort of relentless reductionism of the motives of the psyche is itself a kind of violence, a lusting in one's lusts, so to speak. The relationship between overcharged sexuality and explosive violence is all too familiar in our time.

One might expect a straightforward relationship between anger and violence. The origin of the term points to the constriction and tightening of the psyche. Anger is the buildup of internal pressure before a volcanic eruption. The terms *angst* and 'anxiety' are readily connected to these phenomena. What are less familiar or accepted are the subtler aspects of this contraction or constriction of the nature called anger. Franz Anton Mesmer diagnosed a variety of illnesses directly in terms of such a contraction, while an earlier era bore witness to the unhealthy effects of a choleric disposition. Despite these ideas, which support a fairly continuous judgement in history that anger ought to be dispensed with, there is nevertheless a school of thought which holds that anger is acceptable, if only it is released regularly. Like steam in a boiler, it can do a lot of work, but when it is not put to work, it can accumulate to dangerous levels. In this view, the violence associated with outbursts of anger is not to be held against anger itself, but is seen as the unregulated letting off of otherwise valuable steam. This notion then gives rise to a theory of creativity based upon anxiety, tension and conflict, in effect a refined anger. This outlook is further complicated by the dual meaning of the term *animus*, which is vital energy on the one hand but the basis of animosity on the other. To have a strong *animus* is to have great energy, but also to run a great risk of anger and conflict. Hence the contemporary confusion of aggressiveness, assertiveness and fighting with individuation. The nature and qualities of the energies themselves which flow through the individual and which are reflected in anger must, however, be considered. Since energy, whether physical or psychological, remains a morally neutral category, it is helpful to turn to the Sankhya conception of the three *gunas* — *sattva*, 'light', *rajas*, 'restlessness', and *tamas*, 'darkness'. These three pervade all Nature, including man, and give a definite inherent moral quality to all thought, feeling and action. There may be certain types of psychic energy that are inherently violent in their expression, or inevitably explosive when mixed, no matter how one proposes to handle the relief valves, whether individual or collective.

If anger has to do with violent outbursts, perhaps gluttony may be thought of as a contrasting state of unregulated, even violent, intake. As with many of the other deadly sins, both orthodoxy and modernity seem to have narrowed the associated ancient connotations of the term. Gullibility, the etymological cousin of gluttony, conveys a wider scope and suggests a general lack of discrimination. The image of a fish snapping at the bait and thereby becoming caught has at least as broad a moral application as that of a pig feeding at a trough. There is an obvious relationship between gluttony and inability to follow ascetic discipline — whether in relation to the mind, the heart or the body. The single reference to gluttony in the New Testament is the ironic reference of Jesus to himself, when he drew a contrast to the sternly ascetic John the Baptist. In a similar vein, Gandhi made control of the palate a prerequisite to *brahmacharya*, chastity at every level or the devotion of one's entire being to the realization of *Brahman*. Anyone who has ever attempted to learn, whether about a specific situation or a general idea, has seen the need to narrow the focus of attention, concentrate on essentials, and not snap at everything that comes by. To be a glutton is to fill oneself with inessentials and overwhelm one's power of assimilation, thus doing a good deal of violence to one's constitution.

Envy, on the other hand, is the will to do harm, evil or violence to others. This sin has been almost entirely misunderstood by modernity. It is evident from the original meaning of the term that it is equivalent to the evil eye, an unfortunate but prevalent fact of life, according to many ancient and traditional cultures. Plato, like Patanjali, suggested that there are emanations of the eye involved in vision, along with the reception of external influences. Paracelsus, Mesmer and a host of others elaborated the same point. Indeed, the whole history of healing seems to give direct or grudging acceptance to the power of unspecifiable influences flowing from the physician to the patient. Envy is the other side of the coin. Christian theology early adopted the view that healing was a supernatural and miraculous process, involving divine intervention. It also rejected the notion of the malevolence of envy, attributing its force to possession by the devil. As the entire notion of sin has declined, and hence interest in the devil, the notion of envy has shifted from the idea of active ill-will to the idea of a desire to usurp the possessions of others. Thus, envy is now understood as a desire to have things that belong to others — whether material goods or more abstract ones — and is often conflated with covetousness or greed. This displacement of envy from the other person to their possessions and properties masks the nature of the violence implicit in the older conception. In fact, envy would appear to be the deadly sin most directly connected with violence in the sense of a conscious volition or will to do harm, injury and murder to another. In Gandhian terms, envy comes closer than even anger to pure *himsa*. The contemporary impression that envy has to do with objects, not persons, and that it is a form of desire for some good, masks its vicious and unjustifiable antecedents. From a classical perspective it would be a serious error to dismiss envy as an innocent but understandable disappointment of bourgeois expectations regarding denied access to economic goods.

Turning finally to sloth, it is in its ancient antecedents certainly the most elusive of the seven deadly sins. Sloth itself seems to be almost an aboriginal Teutonic conception. As such, it was rejected by Latin writers who, like Aquinas, preferred the term *acedia*, a neologism from the Greek invented for the purpose. But the term *akedos* clearly represents, at least in Greek, an absence of anxiety, and is thus akin to the absence of anger. Thus there seems to be a dilemma: one must choose between anger and sloth. Later criticism of the idea of religious tolerance as being a form of sloth suggests that there should be righteous anger directed towards wickedness. The Hamlet problem persists in a variety of forms. It has to do with the ability to release the will, and this is perhaps the essence of sloth. On the other side, the Teutonic notion of that which is slow, dull and blunted also conveys an image of the depotentiated will. If it is correct that the old Teutonic 'sloth' is akin to the Greek *laios*, or left, this would connect sloth with classical conceptions of impurity and pollution of the will. This was a powerful idea in the ancient world, but since it has to do with the capacity to invoke divine potencies, it is not a theme upon which Christian orthodoxy encouraged speculation. Hildegard's vision of sloth as lacking a spine is very suggestive to anyone familiar with Patanjali's *Yoga Sutra*. Perhaps the old Celts and Teutons retained an awareness of certain rites and ceremonies which could not be performed if the proper will was lacking in the officiant. From the standpoint of orthodox Christian theory, however, the sacraments could be performed by any officiant properly vested by a consecrated bishop. The success of the ceremony did not depend on the will of the officiant, but was ordained from without. Naturally, the priest was expected to live a pure life and could be defrocked, but so long as he remained a priest in name, all sacraments conducted by him were held to have succeeded. There is here a considerable question of the source and polarity of the forces that are supposed to act through the officiant. In the ancient view, they flow from the inner divinity of the man. In the orthodox view, they are called from without.

Unfortunately, this debate has become almost meaningless to modern thought, though there are remnants of the idea in the contrasts of dependency and self-reliance, slavery and freedom, cowardice and strength.

Put more philosophically, the issue of sloth would have to do with reliance upon the external, the material and the manifest, amounting to a resignation of initiative, will and power of choice. This is much more than laziness. In fact, it is a kind of killing oneself, and in classical terms, it is making oneself the focus of misfortune which can, when given an opening, wreak terrible devastation upon human society and well-being. In this sense, sloth is the deadly sin most allied to the Homeric conception of a violation of that which is *hieros* or holy. The interleaved Greek concepts of *akrasia*, 'a bad mixture', *akrateia*, 'incontinence', *akrates*, 'impotence' and *akratos*, 'unmixed' or 'pure', may be allied with this idea of sloth as an inversion *(anatrope)* and atrophy *(atrophos)* of the will. This is an even more morally vital consideration than the Aristotelian *akrasia* or 'weakness of will'. Jesus declared that the Kingdom of Heaven must be taken by storm, and Dostoievsky's Grand Inquisitor disdainfully remarked that heaven is certainly not for a flock of servile geese.

If many classical conceptions of human moral nature are preserved in the notion of sin and the set of seven deadly sins, others no less important are ignored or reversed. The passage of time has witnessed an erosion of the concept of sin itself. The modern estimate of moral defects and misdeeds is nowhere near as harsh and judgemental as the medieval assessment, nor is it so pessimistic. At the same time, it is much less theoretic and thoughtful, having little or no access to ontology, and hence no secure psychology. Perhaps some of the nostalgia moralists feel for the certainties of sin arise from a recognition that the moral problems of the twentieth century cannot be solved in a way that is psychologically or metaphysically cheap.

Gandhi, the exemplar in the twentieth century who has, more than any other, confronted the gravity of human moral failings in a profound and powerful fashion, found it necessary to elaborate out of Hindu, Buddhist, Muslim and Christian sources, not to mention a great array of secular reformers and theorists, a whole new metaphysic of Truth, enacted and embodied through the master virtue of non-violence. One might expect that the corresponding master vice or sin in such a view would be violence, but it is not. The besetting sin of humanity and civilization is not violence but untruth. Violence is the universal expression of untruth, and all the more specific moral failings of mankind are ultimately traceable to it. Here Gandhi is in agreement with Jesus, who affirmed that knowledge of truth will make men spiritually free. Plato and Shankara taught the same view, attributing moral error to ignorance or *avidya*. The obvious judgemental and retributive concern with sin and its varieties during a large portion of the history of Christian orthodoxy is quite distant from these more compassionate conceptions. In fact, seen from a modern perspective, the net result of European involvement in the concept of sin was a tremendous release of violence in the name of religion. While the future may well require a degree of moral self-consciousness considerably higher than present slothful attitudes, it would be unfortunate, and fortunately unlikely, to resuscitate the seven deadly sins in all their medieval splendour. It is also unlikely that there will be a return to classical modes of culture. Instead, and this is perhaps the lesson to be learnt through twenty centuries of experience of sin, perhaps there will finally be an appreciation of the proposition "Judge not, that you be not judged. For with the judgement you pronounce, you will be judged, and the measure you give will be the measure you get." How could it be any other way in a universe of Law?

III. NON-VIOLENCE AND REGENERATION

The seven deadly sins can be viewed independently of their historical and theological interpretations. They may be seen as an open-textured set of human actions, attitudes and dispositions related to each other through their common participation in an underlying spiritual condition of the soul. In particular, in a Gandhian perspective they may be seen as complex instances and ramifications of violence deriving from untruth. One may leave open the question whether all forms of violence are comprehended within the moral connotations of the seven deadly sins. Certainly, a broad and important range of ethically problematic action does arise through what we understand as pride, avarice, lust, anger, gluttony, envy and sloth. Each of these terms has a rich penumbra of meanings, and each at the core represents the obscuration of an essential aspect of human strength (or virtue, in the classical sense of the word). In a Spinozist analysis they are passions, passive reactions of the human being informed by inadequate ideas — a lack of fullness of spiritual vision of the wholeness of Nature, the wholeness of Man and the wholeness of God. In a Kantian sense they are all fallings off from the ideal of a purely good will. They are forms of moral self-contradiction, inherently non-universalizable, and therefore constituting corruptions of the soul's faculty of reason. In a Pauline sense they are failures of love, of charity and of sympathy. They display the lifelessness, coldness and cruelty that are inescapable so long as the soul lies bound in the coils of mortality and is unable to ascend through an intimate adoration of the divine — that in which we live, move and have our collective being.

All three of these themes — blinded vision, corruption of will and erosion of sympathy — are crucial to an understanding of contemporary moral, psychological, spiritual and social violence, whether one considers the small circle of friends and family, the wider circle of the city and nation or the great circle of the globe.

These three tendencies are like powerful vectors flowing from the centre of one's nature and forming a kind of inverted constellation of force. Where there ought to be vision, strength and love, there is instead blindness, weakness and hatred — a sort of dwarfed and perverted caricature of human nature, a tragic realization of a Hobbesian view of man. This condition is no doubt pervasive in modern civilization, which Gandhi compared to the South American upas tree, a maleficent tree that emanates noxious vapours, choking out life for miles around. But the crucial question is whether this is the natural and inevitable condition of humanity, or whether it is, as Spinoza, Kant, St. Paul and Shankaracharya would affirm, a superimposition upon underlying powers of wisdom, courage and love. The latter view, like its opposite, is unverifiable and therefore also unfalsifiable.

Neither optimism nor pessimism about human nature can be given an unexceptionable warrant on narrowly empirical grounds. Yet as Plato observed in the *Republic*, it makes all the difference in the world whether we tell small children that Nature is inherently consistent with human good and also non-deceptive, or the reverse. We either encourage the child's sense of responsibility and natural capacity to learn, or we cripple them. Where there is a firm optimism about Humanity, Nature and History, there will be a lifelong inclination to learning and self-correction. No man or woman would willingly harbour in the heart an untruth, a falsehood, a lie about the most important things, since this would subvert at the core all one's attempts to realize any good in life. Paradoxically, the worst falsehood one could clutch to one's bosom would be the pessimistic doctrine that evil and ignorance are the inevitable moral condition of man. No matter how ugly the moral visage of humanity may seem in an age obsessed with murder, rapine and deceit, and terrified of mass self-annihilation through foolish or self-righteous misadventure — nevertheless, despair and doubt are the most disabling dangers. Perhaps this is why faith and hope are mentioned before charity, even though charity is greatest of all.

In a similar manner Gandhi displayed a marked reluctance

to begin with an affirmation of the power of love and then to derive from it all other modes of human strength and goodness. Instead, he began like Plato with an affirmation of the centrality of the vision of truth in one's life and the necessity of unwavering adherence to the truth as one knows it in one's heart. Without this devotion to truth, one's life is worth nothing. It is like a vessel with no compass. It cannot lead one to any fair haven. Yet the Gandhian idea of truth is much more than any merely cognitive state of mind. It is first and foremost an ontological precondition. In Indian thought *Sat* is absolute reality, beyond the realm of genesis and corruption. It is the ineffable ground of all truth and existence, the source both of differentiated subjectivity and objectivity. The *satya* in a human being is his or her relative and partial realization of the abstract ideal of Truth, what one might call the tap-root of one's true being. According to many cognate metaphors, the life of true Nature is stifled and choked out by a secondary and sporadic growth. In the *Bhagavad Gita* this is powerfully expressed in terms of the great Ashwatha tree of the world, growing downwards from its roots in heaven and branching out to fill all space with its mayavic or illusionary foliage. To reach wisdom, one must hew down this tree with the sharpened blade of discrimination. In Chaucer's *Parson's Tale* the whole assemblage of the seven deadly sins is seen as the trunk of a great tree from which ramify all the hosts of sinful acts. In either case, what is necessary is to cut this false growth at the root so that the true individual may flourish. The vision, strength and compassion needed to do this are themselves aspects of the higher life of humanity, and their awakening is the obverse of the extinction of spiritual ignorance, impotence and malice.

Like Gautama Buddha, Gandhi held that "Hatred ceaseth not by hatred but by love", and like Jesus Christ he held that the direct measure of one's love, and therefore truth, was in one's daily conduct in relation to others. One treats everyone with whom one comes in contact either with violence, or *himsa*, arising out of one's own untruth or *asatya*, or with *ahimsa*, non-violence, arising out of one's realization of truth or *satya*. There is no intermediate course, according to Gandhi, and thus human nature either sinks or soars at every moment. There is an earnestness to human life, a moral significance that is either sensed and seized through self-discipline, or allowed to slip away through the insidious influence of the elements of untruth in oneself. This is an especially dynamic view of moral life, and whilst perhaps explaining in part the amazing intensity of Gandhi's own life, it also draws attention to the volatility of the various vices and virtues with which moral self-discipline is concerned. Every situation brings with it fresh opportunities for learning and new tests and trials in one's grasp of truth. What one may have understood yesterday is valuable but insufficient to meet the challenge of today. Gandhi, therefore, readily recognized that "sufficient unto the day is the evil thereof", and he often recited the invocation in Cardinal Newman's hymn, "Lead, kindly Light, . . . one step enough for me."

This willingness to take an incremental view of moral growth while holding to the exacting universality of truth and non-violence as twin moral absolutes is the Gandhian key to progressive self-transformation rooted in self-transcendence. In this way, one avoids the Scylla of self-righteousness and the Charybdis of despair. No attainment can exhaust the potentiality of truth and non-violence. Hence, every realized good must point beyond itself. No failing can divest truth and non-violence of their vital relevance to the future. Hence, every misdeed must also point beyond itself. By holding to the possibility of progressive growth, and thereby recognizing the possibility of moral regression, one can avoid the static smugness of those who are too confident of their salvation, as well as the stagnant inertia of those who are too assured of their damnation. Either extreme extinguishes initiative. Unlike any conception of a fixed or homeostatic mean between two extremes, Gandhi sought a dialectical balance between theory and practice, ideal and act, which could release the energies of the soul and of truth itself. No doubt this vision of life is both exacting and elusive. But it holds the promise of the amelioration of human misery, transmitting hope and human dignity to the civilization of the future.

   If the ontological core of *ahimsa* or non-violence is *satya* or truth, then the various forms of violence must be seen as varieties of untruth manifesting with differing degrees of intensity. Just as one can adopt the ideals of truth and non-violence at a minimal or mundane level and also at a maximal or mystical level, one will find that the moral afflictions of human nature have their grosser and subtler forms. One might exemplify truth and non-violence in certain limited contexts and in one's relations, while at the same time one may have far to go inwardly. This is perhaps what Gandhi meant by saying, when asked whether he had no vices, that he had no *visible* ones. Whilst anyone could overcome one or another of the seven deadly sins outwardly, this would be but a preparation for a more intensive internal struggle. This is only common sense, and it is also the essential teaching of every great tradition of spiritual training, such as that of Gautama Buddha and John of the Cross. Both warn against the subtle recrudescence of the sins awaiting the spiritual seeker. One is never safe until the diseases of the soul are removed at the root. It would clearly represent a tremendous improvement in human affairs to remove physical violence, especially rape, murder and warfare. But this advance means little if it is purchased at the price of a psychological reign of terror and the spiritual murder of souls. It is not so much that the contemporary theory of repression is wrong about human nature, which it is, but rather the reason that it is wrong: it is simply another case of treating the symptoms and not the disease. The roots of ignorance, egotism and attachment must be cut if the poisonous tree of deadly sins is to die and the tree of life is to spring up in its place.

   Classically, pride signifies spiritual blindness, overweening self-concern, and arrogant disregard of others in the pursuit of one's own supposed good. Spinoza called pride a species of madness, thereby suggesting that it springs from a fundamentally delusive conception of one's own existence. The image of the tower as the isolated haunt of pride points to its divorce from reality. Pride is the opposite of the sagely posture portrayed in the

Bhagavad Gita, wherein the wise man is said to be content in the Self through the Self — the universal *Atman.* Instead of this divine sufficiency and transcendent unity, the proud man is restlessness incarnate, holding forth against the world but also hopelessly entangled in snares of his own making. The story of Alexander and the Gordian knot is a parable of pride, and so too is Milton's study of *Samson Agonistes,* doomed to toil "eyeless in Gaza". In both cases, pride seizes upon seeming strength to undo the soul. Even the tragic grandeur of such failures has a magnetic attraction for the proud, a higher self-destructiveness or violence of the soul towards itself. According to John of the Cross, spiritual neophytes take pride in their fervour and diligence, taking on a new layer of false identity directly from their sincerest endeavours. This is known in Buddhist practice as the shadow of oneself outside the Path. To become fascinated by it is fatal to inner growth, since it involves turning away from the source of one's being — the metaphorical and noumenal inner light — towards the image cast by oneself on the field of one's awareness. As Patanjali stressed, the underlying ignorance or *avidya* gives rise to the false idea that the ephemeral non-self is the enduring Self. This false sense of identity is subject to myriad vicissitudes, lifted up and cast down by turns through attraction and aversion. Because of this involuted posture, the capacity of the will is subverted and the power of sympathy for others is blocked. What begins in a form of violence towards one's true Self results in an obsessive self-regard which sees others merely as means to one's own selfish ends. As a form of madness, pride is the root of self-destruction.

All the other deadly sins may be seen as arrayed around the core of pride, some related to its subjective and some to its objective manifestations, obscuring the powers of vision, strength and sympathy. Thus, one may think of avarice, anger and envy as a turning outwards of pride into the objective field. Avarice represents the ignorant attempt to compensate for the felt insufficiency of the false self through external goods. Anger represents the impotent assertion of the unregulated centrifugal force of desire turned outward by the ego into the hall of mirrors of the phenomenal world. Envy represents the loveless striving, contention and opposition of the separative personal will against the seeming otherness of other wills in the world. On the other side, lust, gluttony and sloth may be thought of as manifestations of pride turned inward upon the subjective field of awareness. Lust seeks to fill up the void in the centre of one's being that is due to the ignorance of the joy of awareness of supernal unity with a riot of subjective fantasies of pleasure. Gluttony represents the unbalanced operation of the centripetal force of desire turned inward into an all-consuming vortex. Sloth is the careless indifference of will even to one's own well-being, a perverse inattention to the health and purity of the soul, and a sick lovelessness towards oneself that is rooted in the corruption of the will through despair.

In practice, of course, any such systematic conceptualization should function as an aid to reflection and a guide to thought. Nonetheless, it would be useful to trace out the specific relations of the deadly sins to non-violence according to this schema.

Ignorance of the true nature of things, for Plato and Jesus, for Spinoza and Gandhi, is the source of all the futile attempts to fill up life with one or another form of compensatory activity. When these pursuits focus upon external outlets, they involve the acquisition of objective possessions from a deceptive realm wherein to divide is definitely to take away. This striving after external goods is insatiable, since it is a pointless persistence in seeking spiritual fulfilment through material means. Thus, avarice inevitably draws the individual into recurrent conflicts with others. Socrates remarked, after depicting the origin of the luxurious society, that herein lay the cause of expropriation and warfare. Proudhon simply defined property as theft. Gandhi elaborated a similar conception by extolling the virtues of *asteya*, non-stealing, and *aparigraha*, non-possession, as essential to the votary of non-violence. His own individual stance towards personal possessions is well known, but he also put forth a subtle theory of trusteeship for all external goods as an ethically superior alternative to the violence of aggressive capitalism as well as militant communism. When this ontological and psychological sense of deficiency is internalized, there is a futile effort to compensate for it through subjective claims and ideological propaganda. This quest for gross or subtle pleasures is, as contemporary psychology has discovered, extremely malleable and elusive, and is able to adjust itself internally to virtually any external conditions.

Pleasure and pain are not simple terms with stable referents, but amount to a pair of concepts convertible in denotation, depending upon circumstances. In all cases, however, whether one is caught in the attractive or repulsive side of the effort to compensate for a sense of non-being, the direction of attention is away from the centre and towards the elusive focus of desire. For Gandhi, the letting go of all these lustings and longings involved the practice of *brahmacharya*, a term that certainly includes chastity in the ordinary sense, but also means the pursuit of *Brahman*, identical with *Sat*, with one's whole being. True inward chastity is full devotion to the truth, and therefore essential if one is to release the active energy or force of truth through *ahimsa*. According to Patanjali, true *brahmacharya* releases *virya*, inward strength, the strength needed to persevere in one's pursuit of the truth. This strength is vital in the face of the innumerable distractions and snares that trap the ego, annoying and disheartening it. Typically, anger and gluttony are seen as failures of self-control in the face of provocation from without or seduction from within. We sometimes speak of them as connected with sore spots and weak spots in our nature, certain points of vulnerability.

For Gandhi, anger and gluttony, *krodha* and *lobha*, are manifestations of a deceptive reliance upon that which is false. They are essentially opposed to true sovereignty and freedom of the will, *swaraj*, and also true self-reliance, *swadeshi*. Where there is reliance upon the truth, it is possible to release the non-violence of the brave and fearless. Where there is true freedom, there is joyous self-mastery. In their absence one will be beset by anger towards those who seem to threaten one's weakness or by a gluttonous craving for whatever seems to veil it from one's view. The oscillation between these two can itself be quite violent and extreme. As John of the Cross noted, anger at others, owing to their perceived virtues, is the reverse of an impatient ambition to see oneself as a saint. When anything happens to challenge the seductive image of one's own goodness that one has swallowed, this is quickly vented in indignation against the merits of others. At a grosser level, everyone is familiar with the infantile and impotent attitude which says, "If I cannot have it, none else can have it." Whether this is said of a plate of cookies or the entire world, the interplay of anger and gluttony is the same, though the degree and scope of violence involved may differ. Essentially, the forces of violent seeking and grasping are substituted for the harmonious noetic energies of the spiritual will.

The strength of the will cannot be separated from the spiritual and moral texture of one's conception of oneself as an ego or individuality in the world. For Gandhi, the question of the ego resolved itself into two complementary ideals. The first involves the reduction of oneself to a zero or cipher. The second involves training oneself as a champion of truth in the world, an exemplar of heroic non-violence, a *satyagrahi*. Gandhi's conception of beatitude is not a state of exile or stoic aloofness, but rather of incessant striving on behalf of universal welfare, *sarvodaya*. At every point, there are unexpected opportunities for service to others and for relieving their spiritual distress. It is through humility, tolerance, and a willingness to work for the welfare of others that the constructive force of *ahimsa*, or love, is released. To abolish the separative ego is like removing an obscuring disc in front of the sun, allowing its beneficent light to stream forth. The absence of obscuration is not anything to be reified in and of itself, in contrast to the reality of the light released. But from the standpoint of the soul seeking to individuate and realize its true relation to the rest of humanity, the removal of this disc blocking the aperture of the inner light is the crucial task. Every thought of envy towards the light of others, and every trace of slothful indifference to the obscuration of the light within oneself, does violence to the life of the soul. It is perverse, as well as loveless, to deny the light of others. It is suicidal to deny one's own light or, what is the same, to insist that it be kept apart from that of others in the name of the separative ego. True individuation involves the universalization of the heart and the mind in what Spinoza called *amor Dei intellectualis,* the intellectual love of God, and what Jesus called the love of God with all one's soul, heart and mind. This is the existential prerequisite to realization of the concrete ability to love one's neighbour as oneself, as well as the Pauline apotheosis of the finest and fullest love.

Clearly, it is not possible categorically to compartmentalize all the vices, sins and misdeeds that arise out of ignorance and to sharply separate them from their effects upon one's strength of will and one's ability to sympathize with the lives of others. This is part of what is meant by saying that all the seven deadly sins arise through proud ignorance manifesting as egotistic violence. The root of the Ashwatha tree is not to be understood through any set of analytic terms derived from the phenomenal world. It can be known only by rising in consciousness to the noetic realm of pure ideation, sublime tranquillity and universal benevolence that is hidden deep within the heart of every man and woman alike. Then, descending again into the field of moral action (*dharmakshetra*), one may use conceptual tools and categories, not for their own sake or for intellectual sport, but rather as practical tools in the tending, refining and purifying of one's habitual nature. One may see oneself as agitated by many modes and manifestations of violence, arrayed in terms of the seven deadly sins. But all of this, like the physician's diagnosis, is only for the sake of applying curative powers to the soul. Bringing forth all violent tendencies into the light of self-awareness is itself a great therapeutic.

In no case, however, should one allow oneself to become hypnotized by the essentially banal and boring assemblage of one's sins and vices. It is like the story Gautama Buddha told of the man wounded by a poisoned arrow. Instead of pulling it out, he succumbed while asking many questions about the arrow maker, the material of the shaft, the type of poison and the feathers with which the arrow was fletched. In thinking of the seven deadly sins in relation to non-violence, the emphasis should be upon the ability to awaken spiritual vision, to recover the lost virtues of the soul, and to release a current of healing sympathy and love towards all other human beings. This was always the focus and intent of Gandhi's life, and the basis of his indomitable goodwill to all. Rather than make one's failings, however portrayed, the immutable centre of one's metaphysical and psychological perspective, one should instead meditate upon the potential of the good, in oneself, in others and in Nature. Then, even if one cannot at once go forth to sin no more, one can at least go forth to sin less and less.

For Gandhi, however, non-violence or *ahimsa* is an infallible and immediately available means to the arduous task of cutting down the ever-expanding tree of sinfulness with the axe of selflessness in word and act, as well as in thought and feeling. *Ahimsa* becomes no less than the gateway towards *moksha* or emancipation from man-made illusion and delusion.

> Gandhi regarded the aim of human life as *moksha*, liberation from impure thought, and the total elimination of impure thought is possible only as a result of much *tapasya*. The utter extinction of egoism is *moksha* and he who has achieved this will be the very image of Truth or God. 'Government over self is the truest *swaraj* (freedom); it is synonymous with *moksha* or salvation.' He also said that '*ahimsa* means *moksha* and *moksha* is the realization of Truth'. The test of love is *tapasya* and *tapasya* means self-suffering. Self-realization is impossible without service of, and identification with, the poorest. The quest of Truth involves *tapas* — self-suffering, sometimes even unto death. *Satya* then requires the *tapas* of *ahimsa* and this means self-suffering and self-sacrifice in the midst of society. . . .
>
> Gandhi's interpretation of *moksha* as the full

realization of Truth and his justification of *ahimsa* as an exercise in *tapas*, the self-suffering and service needed for the attainment of *satya*, gave traditional values a new meaning and a fresh relevance to politics and to society. In deriving *satya* and *ahimsa* from what were essentially religious notions Gandhi not only gave spiritual values a social significance but also infused into his political vocabulary an other-worldly flavor. His emphasis on suffering as an intrinsic good needed to secure the *summum bonum* is somewhat reminiscent of Kierkegaard's assertion of the concreteness of suffering men against the concept of man as an *animal rationale*. Kierkegaard held that as gold is purified in fire, so is the soul in suffering. Unlike passive and impotent suffering, active and meaningful anguish takes away the impure elements in human nature. It is always man himself that stands in his own way, who is too closely attached to the world, to the environment, to circumstances, to external relationships, so that he is not able to come to himself, come to rest, to have hope, 'He is constantly too much turned outward, instead of being turned inward, hence everything he says is true only as an illusion of the senses'. If a man has love beyond all measure, he has thereby been laboring for all. All the time he was laboring for his own sake to acquire love, he has been laboring for all others. 'It is required of the sufferer that he call a halt to his erring thought, that he reflect what the goal is, that is to say, it is required of him to turn himself about. . . . The difference between man and man is whether they succeed or not in attaining it.'

*The Moral and Political Thought
of Mahatma Gandhi*, pp. 237-239

THE FIRE OF PURGATION

Make a difference between Aether and Ether, the former being divine, the latter physical and infernal. *Ether is the lowest of the septenate division of Akasa-Pradhana, primordial Fire-Substance. Aether-Akasa is the fifth and sixth principles of the body of Kosmos — thus corresponding to Buddhi-Manas, in Man;* Ether *is its Kosmic sediment mingling with the highest layer of the Astral Light. Beginning with the fifth root-race, it will develop fully only at the beginning of the fifth round. Aether is Akasa in its higher aspect, and* Ether *Akasa, in its lowest.*

Transactions of the Blavatsky Lodge, 125

The mirroring of absolute reality in the triadic heart of the unmanifest Logos on the abstract plane of Divine Thought is the archetypal origin of successive births of worlds and men on the noumenal and phenomenal planes of matter. It is the primordial basis of all derivative modes of cognition and causation, and thus the root of relative knowledge and existence in the region of *maya* under the rule of the *nidanas*. Every atom of Monadic life is imbued with an inherent will to self-manifestation, and each is subject to delusion through identification with the illusory forms of the diffused potency of self-ideation. The human Monad, having arrived at the stage of incipient consciousness of its identity with the Logos, is in effect a psychic embryo still trapped in the matrix of astral matter, but capable of a new birth into noetic awareness through the arousal of its Buddhic capacity of intuitive apprehension.

The inward stirrings of higher life within human consciousness presage a golden future for the race as a whole, but under the strictures of universal law this prospect will not be realized by its units until they gain some comprehension of *Buddhi Yoga*, the science of spirituality. The essential factors of this arcane science are hidden within the Mysteries of Divine Wisdom, but they may be sought through fidelity to the inner voice of conscience and the guiding light of intuition. Above all, one must learn the elements of the mathematics of the soul, the art of impersonal computation of karmic causes rooted in relaxed detachment towards personal likes and dislikes on the astral-physical plane.

Philosophical concepts like 'universal unity', 'human solidarity' and 'global interdependence' cannot be grasped through the inverted imagery of the astral light and the imitative ratiocinative responses of *kama manas*. Their hidden meanings must be progressively apprehended by elevating the horizon of one's awareness and the centre of cognition above the limits and inversions of the fourth plane of Spirit-Matter. This is learnt by recognizing that one must replace phenomenal fantasy and concrete images with noumenal awareness and creative imagination through the activation of *Buddhi-Manas*. The noetic science of the generation, transmission and application of thought-energies is exceedingly precise and meta-mathematical. Humanity as a whole is only now becoming prepared to learn this science, but almost every human being has some sense of these immense possibilities through the minor accomplishments of the micro-electronic revolution. In the Victorian age, most people understood neither the telephone nor the telegraph, much less the wireless radio. Today, however, there is no excuse for people not to understand these devices at some elementary level. A growing number of people grasp the logic of these methods because they are involved through micro-electronics in the daily use of complex equipment which enables them to see how instantaneous communication and interaction is possible.

As a beginner, one must discern that all energies, including those of thought, are accompanied by vibrations, whose causal nature is virtually unknown to the individuals who engender them. Those unaware of the potencies and properties of thought-images can at least catch up with those who recognize intuitively that physical modes of electro-magnetic communication are but a material reflection of capabilities and laws inherent in consciousness. This is still easier in simpler societies and more natural cultures than in regions rich in the resources of the earth but poor and backward in the arts of self-discipline. For centuries now the world's peasantry has migrated from farm to town, and from traditional cultures to industrial societies. Hoping to partake of the material prosperity they thought was already there, these restless proletarians soon found themselves mired in the middle class and began to take on bourgeois pretensions. There is nothing new or particularly nefarious in these shared delusions, but many people are trapped by them and squander their spiritual potential. In order to reverse this process, they must be willing to make a fresh start, free from social and economic pretence, free from any false sense of separation from the great masses of the globe, and consecrated to the proper use of the Manasic faculties of concentrated thought, the sacred and priceless, if generally unclaimed, prerogative of every human being.

The effortless mastery of the Adept over manifold energies of potent thought, together with his complete control of the lesser sheaths on the lower planes, is the fruition of an unbroken series of lifetimes of unrelenting discipline and unwavering devotion. The capacity to release the creative light and spiritual genius of the higher Ego as an irresistible impulse for the good of all depends upon the quality and refinement of its instruments. Whilst each Ego is identical to all others in its pristine essence, and each is capable of resonating with the Soundless Sound, no Ego can draw out the harmony of the spheres or transmit noetic energies through an opaque human vesture.

> . . . physical man is the musical instrument, and the Ego, the performing artist. The potentiality of perfect melody of sound, is in the former — the instrument — and no skill of the latter can awaken a faultless harmony out of a broken or badly made instrument. This harmony depends on the fidelity of transmission, by word or act, to the objective plane, of the unspoken divine thought

> in the very depths of man's subjective or inner nature.
> Physical man may — to follow our simile — be a
> priceless Stradivarius or a cheap and cracked fiddle, or
> again a mediocrity between the two, in the hands of
> the Paganini who ensouls him.
>
> H.P. BLAVATSKY

Most people can roughly imagine the enormous discipline involved in becoming a musical genius of the magnitude of Paganini or Caruso. Very few can even remotely imagine the degree of difficulty involved in mastering the transmission of Divine Wisdom, the eternal Harmony of the Pythagoreans, the Self of *Alaya* in the teaching of *The Voice of the Silence*. Though it has always been a vital part of the vast work of the Theosophical Movement to encourage each human being to enquire earnestly into these sacred matters, it has ever been the case that though many are called, few are chosen. And of these, even fewer are chosen for self-training extending over septenates of seven years from the moment of choice to the moment of death. Amongst these, exceptionally few are able to arouse and sustain inner awakening over a lifetime of meditation. Nevertheless, there are such, and the deeper work of the Movement proceeds un-ostentatiously. The ratios now are better than at any time in recorded history and much better than in the eighteenth and nineteenth centuries. But they are still marginal, though even three out of a hundred is a good ratio in these matters. Where there are more than three, this is unusually good, and if there are thirteen, this is excellent.

Given these ratios, individuals could become neophytes at some level if they would come into proper magnetic alignment with those true disciples hidden in their midst. This cannot happen externally; only on the causal plane of the noetic mind. Through deep meditation one must overcome the illusion of the near and the far on the physical plane, and recognize that if through daily meditation one could genuinely use more of the Sacred Teaching, help will be given infallibly. This transmission works too subtly to explain or elaborate, but the Adepts are not here to explain that which can only be comprehended within the sanctuaries of Initiation. They are here to let everyone know that each honest effort helps, that every sincere resolve to do good is invaluable, because the world is in great pain and can use every good impulse that may be generated.

All that is good and true and beautiful can be enhanced because there is hardly enough of it. Wherever it is active in individuals, it can be linked magnetically with the potential good in others, thereby creating living bonds of brotherhood. None of this can be grasped through materialistic psychology and its corrupt handmaiden, the pseudo-science of psychiatry. Apart from the rarefied intuitions of a few constructive psychologists, the contemporary practice of the science of mind is inherently incapable of conceiving the higher noetic function of the Monad or *Manas*. Where psychology has degenerated into nefarious image-mongering and nebulous manipulation through psychiatry, it is worse than worthless. This is recognized in mature cultures, and it is only in adolescent circles obsessed with personal concerns that this shallow rubbish is taken seriously. One drop of the wisdom of the *Bhagavad Gita* is worth more than all such pedantry. Fortunately, psychiatry is pricing itself out of the market, and more and more people are discovering that they can, with little investment in money or pretension, obtain any one of a number of ancient texts in almost any bookshop. Much to the benefit of all, the swarms of ignorant hypnotists and merchants of pathological pessimism are fading away. This itself is part of a larger and more auspicious pattern of events in which exploiters of human need and misery, of human sickness and conflict, are losing their grip upon popular awareness.

It is still true that many middle-class people remain captive to a desperate desire to improve themselves. Nonetheless, many are finding that their former modes of fantasy and compensation are simply unsupportable. They have become tired of the illusion of upward social mobility and dubious of the overblown claims of the supposed virtues of modern life. They are quite happy to become more natural, and relieved to feel free to be simple. They have begun to discover that the purer ideals of youthful innocence, far from having become irrelevant, are relevant and far more fulfilling than the decaying stereotypes of propriety disseminated by self-interested élites. For increasing numbers of individuals one-dimensionality in consciousness is obsolete. People are progressively learning to use what they need and to do what they are able, without worrying about what others are doing. They are learning to live their own lives, not based upon borrowed, bought or rented images and options, but centered upon their own fundamental convictions and intuitions of what is ultimately natural to mankind.

The more one can remain modest and become a true learner, the more the burden of false imagery will fall away from one's consciousness. A mark of becoming a lighter human being is to be able to gaze at the stars with gratitude. When one can look up into the night sky with gladness and realize the infinitude of noumenal abundance behind the veil of shimmering lights, one is beginning to prepare oneself to become a citizen of the cosmos. Without worrying unduly about one's allegiance to any temporal city, one can greet the stars and galaxies that irradiate the canopy of the heavens, but at the same time one should not forget the creatures of the earth. Whilst smiling at the stars one should feel compassion for the ant, because it is the human's privilege to be able to feel the same compassion for the ant that the heavens reflect upon mankind. Whilst raising one's head to the starry vault, bend low and notice the cricket, the frog and the toad, humble creatures that share the earth with man. Learn to show love for all the beings that creep upon the ground whilst one watches the skies. Do not dislike any of the evolving creatures of the earth, neither the scorpion nor the tarantula, neither the mouse nor the mountain lion. To stand as a free citizen of the cosmos, one must first recognize that each and every sentient being in all the seven kingdoms has as much right to exist as oneself. Then one may study and master the obligations and duties of human existence in the cosmic perspective of universal enlightenment.

Out of this renewed and deepened sense of kinship with all

the creatures of the earth, one can prepare oneself to go forth and greet with humility all that lives and breathes. To be worthy of the grand human estate one must display a profound respect for and gratitude towards all the lower kingdoms of nature from which the vestures of incarnation must be drawn. Restoring a pure and healthy relationship with the psychic planes of existence, and becoming a co-worker with Nature in the evolutionary task, one can attempt the removal of every trace and taint of selfishness from one's motivation and conduct. To the extent that this is done, one will no more fall prey to various types of mediumship through karmic involvement with (unconsciously produced) forms in the astral light.

Manasic self-awareness is the potential for cognition of the essential identity of the *sutratman* with the universal *Hiranyagarbha*, but this cognitive capacity has its inverted reflection in ahankaric identification with the projected ray of lower *Manas*. Rather than assimilating the reflection of mind upon the astral planes to a growing Buddhic awareness of noumenal realities, which is the proper use of the *antaskarana* bridge, the Ego under the sway of ignorance diminishes the potency of the Manasic principle in a quixotic attempt to perpetuate ephemeral forms. Philosophically, this can be understood as the confusion of cause with its instrumentality and field of multiple effects. Psychologically, it amounts to a failure to realize that the multivalent term 'self' in human self-consciousness and self-reference is ultimately the *Atman*. Mystically, this error involves the misappropriation of the triadic fire of the Logos, the source of the Spirit, Soul and Body of the cosmos and man, on behalf of its inverted materialized image on the physical plane.

Without noetic discrimination and courageous self-correction, guided by the illumination of selfless meditation, involvement in the astral regions presents a constant danger of dishonesty and self-deception. The astral light has become polluted by the selfish emanations of the pseudo-spiritual, and, whether at death or before, all these matrices of separative consciousness are doomed to be burnt out by the disintegrating fires of karmic retribution. To learn to cooperate self-consciously with Nature one must first learn to cooperate with Karma. Refusing to do so, through attachment to astral forms and images, implies, at this point in evolution, abnormal selfishness and self-annihilation. The universe is sustained by spiritual fire; the world, as the Buddha taught, is a burning house in which all beings are engulfed in a continual conflagration. Impermanence of form is the eternal law of evolution. Identification with shifting shapes in the astral light and attempts to warm oneself by the astral flames can only lead to destruction.

There is nothing inherently wrong with the astral and psychic planes of existence, nor with the various creatures and kingdoms of Nature which are the appropriate evolutionary denizens of those planes. But there is a vital difference between *Akasha* and the astral light, which from the standpoint of the Higher Self is the shadow of a shadow. This difference does not in itself account for the corruption of human consciousness. It is the perverse and unnatural obscuration of noetic awareness through ignorant selfishness and egotism that has made the natural faculties of brain-consciousness and personality productive of evil.

> This brain-consciousness or personality is mortal, being but a distorted reflection through a physical basis of the manasic self. It is an instrument for harvesting experience for the Buddhi-Manas or monad, and saturating it with the aroma of consciously-acquired experience. But for all that the 'brain-self' is real while it lasts, and weaves its Karma as a responsible entity.
>
> H.P. BLAVATSKY

The complex karma created by the brain-minds of human beings returns to them again and again. At certain moments, it cumulatively comes back to them, whether as individuals or as an entire race, in a tremendous mass so that they will be able to confront it and see beyond. To receive such a precipitation of karma is to experience a climactic moment. It is an opportunity for calmness and renunciation, such as one might experience in the mountains when a large boulder falls down. If calm, one would be prepared to accept either the boulder's blessing upon one's head (if this is one's karma), or its passing by (if that is one's karma). One must learn to renounce the will to live, but not out of an escapist wish to die. With calmness, one can be ready to accept and learn from everything, provided one does not exaggerate the importance of one's own survival. Life may be tedious for long stretches of time, but this is no excuse for exaggeration and pretentious self-images. If one cannot accept ordinariness, then nothing will ever seem good enough for more than a brief moment. From a spiritual standpoint, the worst of all delusions is to suppose that one has some exclusive privilege or exalted status through having come into the presence of the sacred Teachings.

What does it mean in consciousness to come closer to the Guru? It is one thing to come closer on the illusory plane of sense-perceptions. It is quite another thing to come closer in noetic consciousness. Pure consciousness has nothing to do with particular desires, wishes and thoughts because it is itself absolute thought, desire and will. Every human being, according to his consciousness of time, emits a certain mental vibration. The degree of awareness of eternity in one's consciousness of time determines the tone, the intensity, the colour and the force of this vibration. Most human beings, preoccupied with today and tomorrow, with this year and the next, are very restricted and fragmented in consciousness. They become prisoners of the external, shifting panorama of human existence, and thereby become victims of history. When they die, they discover they had hardly lived, and in many cases what they called life is what is known to Adepts as living death. But those who are able to transcend the imagery of their immediate perceptions, the narrow horizon of their conceptions of space, time and motion, can think causally in terms of the cosmos and humanity. They resonate with and reflect That which ever was, ever is and ever shall be, for whom the hour shall never strike, the immortal soul within every human being, the

Atman that overbroods each and all. Typically, the *Atman* comes closer to the fontanelle only once in the lifetime of the average human being, at the moment of death. For it to come closer at any other time requires tremendous self-training and effortless self-mastery earned over many lives. Without this self-discipline it is idle to imagine that one has come close to the *Atman* seated in the hearts of all beings.

If it is not part of one's destiny to do this — and there is no room for self-deception or self-dejection here — then it can be a part of one's destiny to serve those who have done so. More beings on earth today have done this very thing than ever before. Largely unknown, many have waited decades for the right moment to receive the call. The world today is in an unusually fortunate position; not only Nirmanakayas, but also numerous disguised Adepts have taken birth in many parts of the world. They are thoroughly prepared in consciousness for the Mysteries, for the City of Man and for the Temple of the Future. And so, the ordinary person who has done none of these things should nevertheless aspire to become part of the future and to find a fitting place in the evolutionary march of humanity. To become part of the solution and not of the problem, to join the future instead of clinging to the past, each must begin by shaving off pretensions and cutting away the obscurations hitherto entertained through ignorance. By becoming natural, straightforward and simple, individuals can enjoy developing a taste for meditation upon pure, unbounded and eternal consciousness. The key is to do *in life* that which one can scarcely do after death (except in an extremely limited sense) and to prepare oneself for future lives of learning.

The secret mysteries of consciousness which underlie the meta-psychological evolution of mankind will remain unspoken to the vast majority of human beings for ages to come. But every man and woman who wishes to make himself or herself worthy of inclusion in that glorious future is invited to engage in philosophic meditation upon the metaphysical propositions of Gupta Vidya. Therein it is taught that all things in the universe are associated with either spirit or matter, one of these being taken as the permanent element of both. Pure Matter is pure Spirit, and neither can be understood by the finite discursive intellect. All pairs of opposites — light and darkness, heat and cold, fullness and the void — are at once pure Matter and pure Spirit. All are manifestations of Spirit-Matter — Aether-*Akasha*. Aether-*Akasha* is consubstantial with the plane of substance constituting *Buddhi-Manas*, the jewel in every heart and the diamond light in every soul. That light is one with the fiery ground of the entire cosmos. It is the origin of the three and seven invisible fires in nature and the forty-nine fires in human consciousness tapped at will by Adepts. These noumenal fires can be invoked infallibly through concentrated thought that reaches to universal good.

Any human being who hungers for universal good and truly wishes that the earth be a better world, out of the intensity of thought and will, draws closer to the sacred fires in the inmost essence of being. It is only in those Akashic fires that there is true rejuvenation. Though they are known to Adepts by other and secret names, they may be viewed by the neophyte as the fires of purification, purgation and resolve. By the sustained ideation of Mahatmas, they are made accessible to all human beings so that each can emit a powerful vibration in consonance with the global current of Aquarian humanity. Anyone willing to take the Teachings of Gupta Vidya as a true talisman can enter the stream of the great endeavour, which is consubstantial with the electric ocean of Life.

Anyone willing to start afresh, without illusions or expectations, but with a new and growing maturity, can forego the compensations of the shadowy past and rediscover a rightful place in the school of universal human evolution. One of the marks of spiritual maturity is a calm recognition that ethical responsibility is self-compelling. Once the resolve is made to grow up, one will recognize that Krishna is on the side of every Arjuna and against none. Then, like Arjuna, one may stand up and be counted amongst heroic souls worthy of the human heritage. Seeing beyond roles and forms, one may learn to breathe the Sacred Sound and the sacred speech: '*Om Mani Padme Hum,* the

Jewel in the Lotus, the God in man? In this spirit the future will draw out and weave together the best, so that all may be on the side of the finest in the human race, allied with the future, under the all-protecting shield of the luminous host of hierophants.

MANASADHARMA

The terms used for the concealed and the unrevealed Principle are many. In the earliest MSS. of Indian literature this Unrevealed, Abstract Deity has no name. It is called generally 'That' (Tad in Sanskrit), and means all that is, was, and will be, or that can be so received by the human mind.

Among such appellations, given, of course, only in esoteric philosophy, as the 'Unfathomable Darkness', the 'Whirlwind', etc. — it is also called the 'It of the Kalahansa, the Kala-ham-sa', and even the 'Kali Hamsa', (Black swan). . . . Many a mysterious sacred name in Sanscrit conveys to the profane ear no more than some ordinary, and often vulgar word, because it is concealed anagrammatically or otherwise. This word of Hansa or esoterically 'hamsa' is just such a case. Hamsa is equal to a-ham-sa, three words meaning 'I am he' (in English), while divided in still another way it will read 'So-ham', 'he (is) I' — Soham being equal to Sah, 'he', and aham, 'I', or 'I am he'. In this alone is contained the universal mystery, the doctrine of the identity of man's essence with god-essence, for him who understands the language of wisdom.

The Secret Doctrine, i 77-78

The fundamental presupposition of Gupta Vidya is that every human being has an innate capacity for selfless action and sacrifice, *anasakti* and *yajna*. Ordinarily, this capacity lies dormant, obscured and unfocussed due to lives of habitual attachment to name and form. Yet, it is the continuous exercise of this capacity that holds together the fabric of human society. Throughout history heroic men and women committed to the service of the spiritually, morally and materially impoverished learnt how to release the Akashic energies implicit in human solidarity. By becoming fearless and selfless, they called forth the strength of the ideal from all those around them. This fearlessness is the prerogative of the immortal soul. It is the identifying mark of those who have merged their being with an ideal, thus gaining the strength that belongs to the ideal and blessing all their actions with its elevating influence. Such ideals are not just vague apprehensions of remote, rarefied possibilities, but living forces rooted on a plane consubstantial with the immortal soul. As soon as a human being is surcharged with an ideal, its living force invokes and involves spiritual will. In essence, it is the energy of the *Atman* that enables one to conquer all fears bound up with name and form, all concern with results or anxiety about events.

During incarnation the powers of human understanding and action necessarily inhere in complex situations. Through an internal slavery to anticipation, even evolved human beings who have given years to meditation and self-discipline may yet be trapped in their own self-image. They may at critical points become fearful, paralysed by a fear of what others are thinking and saying about them on the level of personality. The difficulty of overcoming attachment to the personality lies not in events, but rather in the mind alone. Authentic fearlessness is therefore the deliberate object of mystical and moral striving. To the external observer it sometimes seems that certain souls suddenly discover a new fearlessness, or attain a new level of self-transcendence without effort or warning. In a universe of law, however, this only demonstrates one's ignorance of other beings and the mysteries of the soul. Invariably, such transformations arise not by chance, but out of some profound act of compassion, some pristine response to the world of pain or some fundamental decision about a moral direction. Such acts of the spiritual will cannot be induced or predicted through any mechanical techniques. Yet they can, and will, accelerate an individual's service to his ideals until he becomes more and more fearless, even personally invulnerable.

As self-governed individuals incarnate their ideals, they become inseparable from what they represent and from what they cherish. Thus they become able to tap the spiritual will-energy of other human beings, to touch their deepest hearts, awaken their minds and arouse their latent courage. An extraordinary dialectic takes place in human encounter as soon as it is seen from the standpoint of the forward looking and all-embracing, that which is transcendental and rooted in the plane of *Akasha*. Uncircumscribed by the logic of linearity and limitation, this dialectic is marked by a cool detachment and an unswerving toughness. This all-inclusive resourcefulness in the service of ideals is a characteristic of the *Atman* focussed through Buddhic intuition, sympathy and compassion in the concentrating lens of *Manas*. Once this true basis of ideals is touched, it becomes a potent force in the realm of action, lending immense meaning and richness, dignity and significance, to each and every day and to each responsibility, however modest.

The master key to the release of the spiritual will is the recognition that one's immediate duty is supremely important. To it must be brought all one's energies. Because so many human beings have never really learnt to be whole-hearted or single-minded, they find that they have to act through vestures which are fragmented. This may be experienced as a lack of moral continuity, an inability to concentrate, a liability to forgetfulness, or an appearance of luck or any one of a number of ups and downs. All these, however, reflect only a fundamental misunderstanding of the external and internal state of the soul. Wherever ideals are seen as distant abstractions outside oneself, the energy and motion that belong to a great spiritual conception will be absent. Yet every human soul carries a vast capital acquired in other lives and a tremendous capacity to transcend all fear. Were this not true, there would be no reasonable prospect for the human condition.

What is redemptive about the human scene is that again and again, even amidst cowardice, passivity and inertia, there appear unexpected flashes of fearlessness that cleanse everything around them. Like rainfall — the grace of Nature — the self-sacrificing actions of heroic individuals refresh and regenerate society, quickening the seeds of human growth. Individuals whose entire lives revolve around potent ideas and high ideals can bring total commitment, boundless zeal, complete fearlessness into their every action. Through the performance of their immediate duties, they act upon and touch the spiritual will in others. This fusion of sacrifice (*yajna*) on behalf of ideals with the performance of *dharma* is the hallmark of the highest spiritual confidence.

The basis of the sustained release of the spiritual will is the recognition that human ideals and human nature, *Manasadharma*, as both act and essence, are one. This proposition is the fundamental axiom of all initiations in the Mystery Schools of Gupta Vidya, the Secret Science which is only secret to minds captivated by the projections of the personality. The *Stanzas of Dzyan* teach that the germinal light of the manvantaric dawn of the cosmos is fully present in the lamp of every human soul, and that the spirit of that flame is the highest cosmic foundation of self-existence. This vibrant identity of essence is intimated in the mysterious term *Hamsa*, translated for symbolic purposes as 'the swan', but anagrammatically transformed into *A-ham-sa* and *So-ham*, meaning 'I am he' and 'He is I'. This is the universal enigma of the identity of man's essence with God-essence. It is revealed to those who have deeply contemplated upon the deific principle in the cosmos, and seen it working within themselves and within all beings.

The human being can self-consciously curb identification with all the vestures that keep souls apart. This is the result of deep meditation, and of the action that becomes sacrificial and magical through meditation. The wisdom unfolded by this sacrificial science far transcends the unselfconscious release of heroism by ordinary men and women that leavens the flow of daily human life. Yet, given the confusion and passivity that humanity is now encountering, the Bodhisattvas are truly grateful for every instance of quiet heroism and fearlessness. Certainly, no individual dare neglect the development of authentic moral courage if he wishes to realize that arcane wisdom which is based upon a pervasive and unbroken awareness of the unity of God and man.

It is useless to attempt to explain the mystery in full. Materialists and the men of modern Science will never understand it, since, in order to obtain clear perception of it, one has first of all to admit the postulate of a universally diffused, omnipresent, eternal Deity in Nature; secondly, to have fathomed the mystery of electricity in its true essence; and thirdly, to credit man with being the septenary symbol, on the terrestrial plane, of the One Great UNIT (the Logos), which is Itself the Seven-vowelled sign, the Breath crystallized into the WORD.

Ibid., 78-79

Even among those who call themselves mystics, in the ordinary lay sense, there is a surfeit of unconscious materialism. Few can claim to have fully overcome identification with sense-perceptions and the body, or to have become self-consciously immortal. But this 'spiritual materialism' is ubiquitous because so few spiritually-minded souls have really thought through the fundamental propositions of Gupta Vidya. They have not fully explored the Buddhist axiom regarding the emptiness of substantial forms and the apparent empirical self. So, in appropriating spiritual language, they have merely couched mundane concerns in a metaphysical vocabulary. In truth, they are thereby consolidating a self-image at a more recalcitrant and subtle level. This endemic tendency, which is caused by individual and collective Karma, is rather difficult to overcome. In order to obtain a clear perception of the divine in man, one must first comprehend "the postulate of a universally diffused, omnipresent, eternal Deity in Nature". It is impossible to affirm such a postulate without having grasped its meaning at least at some preliminary level. This in itself requires *dianoia,* the deliberate application of the reasoning power through reflection.

Those who do not question, who will not adopt the humble mental posture of a learner, cannot do any service to ideals and ideas. They are left with little more than verbal repetitions and personal pretensions, the seeds of delusion and dogmatism. Instead, one should begin by asking oneself what it would mean to believe truly that there is divinity in everything. Those allergic to dust may yet conceive that there is divinity in allergy-producing substances in the air. Those afflicted by influenza may still recognize that there is divinity in germs. The universality of Deity in Nature entails that the Mahatmic light of universal ideation is accessible at every single point of space, time and matter. As contemporary scientists have begun to realize, old notions of matter and energy, of space and time, have collapsed; the blinding dualism of subject and object is false. So far from Nature avoiding the vacuum, that vacuum is the All.

If one truly begins to reflect upon the voidness of the seeming full and the fullness of the seeming void, one can think in terms of the universal diffusion of what is called *Akasha*. This represents omnipresent, universally diffused and eternal radiant substance capable of limitless plastic transformation. It is everywhere in Nature, both unmanifest and invisible, as well as manifest and visible. As soon as one has grasped this extraordinary concept, one realizes that there is no particle in one's body which is not divine. The organs of digestion and excretion, one's fingertips and toes, every part of the body is suffused and bathed in the divine essence. This should not be thought of merely in relation to the surface of the body or even in relation to the structures revealed by empirical anatomy. The presence of *Akasha* is an underlying current which cannot be contacted through the senses, but can be felt only through inward ideation. Without deep meditation it is indeed impossible to blast the surface conception of the body and to see it as it really is — as a cosmos, a living temple of a living god.

Once one has touched through meditation the depth of divinity that pervades all Nature, one can begin to fathom the mystery of electricity in its true essence. This will require a transcendence of all finite fields and fixed polarities. The fiery idea of electricity as Fohat must be separated in the mind from its inherence in any particles or units that localize its being and restrict its reality. Seen from the standpoint of the unmanifest, and in relation to the most homogeneous field of primordial substance, essential electricity is an all-powerful vibration. It is the incredible electric potency that is involved in the dawn of manifestation, the emergence of an entire universe out of the Divine Darkness. It is that which may be tapped in the *sandhyas* of dawn and of twilight, glimpsed in the noontide glory of the day as in the fathomless darkness of the night. It is a mystery beyond all conceptions and imaginings, and yet it is the formative agent of the universe and man.

Finally, one must galvanize one's sense of the ubiquity and potency of the divine essence through crediting man "with being the septenary symbol, on the terrestrial plane, of the One Great UNIT". Individuals who give so little credit to themselves or others are asked to credit man with being God. The Logos in the cosmos is the God in man, the Adam Kadmon, the *Purusha* within each and every human being. The Renaissance depiction of this as the man within man, the universal man, pertains to seven different planes and vestures. Even on the terrestrial plane man is the living symbol of the Logos. The Logos is that which can say "I am myself" independent of the existence of the entire universe. If the Logoic intelligence is in every single human being, then every human being can affirm through pure 'I-am-I' consciousness the most transcendental, most active and most living conception of Deity. Yet this 'I' is completely unconnected with all forms and results, with everything that belongs to the world of differentiated perceptions and objects.

The Logos is itself the seven-vowelled sign, the Great Breath crystallized into the WORD. It is OEAOHOO, the Father-Mother of the gods, the single, triple and septenary root from which all proceeds. To credit man as the living septenary symbol of the Logos is to become ready to use the reverberation of OEAOHOO, meditating upon it, becoming one with it and understanding its threefold pronunciations. Those who use so powerful an energy, force, sound and idea in their daily lives can translate metaphysics into magic. By divinizing their breath, they can surrender all compulsive expressions of separateness and selfishness and retreat into the inmost sanctuary where they become the AUM. They become inseparable in consciousness from the universal Logos.

It might seem that an individual who met these requirements would become perfect and so could quit the earthly scene of involuntary incarnation. This is not so. Great and difficult as this transformation in consciousness is, it constitutes only the preliminary discipline of Gupta Vidya. Those whose ideals stop short at this point allow no room for the Bodhisattva, the man of renunciation. To function without bondage to the planes of illusion requires a further practical training. To serve the myriad monads and minds ensnared in the realm of effects, the aspirant who has touched the bed of the Nirvanic stream must re-examine the universe from the standpoint of practical *yajna*. He must consider

> the multiple combination of the seven planets of Occultism and of the Kabala, with the twelve zodiacal signs; to attribute, as we do, to each planet and to each constellation an influence which . . . 'is proper to it, beneficent or maleficent, and this, after the planetary Spirit which rules it, who, in his turn, is capable of influencing men and things which are found in harmony with him and with which he has any affinity'.
>
> *Ibid., 79*

Human beings ordinarily go about their mundane affairs with a mixture of inattention, superstition and self-interest. Though generally aware of the cyclical character of life, they are so subordinated in consciousness to sequential time that they cannot grasp the eternally active potential of its minutest divisions. Thus, for example, through a kind of habitual deference to the wisdom of the ancients, they participate in the seemingly courteous custom of experiencing the days of the week. But one has not fully experienced Wednesday, for example, if one does not think of Wednesday in relation to Woden, Hermes and Budha-Mercury. Yet one must do more than that. While intoning *The Jewel in the Lotus* one should salute, revere and invoke the spiritual Dhyanis that overbrood the planets. The Mercury that one sees in the sky is not itself the planet Mercury, but merely one of its seven globes. Whether one speaks of the solar system or man, one is concerned not only with the physical body, but rather with the whole stream of existence and a set of forces which may ultimately be assigned to presiding spirits. This is true not only of Wednesday, but of every day; each one represents a phase of a spectrum differentiated in what is ordinarily called time.

Adepts live by exquisitely blending a sense of time and a sense of timeliness. They always use the great almanac of Nature, acting with an awareness of all the hierarchies and giving due obeisance to each and every Dhyani and planetary spirit. Through such action one can attract the harmonious influences that are associated with a particular line or stream, and which are connected with centres in oneself. Mercury, for example, is related to the principle of *Buddhi*, spiritual intuition. An inauspicious relationship between Mercury and another planet means that there is a creative tension. In every force in Nature there are possibilities which may correlate in different ways at the micro-level with the entire spectrum of possibilities. These may work themselves out adversely, inhibiting certain kinds of activity and thought. But with a knowledge of these changing correlations, one may transmute each influence, seeing it from a deeper standpoint in relation to its inmost significance and its origins in the one Logos. Those who have already attained a fusion in their hearts between the Logos and the Logoic spark must still acquire the kind of wisdom that belongs within the vast web of complex differentiation. It is a wisdom concerning the archetypal divisions between the seven planets, the twelve signs of the zodiac, the seasons of the year and the days of the week. Adepts are able to use these moments of time because they act with wisdom within the limits of Karma.

Rooted in *anasakti* and *yajna*, ever doing the utmost and the best that one can do, one can use every situation with benevolence and integrity in the service of universal good. Out of one's accumulated experience one may acquire what Gautama Buddha called "skilful means". Mistakes are an essential ingredient in gaining the kind of practical wisdom that applies to all the

planetary forces. Long before an ordinary human being is ready
to engage in this practical training, he must acquire through
self-effort the requisite moral qualifications. This does not at all
mean, however, that one should be indifferent to times and timing.
On the contrary, it is only common sense to make full use of
almanacs and calendars, intimations and aids, made available to
humanity to help ordinary men and women harmonize with the
invisible forces acting upon them.

The foremost of these aids in the constant struggle against
materialism and superstition are the living, enigmatic symbols of
God and man. *Kalahansa*, the divine swan, is such a symbol,
expressing the presence of divine spirit within and beyond the
cosmos and man. Drawing attention to the distinction between
the abstract numinous essence and the manifested creative God
of the cosmos, H.P. Blavatsky declared:

> The 'Swan or goose' (Hansa) is the symbol of that
> male or temporary deity, as he, the emanation of the
> primordial Ray, is made to serve as a Vahan or vehicle
> for that divine Ray, which otherwise could not manifest
> itself in the Universe, being, antiphrastically, itself an
> emanation of 'Darkness' — for our human intellect, at
> any rate. It is Brahmā, then, who is Kala-Hansa, and the
> Ray, the Hansa-Vahana.
>
> As to the strange symbol chosen, it is equally
> suggestive; the true mystic significance being the idea
> of a universal matrix, figured by the primordial waters
> of the 'deep', or the opening for the reception, and
> subsequently for the issue, of that one ray (the Logos),
> which contains in itself the other seven procreative rays
> or powers (the logoi or builders).
>
> *Ibid.*, 80

Kalahansa is the highest conception of self-existence involving
both ideation and substance. It is, therefore, a concept of Deity
that applies both to *Parabrahm* seen in manifestation as well as to
the creative Logos. It is the first principle of spirit-matter,

mysteriously comprehending both. In consciousness the swan symbolizes an omnidirectional vision free from all aberration, a metaphysical potential curiously mirrored in the physical vision of the swan. This state of faultless vision rooted in the androgynous Ray, prior to the differentiations of spirit-matter, is likened, in *The Voice of the Silence*, to "repose between the wings of the GREAT BIRD". This is the *Kalahansa*, "which is not born, nor dies, but is the AUM throughout eternal ages". Its two wings are the *A* and the *U*, and the *M* is its tail, while the *Ardha-matra* — which is like the crescent above the AUM sign — is the head of the swan and represents that element of sound in the pronunciation of the AUM which is its indissoluble unity with the SILENCE.

As a symbol of the hidden Deity in man and Nature, *Kalahansa* is inseparable from Narayana.

> Appearing with every Manvantara as Narayan, or Swayambhuva (the Self Existent), and penetrating into the mundane Egg, it emerges from it at the end of the divine incubation as Brahmā or Prajapati, a progenitor of the future Universe into which he expands. He is Purusha (spirit), but he is also Prakriti (matter). Therefore it is only after separating himself into two halves — Brahmā-Vach (the female) and Brahmā-Viraj (the male), that the Prajapati becomes the male Brahmā.
>
> *Ibid.*, 80-81

Narayana, the One who breathes breathless, is the one who uses Nara, all of humanity, as a vehicle. This metaphysical idea was later trivialized and anthropomorphized in the notion of man as God's footstool. However awe-inspiring to the Victorian preacher, this image is of little help to twentieth century humanity, let alone twentieth century womankind. No amount of tinkering with the language of the Bible will be able to restore the original meaning of the symbol. Instead, one must start to think metaphysically of the entire human race, of all human souls as constituting the limbs of one great universal man-woman, one single being such as the Kabbalistic Adam Kadmon. Then one must see that whole as a vesture of the spirit that breathes breathless, Narayana. To reach the central living core of the identity of God-essence and man-essence, one must grasp the concept of pure self-existence, prior to all manifestation and independent of minds and monads, separate rays and the pregenetic dispersion of the one Ray into the seven rays. At the same time, one must learn to experience in every differentiated atom, in every single point in space, in every vesture of every being, the same ineffable Presence.

If one can begin to realize the identity of essence between God and man through Narayana, one can in meditation enter into a state like that of the swan or the egg. One can brood and incubate ideas and ideals in a condition of extreme abstraction whereby one totally transcends the boundaries of the limit of selfhood. One can experience the activity of Narayana. As above, so below. What applies to the great brooding of Narayana in relation to a whole system of worlds or period of manifestation applies analogously to that same Narayana within each and every *nara*. Each human being who becomes Narayana through mystic meditation re-enacts the process of the formation of a world, provided that the individual has become so secure and invulnerable in reliance upon spirit that he has renounced all the fruits of action.

By renouncing all, one may enjoy all, engaging in the ceaseless sacrificial action of Narayana. It is precisely as difficult to do this as it is difficult to become humble. Before one can become truly humble, one must have something to be humble about. In order to know, one must bestride the Bird of Life, but in order to live, one must give up one's life. So, too, before one can enjoy the universe, one must make a fundamental act of renunciation. This is a continual process, coextensive with the cosmos, and essential to the potentiality of perfectibility inherent in man. True aspirants to the service of ideals, true compassionators of their impoverished brothers and sisters, will begin by renouncing melodrama in the spiritual life. If they wish to contribute to peace on earth, they know that they must steadily strengthen, day by day, the release of spiritual will within themselves out of a benevolence directed towards all men and women. Cherishing authentic beginnings beyond all fanciful dreams of fulfilment, they will treasure *Manasadharma* as the talisman of a life of ideals rooted in selfless service.

LEVELS OF MANIFESTATION

Man ought to be ever striving to help the divine evolution of Ideas, *by becoming to the best of his ability a co-worker with nature in the cyclic task. The ever unknowable and incognizable* Karana *alone, the* Causeless Cause *of all causes, should have its shrine and altar on the holy and ever untrodden ground of our heart — invisible, intangible, unmentioned, save through 'the still small voice' of our spiritual consciousness. Those who worship before it, ought to do so in the silence and the sanctified solitude of their Souls; making their spirit the sole mediator between them and the* Universal Spirit, *their good actions the only priests, and their sinful intentions the only visible and objective sacrificial victims to the* Presence.

The Secret Doctrine, i 280

The ceaseless ideation of the Universal Mind has its most pristine reflection in Dhyan Chohanic thought within the nucleus of the concealed Sun, wherein the most holy and highest self-existent beings initiate the seven rays, the sacred Hierarchies that work throughout the cosmos. Anyone who invokes the *Gayatri* for the sake of universal enlightenment brings his entire being into alignment with benedictory ideation at the most causal and cosmic level. Exempt from the lesser cycles of time, these exalted Logoi are the paradigm of the invulnerable gods, as opposed to lesser genii, venerated in every ancient tradition. They represent universal self-consciousness, the most beneficent power in the universe, and the fullest perfection a human being can attain. In the daily act of consecration to the Spiritual Sun, a disciple is not merely honouring cosmic plenitude, but also solemnly affirming the sacredness of breath, every hint of feeling, thought and word, every atom that makes up the invisible and visible vestures, reaching down and through the physical. All life has the sacred purpose of making the whole of one's being fully available to the highest forces of ideation in the universe for the sake of kindling the spiritual faculties in all human beings.

Anyone who aspires to this holy self-consecration will even initially recognize that it is too sacred to articulate. It seeks to establish a living link between the mind that thinks and the heart that feels on the plane of manifestation, in association with the lesser vestures, bringing these totally into alignment with the inmost core and rootless root in every human being. Therein is the Buddhic essence of the Dhyan Chohanic radiation, corresponding to, consubstantial with, and also analogous to, for the purposes of all spiritual sanctification, the *Atman*. One who calmly contemplates in inward silence can release the immense strength and intense potency of the highest *Itcha* connected with *Itchasakti*, the purest, most profound desire. This is so abstract, holy and selfless in the ordinary sense that it can arise only from the universal Self. But it is recorded, registered and reverberates in each atom of every vesture.

A consummate musician knows that he is only an imperfect instrument of a creative, noetic activity in the supersensuous spheres of the universe. As with music, so with thought and feeling; invocation lends enormous strength and power to any sacred vow. But to realize this latent strength one must repeatedly reaffirm the vow, despite the strain upon the lower mind with its discontinuities and distortions. One must refuse to surrender one's attention and consciousness into the clutches of that parasitic, inefficient and wayward instrument if one is to take hold of one's true nature and become truly worthy of the privilege of incarnation as a human being fit for divine work. As this theurgy is transcendental, as it cannot be expressed in the coinage of conventional speech and thought, it must be nourished and renewed again and again in silence and secrecy. Thus, all the Dhyanis, all the *devas* and the higher potencies, are entitled to the grateful reverence of humanity, and man ought to be ever striving to help the divine evolution of ideas by becoming to the best of his ability a co-worker with Nature in the cyclic task of augmenting self-consciousness.

Philosophically, this work is consonant with the intrinsic logic of manifestation. Patanjali, the great teacher of yoga, declared that the entire universe exists for the sake of the human soul. It is part of the programme of evolution, cosmic and human, that there should be universal enlightenment. Hence, the point and force of taking a vow lies in an individual's becoming fully aware of the inmost purpose of evolution and the privilege of being incarnated. An individual who does this becomes a living link on earth with wise beings who constitute a mighty Fraternity, who are ideating at a level that is sufficiently homogeneous to reach all humanity on the subtlest plane in deep sleep and in deep meditation. But for beings below that level, even to attempt to do this is to help to make possible the percolation into the consciousness of human beings of that universal current which is the impulse of life itself from the standpoint of the immortal soul. If enough people do this, in due course language and thought will change, and, at some point, the modes of human interaction must also change. Human beings must be able to create patterns of life relevant to those future races that will enact at a high level of deliberation and control what was felt intuitively by the earliest races, especially the Third Root Race.

To take a vow is to assist in the divine evolution of ideas. It is to recognize that there is a great deal in oneself which — by atavism, abuse and misuse, the karma of other lives and the karma attached to whole classes of life-atoms over long periods of time — does not want to cooperate intelligently. To overcome these obstructions requires proper attention, the potent power of thought, the spiritual force of the will and the universal energy of feeling. These have become appropriated and dissipated, concretized and wasted, and also, on occasion, badly abused. It is to offset deliberately this downward tendency of the lunar nature that one self-consciously reorients one's attitude of mind, state of being and sphere of magnetic influence around the supernal light of the solar ray which is *Atma-Buddhi*. Thus a vow is made holy. And hence, the ever-unknowable and incognizable *Karana* alone has its shrine and altar on the holy and ever-untrodden ground of the heart. In spiritually developed cultures sacred truths simply could not be uttered indiscriminately by anyone.

Speakers, not speech, bring words to life. For a number of complex reasons connected with the larger purpose of evolution, as against the long-standing exploitation through corrupt and ignorant priestcraft alienated from the true source of wisdom, there is in Kali Yuga the necessary process of widespread access to authentic spiritual teachings. This can give rise to the illusion that one need simply utter certain words to enter into the current of potent ideation. In reality, if one is unfamiliar with the arcane properties of light and sound that are inextricably connected with great ideas, one may actually release a strong force which works as an agent of disintegration, disruption, delusion, decay and death. So one must spend much time in silence, making a repeated and sincere regular effort to enter this state of communion — "invisible, intangible, unmentioned, save through 'the still small voice' of our spiritual consciousness". Only so can one activate the voice of conscience, which in time becomes the voice of spiritual consciousness. At a further stage this becomes the voice of the daimon and at its highest level it is the *chitkala*, the voice which is infallibly and constantly available to the individual. Before one can reach that stage, one must silence other voices. One must draw within; one must "give Nature time to speak". It is a veritable tragedy that when people assemble, they fear silence and ceaselessly transmit to one another mundane, meaningless detail. This needlessly reduces the length of life and restricts the power of the spiritual will. The most crucial training involves deliberate speech and creative silence, that true reverential silence in which all the faculties are at once alert and relaxed, free from any rush to manifest. This is the decisive difference between the sacred and the profane, the holy and the polluted.

One must first learn to listen to that still, small voice of one's spiritual consciousness and the integral teaching of the Gupta Vidya directed towards *Buddhi*, the voice of spiritual intuition in every human being. Because that voice is not initially available, a person may begin by calmly reading and reading again, aloud but also silently, some of the great passages in spiritual texts. This can begin to arouse *Buddhi*. The ordinary mind is in a rush; but *Buddhi* is calm, gentle and assured, like a living spring that flows from the ground. Many people cannot begin this, however, because of a false lower Manasic identification of vitality and wakefulness with manifestation. When they do not manifest, they become drowsy and fall asleep. Unable to keep spiritually awake and Manasically active, they become mediumistic and are taken over by every kind of lower astral force in the elemental universe. They fall prey to a corruption of the faculties because the lunar mind becomes mixed and mingled with anything lurking in the astral light. Many people are imprisoned in a false dichotomy between a loud but weak manifesting tendency and an equally feeble mediumistic tendency.

The aim of true meditation, of developing the mind but also, in time, unfolding the intuition, is to rise above this dichotomy to a relaxed yet heightened awareness that flows in a continuous and steady stream. To be able to do this one has to loosen the hold exercised by the illusion — through ignorance, association of ideas and habits of speech — that there is some entity called the personality. In fact, there is only a vast collection of tendencies. All attempts on the personal plane to gain continuity are only shadowy reflections, a kind of imitative activity that draws fitfully from the true light of awareness of the immortal soul, but which has no chance to manifest continuously because of the overactive personal consciousness. One must see through this illusion at the core to dissociate from it. One must learn through asceticism in speech how one tends to use the personal pronoun, the 'I'; one must see that most of what one views as oneself is merely a set of tendencies, and that by identifying with them one has created a false 'I'. After a point, this aggregate becomes so ossified that one cannot show reverence, be grateful, be calm, or meditate, and hence one cannot withdraw into the inmost sanctuary. One cannot get away from pessimism — a sure sign of corruption of truly human consciousness, which is always marked in its pure form by an inward optimism that is the Buddhic light of awareness of the inner joy of life, behind the veil of manifestation.

The dispelling of the illusion of separateness needs both a preliminary toughness and, ultimately, a readiness to plunge into the stream. *The Voice of the Silence* says, "The pilgrim who would cool his weary limbs in running waters, yet dares not plunge for terror of the stream, risks to succumb from heat." One has to try to withdraw into oneself for the purpose of communion and quiet contemplation, for the purpose of surrender, as many mystics have put it, but also for the purpose of a pure consecration of all energies to this invisible, intangible, unmentioned ground of the altar upon which will shine the flame of the *Karana*. To honour the soul, making one's spirit the sole mediator between oneself and the Universal Spirit, one's good actions the only priests, and one's sinful intentions the only sacrificial victims to the Presence, means having no doubts about the undertaking. Doubts must be thrown into the sacrificial fire of surrender and contemplation. All worries and hesitations are like vermin. They are the encrusted mental deposits made by lower thoughts and emotions that consolidate greedy, hungry, bitter and sour elementals, all of which must be thrown into the fire. In this light one can understand the therapeutic teaching and wise instruction of Jesus, which has to do with authentic initiation, and not with hypocritical public prayer or the mumbo-jumbo of exclusive claims.

> 'When thou prayest thou shalt not be as the hypocrites are . . . but enter into *thine inner chamber and having shut thy door, pray to thy Father which is in secret.*' (Matt. vi) Our Father is *within us*, 'in Secret', our 7th principle, in the 'inner chamber' of our Soul perception. 'The Kingdom of Heaven' and of God *'is within us'* says Jesus, not *outside*.
>
> *The Secret Doctrine*, i 280

There is a direct analogy between the light that shines in the "inner chamber" and the subtle creative light of the first twilight at the dawn of the *Maha-Manvantara*. This Initial Existence is a *conscious spiritual quality* which, in the manifested solar world,

resembles the film of divine breath to the gaze of the entranced
seer. A reflection of the Absolute, it is designated the One Life,
and is a film for creative or formative purposes. Manifesting in
seven states, each with seven subdivisions, it is the basis of the six
shaktis, the highest powers available to the initiated seer, which
exist in germ in every single human being. These six *shaktis* are in
their unity represented by the Light of the Logos, *Daiviprakriti,*
the noumenal light of the dawn of manifestation, also called Vach,
Kwan Yin, Sarasvati, Isis and, in some alchemical texts, the Virgin
of the World. This Initial Existence has an intimate correspondence with the twin twilights that enclose each terrestrial
day. In both the potent hour of readiness before the dawn and
the hour of memory at dusk, human beings can withdraw from
the external physical plane of manifestation and approach their
true spiritual state of being. The universal and cosmic resonances
of these timeless moments remind the soul of forgotten truths
that pertain to the largest cycles and are a permanent presence in
the innermost chambers of the soul. Ancient wisdom has always
taught the use of certain periods of time through which, by
analogy and correspondence, one can come more easily into the
subtle luminous vestures, into the *karana sharira,* and, ultimately,
into the *anandamaya kosha.*

The hidden light-energy and noumenal matter of the highest
principles persist throughout an evolutionary period as the true
raiment of the immortal soul that comes through a vast course
of collective monadic life and over eighteen million years of self-
consciousness and human existence. It is easier to experience this
light through meditation upon the whole host of perfected beings
during certain times because these beings have entered the creative
light of which Jesus spoke. To understand this philosophically, it
is important to think through the metaphysical distinction
between the brute energy inherent in matter and the intelligence
which guides and directs that energy.

> ...what is called 'unconscious Nature' is in reality an
> aggregate of forces manipulated by semi-intelligent

beings (Elementals) guided by High Planetary Spirits, (Dhyan Chohans), whose collective aggregate forms the manifested *verbum* of the unmanifested LOGOS, and constitutes at one and the same time the MIND of the Universe and its immutable LAW.

Three distinct representations of the Universe in its three distinct aspects are impressed upon our thought by the esoteric philosophy: the PRE-EXISTING (evolved from) the EVER-EXISTING; and the PHENOMENAL — the world of illusion, the reflection, and shadow thereof.

The Secret Doctrine, i 277-278

The Ever-Existing is the eternal divine ground of all being. The Pre-Existing is the most subtle, primary, luminous emanation which is totally unmanifest from the point of view of what is called the world, but which is the most potent manifestation. A human being truly concerned to acquire Demiurgic control over the power of thought will deliberate and hold back expression, not in frustration but in order to dwell upon each thought and let it settle. The unmanifest reality of an idea becomes evident only when one can hold an idea for the benefit of others and see that this power of retention truly helps. It will help others far more if silent than if verbalized without having been assimilated through contemplation. Many people sincerely and mistakenly think that by making a slogan out of this they can do it; genuinely to curb the desire to manifest is to have a profound sense of reality in the unmanifest. To live in the causal realm, and in the *karana sharira*, one must see the ideas behind words, and also behind one's own mind. Profound ideas take shape when dwelt upon in the silence and solitude of the immovable mind, far from the noisy speech of the manifesting movable mind. That which is supernally true spontaneously subsists in silence.

Human beings have difficulty realizing this because of mental and moral cowardice. Cheating oneself through life, never really wanting to learn a lesson out of the fear that there is no guarantee of success at the end, they lapse into the habit of never learning anything from life, let alone from the immortal souls within other human beings. This sad but self-inflicted wretchedness comes to those who cannot make proper use of their vast prerogatives as human souls. One must see this in the small, but one can only correct it by comprehension and contemplation in the large.

Pythagoras and Paracelsus taught that the great healer is the Spiritual Sun, and that the best therapy lies in the earnest attempt at daily meditation. One must encounter the seeming dark if one would discover the true light. One must enter the realm of the non-manifest and begin to experience a sense of reality in relation to subliminal states of matter, to root-ideas, but also to the continuity of existence that is untinctured and untrammelled by divisions normally made between past, present and future. The real universe is the invisible, pre-existing reflection of the Ever-Existing, the Dhyan Chohanic thought reflecting the ideation of the Universal Mind; the phenomenal world of brute energies is the world of illusion.

> During the great mystery and drama of life known as the Manvantara, real Kosmos is like the object placed behind the white screen upon which are thrown the Chinese shadows, called forth by the magic lantern. The actual figures and things remain invisible, while the wires of evolution are pulled by the unseen hands; and men and things are thus but the reflections, *on* the white field, of the realities *behind* the snares of *Mahamaya*, or the great Illusion.
>
> *The Secret Doctrine*, i 278

This teaching about the primal triune nature of the universe is connected with the standpoint of the seventh principle, the omnipresent, ever-existing *Atman*. One who reflects this in *Buddhi* and focusses it through *Manas* has truly entered his or her spiritual inheritance. Everything below these three principles — and the highest is really not a principle because it is so universal — should serve merely as a field for calm, deliberate and wise mirroring. Before one can get to that, one must cultivate the power of self-correction in reference to all one's habits and tendencies; one must awaken the capacity to sift within the heart, within the mind, and even within the senses. Those who do this will find that their attitude towards time during the day will change from a linear sequential view to one of subtle cycles of manifestation and withdrawal. This will alter their rates of mental and moral absorption, assimilation and elimination. Most of the blockage to Buddhic illumination comes from retaining unnecessary and irrelevant detail. This atavistic propensity towards the lower realms of manifestation obscures the finer channels of awareness, and compounds itself through a noisy fear of spiritual incapacity. It is like going into a spiritual supermarket, where one is inundated with so many sights, through elemental attraction and repulsion, that one forgets one's original purpose. This happens with the eyes, the ears and all the senses, but it is aggravated when it recoils outward in the form of unregulated speech. If, however, the mind reposes upon elevating concepts, one can take in detail quietly and quickly without becoming embroiled in the habitual, inattentive reactions of the wandering mind.

One can heighten one's power of comprehension significantly as one eschews the wastage of fragmentary consciousness addicted to futile manifestation. But paradoxically, the more one is still, the more one is withdrawn into one's inmost chamber, the more effectively one can consecrate and use all one's instruments on behalf of universal good. Because there is no excess, there is also no overload or wastage. Many beneficent consequences flow from the basic teaching about entering into the stream of uninterrupted consciousness, but one must recognize that every human being is essentially capable of doing this. Each human being is imprisoned by a mass of worn out and corrupted instruments which, although they look difficult to correct, can be corrected fundamentally by first rooting out and replacing the false sense of selfhood. It is a tragedy that many people drawn to the spiritual life do everything else, but forget to do the main thing — to rethink who they are. They specialize in walking backwards. To receive in abundance what is in the universe one must rethink both intellectually and in the deepest and fullest way possible; one must examine oneself and one's relationship to one's instruments. Centering the consciousness correctly will show itself by a heightened power of attention, by greater relaxation and noetic detachment. Drawing inward into the Presence, one will begin to withdraw from excessive allegiance to the manifested. Blending one's will with the universal invocation of the *Gayatri*, one will become an initiator most concerned with the initiating impulse, the ensouling idea behind manifestation. Becoming an alchemical apprentice in the divine evolution of Ideas, one may become truly worthy of the benediction of the Brotherhood of Bodhisattvas.

MAHAT, MANU AND THE AVATAR

Manu is the synthesis perhaps of the Manasa, and he is a single consciousness in the same sense that while all the different cells of which the human body is composed are different and varying consciousnesses there is still a unit of consciousness which is the man. But this unit, so to say, is not a single consciousness: it is a reflection of thousands and millions of consciousnesses which a man has absorbed.

But Manu is not really an individuality, it is the whole of mankind. You may say that Manu is a generic name for the Pitris, the progenitors of mankind. They come, as I have shown, from the Lunar Chain. . . . But, as the moon receives its light from the Sun, so the descendants of the Lunar Pitris receive their higher mental light from the Sun or the 'Son of the Sun.' For all you know Vaivasvata Manu may be an Avatar or a personification of MAHAT, commissioned by the Universal Mind to lead and guide thinking Humanity onwards.

Transactions of the Blavatsky Lodge   H.P. Blavatsky

To understand the relationship between Universal Mind and *Mahat,* and between *Mahat* and Manu, one must first distinguish between Unconditioned Consciousness and Ideation, Eternal Duration and Time, Boundless Space and the subtlest fields of differentiated existence. Though these three hypostases of the Absolute are inconceivable to the finite mind, one may rise, through intuitive intimations, towards that ultimate ground of manifestation which is beyond all boundaries, prior to all beginnings and endings. To do so is to penetrate towards the fathomless Night of non-manifestation, the virtually immeasurable *Maha Pralaya* after the dissolution of the entire solar universe. This is the Divine Darkness wherein Universal Mind "was not", because there were no *Ah-Hi* to contain and reflect the infinite Divine Thought. Within the fundamental substratum of Universal Mind there is neither differentiated consciousness nor the activity of ideation, there are no universes nor any terms of reference, but only the abstract permanent possibility of mental action uncircumscribed by any plane of existence. From this pure potentiality one must pass through Logoic radiation and reflection from the proemally unmanifest ideation of the Universal Mind to its invisible, though unmanifest, embodied potency — *Mahat*, the cosmic Mind. Behind every manifested system of worlds, at the basis of every solar universe, is the manvantaric activity of the cosmic mind directing the Fohatic process whereby Akashic ideation is translated into the concrete prototypes of the astral and physical cosmos. It is through *Mahat* that the highest independent intelligences, one with the Unmanifest Logos, become the Manus, the guiding spirits of thinking humanity.

In the primordial process of unfoldment that precedes the emergence of the cosmos, *Mahat* is the Third Logos. In the arcane teachings of Gupta Vidya and in the derivative philosophical systems of antiquity, the First and the Second Logoi are characterized in a variety of ways to prevent any hard and fast or concretized conceptions of them. This alchemical variation of language is needed because the cosmic process intimated to the intuitive is rather like the passage from midnight through dawn to the day. The dawn of manifestation cannot be thought of in terms of any fixed schema, any multi-dimensional map in space or any series of points of temporal succession; it is something that can only be sensed in deep meditation. The awakening of the three Logoi is coeval with the analogical seventh eternity of *Maha Pralaya*, and it is only with the completion of this process that manvantaric time and space, under the aegis of *Mahat*, may be said to exist. Rather than submit these mysteries to ratiocination, one should contemplate the emergence from midnight darkness of a supple, virginal light. Varying metaphors are given in *The Secret Doctrine* to convey something of the nature of the Unmanifest Logos, the Unmanifest-manifest Logos and the Manifested Logos.

In the Esoteric Philosophy the First is the un-manifested, and the Second the manifested Logos. Ishwara stands for that Second, and Narayana for the unmanifested Logos. . . . In *The Secret Doctrine,* that from which the manifested Logos is born is translated by the 'Eternal Mother-Father'; while in the *Vishnu Purana* it is described as the Egg of the World, surrounded by seven skins, layers or zones. It is in this Golden Egg that Brahmā, the male, is born and that Brahmā is in reality the Second Logos or even the Third, according to the enumeration adopted; for a certainty he is not the First or highest, the point which is everywhere and nowhere. Mahat, in the Esoteric interpretations, is in reality the Third Logos or the Synthesis of the Seven creative rays, the Seven Logoi.

Ibid., 15

Narayana is the Unmanifest Logos, which, like the Pythagorean cosmic *Monas,* radiates only to retire into the Divine Darkness. It is the Three-in-One which gives rise to the primordial seven Logoi, the highest *Ah-Hi.* It is the self-existent and parentless — *Svayambhuva Anupadaka*; it partakes of no differentiation in space or time, but belongs entirely to the undifferentiated noumenal abstract plane of cause. It is synonymous with the last vibration of the seventh eternity. Ishwara, considered as the Second or Unmanifest-manifest Logos, arises as pure potentiality on the plane of the eternal Mother-Father. It represents the potentiality of the differentiation of latent Divine Thought. Still prior to the differentiation of time and space, it is inwardly the reflection of the radiation of Narayana and the latent matrix from which the manifested Ishwara-Brahmā may emerge. It is immaculate space not yet become the immaculate Mother. The emergence of Brahmā at the culmination of the seventh eternity marks the emergence of the Word made flesh on the plane of the immaculate Mother, the commencement of differentiated manvantaric space and time. This is the point of differentiation of the cosmic atoms that become the seeds of solar worlds pervaded by the *Vaishvanara* solar-magnetic fire, the domain of Svayambhuva Manu.

This Logoic process may be better understood if simultaneously seen in terms of the reflection of Divine Thought in the Universal Mind and the ideational activity underlying and sustaining the cosmos.

> In the ABSOLUTE or Divine Thought everything exists and there has been no time when it did not so exist; but Divine Ideation is limited by the Universal Manvantaras. The realm of Akasha is the undifferentiated noumenal and abstract Space which will be occupied by *Chidakasam*, the field of primordial consciousness. It has several degrees, however, in Occult philosophy; in fact, 'seven fields'. The first is the field of latent consciousness which is coeval with the duration of the first and second unmanifested Logoi. It is the 'Light which shineth in darkness and the darkness comprehended it not' of St. John's Gospel. When the hour strikes for the Third Logos to appear, then from the latent potentiality there radiates a lower field of differentiated consciousness, which is Mahat, or the entire collectivity of those Dhyan Chohans of *sentient life* of which Fohat is the representative on the objective plane and the Manasaputras on the subjective.
>
> *Ibid.*, 95-96

Chidakasam is the primary field of ideation of the Absolute Universal Mind. In *Maha Pralaya* there is nothing to contain or perceive *Chidakasam*; hence Universal Mind "is not" *as a manifestation.* In the immutable Be-ness of SAT, *Chidakasam* is eternally present as the abstract and absolute potential of innumerable manifestations and universes. At the dawn of manifestation Divine Thought begins to be reflected and manifested as a primordial light synonymous with the ideation of the highest *Ah-Hi*. Thus *Chidakasam* becomes the substratum of *Chit*. Absolute consciousness becomes relative consciousness periodically at the dawn of manifestation *via* the emergence of a vehicle of Universal Mind. Regardless of the existence or non-existence of manifest worlds, Absolute Mind *is*. It is the immutable, ever-latent and never differentiated ground of that Logoic radiation which eventually gives way to the manifested cosmic mind or *Mahat*. As that Divine Ideation in activity, *Mahat* is neither evolved nor created, but is an aspect of Universal Mind, the periodic potency of the one universal all-potential Law. Put another way, SAT becomes the Three-in-One, SAT-CHIT-ANANDA. Meta-mathematically, SAT over spirit equals SAT; SAT over force equals CHIT; and SAT over matter equals ANANDA. Ordinarily, human beings do not think of matter in terms of *ananda* or force in terms of ideation. Instead, thought, will and act — ideation, volition and joy — are conceived within the prison-house of personal identity. Through the distorting prism of a hyper-fragmented consciousness — mostly refracted through the sensorium and foolishly identified with the corpse or body — it is inherently impossible to conceive of the archetypal relationship between man and *Mahat*.

Clearly, in such a condition one cannot begin to imagine what the states of consciousness associated with the Logoi could be like, let alone the nature of the Universal Mind, which spans *manvantaras* and *pralayas*, witnessing the unfoldment of the cosmos from within without. Yet it is impossible to plumb the depths of human nature without coming to terms with the relationship between *Mahat* and the *Manasaputra*.

> Out of the seven so-called *Creations*, Mahat is the third, for it is the Universal and Intelligent Soul, Divine Ideation, combining the ideal plans and prototypes of all things in the manifested objective as well as subjective world. In the Sankhya and Puranic doctrines Mahat is the first product of *Pradhana*, informed by Kshetrajna, 'Spirit-Substance'. In Esoteric philosophy Kshetrajna is the name given to our informing EGOS.
>
> *Ibid.,* 15

Viewed from the standpoint of Narayana-Ishwara, *Mahat* is an illusion. Viewed from the standpoint of a participant in a world of manifestation, *Mahat* is the seed of all things, the root reality from which all archetypal ideas arise. Symbolically, it resembles a universal golden egg, the *Hiranyagarbha* of the cosmos, brooded over by Narayana and containing the potentiality of manifestation. This potentiality of Mother-Father within the *Brahmanda* is the gestating Brahmā, who is always potentially present in the egg. With the fulfilment of this gestation comes the emergence of the manifested Ishwara, the God of all cultures and religions depicted in so many different ways. But when these primordial realities are experienced through meditation in consciousness, and not rendered into form, image or object, they may be considered as a great galaxy of minds meditating upon a single centre. One may think in terms of Buddhas within Buddhas, and ultimately of the potential of an entire field of Universal Ideation reflected in the cosmic mind.

When thinking of *Mahat* in terms of the seven Logoi, the highest *Ah-Hi* or Dhyanis, one must try to understand the use of generic terms — like *Ah-Hi,* Dhyani, Manu and others — which characterize the entire teaching of the Wisdom-Religion. These terms are like the x's and y's of a complex abstract formula. Whether one puts a capital X or a small x depends upon the level and context being described. Whilst this may seem confusing to the neophyte, the inherent complexity and unity in diversity of manifestation require it. All occult teaching depends upon analogy and correspondence, the serene conviction that what applies in the small also applies in the large, that what is concretely true in the small circle has its archetypal origins in the boundless circle of eternity. Thus, by analogy, Universal Mind may be said to radiate the *Ah-Hi,* its pristine faculty of conscious ideation, through *Mahat,* the cosmic mind which acts as the brain of Universal Mind. Yet the *Ah-Hi* on the highest plane, the primordial containers of Universal Ideation, are *arupa* (formless) breaths. On the second plane they approach to *arupa* nature, and on the third they become the *Manasaputra,* the subjective aspect of the manifestation of *Mahat*. Essentially, they are cosmic forces, not human beings, and in their later differentiations they become the planetary, solar, lunar and finally incarnating Egos. As to their own transformation on the third plane, they become thinkers, able to act with regard to things within and without. Thus, in conceiving of *Mahat* in relation to the architectonic plan of the cosmos, it may be thought of both as pure subjectivity, and also in terms of the seven Logoi, seven colours and seven sounds. In Buddhist iconography this is portrayed in *tankas* which show seven Buddhas, each of whom is in turn at the head of a tree having myriad branches representing manifold Buddhas.

For the embodied human consciousness, captivated by form and largely incapable of abstraction, these unfolding hierarchies with their subjective and objective components may best be intimated through analogy. Imagine a small lantern, containing a candle and a series of mirrors. In the right perspective, the lantern reveals a set of ten candles burning brightly. Surrounding these and seeming to fade into an infinite recurrence are more and more flames extending to the limit of vision. Which of these are real, and which are unreal? If some of them are unreal, then is the glass unreal? One would ordinarily say that the original candle is real in relation to the mirror images, and yet that candle's reality exists only in the flame, the source of light and vision. If this is applied to human life over many incarnations, it is apparent that individuals are generally acted upon from the outside from the manifested objective level of gross matter. Psychical fancies and representations in the imagination result from being acted upon by the subjective side of matter.

When one draws upon abstract ideas, when one experiences fine impulses and noble thoughts, one is in reality experiencing thoughts derived from a higher plane. One is coming closer to a vast collection of invisible beings, who have their ultimate origins in *Mahat* and Universal Mind. Analogy and correspondence require the renunciation of linear ratiocination in favour of alchemical transformation. Abstract ideas can impel the concentrated mind to alter radically its magnetic affinities.

There is no way to approach Divine Wisdom except through a Guru, a living embodiment of realized divine ideation. As there can be no birth without parents, no growth without elders, there can be no spiritual enlightenment without Gurus. For, at the heart of the entire process of manifestation, it is impossible to have a cosmos without Dhyani Buddhas. The failure to recognize this has been the terrible conceit of the West in the modern age.

To some it may seem more scientific to refer to these Dhyanis as rays, and more religious to speak of them as Buddhas. Yet all of this merely arises out of confusion. When, through the experience of meditation, one goes beyond form into a deeper sense of being, one enters a realm of space and time where these polarities and contrasts do not apply. Through meditation one may touch the pure ground of true bliss, the experience of which is the basis of all devotion. Ordinarily, human beings enjoy sleep because, perhaps for a few moments in deep sleep, they experience this state of *ananda*. To experience it self-consciously through meditation requires a breaking away from the false ideation and false sense of subjectivity intrinsic to the *persona*. The true element of subjectivity in a human being is bound up with the *Manasaputra*. The life of the incarnated Ego is itself bound up with more differentiated fields of objectivity and subjectivity connected with differentiated astral and physical matter. From the standpoint of the *Manasa*, the astral and physical fields of force governing the aggregates of matter are themselves the objective manifestations of Mahatic ideation. On the plane of Higher *Manas*, correlative with *Mahat*, though not identical with it, subjectivity and objectivity have to do with fields and entities which precede the gross differentiation of the terrestrial plane. It is only by understanding this through a maturity in consciousness gained through meditation that one is prepared to consider that Vaivasvata Manu may be an Avatar of *Mahat* commissioned by the Universal Mind to guide all humanity.

To discount the conception of Manu as a being, preferring the metaphor of a focussing of rays, suggests that one is threatened by the facts of evolution, foolishly determined to run away from one's spiritual progenitors, preceptors and teachers. And to run away is to cheapen the concept of such beings through the popular notion of an arbitrary personal god. This only arose, and held a hypnotic sway over many people, because it crudely concretized that which is essentially true. Only through the awakened devotional heart may one begin to grasp the indescribable majesty of such beings. Only through a sense of their reality may one begin to apprehend the archetypal meaning of the long pilgrimage of mankind, within which every unit bears fundamental responsibility, but receives divine guidance.

The root principle for comprehending the conception of Manu as the embodiment of a Mahatic plan is that *in Eternal Duration everything is ever present.* In time the vaster the period considered, the closer one comes to ideational prototypes that mirror that which is ever present. Such ideation is philosophically referred to as the plane of *Akasha,* which is like an invisible fire. The highest undifferentiated plane of *Akasha* is correlative to *Buddhi,* which stands in relation to *Manas* as the *Ah-Hi* stand in relation to the *Manasaputra.* The *Ah-Hi* are like a flame proceeding from unity, primary rays streaming forth from a primordial source. The one *Atman* is itself fire, and is the flame of the Flame of *Paramatman.* Speaking of these differentiations of fire, flame and light, as symbolized in Hindu thought by the hosts of Manus and Rishis, H.P. Blavatsky indicated their cosmic origin and cosmic continuity as an expression of the principle of Unity in diversity.

> If all those Manus and Rishis are called by one generic name, this is due to the fact that they are one and all the manifested Energies of one and the same LOGOS, the celestial, as well as the terrestrial messengers and permutations of that Principle which is ever in a state of activity; conscious during the period of Cosmic evolution, unconscious (from our point of view) during Cosmic rest, as the Logos sleepeth in the bosom of THAT which 'sleepeth not', nor is it ever awake — for it is SAT or *Be-ness,* not a Being. It is from IT that issues the great unseen Logos, who evolves all the other *logoi,*

the primeval MANU who gives being to the other
Manus, who emanate the universe and all in it
collectively, and who represent in their aggregate the
manifested Logos.

The Secret Doctrine, ii 310

It is in relation to the unmanifest Logos, symbolized here as the
primeval Manu, that the particular Manus within manvantaric
time may be considered as Avatars of the manifested Logos or
Mahat. The notion of Vaivasvata Manu commissioned by the
Universal Mind with an aspect of the manvantaric plan can only be
understood in relation to states of consciousness and matter
so universal and homogeneous that there is instantaneous
communication amidst a vast field of pre-cosmic and cosmic
ideation.

Within this inconceivably large framework, every human
being can self-consciously invoke the power of protection,
guidance and instruction of the highest Dhyanis, Manus and
Rishis. In his essay on "The Allegorical Umbrella", W.Q. Judge
conveyed this idea through an apt analogy. The ineffable source
of all manifestation may be thought of as a Central Sun, scattering
its rays in every direction. The spokes of an umbrella are the
Dhyanis, the Manus and the Rishis: they simultaneously guide
the supernal light and protect the holder from intense radiation.
The handle of the umbrella represents the channel of communication in consciousness from above below, the awakened
power of *Buddhi-Manas.* In reality, the holder of the umbrella, its
handle, canopy and ribs are all derived from the seven Dhyanis.

Nothing exists which does not come from the seven Logoi.
As they descend, level by level, they emanate the hebdomadic
proliferation of hosts of beings on seven planes. This differentiation is like a fireworks display; an incredible riot and
profusion of sparks and flames, emanations and manifestations
enter into every atom of every being. Because they were lit up as
self-conscious minds by the *Manasaputra* over eighteen million
years ago, human beings have the *sutratman,* the thread-soul, the
sense of consciousness independent of form and personality, prior

to birth and beyond death. There is, in every one, the seed of immortality, the conscious power to invoke the Dhyanis, the capacity to cut through states of consciousness and the alternations of day and night, life and death, *manvantara* and *pralaya*. This ultimate potential of self-conscious immortality is rooted in the Logoic ancestry of the human race, as intimated in the Teachings regarding the Manus and *Manasaputra*.

> Hence we learn in the 'Commentaries' that while no Dhyan Chohan, not even the highest, can realise completely 'the condition of the preceding Cosmic evolution,' 'the Manus retain a knowledge of their experiences of all the Cosmic evolutions throughout Eternity.' This is very plain: the first Manu is called *Swayambhuva*, 'the Self-manifested', the Son of the *unmanifested* FATHER.
>
> *Ibid.*, 310-311

To begin to draw apart from the world of confused personal identity, and to come into contact with truly divine instruction, one must direct one's consciousness upwards and inwards, reverse the polarity of one's perception and action. The supernal states of consciousness, which Gupta Vidya affirms are the birthright of every human being, may be entered only through withdrawal and meditation. At first, it will merely be possible to see a little bit around one's nose, but as one's meditation extends and deepens, the range and depth of vision will increase. Everything depends upon one's courage of selflessness and freedom in generosity towards all other beings. The fundamental measure of one's security as a human being is one's willingness to surrender all, to take a stand in the Divine Darkness. According to one's level of courage and freedom will be one's capacity to draw closer to the primeval vibrations of Logoic consciousness. All of these highest energies are focussed within the resplendent instrument of Vaivasvata Manu as the Avatar. All derive from Maha Vishnu, the seed of all Avatars. Such is the economy of Nature that there is only one Avatar at all times, and only one Avatar at any time.

This is the inscrutable mystery intimated by every divine incarnation, but it may be initially approached by understanding clearly that all human beings are begotten sons of God.

This mystery can never be fully formulated but it may be felt. Indeed, once its vibration is touched, one will become less concerned about formulating, proving and arguing, but more concerned with withdrawing and becoming receptive. The deeper one's realization, the more painful the experience, as those elements in the lower nature that are incompatible with the highest vibration are purged. Through atavistic affinities to those elements which must be let go, one will attract dark forces — the legions of Satan — but through unremitting persistence one may assuredly prevail. The stronger one becomes, the greater one's serenity and the less one's anxiety. Through humility, receptivity grows, and with it the willingness to learn and to love. One may gain the heroic capacity to correct one's errors, the courage painstakingly to retrace one's steps when one has gone wrong, to withdraw harsh words, to forsake regret and, instead, look to the human race and human suffering and for a deepening of pure receptivity to the mirroring of the Universal Mind in Manu. As one awakens the three higher seats of consciousness on the *arupa* planes, connected with *Atma-Buddhi-Manas* and correlative with the three Logoi, one will gain a vivid sense of participation in humanity as a *Manasaputra*, a ray inseparable from the Spirit of Humanity, the Manu whose

> Monad emanates from the never resting Principle in the beginning of every new Cosmic activity: that *Logos* or UNIVERSAL MONAD (collective Elohim) that radiates *from within himself all* those Cosmic Monads that become the centres of activity — progenitors of the numberless Solar systems as well as of the yet undifferentiated *human* monads of planetary chains as well as of every being thereon. Each Cosmic Monad is 'Swayambhuva', the SELF-BORN, *which becomes the Centre of Force, from within which emerges a planetary chain* (of which chains there are seven in our system),

and whose radiations become again so many Manus Swayambhuva (a generic name, mysterious and meaning far more than appears), each of these becoming, as a *Host*, the creator of his own Humanity.

Ibid., 311

Even to begin to contemplate these ideas is to transform one's view of reality, displacing much that one had thought important, whilst discovering the relevance of much that one had previously neglected. A greater attentiveness and skillfulness is brought to the performance of *dharma*, because there is a desire to discharge all obligations to life-atoms, to the elementals of fire, air, water and earth. This may be done through what is called cooking, what is called doing accounts, or what is called earning a living, but these are only words borrowed from a materialistic tongue. All human action involves ideation and has implicit reference to the abiding possibility of lighting up minds and hearts. The inherent function of ideation is to awaken and deepen insight. Once one begins to discover the nature of the ideational potential within the higher principles, one will be filled with an overwhelming love for all beings. One will seek an absolute fidelity and purity of heart towards one's spiritual Guru and express this true *bhakti* through the joyous service of all beings. Thus what one essentially is, what one essentially knows, and what one essentially wants are fused. Thus one may progressively constitute oneself a self-conscious servant of the Manus, Dhyanis and Rishis, who are all born from the mind of Krishna. Themselves the highest intellectual *arupa* Dhyanis, divine souls that have acquired independent conscious existence through traversing the obligatory pilgrimage of manifestation, they are arrayed like a great galaxy around the Unmanifest Logos, ceaselessly serving the Universal Mind through their Mahatmic ideation.

The opportunity to serve, however humbly, the Avatar and the Mahatmas in the dawn of the Aquarian Age is an awesome privilege and a true test of the mettle of the soul. In a time which ends and cancels recorded history, there is no need to prove anything, only to participate in the changing of the vibration of the globe itself. To be a part of this is to be on the side of all that is true and good and beautiful. Therefore, one should have the courage to eliminate with ease whatever is inconsistent with the golden light of the future. Each aspirant should become an apprentice in the continual process of spiritual ingestion, assimilation and absorption, gaining strength and nourishment whilst exemplifying the patience portrayed in the verse:

> Lead, kindly Light, amid the encircling gloom,
>   Lead thou me on;
> The night is dark, and I am far from home,
>   Lead thou me on.
> Keep Thou my feet; I do not ask to see
>   The distant scene; one step enough for me.

Thus, one may loosen the sense of time, discarding anxiety about the future, fear of the past and shame for the present. Experiencing a sense of higher self-forgetfulness, one may change one's dreaming and yet be wide awake, especially at a time when all possible vigilance and compassion are required because of the corpses and shells disintegrating in the field of *Kurukshetra*.

Raising one's sights and moving forward, rooting oneself in the *Kshetragna*, one's life may become like a dance or a song, a sonnet or a symphony. Mirroring the natural flow of great rivers and the unhindered movement of the winds, one may become like the ocean, immovable in its depths, and yet variegated in its colours. By creating a flow, and having the strength to experience it inwardly, without external tokens and signs, one may begin to live an authentic inner life. This life of contemplation is the only life in which one will experience true comradeship. This is the life of the spiritual Path, wherein the heart is filled with love until it overflows with gratitude and reverence, releasing its strength for the benefit of fellow pilgrim souls. Such a life, lived selflessly on behalf of the humanity of the future, will draw deeply upon the inexhaustible well of the grace of the Guru.

TRUTH AND REALITY

It is common to make a sharp separation between knowledge and being, truth and reality, between what we affirm to be true or false and what exists or is non-existent. This distinction, which we have inherited from the Greeks, is valuable in itself and is fundamental to modern thought. On the other hand, in the classical Indian tradition as in pre-Socratic thought echoed in Plato, truth and reality are often used as interchangeable terms and we are taught that there is a higher level of awareness and apprehension beyond the sensory field in which our knowing and what is known are united and even transcended in a sense of immediate vision and absorption in what is seen. This identification of truth and reality was reaffirmed by Gandhi in his insistence that truth is that which *is* and error that which *is not*. Most of what we normally call knowledge has clearly nothing to do with truth as Gandhi understood it, and we are right to distinguish it from being. The modern man is neither willing nor able to grasp reality; he has been trained to develop and use his reason and his feeling in a manner that can give partial formulations of the truth or passing sensations of particular sense-objects. Once we accept the notion that man can be separated and detached from nature, human knowledge and sensation cannot attain to an intuitive insight into the *Tattwas*, the essences of things. If, however, we start with the ancient axiom that man is the microcosm of the macrocosm, then we can see that the extent of truth that is available to any man is connected with the plane of reality on which he functions. Hence the importance of H.P. Blavatsky's advocacy of the Platonic standpoint which was abandoned by Aristotle, who was no Initiate, and who has had such a dominant influence upon subsequent thinking in the West.

In Gupta Vidya, as generally in theosophical thought, the seeker must start with a clear conception of the notion of absolute abstract Truth or Reality, SAT, from which is derived *satya* or truth.

The First Fundamental Proposition of *The Secret Doctrine* urges us to set out with the postulate that there is one absolute Reality which antecedes all manifested, conditioned being, which is attributeless, which is 'Be-ness' rather than Being and is beyond the range and reach of all thought and speculation. *Paranishpanna*, the *summum bonum*, is that final state of subjectivity which has no relation to anything but the one absolute Truth (*Paramarthasatya*) on its plane. Sooner or later, all that now seemingly exists will be in reality in the state of *Paranishpanna*, the state which leads one to appreciate correctly the full meaning of Non-Being or of absolute Being. But there is a great difference between *conscious* and *unconscious* 'being.' "The condition of Paranishpanna, without Paramartha, the Self-analyzing consciousness (Svasamvedana), is no bliss, but simply extinction."

The Greeks were then right to distinguish between reality as it presents itself to finite human minds and reality as it is or would be to the Divine Mind. 'Divine Thought' does not necessitate the idea of a single Divine thinker. The Universe is in its totality the SAT, with the past and the future crystallized in an eternal Present, the Divine Thought reflected in a secondary or manifest cause. However, as man is indissolubly linked with the universe, and his *Manas* is connected with *Mahat*, it is possible for man to bridge the gap between truth and reality, between knowledge and being, by *conscious* effort. As man becomes more and more self-conscious, and less and less passive, in his awareness of the universe, he must abandon the distinction between truth and knowledge and redefine his notion of truth so as to make it identical with reality. The real distinction is between head-learning and soul-wisdom. What the pundit or the ignoramus regards as truth is error to the sage and the Adept. The Adept has realized the non-separateness of all that lives and his own unity with the 'Rootless Root' of all, which is pure knowledge (*Sattva*, which Shankara took to mean *Buddhi*), eternal, unconditioned reality or SAT.

The world in which we live is itself the shadow of a shadowy reflection, twice removed, of the 'World of Truth' or SAT, through which the direct energy that radiates from the ONE REALITY reaches us. That which is manifested cannot be SAT, but is something phenomenal, not everlasting or even sempiternal. This 'World of Truth' is described as "a bright star dropped from the heart of Eternity; the beacon of hope on whose Seven Rays hang the Seven Worlds of Being." The visible sun is itself only the material shadow of the Central Sun of Truth, which illuminates the invisible, intellectual world of Spirit. The ideal conception of the universe is a Golden Egg, with a positive pole that acts in the manifested world of matter, while the negative pole is lost in the unknowable absoluteness of SAT or Be-ness. The first cosmic aspect of the esoteric SAT is the Universal Mind, *Mahat*, 'the manifested Omniscience', the root of SELF-Consciousness. The spirit of archaic philosophy cannot be comprehended unless we thoroughly assimilate the concepts of SAT and *Asat*.

> *Asat* is not merely the negation of *Sat*, nor is it the 'not yet existing'; for *Sat* is in itself neither the 'existent', nor 'being'. SAT is the immutable, the ever present, changeless and eternal root, from and through which all proceeds. But it is far more than the potential force in the seed, which propels onward the process of development, or what is now called evolution. It is the ever becoming, though the never manifesting. *Sat* is born from *Asat*, and ASAT is begotten by *Sat*: the perpetual motion in a circle, truly; yet a circle that can be squared only at the supreme Initiation, at the threshold of Paranirvana.
>
> *The Secret Doctrine*, ii 449-50

The Theosophical Trinity is composed of the Sun (the Father), Mercury or Hermes or Budha (the Son), and Venus or Lucifer, the morning Star (the Holy Ghost, *Sophia*, the Spirit of Wisdom, Love and Truth). To these three correspond *Atma, Buddhi* and *Manas* in man.

It is useful to distinguish between absolute and relative truth, between truth and error, between reality and illusion, between *Paramarthasatya* and *Samvritisatya*. *Paramartha* is self-consciousness and the word is made up of *parama* (above everything) and *artha* (comprehension); and *Satya* means absolute true being, or *esse*. The opposite of this absolute reality, or actuality, is *Samvritisatya*, the relative truth only, *Samvriti* meaning 'false conception' and being the origin of illusion, *Maya*; it is illusion-creating appearance. The two obstacles to the attainment of *Paramarthasatya* are *Parikalpita*, the error of believing something to exist or to be real which does not exist and is unreal, and *Paratantra*, that which exists only through a dependent or causal connection. As a result of *Parikalpita*, we get *tamasic* knowledge or 'truth,' which is based upon an obsession with the sole reality of a single object or thought, which is, in essence, unreal and non-existent. As a result of *Paratantra*, we get *rajasic* knowledge or 'truth,' based upon a concern with the differences between seemingly separate, but inter-dependent and ephemeral, things.

When we have developed the faculties necessary to go beyond *Parikalpita* and *Paratantra*, we begin to get *sattvic* knowledge or truth, based upon the recognition of the unity of all things, their common identity on a single plane of universal, ultimate reality. This is itself only an approximation, imperfect and inadequate, to absolute Truth. Whereas relative truth is ephemeral and can be the subject of controversy and is eventually extinguished, absolute Truth is enduring, beyond dispute and can never be destroyed. Whereas relative truth will triumph over error, absolute Truth ever shines, regardless of whether there are martyrs and witnesses ready to vindicate it and die for it. Hence "the failure to sweep away entirely from the face of the earth every vestige of that ancient Wisdom, and to shackle and gag every witness who testified to it." And yet, in the world of manifestation, every error proliferates other errors rapidly, while each truth has to be painfully discovered. "Error runs down an inclined plane, while Truth has to laboriously climb its way uphill," says an old proverb.

The Theosophist is, in a sense, a Berkeleian phenomenalist and holds to the axiom, *esse est percipi* (to exist is to be perceived), in regard to all relative truths. Everything that exists has only a relative reality since the appearance which the hidden noumenon assumes for any observer depends upon his power of cognition. *Maya* or illusion is an element which, therefore, enters into all finite things. The cognizer is also a reflection and the things cognized are therefore as real to him as he himself is. Nothing is permanent except the one hidden absolute existence which contains in itself the noumena of all realities. Everything is illusion outside of eternal Truth, which has neither form, colour, nor limitation. He who has placed himself beyond the veil of *maya*, the Adept and Initiate, can have no *Devachan*. Whatever plane our consciousness may be acting in, both we and the things belonging to that plane are, for the time being, our only realities. Relative truths are relative to our plane of perception at any given time in any particular situation.

> As we rise in the scale of development we perceive that during the stages through which we have passed we mistook shadows for realities, and the upward progress of the Ego is a series of progressive awakenings, each advance bringing with it the idea that now, at last, we have reached 'reality'; but only when we shall have reached the absolute Consciousness, and blended our own with it, shall we be free from the delusions produced by Maya.
>
> *The Secret Doctrine,* i 40

Ideologies or systems which claim to be the absolute Truth are clearly *tamasic*, static and doomed to atrophy and decay and final extinction. Dogmas and claims to uniqueness are *rajasic*, partial and ephemeral, ever changing and destined to disappear. In ideologies and dogmas are to be contained the seeds of violence because they violate the absolute truth of unity and endow relative truths with the evil aura of the dire heresy of separateness, the greatest of all sins and their common source. When one party or another, when one sect or the other, thinks itself to be the sole possessor of absolute Truth, it becomes only natural that it should think its neighbour absolutely in the clutches of error or of the 'devil', requiring to be redeemed by force or threats or intimidation, *i.e.*, to be shocked into acquiescence by verbal or physical violence. Alternatively, it may attempt to seduce the unwary by subtle propaganda and theological or political bribes.

> But once get a man to see that none of them has the *whole* truth, but that they are mutually complementary, that the complete truth can be found only in the combined views of all, after that which is false in each of them has been sifted out — then true brotherhood in religion will be established.
>
> *The Key to Theosophy*

Further,

> unless every man is brought to understand, and accept as *an axiomatic truth* that by wronging one man we wrong not only ourselves but the whole of humanity in the long run, no brotherly feelings such as preached by all the great Reformers, pre-eminently by Buddha and Jesus, are possible on earth.

That which is true on the metaphysical plane must also be true on the physical plane. *Satya* entails *ahimsa*, and the degree of *ahimsa* that a man possesses is the measure of the *satya* that he embodies.

THEOSOPHIA is identical with SAT or Absolute Truth, and Theosophy is only a partial emanation from it, the shoreless ocean of universal Truth reflecting the rays of the sun of SAT. In *The Secret Doctrine*, H.P. Blavatsky declared that only the outline of a few fundamental truths from the Secret Doctrine of the archaic ages was now permitted to see the light after long millenniums of the most profound silence and secrecy. "That which must remain unsaid could not be contained in a hundred such volumes, nor could it be imparted to the present generation of Sadducees." The great truths, which are the inheritance of the future races, cannot be given out at present, as the fate of every such unfamiliar truth is that, if it falls into the hands of the unready, they will only deceive themselves and deceive others, as the Masters have warned. As esoteric truth is made exoteric, absolute Truth is not only reduced to the illusive plane of the relative, but casts a shadow on the delusive plane of error. Occult Wisdom, dealing with eternal truths and primal causes, becomes almost omnipotent when applied in the right direction; its antithesis is that which deals with illusions and false appearances only, as in our exoteric modern sciences, with their immense power of destruction.

The ancients managed to throw a thick veil over the nucleus of truth concealed by archetypal symbols, but they also tried to preserve the latter as a record for future generations, sufficiently transparent to allow their wisest men to discern that truth behind the fabulous form of the glyph or allegory. The whole essence of truth cannot be transmitted from mouth to ear, nor can any pen describe it, unless man finds the answer in the innermost depths of his divine intuitions. No religious founder invented or revealed a new truth as they were all transmitters.

> Selecting one or more of those grand verities — actualities visible only to the eye of the real Sage and Seer — out of the many orally revealed to man in the beginning, preserved and perpetuated in the *adyta* of the temples through initiation, during the MYSTERIES and by personal transmission — they revealed these truths to the masses. Thus every nation received in its turn some of the said truths, under the veil of its own local and special symbolism.
>
> *The Secret Doctrine*, i xxxvi

Those who do not relish the distinction between esoteric and exoteric truth, the elect and the multitudes, do not really appreciate the tremendous practical potency of pure truths, and the danger of their misuse. In the *Milindapanha* we are told about the magical power of an act of truth, the power of a pure soul who has embodied a truth and enacted it in his daily life and who can work magic by the simple act of calling that fact to witness. In Theosophical literature, we are clearly told that a man must set and model his daily life upon the truth that the end of life is action and not thought; only such a man becomes worthy of the name of a Theosophist. "The profession of a truth is not yet the enactment of it." But truth, however distasteful to the generally blind multitudes, has always had her champions and martyrs. Endless is the search for truth, but we secure it only if we are willing to incarnate it in our own lives. "Let us love it and aspire to it for its own sake, and not for the glory or benefit a minute portion of its revelation may confer on us."

Theosophy thus teaches the transforming power of truth and affirms the teaching of the Gospel, "Ye shall know the Truth and the Truth shall make you free." The early Gnostics claimed that their Science, the GNOSIS, rested on a square, the angles of which represented *Sige* (Silence), *Bythos* (depth), *Nous* (Spiritual Soul or Mind), and *Aletheia* (Truth). The cultists are fighting against divine Truth, when repudiating and slandering the Dragon of esoteric Wisdom. But

> no great truth was ever accepted *a priori*, and generally a century or two passed before it began to glimmer in the human consciousness as a possible verity, except in such cases as the positive discovery of the thing claimed as a fact. The truths of today are the falsehoods and errors of yesterday, and *vice versa*.
>
> *The Secret Doctrine*, ii 442

It is only in the Seventh Race that all error will be made away with, and the advent of Truth will be heralded by the holy 'Sons of Light.' Meanwhile the Golden Age of the past will not be realized in the future till humanity, as a whole, feels the need of it. In *The Key to Theosophy* we are told: —

> A maxim in the Persian 'Javidan Khirad' says: 'Truth is of two kinds — one manifest and self-evident; the other demanding incessantly new demonstrations and proofs.' It is only when this latter kind of truth becomes as universally obvious as it is now dim, and

therefore liable to be distorted by sophistry and casuistry; it is only when the two kinds will have become once more one, that all people will be brought to see alike.

Truth, in the former sense, is identical with reality and cuts across the distinction between knowledge and being. Truth, in the latter sense, presupposes this distinction, but also requires us to transcend it, for we cannot effectively demonstrate truth until we embody and become the truth, until we carry out the injunction: "Become what thou art."

O Teacher, what shall I do to reach to Wisdom?
O Wise one, what, to gain perfection?
Search for the Paths. But, O Lanoo, be of clean heart before thou startest on thy journey. Before thou takest thy first step, learn to discern the real from the false, the ever-fleeting from the everlasting. Learn above all to separate Head-learning from Soul-wisdom, the 'Eye' from the 'Heart' doctrine.

Yea, ignorance is like unto a closed and airless vessel; the soul a bird shut up within. It warbles not, nor can it stir a feather; but the songster mute and torpid sits, and of exhaustion dies.

But even ignorance is better than Head-learning with no Soul-wisdom to illuminate and guide it.

The seeds of Wisdom cannot sprout and grow in airless space. To live and reap experience, the mind needs breadth and depth and points to draw it towards the Diamond Soul. Seek not those points in Maya's realm; but soar beyond illusions, search the eternal and the changeless SAT, mistrusting fancy's false suggestions.

For mind is like a mirror; it gathers dust while it reflects. It needs the gentle breezes of Soul-wisdom to brush away the dust of our illusions. Seek, O Beginner, to blend thy Mind and Soul.

The Voice of the Silence

WISDOM IN ACTION

The atoms emanated from the Central Point emanate in their turn new centres of energy, which, under the potential breath of Fohat, *begin their work from within without, and multiply other minor centres. These, in the course of evolution and involution, form in their turn the roots or developing causes of new effects, from worlds and 'man-bearing' globes, down to the genera, species, and classes of all the* seven *kingdoms (of which we know only four). For 'the blessed workers have received the* Thyan-kam, *in the eternity' (Book of 'The Aphorisms of* Tson-ka-pa').*

'Thyan-kam' is the power or knowledge of guiding the impulses of cosmic energy in the right direction.

The Secret Doctrine, i 635

Every human soul is an apprentice in the sacrificial art of applying cosmic energies for the sake of universal good. Thus, all human evolution is a record of lessons learnt, lost and rediscovered in the arduous practice of *Karma Yoga*. The ragged and uneven tale of recorded history and the glamour of current events are nothing but the distorted image of the pilgrimage of humanity reflected in the inverted lens of egotism. As a result, individuals oscillate between a sense of starvation for meaning in events and a sense of being overwhelmed by their magnitude. Nevertheless, there must be true *Karma Yogins* in disguise on the stage of the world's theatre, individuals with a measure of maturity, from whose sacrificial examples earnest students of human life may learn. Unfortunately, the energy of action is most easily stimulated by egotism, engendering a momentum that is sometimes linked to a grandiose conception of the world and of history, seemingly independent of self. Then through subsuming one's false sense of identity under some vague notion like national destiny, one can view one's life in terms of a false drama. Very often figures in public life are caught up in just such a melodramatic response to chaotic events; they regard their own choices as unique, unprecedented, momentous, fraught with extreme consequences for the future. There is in all of this, of course, an absurd element of unreality. Such illusion is conveyed in the story of the French writer who imagined a poignant meeting of some of the great women of history, including Cleopatra. Gathering together in their old age, and looking back upon their lives, they recognize their relative irrelevance. Plato in his dialogues made much the same point by putting into perspective the presumed importance of what happened in Troy.

In a world of imperfect beings, certain events and actions inevitably assume a much greater magnitude than they truly deserve in the longer view of history. Nature moves gradually, working silently and gestating invisibly under the soil. This is true of the work of sun and fire, sky and earth, air and water; all mirror in time the archetypal realm of Aether-*Akasha*. As Kropotkin pointed out, one could hardly recognize from a study of earthquakes and volcanic explosions the vast geological changes that take place over millions of years, proceeding through minute imperceptible increments. These almost invisible changes can accumulate to set off a shifting in the continents. Thus, massive volcanic eruptions, for example, are the result of a long series of tremors, though they come about as abrupt precipitations filled with fury and force. So long as human beings remain trapped in the realm of effects, seeing only with the physical eye and considering only a very narrow view of time, they will have no sense of the majesty and symphonic resonance of Nature, nor will they feel its resonance in their lives. Instead, they will be caught in what Thoreau called a life of quiet desperation. They will react only to whatever seems to be titanic, dramatic or volcanic, and so reinforce their subservience to the illusion of effects.

Although true of human beings in general, it is especially true of those figures in history who are powerful in a conventional sense. Whether one considers a figure like Alexander or a Genghis Khan, or a more contemporary figure like General Douglas MacArthur, one can see that it is easy for such dedicated and determined individuals to become suddenly caught in the *maya* of the magnification of importance of events. There may have been an element of truth in what General MacArthur saw, at the time of the Korean War, as the tremendous effect upon China of the actions of the United States. At the same time, his judgement isolated China and the United States from the rest of the world. Unlike the more discerning Lord Louis Mountbatten, he was insensitive to the aspirations of millions of souls in many burgeoning nations, great and small.

Whatever the details of an historical judgement, once one leaves out of account large portions of humanity, one can be right at a certain level, though at the expense of being caught in an exaggeration. Yet it was this same sense of the enormity of events that made MacArthur the man he was, a man capable of rendering a far greater service to the nation of Japan than he himself ever realized. As a nation stultified by its immense but wounded pride, Japan required extraordinarily delicate handling. Not only that, it needed to be shown a way out. In doing this, it was necessary to act with a true humanitarian instinct, free from any taint of racism and based on a genuine love for the Japanese people. Out of his soldier's ability to distinguish between the Japanese people and their defeated generals, it was possible for MacArthur to assist in the greatest transformation of Japanese history since the Meiji restoration. If this was evident at the time to some, though perhaps less so now to many observers, its long run and fundamental importance will not emerge until after the end of the present century, when Japan shall have fully worked out all the implications of the route it has taken — breaking with elements of its own tradition, gaining an unprecedented economic ascendancy, and yet feeling itself weighed down by the anxiety that accompanies frenetic success.

The karmic lesson to be drawn is that even the most remarkable figures in history, whether statesmen, military figures or politicians, often cannot gauge the significance of the events they seem to initiate. That man is wise in his time who, without exaggerating or underestimating his own role, understands something of Tolstoy's view in *War and Peace* — that the commanding generals are irrelevant and that in a sense even the vast masses of soldiers are acted upon. There is a mighty force at work in history, moving in mysterious ways through myriad wills. How they all clash and combine and resolve themselves is difficult indeed to know. It certainly cannot be understood if one subscribes to some simplistic Great Man theory of history or military strategy. Here one may learn from the example of General George C. Marshall. As a man, he no doubt took his profession as seriously as did General MacArthur; yet he was fortunate not to have had any other advantage save loyalty to his family, loyalty to what had been done before and loyalty to his teachers. Working hard and well, he at no point found spectacular success, yet he acquired a considerable wisdom in action. For a general or anyone involved in strategic planning, wisdom in action is crucial, less in regard to one's own sphere than in reference to understanding other human beings and in choosing and drawing out their hidden potential. The ability to groom talent innately presupposes some measure of self-confidence and selflessness.

This may be seen clearly in the extraordinary choice made silently and far-sightedly by Marshall of his supreme commander in Europe. At the time Marshall's eye fell on him, Dwight D. Eisenhower was in a position to become the commandant of a military college, in which capacity he could have developed his own deep interest in the profession of military strategy. Marshall wrote to him, suggesting that he might, if he liked, come to Washington and serve in a thoroughly unimportant role as a kind of attaché. Eisenhower wrote frankly of this, remarking that the position of commandant was extremely tempting, but that, out of pure and simple respect for General Marshall, he would take up his offer. What Marshall knew relatively early in the war, but kept to himself, was that there would one day come an extraordinary challenge to selfless coordination among the different allied nations. It would require a quality for which America does not prepare its people — letting others take the credit while standing behind the visible scene. It requires the ability in repetitious and protracted arenas of conflict to be cool and constructive. Marshall knew that any officer who could eventually play this role in the most crucial engagements at the end of the war would have to be trained in anonymity.

If it required a certain karmic insight on the part of Marshall to choose Eisenhower, it required a certain Buddhic intuition on the part of Eisenhower to respond to the call. Hence, he embarked upon a long apprenticeship which featured little of the excitement that he would have enjoyed had he been commandant of a college teaching military strategy. In fact, most of his duties were chores. In effect, Eisenhower merely polished the shoes of his commander, but he was happy to stay put, to watch and learn. Marshall knew that it would require an extraordinary wisdom, when the time came, to match up to the brilliance and force of personality of men like Harold Alexander, Alanbrooke and the other English generals. Most of them were well schooled in a philosophy of true sportsmanship, selflessness and disinterestedness; but at the same time it would also be necessary to cope with MacArthur-like figures on the British side such as General Bernard Law Montgomery. Remarkably, when Eisenhower was appointed as supreme commander, he quickly won the respect of Alexander and all the others, who saw that he could not be drawn into competitive games, let alone the nationalistic rivalries that were part of the high command.

Instead, they found in Eisenhower someone who was willing to learn, willing to stay quiet, but at the same time extremely strong; he was waiting to act and to act with a decisiveness born of deliberation. Eisenhower worked as karma works. When there were critical choices to be made at the end of the war, decisions affecting millions of lives and the concerted effort to bring the war to a close, the last-minute freedom of decision was left in Eisenhower's hands. Under karma he was able to initiate the final move so that World War II in Europe ended on the eighth of May, White Lotus Day, 1945. Here one may discern the *Nirmanakaya* influence at work, affecting selfless and open-minded individuals through their dreams and intuitions, their imagination and ideals.

That larger force may also be discerned in the closure of World War II in Asia on the twelfth of August, 1945, the birth anniversary of H.P. Blavatsky. Thus one finds the most remarkable karma quietly at work; for those who were truly awake and alive to the meaning of events in 1945, it was a time of extraordinary tension, far greater than anything that has taken place since. In the intervening years lesser persons have been dislodged by relatively minor crises. None of them had had a preparation in living through crises, making distinctions and learning from events. Such is the mark of the *Karma Yogin* in the realm of public affairs.

Promethean foresight must be earned through a thorough study of the mistakes, as well as the wise moves, of all who have gone before. Every great military commander has the utmost respect and fascination both for the successful moves but also the avoidable mistakes made by his precursors in the field of battle. This true learning from the past means putting Epimethean wisdom in the service of Promethean forces with reference to the future. What it comes to in practice is that one must study the lives of others well enough to learn how easy it is to be mistake-prone oneself. At the same time, however, one must not let the fear of mistakes come in the way of doing the best that one knows. One's motivation can and should be to lay down as a sacrifice all that one has in the best way one can for the sake of the whole, without drawing attention to oneself. When one can do this, one can become an instrument of a higher law or collective force. In a karmic field, wherein high ideals may be intact but threatened by pollution, such as the peace that follows a horrendous war, it is possible for many people to be touched by such motivations. But to become one with an ideal and so free oneself from all pettiness and residues of personal egotism is to prepare oneself to be used by the wisdom operating through karma. Such detached ardour towards ideals was epitomized by Louis Claude de Saint-Martin at the time of the French Revolution:

> The society of the world in general appeared to
> me as a theatre where one is continually passing one's

time playing one's role and where there is never a
moment to learn. The society of wisdom, on the
contrary, is a school where one is continually passing
one's time learning one's role and where one waits for
the curtain to rise before playing, that is to say, for the
veil which covers the universe to disappear. . . . We are
only here in order to choose.

Mon portrait historique et philosophique

Foresight at that level requires the courage to negate time,
the judgements of the present and also the judgements of posterity.
Too many politicians dance with an eye to posterity. This is foolish.
The greatest men, like Lincoln, were not obsessed with posterity
but with rightness; they understood something of the timeless
nature of the enactment of right in the name of an ideal. At the
same time, one must make full allowance for all the imperfections
in oneself, in the moment and in the act of embodying an ideal.
Therefore, Karma Yoga requires a balance between a capacity to
be strong in a timeless and universal field and a simultaneous
ability to be courageous in that sphere wherein, as Krishna says,
no act is without blame. Put in another way, one must combine a
macro-perspective with a micro-application, see events both in
the large and in the small. The more one is able, through
detachment, to infinitize and so negate the finitizing tendencies
of the human mind, the more one empties oneself into the
boundless, unknown, uncertain and indeterminate ocean of space.
At the same time, to gain efficiency and precision, skill in the
performance of action, one must master concentration, the ability
to bring things to a centre, to an intense, sharp focus. If one can
fuse together this sense of infinitude and a sense of laser-like
precision, one will gain much more than a sense of what is
immediately relevant and essential. One will begin to see the
equilibrizing forces of karma as centered upon an invisible point.
It is like saying that to be able to master attention in reference to
three things, for example, one must focus on some invisible fourth
thing that one may think of as either inside or outside the triad,
but which is, in reality, entirely beyond it.

Karma Yoga depends upon a sense of depth, a sense of that which is infinitesimal and hidden. This is known by the greatest dancers, archetypally represented by Shiva Nataraj, who are concerned not with position but motion, and who at the same time know that there is something mayavic about motion in relation to a field that is homogeneous and immobile. Its pure existence is in the realm of the mind. It is the etheric empyrean of the poets. It is like the sky in which the bird takes wing and floats in a refulgent majesty, remaining in motion, but when seen from a great distance, seemingly motionless. It is difficult indeed to understand or experience this fusion of motion and motionlessness, action and inaction, the micro-perception and the macro-perspective. When one looks at the night sky, one recognizes that boundless space itself is vastly greater than all the possible galaxies and systems. Even the immense voids in intergalactic space that have recently been discovered only give a relative sense of the metaphysical void of absolute space. And when astronomers speculate along the vague lines of the so-called Big Bang theory, this is nothing but a materialized shadow of the teaching of Gupta Vidya regarding the emanation from within without, a version of the Central Point — the one Cosmic Atom — of all the myriad centres of activity in the incipient cosmos.

Without becoming caught up in the unresolved disputes of contemporary cosmology concerning questions of the expanding universe, continuous creation and other mysteries, the ordinary person may learn to look at the sky using the mind's eye. Directing the vision of the hidden eye of the soul through continuous concentration, one will find that what one sees above in the heavens is mirrored within the heart. In particular, one may develop a sense of space in reference to the *Akasha* within the heart. Just as there are chambers in the heart and empty cavities in the brain, so too there is voidness throughout the human body. That voidness, however, cannot be understood in a two-dimensional or three-dimensional sense. Instead, one needs a sense of another level of matter which is consubstantial with the great universal matrix, *Mulaprakriti,* the Divine Darkness or primordial ground and substratum of all manifested matter. On that plane the distinction between matter and mind has no meaning; *Mulaprakriti* is mirrored as the *Akasha* within the heart. It may be symbolized as radiant matter or as a dark luminosity, and mystics have noted the striking analogies between the solar system within which the earth revolves and the miniature solar system within man. As Kropotkin said, every human being is a cosmos of organs, and each organ is itself a cosmos of cells. To be able to experience the cosmos within the empty space in the heart is to discover the seed point or *bindhu* within the lotus of the heart. But to experience it, one must experience the depth of introverted vision. Those who do so are actually much farther from the ordinary terrestrial realm than could ever be reached by traversing what is called outer space.

To reach the heart of action one must rethink one's view of space and time and motion. In the seventeenth chapter of the *Bhagavad Gita*, Krishna gives the mystical key to this meditation upon the heart of action. Having explained to Arjuna the application of the complex doctrine of the *gunas*, or qualities affecting all action, Krishna gives to Arjuna the talismanic mantram vitalizing all true faith and sacrifice:

> OM TAT SAT, these are said to be the threefold designation of the Supreme Being. By these in the beginning were sanctified the knowers of Brahmā, the *Vedas*, and sacrifices.

This is the ancient and sacred mode of consecration of karma or action. The more disinterested one's practice of *Karma Yoga*, the more that action is itself a disinterested flow of benevolence, the more one begins to gain clues into the magical connections of the workings of karma in the large. Freed from a concern with one's own karma, one may begin to discern the karma of nations, continents, races and human beings whom one wishes to serve and help. As one makes inevitable discoveries regarding the cyclic working of karma, one will begin to recognize that the more

complex the karmic mathematics, the more one's practice of
benevolence depends upon strength of mind and clarity of
perception in taking hold of a set of karmic curves and releasing
potent seeds of action.

> Therefore the sacrifices, the giving of alms, and the
> practising of austerities are always, among those who
> expound Holy Writ, preceded by the word OM.

OM is the Soundless Sound in boundless space — space
beyond all subjects and objects, beyond all qualities, space which
is no-thing and the fullness of the void. But OM is also in every
atom, stirring within the minutest centres imaginable and in all
the interstices of empty space. It is also a reverberation of one's
own being, omnipresent in all the vestures, the great keynote of
Nature. To be able to bring it before consciousness and to
consecrate oneself to it as the *Atman* or eternal spirit is to reduce
oneself to a zero, a sphere of light filled with the oceanic pulsation
of the OM at the cosmic level. It encompasses all beginnings,
middles and endings. It includes all creative, supportive and
regenerative action. Most human action is not creative, but
mechanical and routinized, half-hearted and preoccupied, based
upon indirect calculations of consequences in the future or guilt
over the past. Such action is neither free nor one-pointed.
Therefore, it is significant for beings who do not normally
experience creative action to set aside certain times of the day to
engage in action in a deliberate spirit of sacrifice and charity —
yajna and *dana* — for the good of all.

Since all beings must act out of internal necessity or *dharma*,
it makes sense to set aside certain actions — *kriya* — as creative
contributions to the universal good. Far from being grudging or
mechanical, such performance of duty through action flows with
a serene and steady rhythm, rooted in an ability to abstract from
the outward particulars of acts and a freedom from illusion that
is gained through meditation upon the OM. There is an element
of illusion in all action, and hence there are always retrospective

painful lessons to be learnt from it. OM is the destroyer of illusions. Through it one may learn from the flow of action, from past mistakes and illusions. By making oneself a zero, one can regenerate oneself through the OM. The OM is all this and much more. Through it one may get away from particulars, apprehending the whole, entering into the ocean of space and absolute darkness pregnant with the luminosity that contains universes. Reaching beyond the mind, it touches the deepest core of one's being connected with the immortal Self in eternity. Thus Krishna taught:

> Among those who long for immortality and who do not consider the reward for their actions, the word *TAT* precedes their rites of sacrifice, their austerities, and giving of alms.

The moment one consecrates with the OM, one says TAT — That — without past, without limits, the boundless and nameless. To name anything is to limit it. It is not this, it is not that — *neti, neti*. It can never be made an object or a subject. It is prior, and yet also posterior, to the rise of all possible objects and subjects, all possible constellations of entities and atoms, all possible worlds and minds of beings. Thus having in the moment consecrated through the OM, one goes into TAT, totally negating oneself. Having heightened the significance of what one is going to do, one negates it, relinquishing every wish for any fruit of a sacrifice. Through the power of *tapas* one makes the sacrificial act disappear into the totality of TAT. This is a dialectical activity requiring the highest practice and exercise in self-consciousness, self-reference and the interplay of the individuality of the sacrificer and the universality of the cosmic sacrifice. As human beings will naturally experience a sense of satisfaction in an authentic act of creative sacrifice, Krishna pointed to this experience of inner fulfilment, inner freedom and inner recognition of truth:

The word *SAT* is used for qualities that are true and holy, and likewise is applied to laudable actions, O son of Pritha. The state of mental sacrifice when actions are at rest is also called SAT. Whatever is done without faith, whether it be sacrifice, alms-giving, or austerities, is called ASAT, that which is devoid of truth and goodness, O son of Pritha, and is not of any benefit either in this life or after death.

SAT is not a truth, but rather ALL-TRUTH. It may be experienced as truth, goodness, purity, love or a number of other modes familiar to those who are experienced in *tapas*. Thus, having begun by consecrating with the OM, and then emptied all into TAT, which is beyond all possible concepts, worlds, definitions and beings, one reaffirms Being at the level of invisible unity, the level of the One Light of the One Spirit. Through the trinitarian mantram of OM TAT SAT, one may consecrate activity, negate the personal self, and at the same time realize a state of self-consciousness which will give contentment, substance and continuity to a life of service. When this mode of *yajna* becomes as natural as breathing, it infuses creativity, sustenance and regeneration into every action.

Metaphysically, the entire cosmos of manifestation is sacrificial. All existence is sacrifice. All descent from homogeneous planes into planes of greater differentiation is a sacrifice, a kind of grace, an avataric descent of the Logos. The primordial compassion in the One initiates and inaugurates the many. The one white light breaks up into the spectrum and then into the myriads upon myriads of hues that are implicit in the hebdomadic worlds. The entire universe may be understood as a great act of compassion. If this is true of the whole, then by identifying oneself totally, in one's deepest identity, with the Logos, one may find that everything is sacrifice. Once one is attuned to the Logos in this way, then all the tiredness of calculation vanishes, to be replaced by fearlessness with facts and freedom from illusion. One can learn to live in the world, and yet live outside it; one can learn to live only for the sake of sacrifice and benefit to others. By accepting this and cooperating with the cosmic Logoic sacrifice, one frees oneself from virtually all the tension, anxiety and fear that arise out of pseudo-agnosticism, false pride and the inability to recognize that one does not know the karmic mathematics of the universe. One learns to admire the good in others and to adore the wisdom of those who are greater than oneself. As presumption falls away, so too do envy, craving and irritation.

At some point, one can come directly to grips with the twin demons of craving and contempt, like and dislike, attraction and repulsion. Every time one falls prey to the demon of craving, one is equally in the grip of the demon of contempt. So too in the reverse. Once one begins to understand the operation of these shadowy forces in the realm of shadowy selves, one may cut through the pall of murk and gloom that they induce and establish one's mind in the realm of pure light. The shadow world of interaction and action of shadowy fears and hopes is a lie obscuring the dynamic light of true action. That light moves through a dynamic field of endless sacrifice and perpetual motion. It is difficult to root oneself in a consciousness of that realm, but it can be done through training oneself to hold fast to a sense of the heart and a sense of that which is between the eyes. It is possible to create an alignment between the eye of time and the eye of eternity, between the microcosmic and the macrocosmic, between the field of specific sacrificial karma and the boundless fields of universal sacrifice — *Adhiyajna*. To do this is to discover wisdom in action, *Karma Yoga*. If one sets out in dead earnest, one may be confident that things will get worse before they get better. It simply means that each individual has a measure of karma to be worked out. The intense discomfort that one feels in this process is a sign that one is being tested by karma. In fact, one should be grateful that forces are rushing in. It is better to have them precipitate together than to be spread out over a protracted period. And as this happens, one should not advertise it, because it is something that everyone has to do.

Each human being must seize his or her birth, just as, in the Japanese fable, each human being must recognize the donkey of stupidity that he or she is carrying and quietly put it down. These are all elements of past egotism, thoughtlessness, envy, contempt and insensitivity. In the past, one saw people who were blind, deaf and dumb, and instead of saying, "May that be my burden and may I help," one said, "There but for the grace of God go I." Having separated oneself from those who have mysterious karma to bear, these failures will come back to one, and one will have to live out future lives in blindness, deafness and muteness. Whatever the karmic consequences of one's actions, one must accept them as that which is best for the soul, that alone from which one may learn. It requires extraordinary fearlessness, but when one measures up to the test of accepting the truth, one will discover authentic freedom and true humility. Letting go of pride, one will see that everything is a lesson and that one is glad to learn. As one learns this true patience, one will become grateful when one can pause to look through the eyes of other human beings. One will start to feel something about the total saga of the human enterprise, encompassing all the souls living and learning and somewhere in their hearts unconsciously loving.

Inserting one's life into the vast human enterprise, one can become a serene instrument of the cosmic sacrifice, consciously throwing all sense of self and separateness into the fire to be burnt. In the end, this is far wiser than being burnt out because of frenetic action, perversity and allegiance to the tired machinations of the false *persona*. Instead of being an incessant and repetitive victim to excess and deficiency, one may become like the quiet tender of a fire. Discerning the illusive elements in actions, one may gently cast them into the flames of sacrifice, receiving the warmth and joy and light of the fire and freeing oneself from the burden of ignorance. If one can make this a natural way of thinking and breathing, then one will burn out all the dross that would otherwise have formed, at the moment of death, a grotesque *kama rupa*.

Through the initial mastery of sacrificial skill in action, one may purify one's will and desire, minimally assuring oneself that one's actions in life will not be a source of pollution to the human race. When this healthy tropism of the soul has been restored, one is in a position to learn about the positive applications of the Fohatic power of desire. Instead of making an unconscious form or *rupa* out of *kama*, one may enter into the current of joy that accompanies sacrificial participation through meditation and action in the pilgrimage of humanity. One learns to engage in self-study solely for the sake of helping others. One learns to sleep and remain awake, to eat and bathe, to sit and walk, to breathe and think and feel for the sake of others. As this grows natural, one becomes like a station beaming vibrations to vast numbers of human beings in need. Serving as an instrument of the Logos far more than one will ever know, one remains free of the distraction of thinking about how much one may have done. Instead, one is concerned only with maintaining the mental stance and spiritual posture of sacrificial action. This is the central teaching of *Karma Yoga*, which brings about whatever joy, meaning and hope in life is supportable by the universe and is compatible with the joy and hopes of all other beings. *Karma Yoga* is action in accord with the great wheel of the Law, and it is the rightful inheritance of those who have the courage to make experiments with truth on behalf of humanity.

Instead of wasting time in daydreams about others, or about one's regrets and mistakes, one should quicken one's sense of what is necessary to do now. One must learn to stay still and do it. If one can become a one-pointed, whole-hearted person in two or three things done each day, one has embarked on the path of *Karma Yoga*, and the instances will increase with time. The higher cosmic energies guided by the true *Karma Yogin* are the energies of the highest Self — the *Atman* — and they are released only by the power of constructive vows. The mysteries of action and inaction are revealed only to those who bind themselves by sacred vows and commit themselves to the judgement and impartiality of Nature. The selflessness and integrity of Nature is the inward and invisible strength of the *Karma Yogin*. The secret is to work with the Silence residing in the unmanifest, courageously holding to the sacrificial current and welcoming the adjustment whereby distractions are dissolved and one's heart and mind are drawn back to the invisible centre. The more one can learn to shackle the unruly vestures, making them instruments of *Atma-Buddhi-Manas*, the more one can create a stronger karmic matrix for a more glorious future.

EROS AND KAMADEVA

No word has perhaps been so much abused in our age as 'love', thus fulfilling the celebrated prophecy about Kali Yuga in the *Vishnu Purana*. In view of the unfortunate but undeniable fact that 'love' is more loosely used today than 'truth', Gandhi preferred to adopt truth rather than love as the highest value although he repeatedly stressed that the two are inseparable and even identical in the ultimate analysis. Relative truth may masquerade as absolute truth, but the mere existence of contrary claims and the continual violence of controversy cast doubt on the universal validity of all partisan standpoints. On the other hand, when selfish, personal love, often based on passing passion, wears the mask of selfless, impersonal, dispassionate and immortal love, it is far more difficult for deluded victims to discern the true from the false, the everlasting from the ephemeral. Earthly love is indeed an alluring and deceptive shadow, and sometimes a perversion, of ethereal love. Just as untruth invariably requires some form of violence for its instrument, so too blind and selfish love, which contains the seeds of violence and even hatred, is based upon untruth and uses it to further its immediate ends. Our main difficulty here is that, as Socrates points out in *The Symposium*,

> we isolate a particular kind of love and appropriate for it the name of love, which really belongs to a wider whole. . . . The generic concept embraces every desire for good and for happiness; that is precisely what almighty and all-ensnaring love is. But this desire expresses itself in many ways, and those with whom it takes the form of love of money or of physical prowess or of wisdom are not said to be in love, or called lovers, whereas those whose passion runs in one particular channel usurp the name of lover, which belongs to them all, and are said to be lovers and in love.

In *The Secret Doctrine* H.P. Blavatsky explains that Fohat or Eros in the phenomenal world is that "occult, electric, vital power, which, under the Will of the Creative Logos, unites and brings together all forms, giving them the first impulse which becomes in time law. But in the unmanifested Universe, Fohat is no more this, than Eros is the later brilliant winged Cupid, or LOVE."

The universal aspect of Love was embodied in the Puranic conception of Brahmā's 'Will' or desire to create, and it was affirmed in Phoenician cosmogony as the doctrine that desire is the principle of creation. In the *Rig Veda* Kamadeva is the divine personification of that primordial feeling which leads and propels to creation. "Desire first arose in It, which was the *primal germ of mind*; and which sages, searching with their intellect, have discovered to be the bond which connects Entity with Non-Entity." As Eros was connected in early Greek mythology with the world's creation, and only afterwards became the sexual Cupid, so was Kamadeva in his original Vedic character the primeval creative urge, *Atma-Bhu* (self-existent), *Aja* (unborn), sometimes regarded allegorically as the son of *Dharma*, the moral Law, and of *Shraddha*, faith, but elsewhere depicted as *Agni*, the fire-god. Harivansa makes him a son of Lakshmi or Venus. *Aja* is the Logos in the *Rig Veda*. Venus Aphrodite, the Celestial Virgin of the Alchemists and the Christian Virgin Mary, is the personified Sea, the primordial Ocean of Space, *Akasha*, on which *Narayana*, the Self-Born Spirit, moves, together with his consort Lakshmi. Venus is the generator of all the gods, the mother of Kamadeva, the god of Love, Mercy and Charity.

True love is a creative force that emanates from the One Logos and its expression is under the universal law of cosmic and human interdependence. The love of which Christ spoke cannot be grasped without reference to the law of love, which is set forth in *The Key to Theosophy*: "As mankind is essentially of one and the same essence, and that essence is one — infinite, uncreate and eternal, whether we call it God or Nature — nothing, therefore, can affect one nation or one man without affecting all other nations and all other men."

True love can never be a divisive force but always has a universally beneficent and unifying effect. It leads in the end to that love of wisdom, the worship of the Logos, which has been extolled by the Platonists and the great mystics of all ages. This true love was expounded in Porphyry's long letter to his wife, Marcella, when the time came for them to part and for him to resume his wanderings as a pilgrim. He wrote that every disturbance and unprofitable desire is removed by the love of true philosophy.

> In so far as a man turns to the mortal part of himself, in so far he makes his mind incommensurate with immortality. And in so far as he refrains from sharing the feelings of the body, in such a measure does he approach the divine. . . . Neither trouble thyself much whether thou be male or female in body, nor look on thyself as a woman, for I did not approach thee as such. . . . For what is born from a virgin soul and a pure mind is most blessed, since imperishable springs from imperishable. . . . They who do not use their own bodies, but make excessive use of others, commit a twofold wrong, and are ungrateful to nature that has given them these parts . . . it is impossible that he who does wrong to man should honour God. But look on the love of mankind as the foundation of thy piety.

True love is constant and immortal because it springs from the immortal and steadfast nature of the human soul.

Finite love, on the other hand, is born of the perishable part of man and becomes a chain of enslavement rather than an abiding bond of communion and cooperative endeavour. If we are glamoured by the meretricious fascination of this chain of possessive, personal love, we cling to it until we invite unnecessary suffering and inevitable frustration. Dante shows Paolo and Francesca locked in an eternal embrace which is anguish rather than ecstasy, the condign punishment for selfish lovers. Such love is what H.P. Blavatsky calls *égoisme à deux*, an exclusive and destructive love, whether shown between husband and wife, mother and child, between brothers or between friends. Such love may bring temporary pleasure for the personality, but it is displeasing to the Ishwara within all beings. It could sunder the soul from its divine parentage and true mission. It hinders more than it helps the love of Beauty of which Plotinus spoke, the intellectual love of God (*amor dei intellectualis*) of which Spinoza wrote, the constant love of wisdom extolled by ancient sages from Krishna to Shankara, Buddha to Santideva, Pythagoras to Porphyry.

Does this mean that there is no place for the human affections and for the affinities between kindred souls and that we must eliminate every element of personal love? Certainly not, for this can only lead to pure egotism or to spiritual selfishness and the quest for personal salvation. He who loves only himself lives in hell, the hell of loneliness, ambition and despair. On the other hand, he who loves only one other person lives entirely on earth, and all such earthly love must come to an end; at best, it could only correspond to the idealization and illusion which characterize *devachan*. He who loves his fellow men lives on earth in a heavenly condition, but as long as his philanthropy and altruism are purely personal, his only reward is a long *devachan*, a prolonged and beautiful dream, an illusory condition that brings the soul no nearer to its true quest, the love of the SELF of all amidst the conditions of earthly life. Finite, personal love is not bad in itself but it is frustrating and useless to the human soul unless it can gradually purify and make more impersonal and unselfish the force of *kama* in its material manifestations through the incarnated personality. Only thus can love be transformed from a violent and divisive tendency in human relationships into a non-violent, unifying power that produces strength and peace. The evils wrought by lust and selfish love have been nowhere more forcefully depicted than in Tolstoy's indictment of modern marriages in *The Kreutzer Sonata* or in Gandhi's *Self-Restraint versus Self-Indulgence*. The classical Indian ideal of marriage has been clearly stated by W.Q. Judge in "Living the Higher Life" and also hinted at in *The Dream of Ravan.*

In *The Secret Doctrine* H.P. Blavatsky gives the key to the transmutation of finite love when she repeats the ancient teaching that *Manas* is dual — lunar in the lower, solar in its upper portion. It is attracted in its higher aspect towards *Buddhi*, the seat of true love and real compassion, but in its lower aspect it descends into and listens to the voice of its animal soul, full of selfish and sensual desires.

> The human *Ego* is neither Atman nor Buddhi, but the higher Manas: the intellectual fruition and the efflorescence of the intellectual self-conscious *Egotism* — in the higher spiritual sense. The ancient works refer to it as *Karana Sharira* on the plane of *Sutratma*, which is the golden thread on which, like beads, the various personalities of this higher *Ego* are strung.
>
> *The Secret Doctrine,* ii 79

The imperishable thread of radiance which is *Manas* serves man as a medium between the highest and the lowest, the spiritual man and the physical brain. When the lunar aspect of *Manas* is positive, *kama* in man, like the Barhishad Pitris, is possessed of creative fire but devoid of the MAHAT-mic element. When the solar pole of *Manas* is positive, *kama* becomes Agni or divine fire and is capable, like the Agnishwatta Pitris, of conserving its energy as well as of sacrificing itself to the good and salvation of Spiritual Humanity. The distinction here is between finite love and the more enduring love which is a link between passion and compassion and which finally culminates in the highest spiritual love.

When *kama* in man overcomes and enslaves *Manas*, love becomes violent and cunning, or a mere form of sentimental wish-fulfilment. In the former case, it tears the individual to pieces. It becomes a volcanic and tempestuous force, an explosion of all the passions pent up in man; it knows neither law nor restraint and its pressure drives the deepest undercurrents of the animal nature in man to the surface. Love is then a leaping, a devouring fire, but a fire that can be turned to ice, doomed to a tragic end, death-dealing and futile. On the other hand, the love that is romanticized, the love sung by the troubadours, the love of Tristan and Iseult, the love poured forth in the letters of the Portuguese nun, Marianna Alcaforado, is the pathetic attempt of *kama* to masquerade as *Buddhi*, a psychic effusion, a product of delusion and self-pity, a fragile if seductive flower under which the serpent of selfishness is coiled. Tamasic love, as *The Dream of Ravan* points out, is devoid of the light of knowledge and ideality, for it is content with illusions and idealization and could turn into cold indifference and hatred or into self-destructive morbidity. When *kama* influences without overpowering *Manas*, we have rajasic love which can sting the beloved into an emulating pursuit of cherished ends, which is animated by a keen intelligence, and which shows a lofty scorn of every divergence or shortcoming.

Sattvic love has been well depicted in *The Book of Confidences*:

> When thou shalt find true Love, shalt find one homogeneous to thy nature; to whom all Life is consecrate, who will have ardency to take with thee the Bright Track of the Soul. And in that embodiment of thine own love, shalt find all others for thy love, thy joy, thy patience and compassion.

Such love can only arise when kama is under the influence, even if intermittently, of a *Manas* that tends upwards to *Buddhi*. This love is silent rather than clamorous in its expression, marked by inward depth rather than by outward display. The silences of love lie in wait for us, night and day, at our threshold, and those who have loved deeply in this way come to learn many secrets that are unknown to others, the secrets of sharing and sacrifice and duty well done.

Love is the moving power of life itself, and nothing can exist without the love which drives everything towards everything else that is. "He who loves lives." Love is the drive towards the unity of the separated, and separation presupposes an original unity. The restlessness in love is only a dim reflection of the divine discontent of the soul, but it could act as a barrier to the union of the soul with nature if it is channelled merely through personal and material forms of expression. The active and creative element in love is the urge of the human soul to participate in the work of cosmic and human evolution, a form of *Kriyashakti* which enables man to emulate the solar gods, the divine host of creative intelligences known as Dhyani Buddhas or Dhyan Chohans. Human love could become a bridge between the animal and the divine aspects of love provided the desire to ascend through lower to higher forms of love is continually nourished and sustained.

The *Narada Bhakti Sutras* and *The Voice of the Silence* point to the highest kind of love which transcends the three qualities, the constant love of the Absolute, Eternal Truth, the attributeless Compassion which is the Law of laws, embracing the entire universe, ceaselessly filling the world with its benedictory and magical power. We can progress gradually from *Dana*, "the key of charity and love immortal," to *Paramarthasatya* and *Karuna*, the Universal and Absolute Compassion that is rooted in Eternal and Absolute Truth. The *Bhagavad Gita* warns us against the rajasic and downward tendency of *kama*, the constant enemy of man, but it also points to the process by which we could perfect our power of devotion and become worthy of the Divine Grace that flows from the Lords of Love who reflect the Power and the Compassion of the Creative Logos in the cosmos. The *Narada Bhakti Sutras* list the following eleven different forms of *Bhakti* or Divine Love: Love of the glorification of the Lord's blessed qualities, Love of His enchanting beauty, Love of worship, Love of constant remembrance, Love of service, Love of Him as a friend, Love of Him as a son, Love for Him as that of a wife for her husband, Love of self-surrender to Him, Love of complete absorption in Him, Love of the pain of separation from Him. If we wish to go beyond 'love' and 'hate', we must use all our loves as a preparation for *amor dei* or true *Bhakti*, the total and endless Love of the Logos in the cosmos, God in man.

LIGHT, LOVE AND HOPE

*Light is the first begotten, and the first emanation of
the Supreme, and Light is Life, says the Evangelist and the
Kabalist. Both are electricity — the life principle, the* anima
mundi, *pervading the universe, the electric vivifier of all
things. Light is the great Protean magician, and under the
divine will of the architect, or rather the* architects, *the
'Builders' (called* One *collectively), its multifarious,
omnipotent waves gave birth to every form as well as to
every living being. From its swelling electric bosom, spring
matter and spirit. Within its beams lie the beginnings of
all physical and chemical action, and of all cosmic and
spiritual phenomena; it vitalizes and disorganizes; it gives
life and produces death, and from its primordial point
gradually emerged into existence the myriads of worlds,
visible and invisible celestial bodies.*

The Secret Doctrine, i 579

The metaphysical mantram *"Light is Life and both are
electricity"* intimates a profound insight that is realized
only at the highest levels of meditation. Empty the mind
of all objects and subjects, all contrasts and contours, in a world
of names and forms and colours, and one can plunge into absolute
Divine Darkness. Once in this realm of pure potential, one may
apprehend the hidden noumenon of matter, that ultimate
substance or primordial substratum which is the sum-total of all
possible objects of perception by all possible beings. At the same
time, one may apprehend Spirit as the totality of all the possible
expressions, manifestations and radiations of one central divine
energy or Light. In that Divine Darkness, the realm of boundless
potential where no one thing exists, love is like the Light that is
hidden in the Darkness. That Light is the origin of all that is latent,
of all that will ever emerge and persist, all that will depart from
form and yet remain as immaculate rays.

This primordial realm of potential Light and potential Life is also the realm of potential energy. In this pregenetic realm, wherein there is no manifestation, one may apprehend a wholly potential energy which does not produce any interaction between the latent Spirit and noumenal matter. This is not electricity in any manifest sense, nor any force that can be construed in terms of ordinary language or common sense-perception; it is a primordial current. Even the most abstract conceptions of pure science cannot reach this realm, wherein there is a cosmic electrical vibration so fundamental and all-pervasive that it cannot be localized or characterized in any particular way. Out of this Divine Darkness — out of this potential Light, latent Life and hidden energy — there is a coming into manifestation. There is a process of radiation and emanation in which myriad sparks fly. There is a coalescence of the initial primordial ray of light-energy and the latent life-currents which releases pulsations, radiations and currents that flow forth in every direction.

At this stage of the incipient cosmos, Gupta Vidya affirms the presence of great beings, great minds and hearts, great souls perfected in prior periods of evolution. Remaining awake during the long night of non-manifestation — yet having no particular object of reference and no particular conception in the state of *Mahapralaya* — they abided in a state of vigilant, ceaseless, harmonious contemplation of all that was potential. These beings emerge with the burgeoning of primordial Light and Life, the primal reverberation of divine energy throughout the glassy essence of space. They become the focussing instrument in what then comes to be known as Universal Mind or *Mahat*. They become the living lens through which all that is latent within the night of non-manifestation is stirred into active life. These perfected beings, who are later mythified in all the religions of the world as Dhyani Buddhas, Archangels, Lords of Light, become self-conscious agents for the diffusion in every direction of an essence that is otherwise universal, purely potential and entirely homogeneous. For the sake of meditation, they may be thought of as shooting out rays of colour and emitting sounds within transcendental musical scales. One may then, in turn, think of them as belonging to seven classes, each corresponding to a subliminal note or a colour. Each of them corresponds to a particular number or degree of differentiation, and they all work in unison. They may be imagined as having their own differentiated notes, colours and numbers but also as uniting and synthesizing the multiple potencies of the manifested Logos. In that ontogenetically prior state, just before manifestation, there is a pre-cosmic electrical energy that is sometimes called *Daiviprakriti* — the Light of the Logos.

In the world of visible manifestation, the phenomena which are identified as electricity and magnetism, light and heat, are observable effects of this primary Logoic radiation. Gigantic and titanic as they are, they are nonetheless nothing but shadows of supersensuous matter in motion on a noumenal plane prior to the realm of phenomena. The study of light-energy in manifestation involves complex curves and relationships and requires the use of many categories and instruments. This is the realm of diffraction and diffusion, of reflection and refraction, wherein there are complex possibilities owing to the interference and overlapping of waves upon waves of light-energy. It is simultaneously the realm of photons, particles of light-energy travelling at an incredible speed, such that light from the moon arrives at the earth within a second. The notion of light as a complex, though virtually instantaneous, agency having an impact at every level of the cosmos stirs the heart long before it can be truly grasped by the mind. The heart understands the vital significance of life because it resonates to that which is primordial, all-pervasive and instantaneous. Within every human heart there burns a fire of light-wisdom and love-compassion, *Prajna* and *Mahakaruna*. This spark of the One Fire flickers fitfully in the neophyte at first, but it can be stoked into a powerful flame which burns vigorously, steadily and ceaselessly. In its fullness it directs and guides individuals in the expansive and wise application of the boundless energy flowing from the fathomless love-compassion and light-wisdom within the spiritual heart. The monadic heart of every human being is an exact mirror of the heart of the cosmos, that swelling electric bosom from which the dual stream of spirit-matter emerges.

> The Sixth principle in Man (Buddhi, the Divine Soul) though a mere breath, in our conceptions, is still something material when compared with divine 'Spirit' (Atma) of which it is the carrier or vehicle. Fohat, in his capacity of DIVINE LOVE *(Eros)*, the electric Power of affinity and sympathy, is shown allegorically as trying to bring the pure Spirit, the Ray inseparable from the ONE absolute, into union with the Soul, the two constituting in Man the MONAD, and in Nature the first link between the ever unconditioned and the manifested.
>
> *Ibid.,* 119

The presence of this divine Light, Fire and Flame within the secret heart means that every human being is capable of seeing and illuminating a much vaster sphere of existence than he or she is typically prepared to inhabit self-consciously. Similarly, every single human being has a much richer and more profound capacity for effortless love than he or she imagines, love that is spontaneous and selfless, asking nothing and willing to give freely, graciously and generously to all. Yet little of that immense love and light-energy has a chance to come forth in a world of masks and shadows, a world of lies and fears and personal loneliness. Such is the predicament of humanity. Yet this same orphaned humanity, which has barely begun to draw upon a minute fraction of its fathomless boundless potential, can do so if it seeks to sustain a conception of existence that goes beyond all habitual divisions and dichotomies. One must transcend distinctions such as youth and old age, social roles and external labels. Even though the mind has become blunted and the heart tainted, one must unlearn all stifling habits and become able to withdraw the mind and heart from false and fleeting allegiances. Only so can one restore mental resilience.

In diverse societies at different times in recorded history, seekers have tried to meet this challenge by undertaking systematic monastic discipline. They have tried to be helpful to each other and to bind themselves by self-chosen and inexorable rules, vows and pledges. Through a repeated reinforcement of those fundamental resolves, they have sought to develop a way of life aimed at spiritual self-regeneration. Yet in spite of this, again and again in history these monastic institutions, having flourished for a time, invariably degenerated. The vital impulse went out of them and people came to be caught up merely in imitation, in game-playing and in ritual, hollow mimetics. The lesson of this repetitive pattern is that no amount of regimentation on the outside can work unless it is matched by sufficient concentration and continuity of ideation through meditation from within. One cannot force another human being to become a man or woman of meditation. A human being has to sustain a desire to do this which is sufficiently strong to permit him or her to see through the masquerade of that which is false and deceptive in this world.

Each human being must individually come to a deep reflection upon the meaning of death and its connection with the moment of birth. And each must make for himself or herself a decision which enables one to undertake a freely chosen set of spiritual practices. These self-chosen exercises will, now and again, prove extremely taxing, and they can be sustained only by the momentum of a tremendous motivation. As all the greatest benefactors of humanity have taught, we must be ready to give up everything for the sake of the whole. Unless one releases a motivation which is universal, rooted in a love for all humanity, one cannot keep oneself upon the spiritual Path. It is fatal to rush into any pretence that one loves all humanity. Instead, though it will take time, one should dwell again and again upon the sublime and extraordinary nature of that fundamental and all-embracing motivation which is represented by the Kwan-Yin Pledge and the Bodhisattva Vow. Only through that motivation, authentically released and maintained intact, can there be an awakening of the spark of *bodhichitta*.

The redemptive love of the part for the whole springs from the immortal soul. It is deathless in origin and is the individual's share in what is universal and immortal. Behind all the modifications and manifestations of *prakriti* there is *Purusha* — the single indivisible universal Spirit known by many names. It is indestructible, beginningless and endless. It is itself a pristine reflection of the very essence of the Divine Darkness. The spark or ray of that Spirit within every human soul is the power of love. It can illuminate the mind and enlighten the heart so long as one is ready to give up all, willing to be alone and whole-hearted, single-minded and one-pointed. Then that love becomes a form of wisdom, a ray of light, assuring one in the hour of need and seeming gloom and doom that there is hope. It tells one where to go and what to do, it advises whether one should stand and wait. It gives one immense patience whereby one may recognize those tendencies that come in the way of releasing that spiritual energy. There is that in the lower nature which wants to grab and seize, which also at the same time is insecure and fickle, uncertain of itself and desirous of something from outside.

One must learn to wait, to relinquish and wear down that side of oneself which is the weaker, if one is to release the stronger. Meanwhile, before one is able to release the true strength of the heart, and while one is still in the grip of that which is weaker, one can learn. One can discover the patterns, the instabilities and the vulnerabilities of one's nature. This process of diagnostic learning cannot, however, come to fruition unless it is balanced by a deep adoration of those Dhyani Buddhas who sustain the cosmos. One must deliberately place the mind and the heart within the magnetic field of attraction of the ideal, the mighty Host of Dhyanis and Bodhisattvas. One can think of them as galaxies of enlightened beings who are cosmic forces, living facts in invisible Nature, and at the same time shining exemplars to humanity in the visible world. Through hearing about them and through studying the sacred texts and noble traditions that have preserved their teachings, one may begin to assimilate the way of life exemplified by such beings. Thus one can learn to live in a state of learning and letting go, learning joyously and vigorously while at the same time letting go slowly of the fickle, fearful and furtive self. After a point, one cannot even conceive of living in any other way.

One finds a profound satisfaction in this way of life, and as a result one is able to look upon the world not as a receiver but as a giver. In the solitude of one's own contemplation, one will naturally think of hungry hearts and neglected souls to whom one may try to reach out through an ardent longing of the heart and through intense thought. Breathing on behalf of the world's disinherited, one can become a messenger of hope to others. Everyone has had the experience, in dark periods of doubt and despair, of receiving a sudden bright flash of inspiration and hope. Gratitude for this light mysteriously received can become the basis of a faith and confidence that one may give light to others. If one persists in one's solitude in thinking of all those beings who are disinherited, yet worthy of one's compassion, one can reach to them in their deep sleep and in their dreams. Through the strength of what George William Russell called the Hero in Man, one can give to them that hope or saving grace that will sustain them, whatever their condition. Thus one forms invisible magnetic bonds with other human beings, channels of transmission that can move in every direction. To do this is to go beyond any conception of individual salvation or progress based upon a personalized and localized notion of love or light. One learns how to move towards the sun so that one's shadow declines, and one begins to understand what it is to stand directly under the sun and cast no shadow. By freeing oneself from self-concern, one becomes truly confident in one's capacity to reach out and help human beings no matter at what distance. Letting go of all external labels, tokens and pseudo-proofs of love and light, one is prepared to bask, so to speak, in the supernal light and truth, the boundless wisdom and compassion, of the Spiritual Sun.

The entry into this light is to be understood not only in terms of a mystical metaphor. It is also linked up to the presence of actual beings who have become Bodhisattvas of Compassion, rays flowing from a cosmic energy such as Avalokiteshvara. As the lord who looks down from on high, Avalokiteshvara may be envisaged as seated in total contemplation and calmness, wrapped in an extraordinary golden halo of perfect purity and love. He holds within the gaze of his overseeing eye all humanity. To meditate upon this paradigm of all the Tathagatas and Predecessors, Buddhas and Bodhisattvas, is to restore one's sense of the ontological plenty of the spiritual realm. Thus one may transcend confining conceptions of the evolutionary history of humanity or the false notion that human spirituality is entirely dependent upon localized events in the past. Rather, one will come to know humanity as extremely old, extending over millions upon millions of years and sustained throughout in myriads of ways by countless saviours and helpers and teachers. Many of them were humble wanderers in villages who had no external marks, bore no labels and made no claims. Nonetheless, they helped and uplifted the human heart, giving hope to others, and then moving on. Their lives are an uninterrupted and living testimony to the ubiquitous force and presence on earth of the Tribe of Sacred Heroes.

To raise one's sights to this extraordinarily universal perspective is to begin to see that many questions which once were bothersome are no longer difficult. As soon as one thinks of love separatively or in terms of bilateral contexts, one thinks in terms of particularized intentions and externalized concepts of the will. This concretized will is bound up with proving something, showing determination in a context, mostly through verbalizing and acting out. Whereas, if one thinks in terms of vast collective hosts of beings, uniting all humanity through invisible ties, one is drawing closer to an idea of will as a universal and impersonal force. By inserting oneself within the invisible brotherhood of true helpers of humanity, one can learn to do what one can, according to the measure, degree and depth of one's knowledge and feeling, without engendering any false conception of the will.

In whatever one does and in whatever way one releases the higher will, one is merely drawing a certain portion from an inexhaustible and universal source. If one understands this, one will not ask to draw more from it than one in fact can use, or more than one can properly sustain. In other words, one will begin to see through the tricks played by the human mind, which is the great deceiver and the adversary in man, when it tries to escape from what can be done by demanding more. When the mind insists that it must know whether its share of love and light is adequate in relation to its aim or self-conception, it becomes the great deceiver and obscurer of the light and love that are latent in every human soul. Many supposedly philosophical questions and spiritual concerns are really nothing but what the Buddhists call *attavada*, the dire heresy of separateness. They reflect the philosophic error of assuming that all one's tendencies, desires and thoughts make up some kind of entity which is cohesive and persistent and, above all, cut off from the rest of humanity. This is an illusion. There is no such entity. No true sense of selfhood can be located in this aggregate of ever-changing, and second-hand, chaotic tendencies.

Instead, this aggregate of the *skandhas* represents one's karmic share in the collective accumulations of tendencies of all humanity. All human beings, one might say, have contributed to the growing of weeds, and every human being has got his or her share of the world's weeds to take in hand and to cut down. At the same time, every human being has got to find and sow the seeds of wisdom and compassion. This can be done only through cultivating patience and the power of waiting, rooted in the willingness to work with the cycles of Nature. As the prophet teaches in *Ecclesiastes*, there are different seasons, times for sowing and times for reaping, times for living and times for dying. That is true with regard to all the manifestations of love, and the wisest know that the deepest love is beyond manifestation. As Maeterlinck wrote, there are in love silences with so profound a depth that the unexpressed flows with uninterrupted continuity across the barriers of time and space. This deeper love is often forfeited because of a concern with what can be demonstrated, what can be increased, mitigated or compared. To recover the lost potential of the soul, one must rethink what is real. On the one side, there is that which is universal and includes all that is potential. On the other, there is the entire collection of particular, episodic, finite expressions and manifestations. Vast though they are, they are in the end limited in relation to the inexhaustible content of love and light within the immortal soul of every human being and at the heart of the whole cosmos.

By learning to think in this way, one can begin to discern immense beauty in the idea that every human being is, in the simple act of breathing, both living and loving. Most of this is unconscious or unrelated to any particular desires or demands. But in the case of the wisest beings, the most enlightened masters of compassion, this breathing is self-consciously benevolent and universal. Having become conscious of the enormous potential energy within the heart of the cosmos, they are able skilfully to direct and channel that energy to vast numbers of souls. They have learnt how to help particular persons at particular times only through lifetimes of trial and error. They have recognized the proliferating consequences of doing too much or not doing enough. Through practice, over millions of years and myriads of lives, Bodhisattvas become intelligent and skilful in the application of wisdom and compassion, light and love.

To be able even to understand such possibilities in such beings, much less to be able to move in that direction, one must shake off conventional divisions between the head and the heart. Often it is assumed that it is a great thing for the mind to become sharper, smarter and more intelligent. It is also conventional to think of the heart as sentimental. Both these notions are based upon misconceptions. In the subtle vestures of human beings, in what is called the spiritual heart, lies the basis of the highest intelligence, ideation and creativity. Therefore, from the spiritual point of view, one cannot activate any of the higher centres in the brain unless one has first aroused a spark of fire in the spiritual heart. Many human beings are able, sporadically, to release extraordinary powers, skills and flashes of genius. These intermittent abilities represent an unbalanced condition that is a reflection of excess and deficiency in previous lives. They are accompanied by a karmic frustration at not being able to tap and recover knowledge self-consciously, and such individuals have got hard lessons to learn before they can create new and better balances within themselves.

Hence the importance, especially with children, of withdrawing undue emphasis upon the mind and developing instead a sense of the heart. Instead of fostering an obsessive inclination to grade the mind, one should encourage an evolving conception of excellence in relation to the heart. This does not happen automatically; unless one becomes fearless and courageous, one cannot release the potency and spiritual strength in the heart. One must educate the heart in the best truth that one knows. This truth includes the mortality of one's body, the immortality of the soul, and the means of making that immortal soul function within a mortal body. It is crucial to give children some of the fundamental truths of the Divine Wisdom, and in particular to teach them not merely to look at things in terms of today and tomorrow, but rather in terms of their finest impulses and most generous urges. Over a lifetime of learning, these can provide the basis of authentic fearlessness and true universality in compassion and love. One must include in one's heart people whom one does not see. To do this requires an active imagination, ultimately a capacity to visualize the whole of humanity. This involves a dynamic balance between one's contemplation of all the beings that exist on this earth and one's relationships with those who are nearby.

In practice, this requires simplification and a development of precision, which is at the origin of all etiquette and manners. One must learn not to overdo with people who are immediately around oneself. To do less is to do more. Thus one will have a great opportunity to keep oneself intact, without getting into syndromes of excessive expectation and rapid disillusionment. While maintaining a greater steadiness in relationships to those around oneself, one will, at the same time, see beyond them. One will develop a concern to take one's place in the family of man and to become what is called in the Buddhist tradition a son of the Buddha family. Like the Bodhisattvas and Buddhas, one becomes willing to think in terms of serving all beings on earth. This is not something that one can contemplate or emulate in a short time. Instead, it will require a repeated renewal. It will have some impact at the moment of death and also a distinct effect upon the kind of birth one will have in the next life. Not immediately, but eventually, it will change the current and tropism, the tonality and colouring, of one's varied relationships to the vestures and their use.

By gaining this precision, one will become more free, and at the same time the better able to help other human beings. One's mind becomes more willing, vibrant and versatile by becoming an obedient servant of a heart that has found deep peace within itself. Once the heart has discovered within itself its own secret fire, it can, through various forms of daily meditation and oblation, activate that fire. Whether one calls this the fire of devotion, of *tapas*, of wisdom or truth, these are only different aspects of that which is ultimately the fire of the Mysteries. It is the fire that represents the immortal self-subsisting sovereignty of the individual human soul. It is capable in principle of becoming a self-conscious mirror of the whole cosmos. Therefore it is also capable of reaching out from within the inmost sanctuary and affecting, learning from, teaching and helping everything that exists. This requires deliberate and systematic training because of the diverse kinds, speeds and levels of communication between beings based upon the vibrations of the heart realm. The more skilful one becomes in using karmic opportunities to participate in the partial modes of love and learning of this world, the more one learns how to shed a little light for a few human beings upon a few things, while at the same time ceaselessly looking beyond one's horizon towards the limitless potential within all.

Eventually, one can reach a point where one has the great privilege of seeing no more evil and limitation because they have lost their fascination. They are really nothing more than a grotesque representation of muddle, error and delusion, ultimately based upon captivity to illusion. They are futile and short-sighted; they are short-lived. But so long as there are elements in so many beings that are caught up in short-term considerations, evil and limitation are compounded. While at first they may look like an awesome all-potent monster, one later sees that this is not true. This is a form of protection for those who are on the Path and concerned with the real work of the human race. That work is continuous, though hidden by a stream of invisibility, because most people are simply caught up in the external sights and sounds of reality. They are captives to exaggerations of form, limitation and evil. Hence the importance, at the individual level, for each human being to say, like Jesus, "Get thee behind me, Satan." One cannot say this for others; one must do it for oneself.

As long as there is light, there will be shadow. Yet every human being can at any moment turn his face away from the shadow and towards the light of the sun. Whenever one is with other souls, one can ask oneself, "Do I love others more than myself? Do I take less and give more to others? Do I actually reach out within myself, within my mind and heart, and also in my acts, towards other human beings? In the way I look at other human beings, can I salute the Divine within them? Can I shed light and also be grateful for the light that I daily receive from others?" By asking questions of this kind, one will find that all increments of change become significant. Life becomes not only worth living, but worth consecrating. The mind and the heart recapture the immanence of the ideal of boundless Love and Light.

THE DIVINE DIALECTIC

Absolute Truth is not reached by reasoning alone, but by an immediate apprehension that goes beyond any calculus of coherence or correspondence between relative truths. Although Absolute Truth is constant and complete in itself, there are, however, degrees of apprehension, and therefore human awareness of it is a continuous and dynamic process. To find truth completely is fully to realize oneself and one's destiny. It is to become perfect in a Mahatmic sense. Yet, every truth is self-acting and has inherent strength, though this strength lies latent until it is embodied in the actions and thoughts of a perfectible, if still very imperfect, human being. Since truth in the fullest sense is known only by direct perception and immediate apprehension, the intuitionist theory of truth must ultimately subsume the coherence theory of truth, because what is directly and immediately apprehended is also seen as a whole. It can also radically reinterpret the correspondence theory of truth of logical atomism, because one's intuitive perception includes the correspondence of an idea, a statement or a proposition to a fact or a thing or an event. If every truth is self-acting, then the degrees of apprehension of truth must have a direct effect both upon our state of being and upon the world, invisible and visible. If the attainment of the whole truth is equivalent to becoming perfect, then the degrees of apprehension of truth are equivalent to degrees of human imperfection. And, if truth, though self-acting, is latent until and unless it is embodied in thoughts and acts, to affirm the truth in the fullest, deepest and most authentic sense is to actualize it in thought and deed.

Actualization of truth in thought at the highest level is *Kriyashakti*, and belongs to perfected men of meditation. Actualization of truth to the fullest possible extent is the exemplary contribution of the greatest *karma yogins*, the great exemplars of extraordinary, supererogatory acts of renunciation of the self, of love and empathy, in extremely tight and tough situations. But, for all human beings, actualizing truth at some level in thought and deed is a way of affirming and reaffirming the truth and making it come alive. As a living dynamic force, it can both act upon the spiritual will, releasing it in oneself, and also move others to make voluntary but fundamental changes in their lives and their modes of cognition and conduct. Absolute Truth rooted in the one supreme Self-existence must be self-acting as a supreme Fohatic force, the supreme force of universal ideation. It can only be embodied in thought and deed by perfected beings who have gained universal self-consciousness and are the knowers of the Absolute.

The divine descent from the One to the many could not take place without universally self-conscious minds perfected in prior periods of evolution, in previous manvantaras. However, there is also always the presence of a grain or a germ of Absolute Truth in every single relative truth, and in the mists of the ubiquitous relativity of conditions and embodiments that envelop all ordinary states of consciousness. Therefore, Absolute Truth is potentially present in every self-conscious monad. It is dimly apprehended and intermittently, if imperfectly, reflected in the thoughts and acts of all beings, but especially in self-conscious knowers, choosers and agents. It waxes stronger and brighter in knowers, choosers and agents bound by freely chosen but constantly binding resolves, pledges and sacred vows.

A perfected being who identifies with the whole partakes of both absolute and relative truth, so long as there are un-enlightened beings. Yet, through such universal identification with all, a truly wise being would transcend all distinctions between enlightened and unenlightened, and thus be beyond any relative truth, or any relative criteria, however important, of appraisal, classification and grading. Therefore, Absolute Truth is, in a sense, essentially one with those who are perfected in its embodiment. One can speak meaningfully of the perfect embodiment, in thought and deed, of a single relative truth by one individual. This gives the magical power of *saccakriya,* the power that arises when an individual who has realized a single truth invokes it inwardly in consciousness — in thought, word and deed. But those who embody Absolute Truth by becoming one with the Absolute can mirror it perfectly in their minds, which have become attuned to the Universal Mind, whilst fully knowing it cannot be wholly embodied in any finite vesture, in any set or sum total of words and acts, or in any world of unenlightened beings.

One can also see from this that enlightened beings can commune and communicate with each other without words and without any temporal or spatial constraints. They could speak across the ages and across the continents, intimating their presence to unenlightened beings, who have awakened in some degree, by words and by silence, by deeds and by non-action, and thus vindicate the very existence and omnipresence of Absolute Truth. They could not, however, — and being wise, they would not attempt to — compel unenlightened beings to see any truth, let alone the truth in its fullness. Nonetheless, it is always possible to find the possibility of alchemical transmutation and leavening even amidst relative truths, since they themselves are ultimately rooted in the One Absolute. The scriptures speak of this in the image of the imperishable Ashwatta tree, with its roots above and its branches below, with the Vedic hymns as its leaves. He who knows this tree is said to be a knower of the Veda. The relevance of this ancient sacred symbol to the contemporary world can be seen by thinking of every leaf as a human life, every fiber as an act or word, and its boughs as the histories of nations and civilizations. Its branches rustling with the noise of human existence and passion, its trunk unmoved, it grows onward from of old. It is Yggdrasil, the tree of existence. It is the past, the present and the future; what was done, what is doing, what will be done — the infinite conjugation of the verb 'to do'.

The sacred metaphor of the tree points to the tree of knowledge, which finds place for everything. In it, all relative truths have their degrees in relation to the hidden sap and the invisible roots of the tree in *Akasha*, as also their reflections in the region of time. *Akasha* suffuses all and is closer to the wisdom and energy of the Absolute than anything else in this world of differentiation into subjects and objects. It is also potentially present, and may become actively present, within the divine sphere around every immortal soul. Its very existence is the basis of the possibility of communion, communication and contact between all beings, and especially between self-conscious Monads. There is, therefore, deep meaning to sacred communication between souls by means of words, gestures, acts, feelings and thoughts, even by signs and symbols, as well as in the deepest silence of meditation, but also in the deep sleep of *sushupti,* and at all times in the invisible fellowship of all souls.

This also makes possible the conscious and deliberate transmutation of all relativities and relative truths. It is the basis of all willing and concerted efforts to mirror the sacred in the profane, the universal in the realm of particulars, the timeless in the region of time, silence in the midst of sounds, and voidness in the midst of illusions. If all emanations affect gods, Monads and atoms, they can also powerfully affect other minds, other hearts, and other souls, elevating and enriching all consciousness, enlarging and deepening the awareness of those who are receptive and ready. They can bring the flavour of the ineffable beauty, truth and goodness of the flame of Divine *eros* into the midst of human conversation and company, into human relationships and human interactions. What is best in human nature is ever struggling to reach through and beyond the myriad relativities with which we are surrounded. We see this mirrored in the articulation of systems of philosophy, political and social structures, conceptions and modes of justice, educational and ethical ideals, artistic and all creative endeavors using the constructive energies of human souls. In all these arenas of human endeavor we see relative truths struggling to emerge. The best of these point beyond the confines of their specific formulations, and stand out as great utterances which by definition are classic, that is, contemporary in every situation.

This transcendental leavening of relative truths intimates something beyond, something more universal and lasting than anything that can be captured in any word or deed. From the highest standpoint of the divine dialectic, in the Platonic theory of ideal forms and of immortal souls, all knowledge is recognition and soul reminiscence, a recovery of what is ever-present within the soul. In the Platonic conception, the truth is the most potent source of energy and power, volition and causality in the world of time. To see this, but at the highest ontological level, is to grasp the full implication and presuppositions of the proposition that every truth is self-acting. This same idea recurs in the modern Enlightenment in the recognition by the *philosophes* that every human being is, by definition, alive only because every human being is expressing some vital truth. In every human being there is a truth that is struggling to come out, struggling to free itself and surpass the limitations of thought and speech, of time and space, of passion and personality, of prejudice and partisanship.

It is this that lends dignity to being human, and lends divinity to the entire human family, making sacred the pilgrimage of man at all times. It is also what makes the greatest stoics assert that nothing human is ever irrelevant to oneself. Though it is rare, any human being can consciously assume his or her citizenship in the cosmos of *Akasha* — the divine ideation of all the greatest beings who have ever lived. One can constitute oneself a citizen of the invisible cosmos of indwelling intelligence in noumenal nature, behind the visible world that we see. Thereby one can also realize one's full citizenship in the family of all humanity — humanity that is alive, humanity that is gone but remains a factor in our lives, and humanity that is yet to come but still casts its shadow upon all of us in the present. Anybody who does this with full self-consciousness can make the abstract archetypes in the Platonic system of thought the exalted and vital basis for seeing the world from above below.

This is a deliberate counteraction to the common, ubiquitous tendency, in the name of common sense and the lowest common denominator of human life, to look at things from below above. At the same time, it is a standpoint, and certainly not the only standpoint which is possible given the Platonic dialectic or which it was possible for Plato himself to adopt. Indeed, with all the myriad dialogues and the giving of some significance to every utterance, however foolish or muddled by every being, there is a celebration of the eternal conversation of mankind. The dialectic of human encounter has its own glory, beauty and value, regardless of all results, and regardless of the degrees of attainment of truth by different individuals. This was especially important for Plato because, if the philosopher sees the whole of life as a constant practice in the art of dying, and as a deliberate noble preparation for the moment of death, then, what any soul knows at the moment of death, or senses in deep sleep, or knows and yet can never utter or formulate, is far more important to that soul when one lifetime is closed than all the tangible articulations, all the fitful and faint expressions, and all the struggles of a lifetime.

This is not a matter of religious faith, but a philosophical understanding of the connection between the moment of birth, the moment of death, and all the high moments of awakening and awareness, all the peak experiences during human life, and all the lessons learned even in the abyss of suffering and degradation, but in a manner that transcends the possibility of external expression. If this exalted view of Plato is combined with a universal affirmation of the truth working through every human being as a soul, a spectator and agent upon the historical scene of earthy things and limited time, one will then have a basis for inferring an active testable faith in the perpetual victory of truth over falsehood. In fact, this is the true basis of the liberal convictions often associated with John S. Mill and which, in our own time, were expressed with a strange poignancy by Mao in the saying, "Let a hundred flowers bloom". Mill's view is that, as long as there is an open forum in which all truths, half-truths and falsehoods can freely contest without arbitrary or artificial limits, the truth will triumph. Human beings will be ceaselessly educating themselves in regard to the larger, the deeper, the fuller truth, even though outwardly they may be somewhat conditioned by their former captivity and their habitual addiction to partialities, partisanship and limited half-truths.

This liberal view of the inevitable triumph of truth does not, however, provide any assurance or earthly guarantee that any particular set of institutions, immersed in any set of concrete facts about human beings in any particular social structure, will allow true freedom to prevail unhindered over all the subtle devices by which human beings have learnt to subvert freedom in the name of freedom, to narrow life in the name of raising and broadening the human horizon. The moment truth is formulated into any "-ism" or ideology, it will deceive as much as distract people from that which is incapable of being systematized, formulated, and codified. Ideological truth cannot be transmitted externally except by some combination of persuasion, powerful psychological compulsion, and even by the actual use of threats and incentives, and these means only consolidate that self which is weak, furtive, self-protective and susceptible to the blackmail of threats as well as to the false glitter of earthly incentives. This is only another way of saying that, in our total concept of truth within the total context of human history, dialogue and society, there must be a positive and periodic reaffirmation by the greatest minds, echoed at some level by all human beings, of the progressive, the forward-looking, transcendental reaching out toward truth and knowledge. In science, religion and in all human affairs, there is a continual need to raise people's sights beyond the actualities of the present, beyond the memories of the past, and beyond even the ideals of the future projected right now by human beings in terms of their present understanding of the possibilities for the future.

Behind all of this stands the evocative force of what all the spiritual teachers and prophets have affirmed, that the truth can free a human being, that the truth can liberate, that the truth can redeem. In truth lies salvation and in no other thing. And the truth that saves, the truth that redeems, the truth that frees, the truth that liberates, cannot itself be only a scripture or a set of statements, or a set of affirmations or beliefs by any human being. It must be that which acts upon the will. It must be that which sifts among perceptions. It must be that which acts as an engine of restraint in the world of irrational passions, impulses, moods and drives, as well as that which looks beyond and leads beyond, into the realm of that which is truly Promethean in the human being. It must call out that which is capable of foresight, raising one's sights to the stars in the sky, raising them to the empyrean which goes beyond all worlds, and indeed all possible worlds, and yet, at the same time, is closer in its echoes within the human heart than any revealed or formulated truth.

If the truth can free, the truth can also bind, but in a creative, constructive sense. To see a truth, especially in a time of pain and suffering, or after having spent a long, desperate time in the valley of doubt and despondency, is to be quickened, to come alive and to be exhilarated. It is to make an authentic but irrevocable wish to make a new start, to open a new chapter, to write afresh upon the book volume of the brain and the pages of human existence. It is to begin anew in human relationships. But, above all, in one's own self-relationship to all the elements of one's own being, to serve notice on all the tendencies which make up one's lesser fugitive, transient and oppressive self, that lesser self which imprisons the deeper Self that is unmanifest, that is denied expression, denied voice and denied free flow of unfoldment and effortless mastery within the kingdom of the personality.

Therefore, there is great meaning in those affirmations of truth which endow them with the aura of the sacred, placing them beyond the region and the realm of analysis, qualification and rationalization. These thereby become the deepest truths in one's consciousness. Enshrined in noble words, whether coined by oneself or borrowed from those greater than oneself, they serve as a basis for binding oneself in relation to the ever-present tendency to deceive oneself. They help one to see through that which is false, but which can acquire the deceptive glitter of a simulacrum of the truth. This means that there is no other way out of the tinsel and froth of echoed and derivative, emaciated and emasculated truths other than the capacity to charge what is vitally true with the potency of one's own direct declaration, one's own performative support in the realm of acts and one's deepest sense of the sacred. Once the spark is struck, it is the core of that Self to which one will always be true, because to be true to oneself is to be true to those truths that are the most sacred and most inviolable to a human being.

Here one can see the basis of all the pledges, pacts and vows in sacred and secular rites and ceremonies, because one can never dispense with the act of sanctification. This is as relevant in modern law as it was in ancient custom. Emile Durkheim, who was an especially shrewd and perceptive thinker, and the forgotten father of modern sociology, spoke of ideal collective representations in the midst and the minds of all peoples and societies, which give them unity amidst the diversity of all their customs, their codes, their relationships, their rules, their conventions and their rituals. The same binding function is also fulfilled by what we call the eternal verities or the timeless truths — immortalized by poets and playwrights or by spiritual seers as in the great epics, or which sometimes unexpectedly come from the mouths of babes and human beings who are not even aware of the amount of wisdom in their natural utterance, because of deep feeling in a compelling context. These become truths that soon lose all sense of ownership, and, passing among human beings, they contribute to the collective folk wisdom of the human race. They become the common sense of a generation, and, when significantly invoked in the face of everything that is divisive, plausible, meretricious and misleading, they can become the truths that heal human sickness, the truths that reconcile myriad standpoints, the truths that point beyond everything that is existent to that which is beyond.

In the noblest traditions and in the noblest models of society, such as that of Plato, there is a self-conscious inculcation of these verities in at least the finest of human beings available at any given time, those who are willing to test themselves repeatedly over a long period of self-training, and also to become apprentices in learning the true dialectic. The reaffirmation by these beings of those profound truths, which can then become meaningful and relevant to the lives of others around them, is of the highest importance. Just as truth becomes self-acting, when it becomes sanctified in the lives of such exemplars, these truths actually become the hidden vanguard that holds the initiative and in time can cancel and supercede all lesser truths and lesser formulations. Such unacknowledged exemplars or guardians consciously invoke the transcendence of the *Agathon,* the supreme Universal Good that is beyond all description or definition, that is inclusive of, and yet transcends, all possible utterances and formulations in human speech, institutions and the entire gamut of human expression — from art and architecture to philosophy and poetry to music and mathematics.

Now if one recognizes all of this, then one can take a step further and recognize that there is a subterranean fountainhead of truth which ever flows like a hidden stream under the surface noise and utterances, the surface cacophony and harsh violence in the interactions of systems and "-isms". This stream is the ever-present current of Divine Wisdom, which is inscribed in the form of innate ideas given by planetary spirits in the dawn of differentiation during the lighting up of the flame of self-consciousness in all human Monads. It serves as a source that transcends all religions and philosophies, all forms, modes and systems of knowledge, and therefore is the eternal wisdom of humanity recorded in the invisible archives of Nature. As the universal library of human wisdom to which each human being has access within the solitude of his or her own deep, intense, private and personal contemplation, it is that of which great seers and poets have spoken — nobody more than Shakespeare in the modern age. And, it is also the true reference of what is sometimes called the forgotten language of the human soul — the language that lies beyond the Babel of all the known dialects of human speech, the unuttered language that comes out of the immemorial pilgrimage of all humanity.

If we can raise our sights in this way, we can see truth at many levels, and see truth also as that which both liberates and, at the same time, that which can act as a noetic mode of self-restraint. Truth is that which is everywhere, but it is also especially enshrined in certain statements and sayings which only become real for one according to the use to which one puts them in daily life. In the light of so hospitable, so vast and boundless a conception of the horizon of even relative truths, however imperfect and incomplete, one should recognize that to set aside this inheritance in favour of any false and dangerous form of limited certainty is to alienate oneself from one's immortal soul and from the divine purpose of all human life. Given this, tragic numbers of human beings are needlessly ignorant, unenlightened and repeatedly captive to the lowest common denominator of crystallized so-called "worldly wisdom" or inferential truth, which at best is defective and statistical. Inferential truth can never fathom the inexplicable unique situation of each and every human being as a pilgrim soul in the great pilgrimage of Necessity. Yet, there nonetheless arise at times, given the receptivity and the moral and spiritual merits of any group of souls at any given time, those wise, fearless and heroic souls who can become truly alchemical and therapeutic in their speech, able to heal by words invoking the highest, divinest possibilities of uttered sound.

In all the spiritual traditions of the world, there is a recognition that even the greatest recorded statements in the greatest Vedas, in the greatest scriptures of all humanity, however magnificent, are much less vital than the same statements, or any one of them, voiced by human beings who have realized them — those who, from the fount of their own inner experience, love, compassion and wisdom, can voice them and transmit them on the plane on which human beings are captive to the lower astral light and the commonality of vulgar discourse. In the midst of the market-place, by uttering and giving life and form, body and local habitation, to immemorial utterances of ageless truths, they can 'leaven the lump'. They can transmute an entire atmosphere, an entire company of souls, an entire society or generation, and make a difference to the ability of human souls to invite and invoke greater souls than themselves to enter into their midst, to incarnate into the world in the progress of time. From this point of view much depends, for the civilization of the future, upon the deliberate efforts of a few, under the inspiration of the highest auspices conceivable in the cosmos, the Banyan Tree of initiation, to re-learn how to lisp and how to speak the language of the sacred. They could learn how to intone the AUM, how to give life and utterance to what is true and sacred, to what is elevating and capable of therapeutic action upon the life atoms, the vestures, the wills, the minds, the hearts — however mutilated, enslaved, muddled and self-deceived — of human beings within the domain of darkness.

All of this may be understood in terms of the divine dialectic, which serves as a bridge between the Absolute and the relative, and which awakens the self-acting strength of truth at every level, not merely in the lives of isolated souls striving towards perfection, but spanning the entire range of the universal pilgrimage of humanity. Anyone who contemplates the Platonic Divided Line sees at its transcendental apex the union of the knower, the known and the mode of knowing. At the same time, one also sees the thick, seemingly impassable line between the region of becoming and the realm of being. Hence the crucial need, as rapidly as possible, to withdraw and withhold images and lower fancies, beliefs and lower assertions, and to prepare oneself for true, persistent questioning and self-questioning, for the dialogue of the soul within itself, and for the dialogue of the deepest in human beings with what is potentially there lying deep in other human souls. Through the study of mathematics and music, through the awakening of the higher capacities of thought, which rise to the realm of the universal, the general and the abstract, one can find place and lend beauty to everything that reflects the most real, the most general and the most sacred in the vast world of whirling particulars. This is truly to prepare for the highest vision possible for the human soul.

The dialectic, long before it can serve as an available golden bridge between the Absolute and the relative, must first begin in the power to choose decisively within human life. One must draw out from within the self-acting power of truth in the region of that which is inescapable, necessary and unavoidable, the region of that which is capable of being affected and altered for the sake of the universal good by conscious and deliberate choices and acts of freedom. Beginning in the relative freedom that every human being can make real by pitting it against the seemingly vast and inexorable necessities of the world and of living, one then can move through contemplation to a cognition of greater levels of freedom and higher degrees of apprehension of truth. There, the very distinctions between freedom and necessity, between external and internal, become less and less meaningful because everything external is progressively intuited as a partial reflection of what is internal and complete. Everything that is true and free in the highest and fullest sense has the underpinning of the cosmos and of time, of karma and growth, both in history and in individual life. It is also the realm of the highest necessity, the divinest destiny, and the uttermost perfection of each human soul.

OM

APPENDICES

THE THREE FUNDAMENTALS

The Secret Doctrine establishes three fundamental propositions:

(a) An Omnipresent, Eternal, Boundless, and Immutable PRINCIPLE on which all speculation is impossible, since it transcends the power of human conception and could only be dwarfed by any human expression or similitude. It is beyond the range and reach of thought — in the words of Mandukya, "unthinkable and unspeakable".

To render these ideas clearer to the general reader, let him set out with the postulate that there is one absolute Reality which antecedes all manifested, conditioned, being. This Infinite and Eternal Cause — dimly formulated in the 'Unconscious' and 'Unknowable' of current European philosophy — is the rootless root of "all that was, is, or ever shall be". It is of course devoid of all attributes and is essentially without any relation to manifested, finite Being. It is 'Be-ness' rather than Being (in Sanskrit, *Sat*), and is beyond all thought or speculation.

This 'Be-ness' is symbolised in the Secret Doctrine under two aspects. On the one hand, absolute abstract Space, representing bare subjectivity, the one thing which no human mind can either exclude from any conception, or conceive of by itself. On the other, absolute Abstract Motion representing Unconditioned Consciousness. Even our Western thinkers have shown that Consciousness is inconceivable to us apart from change, and motion best symbolises change, its essential characteristic. This latter aspect of the one Reality is also symbolised by the term 'The Great Breath', a symbol sufficiently graphic to need no further elucidation. Thus, then, the first fundamental axiom of the Secret Doctrine is this metaphysical ONE ABSOLUTE — BE-NESS — symbolised by finite intelligence as the theological Trinity.

It may, however, assist the student if a few further explanations are given here.

Herbert Spencer . . . so far modified his Agnosticism as to assert that the nature of the 'First Cause',* which the Occultist more logically derives from the 'Causeless Cause', the 'Eternal', and the 'Unknowable', may be essentially the same as that of the Consciousness which wells up within us: in short, that the impersonal reality pervading the Kosmos is the pure noumenon of thought. This advance on his part brings him very near to the esoteric and Vedantin tenet.†

Parabrahm (the One Reality, the Absolute) is the field of Absolute Consciousness, *i.e.*, that Essence which is out of all relation to conditioned existence, and of which conscious existence is a conditioned symbol. But once that we pass in thought from this (to us) Absolute Negation, duality supervenes in the contrast of Spirit (or consciousness) and Matter, Subject and Object.

Spirit (or Consciousness) and Matter are, however, to be regarded, not as independent realities, but as the two facets or aspects of the Absolute (Parabrahm), which constitute the basis of conditioned Being whether subjective or objective.

Considering this metaphysical triad as the Root from which proceeds all manifestation, the great Breath assumes the character of precosmic Ideation. It is the *fons et origo* of force and of all individual consciousness, and supplies the guiding intelligence in the vast scheme of cosmic Evolution. On the other hand, precosmic root-substance (*Mulaprakriti*) is that aspect of the Absolute which underlies all the objective planes of Nature.

Just as pre-Cosmic Ideation is the root of all individual

---

* The 'first' presupposes necessarily something which is the 'first brought forth', 'the first in time, space, and rank' — and therefore finite and conditioned. The 'first' cannot be the absolute, for it is a manifestation. Therefore, Eastern Occultism calls the Abstract All the 'Causeless One Cause', the 'Rootless Root', and limits the 'First Cause' to the Logos, in the sense that Plato gives to this term.

† See Mr. Subba Row's four able lectures on the Bhagavad Gita, *Theosophist*, February, 1887.

consciousness, so pre-Cosmic Substance is the substratum of matter in the various grades of its differentiation. Hence it will be apparent that the contrast of these two aspects of the Absolute is essential to the existence of the 'Manifested Universe'. Apart from Cosmic Substance, Cosmic Ideation could not manifest as individual consciousness, since it is only through a vehicle* of matter that consciousness wells up as 'I am I', a physical basis being necessary to focus a ray of the Universal Mind at a certain stage of complexity. Again, apart from Cosmic Ideation, Cosmic Substance would remain an empty abstraction, and no emergence of consciousness could ensue.

The 'Manifested Universe', therefore, is pervaded by duality, which is, as it were, the very essence of its EX-istence as 'manifestation'. But just as the opposite poles of subject and object, spirit and matter, are but aspects of the One Unity in which they are synthesized, so, in the manifested Universe, there is 'that' which links spirit to matter, subject to object.

This something, at present unknown to Western speculation, is called by the occultists Fohat. It is the 'bridge' by which the 'Ideas' existing in the 'Divine Thought' are impressed on Cosmic substance as the 'laws of Nature'. Fohat is thus the dynamic energy of Cosmic Ideation; or, regarded from the other side, it is the intelligent medium, the guiding power of all manifestation, the 'Thought Divine' transmitted and made manifest through the Dhyan Chohans,† the Architects of the visible World. Thus from Spirit, or Cosmic Ideation, comes our consciousness; from Cosmic Substance the several vehicles in which that consciousness is individualized and attains to self — or reflective — consciousness; while Fohat, in its various manifestations, is the mysterious link between Mind and Matter, the animating principle electrifying every atom into life.

The following summary will afford a clearer idea to the reader.

* Called in Sanskrit: 'Upadhi'.

† Called by Christian theology: Archangels, Seraphs, etc., etc.

1. The ABSOLUTE; the *Parabrahm* of the Vedantins or the one Reality, SAT, which is, as Hegel says, both Absolute Being and Non-Being.

2. The first manifestation, the impersonal, and, in philosophy, *unmanifested* Logos, the precursor of the 'manifested.' This is the 'First Cause', the 'Unconscious' of European Pantheists.

3. Spirit-matter, LIFE; the 'Spirit of the Universe', the Purusha and Prakriti, or the *second* Logos.

4. Cosmic Ideation, MAHAT or Intelligence, the Universal World-Soul; the Cosmic Noumenon of Matter, the basis of the intelligent operations in and of Nature, also called MAHA-BUDDHI.

The ONE REALITY; its *dual* aspects in the conditioned Universe.

Further, the Secret Doctrine affirms:

(*b*) The Eternity of the Universe *in toto* as a boundless plane; periodically "the playground of numberless Universes incessantly manifesting and disappearing", called 'the manifesting stars', and the 'sparks of Eternity'. 'The Eternity of the Pilgrim'* is like a wink of the Eye of Self-Existence (Book of Dzyan.) "The appearance and disappearance of Worlds is like a regular tidal ebb of flux and reflux."

This second assertion of the Secret Doctrine is the absolute universality of that law of periodicity, of flux and reflux, ebb

---

* 'Pilgrim' is the appellation given to our Monad (the two in one) during its cycle of incarnations. It is the only immortal and eternal principle in us, being an indivisible part of the integral whole — the Universal Spirit, from which it emanates, and into which it is absorbed at the end of the cycle. When it is said to emanate from the one spirit, an awkward and incorrect expression has to be used, for lack of appropriate words in English. The Vedantins call it Sutratma (Thread-Soul). . . .

and flow, which physical science has observed and recorded in all departments of nature. An alternation such as that of Day and Night, Life and Death, Sleeping and Waking, is a fact so common, so perfectly universal and without exception, that it is easy to comprehend that in it we see one of the absolutely fundamental laws of the universe.

Moreover, the Secret Doctrine teaches:

(c) The fundamental identity of all Souls with the Universal Over-Soul, the latter being itself an aspect of the Unknown Root; and the obligatory pilgrimage for every Soul — a spark of the former — through the Cycle of Incarnation (or 'Necessity') in accordance with Cyclic and Karmic law, during the whole term. In other words, no purely spiritual Buddhi (divine Soul) can have an independent (conscious) existence before the spark which issued from the pure Essence of the Universal Sixth principle — or the OVER-SOUL — has (a) passed through every elemental form of the phenomenal world of that Manvantara, and (b) acquired individuality, first by natural impulse, and then by self-induced and self-devised efforts (checked by its Karma), thus ascending through all the degrees of intelligence, from the lowest to the highest Manas, from mineral and plant, up to the holiest archangel (Dhyani-Buddha). The pivotal doctrine of the Esoteric philosophy admits no privileges or special gifts in man, save those won by his own Ego through personal effort and merit throughout a long series of metempsychoses and reincarnations. This is why the Hindus say that the Universe is Brahma and Brahmā, for Brahma is in every atom of the universe, the six principles in Nature being all the outcome — the variously differentiated aspects — of the SEVENTH and ONE, the only reality in the Universe whether Cosmical or micro-cosmical; and also why the permutations (psychic, spiritual and physical), on the plane of manifestation and form, of the sixth (Brahmā the vehicle of Brahma) are viewed by metaphysical antiphrasis as illusive and Mayavic. For although the root of every atom individually and of every form collectively is that seventh principle or the one Reality, still, in its manifested phenomenal and temporary appearance, it is no better than an evanescent illusion of our senses.

The Secret Doctrine, i 14 - 18   H. P. BLAVATSKY

SIX ITEMS OF COSMOGONY

The Secret Doctrine is the accumulated Wisdom of the Ages, and its cosmogony alone is the most stupendous and elaborate system: e.g., even in the exotericism of the Puranas. But such is the mysterious power of Occult symbolism, that the facts which have actually occupied countless generations of initiated seers and prophets to marshal, to set down and explain, in the bewildering series of evolutionary progress, are all recorded on a few pages of geometrical signs and glyphs. The flashing gaze of those seers has penetrated into the very kernel of matter, and recorded the soul of things there, where an ordinary profane, however learned, would have perceived but the external work of form. But modern science believes not in the 'soul of things', and hence will reject the whole system of ancient cosmogony. It is useless to say that the system in question is no fancy of one or several isolated individuals. That it is the uninterrupted record covering thousands of generations of Seers whose respective experiences were made to test and to verify the traditions passed orally by one early race to another, of the teachings of higher and exalted beings, who watched over the childhood of Humanity. That for long ages, the 'Wise Men' of the Fifth Race, of the stock saved and rescued from the last cataclysm and shifting of continents, had passed their lives *in learning, not teaching.* How did they do so? It is answered: by checking, testing, and verifying in every department of nature the traditions of old by the independent visions of great adepts; i.e., men who have developed and perfected their physical, mental, psychic, and spiritual organisations to the utmost possible degree. No vision of one adept was accepted till it was checked and confirmed by the visions — so obtained as to stand as independent evidence — of other adepts, and by centuries of experiences.

2. The fundamental Law in that system, the central point from which all emerged, around and toward which all gravitates,

and upon which is hung the philosophy of the rest, is the One homogeneous divine SUBSTANCE-PRINCIPLE, the one radical cause.

> Some few, whose lamps shone brighter, have been led
> From cause to cause to nature's secret head,
> And found that one first Principle must be. . . .

It is called 'Substance-Principle', for it becomes 'substance' on the plane of the manifested Universe, an illusion, while it remains a 'principle' in the beginningless and endless abstract, visible and invisible SPACE. It is the omnipresent Reality: impersonal, because it contains all and everything. *Its impersonality is the fundamental conception* of the System. It is latent in every atom in the Universe, and is the Universe itself. (See in chapters on Symbolism, "Primordial Substance, and Divine Thought.")

3. The Universe is the periodical manifestation of this unknown Absolute Essence. To call it 'essence', however, is to sin against the very spirit of the philosophy. For though the noun may be derived in this case from the verb *esse*, 'to be', yet IT cannot be identified with a *being* of any kind, that can be conceived by human intellect. IT is best described as neither Spirit nor matter, but both. 'Parabrahmam and Mulaprakriti' are One, in reality, yet two in the Universal conception of the manifested, even in the conception of the One Logos, its first manifestation, to which, as the able lecturer in the "Notes on the Bhagavadgita" shows, IT appears from the objective standpoint of the One Logos as Mulaprakriti and not as Parabrahmam; as its *veil* and not the one REALITY hidden behind, which is unconditioned and absolute.

4. The Universe is called, with everything in it, MAYA, because all is temporary therein, from the ephemeral life of a fire-fly to that of the Sun. Compared to the eternal immutability of the ONE, and the changelessness of that Principle, the Universe, with its

evanescent ever-changing forms, must be necessarily, in the mind of a philosopher, no better than a will-o'-the-wisp. Yet, the Universe is real enough to the conscious beings in it, which are as unreal as it is itself.

5. Everything in the Universe, throughout all its kingdoms, is CONSCIOUS: i.e., endowed with a consciousness of its own kind and on its own plane of perception. We men must remember that because *we* do not perceive any signs — which we can recognize — of consciousness, say, in stones, we have no right to say that *no consciousness exists there.* There is no such thing as either 'dead' or 'blind' matter, as there is no 'Blind' or 'Unconscious' Law. These find no place among the conceptions of Occult philosophy. The latter never stops at surface appearances, and for it the *noumenal* essences have more reality than their objective counterparts; it resembles therein the medieval *Nominalists,* for whom it was the Universals that were the realities and the particulars which existed only in name and human fancy.

6. The Universe is worked and *guided* from *within outwards.* As above so it is below, as in heaven so on earth; and man — the microcosm and miniature copy of the macrocosm — is the living witness to this Universal Law and to the mode of its action. We see that every *external* motion, act, gesture, whether voluntary or mechanical, organic or mental, is produced and preceded by *internal* feeling or emotion, will or volition, and thought or mind. As no outward motion or change, when normal, in man's external body can take place unless provoked by an inward impulse, given through one of the three functions named, so with the external or manifested Universe. The whole Kosmos is guided, controlled, and animated by almost endless series of Hierarchies of sentient Beings, each having a mission to perform and who — whether we give to them one name or another, and call them Dhyan-Chohans or Angels — are 'messengers' in the sense only that they are the agents of Karmic and Cosmic Laws. They vary infinitely in their respective degrees of consciousness and intelligence. . . .

Man, . . . being a compound of the essences of all those celestial Hierarchies may succeed in making himself, as such, superior, in one sense, to any hierarchy or class, or even combination of them. "Man can neither propitiate nor command the *Devas*," it is said. But, by paralyzing his lower personality, and arriving thereby at the full knowledge of the *non-separateness* of his higher SELF from the One absolute SELF, man can, even during his terrestrial life, become as "One of Us." Thus it is, by eating of the fruit of knowledge which dispels ignorance, that man becomes like one of the Elohim or the Dhyanis; and once on *their* plane the Spirit of Solidarity and perfect Harmony, which reigns in every Hierarchy, must extend over him and protect him in every particular.

The Secret Doctrine, i 272-276 H.P. Blavatsky

CLASSIFICATIONS OF HUMAN NATURE

We give below in a tabular form the classifications adopted by the Buddhist and Vedantic teachers of the principles of man:

CLASSIFICATION IN ESOTERIC BUDDHISM	VEDANTIC CLASSIFICATION	CLASSIFICATION IN TARAKA RAJA YOGA
1. Sthula Sarira	Annamaya kosa[1]	Sthulopadhi[3]
2. Prana[2]	Pranamaya kosa	
3. The vehicle of Prana[4]		
4. Kama Rupa	Manomaya kosa	Sukshmopadhi
5. Mind (a) Volitions and feelings, etc.		
(b) Vignanam	Vignanamaya kosa	
6. Spiritual Soul[5]	Anandamaya kosa	Karanopadhi
7. Atma	Atma	Atma

1 Kosa (kosha) is 'Sheath' literally, the sheath of every principle.
2 'Life'.
3 The astral body or Linga Sarira.
4 Sthula-Upadhi, or basis of the principle.
5 Buddhi.

From the foregoing table it will be seen that the third principle in the Buddhist classification is not separately mentioned in the Vedantic division, as it is merely the vehicle of Prana. It will also be seen that the Fourth principle is included in the third Kosa (Sheath), as the same principle is but the vehicle of will-power, which is but an energy of the mind. It must also be noticed that the Vignanamaya Kosa is considered to be distinct from the Manomaya Kosa, as a division is made after death between the lower part of the mind, as it were, which has a closer affinity with the fourth principle than with the sixth; and its higher part, which attaches itself to the latter, and which is, in fact, the basis for the higher spiritual individuality of man.

We may also here point out to our readers that the classification mentioned in the last column is, for all practical purposes, connected with Raja Yoga, the best and simplest. Though there are seven principles in man, there are but three distinct Upadhis (bases), in each of which his Atma may work independently of the rest. These three Upadhis can be separated by an Adept without killing himself. He cannot separate the seven principles from each other without destroying his constitution.

The student will now be better prepared to see that between the three Upadhis of the Raja Yoga and its Atma, and our three Upadhis, Atma, and the additional three divisions, there is in reality but very little difference. Moreover, as every adept in cis-Himalayan or trans-Himalayan India, of the Patanjali, the Aryasanga or the Mahayana schools, has to become a Raja Yogi, he must, therefore, accept the Taraka Raja classification in principle and theory whatever classification he resorts to for practical and occult purposes. Thus, it matters very little whether one speaks of the *three Upadhis with their three aspects* and Atma, the eternal and immortal synthesis, or calls them the 'seven principles'.

The Secret Doctrine, i 157-158   H.P. Blavatsky

THE SYNTHESIS OF
OCCULT SCIENCE

I

The impassable gulf between mind and matter discovered by modern science is a logical result of the present methods of so-called scientific investigation. These methods are analytical and hypothetical, and the results arrived at are necessarily tentative and incomplete. Even the so-called "Synthetic Philosophy" of Spencer is, at best, an effort to grasp the entire method and modulus of nature within one of its processes only. The aim is at synthesis, but it can hardly deserve the name of philosophy, for it is purely speculative and hypothetical. It is as though the physiologist undertook to study the function of respiration in man through the single process of expiration, ignoring the fact that every expiratory act must be supplemented by inspiration or respiration cease altogether.

Taking, therefore, the facts of experience derived from the phenomena of nature and viewing both cosmic and organic processes purely from their objective side, the "missing links", "impassable gulfs", and "unthinkable gaps" occur constantly. Not so in Occult Science. So far as the science of occultism is concerned, it is both experimental and analytical, but it acknowledges no "missing links", "impassable gulfs", or "unthinkable gaps", because it finds none. Back of occult science there lies a complete and all-embracing Philosophy. This philosophy is not simply synthetical in its methods, for the simplest as the wildest hypothesis can claim that much; but it is *synthesis itself*. It regards Nature as one complete whole, and so the student of occultism may stand at either point of observation. He may from the stand-point of Nature's wholeness and completeness follow the process of segregation and differentiation to the minutest atom conditioned in space and time; or, from the phenomenal display of the atom, he may reach forward and upward till the atom becomes an integral part of cosmos, involved in the universal harmony of creation. The modern scientist may do this incidentally or empirically, but the occultist does it systematically and habitually, and hence philosophically. The modern scientist is confessedly and boastfully *agnostic*. The occultist is reverently and progressively *gnostic*.

Modern science recognizes matter as "living" and "dead", "organic" and "inorganic", and "Life" as merely a phenomenon of matter. Occult science recognizes, "foremost of all, the postulate that there is no such thing in Nature as *inorganic* substances or bodies. Stones, minerals, rocks, and even chemical *'atoms'* are simply organic units in profound lethargy. Their coma has an end, and their inertia becomes activity." (*Secret Doctrine*, Vol. I, p. 626 fn.) Occultism recognizes ONE UNIVERSAL, ALL-PERVADING LIFE. Modern science recognizes life as a special phenomenon of matter, a mere transient manifestation due to temporary conditions. Even logic and analogy ought to have taught us better, for the simple reason that so-called "inorganic" or "dead" matter constantly becomes organic and living, while matter from the organic plane is continually being reduced to the inorganic. How rational and justifiable, then, to suppose that the capacity or "potency" of life is latent in all matter!

The "elements", "atoms", and "molecules" of modern science, partly physical and partly metaphysical, though altogether hypothetical, are, nevertheless, seldom philosophical, for the simple reason that they are regarded solely as phenomenal. The Law of Avogadro involved a generalization as to physical structure and number, and the later experiments of Prof. Neumann deduced the same law mathematically from the first principles of the mechanical theory of gases, but it remained for Prof. Crookes to perceive the philosophical necessity of a primordial substratum, *protyle*, and so, as pointed out in *The Secret Doctrine*, to lay the foundations of *"Metachemistry"*; in other words, a complete philosophy of physics and chemistry that shall take the place of mere hypothesis and empiricism. If one or two generalizations deduced as logical or mathematical necessities from the phenomena of physics and chemistry have been able to work such revolutions in the old chemistry, what may we not expect from a complete synthesis that shall grasp universals by a law that compasses the whole domain of matter? And yet this complete synthesis has been in the possession of the true occultist for ages. Glimpses of this philosophy have been sufficient to give to minds like Kepler, Descartes, Leibnitz, Kant, Schopenhauer, and, lastly, to Prof. Crookes, ideas that claimed and held the interested attention of the scientific world. While, at certain points, such writers supplement and corroborate each other, neither anywhere nor altogether do they reveal the complete synthesis, for none of them possessed it, and yet it has all along existed.

> Let the reader remember these 'Monads' of Leibnitz, every one of which is a living mirror of the universe, every monad reflecting every other, and compare this view and definition with certain Sanskrit stanzas (*Slokas*) translated by Sir William Jones, in which it is said that the creative source of the Divine Mind, . . . 'Hidden in a veil of thick darkness, formed *mirrors of the atoms* of the world, and *cast reflection from its own face on every atom*.'
>
> *The Secret Doctrine*, i 623

It may be humiliating to "Modern Exact Science" and repugnant to the whole of Christendom to have to admit that the Pagans whom they have despised, and the "Heathen Scriptures" they long ridiculed or ignored, nevertheless possess a fund of wisdom never dreamed of under Western skies. They have the lesson, however, to learn, that Science by no means originated in, nor is it confined to, the West, nor are superstition and ignorance confined to the East.

It can easily be shown that every real discovery and every important advancement in modern science have already been anticipated centuries ago by ancient science and philosophy. It is true that these ancient doctrines have been embodied in unknown languages and symbols, and recorded in books inaccessible to western minds till a very recent date. Far beyond all this inaccessibility, however, as a cause preventing these old truths from reaching modern times, has been the prejudice, the scorn and contempt of ancient learning manifested by the leaders of modern thought.

Nor is the lesson yet learned that bigotry and scorn are never the mark of wisdom or the harbingers of learning; for still, with comparatively few exceptions, any claim or discussion of these ancient doctrines is met with contempt and scorn. The record has, however, been at least outlined and presented to the world. As the authors of *The Secret Doctrine* have remarked, these doctrines may not be largely accepted by the present generation, but during the twentieth century they will become known and appreciated.

The scope and bearing of philosophy itself are hardly yet appreciated by modern thought, because of its materialistic tendency. A complete science of metaphysics and a complete philosophy of science are not yet even conceived of as possible; hence the ancient wisdom by its very vastness has escaped recognition in modern times. That the authors of ancient wisdom have spoken from at least two whole planes of conscious experience beyond that of our every-day "sense-perception" is to us inconceivable, and yet such is the fact; and why should the modern advocate of evolution be shocked and staggered by such a disclosure? It but justifies his hypothesis and extends its theatre. Is it because the present custodians of this ancient learning do not scramble for recognition on the stock exchange, and enter into competition in the marts of the world? If the practical outcome of such competition needed illustration, Mr. Keely might serve as an example. The discoveries of the age are already whole centuries in advance of its ethical culture, and the knowledge that should place still further power in the hands of a few individuals whose ethical code is below, rather than above, that of the ignorant, toiling, suffering masses, could only minister to anarchy and increase oppression. On these higher planes of consciousness the law of progress is absolute; knowledge and power go hand in hand with beneficence to man, not alone to the individual possessors of wisdom, but to the whole human race. The custodians of the higher knowledge are equally by both motive and development almoners of the divine. These are the very conditions of the higher consciousness referred to. The synthesis of occult science becomes, therefore, the higher synthesis of the faculties of man. What matter, therefore, if the ignorant shall scout its very existence, or treat it with ridicule and contempt? Those who know of its existence and who have learned something of its scope and nature can, in their turn, afford to smile, but with pity and sorrow at the willing bondage to ignorance and misery that scorns enlightenment and closes its eyes to the plainest truths of experience.

Leaving, for the present, the field of physics and cosmogenesis, it may be profitable to consider some of the applications of these doctrines to the functions and life of man.

> The intellect derived from philosophy
> is similar to a charioteer; for it
> is present with our desires, and
> always conducts them to the beautiful.
>
> DEMOPHILUS

II

"In reality, as Occult philosophy teaches us, everything which changes is organic; it has the life principle in it, and it has all the potentiality of the higher lives. If, as we say, all in nature is an aspect of the one element, and life is universal, how can there be such a thing as an inorganic atom!" * Man is a perfected animal, but before he could have reached perfection even on the animal plane, there must have dawned upon him the light of a higher plane. Only the perfected animal can cross the threshold of the next higher, or the human plane, and as he does so there shines

* Quotations are from The Secret Doctrine and other writings of H.P. Blavatsky.

upon him the ray from the supra-human plane. Therefore, as the dawn of humanity illumines the animal plane, and as a guiding star lures the Monad to higher consciousness, so the dawn of divinity illumines the human plane, luring the monad to the supra-human plane of consciousness. This is neither more nor less than the philosophical and metaphysical aspect of the law of evolution. Man has not one principle more than the tiniest insect; he is, however, "the vehicle of a fully developed *Monad*, self-conscious and deliberately following its own line of progress, whereas in the insect, and even the higher animal, the higher triad of principles is absolutely dormant." The original *Monad* has, therefore, locked within it the potentiality of divinity. It is plainly, therefore, a misnomer to call that process of thought a "Synthetic Philosophy" that deals only with phenomena and ends with matter on the physical plane. These two generalizations of Occult philosophy, endowing every atom with the potentiality of life, and regarding every insect or animal as already possessing the potentialities of the higher planes though these powers are yet dormant, add to the ordinary Spencerian theory of evolution precisely that element that it lacks, *viz.* the metaphysical and philosophical; and, thus endowed, the theory becomes synthetical.

The *Monad*, then, is essentially and potentially the same in the lowest vegetable organism, up through all forms and gradations of animal life to man, *and beyond*. There is a gradual unfolding of its potentialities from "Monera" to man, and there are two whole planes of consciousness, the sixth and the seventh "senses," not yet unfolded to the average humanity. Every monad that is enclosed in a form, and hence limited by matter, becomes conscious on its own plane and in its own degree. Consciousness, therefore, no less than sensitiveness, belongs to plants as well as to animals. Self-consciousness belongs to man, because, while embodied in a *form*, the higher triad of principles, Atma-Buddhi-Manas, is no longer dormant, but active. This activity is, however, far from being fully developed. When this activity has become fully developed, man will already have become conscious on a still higher plane, endowed with the sixth and the opening of the *seventh* sense, and will have become a "god" in the sense given to that term by Plato and his followers.

In thus giving this larger and completer meaning to the law of evolution, the Occult philosophy entirely eliminates the "missing links" of modern science, and, by giving to man a glimpse of his nature and destiny, not only points out the line of the higher evolution, but puts him in possession of the means of achieving it.

The "atoms" and "monads" of the Secret Doctrine are very different from the atoms and molecules of modern science. To the latter these are mere particles of matter endowed with blind force: to the former, they are the "dark nucleoles," and potentially "Gods," conscious and intelligent from their primeval embodiment at the beginning of differentiation in the dawn of the Manvantara. There are no longer any hard and fast lines between the "organic" and the "inorganic"; between the "living" and "dead" matter. Every atom is endowed with and moved by intelligence, and is conscious in its own degree, on its own plane of development. This is a glimpse of the *One Life* that —

> Runs through all time, extends through all extent,
> Lives undivided, operates unspent.

It may be conceived that the "Ego" in man is a monad that has gathered to itself innumerable experiences through aeons of time, slowly unfolding its latent potencies through plane after plane of matter. It is hence called the *"eternal pilgrim."*

The *Manasic*, or mind principle, is cosmic and universal. It is the creator of all forms, and the basis of all law in nature. Not so with consciousness. Consciousness is a condition of the monad as the result of embodiment in matter and the dwelling in a physical form. Self-consciousness, which from the animal plane looking upward is the beginning of perfection, from the divine plane looking downward is the perfection of selfishness and the curse of separateness. It is the "world of illusion" that man has created for himself. "Maya is the perceptive faculty of every Ego which considers itself a Unit, separate from and independent of the One Infinite and Eternal Sat or 'be-ness'." The "eternal pilgrim" must therefore mount higher, and flee from the plane of self-consciousness it has struggled so hard to reach.

The complex structure that we call "Man" is made up of a congeries of almost innumerable "Lives." Not only every microscopic cell of which the tissues are composed, but the molecules and atoms of which these cells are composed, are permeated with the essence of the "One Life." Every so-called organic cell is known to have its nucleus, a center of finer or more sensitive matter. The nutritive, all the formative and functional processes consist of flux and re-flux, of inspiration and expiration, to and from the nucleus.

The nucleus is therefore in its own degree and after its kind a "monad" imprisoned in a "form". Every microscopic cell, therefore, has a consciousness and an intelligence of its own, and man thus consists of innumerable "lives". This is but physiological synthesis, logically deduced no less from the known facts in physiology and histology than the logical sequence of the philosophy of occultism. Health of the body as a whole depends on the integrity of all its parts, and more especially upon their harmonious association and cooperation. A diseased tissue is one in which a group of individual cells refuse to cooperate, and wherein is set up discordant action, using less or claiming more than their due share of food or energy. Disease of the very tissue of man's body is neither more nor less than the "sin of separateness." Moreover, the grouping of cells is upon the principle of hierarchies. Smaller groups are subordinate to larger congeries, and these again are subordinate to larger, or to the whole. Every microscopic cell therefore typifies and epitomizes man, as man is an epitome of the Universe. As already remarked, the "Eternal Pilgrim", the Alter-Ego in man, is a monad progressing through the ages. By right and by endowment the ego is king in the domain of man's bodily life. It descended into matter in the cosmic process till it reached the mineral plane, and then journeyed upward through the "three kingdoms" till it reached the human plane.

The elements of its being, like the cells and molecules of man's body, are groupings of structures accessory or subordinate to it. The human monad or Ego is therefore akin to all below it and heir to all above it, linked by indissoluble bonds to spirit and matter, "God" and "Nature". The attributes that it gathers, and the faculties that it unfolds, are but the latent and dormant potentialities awaking to conscious life. The tissue cells constitute man's bodily structure, but the order in which they are arranged, the principle upon which they are grouped, constituting the human *form*, is not simply an evolved shape from the lower animal plane, but an *involved* principle from a higher plane, an older world, *viz.* the "Lunar Pitris". "Hanuman the Monkey" antedates Darwin's "missing link" by thousands of millenniums. So also the *Manasic*, or mind element, with its cosmic and infinite potentialities, is not merely the developed "instinct" of the animal. *Mind* is the latent or active potentiality of *Cosmic Ideation*, the essence of every form, the basis of every law, the potency of every principle in the universe. Human thought is the reflection or reproduction in the realm of man's consciousness of these forms, laws, and principles. Hence man senses and apprehends nature just as nature unfolds in him. When, therefore, the Monad has passed through the form of the animal ego, involved and unfolded the human form, the higher triad of principles awakens from the sleep of ages, over-shadowed by the "Manasa-putra" and *built into* its essence and substance. How could man epitomize Cosmos if he did not touch it at every point and involve it in every principle? If man's being is woven in the web of destiny, his potencies and possibilities take hold of divinity as the woof and pattern of his boundless life. Why, then, should he grow weary or disheartened? Alas! why should he be degraded, this heir of all things!

> The peculiarity also of this theology, and in which its transcendency consists, is this, that it does not consider the highest God to be the principle of beings, but the *principle of principles*, i.e. of deiform processions from itself, all which are eternally rooted in the

unfathomable depths of the immensely great source of
their existence, and of which they may be called
supersensuous ramifications and superluminous
blossoms.

Introduction to   THOMAS TAYLOR
Mystical Hymns of Orpheus

III

It has often been thought a strange thing that there are no
dogmas and no creed in Theosophy or Occultism. Is theosophy a
religion? is often asked. No, it is *religion.* Is it a *philosophy?* No, it is
philosophy. Is it a science? No, it is *science.* If a consensus of religion,
philosophy, and science is possible, and if it has ever been reached
in human thought, that thought must long since have passed the
boundaries of all creeds and ceased to dogmatize. Hence comes
the difficulty in answering questions. No proposition stands apart
or can be taken separately without limiting and often distorting
its meaning. Every proposition has to be considered and held as
subservient to the synthetic whole. Really intelligent people,
capable of correct reasoning, often lack sufficient interest to
endeavor to apprehend the universality of these principles. They
expect, where they have any interest at all in the subject, to be
told "all about it" in an hour's conversation, or to learn it from a
column in some newspaper; all about man, all about Nature, all
about Deity; and then either to reject it or to make it a part of
their previous creed. These are really no wiser than the penny-a-
liner who catches some point and turns it into ridicule, or makes
it a butt for coarse jest or silly sarcasm, and then complacently
imagines that he has demolished the whole structure! If such
persons were for one moment placed face to face with their own
folly, they would be amazed. The most profound thinker and the
most correct reasoner might well afford to devote a life-time to
the apprehension of the philosophy of occultism, and other lifetimes to mastering the scientific details, while at the same time
his ethics and his religious life are made consistent with the

principle of altruism and the Brotherhood of man. If this be regarded as too hard a task, it is, nevertheless, the line of the higher evolution of man, and, soon or late, every soul must follow it, retrograde, or cease to be.

Man is but a link in an endless chain of being; a sequence of a past eternity of causes and processes; a potentiality born into time, but spanning two eternities, his past and his future, and in his consciousness these are all one, *Duration,* the *ever-present.* In a former article man was shown to be a series of almost innumerable "Lives", and these lives, these living entities called "cells", were shown to be associated together on the principle of hierarchies, grouped according to rank and order, service and development, and this was shown to be the "physical synthesis" of man, and the organic synthesis as well. Disease was also shown to be the organic nutritive, or physiological "sin of separateness". Every department of man's being, every organ and cell of his body, was also shown to possess a consciousness and an intelligence of its own, held, however, subordinate to the whole. In health every action is synchronous and rhythmical, however varied and expanded, however intense and comprehensive. Enough is already known in modern physics to justify all these statements, at least by analogy. The principle of electrical induction and vibration, the quantitative and qualitative transmission of vibration and its exact registration, and their application to telegraphy, the telephone, and the phonograph, have upset all previous theories of physics and physiology. "A metallic plate, for instance, can that talk like a human being? Yea or nay? Mr. Bouillard — and he was no common man — said No; to accept such a fact were to upset all our notions of physiology. So said Mr. Bouillard, right in the face of Edison's phonograph in full Academy, and he throttled the luckless interpreter of the famous American inventor, accusing it of ventriloquism." *

Occultism teaches that the Ego both precedes and survives the physical body. The phenomena of man's life and the process

* Dr. J. Oehorowicz, "Mental Suggestion", p. 291.

of his thought can be apprehended and explained on no other theory. Modern physiology teaches in detail certain facts regarding the life of man. It, moreover, groups these facts and deduces certain so-called principles and laws, but such a thing as a synthesis of the whole man is seldom even attempted. "Psychology" is mere empiricism, represented by disjointed facts, and these, of course, but little understood, and more often misinterpreted.

Ask the modern physiologist if man can think when unconscious, and he will answer No; and if asked if man can be conscious and not think, he will as readily answer No. Both answers will be based on what is known, or supposed to be known, of memory. The idea that the real man, the Ego, is always conscious on some plane, and that it "thinks", as we ordinarily use the term, only on the lower plane through the physical brain, in terms of extension and duration, or space and time, is seldom in the least apprehended by the modern physiologist. If, however, one grasps the idea of the ego as the real man dwelling in the physical body and using it as its instrument through which it is related to space and time, perception, sensation, thought, and feeling, the gaps in physiology and psychology begin to disappear. Here again it should be particularly borne in mind that this doctrine of the ego must be considered in the light of the complete synthesis of occultism, and just to the extent that this is intelligently done will the significance of the ego appear.

The brief and concise outline of the philosophy of occultism given in the Introduction to *The Secret Doctrine* is therefore very significant, and the student who desires to apprehend that which follows in these two large volumes ought to study this outline very carefully. No subsequent proposition, no principle in the life of man, can be correctly understood apart from it. The subject-matter following is necessarily fragmentary, but the outline is both inclusive and philosophical, and if one reasons logically and follows the plainest analogies he can never go far astray. The relation of mind to brain, of thought to consciousness, of life to matter, and of man to Nature and to Deity, is there clearly defined; not, indeed, in all its details, but in a philosophical modulus, to be worked out in reason and in life. The all-pervading Life, the cyclic or periodical movements, the periods of action and of repose, and the intimate relations and inter-dependences of all things apply to Cosmos, and equally to every atom in its vast embrace.

Students sometimes complain that they cannot understand, that the subject is so vast, and so deep and intricate, and not made clear. It is because they do not realize what they have undertaken. Occultism can neither be taught nor learned in "a few easy lessons." The "object lessons" sometimes given by H.P.B., almost always misunderstood and misapplied, though often explained at the time, served as often to excite vulgar curiosity and personal abuse as to arrest attention and study. If, before the advent of the T.S. in the face of the creeds of Christendom, the materialism of science, the indifferences and supercilious scorn of Agnosticism, and the babel of spiritualism, it had been proposed to begin at the foundations and reconstruct our entire knowledge of Nature and of man; to show the unity and the foundations of the world's religions; to eliminate from science all its "missing links"; to make Agnosticism gnostic; and to place the science of psychology and the nature and laws of mind and soul over against "Mediumship"; it would have been held as an herculean task, and declared impossible of accomplishment. Now that the thing has virtually been accomplished and this body of knowledge presented to the world, people think it strange that they cannot compass it all, as the poet Burns is said to have written some of his shorter poems, "while standing on one leg!"

Again, people complain at the unfamiliar terms and the strange words imported from foreign languages. Yet if one were to undertake the study of physics, chemistry, music, or medicine, quite as great obstacles have to be overcome. Is it a strange thing, then, that the science that includes all these, and undertakes to give a synthesis of the whole realm of Nature and of life, should have its own nomenclature?

Beyond all these necessary and natural obstacles, there is another, *viz.*, that contentious spirit that disputes and opposes every point before it is fairly stated or understood. Suppose one ignorant of mathematics were to proceed in the same manner and say, "I don't *like* that proposition," "I don't see *why* they turn a six upside down to make a nine," "Why don't two and two make five?", and so on, how long would it take such a one to learn mathematics? In the study of the Secret Doctrine it is not a matter of likes or dislikes, of belief or unbelief, but solely a matter of intelligence and understanding. He who acknowledges his ignorance and yet is unwilling to lay aside his likes and dislikes, and even his creeds and dogmas, for the time, in order to see what is presented in its own light and purely on its merits, has neither need nor use for the Secret Doctrine. Even where a greater number of propositions are accepted or "believed" and a few are rejected, the synthetic whole is entirely lost sight of. But, says some one, this is a plea for blind credulity, and an attempt to bind the mind and the conscience of man to a blind acceptance of these doctrines. No one but the ignorant or the dishonest can make such an assertion in the face of the facts. Listen to the following from p. xix, Introduction to *The Secret Doctrine*. "It is above everything important to keep in mind that no theosophical book acquires the least additional value from pretended authority." If that be advocating blind credulity, let the enemies of the T.S. make the most of it. If any authority pertains to *The Secret Doctrine*, it must be sought inside, not outside. It must rest on its comprehensiveness, its completeness, its continuity and reasonableness; in other words, on its *philosophical synthesis,* a thing missed alike by the superficial and the contentious, by the indolent, the superstitious, and the dogmatic.

> O wise man: you have asked rightly. Now listen carefully. The illusive fancies arising from error are not conclusive.
>
> The great and peaceful ones live regenerating the world like the coming of spring, and after having themselves crossed the ocean of embodied existence, help those who try to do the same thing, without personal motives.
>
> *Crest Jewel of Wisdom*

IV

In the foregoing articles, necessarily brief and fragmentary, a few points have been given to show the general bearing of *The Secret Doctrine* on all problems in Nature and in Life.

Synthesis is the very essence of philosophy — "the combination of separate elements of thought into a whole" — the opposite of analysis, and analysis is the very essence of science.

In the "Outline of the Secret Doctrine" by "C.J.," now running through the pages of *Lucifer,* this philosophy or synthesis of the whole is made very clear.

There have been many *philosophizers* in modern times, but there can be but one philosophy, one synthesis of the *whole* of Eternal Nature. With the single exception of the writings of Plato, no one in modern times had given to the Western world any approximation to a complete philosophy, previous to the appearance of H.P. Blavatsky's *Secret Doctrine.* The writings of Plato are carefully veiled in the symbolical language of initiation. *The Secret Doctrine,* coming more than two millenniums later, and in an age of so-called Science, is addressed to the Scientific thought of the age, and hence considers the whole subject largely from the stand-point of Science. The present age is as deficient in philosophy as was the age of Plato in knowledge of science. It follows, therefore, that while the Secret Doctrine itself apprehends equally both philosophy and science, in addressing itself to the thought of an age it must recognize here, as it does everywhere, the *law of cycles* that rules in the intellectual development of a race no less than in the revolutions of suns and worlds, and so address the times from that plane of thought that is in the ascendant. It is just because analytical thought is in the ascendant, because it is the *thought-form* of the age, that the great majority of readers are likely to overlook the broad synthesis and so miss the philosophy of the Secret Doctrine. The only object of these brief and fragmentary papers has been to call attention to this point.

We are now in a transition period, and in the approaching

twentieth century there will be a revival of genuine philosophy, and the Secret Doctrine will be the basis of the "New Philosophy." Science today, in the persons of such advanced students as Keely, Crookes, Lodge, Richardson, and many others, already treads so close to the borders of occult philosophy that it will not be possible to prevent the new age from entering the occult realm. H. P. Blavatsky's *Secret Doctrine* is a storehouse of scientific facts, but this is not its chief value. These facts are placed, approximately at least, in such relation to the synthesis or philosophy of occultism as to render comparatively easy the task of the student who is in search of real knowledge, and to further his progress beyond all preconception, provided he is teachable, in earnest, and intelligent. Nowhere else in English literature is the Law of Evolution given such sweep and swing. It reminds one of the ceaseless under-tone of the deep sea, and seems to view our Earth in all its changes "from the birth of time to the crack of doom." It follows man in his triple evolution, physical, mental, and spiritual, throughout the perfect circle of his boundless life. Darwinism had reached its limits and a rebound. Man is indeed evolved from lower forms. But *which* man? the physical? the psychical? the intellectual? or the spiritual? The Secret Doctrine points where the lines of evolution and involution meet; where matter and spirit clasp hands; and where the rising animal stands face to face with the fallen god; for *all natures* meet and mingle in man.

Judge no proposition of the Secret Doctrine as though it stood alone, for not one stands alone. Not "independence" here more than with the units that constitute Humanity. It is *interdependence* everywhere; in nature, as in life.

Even members of the T.S. have often wondered why H.P.B. and others well known in the Society lay so much stress on doctrines like Karma and Reincarnation. It is not alone because these doctrines are easily apprehended and beneficent to individuals, not only because they furnish, as they necessarily do, a solid foundation for ethics, or all human conduct, but because they are the very key-notes of the higher evolution of man. Without Karma and Reincarnation evolution is but a fragment; a process whose beginnings are unknown, and whose outcome cannot be discerned; a glimpse of what might be; a hope of what should be. But in the light of Karma and Reincarnation evolution becomes the logic of what *must* be. The links in the chain of being are all filled in, and the circles of reason and of life are complete. Karma gives the eternal law of action, and Reincarnation furnishes the boundless field for its display. Thousands of persons can understand these two principles, apply them as a basis of conduct, and weave them into the fabric of their lives, who may not be able to grasp the complete synthesis of that endless evolution of which these doctrines form so important a part. In thus affording even the superficial thinker and the weak or illogical reasoner a perfect basis for ethics and an unerring guide in life, Theosophy is building toward the future realization of the Universal Brotherhood and the higher evolution of man. But few in this generation realize the work that is thus undertaken, or how much has already been accomplished. The obscurity of the present age in regard to genuine philosophical thought is nowhere more apparent than in the manner in which opposition has been waged toward these doctrines of Karma and Reincarnation. In the seventeen years since the Theosophical movement has been before the world there has not appeared, from any source, a serious and logical attempt to discredit these doctrines from a philosophical basis. There have been denial, ridicule, and denunciation *ad nauseum*. There could be no discussion from such a basis, for from the very beginning these doctrines have been put forth and advocated from the logical and dispassionate plane of philosophy. Ridicule is both unanswerable and unworthy of answer. It is not the argument, but the atmosphere of weak minds, born of prejudice and ignorance.

The synthesis of occultism is therefore the philosophy of Nature and of Life; the full — or free — truth that apprehends every scientific fact in the light of the unerring process of Eternal Nature.

The time must presently come when the really advanced thinkers of the age will be compelled to lay by their indifference, and their scorn and conceit, and follow the lines of philosophical investigation laid down in *The Secret Doctrine.* Very few seem yet to have realized how ample are these resources, because it involves a process of thought almost unknown to the present age of empiricism and induction. It is a revelation from archaic ages, indestructible and eternal, yet capable of being obscured and lost; capable of being again and again reborn, or like man himself — reincarnated.

> He who lives in one color of the rainbow is blind to the rest. Live in the Light diffused through the entire arc, and you will know it all.
>
> *The Path*

> He who knows not the common things of life is a beast among men. He who knows only the common things of life is a man among beasts. He who knows all that can be learned by diligent inquiry is a god among men.
>
> PLATO

The Path, November 1891,   W. Q. JUDGE
February, March & May, 1892

UNITY AND DIFFERENTIATION

It is a trite axiom that truth exists independent of human error, and he who would know the truth must rise up to its level and not try the ridiculous task of dragging it down to his own standard. Every metaphysician knows that Absolute Truth is the eternal Reality which survives all the transient phenomena. The preface to the *Isis Unveiled* expresses the idea very clearly when it says: — "Man and parties, sects and schools are but the mere ephemera of the world's day. TRUTH, high-seated upon its rock of adamant, is alone eternal and supreme." Language belongs to the world of relativity, while Truth is the Absolute Reality. It is therefore vain to suppose that any language, however ancient or sublime, can express Abstract Truth. The latter exists in the world of ideas, and the ideal can be perceived by the sense belonging to that world. . . . Words can merely clothe the ideas, but no number of words can convey an idea to one who is incapable of perceiving it. Every one of us has within him the latent capacity or a sense dormant in us which can take cognizance of Abstract Truth, although the development of that sense or, more correctly speaking, the assimilation of our intellect with that higher sense, may vary in different persons, according to circumstances, education and discipline. That higher sense which is the potential capacity of every human being is in eternal contact with Reality, and every one of us has experienced moments when, being for the time *en rapport* with that higher sense, we realize the eternal verities. The sole question is how to focalize ourselves entirely in that higher sense. Directly we realize this truth, we are brought face to face with occultism.

Occultism teaches its votaries what sort of training will bring on such a development. It never dogmatizes, but only recommends certain methods which the experience of ages has proved to be the best suited to the purpose. But just as the harmony of nature consists in symphonious discord, so also the harmony of occult training (in other words, individual human progress) consists in discord of details. The scope of Occultism being a study of Nature, both in its phenomenal and noumenal aspects, its organization is in exact harmony with the plan of Nature. Different constitutions require different details in training, and different men can better grasp the idea clothed in different expressions. This necessity has given rise to different schools of Occultism, whose scope and ideal is the same, but whose modes of expression and methods of procedure differ. Nay, even the students of the same school have not necessarily a uniformity of training. This will show why it is that until a certain stage is reached, the *Chela* is generally left to himself, and why he is never given verbal or written instructions regarding the truths of Nature. It will also suggest the meaning of the neophyte being made to undergo a particular kind of sleep for a certain period before each initiation. And his success or failure depends upon his capacity for the assimilation of the Abstract Truth his higher sense perceives. However, just as unity is the ultimate possibility of Nature, so there is a certain school of Occultism which deals only with the synthetic process, and to which all the other schools, dealing with analytical methods wherein alone can diversity exist, owe their allegiance.

A careful reader will thus perceive the absurdity of a dogmatism which claims for its methods a universal application. What is therefore meant by the Adwaitee Philosophy being identical with the Arhat Doctrine, is that the final goal or the ultimate possibility of both is the same. The synthetical process is one, for it deals only with eternal verities, the Abstract Truth, the noumenal. And these two philosophies are put forth together, for in their analytical methods they proceed on parallel lines, one proceeding from the subjective and the other from the objective standpoint, to meet ultimately or rather converge together in one point or centre. As such, each is the complement of the other and neither can be said to be complete in itself. It should be distinctly remembered here that the Adwaitee Doctrine does not date from Shankaracharya, nor does the Arhat Philosophy owe its origin to Gautama Buddha. They were but the latest expounders of these two systems which have existed from time immemorial as they must. Some natures can better comprehend the truth from a subjective standpoint, while others must proceed from the objective. These two systems are therefore as old as Occultism itself, while the later phases of the Esoteric Doctrine are but another aspect of either of these two, the details being modified according to the comprehensive faculties of the people addressed, as also the other surrounding circumstances.

Attempts at a revival of the knowledge of this Truth have been numberless, and therefore to suggest that the present is the first attempt in the world's history is an error which those whose sense has just been awakened to the glorious Reality are apt to commit. It has already been stated that the diffusion of knowledge is not limited to one process. The possessors of it have never jealously guarded it from any personal or selfish motives. In fact such a frame of mind precludes the possibility of the attainment of knowledge. They have at every opportunity tried all available means to give its benefit to humanity. Times there were undoubtedly when they had to rest content with giving it only to a few chosen pupils, who, it should be remembered, differ from ordinary humanity only in one essential particular, and that is, that by abnormal training they bring on a process of self-evolution in a comparatively very short period, which ordinary humanity may require numberless ages to reach during the ordinary course of evolution.

Those who are acquainted with the history of Count de St. Germain and the works of the late Lord Bulwer Lytton, need not be told that even during the past hundred years constant efforts have been made to awaken the present races to a sense of the knowledge which will assist their progress and ensure future happiness. It should not be forgotten, moreover, that to spread a knowledge of philosophical truths forms but a small fraction of the important work the occultists are engaged in. Whenever circumstances compel them to be shut out from the world's view, they are most actively engaged in so arranging and guiding the current of events, sometimes by influencing people's minds, at others by bringing about, as far as practicable, such combinations of forces as would give rise to a higher form of evolution and such other important work on a spiritual plane. They have to do and are doing that work now. Little therefore do the public know what in reality it is that they ask for when they apply for *Chelaship*. They have to thus pledge themselves to assist the MAHATMAS in that spiritual work by the process of self-evolution, for the energy, expended by them in the act of self-purification, has a dynamic effect and produces grand results on a spiritual plane. Moreover, they gradually fit themselves to take an active share in the grand work. It may perhaps be now apparent why "THE ADEPT BECOMES; HE IS NOT MADE," and why he is the "rare efflorescence of the age."...

The great difficulty which an ordinarily philosophic mind has to contend against is the idea that consciousness and intelligence proceed out of non-consciousness and non-intelligence. Although an abstruse metaphysical intellect can comprehend or rather perceive the point subjectively, the present undeveloped state of humanity, at any rate, can conceive the higher truths only from an objective standpoint. Just as, therefore, we are obliged to talk of the setting of the sun, in common parlance, although we know that it is not the movement of the sun that we really refer to, and just as in the geocentric system we have to speak as though the earth were a fixed point in the centre of the universe so that the unripe mind of the student may understand our teachings, so in the same manner the Abstract Truth has to be presented from an objective point of view, so that it may be more easily comprehended by minds with not a very keen metaphysical intellect. Thus one may say that Buddhism is rational Vedantism, while Vedantism is transcendental Buddhism...

The one Life permeates ALL. Here it may be added that consciousness and intelligence also permeate ALL. These three are inherent potentially everywhere. But we do not talk of the life of a mineral, nor of its consciousness or intelligence. These exist in it only potentially. The differentiation which results in individualization is not yet complete. A piece of gold, silver, copper or any other metal, or a piece of rock, etc., has no sense of separate existence, because the mineral monad is not individualized. It is only in the animal kingdom that a sense of personality begins to be formed. But for all that, an occultist will not say that life, consciousness or intelligence do not potentially exist in the minerals. Thus it will be seen that although consciousness and intelligence exist everywhere, all objects are not conscious or intelligent. The latent potentiality when developed to the stage of individualization by the Law of Cosmic Evolution separates the subject from the object, or rather the subject falls into *Upadhi* and a state of personal consciousness or intelligence is realized. But the absolute consciousness and intelligence which has no *Upadhi* cannot be conscious or intelligent for there is no duality, nothing to wake intelligence or to be conscious of. Hence the *Upanishads* say that *Parabrahm* has no consciousness, no intelligence, for these states can be cognized by us only on account of our individualization, while we can have, from our differentiated and personal state, no conception of the undifferentiated, non-dualistic consciousness or intelligence. If there were no consciousness or intelligence in Nature, it were absurd to talk of the Law of Karma or every cause producing its corresponding effect.

The MAHATMA, in one of the letters published in *The Occult World,* says that matter is indestructible, but enquires whether the modern Scientist can tell why it is that Nature *consciously* prefers that matter should remain indestructible under organic rather than inorganic form. This is a very suggestive idea in regard to the subject under notice. At the beginning of our studies we are apt to be misled by the supposition that our earth, or the planetary chain, or the solar system, constitutes infinity and that eternity can be measured by numbers. Often and often have the MAHATMAS warned us against this error, and yet we do, now and then, try to limit the infinity to our standard instead of endeavouring to expand ourselves to its conception. This has led some naturally to a sense of isolation, and to forget that the same Law of Cosmic Evolution which has brought us to our present stage of individual differentiation is tending to lead us gradually to the original undifferentiated condition. Such allow themselves to be imbued so much with a sense of personality that they try to rebel against the idea of Absolute Unity.

Forcing themselves thus in a state of isolation, they endeavour to ride the Cosmic Law which must have its course: and the natural result is annihilation through the throes of disintegration. This it is which constitutes the bridge, the dangerous point in evolution referred to by Mr. Sinnett in his *Esoteric Buddhism*. And this is why selfishness, which is the result of a strong sense of personality, is detrimental to spiritual progress. This it is that constitutes the difference between white and black magic. And it is this tendency to which reference is made when talking of the end of a Race. At this period, the whole humanity splits up into two classes, the Adepts of the good Law and the Sorcerers (or *Dugpas*). To that period we are fast rushing; and to save humanity from a cataclysm which must overtake those who go against the purposes of Nature, the MAHATMAS, who are working with her, are endeavouring to spread knowledge in a manner to prevent its abuse as far as possible.

We should therefore constantly remember that the present is not the apex of evolution, and that if we would not be annihilated, we must not allow ourselves to be influenced by a sense of personal isolation and consequent worldly vanities and shows. This world does not constitute infinity, nor does our solar system, nor does the immeasurable expanse our physical senses can take cognizance of. All these and more are but an infinitesimal atom of the Absolute Infinity. The idea of personality is limited to our physical senses which, belonging as they do to the *Rupa Loka* (world of forms), must perish, since we see no permanent form anywhere. All is liable to change, and the more we live in transient personality, the more we incur the danger of final death, or total annihilation.

It is only the seventh principle, the *Adi Buddha*, that is the

Absolute Reality. The objective standpoint, however, adds further that *Dharma*, the vehicle of the seventh principle or its Upadhi, is co-existent with its Lord and Master, the *Adi Buddha*, because it says nothing can come out of nothing. A more correct form of expressing the idea would be that in the state of *Pralaya* the sixth principle exists in the seventh as an eternal potentiality to be manifested during the period of cosmic activity. Viewed in this light both the seventh and the sixth principles are Eternal Realities, although it would be more correct to say that the seventh principle is the only Reality, since it remains immutable both during cosmic activity as also during cosmic rest, while the sixth principle, the Upadhi, although absorbed into the seventh during *Pralaya*, is changing during Manvantara, first differentiating to return to its undifferentiated condition as the time for *Pralaya* approaches. . . .

Now the Vedantin doctrine says that *Parabrahm* is the *Absolute Reality* which never changes and is thus identical with the *Adi Buddha* of the Arhats, while *Mulaprakriti* is that aspect of *Parabrahm* which at the time of *Manvantara* emanates from itself *Purusha* and *Prakriti*, and which thus undergoes change during the period of cosmic activity. As *Purusha* is force, which remains immutable throughout, it is that aspect of *Mulaprakriti* which is identical with *Parabrahm*. Hence it is that *Purusha* is said to be the same as *Parabrahm*, or the *Absolute Reality*, while *Prakriti*, the differentiated cosmic matter, constantly undergoes change, and is thus impermanent, forming the basis of phenomenal evolution. This is a purely subjective standpoint from which Mr. Subba Row was arguing with the late Swami of Almora who professed to be an Adwaitee. A careful reader will thus perceive that there is no contradiction involved in Mr. Subba Row's statements, when he says from the objective standpoint that *Mulaprakriti* and *Purusha* are eternal, and when again from a subjective standpoint he says that *Purusha* is the only eternal Reality. His critic has unconsciously mixed up the two standpoints by culling extracts from two different articles written from two different points of view and imagines that Mr. Subba Row has made an error.

Attention must now be turned to the idea of the *Dhyan*

Chohans. It has been already stated above that the sixth and the seventh principles are the same in all, and this idea will be clear to everyone who reads carefully the foregoing remarks. It has also been added that the sixth principle, being a differentiation of *Mulaprakriti*, is personal, however exalted and ubiquitous that personality may be. In the Adwaitee Philosophy the *Dhyan Chohans* correspond to *Iswara*, the Demiurgos. There is no *conscious Iswara outside* of the 7th principle of Maya as vulgarly understood. This was the idea Mr. Subba Row meant to convey when he said: "expressions implying the existence of a conscious *Iswara* which are to be found here and there in the Upanishads, are not to be literally construed." Mr. Subba Row's statement is therefore neither "perfectly inexplicable," nor "audacious," as it is consistent with the teaching of Shankaracharya.

The *Dhyan Chohans*, who represent the aggregate cosmic intelligence, are the immediate artificers of the worlds, and are thus identical with *Iswara* or the Demiurgic Mind. But their consciousness and intelligence, pertaining as they do to the sixth and the seventh states of matter, are such as we cannot cognize, so long as we prefer to remain in our isolation and do not transfer our individuality to the sixth and the seventh principles. As artificers of the worlds, they are the primary principle of the Universe, although they are at the same time the *result* of Cosmic Evolution. It is an incorrect understanding of the consciousness of *Dhyan Chohans* that has given rise to the current vulgar notion of God. Little do the dogmatic theists realize that it is within their power to become *Dhyan Chohans* or *Iswara*, or at least they have the latent potentiality in them to rise to that spiritual eminence if they will but work *with* Nature. They know not themselves, and thus allow themselves to be carried away and buried under a sense of personal isolation, looking upon Nature as something apart from themselves. They thus isolate themselves from the *spirit* of Nature, which is the only eternal Absolute Reality and hurry towards their own disintegration. . . .

Speaking from a subjective standpoint, to talk of locality and time is absurd, since the latter are mere relative terms and as such restricted only to the phenomenal. Abstract space and eternity are indivisible; and therefore to try to fix time and place, as though they were absolute realities, is neither metaphysical nor philosophical. However, an objective standpoint is essential, as has been already pointed out. In the economy of Nature, everything is right in its place, and to ignore a certain plane is just as illogical as to over-estimate it. True knowledge consists in a right sense of discrimination: to be able to perceive what phenomenon performs what function, and how to utilize it for human progress and happiness. Both the objective and subjective standpoints, as much as the inductive and deductive methods, are therefore essential for the attainment of *true* knowledge which is *true* power. . . .

A few words may now be said in connection with the idea of *Buddha*. When Mr. Subba Row talks of the historical aspect of Buddha, he probably refers to *Gautama Buddha*, who was an historical personage. It must, of course, at the same time be remembered that every entity that identifies itself with that ray of the Divine wisdom which is represented by Gautama, is a Buddha; and thus it will be evident that there can be but one Buddha at a time, the highest type of that particular ray of Adeptship.

The Theosophist, May 1884   D.K. MAVALANKAR

ARUPA BRAHMA

Rama said: You have declared the mind to be a pure essence, unconnected with this earth or matter, and verily Brahmā itself.

Tell me, O Brahmin, why remembrance of former births is not the cause of Brahmā's birth, as it is with you and me.

Vasishtha replied: Whoever has had a body accompanied by acts in a prior existence retains its reminiscence, and this is the cause of rebirth.

But Brahmā is known to have had no prior acts and thus cannot have any reminiscence.

Existing by its own mind alone, Divine Spirit is Self-born and is its own cause.

Everlasting, with body born of itself from the Self-existent Brahman, the Self-born Brahmā has no body except the subtle *ativahika*.

Rama said: The everlasting subtle body or *sukshma sarira* and the mortal body or *sthula deha* are distinct. Do all created beings have a subtle body like that of Brahmā?

Vasishtha replied: All beings produced by a cause have *sukshma* and *sthula* bodies. But the Unborn Causeless has only one body —the *ativahika* or everlasting spiritual body.

The uncreated Brahmā, the cause of all created beings, having no cause of itself, has only one body.

The prime Lord of creatures has no material body but manifests in the aerial forms of his spiritual body.

This body, composed of mind alone, is without contact with earth or matter. From it the first Lord spreads forth the world.

All creatures are but forms of the ideas in that mind, being without other basis and coeval in essence with their cause.

That uncreated Being of perfect intelligence is purely of the form of mind, having intellectual but not material body.

This First Cause of all productions in the material world is Self-born through the prime moving force in the form of mind.

By the first impulse of that force the expanse of creation was spread out, as wind and wave move in proportion to the impetus they receive.

This shining creation, brilliant to sight, derives its light from the luminous mind of *Arupa* Brahmā, and appears real only to our conception.

As in a dream vision of enjoyment of connubial bliss, unreal objects of desire present themselves as actualities to our false and fond imagination.

The empty, immaterial and formless Spirit is represented as the Self-born manifest Lord of creatures, existing in the form of the First Male.

Undiscerned as pure intelligence, It manifests to all by the evolution of its volition. Indistinct as absolute rest, It is resplendent in the display of its nature.

Brahmā is the divine power of volition and is personified as the Protogonos devoid of material body. Purely of the form of mind, it is the sole cause of the triple worlds.

Its volition produces the exertion of the energies of the Self-born, just as human desires impel mankind to action and the vacuous mind manifests as a mountain of desires.

Forgetting its everlasting and incorporeal nature, it assumes a solid material body, showing itself as delusive appearances.

But Brahmā of unsullied understanding is not involved in self-oblivion by transformation from the *nirguna* to the *saguna* state.

Unborn of matter, Brahmā sees no apparition, unlike those exposed by their ignorance to misleading errors of falsehood looming as mirages before them.

Brahmā is purely of the form of mind, and not composed of matter. The world as the product of Eternal Mind is of the same nature as its archetype.

Just as the uncreated Brahmā is without secondary cause, so the creation is without any cause but Brahmā.

There is no difference of product and producer, for works are as perfect as their authors.

No cause and effect are to be found within this creation, because the three worlds are but prototypes of the archetype of Divine Mind.

Stretched out upon the model of Divine Mind, and unformed by any other spirit, the world is immanent in that Mind like fluidity in water.

Mind spins out the extended unreality of the world like a castle in the air or a utopian city.

There is no materiality. It is as false as the snake in the rope. Hence it is in no way possible for Brahmā or other things to exist as individual bodies.

Even spiritual bodies are non-existent to those of enlightened understanding. Material bodies are totally unreal.

Man or *manu* derives from *manas* and is a form of the volitional soul *virinchi* with dominion over the mental world — *manorajyam*.

Manas is Brahmā called *virinchi* by the exercise of its inherent *sankalpa sisriksha* or incipient creative volition. It displays itself as the visible world through development of its own essence.

This *virinchi*, or creative power, and *manas* are consubstantial and unconnected with matter which is a mere creation of fancy.

All visible things are contained in the bosom of mind, just as the lotus bud and blossom reside in the lotus seed. Hence the mental and visible existence of things are the same.

The objects of your dreams, the desires of your heart, the ideals of your imagination, together with your ideas, notions and impressions of visible things — know them all to be within the receptacle of mind.

But visible things bound up with mental desire are as baneful to their beholder as an apparition to a child.

The ideal origin of phenomena develops itself like the germ in the seed which becomes a great tree.

Without reliance on the Self, there can be no peace with phenomena full of troubles, nor solace for the mind. The feeling of perception of visibles will never be lost to the perceiver. Abstraction from it alone is liberation.

Yoga Vasishtha Maharamayana Utpatti Khanda, III   RISHI VASISHTHA

The great and peaceful ones live regenerating the world like the coming of spring; having crossed the ocean of embodied existence themselves, they freely aid all others who seek to cross it. The very essence and inherent will of Mahatmas is to remove the suffering of others, just as the ambrosia-rayed moon of itself cools the earth heated by the intense rays of the sun.

SHANKARACHARYA

EVOLUTIONARY PROGRESS

Two factors must be kept in view — (a) a fixed period, and (b) a fixed rate of development nicely adjusted to it. Almost unthinkably long as is a *mahayug*, it is still a definite term, and within it must be accomplished the whole order of development, or to state it in occult phraseology, the descent of Spirit into matter and its return to the re-emergence. A chain of beads, and each bead a world is an illustration already made familiar to you. You have already pondered over the life impulse beginning with each *manvantara* to evolve the first of these worlds; to perfect it; to people it successively with all the aerial forms of life. And after completing on this first world seven cycles — or evolutions of development — in each kingdom, as you know — passing forward down the arc — to similarly evolve the next world in the chain, perfect it, and abandon it. Then to the next and next and next — until the sevenfold round of world-evolutions along the chain is run through and the *mahayug* comes to its end. Then chaos *again* — the *pralaya*. As this life-impulse (at the seventh and last round from planet to planet) moves on it leaves behind it dying and — very soon — 'dead planets'.

The last seventh Round man having passed on to a subsequent world, the precedent one with all its mineral, vegetable and animal life (except man) begins to gradually die out, when with the exit of the last *animalcula* it is extinguished, or as H.P.B. has it — snuffed out (*minor* or partial *pralaya*). When the Spirit-man reaches the last bead of the chain and passes into *final nirvana*, this last world also disappears or passes into subjectivity. Thus are there among the stellar galaxies births and deaths of worlds ever following each other in the orderly procession of natural Law. And — as said already — the last bead is strung upon the thread of the *'mahayuga.'*

When the last cycle of man-bearing has been completed by that last fecund earth, and humanity has reached in a mass the stage of Buddhahood and passed out of the objective existence into the mystery of *nirvana* — then 'strikes the hour'; the seen becomes the unseen, the concrete resumes its pre-cyclic state of atomic distribution.

But the dead worlds left behind (by) the on-sweeping impulse *do not* continue *dead*. Motion is the eternal order of things and affinity or attraction its handmaid of all works. The thrill of life will again re-unite the atoms, and it will stir again in the inert planet when the time comes. Though all its forces have remained *in status quo* and are now asleep, yet little by little it will — when the hour *re*-strikes — gather for a new cycle of man-bearing maternity, and give birth to something still higher as moral and physical types than during the preceding *manvantara*. And its "cosmic atoms already in a differentiated state" (*differing* — in the producing force, in the mechanical sense, of motions *and* effects) remains *in statu quo* as well as globes and everything else in the process of formation". . . . For, as planetary development is as progressive as human or race evolution, the hour of the *pralaya's* coming catches the series of worlds at successive stages of evolution; (i.e.), each has attained to some one of the periods of evolutionary progress — each stops there, until the outward impulse of the next *manvantara* sets it going from that very point — like a stopped time-piece rewound. Therefore, have I used the word 'differentiated'.

At the coming of the *pralaya* no human, animal, or even vegetable entity will be alive to see it, but there will be the earth or globes with their mineral kingdoms; and all these planets will be physically disintegrated in the *pralaya*, yet not destroyed; for they have their places in the sequence of evolution, and their 'privations' coming again out of the subjective, they will find the exact point from which they have to move on around the chain of 'manifested forms'. This, as we know, is repeated endlessly throughout ETERNITY. Each man of us has gone this ceaseless round, and will repeat it for ever and ever. The deviation of each one's course and his rate of progress from *nirvana* to *nirvana* is governed by causes which he himself creates out of the exigencies in which he finds himself entangled. . . .

We know that periods of action and rest follow each other in everything in Nature from the macrocosm with its Solar Systems down to man and its parent-earth, which has its seasons of activity followed by those of sleep; and that in short all Nature, like her begotten living forms has her time for recuperation. So with the spiritual individuality, the Monad which starts on its downward and upward cyclic rotation. The periods which intervene between each of the great *manvantarian* 'Rounds' are proportionately long to reward for the thousands of existences passed on various globes; while the time given between each 'race birth' — or *rings* as you call them — is sufficiently lengthy to compensate for any life of strife and misery during that lapse of time passed in conscious bliss after the rebirth of the *Ego*. To conceive of an *eternity* of bliss or woe, and to offset it to any conceivable deeds of merit or demerit of a being who may have lived a century or even a millenium in the flesh, can only be proposed by one who has never yet grasped the awful reality of the word Eternity, nor pondered upon the law of perfect justice and equilibrium which pervades Nature. . . .

Let us see what your Science has to tell us about Ethnography and other matters. The latest conclusions to which your wise men of the West seem to have arrived briefly stated are the following. The theories even approximately correct I venture to underline with blue.[†]

1. The earliest traces of man they can find disappear beyond the close of a period of which the rock-fossils furnish the only clue *they possess*.

[†] Ed. Note: blue underlining is indicated by italics in the remaining passages.

2. Starting thence they find four Races of men who have successively inhabited Europe: (a) The Race of the river Drift — mighty hunters (perchance Nimrod?) *who dwelt in the then sub-tropical climate of Western Europe,* who used chipped stone implements of the most primitive kind and *were contemporary with the rhinoceros and the mammoth;* (b) the so-called cavemen, a Race developed during the glacial period *(the Esquimaux being now, they say, its only type)* and which possessed finer weapons and tools for chipped stone since they made with wondrous accuracy pictures of various animals they were familiar with, simply with the aid of sharp pointed flints on the antlers of reindeer and on bones and stones; (c) the third Race — the men of the Neolithic age are found already *grinding* their stone implements, building houses and boats and making pottery, in short — the lake dwellers of Switzerland; and finally (d) appears the fourth Race, coming from Central Asia. These are the fair complexioned Aryans who intermarry with the remnant of the dark Iberians — now represented by the swarthy Basques of Spain. This is the Race which they consider as the progenitors of you modern peoples of Europe.

3. They add, moreover, that the men of the river Drift preceded the glacial period known in geology as the *Pleistocene,* and originated some 240,000 years ago, while human beings generally (see Geikie, Dawkins, Fiske and others) inhabited *Europe at least 100,000 years earlier.*

With one solitary exception they are all wrong. They come near enough yet miss the mark in every case. There were not *four* but *five* Races; and we are that fifth with remnants of the fourth. (A more perfect evolution or Race with each maha-cyclic Round); while the first Race appeared on earth not half a million of years ago (Fiske's theory) — but several millions. The latest scientific theory is that of the German and American professors who say through Fiske: "we see man living on the earth for perhaps half a million years to all *intents and purposes dumb.*"

He is both right and wrong. Right about the Race having been 'dumb', for long ages of silence were required for the evolution and mutual comprehension of speech, from the moans and mutterings of the first remove of man above the highest anthropoid (a Race now extinct since "Nature shuts the door behind her" as she advances, in more than one sense) — up to the first monosyllable-uttering man. But he is wrong in saying all the rest.

By the bye, you ought to come to some agreement as to the terms used when discussing cyclic evolutions. Our terms are untranslatable; and without a good knowledge of our complete system (which cannot be given but to regular Initiates) would suggest nothing definite to your perceptions but only be a source of confusion as in the case of the terms 'Soul' and 'Spirit' with all your metaphysical writers — especially the Spiritualists.

MAHATMA M.

GLOSSARY

abhyasa	Constant practice; exertion
Adhibhuta	Primordial element
Adhidaivata	Substratum of divine intelligences
Adhiyajna	Primordial sacrifice; region of sacrifice
Adipurusha	The primordial cosmic being or spirit
Aditi	Vedic name for *Mulaprakriti*; the abstract aspect of *Parabrahman*, though both manifested and unknowable
Agnishwatha Pitris	*Also* Solar Pitris. A class of dhyanis who lit up the principle of manas in the third race; our solar ancestors
ahankara	Egoism; the sense of 'I', self-identity
Ain-Soph	The Absolute, Endless, No-Thing; "Boundless" or Limitless Deity
Akasha	Space, universal solvent, spiritual substance, the *upadhi* of Divine Thought
Alaya	Universal Soul; identical with *Akasha* in its mystic sense, and with *Mulaprakriti* in its essence, as it is the basis or root of all things
Amitabha	Cosmic Buddha, the "Boundless Age," the Dhyani Buddha of Gautama Buddha
ananda	Bliss, joy
Anima Mundi	The seven-fold Universal Soul and material source of all life, the divine essence which permeates, animates and informs all, the essence of seven planes of sentience, consciousness and differentiation; *Alaya*
antaskarana	The bridge between the lower mind (head) and the higher mind (heart), between the divine Ego and the personal soul of man
anu	Atom; point
Anupadaka	Parent-less, self-existing
Ashwatha	Sacred tree used to kindle the sacrificial fire: the Bo tree; the Tree of Knowledge, *ficus religiosa*
asuras	Class of celestial beings born from the breath—*Asu*—of Brahmā-Prajapati; the spiritual and divine ancestors of Manasic humanity
Atma	The Universal Spirit, the divine Monad, the seventh Principle in the septenary constitution of man; the Supreme Soul
Atman	SELF; divine breath; the universal Self
AUM	The sacred syllable, eternal vibration

avidya	Fundamental ignorance, any failure to discern the truth
Barhishad Pitris	*Also* Lunar Pitris. Lunar Gods, those who evolved astral prototypes of the human form; called in India the Fathers, "Pitris" or the lunar ancestors, and subdivided into seven classes or hierarchies
bhakti	Devotion
Bodhi	Wisdom
bodhichitta	*Lit.* 'seed of enlightenment'; embryo of spiritual man
Bodhisattva	*Lit.* 'he whose essence *(sattva)* has become Wisdom *(Bodhi)*'; enlightened being who remains in *samsara* to serve and help humanity
Book of Dzyan, The	*Also* 'The Stanzas of Dzyan'. An ancient, esoteric text written in an unknown language upon which *The Secret Doctrine* and *The Voice of the Silence* are based; *see* Dzyan
Brahmā	The creative Logos; the creator of the manifest universe in the Indian pantheon, the first of the Trimurti (three forms) of Brahmā, Vishnu and Shiva (creator, sustainer and destroyer/regenerator) existing periodically in manifestation then returning to *pralaya* (dissolving into non-manifestation) at the end of this cycle
Brahma	*Also Brahman.* The impersonal, supreme and incognizable principle of the universe; the Ultimate Reality; the attributeless Absolute
Brahma Vach	Divine wisdom; divine speech
Buddhi	Intellection, intuitive discernment, direct perception, resolute conviction, wisdom; the Universal Soul; the spiritual soul in man (the sixth principle), vehicle of *Atman*; divine discernment; Universal Intelligence
chela	Disciple, especially the initiated disciple
chit	Thought, ideation, intellect
daimon	Inner voice of conscience and intuition; an aspect of the human soul
Daiviprakriti	Divine Nature; primordial, homogeneous light; the Light of the Logos
deva	God, celestial being, resplendent deity
devachan	A post-mortem state of heavenly bliss wherein the Ego assimilates and enjoys the fruition of the good karma and harvest of most universal thought and intuition of the last life
dharma	Duty, moral law; social and personal morality; natural law, natural obligation; teaching, essence
Dhyan Chohan	*Lit.* 'Lord of Light'; one of the the highest gods; *pl.* the primordial divine intelligences and agents of divine law through which *Mahat* manifests and guides the Kosmos

dhyana	Contemplation, meditation; state of abstraction
Dhyani	Divine embodiment of ideation; man of meditation
Dzyan	*Lit.* 'to reform one's self by meditation and knowledge'; *see The Book of Dzyan*
Ego, the higher	SELF; the consciousness in man of "I am I" or the feeling of "I-am-ship"; Esoteric philosophy teaches the existence of two Egos in man, the mortal or personal, and the Higher, the Divine and the Impersonal, calling the former "personality" and the latter "Individuality."
Epimethean	Of Epimetheus: Greek Titan. *Lit.,* 'Afterthought'; brother to Prometheus ('Forethought')
Eros	The third personage of the Hellenic primordial trinity of Ouranos, Gaea and Eros; the abstract and universally beneficent creative force in nature, degraded by later attributions; *see also kama*
Fohat	The active (male) potency of the *Sakti* (female power) in nature; Higher Eros or *Kamadeva,* the essence of cosmic force or electricity; *Daiviprakriti;* the link between spirit and matter
Gelukpa	*Lit.* 'Yellow Caps', the highest and most orthodox Buddhist sect in Tibet. The Dalai Lama, responsible for all Tibetan Buddhist traditions, is a Gelukpa.
gnosis	Spiritual, sacred Knowledge; the technical term used by the schools of religious philosophy before and during early Christianity
Great Breath	Symbolizing eternal ceaseless Motion; the One Life, eternal yet periodic in its regular manifestations; Absolute, omnipresent Consciousness
guna	Propensity; quality; constituent
Gupta Vidya	Secret Wisdom, highest knowledge
guru	Venerable teacher; religious preceptor; spiritual teacher
Guruparampara	Sacred lineage of teachers
Hermes Trismegistus	A lineage of Initiators in ancient Egypt, ultimately traceable to Shiva as Dakshinamurti, Initiator of Initiates; Initiates who transferred from latent to active potency a precise and comprehensive knowledge of the complex laws governing the seven kingdoms of Nature, constituting a divine gnosis
Hiranyagarbha	The radiant or golden egg or womb; esoterically, the luminous 'fire mist' or ethereal stuff from which the universe was formed
Ishwara	The sovereign Lord; the omnipresent Spirit; the controller of maya
jiva	Life, life-essence; individual soul; the Monad or *Atma-Buddhi;* Life as the Absolute

jnana yajna	Wisdom-sacrifice
jnana yoga	Yoga of knowledge; communion through wisdom
Kali Yuga	The dark age; the fourth age; the iron age that began in 3102 B.C.
kalpa	Cosmic cycle, day of Brahmā
kama	Desire, attraction, passion; cleaving to existence; creative impetus and longing; *see also* Eros
kama manas	The desire mind, the lower *Manas* or human animal soul, the reflection of the higher *Manas*
kamaloka	The semi-material plane, to us subjective and invisible, where the disembodied "personalities" or human astral remains gradually disintegrate
kamarupa	The form of desire; the assemblage of cravings
karana	Instrument of action; basis of causation
karana sharira	The causal body; the inmost sheath
karma	Act, action; the law of ethical equilibrium
kosha	Sheath; body
Krishna	The eighth Avatar of Vishnu
Kriyashakti	Creative imagination; a cosmic and human power
Kundalini-shakti	The power of life; one of the forces of Nature; a power known only to those who practice concentration and Yoga
Kwan Yin	The female logos, the "Mother of Mercy"
lanoo	A disciple; *see also* chela
laya	Absorption, dissolution, repose; resting place; motionless point, still center; zero point
linga sharira	Astral body, aerial vesture, prototypal, vital body; *eidolon;* doppelgänger
Logos	The 'Verbum'; the 'Word'; the manifested Deity, the outward expression of the ever-concealed Cause
loka	Abode, circumscribed place; world, sphere; plane
Lunar Pitris	*See* Barhishad Pitris
Madhyamika	The "middle way" school of Buddhism
Maha Chohan	The chief of a spiritual Hierarchy, or of a school of Occultism; the head of the trans-Himalayan mystics
Mahakalpa	Great age
mahamanvantara	The manifestation of cosmos from *mahapralaya;* out-breathing of the Great Breath
Mahapurusha	Equivalent term for *Paramatman,* the Supreme Spirit

Mahat	The first principle of universal intelligence and consciousness; the primal basis of individuation; cosmic ideation; the cosmic Mind behind manifested Nature and the great hebdomadal Heart of all humanity
Mahatma	Great soul; exalted exemplar of self-mastery and human perfection
Manas	Mind; the faculty of cognition, choice and self-awareness
Manasa	"The efflux of the divine mind"; the divine sons of Brahmā-Viraj, identical with the Kumara, the Manasaputra, and are identified with the human "Egos"
Manasaputras	The sons of (universal) Mind; human "Egos"; spiritual individuality of each human being
manvantara	Cosmic cycle of manifestation
maya	Illusion, appearance; the cosmic power behind phenomenal existence
moksha	Deliverance, emancipation
Monad	The Unity, the One; the unified triad *(Atma-Buddhi-Manas)*, or the duad *(Atma-Buddhi)*; the immortal part of man
Mulaprakriti	Root Nature; undifferentiated primordial substance; unmanifested matrix of all forms
Nadabrahman	Transcendental Sound or Vibrations; the Unmanifested Logos; *also Sabdabrahman*
namarupa	The fourth link in the chain of twelve *nidanas*; *nama* or mind, and *rupa* or form; *see nidana*
nidana	The twelve links in the chain of dependent origination, a concatenation of causes and effects; the cycle of birth, life, death and rebirth
nirguna	Without attributes; devoid of relations and qualities; unmodified; unbound
Nirguna Brahman	Brahma without attributes; Brahma (neuter); *see nirguna*
nirvana	Unalloyed bliss; the entire 'blowing out' of separateness; absolute consciousness
nitya pralaya	One of four kinds of *pralaya*, the stage of chronic change and dissolution, of growth and decay; the constant and imperceptible changes undergone by the atoms which last as long as a *mahamanvantara*, a whole age of Brahmā
nous	A Platonic term for the Higher *Manas* or Soul; Spirit as distinct from animal soul or psyche; divine consciousness or mind in man
OM	The mystic monosyllable; the soundless sound; the Word
OM TAT SAT	The triple designation of *Brahman*
para	*Lit.* 'beyond' or 'above'
Parabrahman	Supreme *Brahman;* the attributeless Absolute

Paramartha	Absolute existence and universal self-consciousness
Philosophia Perennis	The perennial philosophy; the source of all true religions and philosophies; sometimes equated with the Secret Doctrine
Pitris	The ancestors or creators of mankind, of seven classes, three incorporeal (*arupa*), and four corporeal; *see* Solar Pitris and Lunar Pitris
prajna	A synonym of *Mahat*, the Universal Mind; the capacity for perception; Consciousness; wisdom
prakriti	Nature in general; spiritual nature, as distinct from *purusha*, Spirit; together the two primeval aspects of the One Unknown Deity
pralaya	A period of obscuration or repose — planetary, cosmic or universal — the opposite of *manvantara*
prana	Life-Principle; the breath of life
Pranava	The sacred Word, OM
Raja Yoga	System of developing spiritual powers through union with the Supreme Spirit; regulation and concentration of thought
rajas	One of the three *gunas* which constitute the qualities or divisions of matter; activity and change
Ṛg Veda, Rig Veda	The first and most important of the four Vedas; recorded in Occultism as having been delivered by great sages on Lake Manasarovar beyond the Himalayas
Root Race	The human Race has been compared to a tree — the main stem may be compared to the Root-Race, its larger limbs to seven Sub-Races
Ṛta, rita	Cosmic order, divine law; righteousness
Sabdabrahman	The Unmanifested Logos of the Vedas; ethereal vibrations diffused throughout Space; *also Nadabrahman*
Saguna Brahman	With attributes and all perfections; Brahman
samadhi	*Lit.* 'self-possession'; the highest state of yoga; ecstatic meditation; supreme self-control
samsara	Conditionality, as contrasted with *nirvana*; realm of becoming, in contrast to Being; birth and death; conditioned existence; illusion
SAT	The ever-present Reality, absoluteness, Be-ness
Sat-Chit-Ananda	Abstract reality, consciousness and bliss
sattva	One of the three *gunas* which constitute the qualities or divisions of matter; the quality of goodness or purity
satya	Supreme truth
shakti	The feminine, active creative forces in nature, mirrored in the seven forces in man

Shankaracharya	The great religious teacher and legendary reformer of India, the founder of Advaita Vedanta philosophy; *also* Shankara
sharira	Body
Solar Pitris	*See* Agnishwatha Pitris
srotapatti	One who has entered the stream leading to enlightenment
sthula sharira	In metaphysics, the physical body
sutratman	Thread soul; reincarnating individuality
Svabhavat	The spirit and essence of Substance; from the root word *Subhava: su* — good, perfect; *sva* — self, and *bhava* — being or state of being; the "Father-Mother"
svasamvedana	*Lit.* the 'reflection which analyses itself'; *see paramartha*
tamas	The lowest of the three *gunas* which constitute the qualities or divisions of matter; the quality of darkness, foulness, inertia, and ignorance
tanha	The thirst for life; desire to live; clinging to life on this earth which causes rebirth or reincarnation; *also trishna*
TAT	*Lit.* 'That'; *Brahman;* beyond the three worlds; the pre-existent
tattva	Truth, reality; principle, essence
Theosophia	"Divine Wisdom," the substratum of truth and knowledge which underlies the universe, from which of all the great world-religions and philosophies were derived; pure divine ethics. While *Theosophia* cannot be put entirely in words, Theosophy is what can be expressed at this time.
Theosophy	The maximal expression of *Theosophia* at this time in history; *See Theosophia*
trishna	*Lit.* 'thirst' or 'craving', the cause of suffering; *also tanha*
Tsong-Kha-Pa	1357-1419 A.D. The 'model of virtue': Tibetan Buddhist founder of a new reformed order, the Gelugpa, to which all Dalai Lamas belong; stated by H.P. Blavatsky to have initiated a Seven Century Plan to infuse the Wisdom current into Western consciousness through various agents of the Society of Sages
turiya	Spiritual wakefulness; the fourth or highest state of the soul
upadhi	Basis; the vehicle, carrier or bearer of something less material than itself
Upanishads	Esoteric doctrines; interpretations of the Vedas by the methods of Vedanta
Vaikari	Human speech; the lowest of four levels of speech
Vak, Vach	From *vach, vacha*: voice, word, speech; mystic personification of speech; the female Logos

Vedas	The most ancient and sacred Sanskrit works: the *Rig, Atharva, Sama, Yajur Vedas;* from the root *vid* 'to know' or 'divine knowledge'
Verbum	The Word; the manifested Deity, the outward expression of the ever-concealed Cause; *see* Logos
Word, the	*See* Verbum
Yggdrasil	World Tree of Norse cosmogony; tree of the Universe, of time and of life
yoga	Unswerving concentration; fusion, integration; union with the divine; skill in action
yogin	Practitioner of yoga; proficient in yoga
Zarathustra	*Lit.* 'the star who sacrifices to the Sun'; the founder of Zoroastrianism; a title which some traditions give to thirteen Magus-Teachers

BIBLIOGRAPHY

Arnold, Sir Edwin. *The Light of Asia.* David McKay Co.,
   Philadelphia 1932.

Bellamy, Edward. *The Religion of Solidarity.* Concord Grove
   Press, Santa Barbara 1977. Originally published
   in 1874.

Blavatsky, Helena Petrovna. *Isis Unveiled.* Theosophy Co., Los
   Angeles 1982. Originally published in 1877.

———— *The Key To Theosophy.* Theosophy Co., Los Angeles 1987.
   Originally published in 1889.

———— *Lucifer,* 1887-1890. H.P. Blavatsky and Mabel Collins,
   London.

———— *The Secret Doctrine.* Theosophy Co., Los Angeles 1947.
   Originally published in 1888.

———— *Theosophical Articles, Vols. I - III.* Theosophy Co., Los
   Angeles 1981. Originally published in 1886-96.

———— *The Theosophical Glossary.* Theosophy Co., Los Angeles
   1973. Originally published in 1892.

———— *Transactions of the Blavatsky Lodge.* Theosophy Co., Los
   Angeles 1987. Originally published in
   1890-91.

———— *The Voice of the Silence.* Concord Grove Press, Santa
   Barbara 1989. Originally published in 1889.

Collins, Mabel. *The Gates of Gold.* Concord Grove Press, Santa
   Barbara 1982. Combined volume: *Through the
   Gates of Gold* (1887) and *Light on the Path* (1885).

Crosbie, Robert. *The Friendly Philosopher.* Theosophy Co., Los
   Angeles 1934.

———— *The Language of the Soul.* Concord Grove Press, Santa
   Barbara 1982. Originally published in 1919.

Iyer, Raghavan, ed. *In the Beginning (Zohar)*. Concord Grove Press, Santa Barbara 1979.

———— *The Golden Verses of Pythagoras*. Concord Grove Press, Santa Barbara 1980.

———— *The Gospel According to Thomas*. Concord Grove Press, Santa Barbara 1976.

———— *Hermes*, 1975 - 1989. Concord Grove Press, Santa Barbara.

———— *Return to Shiva (Yoga Vasishtha)*. Concord Grove Press, Santa Barbara 1977.

———— *Tao Te Ching*. Concord Grove Press, Santa Barbara 1978.

———— *The Jewel in the Lotus*. Concord Grove Press, Santa Barbara 1983.

Judge, William Quan. *The Bhagavad Gita: The Book of Devotion*. Theosophy Co., Los Angeles 1971. Originally published in 1890.

————*"Forum" Answers by William Q. Judge*. Theosophy Co., Los Angeles 1982. Originally published 1889-96.

———— *The Ocean of Theosophy*. Theosophy Co., Los Angeles 1962. Originally published in 1893.

———— *Theosophical Articles*. Theosophy Co., Los Angeles 1980.

Mavalankar, Damodar K. *The Service of Humanity*. Concord Grove Press, Santa Barbara 1982. Originally published in 1884.

Patanjali. *Yoga Aphorisms*. Theosophy Co., Los Angeles 1951.

Plato. *The Banquet*. Translation by P.B. Shelley, Concord Grove Press, Santa Barbara 1981.

Plotinus. *The Enneads*. Translation by S. Mackenna. Faber and Faber, London 1966.

Russell, George William. *The Descent of the Gods, The Mystical Writings of A.E.* Ed. by Raghavan and Nandini Iyer. Colin Smythe, London 1983.

Shankar, Bhavani. *The Doctrine of the Bhagavad Gita.* Concord Grove Press, Santa Barbara 1984. Originally published in 1966.

Shankaracharya, Shri. Shankara's *Crest-Jewel of Discrimination: Timeless Teachings on Nonduality — The Viveka-chudamani.* Translated by Christopher Isherwood and Swami Prabhavananda. Vedanta Press, UK 1978.

Taimni, I.K. *The Gayatri.* The Theosophical Publishing House, Madras 1974.

Wadia, B.P. *The Grihastha Ashrama.* Concord Grove Press, Santa Barbara, 1981. Originally published in 1941.

——— *The Law of Sacrifice.* Concord Grove Press, Santa Barbara, 1981. Originally published in 1961.

INDEX